MW00489904

Foundations
of Social Policy

Foundations of Social Policy

Social Justice, Public Programs, and
the Social Work Profession

AMANDA SMITH BARUSCH
University of Utah

THOMSON

BROOKS/COLE

Australia • Canada • Mexico • Singapore • Spain
United Kingdom • United States

Advisory Editor in Social Work
Donald Brieland

Edited by Janet Tilden
Production supervision by Kim Vander Steen
Designed and typeset by Lucy Lesiak Design
Printed and bound by Quebecor World/Fairfield

Cover illustration © David Ridley/SIS

ISBN: 0-87581-447-6
Library of Congress Catalog Card No. 2001 135874

COPYRIGHT © 2002 Brooks/Cole, a division of Thomson Learning, Inc.
Thomson Learning ™ is a trademark used herein under license.

ALL RIGHTS RESERVED. No part of this work covered by the
copyright hereon may be reproduced or used in any form or by any
means — graphic, electronic, or mechanical, including photocopying,
recording, taping, Web distribution, or information storage or retrieval
systems — without the written permission of the publisher.

Wadsworth/Thomson Learning
10 Davis Drive
Belmont CA 94002-3098
USA

For information about our products, contact us:
Thomson Learning Academic Resource Center
1-800-423-0563
http://www.wadsworth.com

For permission to use material from this text, contact us by
Web: http://www.thomsonrights.com
Fax: 1-800-730-2215
Phone: 1-800-730-2214

Printed in the United States of America
10 9 8 7 6 5 4 3 2

To
Phyllis Roos Barusch
An extraordinary advocate

Contents in Brief

Contents

PART II

COLLECTIVE RESPONSES TO SOCIAL PROBLEMS

Mobilizing Factors 73

PART III

VULNERABLE POPULATIONS
Discrimination and Oppression   193

PART IV

POLICY PRACTICE AND THE SOCIAL WORK PROFESSION
Cycles of Liberation   367

Preface

"Social workers promote social justice...."

Preamble to *NASW Code of Ethics* (1996)

Social justice is central to the mission of social work and the focus of intense debates throughout the nation. Social policies reflect decisions about what constitutes justice and how it can be achieved. Social work professionals can contribute to debates over social justice by providing a deeply personal and empathetic understanding of the consequences of injustice.

Like most people, social workers (and social work students) understand justice in terms of events and conditions that affect individuals. In this text, we use case examples as tools for the analysis and critique of contemporary U.S. social policy, helping students to draw connections between individual problems and public policies. We present a policy analysis framework that uses a social justice perspective to examine the fairness of policies. Policy development and implementation are presented as integral aspects of social work practice, and the role of social work professionals is discussed in each chapter.

ABOUT THE BOOK

This book is designed for use in foundation policy courses at the master's level. It may also be appropriate for advanced students at the bachelor's level. It has four parts. Part I provides an introduction to U.S. social policy. In Chapter 1, philosophical conceptions of social justice are examined for their relevance to contemporary U.S. social policy. Next, we introduce a framework for policy analysis designed to help students examine social justice issues through diverse philosophical perspectives. The role of government in promoting social justice is the focus of Chapter 2, which offers a brief description of the structure and function of the U.S. government and an introduction to the nation's tax system. Chapter 3 covers the Social Security Act as the legislative framework for most U.S. social policies. Discussion topics, suggested readings, and interesting web sites are included at the end of each chapter in Parts I through IV.

Part II introduces a framework for determining when a society will develop collective responses to social problems. Chapters in this part of the book examine problems that have been approached through collective action in the United States: poverty (Chapter 4), physical illness (Chapter 5), and mental illness (Chapter 6). Each chapter opens with a case study. The case studies are based on interviews with people chosen to illustrate the complexity of each area of study. We explore the development of policies and services, as well as contemporary policy issues and debates. These chapters provide background material necessary for students to apply the social justice framework introduced in Chapter 1.

Part III introduces theories of oppression. Each chapter explores a population that has experienced oppression in the U.S.: children, women, the elderly, racial and ethnic minorities, and gays and lesbians. The structure of these chapters mirrors that in Part II, with the addition of major social/demographic trends affecting each population.

Part IV closes the book with a focus on policy practice. Chapter 12 begins with a case study in advocacy, then addresses philosophical and tactical considerations in policy practice, providing suggestions to beginning advocates. Chapter 13 returns full-circle to the philosophical perspectives presented in Chapter 1, using these perspectives to analyze the implications of globalization and rising inequality for the social welfare state and the social work profession.

ACKNOWLEDGMENTS

This book benefited from the talents and energies of many colleagues and friends. Mary Jane Taylor, David Derezotes, Mary Ann Overcamp, and Mary Duffy (all of the University of Utah) reviewed chapters, as did Terry Peak (Utah State University), Jim Hinterlong (Washington University), and Bill Walsh and Shirley Weathers (Walsh & Weathers Policy Studies). Brian Simmons (California State University, Monterey) taught me about child welfare policy and gave an early version the most thoughtful review a draft ever saw. Martha Anderson (Utah Division of Mental Health) helped with both the substance and style of Chapter 6. Russ Van Vleet (University of Utah) oriented me to the juvenile justice system. Irene Fisher and Bill Crim (Utah Issues) educated me about the advocacy efforts described in Chapter 12. Hank Liese (University of Utah) and his red pen improved the readability of Part I. Jamelle Chadwick spent days and nights tracking down lists of articles that never seemed to end.

Early drafts were reviewed by Rob Hudson (Boston University), Paul Stuart (University of Alabama), Ray Engle (University of Pittsburgh), and Sanford Schram (Bryn Mawr), who improved both content and the organization. Each page of this book was enhanced by Janet Tilden who, along with Dick Welna and Don Brieland, provided the best editorial review I've ever experienced.

Masters and doctoral students at the University of Utah and Washington University served as the testing ground for ideas and text.

Nine people from various walks of life shared their experiences with me in the hope of enriching the educational backgrounds of professional social workers. I can't name them here, but I will always be grateful for the time we spent together.

Finally, my family made allowances for the demands of book preparation and reminded me of the things that really matter.

PART I

Policy Analysis Frameworks

SOCIAL JUSTICE DEFINED

The notion of social justice may seem alien to social work students. Many enter the profession with a strong desire to help people and a personal inclination to avoid conflict. The language of social justice and policy practice may seem hostile to both impulses, yet the pursuit of social justice stems from the urge to help and the desire to get along. This book (like the social work profession) reflects the belief that justice is "good for human beings." Individuals flourish and societies endure when justice "flows down like water" (M. L. King).

But what is social justice? Chapter 1 offers a deceptively simple definition: "the fair allocation of costs and benefits of group membership." The complexities begin to emerge as we examine four philosophical conceptions of social justice. Understanding these divergent perspectives will strengthen students' analytic skills, enabling them to recognize assumptions underlying arguments of others and to frame their own arguments in terms more likely to persuade. The discussion then turns to social work. We will identify major themes in policy practice, present a brief biography of one of the profession's early policy practitioners, and examine the role of the profession in America's pursuit of social justice. A framework for policy analysis based on the social justice perspective is also introduced in this chapter.

Government is an important vehicle for defining and promoting social justice. Chapter 2 offers a general description of the structure and processes of the U.S. government, organized around the "levels" and "branches" of government. The tax system is introduced as an important vehicle for promoting justice. It is vital that social workers be "tax literate" in the twenty-first century, as taxes are increasingly used to advance social goals. Toward that end, this chapter offers a brief introduction to the nation's tax system that considers not only the mechanics, but also the philosophical assumptions that drive the system. For some readers, this chapter will be review, but for most it will provide useful reminders and reference material.

The Social Security Act, our focus in Chapter 3, defines the framework for most social programs that advance social justice in the United States. We will examine the role of Social Security in building the nation-states of Europe, and then trace the history of Social Security in the United States. Three types of programs will be described: social insurance programs, public assistance programs, and health and social service programs. We will review major reform proposals, then conclude by looking at the philosophical foundations of Social Security in the United States.

1

Social Justice
and Social Workers

Our focus in this chapter is on the search for social justice. The chapter begins with a case study involving domestic violence. Next, we will provide a working definition of social justice, introduce a framework for analyzing policy from a social justice perspective, and then examine four distinct philosophical conceptions of justice: oligarchy, libertarianism, liberalism, and socialism. The chapter concludes with an exploration of the role of the social work profession in the search for social justice. We will review the life and achievements of a leading social worker, Bertha Reynolds, and then examine the practice of social work from a social justice perspective.

CASE STUDY ♦ MELISSA WILLIAMS

In June 1996, 150 people, mostly women, met in a hotel to discuss welfare and domestic violence. The program was led by a social worker and attended by state legislators, social workers, welfare administrators, academicians, advocates, and religious leaders. In the context of a national debate about welfare reform, this session was designed to raise awareness of the importance of welfare as a resource for women leaving abusive homes. One such woman was Melissa Williams. During the luncheon she and three other women told their stories.

Melissa is an attractive young woman with flowing blond hair and a gentle, reflective way of speaking. Clearly intimidated by the size of the group and the lectern in front of her, she spoke haltingly of her experiences with welfare and domestic violence.

Melissa grew up in a working-class family. Her father worked for a mining company and had little interest in children, let alone female children. Her mother was a silent woman, struggling to raise a large family on a miner's salary. Neither parent was physically abusive, but both reminded the children repeatedly that they were "worth less than nothing." For Melissa this emotional abuse intensified during puberty. Miserable in her own family, Melissa saw marriage to her boyfriend, Will, as a way out.

Will was strong, energetic, and determined. He seemed to have the world by the tail and promised a kind of protection and appreciation Melissa had never enjoyed. At 16, she married him. She laughed, recalling that "Everyone thought we had to get married, but I wasn't even pregnant!"

Melissa did get pregnant immediately and left high school. Her husband finished high school and found a "good job"—one with health benefits. They rented an apartment and settled in. Three children were born in rapid succession. Will's job began to feel more and more like a dead end, and he took to hanging out in bars with old high school friends. He'd come home drunk and take out his anger on Melissa. Her medical records show three visits to the emergency room with facial bruising, lacerations, and a broken arm.

Suffering from a debilitating depression, Melissa was not roused to action until Will attacked one of the children. It was just a slap, but it was enough to send Melissa back to her parents' home. At home her depression worsened. Her parents encouraged Melissa to stay away from her husband, but they could not afford to support Melissa and her three children. So, one day, Melissa and her mother took the bus to the welfare office. Melissa was enrolled in the "self-sufficiency program" and awarded emergency housing assistance. Depression was identified as a barrier to employment, and her caseworker arranged for counseling and medication. She also introduced Melissa to a women's advocacy group called JEDI Women (Justice, Economic Dignity, and Independence for Women).

At the time of the conference, Melissa was living independently with her children. She had divorced her husband and did not expect to re-marry. Anti-depressants and a support group were critical to her ongoing success. Her children had residual health and behavioral problems from witnessing domestic violence.

Deeply moved by Melissa's experience, her audience resolved to ensure that welfare reform in their state would not eliminate a key resource for women leaving abusive relationships. A few weeks later, President Clinton signed an executive order establishing a national hotline for victims of domestic abuse. Today the state exempts victims of domestic violence from lifetime limits on public assistance.

This commitment to devote public resources to protect abused women reflects personal and public decisions about what constitutes social justice in today's society. In a nutshell, it reveals a belief that the suffering caused by domestic violence is not a cost that women should be asked to bear alone, but that it is fair to organize a collective response.

SOCIAL JUSTICE DEFINED

In August 1996, the Delegate Assembly of the National Association of Social Workers approved a new code of ethics. The preamble to this document states that "Social workers promote social justice" (NASW, 1999). What is social justice?

The terms "social justice," "social and economic justice," and "distributive justice" are often used interchangeably. They refer to the way a group (of any size) allocates the costs and benefits of membership. If the rules of allocation used by the group are considered "fair" by members of that group, then the group has achieved a measure of social justice. Analysis of a group's efforts to achieve justice must be informed by two concepts: "membership" and "voice." Membership refers to the group's boundaries for distinguishing between "us" and "them." Voice refers to an individual's ability to influence decision-making within the group.

Social justice issues arise in families; for example, new parents struggle to decide how to divide the responsibilities of rearing their baby. These issues also arise in societies; for example, members of the U.S. Congress debate tax reform proposals. Disputes about how many diapers a father should change or how much tax a corporation should pay are fundamentally debates over how to allocate the costs of group membership. Disputes about membership arise when a sub-group's right to the benefits of group membership is questioned. For example, a family may question its obligation to provide care to an elderly grandparent on the grounds that he or she is not *really* a member of the family. A nation may question the delivery of cash benefits to immigrants who are not *really* citizens. Similarly, at all levels of social organization, an individual's voice will be determined by the extent to which others hear and attend to his or her concerns.

Benefits of group membership are also allocated through social justice mechanisms. Mundane decisions about who gets to use the family car reflect fundamental beliefs about what is a "just" or "fair" distribution of this benefit. In the United States, the benefits of citizenship include entitlements such as Social Security, tax deductions for home mortgage interest, and Medicaid. Distribution of these benefits is often the subject of extensive debate.

This book offers five sets of questions that serve as a framework for analyzing social policy. These questions are discussed below and summarized in Table 1.1.

TABLE 1.1 FRAMEWORK FOR POLICY ANALYSIS

QUESTION 1: *What are the costs and/or benefits under consideration?*

QUESTION 2: *Who bears the cost, who receives the benefits, and what is the relationship between these two entities?*

QUESTION 3: *Is anyone who is affected by this policy being labeled "other," and does everyone affected by this policy have an equal voice?*

QUESTION 4: *What are the rules, both formal and informal, that govern who receives and who pays?*

QUESTION 5: *Is this policy fair?*

QUESTION 1   The first step in analyzing social policies within a social justice framework is to ask, "What are the costs and/or benefits under consideration?" Costs may be specific and easy to measure, such as a person's tax obligation. Or they may be more abstract, such as the risk of catastrophic illness or poverty. These costs may appear to be only loosely related to group membership. To the extent that they are not influenced by social allocation mechanisms they may not be the direct result of group membership. But, as we will see in later chapters, many risks are not randomly distributed in the population and instead are directly influenced by our social structure and public policies. Like costs, benefits can be specific and concrete, such as tax deductions, or more difficult to measure, such as physical safety or access to care.

QUESTION 2   The second question in our framework for policy analysis asks, "Who bears the costs, who receives the benefits, and what is the relationship between these two entities?" Sometimes benefits for some persons represent costs for others. When policy-makers decide to use tax funds for social programs, they are imposing costs on some taxpayers in order to provide benefits to the programs' clients. Discussions about social justice should include not only simple considerations of *how much* cost or benefit one should incur, but also *who* should bear the cost of someone else's benefit. An example of this more complex debate arises when we consider Social Security. Advocates of means testing for recipients of Social Security benefits argue that it is unfair to ask low- and middle-income workers to pay taxes so the affluent can enjoy comfortable retirement incomes. While this scenario grossly oversimplifies the dynamics of Social Security financing (see Chapter 3), it illustrates this added dimension of social justice. Allocation debates often concern the *relationship* between the person who bears the cost and the one who enjoys the benefits of membership in a group.

QUESTION 3   The third question asks whether anyone's membership in the collective, or group, is under dispute and whether the views of all affected parties are being heard: "Is anyone affected by this debate being labeled 'other,' and does everyone affected by this policy have an equal voice?" The principle "One person, one vote" is pivotal in a working democracy. When the voices of affected parties are silenced, the likelihood of an unjust result is high. Thus, a central role of social workers is speaking on behalf of those who cannot speak for themselves. The profession becomes more powerful when it empowers those who are silent to speak on their own behalf.

QUESTION 4   The fourth question in our policy analysis framework considers the distributive principles governing the allocation of costs and benefits, asking "What are the rules, both formal and informal, that govern who receives and who pays?" Formal rules are codified in laws and regulations. They might consist of the eligibility requirements of a program, or the rules governing use of a tax deduction. Informal allocation rules are not written and seldom discussed. They can be derived through careful examination of how benefits and costs are allocated. For example, when clients who are combative receive less time with their case managers, or when people of color are discouraged from voting by hostile precinct workers, informal allocation rules are in operation. Understanding and articulating these distributive principles will reveal the philosophical underpinnings of a policy, or a policy proposal, as well as its impact on social justice.

QUESTION 5 This brings us to the final, and most difficult, question in a social justice analysis: "Is this policy fair?" Usually, as Aristotle and others have observed, humans have a simple, gut-level reaction that says either "Yes!" or "No!" This initial reaction is an important tool for policy analysis, but it is certainly *not* the whole story. The story is much longer and more complicated, and the answer will vary depending on a person's philosophy, perspective, and assumptions. The challenge for policy practitioners is to consider the perspectives of those involved, to review the background of the policy under consideration, and to arrive at a tentative conclusion about its fairness. In the following section we will consider the ways in which adherents of major philosophical perspectives have approached the question of fairness or justice.

PHILOSOPHICAL APPROACHES

Justice revolves around a simple question: "Is this fair?" Lee Ann Bell offers a clear vision of a just society: ". . . a society in which the distribution of resources is equitable and all members are physically and psychologically safe and secure. We envision a society in which individuals are both self-determining (able to develop their full capacities), and interdependent (capable of interacting democratically with others)" (Bell, 1997, p. 3). Like Bell, others from Plato to Ayn Rand have shared their visions of just societies. Some of these visions strike us as Utopian, and others as the reverse.

In this book we will not offer an objective definition of what constitutes a "just society," arguing instead that the answer to our fifth question is socially constructed. That is, conceptions of justice change from group to group and vary throughout the history of societies, families, and individuals. There may not be an objective end-point when absolute justice is achieved. Instead, in the process of striving for justice we continually redefine the goal. Within this "post-modern" framework, it is nonetheless useful to consider what major philosophers have said about what constitutes social justice.

Most philosophical conceptions of justice stem from or elaborate upon Aristotle's views. Aristotle described "distributive justice" as the equal distribution of shares among people who are equal, and unequal distribution among people who are unequal. Like policy-makers and family members, philosophers have struggled with the dynamics of inequality, and their conceptions of social justice differ in their approaches to inequality.

Four major philosophical perspectives are summarized below.[1] Each is based on a central distributive principle, and within each we find concepts and arguments with direct implications for social policy in the United States.

OLIGARCHY AND SOCIAL JUSTICE

Distributive Principle: From each according to his status;
to each according to his status.

Aristotle noted that "adherents of oligarchy take it [merit] to mean wealth or noble birth, . . . aristocratic excellence" (Aristotle). From the perspective of an "oligarchist," individuals are born to a station in life that is divinely ordained and entails well-established benefits and responsibilities. Justice involves providing and receiving your due. Inequality is the natural and perhaps intended result. The basic premise of this view often stems from a belief that God created an orderly world and humanity's challenge is not to improve upon but to understand and accept God's work.

Americans have long rejected the notion of a divinely ordained aristocracy, but we find remnants of oligarchy in the view that human nature and abilities are determined by innate factors. Here the idea of genetic destiny or predisposition has replaced that of divine ordination in explaining what is "just" or "expected." Scholars who link IQ with race or ethnicity often make this argument. For example, Eysenck argued that 80 percent of IQ is genetically determined, and that social class is "determined quite strongly by IQ" (Eysenck, 1973, p. 159). Jensen took the argument a step further, suggesting that American whites and blacks differ markedly in their IQ scores and that "something between one-half and three-fourths of the average IQ difference between American Negroes and whites is attributable to genetic factors, and the remainder to environmental factors and their interaction with the genetic differences" (Jensen, 1973, p. 363). Richard Herrnstein and Charles Murray achieved notoriety by making the same argument in their 1994 book *The Bell Curve*.

Some have gone further, arguing that in human society inequality is not only inevitable, but desirable. For example, Davis and Moore (1967) offered a "functionalist theory of stratification," arguing that society's most important positions require scarce talents and that higher rewards are required to recruit people with such talents into these positions. "Social inequality is thus an unconsciously evolved device by which societies insure that the most important positions are conscientiously filled by the most qualified persons" (Davis & Moore, 1967, p. 47).

---

[1]Summaries of the philosophical approaches are provided by Sterba in *Justice: Alternative Political Perspectives* (Belmont, CA: Wadsworth, 1980).

Social Darwinism is closely related to this outlook. The principle of "survival of the fittest," when applied to social and economic relations, implies that those who have great wealth are in some way superior to those who have been less successful. A natural consequence of this perspective is the exclusion of welfare recipients from debates that vitally affect them. Social work policy practice can counter this tendency by bringing the voices of the vulnerable back into the dialogue.

From the perspective of oligarchy, Melissa's experience may reflect her status as a woman of working-class background who married a man of limited means. This status is fixed and brings with it certain costs and rewards. At one time in the United States, marital status carried with it the risk of physical abuse for women. That risk was simply one of the costs endured. Today our understanding of the status of wives has changed. Americans no longer expect wives to submit to physical or emotional abuse.

LIBERTARIAN CONCEPTIONS OF SOCIAL JUSTICE

Distributive Principle: From each according to his choice;
to each according to his product.

Allocation of resources according to product is central to a libertarian understanding of justice. Emphasizing liberty over equality, libertarians argue that inequality is acceptable and promotes social well-being. Oliver Wendell Holmes exemplified this view when he said, "I have no respect for the passion for equality, which seems to me merely idealizing envy" (Hayek, 1960, cited on p. 126 of Sterba). Hayek argued that the only form of equality that does not interfere with liberty is equality before the law. With respect to the role of government, a libertarian view would hold that there is no justification for the state to treat people differently. "Before the law . . . people should be treated alike in spite of the fact that they are different . . ." (Ibid., p. 127).

Equal treatment under the law inevitably leads to unequal distribution of resources. For libertarians, this is the price of freedom, and does not require correction by the government. Libertarians typically view taxes as coercive taking of private property. Thus, for example, Hayek argued that ". . . economic inequality is not one of the evils which justify our resorting to discriminatory coercion or privilege as a remedy" (Ibid., p. 128). This general objection to the use of government coercion to achieve equality leads libertarians to oppose taxation and policies designed to promote equal opportunity in education and job opportunity, such as affirmative action. The pursuit of equality is seen as antithetical to individual freedom and hence an inappropriate goal for government.

Robert Nozick's 1974 work, *Anarchy, State and Utopia*, exemplifies the libertarian perspective. Nozick argues that inequality is not necessarily an indication of injustice if it results from a process that treats people fairly and equally. The fact that a free market results in disparate incomes is not cause for intervention. Nozick disputes the notion of communal responsibility for poverty, offering an example involving ten Robinson Crusoes on ten separate islands. If these men have different levels of well-being, these differences result from variation in their abilities or the availability of natural resources on the islands. In Nozick's view, since none of the Crusoes is responsible for any other Crusoe's disadvantages, none would be justified in demanding that the others transfer resources to him.

In a similar vein, one of President Reagan's economic advisors, Milton Friedman, argued that failure to allocate resources on the basis of product under-mines the prosperity of society. He suggested that the appropriate ethical principle for distribution of income in a free society is "To each according to what he and the instruments he owns produces." Under this view, wealth and high incomes come to those who are fortunate (inheritance) and who take risks (speculation). The community as a whole benefits from the presence of the wealthy, in part because they provide "independent foci of power to offset the centralization of political power" (Friedman, 1962, cited on p. 145 of Sterba) and in part because they become "patrons" of experimentation, novel ideas, and the arts.

Libertarians emphasize the benefits of the free market, arguing that a free-market society enjoys greater productivity among its workers and greater incentive to accumulate capital and pass it on to the next generation. A by-product of this capital accumulation is lower interest rates. Further, the free market encourages innovation and risk-taking by offering high rewards for success in uncertain ventures, such as speculative investment. Finally, proponents of this view argue that the free market is preferable to government coercion in the allocation of resources because it does not interfere with individual liberty.

Several aspects of the libertarian view have direct implications for welfare policy. With its general opposition to taxation, a libertarian perspective on social justice would clearly oppose the use of public funds to redistribute income toward the poor. The value placed on a free-market economy would suggest that welfare, as an alternative to paid work, should be made available only as a last resort. Finally, the emphasis on personal freedom, when extended to welfare recipients, would oppose coercion as a means of social control.

A libertarian perspective would emphasize Melissa's free choice in marrying Will and having children. Libertarians would note that Will chose his job. While acknowledging the problems that resulted from these choices, the libertarian perspective would not condone the use of tax funds to help Melissa improve her situation.

LIBERAL CONCEPTIONS OF SOCIAL JUSTICE

Distributive Principle: Economic liberty and political equality for all.

Central to most liberal conceptions of social justice is the attempt to combine liberty and equality, specifically economic liberty and political equality. Liberal thinkers have taken two different approaches to defining justice: the contractual and the utilitarian. The contractual tradition views the just state as one based on an unwritten contract between free and independent citizens. In contrast, the utilitarian tradition rejects the centrality of a social contract, defining justice as that which optimizes the total well-being of a society. John Rawls is widely cited for his contractual approach, while John Stuart Mill's work exemplifies the utilitarian tradition.[2]

A CONTRACTUAL APPROACH (JOHN RAWLS). John Rawls developed what he considered "a procedural interpretation" of Immanuel Kant's theories in his classic book, *A Theory of Justice.* According to Rawls, justice is a rational choice made behind a "veil of ignorance." Rawls's veil of ignorance represents a hypothetical position in which individuals ignore their personal advantage in making decisions, because "no one knows his place in society, his class position or social status; nor does he know his fortune in the distribution of natural assets and abilities, his intelligence and strength and the like" (Rawls, 1971, p. 137).

Rawls reasons that behind this veil people would rationally choose distributive rules that employ a "maximin" strategy—rules that would maximize the welfare of the least well-off. This conservative or cautious strategy, Rawls argues, would naturally be adopted if one were unaware of the chances that he or she might be among the least well-off.

For Rawls, distributive justice includes not only the fair distribution of economic goods and services but also nonmaterial "social goods," including opportunity, power, and the social bases of self-respect. He argues that a "social minimum" in all of these should be established, below which citizens of a state would not be allowed to fall. One general rule for determining the social minimum is that it be set as high as possible consistent with maintaining an efficient economic system (this condition being essential to the long-term well-being of the least advantaged).

Also central to Rawls's conception is the "just savings principle." Arguing that the veil of ignorance would deprive people of knowledge about the generation or cohort to which they belonged, Rawls suggests that "the just savings principle applies to what a society is to save as a matter of justice" (p. 288) to ensure the economic and cultural well-being of successive generations. This insures against one generation spending all of society's resources and leaving the next generation impoverished.

Rawls formulates two principles of justice that he believes would be derived by individuals operating behind the veil of ignorance:

Principle I: Special Conception of Justice
1. Each person is to have an equal right to the most extensive total system of equal basic liberties compatible with a similar system of liberties for all.

2. Social and economic inequalities are to be arranged so that they are both

---

[2]See Locke's *Second Treatise of Government,* Rousseau's *The Social Contract,* and Kant's *The Foundations of Metaphysics* for examples of the contractual tradition. For the utilitarian tradition, see John Stuart Mill's *Utilitarianism.*

(a) to the greatest benefit of the least advantaged, consistent with the just savings principle, and (b) attached to offices and positions open to all under conditions of fair equality of opportunity.

Principle II: General Conception of Justice
All social goods—liberty and opportunity, income and wealth, and the bases of self-respect—are to be distributed equally unless an unequal distribution of any or all of these goods is to the advantage of the least favored.

Suggesting that Rawls is "perhaps the most instrumental [writer] in widening the scope of the concept of distributive justice," Jerome Wakefield has applied Rawls's concepts to the practice of psychotherapy by social workers (Wakefield, 1988, p. 193). His conclusions are discussed below, in the section on Social Work and Social Justice.

Rawls's concept of social justice contrasts sharply with the libertarian view in its treatment of the disadvantaged. Under this general conception of justice, inequality is tolerable only when it benefits the least-advantaged members of society. For Rawls, the welfare problem would be turned on its head. Welfare mothers themselves would not be seen as "the problem." Instead, concern would focus on the presence of extreme wealth that does not contribute to the well-being of the poor.

A UTILITARIAN APPROACH (JOHN STUART MILL). In his essay "On the Connection Between Justice and Utility," John Stuart Mill sought to describe justice (Mill, 1863). He began with the premise that humans have a natural "feeling of justice"—that we intuitively recognize and respond negatively to injustice. But that feeling of justice stems from the pursuit of social well-being. Mill argues that justice must be understood as that which is most "useful" to society as a whole or, to use his terms, that which generates the highest "utility"—the greatest good or well-being—for the greatest number.

A sub-group of utilitarian liberals called "Egalitarians" argue that the highest utility is achieved through equal distribution of wealth and income. This conclusion is based on a "diminishing returns" argument, which holds that the satisfaction arising from possessing a good diminishes as the good becomes less scarce. Stated more concretely, a poor man will value an additional $50 per month more highly than a rich one. So, as Dalton argued, "unequal distribution of a given amount of purchasing power among a given number of people is . . . likely to be a wasteful distribution from the point of view of economic welfare" (Dalton, 1925, p. 84). In other words, giving the additional $50 to the rich man produces less overall well-being than giving it to the poor man.

Central to the utilitarian argument is the principle that the happiness of each person is valued equally. For Mill, this "involves an equal claim to all the means of happiness except insofar as the inevitable conditions of human life *and the general interest in which that of every individual is included set limits to the maxim*" (Sterba, 1980, p. 103, italics added). Mill argued that unequal access to "the means of happiness" is justified only when it is in the interest of society as a whole—unlike Rawls, who argued that inequality must favor the least advantaged members of that society.

Mill suggested that our perception of social inequalities as "unjust" stems from their lacking social expediency. Writing in 1863, he stated:

> The entire history of social improvement has been a series of transitions by which one custom or institution after another, from being a supposed primary necessity of social existence, has passed into the rank of a universally stigmatized injustice and tyranny. So it has been with the distinctions of slaves and freemen, nobles and serfs, patricians and plebeians; and so it will be, and in part already is, with the aristocracies of color, race, and sex (Mill, 1863, cited on p. 104 in Sterba).

While both contractual and utilitarian approaches would place limits on inequality in a just society, utilitarians might tolerate inequality if it produced greater good for society, regardless of its implications for the poor. Nonetheless, both perspectives place a high value on providing benefits to the disadvantaged.

In Melissa's case, both liberal approaches (contractual and utilitarian) would support intervention. From the viewpoint of a contractual liberal such as Rawls, Melissa's depression and abuse would place her below an acceptable social minimum. His philosophy would support the use of community resources to bring her above that minimum. A utilitarian liberal would emphasize Mill's concept of an intuitive feeling of justice. Within this perspective, our abhorrence to domestic violence is a clear indicator of injustice. Further, since a utilitarian liberal perspective values the happiness of each individual equally, relief of Melissa's suffering would merit the use of community resources.

SOCIALIST CONCEPTIONS OF SOCIAL JUSTICE

Distributive Principle: From each according to his ability;
to each according to his need.

Describing his vision of a communist utopia, Marx wrote, "In place of the old bourgeois society, with its classes and class antagonisms, we shall have an association, in which the free development of each is the condition for the free development of all" (Marx, 1888, cited on p. 195 in Sterba). Under socialism, justice would consist of each person contributing to the communal well-being to the extent of his or her ability. Free from the alienation imposed by a capitalist system, labor would become not a means, but an end—an activity done for its own sake.

In its ultimate form, justice under socialism would involve distribution "to each according to his need," but this goal would be reached only after a generation of workers had been raised in a cooperative society. For Marx, communist society "emerges from capitalist society" and thus is "still stamped with the birthmarks of the old society from whose womb it emerges" (Ibid., p. 197).

During the early phases of socialism, distributive justice would consist of returning to each according to his contribution. Several costs would first be subtracted from the "total social product," including (1) replacement of the means of production used up; (2) costs of expansion of production; (3) a reserve or insurance fund to provide against "misadventures, disturbances through natural events, etc.;" (4) costs of administration not belonging to production; (5) costs of meeting communal needs, such as schools and health services; and (6) funds for those unable to work.

The remainder, called the "diminished proceeds of labor," would be distributed to workers according to their work effort. Marx acknowledged that this would be an unequal distribution. Workers with greater strength or natural abilities contribute more work effort than those less fortunate. Also, workers who were supporting families would receive less per capita. But in Marx's view, "these defects are inevitable in the first phase of communist society. Right can never be higher than the economic structure of society and the cultural development thereby determined" (Ibid., p. 198).

A purely Marxist perspective would hold that the current status of the poor in America is the direct result of the oppression of laborers by those who own the means of production. In this view, welfare is yet another means of controlling the disadvantaged while maintaining the labor pool at a subsistence level. Debates regarding the welfare system are irrelevant, as this stage of societal development will inevitably yield to a higher one in which welfare will be obsolete.

A Marxist analysis of Melissa's situation might see her abuse as the natural result of the oppression of laborers. Growing up in a working-class setting, Melissa was systematically taught to devalue herself, just as a capitalist society devalues laborers. Similarly, Will's violence can be seen as a response to alienating work and limited opportunities. Indeed, this violence may be viewed by some Marxists as a harbinger of revolution. Intervention simply to alleviate the suffering would serve only to continue the oppression. A Marxist viewpoint would support intervention that would teach Melissa and Will to view their situation as part of a broader socio-economic context.

SUMMARY OF PHILOSOPHICAL APPROACHES

The distributive principles associated with each of these philosophical perspectives, as well as their implications for Melissa's situation, are summarized in Table 1.2.

The labels commonly assigned to these conceptions of social justice are best applied to ideas, not people. Each approach described here represents a pure type seldom found in human form. A "neo-Marxist" who publicly espouses the equality of humanity may dominate a household marked by rigid gender roles. A "libertarian" who values distribution of benefits on the basis of production may contribute generously to a favorite charity. Meanwhile, those of less clear-cut ideological persuasions may leapfrog from one philosophy to another as issues or personal interests dictate.

Effective policy practice requires the analytic capacity to respond to arguments stemming from these philosophical approaches. Equally important is the ability to communicate and argue without polarizing, rejecting, or demonizing those of divergent views. Social workers who are familiar with these conceptions will be able to "speak the language" of those whose world views differ from theirs. So, for example, when talking with a libertarian, an advocate for public assistance might find it more effective to emphasize the libertarian's loss of freedom when extremely poor people roam the streets. Utilitarian liberals might be persuaded by a presentation that simply articulates the suffering experienced by the disadvantaged. Contractual liberals are likely to respond to an explanation that emphasizes how deprivation reduces people to a level that is below certain acceptable standards (social minimums). A socialist audience may be attuned to the impacts of oppression but unsupportive of interventions that would perpetuate the status quo. Finally, while it is difficult to dispute an oligarchist's conviction that the social order is divinely (or genetically) controlled, it might be possible to persuade such a person that mercy toward those who are suffering is part of the divine plan.

We rarely find a distributive principle clearly labeled as such. Instead, as we listen to arguments and examine how policies work, we are able to identify their philosophical underpinnings. Thus, for example, when a legislator argues that "It is not fair that our tax dollars support women just because they are mothers—welfare mothers should work for their money like the rest of us," the leg-

TABLE 1.2 SUMMARY OF PHILOSOPHICAL APPROACHES TO SOCIAL JUSTICE

Philosophical Perspective	Distributive Principle	Approach to Melissa
Oligarchy	"From each according to his status; to each according to his status."	Melissa's working-class status defines her opportunities and assigns her burdens. Abuse may be one of those burdens.
Libertarianism	"From each according to his choice; to each according to his product."	Melissa chose to marry Will. Will chose his job. Tax funds that are taken coercively from others should not be used to intervene in their lives.
Liberalism	"Economic liberty and political equality for all."	Intervention to bring Melissa above a social minimum is in order. Relief of her suffering will enhance community well-being.
Socialism	"From each according to his ability; to each according to his need."	Melissa's abuse is the natural result of capitalistic oppression of laborers. Intervention should educate her about the societal roots of her suffering.

islator is rejecting an oligarchic principle that says benefits should flow directly from status as a mother, and taking a libertarian perspective that one should be paid for economic productivity. An advocate who argues, "Welfare mothers are not able to work; we should support them because they need help!" is presenting a distributive principle drawn from a socialist philosophy. Finally, the student who argues that "It doesn't hurt Bill Gates to pay his taxes, and public programs make a huge difference in the quality of life of the poor" is taking a liberal (utilitarian) perspective.

In the remaining sections of this chapter we will focus on policy practice. We will begin by exploring three pervasive themes in policy practice. Next, we will present a brief biography of a leading policy practitioner. We will conclude the chapter by examining social justice as a defining mission for the social work profession.

SOCIAL JUSTICE APPLIED: THEMES IN POLICY PRACTICE

Three themes permeate policy practice by social workers:

1. Social justice is personal and political.
2. Social justice issues are ubiquitous.
3. Injustice undermines social bonds and nation-states.

These themes are discussed in greater detail below, with reference to Melissa's case.

SOCIAL JUSTICE IS PERSONAL AND POLITICAL

In response to cultural and historical pressures, many social workers "psychologize" human misery and ignore or avoid the political and economic dimensions of their clients' pain. They provide opportunities for introspection and personal change but fail to offer transformative insights rooted in understanding of broader social forces (Specht & Courtney, 1994; Saleebey, 1990). A therapist working in this vein might lead Melissa to see how her selection of a spouse was conditioned by childhood experiences, or encourage her to view her response to abuse as a symptom of low self-esteem.

Yet, as Dennis Saleebey noted, "Even the most private problems of relationship and consciousness have political and social dimensions" (1990, p. 38). A social worker might empower Melissa to seek transformative change by encouraging her to participate in an advocacy group such as JEDI Women. Participation in the group could increase Melissa's awareness of the social and political forces that contributed to her abuse, and she could begin to experience herself as a capable change agent. Failure to acknowledge the social and political roots of individual misery can leave professionals as well as their clients in what Jacoby

(1975) termed "the isolation that damns the individual to scrape along in a private world" (p. 44).

Social, economic, and political forces have influenced Melissa's life in many ways:

1. She was born into a society that does not provide universal family planning services. Melissa's parents had a large family. Melissa, herself, bore three children she could ill afford. Nor does the United States offer direct financial support to parents. Nations such as Germany and Sweden offer limited financial support to all parents in the form of children's allowances. This is a "universal" approach to the income maintenance needs of children. The U.S. has adopted a "residual" approach, providing public assistance only for the most needy.

2. Melissa's decision to leave high school during her first pregnancy may reflect a lack of support for education of pregnant teens. Although programs for teenage mothers have increased in recent years (see Chapter 8), they remain limited to major metropolitan areas where they serve only a small proportion of teen mothers.

3. Will's "good job" provided health benefits but did not offer career mobility. Lack of universal access to health care often traps workers in unrewarding jobs. The resulting tension may have contributed to Will's abuse of Melissa and the children.

4. Recent welfare reforms provided for treatment of Melissa's depression. Although depression often goes untreated (see Chapter 6), Melissa was fortunate that her state's welfare program supported identification and treatment of barriers to employment. With anti-depressant medication and counseling, Melissa can remain in transitional employment. Her ability to support her family will depend on continuing support through her state's welfare program. Mandates at either the state or the federal level might cut off that support through time limits on welfare (see Chapter 4).

5. Entering the labor market as an unskilled worker, Melissa will encounter the effects of discrimination against women (see Chapter 8). She may find employers who pay her 70 cents for work of "comparable worth" to that done by a man for a dollar. Or she may be unable to care for her children when they are ill because federal legislation exempts small companies from providing medical leave (see Chapter 5).

Clearly, social policies significantly influence the lives of Melissa and her family. Conversely, Melissa herself has affected public policy. By sharing her experiences, she helped mobilize key stakeholders to protect welfare in her state. She has also become active in a women's organization, thereby joining an emerging grassroots effort to give voice to the concerns of vulnerable women like herself. For Melissa this involvement triggered a transformation—she began to see herself not as a victim but as an agent of change.

Charity or Justice?

President George H. Bush promoted the concept of "a thousand points of light," arguing that volunteerism and charity should substitute for professional assistance and entitlement. In making this suggestion, the president articulated the view that instead of demanding their right to assistance the poor should ask for charitable support. This is compatible with a libertarian understanding of social justice, as it preserves the freedom of donors to deny aid—a liberty not enjoyed by taxpayers who are coerced into paying for entitlements. Charity also substitutes the warm glow of beneficence and personal gratitude for the cold bureaucratic exchange and the stigma associated with public assistance. Rather than demanding their rights, recipients of charity ask for help—behavior that the donors view as being much more appropriate from the lower classes.

Justice, on the other hand, confers rights—rights that society is obliged to defend. Recipients of assistance emerge, not as sympathetic individuals humbly asking for relief, but as members of an interest group using the politics of protest and the tools of jurisprudence to enforce public obligations. Bertha Reynolds and others have suggested that justice confers greater dignity on the recipient of assistance. For example, during the Depression she noted that to social workers' surprise, "They [clients] did not seem to feel the 'stigma' which social workers attached to assistance, and some, indeed, came to prefer public aid . . . to which they felt they were entitled, to private 'charity'" (Reynolds, 1963, p. 140).

SOCIAL JUSTICE ISSUES ARE UBIQUITOUS

In her feminist critique of major political theories of justice, Susan Okin argued that (with the rare exception of John Stuart Mill) philosophers from Aristotle to Marx have confined their discussions to the public sphere, from which women historically have been excluded. Yet, as Okin, Rousseau, Mill, and others have observed, the moral development of children takes place in families, not in courts or legislatures. It is primarily in families that we "learn to be just" (Okin, 1989, p. 297). Indeed, politicians and developmental psychologists alike have linked the structure and operation of families to the broader structure and operation of nations.

Clearly, social justice is a significant concern within families, just as it is in the workplace and in national policy. Indeed, social workers will find groups of various sizes struggling with the allocation of membership's costs and rewards. Social workers who promote social justice in a family context may have as much impact on the nation's well-being as those who confine themselves to legislative advocacy.

INJUSTICE UNDERMINES SOCIAL BONDS AND NATION-STATES

People often disagree when defining what is just. Like children, adults find it difficult to transcend self-interest and consider the well-being of the group as a whole. Central to this task is long-term commitment to the group. This commitment stems first from receiving the benefits of group membership, then from recognizing them as such, and later from observing that the benefits and costs of membership are fairly allocated. On a personal level, the thrill of newfound intimacy brings two individuals into a committed couple relationship. That relationship is sustained in large part by the partners' belief that the relationship is just—that costs and benefits are fairly allocated. On a broader level, nation-states do not endure when a significant number of their citizens view them as unjust. We have seen examples of this as autocratic regimes such as the Marcos reign in the Philippines have been overthrown by popular uprisings. By promoting social justice, social workers enhance the long-term stability of groups and nations.

SOCIAL WORKERS AS PROMOTERS OF SOCIAL JUSTICE

Bertha Capen Reynolds (1885–1978) was instrumental in promoting social justice both within and outside her profession. After examining Reynolds's contributions, we will discuss how social work professionals can continue to carry out her mission of working toward a just society.

BERTHA CAPEN REYNOLDS: A PROFILE

The Bertha Reynolds Society was established in 1985 to honor a singular figure in the social work profession. Bertha Capen Reynolds was one of the nation's first professionally trained social workers, with experience spanning the first half of the twentieth century. Her autobiography chronicles the personal development of an inquiring and sensitive practitioner who entered the profession determined to master the psychiatric techniques she and her peers believed were the key to unlocking human potential. After graduating from Smith College in 1918, Reynolds spent most of her career as Associate Director of the school's social work program. But her practice ranged from academic pursuits to serving and residing in residential facilities for the mentally ill, supervising social workers providing relief during the Depression, and serving the seamen's union during World War II.

During the Depression, Reynolds joined the "rank-and-file" social workers of her time to call for a new social order. Dissatisfied with the "passivity" she observed among caseworkers, Reynolds began to call for a professional commitment to community development. She noted that "the community is always involved in any professional relationship" (Reynolds, 1963, p. 147) and argued that "the future of social work is bound up with the coming of a sounder social order . . . the members of this profession have not only the obligation to work for justice which good citizenship applies, but the professional duty" (Ibid., p. 141).

Reynolds saw in Marxism the key to establishment of a sounder social order. At a student's suggestion she read the works of Marx and Engels and was persuaded that their theory of dialectical materialism accurately reflected the inevitable progress of society. She watched the development of the USSR with interest. Unfortunately, she did not live to observe its dissolution. Her intellectual response to today's events would undoubtedly enrich and inspire the profession.

With her own brand of "brilliant common sense," Reynolds observed a parallel between the psychodynamic theory of her early training and the Marxism she discovered later in life. Both saw conflict as a necessary prerequisite to growth, and both relied on the clash of opposites (id-ego and capitalist-proletariat) to produce a synthesis that represented a higher order of development.

Reynolds never married. She cultivated and treasured her close relationships, in some cases carrying on enduring correspondence with people she had never met. She said, "If one word is needed, then, to begin to sum up what fifty years of living have taught me, that word is *relatedness* . . . many people do not know that they stand in any particular place in society, and so they judge their viewpoint to be the only one possible for anybody. I believe it indispensable to a sound *relatedness* to others to know where one is to start with, for what biases and blind spots to make allowance, and to know that there exist other and quite different viewpoints" (Reynolds, 1963, pp. 314–315).

SOCIAL WORK AND SOCIAL JUSTICE

Bertha Reynolds saw social justice as the hallmark of the profession and argued that social work techniques are authentic only to the extent that they serve this mission. She suggested that activities that focus exclusively on what she called the "mental hygiene" of the client should not be considered social work. For Reynolds, the proper clients for social work were the needy. She offered principles for social work practice during the Depression, saying, "They were, first of all, that social work exists to serve people in need. If it serves other classes who have other purposes it becomes too dishonest to be capable of either theoretical or practical development" (Reynolds, 1963, p. 173).

Jerome Wakefield pursued the same line of reasoning to arrive at a more elaborate conclusion. He agreed that distributive justice is the "organizing value" of the profession and that "the purpose of social work is to see to it that anyone falling below the social minimum in any of the social primary goods is brought above that level in as many respects as possible" (Wakefield, 1988, p. 205).

But, as Wakefield noted, "for better or worse, social work has become one of the mental health professions" (Wakefield, 1988, p. 187). Noting that "Social workers probably provide more care for the severely mentally ill than any other professional group," The National Institute of Mental Health acknowledged social workers as important providers of mental health services in the United States (NIMH, 1992, p. 5; *see also* Task Force on Social Work Research, 1991). Further, the growth of private practice in social work is one of the most significant trends in the recent history of the profession. Between 1975 and 1985, the number of social workers in full-time private practice increased dramatically, so that in 1985, more than a third of the members of the National Association of Social Workers were engaged in private practice (Hardcastle, Social Work Labor Force, cited by Specht & Courtney, 1994).

Wakefield sought to integrate this trend with the overall mission of the profession by specifying the conditions under which psychotherapy promotes social justice. Relying on Rawls's conceptualization, Wakefield argued that "It is the focus on minimal distributive justice that differentiates clinical social work from traditional psychotherapy" (Wakefield, 1988, p. 206). Social workers focus on clients who are deprived, or who fall below a basic social minimum. So, for example, a professional woman whose fear of flying interferes with her advancement is not an appropriate target for social work intervention. Even with the fear of flying, she enjoys social benefits well above any social minimum.

But, as numerous authors have noted (e.g., Leighninger, 1990), the status and credibility of a profession are largely determined by the power and affluence of the people it serves. Social workers who focus on the concerns of the middle and professional classes enjoy a measure of security and stature. This is the case for social workers in private practice and those who work in Employee Assistance Programs (EAPs).

Indeed, social workers in these settings often struggle to integrate their professional mission of service to the needy with their day-to-day activities. Social workers in EAPs must regularly confront the reality that their paychecks depend on their ability to satisfy the members of the managerial ranks. Similarly, social workers in managed care environments increasingly confront the conflict between cost-containment goals and the care and treatment needs of patients. The ethical practice of social work requires that the needy individual, not his or her employer or health care provider, be the focus of concern.

SOCIAL JUSTICE AND POLICY ANALYSIS

A social justice perspective on policy analysis must be distinguished from an "interest group" approach. A social justice perspective asks, "Are the costs and benefits of group membership allocated fairly?" In contrast, an interest group perspective asks, "Is this a good deal for the people I serve?"

The social justice perspective requires a broad approach to analyzing social policy. Under this view, a policy that is beneficial for one needy group may not be just if it is financed through an oppressive tax on another vulnerable group. An interest group perspective might not concern itself with the financing mechanism, but simply with the benefits to the specific group.

An illustrative example: Shortly after completing a book on low-income older women I was asked to endorse a proposal to finance an increase in Medicare benefits by raising the payroll tax. The colleague who made the request was sure I would be sympathetic because I was worried about the status of older

TABLE 1.3 APPLICATION OF POLICY ANALYSIS FRAMEWORK

QUESTION 1: *What are the costs and/or benefits under consideration?* Benefits included prescription drug coverage. Costs were higher payroll taxes.

QUESTION 2: *Who bears the cost, who receives the benefits, and what is the relationship between these two entities?* Working Americans would bear the costs, and retirees would receive the benefits.

QUESTION 3: *Is anyone who is affected by this policy being labeled "other," and does everyone affected by this policy have an equal voice?* I do not believe membership is at issue here. Clearly the elderly have a strong voice in their representative organizations and the widespread perspective of their political clout. We would expect unions to represent the views of working Americans, but they do not seem to be weighing in on the issue. It is unclear whether the elderly and working Americans share equal voices on this issue. Low-wage workers seem to have less voice collectively than do the elderly.

QUESTION 4: *What are the rules, both formal and informal, that govern who receives and who pays?* Payroll taxes are paid on all income up to a cap. They are borne by low- and middle-income workers. Medicare benefits are received by all retirees, regardless of income.

QUESTION 5: *Is this policy fair?* Medicare beneficiaries would enjoy the benefit. Low-income beneficiaries certainly *need* the benefit. But wages have eroded in recent decades, and the payroll tax weighs heaviest on low-income workers and their families, millions of whom do not even have health insurance. My tentative conclusion was: "No, the proposed policy is not fair."

women, and they would clearly be better off with enhanced Medicare benefits. Indeed, she felt a little betrayed by my lack of enthusiasm for the proposal. My concerns stemmed from policy analysis using a social justice perspective. This analysis is outlined in Table 1.3.

SUMMARY: SOCIAL JUSTICE CONCEPTS

The pursuit of social justice resembles the quest for the Holy Grail. It is time-consuming and hazardous, its goal is ephemeral at best, and it is an integral part of the human experience. Policy practice, with its alternating victories and setbacks, brings social workers into this quest. Effective policy practice requires a clear vision of social justice and the ability to operate within existing social, economic, and political frameworks to promote that vision.

We began this chapter by providing a working definition of social justice: "the fair allocation of costs and benefits of group membership." To facilitate policy analysis, we presented a framework based on five questions. We introduced four philosophical perspectives on social justice, suggesting that familiarity with these approaches can help us analyze the basic assumptions underlying most social policies. Three themes of policy practice were discussed: social justice issues are personal and political, they are found at every level of human social organization, and failure to correct injustice can break up families and topple governments. Finally, we explored the role of social work and social workers in the search for social justice.

DISCUSSION TOPICS

1. Use an argument from a contemporary policy debate to illustrate one of the philosophical conceptions of social justice presented in this chapter. How might you refute that argument in a way that "speaks the language" of the person who holds this view?

2. Which of the four philosophical approaches is most congruent with your world view? Do your classmates differ in this regard? Are some conceptions not represented among them?

3. Identify a personal conflict or negotiation that involves the allocation of costs and/or rewards of group membership.

4. What if the members of a group agree that a practice (such as genital mutilation of young girls) is acceptable but an outside observer finds it abhorrent. Is the practice just? Does the outsider, a social work professional, have the responsibility to intervene if no one who is involved objects to the practice? What about the young girls? Do they have a voice?

SUGGESTED RESOURCES

Aristotle. *Nicomachean Ethics*. Chapter V: The Varieties of Justice. Translated by D. Bostock. New York: Oxford University Press, 2000.

Mill, J. S. (1863). *Utilitarianism*. Released in 1998 by R. Crisk (Ed.). New York: Oxford University Press.

Reynolds, B. C. (1963). *An Uncharted Journey: Fifty Years of Growth in Social Work*. New York: Citadel Press.

Sterba, J. P. (1998). *Justice for Here and Now*. New York: Cambridge University Press.

2

The Government's
Role

In Chapter 1 we noted that the central mission of the social work profession is to promote social justice. Our focus in this chapter will be the role of government in advancing social justice. The structure of the U.S. government will be described along two dimensions: "levels" and "branches." We will emphasize that despite its complexity, the U.S. government must be seen, not as an end-point for democracy, but as the latest stage in a continuing evolutionary process. The chapter closes with a brief overview of U.S. tax policy. It is vital that social workers understand the tax system. Taxation is an important tool of social policy, not only because it usually represents the "cost" side of the social justice equation, but also because tax policy is used with increasing frequency to accomplish social policy goals. Taxes provide the resources that permit collective responses to individual problems.

LEVELS OF GOVERNMENT

Governance in the U.S. is shared among three levels of government: federal, state, and local. At the federal level, Congress is vested by the Constitution with the power to tax, provide for the common defense and general welfare, borrow money, regulate interstate commerce, manage immigration and naturalization, regulate bankruptcies, coin money, set standards for weights and measures, establish post offices, issue patents and copyrights, establish courts, declare war, raise and support military forces, and protect civil rights.

The structures of state governments mirror those of the federal government. Like the federal legislative branch, nearly all states have bicameral legislatures (that is, legislatures made up of two houses, such as a Senate and a House of Representatives).[1] Similarly, the federal courts have parallel entities in the various

---

[1] At the time of this writing, only Nebraska has a unicameral legislature, but Minnesota is considering a proposal to establish one.

---

state judicial systems. Finally, at both federal and state levels the executive branch consists of a head of state (the president or governor), an appointed cabinet, and a cadre of civil servants who implement policy. Governments at county and city levels typically consist of two branches, with legislative entities such as county commissions or city councils, and an executive branch consisting of a mayor or city manager and the employees of various city or county agencies.

Overlapping areas of authority among the various levels of government can create confusion about which entity is responsible for addressing a given problem. A recurring theme in U.S. history has been the struggle to determine the nexus of authority for social policy. As we will see in Chapter 10, the civil rights movement often called upon federal authority to restrict state discretion. Nevertheless, the federal government enjoys no *authority* over state governments except that which pertains to constitutional violations. In a vivid example of this tension between federal control and state or local control, the Social Security Act of 1935 was subjected to court challenge on the grounds that it represented abuse of federal taxing authority (see Chapter 3). Today, state officials frequently claim the federal government has exceeded its constitutional authority or placed unmanageable demands (such as "unfunded mandates") on state governments. This complaint is often lodged in relation to federal grant-in-aid programs.

A "grant-in-aid" or "block grant" extends the capacity of the federal government to pursue a social agenda. Through grants-in-aid, the federal government offers money to states on the condition that they abide by federal regulations governing these programs. In this way the federal government can expand social programs that might arguably extend beyond its constitutional authority. For example, states elect to participate in the Medicaid program and receive federal funding to provide medical care to low-income residents. The medical care that is provided must conform to the requirements of federal law. Thus, the federal law has expanded and regulated health care for the needy. At the same time, participating states must pay part of the costs of their Medicaid programs. This required "match" fuels governors' protests that the federal government is imposing on states' authority. In the late 1990s, an emerging (or *re*-emerging) "states' rights" movement exerted considerable pressure to reduce the federal regulations governing Medicaid and to assign greater power to state governments (see Chapter 5).

Just as there is often tension between *levels* of government, there is also dispute about the proper roles of the legislative, executive, and judicial *branches* of government in social policy development. For example, some argue that the *Roe v. Wade* decision that established a woman's right to abortion moved the Supreme Court into an "activist" role in which it legislated social policy rather than simply interpreting the laws. In the following section we will describe the operations of the three branches of government at the federal level and discuss the processes through which they establish social policy.

BRANCHES OF GOVERNMENT

Social workers—indeed, anyone interested in influencing policy—must be conversant with how the branches of government operate, because each of these entities plays a role in social policy. Put simply, the legislative branch passes the laws that we think of as social policies. The executive branch issues regulations that determine how laws will be implemented and, in many cases, directly implement social policy. The judicial branch issues opinions that interpret laws and create a body of case law that also constitutes social policy. Thus, in-depth research of a social policy should address the contributions of all three branches of government: legislation (legislative branch), regulations (executive branch), and opinions (judicial branch).

THE LEGISLATIVE BRANCH

"All Legislative Powers herein granted shall be vested in a Congress of the United States, which shall consist of a Senate and House of Representatives" (Article I, Section 1, *United States Constitution*).

The U.S. Congress consists of a Senate and a House of Representatives. The Senate has 100 members, two from each state. Members of the Senate serve six-year terms. The House of Representatives has 435 members, with each state's representation being proportionate to the size of its population. At the time of this writing, the most populous state in the U.S. is California, which has 52 members in the House. The smallest delegations come from the states of Delaware, Montana, North Dakota, South Dakota, Vermont, and Wyoming, which have one representative apiece. Members of the House serve two-year terms. The primary functions of the U.S. Congress are legislation (creation of laws) and budgeting (collection and allocation of public funds).

LEGISLATION. Legislation begins with a proposal in the form of a bill or a resolution.[2] A bill is used for most legislation. Bills originating in the House of Representatives are designated by the letters "H.R.," while those originating in the Senate begin with "S." These letters are followed by a number that the bill retains until it is enacted into law.

Any House member may introduce a bill at any time while the House is in session. Traditionally, a receptacle known as the "hopper" is provided for this purpose beside the clerk's desk in the House chamber, hence the expression "put it in the hopper," which means to introduce an idea or proposal. The sponsor's signature must appear on the bill. A bill may have an unlimited number of

---

[2]Most of the information presented in this section is found in a congressional document called *How Our Laws Are Made*, available through the U.S. House of Representatives.

co-sponsors. It is assigned a number by the clerk and referred to the appropriate committee by the Speaker of the House. The bill is then printed.

The Speaker of the House enjoys some discretion in deciding which committee will receive a bill, and thus can greatly influence its fate. For example, the Speaker can slow a bill's progress by forwarding it to a committee that is hostile to its intent. Consideration by committees is an important phase of the legislative process. It is the time when the public has an opportunity to be heard. Usually the first step in this process is a public hearing in which committee members hear testimony from witnesses representing diverse viewpoints. Each committee publicly announces the date, place, and subject of any hearing it conducts. A transcript of testimony taken at the hearing is frequently printed and distributed by the committee.

After the hearings are completed, the bill is reviewed in what is popularly known as a "mark-up" session. Here members of the committee study the bill and review related testimony. Amendments may be offered, and committee members vote to accept or reject these changes.

When the committee has finished its deliberations, a vote is taken to determine what action to take on a bill. The bill may be reported, with or without amendment, or tabled, which means no further action will occur. If the committee has approved extensive amendments it may decide to report a new bill. This is known as a "clean bill," which will have a new number. If the committee votes to report a bill, the report is written by a committee staff member. It describes the measure and reasons for approval. Committee reports are excellent sources of information for students and policy members interested in studying Congressional intent.

Although consideration of a bill generally occurs only after it is reported out of committee, some measures are brought directly to the floor by the Speaker. Consideration of a bill may be governed by a resolution that sets out the debate procedures for the specific measure. Specific aspects, such as the amount of time allowed for debate and whether amendments can be offered, may be determined at this time. Debate time for a measure is usually divided between proponents and opponents. Each side yields time to members who wish to speak on the bill. When amendments are offered, these are also debated and voted on. After debate is concluded and amendments determined, the House votes on final passage. In some cases, a vote to "recommit" the bill to committee is requested. This is usually an effort by opponents to change or table the measure. If a vote to recommit fails, a final vote is ordered.

The standing rules of the Senate differ from those of the House in that they permit Senators to debate at length. Debate cannot be ended by a simple majority. This right of extended debate permits filibusters that can be brought to an end only if "cloture" is invoked through a vote of three-fifths of all Senators. Senators also enjoy the right to propose floor amendments that are not germane to the matter under consideration. Thus, individual senators can raise issues and subject them to vote even if they have not been reviewed by a standing committee.[3] Although it is within their rights, Senators do not filibuster every measure they oppose. To do so would seriously impede the Senate's functioning. Filibusters are reserved for issues on which Senators hold strong opinions.

After a measure passes in its originating chamber (either the House or the Senate) it passes to the other chamber. It must pass both bodies in the same form before it can be presented to the President for signature. If either chamber changes the measure, it must return to the originating chamber for concurrence or additional changes. This negotiation may occur on the Floor. Often a conference committee will be appointed with both House and Senate members. This group will resolve differences and report identical versions to both sides for a vote. Conference committees also issue reports outlining the final version of the bill.

After a bill has passed both the House and Senate, it is considered "enrolled" and is sent to the President, who may (1) sign the measure into law; (2) veto it and return it to Congress (where a two-thirds vote is required to override his veto); (3) let it become law without signature; or (4) if the bill arrives at the end of a session, give it a "pocket-veto"—that is, if Congress has adjourned and the President does not sign a bill, it is automatically vetoed.

RESOLUTIONS. Generally speaking, a resolution differs from a bill in that it does not become law, but is either an expression of the opinion of Congress or an administrative act governing the operation of Congress. Resolutions may originate in either the House of Representatives or the Senate. Like bills, resolutions are numbered sequentially, with a brief designation that reflects their origins. Those introduced in the House of Representatives are numbered with the designation "HRES," which stands for "House Resolution." Those originating in the Senate are designated "SRES," for "Senate Resolution." Joint resolutions (designated "HJRES" or "SJRES") become law in the same manner as bills. The only exceptions to this rule are joint resolutions proposing an amendment to the Constitution. Upon approval of such a resolution by two-thirds of both House and Senate, it is not sent to the President, but to the Administrator of General Services for submission to the individual states for ratification. Such was the case with the Equal Rights Amendment, discussed in detail in Chapter 8.

BUDGETING.[4] Budgeting is a gargantuan task in the United States, involving both executive and legislative branches. The calendar complicates public understanding of the process. The federal budget year or "fiscal" year extends from October 1 through September 30 (see Table 2.1). The President is required by

---

[3]I am grateful to Stanley Bach, Senior Specialist in the Legislative Process, Government Division, for his discussion of the rights of Senators and his introduction to Senate processes.

[4]Much of the content in this section is drawn from *A Citizen's Guide to the Federal Budget*, available through the Office of Management and Budget.

law to submit his proposed federal budget for the next fiscal year to Congress by the first Monday in February. This proposed budget is prepared by the White House Office of Management and Budget (OMB), under the President's direction and with consultation from Cabinet members and other senior officials. The President's budget typically consists of several volumes, covering thousands of pages. But it is only a proposal, and it is subject to Congressional approval.

Congress first passes a "budget resolution" that outlines the framework for budget decisions. It includes total spending targets, revenue projections, deficit figures, and spending targets for two types of spending: discretionary and mandatory (OMB, 2001a). *Discretionary spending* represents about a third of all federal spending, the portion that the President and Congress may spend through 13 annual appropriations bills. *Mandatory spending*, roughly two-thirds of federal spending, is authorized by permanent laws. It includes entitlements, such as Social Security, Medicare, veterans' benefits, and food stamps. It also includes interest on the national debt. Changes in mandatory spending require revisions in the laws governing these programs.

Current legislation restricts the power of Congress to increase the deficit. As a result, increases in mandatory spending or tax reductions must be offset by spending cuts. This requirement, called "pay-as-you-go," is designed to prevent further increases in the deficit. Congressional examination of the President's budget consists of hearings and meetings by scores of committees and subcommittees.

It is important to remember that despite a plethora of technical details, budgeting is a political process characterized by negotiation. Budget negotiations are

TABLE 2.1 Major Steps in the Federal Budget Process

Budget Step	Budget Activities	Time Frame
1. President formulates budget for FY 2002.	Agencies in Executive Branch develop their budget requests for submission to Office of Management and Budget. President reviews requests and develops budget.	February – December 2000
2. Budget is transmitted.	Budget documents are prepared and sent to Congress by OMB.	December 2000 – February/March 2001
3. Congress reviews and approves budget.	Congress reviews the President's proposals, passes its "budget resolution," holds hearings and approves annual appropriations bills.	March – September 2001
4. The fiscal year begins.		October 1, 2001
5. The budget is implemented.	Under supervision of the OMB and General Accounting Office, agencies use the funds appropriated.	October 1, 2001 – September 30, 2002
6. Actual spending and receipts are tabulated.	Agencies and OMB prepare reports on outlays and receipts.	October – November 2002

carried out under time pressure, and failure to reach compromise can produce massive disruption. Such was the case in 1995, when federal agencies closed temporarily because of the lack of an approved budget.

WHERE THE MONEY GOES. In 2001, the federal government budget authorized approximately $1.8 trillion in expenditures (OMB, 2001a). Mandatory spending, described above, accounts for most federal spending. The largest federal program is Social Security. In 2001, this program, which provides monthly benefits to more than 45 million Americans, accounted for 23 percent of federal spending. The next largest mandatory spending category is interest on the national debt. In 2001, interest accounted for 11 percent of federal spending. Interest on the debt increased dramatically in the 1980s. From an average 7 percent of federal spending during the 1960s and '70s, the deficits of the 1980s quickly doubled this proportion. The budget surpluses of the late '90s lowered the amount of the budget that is devoted to interest payments. Medicare, which provides health coverage for more than 40 million Americans, is the third largest expenditure. In 2001 it represented 12 percent of federal spending. Medicaid, which provided health care to more than 34 million Americans, is jointly funded by state and federal governments. The federal share of Medicaid funding represented 7 percent of federal spending in 2001. Other means-tested entitlements, including Food Stamps, Aid to Families with Dependent Children, Supplemental Security Income, Child Nutrition, the Earned Income Tax Credit, and veterans' pensions, accounted for another 6 percent of federal spending in 2001. Other entitlements, mainly consisting of federal retirement programs and payments to farmers, amounted to 6 percent of 2001 spending.

Discretionary spending is usually divided into two categories. *National defense* discretionary spending amounted to approximately $292 billion in 2001, comprising 16 percent of federal spending and half of all discretionary spending. *Non-defense* discretionary spending funds a wide array of programs, including education, training, science, technology, housing, transportation, and foreign aid. This category accounted for an estimated 19 percent of 2001 federal spending, down from 23 percent in 1966. See Figure 2.1.

After the President and Congress approve a budget, it is monitored by agency managers and budget officials, the OMB, congressional committees, and the General Accounting Office, an auditing arm of Congress.

THE EXECUTIVE BRANCH

Headed by the Chief Executive (the President), the executive branch is organized into 14 departments, each represented by a member of the President's Cabinet.

Among the cabinet-level departments, social workers are most familiar with the **Department of Health and Human Services**. This department includes the Administration for Children and Families, Administration on Aging, Health Care Financing Administration, Centers for Disease Control and Prevention, Food and

Drug Administration, National Institutes of Health, National Institute of Mental Health, and National Library of Medicine. Social programs and programs with social implications are also housed in other departments, often for historical reasons.

For example, the Food Stamp program is administered by the **Department of Agriculture**, which oversees the Forest Service, Natural Resources Conservation Service, Food and Consumer Service, National Agricultural Library, and National Agricultural Statistics Service. Other programs in this department with implications for social policy include farm subsidies, commodities distribution, and food price supports. The Food Stamp program, which will be described in detail in Chapter 3, is located in the Department of Agriculture because it was designed, not primarily as a nutritional supplement, but as a vehicle for stabilizing the demand for agricultural products.

The **Department of the Interior** is also involved in the direct provision of social services and health care through the Bureau of Indian Affairs (BIA). This department also includes the Bureau of Land Management, U.S. Bureau of Mines, Bureau of Reclamation, Minerals Management Service, National Biological Service, National Park Service, Office of Surface Mining, U.S. Fish and Wildlife Service, and U.S. Geological Survey. Health and social programs for Native Americans are generally implemented by the BIA. Issues related to the BIA are discussed in more depth in Chapter 10.

Although military and social spending are often viewed as being separate from each other (a popular bumper sticker reads: "Won't it be nice when schools have plenty of money and the Army has to hold a bake sale to build a bomber?"), the **Department of Defense** provides a wide range of social and health services for

FIGURE 2.1 THE FEDERAL GOVERNMENT DOLLAR—WHERE IT GOES

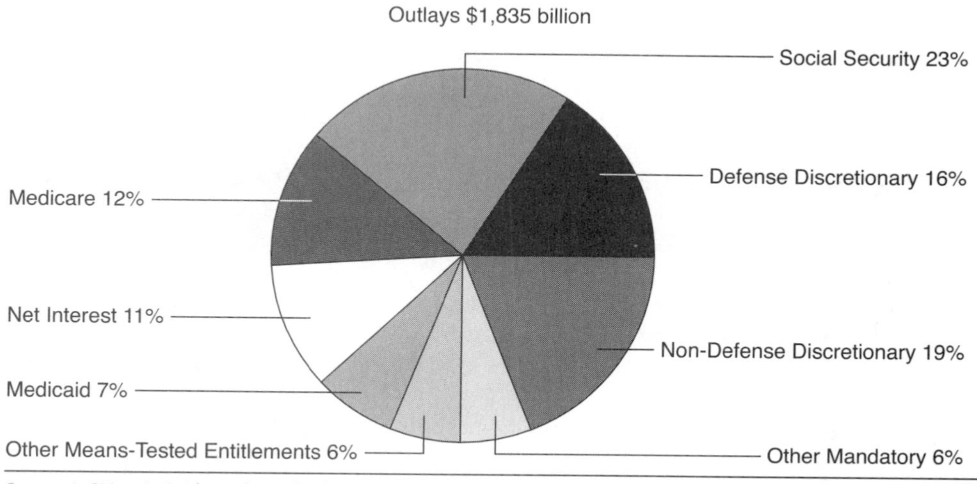

Outlays $1,835 billion

Social Security 23%

Defense Discretionary 16%

Medicare 12%

Net Interest 11%

Non-Defense Discretionary 19%

Medicaid 7%

Other Means-Tested Entitlements 6%

Other Mandatory 6%

Source: A Citizen's Guide to the Federal Budget, http://w3.access.gpo.gov/usbudget/FY2001/guide02.html.

military personnel and their dependents, and it is a major employer of professional social workers in many jurisdictions. The Department of Defense includes the
Joint Chiefs of Staff, Army, Navy, Air Force, and Marine Corps. Similarly, the **Department of Veterans Affairs**, only recently advanced to the Cabinet level, offers
services (primarily health care) to veterans of the armed services.

The **Department of Commerce** includes the Census Bureau, Bureau of
Economic Analysis, Economic Development Administration, Minority Business
Development Agency, Patent and Trademark Office, and National Technical Information Service. Decisions made about the Census often affect the nature of
the information on which social policy is based. For example, the Census treatment of ethnic minorities in the U.S. has changed in recent decades to reflect
broader changes in our understanding of the role of culture in individual lives.
Sampling techniques used by the Census are often controversial because they
may under- or over-represent certain groups.

The **Department of Housing and Urban Development (HUD)** has a
mandate to address issues related to community planning and development and
fair housing, but increasingly finds itself addressing social policy issues through
its attempts to meet the needs of residents of public housing. Programs under
HUD are described in detail in Chapter 4. Its agencies include the Federal
Housing Administration and the Government National Mortgage Association
("Ginnie Mae").

The **Department of Education** is charged with implementing national educational policy. The **Department of Justice** includes the Office of the Attorney
General of the U.S., Federal Bureau of Investigation, Drug Enforcement Administration, Federal Bureau of Prisons, Immigration and Naturalization Service, and
the U.S. Marshals Service. The **Department of Labor** includes the Bureau of
Labor Statistics, Occupational Safety and Health Administration, Office of Small
Business and Minority Affairs, and the Women's Bureau.

A few of the Cabinet-level departments have relatively little direct involvement in social policy. The **Department of State** is charged with carrying out foreign policy and diplomatic efforts. The **Department of Energy** provides scientific and technical information and educational support to encourage efficient
energy use and diversity in energy sources. The **Department of the Treasury**
includes the Internal Revenue Service; Customs Service; Bureau of Engraving and
Printing; Secret Service; U.S. Mint; and Bureau of Alcohol, Tobacco and Firearms.
The **Department of Transportation** includes the Bureau of Transportation
Statistics, Federal Aviation Administration, Federal Highway Administration,
National Highway Traffic Safety Administration, and U.S. Coast Guard.

The **Social Security Administration** and the **U.S. Postal Service** are
among twenty-three independent agencies that are not represented by a Cabinet-
level official.

The executive branch is far and away the largest employer in the federal system. As of 1996, nearly 3 million people (2,767,480) worked as civilian employ-

ees of this branch. Nearly one-third of these (31 percent) worked for the U.S. Postal Service. After the Postal Service, the Department of Defense is the second largest employer, with a civilian work force of 779,458 in 1996. The Department of Veterans Affairs comes next, employing 249,902 civilians in 1996. Health and Human Services pales by comparison, with 58,543 in its 1996 payroll, as does the Social Security Administration, with 65,984 employees in the same year (U.S. Office of Personnel Management, 1997).

THE REGULATORY PROCESS. While many assume that the executive branch simply "executes" but does not "create" policy, this perception is inaccurate. Through the regulatory process the executive branch translates legislation into services, resources, and decisions that directly affect individuals. Rules and regulations established by executive agencies have the force of law.

At the federal level[5] rulemaking is primarily governed by the Administrative Procedures Act (APA), which has several provisions that allow for public participation. Usually rulemaking is initiated in response to legislative action, but the APA does allow for the public to petition an agency to begin rulemaking. Once the process begins, the APA requires that departments develop a "rulemaking record" that reflects both public participation and the factual conclusions on which the rule is based. Rulemaking must begin with a period of "notice and comment." Agencies provide public notice of their intent to begin rulemaking by publishing a statement in the Federal Register. Often this statement is accompanied by press releases, as well as targeted electronic notices. Agencies must allow a reasonable period for public comment. While not specified by law, the public comment period is usually at least 60 days. At the end of this period, the agency prepares a summary of comments received and its response to those comments. This summary is followed either by a new cycle of notice and comments or by publication of the rule (Lubbers, 1998).

Since 1990, a procedure known as "negotiated rulemaking" (or "neg reg") has been allowed. This involves bringing interested parties into the process at an early stage and involving them in the drafting of the rule. Agencies that anticipate controversy over a regulation might use "neg reg" to reach a compromise among key players before the period of public comment.

An advocate's participation in rulemaking can take three forms. First, the advocate may petition an agency to begin rulemaking. Second, during the notice and comment period, an advocate can comment on a proposed rule and offer revisions. Finally, an advocate who is identified as an interested party can participate in negotiated rulemaking. Social work advocates naturally pay close attention to the legislative process. But failure to participate in the regulatory process can seriously undermine an advocacy effort.

---

[5]States have their own laws that govern rulemaking by state agencies. These laws are typically called Administrative Procedures Acts.

The Judicial Branch[6]

"The Judicial Power of the United States shall be vested in one Supreme Court, and in such inferior courts as the Congress may from time to time ordain and establish" (Article III, *United States Constitution*).

There are two judicial systems in the United States: the *Supreme Court and federal court system* created by Congress under the authority of the Constitution and the *state and local courts* established by state governments.

The structure of the federal court system has varied throughout the nation's history. Under the Constitution, the only indispensable court is the Supreme Court, and Congress has established and abolished other courts over time. The current federal system includes the Supreme Court, 13 U.S. Courts of Appeals, and 94 U.S. District Courts and specialized courts. The U.S. Courts of Appeals serve 12 regions (in addition to the 12 regional courts, there is a "federal court of appeals") and for historical reasons they are often referred to as "circuit" courts. In the nineteenth century, judges in courts of appeals rode "circuit" on horseback, visiting courts in the region.

Most controversies are decided in the state courts, because the power of federal courts is restricted. Under Article III of the Constitution, federal courts may decide "Controversies between two or more states; between a State and Citizens of another State; between Citizens of different States; [or] between Citizens of the same State claiming Lands under Grants of different States." Federal courts also hear cases in which the U.S. government or one of its officers is suing someone or being sued, as well as cases for which state courts might be biased or inappropriate.

Federal cases originate in District Courts, and may be reviewed by courts of appeals upon the request of one party. The final appeal in a few cases is heard in the Supreme Court. For example, the case of *Roe v. Wade* involved a class action suit challenging criminal abortion laws in Texas. A three-judge District Court from the Northern District of Texas declared the state's abortion statutes void. The case was argued in 1971 before the Supreme Court, which also declared the Texas statutes unconstitutional. This case is discussed in more detail in Chapter 8.

The Supreme Court of the United States consists of nine justices appointed for life by the President, with advice and consent of the Senate. In the nation's history, all but 27 Supreme Court justices nominated by a President have secured Senate confirmation. Each justice is assigned to one of the district courts of appeals for emergency responses (urgent appeals that cannot wait until the full court is in session), and the Chief Justice assumes additional administrative responsibilities. The Supreme Court convenes each year on the first Monday in October and usually remains in session until the end of June. During this period, the Court reviews about 5,000 cases annually. In most, a brief decision is

---

[6]Much of the material in this section is drawn from *Understanding the Federal Courts*, available through the Judicial Council.

offered, indicating that the case is not of sufficient importance to warrant review. Each year about 150 cases of great national importance are reviewed by the entire court.

While officers of the Supreme Court are called "justices," those presiding over courts of appeals, district courts, and other courts are called "judges." All federal judges are appointed by the President with the advice and consent of the Senate. Most judicial appointments are for life or, in the language of the Constitution, they "hold their Offices during good Behavior." These judges may be removed from office against their will only through "impeachment for, and conviction of Treason, Bribery, or other high Crimes and Misdemeanors." Between 1789 and 1992, 2,627 men and women served as federal judges. Of those, 184 or 7 percent resigned for reasons other than health or age. In the last 200 years, Congress has removed seven federal judges following contested impeachment proceedings. Further, between 1818 and 1980, at least 22 judges have resigned or retired following allegations of misbehavior (Van Tassel, Wirtz, & Wonders, 1993).

The judicial system, like the executive branch, often plays an important role in social policy development. For example, efforts to establish federal programs have often been subjected to challenge in federal courts. These efforts have included the Child Labor Act, which was twice declared unconstitutional, and the Social Security Act, which was successfully defended against a constitutional challenge. Disputes over federal entitlements such as Supplemental Security Income have typically been heard by federal courts. Indeed, some opponents of federal entitlements have argued that they clog the federal courts with disputes between citizens and states.

In this section we have examined the basic structure of the U.S. government in terms of both "levels" and "branches." It takes only a basic level of understanding of human behavior to see that there are inevitable tensions among these levels and branches. The authors of the Constitution understood and anticipated these tensions and crafted "checks and balances" to prevent the concentration of power in any single individual or entity. In the following section we will consider one of the most basic uses of governmental power: taxation.

THE U.S. TAX SYSTEM: A BRIEF INTRODUCTION[7]

Benjamin Franklin is often quoted as saying that only two things are inevitable: death and taxes. The two are sometimes approached with equal dread! No one likes to pay taxes. Indeed, public polls have revealed that a majority of Americans have cheated on their tax returns. Some of us spend more money on

---

[7]This section draws heavily from the third edition of a law text by Michael J. Graetz and Deborah Schenk, *Federal Income Taxation: Principles and Policies*, and the advice of a singular tax attorney, Lawrence Barusch.

tax-avoidance schemes than the schemes ever save us in taxes. There is something intrinsically satisfying about avoiding taxes. Throughout the nation's history, policy-makers have tapped into this mind-set, using it to advance social agen-
das through the judicious use of tax credits and deductions. In this section we
will first examine the basic structure of the U.S. tax system and then describe the
use of taxation to accomplish social goals.

STRUCTURAL AND PHILOSOPHICAL CONSIDERATIONS

Americans pay taxes to each level of government. As with legislative processes,
taxes at lower levels generally mirror those at the federal level. There is one
exception to this general rule: sales taxes, which are not applied at the federal
level but are levied at state, county, and even city levels.

With the exception of one clause (Article I, Section 2, Clause 3) requiring that
taxes be fairly apportioned among the states, there are few constitutional limits
on the taxation authority of the federal government. Congress has the power to
"lay and collect Taxes, Duties, imposts and excises, to pay the Debts and provide for the common Defence and general Welfare of the United States" (Article
I, Section 8, clause 1). Nonetheless, both income and Social Security taxes have
been subjected to constitutional challenges. The Sixteenth Amendment, passed
in 1913, affirmed the authority of the federal government to levy income taxes.
Two Supreme Court cases upheld the constitutionality of the Social Security tax
(see Chapter 10).

The utilitarian liberal philosophical perspective introduced in Chapter 1
emphasizes the distinction between "regressive" and "progressive" taxes. A regressive tax is one that falls most heavily on the poor. For example, a head tax exacts
the same amount from each person. Since poor people have less money, the tax
represents a greater proportion of a poor person's resources. The rate of a progressive tax increases as a person's affluence increases, and so the amount of tax
paid is greater for the wealthy. Simply put, progressive taxes are based on the taxpayer's ability to pay. The federal income tax is a progressive tax, while sales and
payroll taxes are regressive.

The rationale for progressive taxation stems directly from a liberal, utilitarian tradition. Under this philosophy, the goal of policy is to optimize well-being,
or (since we're talking about taxes here) to minimize distress. If an individual is
at, or very close to, a social minimum, taking 30 percent of his or her income
will place the person at a significant disadvantage. But if someone is well above
a social minimum, taking 30 percent of his or her income will create much less
distress. Or, to put it more simply, if you have two dollars and I take one of them,
you will be unable to buy a half-gallon of milk. But if you have two hundred
dollars and I take $100, or even $125, you will be able to buy much more than
a half-gallon of milk. Under this view (which dominates federal, and to a lesser
extent, state income tax structures), the community as a whole experiences less
distress with a progressive tax than with a regressive one.

John Rawls's concept of a social minimum offers a second argument in favor of progressive taxation. Under this view, a regressive tax puts a larger proportion of the population below an acceptable minimum standard of living than a progressive tax would.

FEDERAL INCOME TAX. The federal income tax is a progressive tax: the proportion of income subject to tax increases as a taxpayer's income rises. A simplified illustration: Consider five taxpayers. In 2000, taxpayer A had $25,000 in taxable income, taxpayer B had $50,000, taxpayer C had $100,000, taxpayer D had $200,000, and taxpayer E had $400,000. Taxpayer E would not only pay the highest absolute dollar amount in income tax, but also a higher *proportion* of his or her income.

Each person's tax would be assessed by dividing the income into steps or "brackets." The 2000 Tax Rate Schedule included five brackets. These are illustrated in Figure 2.2.

Federal income tax brackets are adjusted annually for inflation. From time to time, they are also changed through tax legislation. By the time you read this chapter, the brackets for federal income tax will no doubt be different. Nonetheless, these specific figures should help you understand the general concepts. In 2000, taxpayer A would have paid 15 percent of taxable income, or $3,750, in taxes. On the first $26,250 of income, taxpayer B would pay the same proportion as A. For income in the next bracket, B would pay the next higher rate, 28 percent. So B would pay $3,938 (15 percent of $26,250) plus $6,650 (28 percent of the remaining $23,750). Taxpayer B's total tax bill would be $10,588, or 21 percent of his or her total income of $50,000. Taxpayer E would pay the most tax and the highest rate. Taxpayer E's tax is computed using all five of the steps in the above illustration: $3,938 (15 percent of 26,250) plus $10,444 (28 percent of $37,300) plus $21,592 (31 percent of 69,050) plus $56,070 (36 percent of $155,750) plus $44,213 (39.6 percent of the remaining income over $288,350, or $111,650). Taxpayer E's total tax bill would amount to $136,257, or 34 percent of the total taxable income of $400,000. Thus, E's *average rate* of taxation, 34 percent, is the rate paid on each dollar of income. E's *marginal rate* would be 39.6

FIGURE 2.2 FEDERAL INCOME TAX BRACKETS (**2000** RATES)

Taxable Income	A	B	C	D	E
	\multicolumn{5}{c}{Hypothetical Taxpayer}				
$288,350 and over					39.6%
$132,600 to $288,350				36%	36%
$63,550 to $132,600			31%	31%	31%
$26,250 to $63,550		28%	28%	28%	28%
Taxable income to $26,250	15%	15%	15%	15%	15%

percent, which was paid on each additional dollar of income above $283,150. In a progressive tax, the marginal rate (highest rate paid on the last taxable dollar) is always higher than the average rate (rate paid on all taxable dollars).

Of course, a person's federal income tax obligation does not begin with his or her first dollar of income. Taxpayers are entitled to both a "standard deduction," and "personal exemptions" for themselves and their dependents. In 2000, a single parent with one child would not incur federal income tax obligation for income below $12,050 (computed by adding the standard deduction of $6,450 to two personal exemptions valued at $2,800 each). The standard deduction is higher for people over 65 years of age and those who are blind. Like the tax brackets, the standard deduction and personal exemptions are adjusted annually for inflation.

The United States has not always had a federal income tax. George Washington and his Secretary of the Treasury, Alexander Hamilton, imposed the nation's first taxes on "distilled spirits and carriages." The money was needed to pay debts from the Revolutionary War. But, more importantly, Washington felt the tax was needed to establish the power of the new government. Like many of its successors, the nation's first "sin tax" met with protests. In 1794, protestors burned a tax collector's home, leading the President to send 13,000 troops into the area. This action effectively suppressed the rebellion and secured the taxation power of the federal government.

The first federal income tax was proposed in 1862 by Abraham Lincoln to finance the Civil War. The tax affected relatively few Americans. It applied only to those with annual incomes over $600. Up to $10,000, these incomes were taxed at a rate of 3 percent. Income over $10,000 was taxed at 5 percent. The tax was subjected to a constitutional challenge, and in 1880 the Supreme Court upheld it (*Springer v. United States*, 102 U.S. 586). In subsequent years, the tax was raised and lowered, eliminated and reinstated. In 1895, the Supreme Court reversed its earlier decision and declared the income tax unconstitutional (*Pollock v. Farmers' Loan and Trust Co.*, 158 U.S. 601). This judicial decision led to the adoption of the Sixteenth Amendment, which allows Congress to tax income. Still, it was not until the World War II era that income taxes were applied to most Americans. The tax rates peaked at a *marginal* (not average) rate of 94 percent during this period, as funds were needed to cover wartime expenses.

Since the 1950s, individual income taxes have provided nearly half of the revenues collected by the federal government. In 1953, individual income taxes accounted for 42.8 percent of federal revenues. That figure ranged between 44.1 and 48.1 percent between 1983 and 1993 (Graetz & Schenk, 1995). In contrast, the contribution of corporate income taxes diminished considerably during the same period, from 30.5 percent in 1953 to about 10 percent since 1986 (Graetz & Schenk, 1995).

SOCIAL SECURITY TAX. The 1935 passage of the Social Security Act financed the nation's retirement, disability, and unemployment insurance systems using a tax on wages. This tax was originally set at 1 percent of wages, and was expected to increase to 5 percent as the program grew. The payroll tax was equally divided between employees and employers. It was immediately subjected to a constitutional challenge, and the Supreme Court upheld the payroll tax (*Chas. C. Steward Machine Co. v. Davis*). Today the payroll tax amounts to 15 percent of the nation's wages, up to a limit called a "cap." In 2000, income over $6,200 per month was not subject to the payroll tax. Half of the tax is taken directly from workers' paychecks, and half is paid quarterly by employers. It is usually listed on pay stubs as the "FICA contribution," with FICA standing for "Federal Insurance Contribution Act." In addition to the FICA tax, wages are taxed at 2.9 percent (again split between employer and employee) to finance Medicare's hospital insurance program.

The proportion of federal revenues drawn from payroll taxes has increased dramatically in recent decades. In 1953, payroll taxes contributed 10 percent of federal revenues. That figure had increased to 40 percent by 1994 (Graetz & Schenk, 1995). See Figure 2.3.

STATE TAXES. Most state revenues are drawn from state income taxes, property taxes, and sales taxes. State income taxes generally mirror those at the federal level, except for the fact that state tax rates are lower. Sales taxes are col-

FIGURE 2.3 SOURCES OF FEDERAL REVENUE

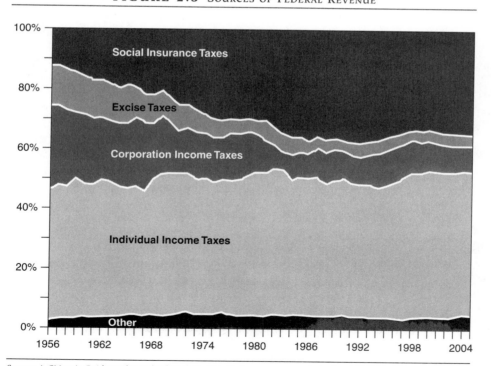

Source: A Citizen's Guide to the Federal Budget, http://w3.access.gpo.gov/usbudget/FY2001/guide02.html.

lected by vendors at the point of sale. They range from about 3 percent to 10 percent. Some states try to reduce the regressivity of their sales taxes by exempting essential items, such as food or medicine.

LOCAL TAXES. Traditionally, most local governments have collected the bulk of revenues through property taxes. Tax rates on real property (e.g., land and some personal property, such as cars) can vary tremendously within a state, and from state to state. The tax is based on a formal appraisal of value. The timing of this appraisal can vary. Jurisdictions experiencing rapid changes in property values may conduct appraisals on a regular basis, such as every three to five years. In other areas property is appraised only when it is sold. The proportion of local revenues drawn from property taxes declined from 90 percent in 1960 to 74 percent in 1984 (Graetz & Schenk, 1995). The property tax is the primary source of funding for most public schools.

With declining revenues from property taxes, local governments are relying more heavily on sales taxes for revenue. Local sales tax rates can vary from 1 to 3 percent. Local sales tax revenues may be used to finance specific services, such as parks or cultural activities, or may be applied generally to fund local government activities.

TAX REVOLTS. In the preceding sections we noted some recent trends in U.S. government revenues. At the federal level, a growing proportion of revenue has been drawn from payroll taxes during the past five decades. The contribution of federal income taxes has remained fairly constant, and that of corporate income taxes has diminished. At the local level, we have seen a diminished contribution from property taxes, coupled with increased reliance on sales taxes. These trends reflect the influence of a popular movement known as the "tax revolt."

While corporate lobbyists have worked quietly to reduce the corporate income tax burden, citizens' groups have publicly focused on reducing property tax obligations (Dworak, 1980). California has led the nation in tax protests. After nearly a decade of dramatic increases in property values (and property taxes), in June 1978 the state's residents voted to support "Proposition 13," a constitutional amendment that would dramatically alter the state's tax system and set the stage for a new era of citizen involvement in tax policy. Proposition 13 limited residential property taxes to 1 percent of value and required a two-thirds legislative majority to pass tax increases. As a result, local revenues diminished by nearly a third, and the state's educational and municipal institutions suffered.

Other states followed California's lead, and during the late 1970s property tax limitation measures passed in Idaho, Nevada, Oregon, Michigan, Alabama, Massachusetts, and Missouri (Dworak, 1980). President Bush took the tax revolt nationwide in his 1988 campaign when he issued the disastrous statement, "Read my lips: no new taxes!" Since then, few politicians have dared to suggest a tax increase. Anti-tax organizations, such as the National Taxpayers Union, are quick to oppose any measure that might raise taxes.

The irony of a tax revolt in the United States is not lost on our trading partners. U.S. citizens pay considerably less in taxes than do our competitors in the global market. Graetz and Schenk (1995) examined tax revenues as a percent of Gross Domestic Product (GDP) for the U.S. and its trading partners. In 1991, tax revenues in the U.S. were about 30 percent of GDP. The average for countries in the Organization for Economic Cooperation and Development (OECD) was about 38 percent. Comparable figures for similar nations in 1991 were as follows: United States (29.8), Canada (37.3), France (44.2), Germany (39.2), Italy (39.7), Japan (30.9), and United Kingdom (36.0).

Still, as Rubin (1998) pointed out, tax revolts are not about relative levels of taxation, but about *the consent of the governed.* In the face of rapidly increasing government spending, citizens resist taxation. Uncontrollable economic events, such as inflation, also contribute to tax revolts. Finally, and perhaps most importantly, government spending on ineffective or unpopular programs can trigger popular resistance. Thus, the challenge in a democracy is to maintain a level of consensus, both about the fairness of the tax system and about the social goals that it advances. Social workers are familiar with the social programs that are financed through tax revenues. We are less familiar with the direct use of taxation to accomplish social policy. This aspect of taxation is examined in the next section.

TAXATION AS SOCIAL POLICY. Taxes have long been used to influence social trends in the U.S. As Graetz and Schenk (1995, p. 1) observed:

> Today's income tax provisions, for example, favor new development of natural resources over recycling, tell people it is far better to own their own homes than to rent, give a break to families that have one spouse who stays at home rather than those that have both husband and wife in the job market, and make it cheaper for some people to marry, cheaper for others to divorce or remain unmarried. Federal alcohol taxes favor wine drinkers over beer drinkers, and both over those who prefer whiskey. Shortly after his inauguration, President Clinton proposed a new energy tax that would have given economic force to fathers' eternal admonitions to their children to turn off the lights, but Congress refused to enact it.

In addition, corporate income tax provisions favor companies that provide pension and health coverage to employees.

Tax policy attempts to influence social behavior in both the imposition and the withdrawal of tax obligations. We are most familiar with the imposition of taxes to discourage or limit certain kinds of behavior. Thus, for example, we impose taxes on the purchase of tobacco, alcohol, and gasoline. On the flip side, desirable behavior can reduce a person's tax liability. The nation's tax code provides tax deductions or exemptions. Home ownership is encouraged by laws that provide for a "home mortgage deduction." More recently, tax deductions have been used to encourage home care of the elderly. The medical expenses associated with such care can be deducted from one's income. To encourage some kinds of investment, income from these sources can be declared "tax exempt." For example, a state may declare that interest paid by municipal bonds will be exempt from state income tax.

Deductions and exemptions represent "forgone revenue" to the federal government, and should be considered with the same deliberation as proposals for new expenditures. To encourage this view, the President is required to submit an annual "Tax Expenditure Budget" to Congress. Also known as "The Green Book," this budget is a useful document for policy analysts interested in the use of taxes for social policy.

Oddly enough, Americans seldom subject tax expenditures to the level of scrutiny that is applied to revenue expenditures. The nation's politicians find it easier to exempt someone from taxes than to establish a new social program. Tax exemptions and deductions are politically popular because Americans hate taxes. However, these exemptions and deductions favor the wealthy and do little or no good for the poor, because exemptions and deductions operate by reducing a person's income tax obligation. Given the progressive nature of the federal income tax, this reduction has the greatest value to those with the greatest tax obligation—the affluent (see Barusch, 1995).

This problem does not hold for tax credits, which can result not only in reduced taxes but in a refund from the IRS. A refund that is the result of a tax credit is not the same as a refund that comes because you have overpaid your taxes. The refund most people are familiar with is not based on their deductions per se, but on the fact that they have had more money withheld than they owed. A tax credit actually changes the amount that the taxpayer owes. For that reason, the Earned Income Tax Credit (EITC) provides significant benefits to the nation's working poor. The EITC, discussed in detail in Chapter 4, provides a refund to low-income workers with children. In essence, it is an anti-poverty measure embedded in the U.S. tax code.

Few of us make personal decisions on the basis of tax consequences. Taxes operate in the background, punishing and rewarding behavior in ways that may influence us without our awareness. But the U.S. tax system is an important tool for achieving social justice. It allocates billions of dollars every year, and thus it plays a significant role in allocating the costs and benefits of citizenship.

SUMMARY: GOVERNMENTAL INFLUENCES ON SOCIAL POLICY

We have argued in this chapter that government is a vehicle for orchestrating a collective response to individual problems. Government evolved because we needed an organization to carry out this collective enterprise. The U.S. government can be seen as having both "levels" (federal, state, and local) and "branches" (legislative, executive, and judicial). Each of these entities plays an important role in the creation and implementation of social policy.

Near the end of the chapter, we explored the U.S. tax system and considered its roles in funding governmental activities and influencing social policy.

It is easy to become overwhelmed by the complexity of the U.S. government. By achieving a basic understanding of its structure, as well as the knowledge that in a democracy the central role of government is to carry out the will of the people, a social worker can engage effectively in policy practice on behalf of his or her clients.

The Social Security Act is a vital part of Americans' search for social justice. Indeed, as we will see in the next chapter, the establishment of social insurance programs in Europe and the U.S. provided a significant impetus for the growth of governments. Chapter 3 is the last chapter in the introductory part of this book. It describes the background and current structure of Social Security, which is the legislative framework for most U.S. social policy.

DISCUSSION TOPICS

1. List three arguments in favor of having the states, not the federal government, operate a major social program such as Social Security. Now list three arguments opposing state management. We are all familiar with constitutional limits on the federal government. Does the Constitution limit the powers of the states?

2. What is the largest tax expenditure in the current Tax Expenditure Budget? What social goals does it serve?

3. Has your community used tax exemptions to attract business in the past year? What were the terms of those exemptions? Who benefited?

4. What is taxpayer C's *average* tax rate? What is his or her *marginal* rate?

SUGGESTED RESOURCE

www.thomas.loc.gov — This site is maintained by the Library of Congress "in the spirit of Thomas Jefferson." It provides a searchable database with the text and status of bills going back several years. It is an excellent source of up-to-date information on Congressional proposals.

3

The
Social Security
Act

Most Americans think of the Social Security Act as a retirement program for the nation's elderly. In fact, as this chapter will reveal, three types of programs are authorized under the Act: social insurance, public assistance, and health and social services. These programs serve Americans of all ages and income levels. The retirement program, known as "Old-Age Insurance" (OAI), was part of the original Social Security Act, along with unemployment insurance, public assistance programs for the aged, the blind, and dependent children, and health services for mothers and children. The titles of the 1935 act are presented in Table 3.1.

Subsequent amendments added survivors insurance, disability insurance, medical insurance for the aged, and two means-tested programs: Medicaid and Supplemental Security Income. Other, less-well-known programs administered under the Social Security Act include the Maternal and Child Health Services Block Grant, the Social Services Block Grant, and the Children's Health Insurance Program. The titles of the Social Security Act in 2000 are presented in Table 3.2.

In this chapter we will trace the emergence of social security in Western Europe and the United States, then discuss the major programs authorized under the Social Security Act: old-age and survivors insurance, disability insurance, unemployment insurance, medical insurance, Supplemental Security Income, and health and social services. In each section we will consider the background of the program, then discuss its current status. Major reform proposals will be presented as well. Perhaps the most urgent of these proposals are designed to address concerns about the solvency of Old-Age and Survivors Insurance (OASI). Other proposals, such as Earnings Sharing and Caregiver Credits, address the program's treatment of women. The chapter concludes with a brief consideration of the philosophical underpinnings of Social Security in the United States, and a look at the role of Social Security in advancing social justice.

TABLE 3.1 CONTENTS OF THE SOCIAL SECURITY ACT OF 1935

Preamble: *An act to provide for the general welfare by establishing a system of Federal old-age benefits, and by enabling the several States to make more adequate provision for aged persons, blind persons, dependent and crippled children, maternal and child welfare, public health, and the administration of their unemployment compensation laws; to establish a Social Security Board; to raise revenue; and for other purposes.*

Title I	Grants to States for Old-Age Assistance
Title II	Federal Old-Age Benefits
Title III	Grants to States for Unemployment Compensation Administration
Title IV	Grants to States for Aid to Dependent Children
Title V	Grants to States for Maternal and Child Welfare
Title VI	Public Health Work
Title VII	Social Security Board
Title VIII	Taxes with Respect to Employment
Title IX	Tax on Employers of Eight or More
Title X	Grants to States for Aid to the Blind
Title XI	General Provisions

TABLE 3.2 TITLES OF THE SOCIAL SECURITY ACT (2000)

Title I	[Grants to States for Old-Age Assistance] (Supplemental Security Income)
Title II	Old-Age, Survivors, and Disability Insurance Benefits
Title III	Grants to States for Unemployment Compensation
Title IV	Grants to States for Aid and Services to Needy Families with Children and for Child Welfare Services
Title V	Maternal and Child Health Services Block Grant
Title VII	Administration
Title VIII	Special benefits for Certain World War II Veterans
Title IX	Miscellaneous Provisions Relating to Employment Security
Title X	[Grants to States for Aid to the Blind] (Supplemental Security Income)
Title XI	General Provisions
Title XII	Advances to State Unemployment Funds
Title XIII	Special Benefits for Certain World War II Veterans
Title XIV	[Grants to States for Aid to the Permanently and Totally Disabled] (Supplemental Security Income)
Title XVI	Supplemental Security Income for the Aged, Blind and Disabled
Title XVII	Grants for Planning Comprehensive Action to Combat Mental Retardation
Title XVIII	Health Insurance for the Aged and Disabled
Title XIX	Grants to States for Medical Assistance Programs
Title XX	Block Grants to States for Social Services
Title XXI	State Children's Health Insurance Program

Titles VI and XV have been repealed.

SOCIAL INSURANCE IN WESTERN EUROPE

Early social insurance schemes developed in Western Europe addressed the "three fears" of industrial workers: poverty in old age, illness, and unemployment. As several historians have pointed out, the social security programs established during the nineteenth century were adopted by authoritarian, rather than democratic, regimes (Flora, 1983; Flora & Heidenheimer, 1981; Rimlinger, 1971).[1] An important motivation was undoubtedly the government's need to secure the loyalty of the growing number of industrial wage-earners.

The regime of Otto Von Bismarck is credited with establishing Europe's first social insurance program through a series of acts passed in the 1880s. Popular myth holds that Bismarck's motivation for establishing this program was a desire to force his political foes into retirement. A more likely explanation is that the social insurance program, "Sozialversicherung," was established as part of an effort to strengthen the German state by securing the allegiance of the industrial working class. Sozialversicherung was successful in this regard. It offered workers a stake in the political order and gained enough popular support to survive two world wars, National Socialism, and foreign occupation to continue as a central feature of the German welfare state (de Swaan, 1988).

Oddly enough, leaders of the German labor movement opposed the establishment of Sozialversicherung. Drawing on Marxist doctrine, labor leaders believed that workers should have global allegiance to other members of the proletariat rather than to a nation-state. Leaders of workers' parties may have also seen the program as another tactic in the government's ongoing repression of their organizing efforts. Despite their initial opposition, labor leaders were effectively co-opted by the program. As de Swann (1988) noted, union leaders and socialist party officials were quickly "integrated into the state's fabric as executives of the national insurance system" (p. 188).

In England, the elaborate system for relief created by the Elizabethan Poor Law (see Chapter 4) was a barrier to the development of social insurance. Charity Organization Societies that provided aid to the indigent were adamant in their belief that poverty was the result of personal failings and that efforts to relieve it should focus on moral reform of individuals. But as industrialization advanced, local authorities were overwhelmed by the needs of older workers. With the 1906 election of a Liberal Government, Lloyd George and Winston Churchill formed an activist regime that, with the support of organized labor, passed social insurance legislation in the form of the Pension Act of 1908.

The French social security system was established in 1930. Small property owners had effectively opposed social insurance for several decades. These members of the "petit bourgeoisie" feared that government control of the large sums of capital accumulated in national insurance funds would increase govern-

---

[1]Germany, Austria, Finland, Sweden, and Italy had established compulsory social insurance programs for workers by the end of the nineteenth century (de Swaan, 1988).

ment control of the capital market, disrupting their businesses. They also argued that social security taxes would undermine workers' ability to accumulate personal savings. The establishment of the French program has been attributed to the erosion of the bourgeois power base and the support of moderate labor organizations (de Swaan, 1988).

France's position on social insurance was unusual, since most European nations had mandatory old-age insurance programs in place prior to World War I (1914–1918). Throughout the continent, these new programs served a state-building function, converting wages into accumulated capital through a mandatory system operated by a public administrative apparatus. These programs enhanced workers' loyalty to the state by giving laborers a stake in the government even if they were not landowners.

SOCIAL SECURITY IN THE UNITED STATES

Like the French, Americans established social insurance for workers later than most European nations. Despite growing recognition of old-age dependency as a social problem, the belief that poverty was caused by individual inadequacies effectively precluded comprehensive federal legislation. Workers were expected to set aside sufficient personal savings to ensure their security in old age.

Many workers bought private insurance against accidents and illness. In 1910, roughly half of the work force had such insurance (Achenbaum, 1986). These workers typically filed disability claims if old age forced them to retire. Those who failed to provide for their old age were left first to the mercies of their families, and second to the limited public and charitable assistance that was available.

After the 1920s, large companies (public utilities, railroads, and manufacturing firms) established private pension plans for their employees. Retirement insurance was made available to federal employees in 1920 through the establishment of the Federal Employees Retirement Program. By 1931, 18 states had established compulsory old-age insurance programs for workers (Piven & Cloward, 1971). By 1933, 21 states and the territories of Alaska and Hawaii operated relief programs for dependent elderly people (Achenbaum, 1986).

In this context, proposals to establish social insurance against old-age dependency were unsuccessful. They surfaced periodically during the Progressive Era, promoted by advocates such as Abraham Epstein and I. M. Rubinow. Epstein founded the "American Association for Old-Age Security" in 1927 to advance his social insurance scheme. But for the most part, these proposals did not have the support of workers or federal politicians, and there was widespread belief that a mandatory social insurance program would be declared unconstitutional by the Supreme Court (Kingson & Berkowitz, 1993).

The Great Depression was not the first major economic upheaval in the U.S., but its duration and intensity were overwhelming. Andrew Achenbaum (1986, p. 16) described the economic impact:

Between October 1929 and June 1932, the common-stock price index dropped from 260 to 90. The nation's real GNP, which had risen 22 percent between 1923 and 1929, fell 30.4 percent over the next four years. Nearly 5,000 banks, with deposits exceeding $3.2 billion, became insolvent; 90,000 businesses failed. Aggregate wages and salaries in 1933 totaled only 57.5 percent of their 1929 value. The gross income realized by farmers was cut nearly in half; the farm-product index took a dive from 105 to 51 between 1928 and 1932. More than a thousand local governments defaulted on their bonds. . . . Insecurity pervaded the land.

Widespread insecurity undermined the popular belief that poverty was the result of personal irresponsibility. No longer could middle-class Americans feel confident that hard work would insulate them from insecurity. Job loss and destitution, once seen as individual problems, now seemed to call for collective action. The external impacts of insecurity were evident in the domino effects of bank and business closures. Individual remedies, from personal initiative to private insurance, had little effect. Finally, no one really knew who would be singled out for unemployment. The Depression also overwhelmed local and state relief programs.

A wide range of reform proposals came to the fore. Most involved the use of taxes to fund guaranteed incomes in old age. Francis E. Townsend, a retired doctor living in California, organized "Townsend Clubs" to support his proposal that everyone over 60 who was unemployed[2] be given $200 a month on the condition that they spend the amount within 30 days. The program was to be funded through a tax on business transactions. Others, including Upton Sinclair and Senator Huey P. Long, advanced similar ideas.

The 1932 presidential election brought Franklin Delano Roosevelt into office with a clear mandate to "do something." His opponent, incumbent Herbert Hoover, argued that the market should be left alone to correct itself. Roosevelt and his colleagues supported the establishment of a government insurance program to protect the unemployed and the aged. Roosevelt established a cabinet-level Committee on Economic Security (CES), under the direction of Edwin E. Witte, to draft proposals for the New Deal programs in collaboration with Francis Perkins, a social worker who was appointed to serve as Secretary of Labor. In January 1935, Roosevelt presented Congress with "the most comprehensive social welfare bill that any president had ever asked Congress to consider" (Kingson & Berkowitz, 1993, p. 35). It combined programs for the unemployed, children, and the elderly within a single piece of legislation, the Social Security Act. Table A.1 in the Appendix presents a list of milestones in the history of Social Security in the United States.

The Act that was passed in 1935 was only a skeleton of the Social Security Act as we know it today. Its old-age insurance offered benefits only to retired

---

[2]The requirement that Social Security recipients be unemployed was an integral part of the Act. Some have argued that this "retirement test" evolved in an effort to reduce unemployment. It effectively moved the elderly out of the labor force to make jobs available to younger workers.

workers, not to their survivors or to workers with disabilities. Further, the original program covered only about half of the labor force, excluding many farm and domestic workers, state and local employees, and the self-employed. It was financed by joint contributions from employees and employers.

The Social Security Act was subjected to two constitutional challenges heard by the Supreme Court in 1937. In the first case (*Chas. C. Steward Machine Co. v. Davis*), the Charles C. Steward Machine Company of Alabama sued to recover its share of Social Security taxes, claiming it was an illegal excise tax. The Court upheld the constitutionality of the tax, holding that the magnitude of the emergency presented by the Depression justified federal intervention. In the second case (*Helvering et al. v. Davis*), a shareholder with Edison Electric Illuminating Company of Boston argued that deduction of Social Security taxes from wages would produce unrest among employees and "would be followed by demands of increases in wages and that corporation and shareholders would suffer irreparable loss" (Supreme Court, 1937). In rejecting this argument, the court relied on the concept of general welfare:

> Congress may spend money in aid of the general welfare. . . . The purge of nation-wide calamity that began in 1929 has taught us many lessons. Not the least is the solidarity of interests that may once have seemed to be divided. Unemployment spreads from state to state, the hinterland now settled that in pioneer days gave an avenue of escape. . . . The hope behind this statute is to save men and women from the rigors of the poorhouse as well as from the haunting fear that such a lot awaits them when journey's end is near (Supreme Court, 1937, p. 640).

The constitutional challenges to the Social Security Act focused on its only compulsory element, old-age insurance. Having survived these challenges, the program was put in place. Retirement benefits were financed by employer and employee contributions of 1 percent each on a wage base of $3,000, with a maximum contribution of $30 per year. Benefits were paid out at age 65, and amounted to about $22 per month for single workers and $36 per month for couples. To allow a reserve to accumulate, no benefits were paid until 1940. The first benefit paid was $22 per month to Miss Ida Fuller, a retired secretary. Miss Fuller lived to be over 100. She paid less than $100 in Social Security taxes and collected about $21,000 in benefits (Schulz, 1995). Other women have fared less well through Social Security, as we will see later in this chapter.

Old-Age Insurance (OAI) was not the only program established through the Social Security Act of 1935. The Act included eleven titles (see Table 3.1). Title I, "Grants to States for Old-Age Assistance," established a federal-state partnership to offer relief to the elderly poor. Title II, "Federal Old-Age Benefits," included the Act's pension provisions. Title III established a grant-in-aid for states to provide unemployment insurance. Title IV provided a grant-in-aid for states to provide public assistance to dependent children. Title V provided a grant-in-aid for health services to mothers and children. Title VI established a public health authority. Title VII created a governing board for Social Security. Title VIII levied taxes on employers and employees and created the Old-Age Reserve Account, later renamed the Old-Age and Survivors Insurance (OASI) Trust Fund. Title IX further elaborated on Social Security taxes. Title X established a grant-in-aid for states to provide public assistance to the blind. Title XI contained general provisions related to administration of Social Security.

In the following sections of this chapter, we will trace the development of five programs authorized through the Social Security Act of 1935 and its later amendments: Old-Age and Survivors Insurance (OASI); Disability Insurance (DI); Unemployment Insurance (UI); Medical Insurance; Public Assistance for the Aged, Blind, and Disabled (SSI); and health and social services.

OLD-AGE AND SURVIVORS INSURANCE FOR WORKERS

In the 1936 election, Franklin Roosevelt roundly defeated his Republican contender for President. In its second term, the Roosevelt Administration set out to expand the Social Security Act. The 1939 amendments expanded Social Security coverage by adding benefits for workers' survivors and dependents. Widows of both active and retired workers received a portion of the benefits to which the workers were entitled, as did other dependents of retired workers.

Subsequent years saw continued expansion of Social Security coverage. In 1950, farm workers and the self-employed were added, bringing coverage to about 90 percent of the labor force. Later, provision for early retirement was added, allowing workers to retire at the age of 62 with 80 percent of the monthly benefit they would have received at 65. In 1972, the Cost of Living Adjustment (COLA) was established to raise benefits at rates linked to inflationary increases in the Consumer Price Index (CPI). In 1977, procedures for "indexing" earnings were put in place. Indexing adjusts earnings for inflation in benefit computations, resulting in a more generous treatment of earnings from the early years of a worker's career.

The 1980s marked the beginning of a retrenchment period for Social Security. By this time, program expansions had eroded reserves, and the Old-Age and Survivors Insurance (OASI) Trust Fund was on the verge of bankruptcy. Anticipating the demands that would be presented by the baby boomer cohort, in 1981 President Reagan appointed a bipartisan commission, the National Commission on Social Security Reform, chaired by Alan Greenspan, to recommend measures to restore the program's solvency. The following measures were implemented in subsequent amendments:

1. **Revisions in the Cost of Living Adjustment (COLA).** These included a one-time delay of the COLA and "stabilizer" on future COLAs. When the trust fund falls below certain measures, the COLA is automatically indexed,

not to the Consumer Price Index, but to the average increase in wages (if it is lower).

2. **Taxation of benefits.** For retirees with incomes above $25,000 per year for individuals or $32,000 for couples, up to half of their benefits were made subject to federal income tax.

3. **Increased retirement ages.** Starting in 2003, the age for receipt of full retirement benefits was to rise gradually. By 2027, the retirement age for full benefits would be 67. Early retirement would bring 70 percent of the regular benefits, not the 80 percent previously provided.

4. **Work incentives.** These provisions increased the amount beneficiaries could earn through employment before their Social Security benefits were reduced, and also eliminated the reduction of benefits for earnings of workers over the age of 70.

The work of the National Commission became law in the 1983 amendments to the Social Security Act. The National Commission's work was pivotal in two ways. First, its recommendations greatly enhanced the program's solvency; and second, the process of reform undertaken by the Commission greatly reduced the influence of partisan politics and enhanced the quality of technical information that was used in the Social Security debate. These reforms also represented fundamental shifts in the approach of Social Security. First, by subjecting Social Security benefits to income tax, the reforms introduced another progressive element into the program. As discussed in Chapter 2, the income tax draws a higher proportion of income from high-income Americans than it does from the poor. Second, the introduction of work incentives represented a significant departure from earlier policies requiring retirement as a condition for receiving benefits. This change suggests that the policy goal of removing older workers from the labor force had become less compelling.

The 1983 Amendments set the stage for subsequent revisions, primarily designed to maintain system solvency through the retirement of the nation's baby boomer generation. In 1999, President Clinton called for partial privatization of Social Security to increase trust fund income. The next year, in rare unanimous votes in both houses, Congress eliminated the retirement test altogether. Social Security beneficiaries would no longer be required to leave the work force in order to receive full benefits.

HOW OASI OPERATES

To understand current proposals to reform Social Security, it is important to have some basic knowledge of how the program operates.

Old-Age and Survivors Insurance (OASI) is the primary source of retirement income in the U.S., supporting over 40 million retired workers and their families in 2002 (OMB, 2001b). Although it was not conceived to be the sole support of elderly recipients (savings and pension income were seen as equal contributors), many low-income elders depend entirely on Social Security. In 1992, low-income elderly households received 77 percent of their total income from Social Security. This compares to 22 percent of the income received by upper-income elderly households during the same year (AARP Public Policy Institute, 1993).[3]

Old-Age and Survivors Insurance (OASI) is a carefully crafted compromise between two objectives, offering "welfare" to low-income seniors and "investment " to others. Thus, the program integrates the principles of "adequacy" and "equity." Equity is achieved when benefits drawn are based on contributions paid—in other words, when an individual receives a return that is proportional to his or her investment in the program. Under the principle of adequacy, benefits should be sufficient to maintain a decent standard of living, regardless of individual contributions.

To achieve equity, an individual's benefits are computed on the basis of prior contributions. Benefits are based on a person's "Average Indexed Monthly Earnings" (AIME). Earnings between ages 21 and 62 that were subject to the payroll tax (as of 2001, earnings under $80,400 per year) are adjusted for inflation. Then the five years with lowest earnings are dropped. The resulting total is averaged to produce the AIME. To be eligible to draw Social Security benefits, an individual must have worked in covered employment for at least 40 quarters (i.e., 10 years).

"Adequacy" refers to the guarantee of sufficient income for a modest existence in old age. The "replacement rate" under OASI is designed to ensure adequacy. Benefit computations replace lower earnings more generously than high earnings. As of 2001, the first $561 of AIME were replaced at the rate of 90 percent; earnings from $561 per month to $3,381 per month were replaced at the rate of 32 percent; and earnings between $3,381 and the maximum ($6,700) were replaced at 15 percent (Social Security Administration, 2001c). Thus, an individual retiring with low lifelong earnings enjoys a higher replacement rate than one retiring with high earnings. This does not mean his or her Social Security check will be larger, but that the difference between working income and Social Security income will be less than it would be for someone with high earnings.

OASI is financed through a payroll tax authorized under the Federal Insurance Contributions Act (FICA). This tax totals 15.30 percent of wages up to a cap. In 2001 this wage cap was set at $80,400 per year. Half of the tax is paid by the employer and half by the worker. The largest portion of these combined contributions (12.4 percent of wages) is allocated to Old-Age, Survivors, and Disability Insurance (OASDI). The remainder (2.9 percent of wages) goes to finance Medicare. High-income workers pay more tax, and low-income workers receive more generous replacement income. This aspect is sometimes described as a "redistributive feature" of the Social Security program.

---

[3]"Low-income" refers to households with less than $6,570 per year; "upper-income," to those with over $28,714.

The "minimum monthly benefit" is another redistributive feature. At the inception of Social Security, the minimum monthly benefit was set at $10 per month (Achenbaum, 1986). Under the 1972 amendments to the Social Security Act, Congress indexed the minimum benefit to inflation. By 1981 it had increased to $170.31 per month for a worker retiring at age 65. Faced with rising Social Security costs, Joseph A. Califano, then Secretary of Health, Education and Welfare, proposed repealing the minimum benefit. The primary argument for repeal was that SSI effectively eliminated the need for a minimum benefit. In 1981, the Reagan Administration repealed the minimum benefit. The next year it was reinstated for current retirees. Today, the minimum benefit is provided only to workers who were 62 years old before 1982 and is approximately $244 per month (Schulz, 1995).

Social Security is a "pay as you go" program. That is, most of the revenue collected through payroll taxes is used to pay for the benefits of current recipients. The remainder goes into four separate reserve funds: OASI; Disability; Hospital Insurance (Medicare Part A); and Supplementary Medical Insurance (Medicare Part B). Until the early 1980s, revenue matched benefits paid, at approximately $200 billion per year. Since passage of the 1983 amendments developed by the National Commission on Social Security Reform, the OASI and DI trust funds have been accumulating reserves. In 2000, these reserves increased by $153.3 billion, so that at the end of 2000 the combined trust funds held a balance of more than $1 trillion (Social Security Administration, 2001a).

Long-term projections suggest that, despite today's generous surplus, the OASI trust fund will begin to show a revenue shortfall during the first half of this century.[4] That is, the surplus will be exhausted, and benefit payments will exceed the amount collected through payroll taxes, assuming no change in either taxes or benefits. The projected deficit will average 2.2 percent of projected payroll taxes. Thus, an increase of 2.2 percentage points in the payroll tax (from 12.4 percent of earnings to 14.6 percent) could restore the system's solvency. Other proposals to restore solvency will be discussed after we examine the treatment of women by the Social Security system.

WOMEN AND OASI

Early debate about the Social Security Act often referred to "men and women" workers, lending an impression of gender neutrality. But in its original form, Social Security reflected the dominant family structure of the day, in which nearly all women depended on working men for income. In fact, as mentioned ear-

---

[4]The OASDI Trustees issue annual reports that estimate the date when the Social Security surplus will be depleted and expenditures will exceed revenues, sometimes called the date of "insolvency." The "intermediate" estimate of that date in the 1998 Trustees report was 2032. In the 2001 report, insolvency was projected for the year 2038 (Kijakazi, Primus, & Greenstein, 1998; Social Security Administration, 2001a). The 2001 report also estimated that revenues would exceed expenditures until 2016.

lier, the program did not address the income needs of these non-wage-earning women at all until the 1939 amendments added coverage for dependents and survivors. Further, until 1977, men seeking to receive survivors' benefits were required to demonstrate financial dependency.

As a dependent, a woman is now entitled to 50 percent of the benefit her husband receives upon his retirement. As a survivor, or widow, she receives 100 percent of his benefit. Thus, during her husband's lifetime, a wife receives benefits as a dependent (half of the husband's benefit) so that a couple receives 150 percent of his benefit (100 percent for him and 50 percent for her); upon his death, she receives benefits as a survivor (100 percent of the husband's benefit).[5] Widows may not claim benefits until they reach the age of 60. If they do choose to draw benefits at that age, the benefit is reduced by almost one-third (28.5 percent). Those who apply for benefits at the age of 62 experience a smaller, but still substantial, reduction (17.1 percent) (Quadagno & Meyer, 1990).

With rising divorce rates, provisions for widows left out a growing proportion of women: divorcees who had been dependent on their husbands for support. Therefore, in 1965 provision was made for women who had been married for at least 20 years. In 1977 that period was decreased to 10 years. Today, a woman who was married to a worker for at least 10 years is eligible to receive half of her husband's (or ex-husband's) benefit, as long as she has not remarried. She cannot receive benefits until she reaches the age of 60. Further, she cannot receive her benefits until her former husband applies to receive his.

Women are more likely than men to rely on Social Security as their sole source of income (Kammerman & Kahn, 1987). But the benefits paid to women are less than those paid to men. In 1998, the average monthly benefit paid to men was $877, compared to a mean of $731 for women. The average benefit paid to African-American men that year was $679; to African-American women, $604 (U.S. Department of Health and Human Services, 1999).

The Social Security system is facing criticism for its treatment of dual-earner couples. Generally, because of departures from the work force and lower lifetime wages, most working women receive larger benefits as dependents than they would on the basis of their own work histories. Thus, they receive no benefit for the payroll taxes they paid during their working years. This violates the principle of equity, since these working women receive no return on their investment in the program.

Another significant inequity is the fact that dual-earner couples with low to moderate incomes receive lower retirement benefits than couples in which one partner earns a high income and the other is not employed. Benefits are based on the income of the higher-earning partner. Figure 3.1 illustrates the effects on

---

[5]While this may seem (and is intended to be) fairly generous treatment of widows, in essence it means they are expected to live on two-thirds of the amount they had been receiving while they were part of a married couple. For low- and moderate-income couples, this reduction often leaves the widow in poverty.

FIGURE 3.1 DIFFERENTIAL TREATMENT
OF DUAL-EARNING COUPLES

	Couple A	Couple B	Couple C
Monthly earnings 1	$6,000	$5,000	$3,000
Monthly earnings 2	0	1,000	3,000
Monthly OASI Tax (12.4%)	744	744	744
Benefit base 1	6,000	5,000	3,000
Benefit base 2	3,000	2,500	3,000
Combined base:	9,000	7,500	6,000

couples in three different situations. Each of the couples earns the same total monthly income, $6,000.

In Couple A, one partner earns a monthly salary of $6,000 and the other partner is not employed. The wage-earner's retirement benefits are based on 100 percent of earnings, and the spouse's benefits are based on 50 percent of the same earnings. Thus, the couple's combined retirement income is based on 150 percent of the wages earned, or a combined wage base of $9,000.

Dual-earning couples fare less well. In Couple B, both spouses are employed. The first earner makes $5,000 per month, and the second makes $1,000 per month. The first earner is entitled to benefits based on $5,000. The second earner will draw retirement benefits based on 50 percent of the wages of the higher-earning partner. Thus, Couple B receives benefits based on a combined wage base of $7,500, even though their total income was the same as Couple A.

Couple C includes two earners with equal monthly salaries. Each partner earns $3,000 per month. Their retirement benefits are based on 100 percent of each person's wages, or $6,000,[6] the lowest wage base of the three couples in our comparison.

PROPOSED OASI REFORMS

Generally, efforts to reform OASI produce "winners" (those whose benefit status would be improved) and "losers" (those who would receive fewer benefits). Because reform is largely dictated by political considerations, the clout of the winners as compared to that of the losers can give an indication of the probability that a reform will be enacted. Reform proposals discussed in this section are designed to address two concerns. The first is the need to restore the solvency of the OASI fund. "Privatization" proposals dominate recent debates in this

---

[6]For another explanation of this phenomenon, with benefit computations, see Schulz, 1995.

area. The second concern is Social Security's treatment of women. Earnings sharing and caregiver credits have been proposed as ways to address this issue.

"PRIVATIZING" OASI. In 1979, José Pinera, then labor minister of Chile,
oversaw the final stages of "privatizing" that nation's pension system. The results
were satisfactory, and at the end of his term in Chile's government Mr. Pinera
came to the United States to co-chair a project funded by the conservative Cato
Institute to advance the case for privatizing the U.S. Social Security system
(Dreyfuss, 1996). These efforts were successful in persuading President Clinton
to include partial privatization of OASI on the policy agenda presented in his
1999 State of the Union address. While the specifics of proposals vary, the theme
of privatization simply means moving the money in the OASI trust fund away
from government treasury bonds into the stock market.

Why has privatization become the subject of national debate? The rhetoric of
the debate focuses on the system's impending insolvency and suggests that
younger workers have no faith in the system.[7] But an underlying cause may be
found in the system's changing economics. As Quinn and Mitchell (1996) argue,
"Social Security is newly vulnerable because it is no longer a good deal for all" (p.
78). In the system's early decades, all workers could expect to receive more in
benefits than they would have received if they had taken the amount they paid in
Social Security taxes and invested it themselves. But as the ratio of workers to beneficiaries has declined, payroll taxes have increased and benefits for upper-income
retirees have been taxed. So for workers (primarily high earners) expecting to
retire in one decade or more, OASI benefits will be less than what they would
have received had they put their payroll taxes in low-risk investments. One-earn-
er couples and recipients with incomes in the bottom half of the earnings distribution will continue to receive more from Social Security than they would have
received from private investments. But, for the first time in the system's history, a
sizeable number of workers will not. This prospect not only has made the redistributive aspect of the program explicit, but it has also undermined political support for Social Security among high earners (Kingson & Quadagno, 1997).

Three "privatization" proposals surfaced in President Clinton's Social Security
Advisory Council. The first, advanced by Robert Ball (former Social Security
Commissioner) is called the "Maintenance of Benefits Plan." This proposal had
the support of six members of the 13-person council. It would raise revenues to
restore the system's solvency. A proportion of this increase would be achieved
by investing up to 40 percent of trust fund reserves in private capital markets.
Ball's plan would also entail a two-point increase in payroll taxes beginning in

---

[7]The "Third Millennium" is a group of about 1,700 members that claims to represent the interests of younger workers or "Generation X." In the early 1990s, this group organized a poll, conducted by Frank Luntz, that reported that more young Americans believe in flying saucers than in
the future of Social Security. While the results of the poll have been widely disseminated, its methods have been questioned (see McLeod, 1995).

2050. The second proposal to establish "Individual Accounts" had the support of two council members. This proposal would reduce benefits and increase revenues in part by establishing individual contribution accounts, funded by an increased payroll tax. Participants would have some (limited) discretion in investing their accounts. The third and most radical proposal would establish "Personal Savings Accounts" (PSAs) that would replace the Social Security system. This proposal was supported by five members. It would replace Social Security with a two-tiered system. The first tier would provide a low flat-rate benefit to all workers with at least 10 years of contributions, regardless of their earnings history. The benefit would be prorated to provide higher incomes to those with 35 or more years of contributions. At its maximum, this flat benefit would amount to about two-thirds of the poverty level for an elderly individual. The second tier would consist of mandatory personal savings accounts (PSAs), that would be held and managed by the individual retiree. These accounts could be withdrawn as lump sum payments after the age of 62.

The similarities among these plans are striking. As Quinn and Mitchell (1996) noted, "They all recommend the maintenance of a mandatory, universal, public social insurance program, with retirement, survivor, and disability benefits" (p. 80). Also striking in the privatization debate is the extent to which the redistribution function of Social Security is maintained. None of the plans suggests turning Social Security into a welfare system through means-testing of beneficiaries. There is some concern, though, that the two-tiered system will result in eroded support for the flat-rate benefit and undermine the anti-poverty function of Social Security.

Opposition to privatization came from a surprising source when Alan Greenspan, Chair of the Federal Reserve Board, testified before the Senate Banking Committee in 1999. Greenspan argued that it would be impossible to keep politics out of the stock market if huge amounts of public dollars were invested there by the Social Security system. In essence, he suggested that a dominant public presence in the market would diminish returns, not only reducing the supposed benefits of privatization but weakening the market as a whole.

EARNINGS SHARING. Proposals to establish "earnings sharing" essentially would combine the earnings of a married couple and allocate half of the combined total to the husband and half to the wife for the duration of the marriage. This change would benefit divorced persons who had less than 10 years of marriage, giving them credit for their husbands' (or wives') earnings. It would also eliminate the inequities experienced by dual-career couples. To keep the system revenue neutral, the gains experienced by these two groups would be offset by losses to another group, in this case women (and a few men) who receive benefits as dependents without a work history.

CAREGIVER CREDITS. Another growing concern is lack of recognition for the non-waged labor of women caring for children and disabled or elderly family members. Women's caregiving responsibilities often require them to stop working, thereby jeopardizing their retirement benefits. Several proposals to allow Social Security credit for caregiving years have been introduced in the U.S. Congress. Typically, these proposals would provide Social Security credit for up to five years of no or minimal earnings while a worker is living with a young child or caring for a disabled family member. Caregiver credits attempt to address the difficulties experienced by women who leave work to care for family members. They have been criticized as being unfair, since they offer no benefits to those who take on double duty, meeting family care responsibilities without leaving the work force.

In this section we have traced the development of old-age insurance in the U.S. Social Security system. In the following sections we will consider two other types of social insurance: Unemployment Insurance and Medical Insurance.

UNEMPLOYMENT INSURANCE

When the Social Security Act was developed in 1934 and 1935, unemployment was an overwhelming concern. An estimated 11 to 15 million workers were out of work, and the resulting pressure on relief programs was staggering. A few states, most notably Massachusetts and New York, had attempted to pass unemployment insurance legislation prior to the Depression. But, until the Depression, these bills had consistently failed in state legislatures (Altmeyer, 1963).

Unemployment Insurance (UI) was an integral part of the Social Security Act of 1935. It was one of two social insurance programs the President and his advisors felt should be enacted immediately; the other was old-age insurance. The Committee on Economic Security debated extensively whether Unemployment Insurance should be operated as a federal-state partnership or as a strictly federal program. Ultimately, unlike OAI, Unemployment Insurance was established as a federal-state partnership. Under Title III of the 1935 Social Security Act, the role of the federal government was limited to making grants available to states interested in administration of UI. Funds for these grants were provided through a federal payroll tax paid by employers. A tax credit was made available to employers whose states met federal guidelines for UI. Within two years, unemployment insurance extended nationwide, with programs established in all the states. Originally, UI applied only to workers in firms with eight or more employees. Later, coverage was extended to those in firms with at least four employees.

Financing for UI at the state level is provided through a tax on payrolls. The state unemployment tax rate varies, depending on the firm's use of unemployment compensation during previous years. This is known as "experience rating." Under this approach, firms that have had high rates of unemployment pay higher unemployment taxes than those who have had lower unemployment rates. The use of experience rating was designed to reduce unemployment by giving employers an incentive to stabilize their work force. Alternatively, some considered it a fair way to allocate the social cost of unemployment (Altmeyer,

1963). Funds for UI are placed in an Unemployment Trust Fund. A state agency known as the State Employment Security Agency is charged with administration of the program.

Unemployment Insurance was designed to provide temporary replacement of lost wages for workers who had strong attachment to the labor force. As a result, eligibility for UI is based on three factors: the worker's earnings history, the reason for unemployment, and the worker's availability for work. Within these categories, specific requirements vary from state to state. Most states require that a worker be in covered employment for the first four of the last five calendar quarters prior to filing a claim. Earnings must be above a minimum that is set by the state. Second, the job loss must be due to factors beyond the worker's control. Workers who choose to leave their jobs are not eligible for unemployment benefits. Finally, recipients of unemployment benefits must actively seek employment and must accept suitable employment if it is offered. Most states also require that workers be unemployed for at least one week before filing for UI benefits.

Like eligibility requirements, benefit levels vary from state to state. Most states provide half of a worker's salary for up to 26 weeks. Most states have maximum benefits, and some argue that inflation has eroded the value of unemployment compensation (Altmeyer, 1963; McMurrer & Chasanov, 1995). Another concern has been the disparity of benefits paid from state to state. Since state unemployment taxes are based on benefits paid, firms in states with high benefit rates suffer from a competitive disadvantage. This situation can lead to a "race for the bottom," in which states compete for the lowest unemployment tax rates. One way to succeed in this race is to keep benefits as low as possible.

Since UI's inception, the role of the federal government has expanded. In 1970, the Extended Unemployment Compensation Act was passed to allow the use of federal funds to provide benefits beyond state time limits during periods of high unemployment. Federal funds collected under the Federal Unemployment Tax Act finance 50 percent of the Extended Benefits Program. The other half is funded through state revenues. States may access this program to provide extended benefits in times of high unemployment.

The federal government finances 100 percent of the costs of the Emergency Unemployment Compensation program through general revenues. This Emergency Benefit Program was established in 1991 to supplement state coverage during times of high unemployment (McMurrer & Chasanov, 1995).

Financing for the federal share of the UI program is provided through a payroll tax paid by employers. In 2000, that tax amounted to 6.2 percent of the first $7,000 of covered employee wages. Employers in states with insurance programs that met federal requirements received credits against this tax of up to 5.4 percent of covered wages. The Department of Labor has administrative responsibility for the federal component of the UI program.

Nearly all workers in the U.S. are covered by unemployment insurance. Indeed, in 2000 the Department of Labor reported that 97 percent of employees were covered (OMB, 1997). Only workers on "small" farms and the self-employed are not covered. Despite this growth in coverage, the proportion of workers who actually receive benefits has declined, with significant drops in the 1980s (Burtless & Saks, 1984). The proportion of unemployed workers who received unemployment compensation bottomed out in 1984 at 28.5 percent. In the mid-1990s, the proportion stood at about 43 percent (McMurrer & Chasanov, 1995).

Reduced participation in the unemployment insurance program has been attributed in part to changes in federal and state policies. First, federal loans to states for their unemployment insurance trust funds were changed in 1982, when states were required to repay the loans with interest. Prior to 1982, the loans had been interest-free. This change created an incentive for states to tighten their eligibility requirements, and many did so. Denial rates increased significantly, as did minimum earnings requirements. Many states have reduced both the amount and duration of UI benefits. Federal laws also changed the value of benefits. In 1979, UI benefits were partially taxed, and in 1986 all UI benefits were subject to federal income tax. States were also required to reduce or eliminate UI payments to workers who received pensions or Social Security payments (Corson & Nicholson, 1988).

DISABILITY INSURANCE

The Social Security Act of 1935 did not provide for Disability Insurance (DI). Although there was some concern about workers who lost earnings due to disability, the overriding concern was potential malingering. As one member of the Social Security Advisory council put it, "You will have workers like those in the dust bowl area, people who have migrated to California and elsewhere...who will imagine they are disabled" (Berkowitz, 2000).

In 1956, the Social Security Act was amended to provide monthly benefits to "permanently and totally disabled" workers aged 50 to 64 and to adult disabled children of deceased or retired workers through the OASI program. With this addition, OASI came to be known as "OASDI." Congress passed Disability Insurance by "the barest of margins" (Berkowitz, 2000) despite opposition from the American Medical Association, private insurance companies, and employers' organizations. Even the Eisenhower Administration opposed disability coverage (Altmeyer, 1963).

Opposition to DI stemmed from concerns that it would reduce a worker's incentive to work. In response to this concern, coverage did not extend to temporary disability, but to workers who were "permanently and totally disabled." The disability determination requirements were quite stringent. Eligibility for disability payments, like OASI eligibility, was based on a worker's past participation in covered employment.

In subsequent years, DI was liberalized. In 1958, benefits were provided for dependents of disabled workers. During the same year, coverage was extended to disabled workers of all ages. Disability coverage is financed through the payroll tax, so with these additions the payroll tax (originally 1 percent) was increased to 2.25 percent each for employees and employers.

The liberalization of the program did not apply to disability determination, which remains stringent. Under current law,

> "Disability" means inability to engage in any substantial gainful activity by reason of any medically determinable physical or mental impairment which can be expected to result in death or which has lasted or can be expected to last for a continuous period of not less than 12 months. An individual shall be determined to be under a disability only if his physical or mental impairment or impairments are of such severity that he is not only unable to do his previous work but cannot, considering his age, education, and work experience, engage in any other kind of substantial gainful work . . . (Social Security Administration, 1999).

Today, DI beneficiaries make up just over half of the nation's disabled population. An estimated 17 million working-age adults have a disability that could limit their ability to work. Among them, about 4.7 million received DI in 1999 (SSA, 1999). Recent years have seen increases in the number of female beneficiaries and individuals with mental impairments. In 1999, DI beneficiaries received an average of $733 per month, resulting in an income well below the poverty threshold (Social Security Administration, 1999).

In recent years, concern about the DI program's effect on the incentive to work has led to several initiatives. The "ticket to work" program was announced in 1999. Under the Ticket to Work and Work Incentives Improvement Act of 1999, the Social Security Administration must offer recipients of Social Security disability payments or SSI the opportunity to participate in rehabilitative services. These services are designed to enhance their ability to be self-supporting. The Act also removes two major disincentives to work. First, it allows participants who do enter the work force to retain their Medicare or Medicaid coverage for an extended period. Second, it allows for an expedited eligibility determination if their effort to work is not successful. Thus, while disability beneficiaries who go to work would lose their cash payments, they would retain medical coverage and be assured that their cash assistance could be easily reinstated.

ADDICTION AS DISABILITY

Prior to 1996, severe drug addiction or alcoholism was considered an appropriate basis for receiving disability benefits under OASDI or SSI. As the number of individuals whose disability stemmed from drug addiction or alcoholism increased, there was rising concern that they were abusing federal disability programs. As a result, the 1972 Social Security Act Amendments required that SSI beneficiaries whose disability was caused by addiction receive payments through a representative payee and participate in treatment. These amendments included no restrictions on DI recipients.

Twenty-two years later, the Social Security Independence and Program Improvements Act of 1994 placed a three-year time limit on both SSI and DI benefits to people who were disabled by virtue of addiction. The act also extended treatment requirements to DI recipients. It reflected what many in Congress saw as "inappropriately diverting scarce federal resources from severely disabled individuals" and "providing a perverse incentive, contrary to the long-term interest of alcoholics and addicts, by providing them with cash payments so long as they do not work" (Committee on Finance, 1995, from Lewin Group, 1998).

Finally, all Social Security benefits to victims of addiction were cut off. The Contract with America Advancement Act of 1996 eliminated eligibility for DI, SSI, Medicare, and Medicaid for individuals whose drug addiction or alcoholism was material to their disability. This prohibition applied to just over 200,000 SSI and DI beneficiaries (Lewin Group, 1998).

MEDICAL INSURANCE

With the exception of the United States and South Africa, all developed countries provide some form of national health insurance to working-age adults. In the United States, health insurance is available to the elderly through Title XVIII of the Social Security Act (Medicare).

THE DEVELOPMENT OF NATIONAL HEALTH INSURANCE IN EUROPE

Medical insurance had its origins in the "sickness insurance" that was initially provided to craftsmen in sixteenth- and seventeenth-century Europe. The craft guilds collected dues from members to establish funds to assist sick and disabled colleagues. With industrialization, "sickness insurance" was extended to factory workers. Industrial laborers joined "krankenkassen" or sickness insurance societies, often operated under the auspices of their unions. In 1854, Prussian legislators made sickness insurance compulsory for low-wage workers.[8]

Otto von Bismarck, once Prime Minister of Prussia, became Chancellor of the German Empire in 1871. Bismarck viewed sickness insurance, like pension insurance, as a vehicle for cementing workers' loyalty to the German state. During a two-year period, from 1881 to 1883, Bismarck spearheaded the passage of a law that required low-wage workers in certain occupations to join a sickness insurance fund. Two-thirds of the cost of premiums was paid by the worker, with one-third contributed by the employer. As Roemer (1993) observed, "It is noteworthy that physicians raised no objections to this legislation; it ensured payment for their services to low-income patients; more affluent middle-class patients remained in the private market" (p. 92). Passage of this law set the stage for subsequent expansion of national health insurance throughout Germany and the rest of Europe.

---

[8]Prussia was one of 30 German states at the time.

In Britain, the "National Health Insurance" law passed in 1911 under Prime Minister Lloyd George. Based on the German model, this legislation established compulsory health insurance coverage for low-wage workers. "Friendly societies" were established as the British equivalent of Germany's sickness insurance funds. They covered prescription drugs and general practitioner services, since hospital and specialist care were offered through public and charitable hospitals. After World War II, the British Labour Party enacted the National Health Service (NHS) Act of 1946, establishing the program of national health insurance that currently operates in Great Britain. Rather than simply covering drugs and general practitioner care, the NHS offered broad coverage to all British residents, with financing through general revenues. It became a model for post-WWII health insurance reform in other European nations.

France was the last major European nation to establish national medical insurance for industrial workers. As in most nations, autonomous sickness insurance societies had proliferated. French physicians were politically powerful, and they insisted that insurance operate on an "indemnity" basis, under which the patient pays the doctor's fee and then seeks reimbursement from the insurance provider. During times of economic hardship, physicians agreed to charge a negotiated fee schedule (Roemer, 1993).

MEDICAL INSURANCE IN THE UNITED STATES

Discussion of national health insurance in the United States began as early as 1912, with a proposal from Theodore Roosevelt's Bull Moose Party. In 1935, the reformers who developed the Social Security Act were concerned about medical costs, but most believed that unemployment and old age were more immediate risks to workers than inability to pay for medical care. There was also concern that physicians would oppose social insurance for health care.

In the 1940s, President Truman made national health insurance a legislative priority. But he was less effective than Roosevelt at working with Congress, and the American Medical Association effectively derailed his proposal. In addition, the post–World War II expansion in employee benefits meant that a growing number of workers were covered by private health insurance through their unions or employers. Consequently, Medicare was not enacted until 1964.

Pressure for Medicare came in part from the recognition by Social Security officials and others that the elderly had been left behind during the expansion of private helth insurance. Retired workers were usually unable to obtain group insurance through a former employer; and insurance companies were reluctant to insure them as individuals, viewing the aged as "bad risks." As President Johnson put it, "Many of our older citizens are still defenseless against the heavy medical costs of severe illness."

Robert Ball (Commissioner of Social Security under Presidents Kennedy, Johnson, and Nixon) explained that advocates for Medicare saw it as "a first step toward universal national health insurance" (Ball, 1996). The American Medical

Association (AMA) had favored national health insurance in 1916, but by the time Medicare came up for debate, the AMA vigorously opposed any government-sponsored health insurance. Most business groups, especially those in the insurance industry, joined the opposition to Medicare (Ball, 1996). Medicare's strongest advocates were leaders of the labor movement, who started to push for enactment in 1957 and made the final push during the expansion of Lyndon Johnson's Great Society programs.

As initially conceived, Medicare was to provide only hospital insurance. This limitation was intended to defuse AMA opposition by minimizing federal involvement in the patient-physician relationship. But the original legislation was amended in Congress to include doctors' services. The program now offers both hospital insurance (Part A) and optional coverage for physician services (Part B).

Today Medicare benefits are provided through two separate programs, Part A and Part B. Part A is "free" to the beneficiary and covers many services provided within hospitals and nursing homes, as well as home health services and some hospice services. Part B is purchased through a monthly premium. Unless a beneficiary notifies Social Security that he or she does not want Part B, the premium ($43.80 per month in 1999) is automatically deducted from each Social Security check. Part B covers doctors, therapists, ambulance, and diagnostic services as well as prostheses, medical equipment, and certain other medical services and supplies. Medicare offers limited coverage of nursing home care, paying some expenses associated with stays of up to 90 days. As originally conceived, Medicare operates the same as private indemnity insurance, paying reasonable fees for all covered services.

MEANS-TESTED PROGRAMS UNDER THE SOCIAL SECURITY ACT

Three programs under the Social Security Act are not social insurance: Aid to Dependent Children (now known as Temporary Assistance to Needy Families, or TANF); Supplemental Security Income; and Medicaid. All of these programs are operated as federal-state partnerships. They are means-tested, with eligibility based on income and assets.

PUBLIC ASSISTANCE FOR DEPENDENT CHILDREN

Title IV of the Social Security Act of 1935 provided for federal grants to states choosing to provide public assistance to dependent children (ADC). In 1955, Nevada was the last state to provide ADC benefits. By that time, provisions of the Social Security Act of 1950 had taken effect. These allowed grants under the program to take into account not only the needs of the dependent child(ren), but also those of the caretaker, usually the mother.

In 1962, the Kennedy Administration proposed several revisions to ADC. Most noticeably, the program's name was changed to "Aid to Families with Dependent Children" in an effort to emphasize the family context. The same year, Amendments to the Social Security Act called for the delivery of social services to AFDC recipients. This change was to be the last major expansion of public assistance to dependent children under the Social Security Act.

During the 1970s and 1980s, growth in the welfare rolls exceeded population growth. At the same time, real wages eroded, and public support for welfare deteriorated. With the election of Ronald Reagan in 1982, the call to "end welfare as we know it" was popularized. Responding to this call, Congress and the President enacted the Family Support Act of 1988, which added a work requirement to AFDC. Harshly criticized as "work-fare" by advocates for the poor, this measure was only a hint of what was to follow.

The 1996 Personal Responsibility and Work Opportunity Reconciliation Act (PRWORA) effectively dismantled the New Deal guarantee of a minimum income for needy children. The Act abolished the AFDC entitlement, substituting a block grant to the states. Federal guidelines required states to enforce work participation requirements and established a five-year lifetime limit for assistance under the new program, called "Temporary Assistance to Needy Families." PRWORA also restricted non-citizens' access to SSI, although some of the more draconian measures were later softened.

Supplemental Security Income (SSI)

The Supplemental Security Income (SSI) program was established in 1972 (implemented in 1974) to provide a minimum guaranteed income to elderly, blind, and/or disabled persons. SSI combined several state-administered, categorical programs (Aid to the Blind; Aid to the Disabled; and Old-Age Assistance) into a single entity. Eligibility is based on categorical status (recipients must be either aged, blind, or disabled) and financial resources. The program is administered as a federal-state partnership. State agencies manage eligibility determination and may supplement SSI payments, and the Social Security Administration manages federal contributions and regulation of the program. Since its inception, SSI has been remarkably unchanged, but it has seen considerable enrollment growth in the past two decades (U.S. General Accounting Office, 1995).

In 1990 the Commissioner of Social Security appointed the "SSI Modernization Panel" to review the program and suggest modifications. Chaired by Dr. Arthur Flemming (former Social Security Commissioner), the panel undertook an exhaustive study of the program. The panel's report, released in 1992, identified major weaknesses in SSI and recommended a series of reforms. These included increasing benefits to 120 percent of the poverty threshold, adding staff to reduce delays in eligibility determination, eliminating the reduction in benefits for recipients who lived with family members, and increasing the program's asset limits (U.S. Department of Health and Human Services, 1992).

The recommendations of the Modernization Panel were largely ignored, yet SSI was revised, along with other welfare programs, through the 1996 Personal Responsibility and Work Opportunity Reconciliation Act. Under this welfare reform legislation, legal immigrants lost access to both SSI and food stamps unless they and/or their spouses had worked for 10 years and not received benefits. Following implementation of the 1996 reforms, an estimated 500,000 immigrants (more than half of them elderly) became ineligible for SSI. Another 940,000 immigrants (many of them elderly) lost their eligibility for food stamps (www.gao.gov/AIndexFY98/abstracts/he98132.htm).[9] SSI benefits for most of these immigrants were restored by the Balanced Budget Act of 1997; however, this act did not restore benefits for immigrants who arrived in the United States after August 1996.

Currently, SSI has a strict means test. In 2001, income limits for eligibility were $531 per month for individuals and $796 per month for couples. In-kind income, including food, clothing, or shelter (or "something" that can be exchanged for food, clothing, or shelter) is considered when determining eligibility. If a person lives with a family member who provides shelter and food, his or her income is adjusted through addition of one-third of the federal SSI benefit amount. When this "in-kind" contribution is taken into account, some people become ineligible for SSI. Resource limits for SSI were subject to a one-time adjustment in 1984. Current asset limits are $2,000 for individuals and $3,000 for couples. Homes, adjoining land, and automobiles are not counted as assets in determining SSI eligibility, but life insurance policies with cash values in excess of $1,500 per person are considered (Social Security Administration, 1999).

Benefit levels vary from state to state. Although the federal monthly benefit is fixed (in 1999 it was $494 for an individual and $741 for a couple), some states supplement this amount with contributions from state funds. All but five states (Kansas, Mississippi, Tennessee, Texas, and West Virginia) provide a supplement. Some provide a token amount, ranging from $1.90 to $5.30 per month for an individual (Hawaii, Oregon, Utah). The most generous supplements were found in Alaska ($320 for an individual and $528 for a couple) and California ($223 for an individual and $557 for a couple) (Social Security Administration, 1999).

The SSI program, while "ideally suited to serve as a vehicle for reducing poverty among the elderly" (Zedlewski & Meyer, 1987, p. 14), fails to fulfill its promise for two reasons: non-participation and inadequate benefits. Only half of the aged who are eligible for SSI benefits participate in the program (Zedlewski & Meyer, 1987). A 1979 study conducted by the Social Security Administration concluded that women were more likely than men to be non-participants (Menefee, Edwards, & Schieber, 1981). Concern over access problems led the

---

[9]Although states were allowed to prohibit legal immigrants from participating in Medicaid, most have consented to continue to provide Medicaid benefits to immigrants who were on the program before welfare reform as well as to new immigrants after five years of U.S. residency.

U.S. Administration on Aging (AOA) to fund outreach demonstration efforts designed to raise public awareness of the program and to simplify the application process.

Those who do participate in SSI find that the program's benefits do not raise them above the poverty level. For example, in 1999 an elderly individual living in a state that did not supplement SSI would receive $514 per month, for an annual income of $6,168. The federal poverty threshold for that person was $652 per month, or $7,818 per year. Moon (1990) based her critique of SSI on this difference between benefit levels and the poverty threshold and further argued that the program was unfair to women. Benefits for couples are more generous than those for individuals. Individuals are most often women living alone. In 1998, older individuals received benefits amounting to 79 percent of the poverty threshold, while older couples received 90 percent.

MEDICAL CARE FOR THE INDIGENT: MEDICAID

In 1950, the first federal program of medical care for indigent Americans was established as a grant-in-aid program. Established as part of the Social Security Act Amendments of 1950, this program offered a federal match to states wishing to provide medical care to participants in other public assistance programs; however, not all states elected to participate.

In 1965, with an Administration committed to medical insurance, Medicaid was established as Title XIX of the Social Security Act. Like the program of medical care for the indigent, Medicaid would operate as a federal-state partnership, with the federal match determined on the basis of poverty levels in the state. The Medicaid program was more generous than the previous program. Nonetheless, it would be 17 years before all states had established such programs. Arizona was the holdout, waiting until 1982 to participate in Medicaid.

Unlike Medicare, Medicaid is means-tested and serves clients of all ages. Medicare is administered by the Social Security Administration, whereas direct administration of Medicaid is carried out by each state. States vary in their eligibility requirements and in medical services covered, although coverage of some services is required by federal law. This mandatory coverage includes inpatient and outpatient hospital services; physician, midwife, and nurse practitioner care; laboratory and X-ray services; nursing home and home health care; and rural health clinic services. States may provide additional services. These commonly include prescription drugs, clinic services, hearing aids, dental care, prosthetic devices, and long-term care for the mentally retarded.

Medicaid provides health care to millions of Americans. Eligibility requirements are both means-tested and categorical. In addition to having limited income and assets, clients must belong to a covered group. These groups include children, pregnant women, the elderly, and people with disabilities. In 1996, the program served 41.3 million people at a cost of $155.4 billion (Kaiser Family

Foundation, 1998). Medicaid has absorbed a growing proportion of state budgets in recent decades, leading state and federal policy-makers to focus on cost-containment strategies.

The elderly and disabled are a minority of those served by Medicaid, but they account for most program costs because of their more intensive use of health care services. In 1996, for example, 9.9 percent (4.1 million) Medicaid clients were elderly and 16.2 percent (6.7 million) were blind or disabled; yet these groups accounted for 64 percent of program spending (Kaiser Family Foundation, 1998). Unlike Medicare, Medicaid covers custodial care in a skilled nursing facility. As a result, the program is the primary public financing mechanism for long-term care of the elderly. Medicaid covers about half of the nation's nursing home costs, which amount to more than one-third of the program's expenditures (35.8 percent in 1996).

HEALTH AND SOCIAL SERVICES

In addition to social insurance and public assistance, the Social Security Act allows for the use of federal funds to provide some health and social services. Four of the Act's titles authorize services: Title IV allows for child welfare services, Title V establishes maternal and child health services, Title XX authorizes social services, and Title XXI creates the Child Health Insurance Program. Although federal staff are employed under these titles, they do not provide direct services, as doing so would be incompatible with constitutional limitations on the power of the federal government. Instead, federal staff members administer grants to the states. States then deliver services or arrange for their delivery in ways that are compatible with federal regulations governing each program.

CHILD WELFARE SERVICES UNDER TITLE IV

Title IV of the 1935 Social Security Act established a program of grants-in-aid for states to set up their ADC programs. The Act also allowed for child welfare services, allocating $1.5 million for that purpose (Lenroot, 1960). An initial focus was on development of child welfare services in rural areas, though states had considerable latitude in using their child welfare allocations. Katharine Lenroot, Director of the Children's Bureau in 1935, explained that

> The basic principle followed in planning programs, especially in child welfare, was that of taking each state where it was, and encouraging initiative and flexibility, with great emphasis on local responsibility. . . . The term "child welfare service" was seen for the first time, in many states, as extending far beyond institutional care, or foster home care, or protective services, or cooperation with juvenile courts, to include a variety of measures, such as casework service, homemaker service and day care to strengthen and supplement the child's own home so that he could remain in it (Lenroot, 1960, p. 2).

Just as the 1950s were a time of expansion for other Social Security Act programs, child welfare experienced tremendous growth and increased federal appropriations. With the shift from a rural to an urban emphasis, child welfare services reflected the broad social transition into an urban, industrialized nation.

Today, child welfare services under Title IV include federal payments for foster care and adoption assistance, preventive services designed to keep children in their homes, services to develop alternative placements for children for whom foster care or adoption are not feasible, and family reunification services. Family preservation services are authorized under this Title to provide intensive support to maintain children in their homes. Funds are also provided for training of child welfare professionals and research in methods of improving services in the field. States receive fixed allocations under these statutes, although some must meet matching requirements.

MATERNAL AND CHILD HEALTH SERVICES (TITLE V)

Title V of the 1935 Social Security Act allowed for grants to states in support of maternal and child health services. This program enabled the U.S. Children's Bureau to continue the work it had begun in establishing clinics for mothers and children throughout the nation. Grants for maternal and child health did not require states to provide matching funds, but the program's regulations did stipulate that states had to use funds to extend or improve upon existing services (not to replace them) and that states must focus on needy areas (typically rural areas) and groups with severest hardships.

Today, these services are provided in each state under the Maternal and Child Health Services Block Grant. With a focus on low-income mothers and those in rural areas, these block grant funds are used to meet the health objectives established under the Public Health Service Act of 2000. States have considerable latitude in allocating these funds. Typical services provided include immunizations, visiting nurse activities, rehabilitative services for blind and disabled children, and case management for children with special health care needs. In addition to the state allocations, federal funds are available under Title V for training health personnel and conducting research on health care delivery, genetic testing and counseling, hemophilia, and early interventions.

SOCIAL SERVICES BLOCK GRANT (TITLE XX)

Title XX of the Social Security Act was passed in 1975 to provide social services to vulnerable Americans. A funding cap of $2.5 billion was established, making the program a "capped entitlement." It was converted to the "Social Services Block Grant" through the Omnibus Budget Reconciliation Act of 1981. The SSBG provides funds to states for social services directed toward achieving economic self-sufficiency; preventing or remedying neglect, abuse, or exploitation of children or adults; preventing or reducing inappropriate institutionalization; and securing referrals for institutional care. Within these broad goals, states have latitude in deciding what services they will provide. SSBG funds are typically used to provide day care for children, home-based services for the elderly or disabled, and protective services. Each states's allocation is based on its population. The SSBG does not have a state matching requirement.

CHILDREN'S HEALTH INSURANCE PROGRAM (TITLE XXI)

In 1995, an estimated 10 million children, 13.8 percent of Americans under the age of 18, were not covered by medical insurance (Weil, 1997). Concern for these vulnerable children led to the creation, through the 1997 Balanced Budget Act, of the State Children's Health Insurance Program, known as S-CHIP, or CHIP. The program authorizes funding for states to provide health coverage to uninsured, low-income children. It is targeted to children who are not eligible for Medicaid, but whose families are unable to purchase private insurance (i.e., children in families with incomes below 200 percent of the federal poverty threshold). States enjoy broad latitude in designing their CHIP programs. They may either expand their existing Medicaid coverage or establish separate programs. The CHIP program limits enrollee costs by prohibiting deductibles and limiting copayments to nominal amounts. Usually premiums are not allowed.

A TOOL FOR SOCIAL JUSTICE: THE PHILOSOPHIES OF SOCIAL SECURITY IN THE UNITED STATES

The Social Security Act is the foundation of America's safety net and a central vehicle for promoting social justice. It applies three broad strategies: (1) individual insurance financed through payroll taxes and user premiums; (2) public assistance financed through federal grants-in-aid using federal and state general revenues; and (3) health and social services financed through general revenues.

Social Security is a pivotal mechanism for allocating the costs and benefits of U.S. citizenship. Perhaps the most controversial of the Act's provisions stem from the costs it has imposed on citizens. This controversy is seen, for example, in the constitutional challenges that were raised concerning the OAI program's compulsory payroll tax. The payroll tax has risen considerably in recent decades, from 2 percent of wages and a $3,000 cap to more than 15 percent of wages and a $74,400 cap in 2000. Thus, OAI absorbs a significant proportion of the incomes of low- and middle-income workers. Proposals to increase the payroll tax continue to fuel the controversy.

Other costs imposed by the Social Security Act are tied less directly to the Act itself but are every bit as controversial as the payroll tax. The public assistance and service programs funded under Social Security are financed through general revenues, often at both federal and state levels. As indicated in Chapter

2, these revenues are generated through individual and corporate income taxes. Since these taxes are progressive, Social Security's public assistance and service programs represent a significant redistribution of income from the affluent to the needy. Movements to dismantle these programs, most recently through the elimination of AFDC, enhance the economic standing of affluent Americans while imposing hardships on the vulnerable.

Social Security represents a distinctly American approach to vulnerability and social justice. The program borrows little from oligarchic and socialist philosophies. Instead, it reflects the two philosophical perspectives on social justice most compatible with American political and economic thought: libertarianism and liberalism.

The Social Security Act was carefully crafted to minimize libertarian objections. The imposition of compulsory taxes was minimized, as was the role of the federal government in providing assistance and services. The increasing use of block grants to fund Social Security Act programs responds to the call for "states' rights," or moving decision-making as close as possible to the individual level. This movement is an indirect outgrowth of the libertarian emphasis on personal freedom. The Social Security Act defers to the private market in several areas— for example, when it establishes benefit levels that are well below the poverty threshold. No able-bodied worker would be motivated to forego employment with the promise of such minimal sustenance. This unwillingness to provide an alternative to private employment illustrates the principle of "less eligibility," which will be discussed in Chapter 4.

The contribution of liberal philosophies to Social Security in the United States is readily apparent. The Act established a "social minimum" for income below which Americans in some vulnerable categories (the deserving poor) should not fall. Thus, the SSI program provides a social minimum for the aged, blind, and disabled. The public assistance and health and social service programs under Social Security may be viewed from a utilitarian perspective as optimizing social well-being. Financed through progressive taxes, they transfer income from those who can afford it most easily to enhance the well-being of those who are most in need of assistance.

SUMMARY: SOCIAL SECURITY PROGRAMS

In this chapter we have explored programs established through the Social Security Act of 1935 and its amendments. From a historical perspective, Social Security is seen, not simply as a tool for improving workers' well-being, but as a political vehicle for securing loyalty to a State. Even as it secures worker loyalty, it presents tremendous administrative demands, essentially requiring the construction of a government administrative apparatus. Contemporary programs established through the Act reflect three models: (1) social insurance programs financed through payroll taxes and premiums; (2) public assistance programs financed through federal and state general revenues; and (3) health and social service programs delivered through grants-in-aid to the states. Several proposals to reform the OASI program were reviewed here: privatization, earnings sharing, and caregiver credits. These proposals can be seen as efforts to shift the costs and benefits of citizenship, thereby directly influencing social justice within the nation.

DISCUSSION TOPICS

1. The Social Security Act of 1935 was carefully crafted to comply with constitutional provisions restricting the role of the federal government. Compare the Act's insurance programs with its means-tested programs. Do they differ in the roles assigned to the states? How and why?

2. Social Security developed in Europe during the latter part of the nineteenth century. What was happening in major Asian countries during this period? What type of insurance did workers in these countries have against "the three fears" of poverty and illness in old age and unemployment? What forms of social insurance are offered by Asian nations today?

3. What are the consequences should a state fail to adhere to federal laws and regulations governing a grant-in-aid program? Have these consequences ever been applied to your state?

4. Analyze a proposal to revise a Social Security Act program using the five questions presented in Chapter 1.

    (a) What are the costs and/or benefits under consideration?

    (b) Who bears the cost? Who receives the benefit? What is the relationship between these two entities?

    (c) Are issues of membership and voice relevant? Does everyone affected by this proposal have an equal voice in the decision?

    (d) What are the distributive principles governing the allocation of costs and benefits?

    (e) Is this proposal fair?

SUGGESTED RESOURCES

Achenbaum, W. A. (1986). *Social Security: Visions and Revisions.* Cambridge: Cambridge University Press.

Kingson, E. R., & Berkowitz, E. D. (1993). *Social Security and Medicare: A Policy Primer.* Westport, CT: Greenwood Publishing Group.

www.ssa.gov—Maintained by the Social Security Administration, this site offers outstanding historical material on the Act, as well as the opportunity to subscribe to a free e-mail newsletter that gives updates on news affecting Social Security.

PART II

Collective Responses to Social Problems

MOBILIZING FACTORS

During the Paleolithic Era, humans banded together to hunt mammoth. In the twentieth century, they paid Social Security taxes. Since the dawn of our species, humans have used collective action to meet individual needs, but no human society responds collectively to *every* individual problem. How can we determine whether or not a problem will be addressed collectively?

Abram de Swaan (1988)[1] identified three conditions that encourage collective solutions to individual adversity. First, the *external effects* of the adversity must be recognized. One person's suffering must affect another, and the "other" must recognize that effect. This recognition is particularly effective when the other person has the resources to do something about the adversity. Second, *individual remedies* must be of limited effectiveness. Attempts by indi-

---

[1]De Swaan's book, *In Care of the State*, serves as the basis for much of this discussion. Drawing from two distinct intellectual traditions, welfare economics and historical sociology, de Swaan asked, "How and why did people come to develop collective, nation-wide and compulsory arrangements to cope with deficiencies and adversities that appeared to affect them separately and to call for individual remedies?" The result is a compelling work.

viduals to escape the external effects or to avoid the problem must prove ineffective. Finally, when adversity as well as its external effects can strike at any time with unpredictable magnitude (*uncertainty of moment and magnitude*), collective responses are more likely.

In the nineteenth century, cholera epidemics devastated many European cities. The 1832 wave of cholera took 18,000 victims in England and a similar number in Paris. Nineteenth-century scientists quickly linked the infection to lack of fresh water and inadequate sewage removal. Those who could apply individual solutions (the rich) removed themselves to healthier (usually higher) quarters. After the disease was established among the poor, however, it began to invade the quarters of the rich. As de Swaan noted, "mass epidemics provided a striking image of interdependency between fellow city-dwellers, poor and rich, established and newcomers, ignorant and cultivated alike" (p. 124). As the failure of individual solutions became evident, there was widespread agreement that a collective approach was in order.

Experts soon decided that citywide sanitation systems were the best solution, but such systems were disruptive and expensive. Initially they were built in wealthy neighborhoods and financed through what we now call "user" or "connection" fees. As soon as wealthy neighborhoods were saturated with pipes, the "venous-arterial system" of sanitation networks was extended throughout the city—a "public good" supported by compulsory taxes and fees. Sanitation departments were established to collect these fees and maintain the systems.

Thus, modern plumbing, the collective approach to managing fresh water and removing sewage, emerged because of the external effects of the adversity experienced by the poor (the wealthy were exposed to cholera); the failure of individual remedies (moving to higher ground did not ensure protection against the disease); and uncertainty regarding the moment and magnitude of adversity (one never knew whether or how badly one might be affected by the disease).

In Part II of this book, we will trace the development of policies and programs to address three individual problems: poverty (Chapter 4), physical illness (Chapter 5), and mental illness (Chapter 6). In each case, society's collective response can be traced to some of the conditions we have just examined: external effects, failure of individual remedies, and uncertainty of moment and magnitude of adversity. In each chapter we will focus on the problem under consideration, beginning with a case study and then examining definitional issues, the development of policies and services, and emerging policy issues. In each chapter, we will include the background material necessary for students to apply the social justice framework described in Chapter 1 to emerging policy issues in the field.

The problems under consideration in these chapters represent risks that are shared, to various degrees, by all Americans. Each meets de Swann's three criteria for collective action (external effects are recognized, individual remedies are of limited effectiveness, and there is uncertainty of moment and magnitude); and each of these problems has mobilized governmental action to allocate benefits and resources. Progress toward social justice is achieved by the development of collective responses to these problems through governmental policies and programs.

4

Poverty and
Income Support

Poverty is the parent of revolution and crime.

ARISTOTLE

Considerable time and effort have been devoted to identifying the causes of
poverty and quantifying its toll on individuals and families. In the United
States we tend to attribute poverty to individual flaws such as laziness or intemperance, or to cultural weaknesses such as inability to defer gratification. But the
nation's most effective anti-poverty program, Social Security, grew out of a
national event—the Great Depression—that persuaded millions of Americans
that poverty could be addressed effectively through collective action.

This chapter begins with a case study involving Emily Morrison, a welfare
mother raising five children. Next, we will explore the problem of defining
poverty, then move on to examine divergent values and beliefs about poverty
and the poor. These beliefs include religious explanations of poverty, as well as
economic and sociological theories about its causes. To provide some historical
background, we will trace the development of interventions to prevent or alleviate poverty. The 1996 welfare reforms will be examined, along with other contemporary programs and policies, including the Food Stamp Program, the Earned
Income Tax Credit, and the Minimum Wage. We will look at the contemporary
realities of poverty in this nation, examining populations at risk, recent trends in
inequality, and three "secondary risks" associated with poverty: homelessness,
violence, and fraud. The chapter will close with a brief consideration of the
future prospects of America's poor.

CASE STUDY ♦ EMILY MORRISON

In some ways, Emily Morrison does not fit anyone's stereotype of a welfare mother. She is bright and articulate. Her home is clean. Her children are healthy and well-groomed. And therein lies her difficulty. Caseworkers at the Welfare Department view her as a problem client who is "working the system." I was warned before my interview with Emily that she was "manipulative" and "not an ideal client."

Emily lives in a working-class neighborhood. Her tiny home was freshly painted bright blue with lime green trim when I arrived to meet with her. The screen door was new, and let the visitor straight in to her small, warm living room. There were two wooden bookshelves, overloaded with books about Native Americans and the law. The living room also held a playpen, an automatic baby rocker, an afghan-covered couch, and a rocking chair. Two babies were at home during our interview, yet the house was remarkably quiet.

Emily is 34 years old, small and heavy-set, with long, dark hair. Even minimal activity can leave her breathing hard, with a wheeze that comes from lifelong asthma. She has some Native American blood, and explained that she was the only one in her family whose looks hinted at her Indian roots. She and her mother are exploring the possibility of registering as members of her tribe.

Emily's second son (age 17) and a few of his friends came home in the middle of our conversation. He was a handsome boy, with jet-black hair slicked back and stylish baggy pants. The boys headed straight for the babies, picking them up and cooing fondly. They had just returned from a classmate's funeral. As Emily explained, "This is a kid. He wasn't involved in anything. Apparently this other boy's house got shot up, and for some reason he thought this kid had done it and he just came up to him . . . in these people's house and held a gun to him and shot . . . they had both just turned 17."

Both of Emily's parents were high school graduates. Her mother taught dance to children in the neighborhood and her father worked for an employment service. Emily is the oldest of her parents' four children, and has fond memories of the foster children her parents helped to raise. Her father wrote and self-published two books during his retirement.

Emily describes herself as a "child of the sixties," explaining that her two oldest children were born out of wedlock. She lived with her first partner for three years. He was half African-American and half Native American, and is the father of her first son, who is now 19 years old. Her second relationship was with a man she now believes was mentally ill. She was living as a single mother and attending college when she became pregnant with her second son.

When her children were babies, Emily attended the local state university with support from Aid to Families with Dependent Children (AFDC). Of her second son, she said, "I went back to school with him. He was four days old. I carried him in a little front pack. I was always in school or working. I've never been on assistance when I wasn't doing something productive."

A social worker told Emily that she was not eligible for food stamps. Then, "One day I was in the library and I came across this code of federal regulations, and I was like, 'Oh wow. What are these?' Cause I didn't know anything about the law books and things like that at the time. And this guy that was in there started showing me how it worked and I said, 'Well, are there rules for welfare?' and he said, 'Well, of course there are.' And so I started looking it up and come to find out from what I read I was being [inappropriately] denied food stamps . . ." So Emily went to legal services and ended up getting retroactive food stamps. "That was the first time that I realized that I had rights. I was a human being you know . . . and that you didn't just have to go beg on your knees to these people for, you know, whatever little bit they'd give you. That you had legal rights, you know. People didn't want to give you information back then. It was like these big secrets."

After her food stamp victory, Emily worked for legal services, an experience that inspired her current desire to become a lawyer representing disadvantaged individuals. She spent several years in college, accumulating thousands of dollars in student loans, but quit school without completing graduation requirements. She had met a man she wanted to marry. "He was definitely the kind of husband that I wanted, and he was a hard worker and a good provider, you know. And initially my kids really liked him, and we did a lot of fun things together, you know? And he was just very loving and caring."

Emily's husband was from Tonga. Shortly after the wedding he brought his mother to live with them. Not long after his mother's arrival, he began to physically abuse Emily. The violence escalated, until, as Emily explained, "The last time he beat me up . . . I faked that I passed out because I knew if he hit me again, I knew I would die . . . it broke my nose and I had a concussion . . . I was out of it basically, completely out of it. I had a lot of blood, I guess, gush out of my nose and mouth and he stopped. His mother was there and she just, you know, went nuts on him." Emily was divorced from him "in 45 days."

While she was married, Emily worked as a clerk-typist. She later became the manager of an Indian Alcohol Recovery Center. After that she worked as a housing advocate for several years, writing construction grants for migrant housing and advocating for low-income housing. None of these jobs provided health insurance. She struggled with child care, and during most of their school-age years her boys came home to an empty house. "They were latchkey kids. We had some rules about what had to happen. They couldn't go out and play until I got home from work. I think the hardest thing that I remember from that . . . was that I didn't have a phone. They always had a quarter, and there is a pay phone down at the little market and if there was an emergency there was always an emergency quarter so they could call me."

When her oldest child was 13, Emily's asthma became so serious that she could no longer afford to live without health insurance. "I went and applied for AFDC. It was more than the financial part. I really needed the medical card. My medications alone ran me over a hundred a month. If I didn't get anything on the AFDC as long as I could get that medical card that was the most important thing to me, because you just never know with asthma. I've been in the hospital a couple of times, in emergency, you know. When

I couldn't breathe I had to go by ambulance one morning. That to me is the scary thing. Because even if I were to go back to work full-time now, I probably wouldn't be able to get picked up on insurance for six months to a year because of pre-existing conditions, and I don't know if I could go that long without having a health crisis."

Emily became a foster mother when a Native American friend asked her to get licensed so she could take his daughter, who was then living with a white foster family. She has since adopted one "special needs" child and become a legal guardian for two Native American children. Most of her income comes from foster care reimbursements of $15 per day and the adoption subsidy of $470 per month. Other income comes from Temporary Assistance to Needy Families (TANF) ($342 per month for herself and one child) and monthly disability payments from Supplemental Security Income (SSI) of about $484 for her son. He is eligible for disability payments because his father is terminally ill.

For the time being, Emily is comfortable (a violation of the principle of "less eligibility" described later in this chapter). She has lived in the same house for 11 years, and her payments are only $277 per month. But SSI is reviewing her son's eligibility, and lifetime limits on TANF will soon eliminate that source of income. Emily is struggling to create a "self-sufficiency plan." Without one, her TANF aid will be terminated. But often the activities her caseworker proposes for the plan are either unattractive or unfeasible. Emily would like to stay home and care for all five of her children. But doing so would not result in "self-sufficiency," so it is not an acceptable plan. She is reluctant to take a job, fearing that her health will suffer and her children will not receive adequate care.

Reflecting on her life, Emily has mixed feelings. "Maybe there's something really wrong with me, and I really can't be successful. You know what I mean?" But when reminded of her ability to promptly leave an abusive relationship, something many women struggle to do, she said, "Well, there was no question about it, you know. I think I know that I'm a survivor. I am definitely a survivor."

But she does not apologize for receiving public assistance. "Why it is that I don't feel ashamed if I am on welfare? The one thing that I feel really, really strongly about is that our society has devalued the role of family and mother so much . . . that's why so many of these kids have trouble. Because their mothers, a lot of them, are working in low-wage jobs . . . are divorced . . . and they don't see their dads that often or, you know, at all. There is just no structure left in the family. I've been really blessed. My boys are just terrific kids. They're not in trouble. They're good students. My oldest boy is gifted in music and art. I'm really proud of him cause he's very talented. He knows where he's going. My other boy, he's really involved in sports and he's a good student. He's in his second year as commanding officer of the ROTC program at his high school, and I think he's probably going to enlist right after he graduates. He'll graduate early."

Of course, Emily has secrets. She provides child care for a neighbor and would rather the welfare office not be aware of that fact. The father of her second son suffers from a debilitating mental illness, and she would rather no one knew about that. She has persuaded her caseworker that she is no longer "working the system." The worker said, "She used to work the system. But now she has seen the light in a sense. She is now working toward self-sufficiency." And, of course, "working toward self-sufficiency" is precisely what Emily must do for the next three years if she is to retain her TANF eligibility. After that, of course, the welfare system that she has relied on for so long will no longer be available to Emily and the three youngsters she has undertaken to raise.

DISCUSSION   Emily is probably not a typical "welfare mother." She has some college. She understands the system that provides income for her family—perhaps better than her caseworker. She maintains an oasis of comfort for her children in a neighborhood troubled by deteriorated housing and gang violence. Perhaps more important, she does not apologize for receiving public assistance, viewing the job of raising five children as a contribution that exceeds the value of funds she has received through public assistance.

But Emily's world has changed. Child-rearing is no longer sufficient to receive public support. The rug has been pulled out from under this "sixties-style advocate." The rights she was so delighted to discover in college are gradually being eliminated. AFDC was an entitlement, but TANF is not. Her caseworker and the state welfare agency now have discretion in deciding whether or not to continue her benefits. Her caseworker may become disillusioned with Emily's "self-sufficiency" planning and terminate her TANF benefits for what the agency calls "non-participation." Even if benefits are not terminated, her state's lifetime limit on TANF benefits means that the clock is ticking. Much will depend on how her state decides to allocate the slots for individuals exempted from its lifetime limit. Under federal law, states can exempt up to 20 percent of their caseloads. If Emily's asthma qualifies her as a "disabled parent," she may be eligible for extended assistance. But it is unclear whether she will meet criteria that her state has yet to establish. Emily may find that foster care payments and adoption subsidies are her sole sources of income.

DEFINING POVERTY

Poverty can be understood in both absolute and relative terms. "Absolute poverty" is based on a fixed level of resources, or "threshold." If a person's resources fall below the threshold, he or she is viewed as experiencing "absolute" poverty. Eligibility requirements for public poverty programs such as TANF involve the concept of absolute poverty. "Relative poverty" is based on comparison. If an individual's situation is disadvantaged compared to someone else's, or compared to what it was in the past, he or she is viewed as experiencing "relative" poverty. Compared to her siblings, Emily experiences relative poverty, but because of her other sources of income she is relatively advantaged compared to other TANF recipients. Some have argued that relative measures of poverty are superior to absolute measures because the self-images, expectations, and prospects of poor families are relative to others in their culture, regardless of their actual level of deprivation.

TABLE 4.1 2001 U.S. DEPARTMENT OF HEALTH AND
HUMAN SERVICES POVERTY THRESHOLDS

Family Size (no. of persons)	Threshold*
1	$ 8,590
2	11,610
3	14,630
4	17,650
5	20,670
6	23,730

For each additional person, add $3,020.

*Note: For Hawaii, multiply this figure by 1.15; for Alaska, multiply by 1.25.

The most common definition of poverty used in the United States, the Federal Poverty Threshold, is an absolute measure. It is used by the Census Bureau to gauge the level of poverty in the nation, and serves as the basis for official allocation of several means-tested programs, including the Food Stamp Program, Supplemental Security Income, and TANF.

The Federal Poverty Threshold was developed in the 1960s, by economist Mollie Orshansky, who worked for the Social Security Administration. Charged by the Kennedy administration with the task of developing an effective measure of poverty, Ms. Orshansky found that the only existing measure of family needs was based on food. She used a measure called the "Economy (or 'Thrifty') Food Plan" that had been developed by the U.S. Department of Agriculture. This plan estimated the cost of food required to sustain nutritional adequacy during a temporary emergency or shortage of funds. Since it was believed that food costs represented one-third of a family's budget, the total budget was set by multiplying the Economy Food Plan by three. Initially the poverty threshold for farm families, female-headed households, and the elderly was set lower than the standard amount. This was based on consumption studies conducted by the Department of Agriculture that revealed lower food expenditures among women than among men, and among the elderly than among younger groups. Farm families were believed to have access to inexpensive produce through their gardens, and the elderly had lower caloric requirements (Orshansky, 1965).

The poverty threshold has been changed in two ways. In 1969 the measure was "indexed" to the Consumer Price Index (CPI—a measure of inflation). As a result, it rises annually based on increases in the CPI. Then in 1981, in response to political pressure and technical arguments, the thresholds for farm families and female-headed households were raised to the standard level (Fisher, 1997). The threshold for those older than 65 remains 8 to 10 percent below that of other households.

Each year, the Department of Health and Human Services publishes the latest poverty thresholds in the Federal Register and on its web site (http://aspe. hhs.gov/poverty/01poverty.htm). The poverty thresholds for 2001 are listed in Table 4.1.

CRITIQUES OF THE POVERTY THRESHOLD

Some people have argued that the federal poverty threshold *over*estimates the extent of poverty in the United States because it does not count "in-kind" benefits such as food stamps, housing assistance, and medical programs as income (Friedman & Friedman, 1979; Murray, 1994). According to this view, the in-kind benefits available to the poor should be counted as income, based on their market value. Charles Murray argued that the many benefits available to poor people made it "possible for almost anyone to place themselves (sic) above the official poverty level" (Murray, 1994, p. 64). Going even further with this argument, Gilder (1981) suggested that the poor receive benefits every bit as valuable as a middle-class job because they have more leisure time and they work "off the books." Others have argued that the poverty threshold should be revised to include assets, as well as income, because some poor people own their homes (see Oliver & Shapiro, 1990).

Others argue that the federal poverty threshold *under*estimates financial hardship. Mollie Orshansky, the economist who developed the poverty threshold, suggested that it was at least 40 percent too low because the "multiplier" used to estimate total costs as three times food costs was too small (Chambers, 1982). Other critics of the poverty threshold focus on the Economy Food Plan itself. Some note that it was intended as a *temporary* budget and is inadequate for sustaining health over an extended period. The plan also places heavy demands on homemakers. It requires that a shopper know where to buy the least expensive commodities, be able to transport and store large quantities of food, and have the time, energy, and ability to prepare meals from basic staples (Chalfant, 1985; Wilson, 1987).

Another problem with the federal poverty threshold is its failure to take into account regional differences in the cost of living. A family of four would be hard-pressed to live on $17,050 (the 2000 poverty threshold) in New York City, but they might find it possible in rural Alabama.[1] The threshold does not take into account other circumstances, such as chronic illness or disability, that might affect a family's needs. Finally, multiplying a food budget by three to arrive at a total budget is unrealistic. Recent estimates suggest that low-income families in the United States spend roughly one quarter of their income on food, compared to a national average of about 12 percent. This would suggest a multiplier of 4, rather than 3 (see Patricia Ruggles, 1990).

Several authors have suggested alternative approaches to the measurement of financial hardship. Holden and Smeeding (1990) identified five sources of financial vulnerability among the elderly: lack of health insurance, lack of assets, social security benefits that preclude Medicaid eligibility, high housing costs, and

---

[1]This issue has been at least partially addressed, as the current threshold distinguishes between Alaska and Hawaii and the 48 contiguous states. The poverty threshold for Alaska is 1.25 times the threshold for the 48 states, while that of Hawaii is 1.15 times the mainland threshold.

chronic disability. They concluded that 35 percent of older persons experienced at least two of these sources of insecurity. Robert Binstock (1985) suggested that valid measures of poverty incorporate household expenditure patterns, as well as an individual's ability to cope with hardship. Either of these measures would involve a complex assessment process. In contrast, the federal poverty threshold is attractive because of its historic consistency and its administrative convenience. Thus, it will probably continue to be used as the dominant measure of financial hardship in this country.

VALUES AND BELIEFS ABOUT POVERTY AND THE POOR

Cultural values and beliefs about poverty and the poor influence the methods that are chosen to prevent or mitigate poverty. These values and beliefs can be grouped into seven broad categories: religious teachings about charity; punitive responses to the poor; poverty as motivation; "human capital" approaches; "culture of poverty" explanations; "restricted opportunity" explanations; and "pauperization" arguments. These ideas emerged at different times in the history of Western thought about the causes and treatment of poverty. Each belief offers a distinct outlook on the individual and structural factors that contribute to poverty, and each supports a distinct approach to poverty interventions.

RELIGIOUS BELIEFS ABOUT CHARITY

Charity is an essential part of the teachings of most world religions. The Code of Hammurabi, written two thousand years before the birth of Christ, called for protecting the weak from the strong. Buddhism teaches that "emancipation of the heart through love and charity" is the most important form of righteousness. Islamic teachings view charity, not as a "favor done by the giver," but as "spending for the cause of Allah . . . as a means to purify the soul of the giver and to . . . unite him with his poor brother" (http://ourdialogue.com/charity.htm).

Ancient Jewish doctrines moved care of the poor from the realm of charity to that of justice. They taught that not only did the well-off have a duty to give charity, but the poor had a right (and even a duty) to receive it. The Talmud, a collection of biblical texts accompanied by rabbinical commentaries, prescribes in careful detail how relief is to be administered. Under Talmudic law, a poor man should receive "Sufficient for his needs in that which he wanteth . . . [if he is hungry] he should be fed; if he needs clothing, he should be clothed; if he lacks household utensils, they should be purchased for him" (Trattner, 1989, p. 3).

Christianity emerged from the Jewish tradition and retained its emphasis on care of the poor. The New Testament emphasizes that the soul's entry into heaven depends on deeds of mercy and charity. Most telling in this regard is the description of Judgment Day in the Gospel of St. Matthew: "And the King shall answer and say unto them, Verily, I say unto you, Inasmuch as ye have done it unto one of the least of these my brethren, ye have done it unto me" (Matt. 25:40). Under Christian teachings, care of the poor is a matter of both justice and charity. The needy have a right to assistance; and the spiritual well-being of the rich depends on their providing charity. The Christian notion of salvation requires the faithful to care for the poor, not for altruistic reasons, but for the benefit of their own souls.

As early as the sixth century AD, care of the poor was an integral part of Christian monastic traditions. Using income from land holdings and donations, monks cared for the needy who came to their doors, as well as those who lived in nearby communities. Medieval hospitals, many of which were attached to monasteries, also provided services to the needy.[2]

Later, during the Middle Ages, the Catholic Church organized the first comprehensive system of relief in Europe. From the twelfth through the fourteenth centuries, relief for the poor operated under the direction of the Medieval Poor Law, a set of policies developed by church leaders to specify relief measures for the indigent. Under this system, "a poor man was considered an honorable man, and the only test for aid was need" (Segalman & Basu, 1981, p. 60).

Thus, religious approaches to poverty do not attempt to explain why some people are poor and others are not. Poverty is viewed as neither an individual nor a societal failure, but as an integral part of the human condition, offering the opportunity, requirement, or possibility of personal charity. This view stands in sharp contrast to approaches that treat poverty as a crime.

POVERTY AS CRIME

Punitive responses to poverty are based on the belief that at least some of the poor are lazy and need punishment to overcome their evil ways. Most obvious among these "undeserving" poor are individuals who are able-bodied but do not work. But their ranks also include people whose disabilities might be considered their own fault, such as alcoholics and spendthrifts.

One of de Tocqueville's remarks after visiting America was that in the new nation there was only one crime: being poor. But Americans were not the first to assume a punitive stance vis à vis the poor. Laws in sixteenth-century England assigned severe punishments to able-bodied beggars. As Trattner reported, "They were to be brought to the market place and 'there to be tyed to the end of a carte naked and be beten with whyppes throughe out . . . tyll [their bodies] . . . be blody by reason of suche whypping'" (p. 7).

Modern approaches to the poor are seldom as harsh as these, but are often nonetheless punitive. The poor are no longer subjected to whipping but to shame and indifference. Lengthy waits are one form of punishment. In *Tyranny*

---

[2]This discussion draws heavily from Walter Trattner, *From Poor Law to Welfare State: A History of Social Welfare in America* (New York: Free Press, 1989).

of Kindness, Theresa Funiciello noted a sign in a New York welfare office that said, "NO MATTER WHAT TIME YOUR APPOINTMENT IS, IF YOU ARE NOT HERE BY 8:30 AM YOU WILL NOT BE SEEN" (Funiciello, 1993, p. 3).

POVERTY AS MOTIVATION

Some have argued that in pre-industrial nations there is no individual poverty. Families, communities, and even nations as a whole may experience severe deprivation. But individuals are not left to experience poverty alone, and the poor are not isolated as "other" or "different." According to this view, capitalist industrial economies require the existence of poverty, because they need a large, unemployed segment in their labor force. The poverty and embarrassment associated with unemployment are seen as necessary motivators because they make workers willing to labor for low wages in difficult conditions and to leave their homes and seek employment in industrial centers. Herbert Gans noted that poverty could be eliminated if the wealthy chose to do so. The fact that they choose not to do so indicates their need for a reliable source of cheap labor (Gans, 1971).

The regulation of charity in the interests of maintaining a labor force pre-dates the industrial revolution. In 1348 an outbreak of "Black Death" (bubonic plague) decimated the population of England. In response to a shortage of laborers, parliament enacted the "Statute of Labourers," which forbade giving charity to able-bodied beggars. Later on, the Elizabethan Poor Law would require anyone capable of working to do so, if only to earn the right to receive assistance.

The principle of "less eligibility" illustrates the belief that poverty is an important motivator. Under this view, no one on relief should be as well off as the lowest-paid laborer. This principle is an integral part of poverty interventions. It is manifest in the low level of benefits provided by public assistance programs and by humiliating administrative practices such as those described above.

HUMAN CAPITAL EXPLANATIONS OF POVERTY

Human capital explanations of poverty focus on the skills, education, and experience ("human capital") that an individual brings to the marketplace. According to this view, the poor simply have inadequate or outdated skills and work experience. Neither the individual nor the system is held responsible for poverty, which is viewed as an inevitable consequence of a dynamic economy. Interventions based on this outlook are likely to incorporate job training and education for the poor. They might also include subsidized employment.

CULTURE OF POVERTY EXPLANATIONS

The term "Culture of Poverty" was coined by Oscar Lewis, an anthropologist who studied poor families in Mexico and Puerto Rico. As he defined it, "The culture of poverty is both an adaptation and a reaction of the poor to their marginal position in a class-stratified, highly individuated, capitalistic society. It represents an effort to cope with feelings of hopelessness and despair which develop from the realization of the improbability of achieving success in terms of the values and goals of the larger society" (Lewis, 1965, p. xliv).

The culture of poverty is seen as a distinct set of values that arise in the context of hopeless disadvantage. These values include a present-time orientation that seeks immediate gratification and precludes long-term planning or deferred reward. For example, according to this view, a person raised in poverty would prefer the instant rush of intoxication to the sustained effort of education. They may be seen as improvident or lazy, when in fact they have learned (or been taught) that effort is not rewarded, life is short, and pleasures are rare. Their behavior represents an effort to adapt to lifelong—even intergenerational— poverty. Drug addiction or teenage pregnancy can be understood as the natural consequence of growing up in poverty. Crime may be the logical reaction to repeated failure, and family break-up the inevitable result of a chaotic and unrestrained social milieu. Yet, as Segalman and Basu noted, "The coping mechanisms by which the poor adjust to their state also serve to prevent them and their children from ever moving out of poverty" (1981, p. 13). An important component of this view holds that victims of poverty cannot make use of opportunities that present themselves later in life because they have been irreparably damaged by their culture.

In 1968, Edward C. Banfield of Harvard University described his vision of the culture of poverty. He argued that poverty creates a "present-orientedness" that leaves individuals unable to plan for the future or to defer gratification. Acknowledging that some people become poor through accidents or misfortunes that are short-lived, he argued that others will be poor regardless of their circumstances. Such people lack the values and strengths necessary to succeed. Giving them money would be pointless, because they would squander it on frivolous nonessentials.

Others have described the culture of poverty. Among them, Nicolas Lemann (1986) suggested that residents of black ghettos in inner cities inherited the values and traits of sharecroppers. Most of them, he noted, come from rural Southern roots, where sharecroppers could neither own property nor save money and thus failed to learn the values necessary to preserve family stability and accumulate financial reserves (see Segalman & Basu, 1981). In 1969, Senator Daniel Patrick Moynihan endorsed the culture of poverty argument in his controversial book *Maximum Feasible Misunderstanding*, which argued that poverty among African-Americans reflected the failure of African-American family life.

"Culture of poverty" explanations apply only to individuals who experience lifelong, intergenerational poverty. Interventions based on such explanations attempt to change the values of poor adults or to inculcate a different set of values in their children. Historically, the latter objective was used to justify removing poor children from their homes and placing them in middle-class settings where they were expected to learn the values of thrift, abstinence, and productivity.[3] Other interventions based on this viewpoint simply exposed poor adults to middle-class role models in the hope that they would absorb new habits and values.

RESTRICTED OPPORTUNITY THEORIES OF POVERTY

Like "culture of poverty" explanations, "restricted opportunity" theories about poverty surfaced in the twentieth century. But where the culture of poverty explanation attributes poverty to personal attributes, restricted opportunity explanations focus on structural barriers that prevent individuals from securing the education and/or jobs necessary to succeed financially. According to this view, traits such as gender, race, and class expose an individual to institutional discrimination that restricts opportunities and increases the risk of poverty.

Proponents of this view often note that poverty is not randomly distributed within the population of the United States. Female-headed households are more vulnerable than households headed by men; people of color are more likely to be poor at any age than Caucasians; and those who grew up in impoverished households are exposed to a whole host of risks, including the strong likelihood of spending their lives in poverty.

This greater risk of poverty can be explained with reference to discriminatory practices in education and in the workplace. Some of the programs established under President Lyndon Johnson's War on Poverty during the 1960s reflected this perspective, attempting to increase the educational, employment, and political opportunities available to the poor. Civil rights laws designed to increase opportunities for women and minorities also represent interventions based on the restricted opportunity explanation of poverty.

THE PAUPERIZATION ARGUMENT

In 1994, President Clinton promised to "end welfare as we know it." He was certainly not the first U.S. policymaker to make this promise, which reflected a widespread belief that welfare did not relieve poverty but caused it by fostering dependence on a system that destroyed incentives to work. The welfare system created "paupers" (or permanent poor) from those who might otherwise succeed. If there were no welfare, the pauperization argument held, those who were receiving public assistance would be motivated to find jobs and pull themselves out of poverty.

---

[3]Two striking examples of this practice are found in the history of child welfare in the United States. During the nineteenth century, Charles Loring Brace of the Children's Aid Society removed children from urban tenements and placed them with middle-class farm families. During the nineteenth and twentieth centuries, Native American children were removed from their homes on reservations and placed with middle-class white families.

In itself, this idea is not unique to the twentieth century. Nineteenth-century advocates of poorhouses raised the specter of pauperization to criticize the existing practice of "outdoor relief" (providing financial support to poor people in their homes, rather than requiring them to enter a poorhouse). Indeed, the pauperization argument has been used by critics of most established systems of cash assistance for the poor.

PUBLIC INTERVENTIONS TO PREVENT OR ALLEVIATE POVERTY

In most capitalist nations, poverty interventions encounter deep-seated ambivalence. The allocation principle used in most programs ("to each according to his need") is incompatible with that of a capitalist economy ("to each according to his product"). Thus, poverty programs are often criticized for their socialist underpinnings. Further, the history of poverty interventions frequently intersects with that of labor policies. A nation's willingness to support the poor may fluctuate according to the labor needs of its economy.

BRITISH APPROACHES

In 1348, an outbreak of "Black Death" (bubonic plague) decimated the populations of England and other European nations. In England a labor shortage led to the passage of the "Statute of Labourers," which forbade giving charity to able-bodied beggars. The law also set maximum wages and imposed travel restrictions, ensuring that laborers would stay within their home parishes and accept employment there, rather than traveling to pursue opportunities elsewhere. This law is a striking illustration of the use of poverty policies to control the labor force, based on the idea of poverty as a motivator. It also represented the first constraint on private relief efforts.

Two hundred years later, during the sixteenth century, a series of laws were passed in England to regulate begging. These laws established a clear distinction between the "deserving" and the "undeserving" poor. Severe punishment was allotted to able-bodied people who were not inclined to work, but those who were unable to work were assigned areas where they could beg. In 1536, the Act for the Punishment of Sturdy Vagabonds and Beggars elaborated both the punishments for undeserving beggars (which extended to branding, enslavement, and execution) and government relief for the deserving poor. The Act directed local public officials to collect donations from the churches for poor relief. This legislation changed the role of government from the regulation of beggars to the administration of relief in partnership with the church. The Act also reflected the human capital explanation of poverty, as it provided for training of indigent youth and community service employment for unemployed adults.

Later in the sixteenth century, the parish system became unable to collect sufficient voluntary donations to meet the demands for poor relief. A new statute called the "Elizabethan Poor Law" was passed to levy a tax for the care of the poor and create an administrative structure for the management of relief efforts.

The statutes passed during the sixteenth century established the basic principles that were later codified in the Poor Law of 1601 (also known as the "Elizabethan Poor Law"). This law remained essentially unchanged for 250 years, and was the foundation of the measures European colonists put in place when they came to the New World. Its basic principles included:

- **Family responsibility:** Parents were legally responsible for supporting their children and grandchildren, and conversely, children were responsible for their aged parents and grandparents.

- **Local responsibility:** Aid was managed through local units of government called "parishes," and strict residency requirements were in place to discourage vagrancy. Indigents who did not meet residency requirements were returned to their home parishes. Community relief efforts provided for needy neighbors, not for roving strangers.

- **Differential treatment:** The law distinguished between the "deserving" and the "undeserving" poor. Among the deserving, it established three major categories: children, the able-bodied unemployed, and those incapacitated by disability or age (the "impotent"). The undeserving included those who were too lazy, shiftless, or drunk to support themselves.

- **Work preference:** Public relief was *not* intended as an alternative to paid employment. Those who could work were expected to do so. Children were employed in apprenticeships, the able-bodied unemployed were given jobs, and the undeserving were sent to workhouses for forced labor. Only the "impotent" were excused from the work requirement.

- **Public assistance through compulsory taxation:** Under the Poor Law of 1601, mandatory taxes were collected to finance the relief of poverty. Every household in a parish was taxed, and the money was collected by overseers of the poor. Those who did not pay the tax were threatened with imprisonment.

The Elizabethan Poor Law provided the foundation for later U.S. interventions designed to alleviate poverty and maintain social equilibrium.

AMERICAN APPROACHES TO POVERTY IN THE EIGHTEENTH AND NINETEENTH CENTURIES

In the following sections we will trace the development of American relief from its origins in the colonies to the present. As we will see, relief in colonial times was a chancy affair—an individual's care depended not only on the town in which he or she lived, but on his or her relationships with community leaders. The nineteenth century was marked by widespread intolerance for public relief and contempt for the poor. These attitudes led to diminished "outdoor relief" and the growth of poorhouses. Social work's origins in this time reveal two contradictory approaches to poverty: the Charity Organization Societies and the Settlement Movement. It took the Great Depression to convince twentieth-century Americans of the need for a federal system of relief. In recent years it has become important, and sometimes difficult, to separate rhetoric from reality, and message from messenger. For example, President Lyndon Johnson declared an "unconditional war on poverty," yet his Great Society programs did little to expand relief for the poor. President Nixon spoke ardently against welfare, yet his administration was marked by significantly expanded benefits for the poor. Presidents Reagan and Bush were at the forefront of anti-welfare rhetoric, but it took a Democrat (Bill Clinton) to dismantle the federal relief entitlement.

POVERTY INTERVENTIONS IN EARLY AMERICA. America was not colonized as a refuge for Europe's poor. Instead, the New World was a haven for adventurers and religious minorities. The first permanent settlement was established at Jamestown in 1607. The Virginia Company sent a group of adventurers to identify ways of exploiting the region's natural wealth. Women joined the settlement later, in 1608. The pilgrims didn't come to New England until the development of forces that would lead to the English civil war. Refugees from that conflict, the pilgrims were people of limited means—craftsmen, small shopkeepers, and farmers—but they were hardly destitute.[4] Later, colonists who could not pay for their passage financed their trips by selling their labor as indentured servants. While these servants entered the colonies without resources, the terms of their indenture were generous, and in at least one state (Pennsylvania) they received land grants at the end of their service.

During the early years of shared deprivation, government programs to alleviate poverty were a luxury the colonies could ill afford. Individual misfortune, such as disease or bereavement, met with neighborly kindness—or at least, assistance.[5] But the poor, including widows and orphans, those disabled by age or disease, and others, rapidly increased in number. By the mid-seventeenth century most of the colonies had initiated formal provisions that made local taxpayers responsible for the support of their poor neighbors. Measures adopted by the colonies were modeled on the Elizabethan Poor Law and included the principles of family and local responsibility.

Care of the poor was undertaken by the town in which they resided. Towns used three approaches. The most straightforward approach was to send poor individuals to live in private homes. Another approach involved placing the poor

---

[4]During the nineteenth century the British shipped prisoners and beggars to Australia, but this practice was not widespread in North America. Nonetheless, it was a significant concern to the colonial leaders. In 1776, Benjamin Franklin was sent to England to protest the transportation of criminals to the colonies.

[5]A possible exception to this neighborly assistance was the treatment of witches, who were usually single older women of limited means who violated community norms.

in private homes at public expense. The fee was usually set through an auction where those in need were offered to the lowest bidder, with the fee paid by the town. A third approach was sometimes used when people needed only temporary aid. In this practice, called "outdoor assistance" or "outdoor relief," payments were given directly to the person in need.

The principle of local responsibility for local residents meant that people who were displaced or had left their original homes were not entitled to receive aid. Most towns developed elaborate policies to discourage needy strangers from staying. Some of these involved "warning away" visitors who might become a burden; prohibiting the sale of land to strangers without official permission; and requiring residents who brought in servants to support them if they became needy. Port towns, troubled by the arrival of needy immigrants, required captains of vessels to post bonds for each passenger they discharged. In some cases, the towns forced captains to return the destitute to their points of origin. Another source of trouble for local governments was refugees from Indian wars, who arrived in towns with little more than the clothing on their backs.

Ultimately, these "unsettled poor" proved to be the undoing of the principle of local responsibility. Wars and migration overwhelmed the towns' ability to provide assistance. Eventually towns asked colonial authorities for funds to provide relief for these strangers. Thus, the colonial treasury was used to reimburse towns for the care of the "unsettled poor."

RELIEF IN THE NEW NATION. The War of Independence left many of the new nation's residents widowed, orphaned, or disabled, and seriously disrupted economic ties to England and other European nations. Although private philanthropy supplemented public relief efforts, local relief organizations were overwhelmed by requests for assistance. Many of these requests came from people who did not meet local residency requirements. As a result, one of the first actions undertaken by the new states was the establishment of administrative structures for handling poor relief. New York was the first state to do so, setting up "the Committee on Superintendence of the Poor."[6]

Despite the "general welfare" clause of the U.S. Constitution (Article I, Section 8), the United States did not pass national legislation governing the provision of relief. In this respect the Americans deviated from European tradition. In the United States, responsibility for the relief of poverty was left to state and local governments.

RELIEF IN NINETEENTH-CENTURY AMERICA. The nineteenth century was a time of great industrial expansion in both England and the United States. The demand for industrial workers triggered a new approach to relief of poverty, and outdoor relief was harshly criticized.

---

[6]The state of New York was at the forefront of poverty relief for several decades. New York is the only state in the U.S. that addresses relief of poverty in its constitution, and it led the nation in establishing relief during the Depression of 1929.

Several arguments were made against outdoor relief. Economists argued that relief interfered with the natural relationship between capital and labor. By providing an alternative to industrial labor, it reduced the pool of available workers. Other critics argued that outdoor relief created dependency. Still others noted that the needy were embracing the idea that they had a "right" to relief. This ingratitude on their part, along with the compulsory taxation required to finance relief efforts, was seen as interfering with private charity.

These arguments were effective both in England and in the United States. In England, the "Poor Law Reform Bill" was passed to eliminate outdoor relief and relegate the nation's disadvantaged to almshouses and workhouses. Unlike their counterparts across the Atlantic, American poverty officials did not completely dismantle the system of outdoor relief. But they did expand "indoor relief," sending many of the nation's poor to institutions.

Most states assigned responsibility for poorhouses to the counties. For example, in 1824, New York enacted the County Poorhouse Act, calling for the construction of one or more poorhouses in each county in the state. These institutions proliferated. For most people they were not permanent addresses but temporary shelters in times of need. Families might move into poorhouses during an especially harsh winter, or stay there during periods of temporary unemployment. Over time, more and more elders spent their final months in poorhouses, turning these facilities into precursors for today's nursing homes.

The end of the Civil War saw a new population in need of assistance—newly freed African-American men and women in southern states. For several million former slaves, the abrupt change in status brought with it a need for education, employment, and assistance. To address their needs, a Bureau of Refugees, Freedmen, and Abandoned Lands was established in the U.S. War Department two months before the war ended. This agency, usually called the "Freedmen's Bureau," took what today would be called a "holistic" approach to the relief needs of the freedmen. As Trattner (1989) pointed out,

> [The Freedmen's Bureau] served as a relief agency on an unprecedented scale, distributing twenty-two million rations to needy persons in the devastated South. It served as an employment agency . . . a settlement agency, leasing certain abandoned properties to black cultivators . . . it employed doctors and maintained hospitals . . . it encouraged the founding of black schools and then provided them with financial aid . . . it served as legal agency, maintaining courts in which both civil and criminal cases involving ex-slaves were dealt with in an informal and just manner (p. 79).

In its second year of operation, the Freedmen's Bureau became part of a controversy between President Andrew Johnson (himself a Southerner) and the U.S. Congress.[7] Congress voted to extend the Bureau, but Johnson vetoed the

---

[7]Johnson's ongoing battles with Congress eventually led to the nation's first presidential impeachment hearings.

measure, arguing that the Constitution did not allow for a federal system of relief. Congress overrode his veto, and the Bureau continued to operate for six years. In 1876, the Freedmen's Bureau was closed, having demonstrated that the federal government could deliver comprehensive relief to needy individuals for whom states either could not or would not provide.

By the end of the nineteenth century, the United States had been transformed from a small localized economy to a world-class manufacturer. This industrialization brought an explosion of jobs in settings that can only generously be described as "sweatshops." The textile mills that moved into the newly reconstructed South offered much-needed jobs to poor whites and African-Americans, but they were jobs with low pay and abysmal working conditions. Dramatic economic growth created massive fortunes, such as those enjoyed by William Henry Vanderbilt, John D. Rockefeller, and J. P. Morgan, and raised the general standard of living. Reflecting the growing need for a large labor force willing to endure periodic unemployment and difficult working conditions, public support for government relief efforts waned.

The dominant economic philosophy of the times was Social Darwinism. According to this view, those who did not flourish in the booming economy could only be inferior specimens. Public care for them not only undermined private charity but weakened the human race by permitting the "unfit" to survive and reproduce. Members of the economic elite found in Social Darwinism a philosophy that was closely aligned with their interests. As a result, public relief efforts were reduced during this era.

The reduction of public relief was not accompanied by a drop in destitution. The nineteenth century saw a series of financial crises occurring at ten- to twenty-year intervals that led John Kenneth Galbraith to remark later that the intervals between crises corresponded "roughly with the time it took people to forget the last disaster" (Strouse, 1998, p. 66). Panics disrupted the stock market and threw millions out of work. Private charities raced to respond to massive need, and the result was a chaotic proliferation of organizations, all serving the same pool of indigents.

This disorganization horrified many charity workers, who argued that private relief efforts needed to be rationalized along "scientific" lines. Thus, when the Reverend Stephen Humphreys Gurteen proposed the creation of a Charity Organization Society (COS) for Buffalo, New York, his suggestion met with eager acceptance. Indeed, charity organization societies, going by names such as "Society for Organizing Charity," "Associated Charities," and "Bureaus of Charities" proliferated rapidly.

Charity organization societies did not provide relief. Instead, they conducted detailed investigations to distinguish the worthy from the unworthy poor, then referred those deemed worthy to the proper relief agencies. The goal was to raise the morals of the poor by exposing them to well-intentioned volunteers from middle- and upper-class backgrounds. Long before the term "culture of poverty" was coined, this intervention reflected the belief that upright role models could improve the values of the poor. Thus, "friendly visiting" was born. Mary Richmond's 1917 book, *Social Diagnosis*, which is widely considered the first systematic description of social casework, grew out of the experiences of COS friendly visitors.

The movement was not without its critics. Jane Addams, the founder of Hull House, was one of the most vocal. She argued that charity organization societies were "cold and unemotional, too impersonal, and stingy . . . pervaded by a negative pseudo-scientific spirit." Their vocabulary, she argued, was one of "don't give," "don't act," "don't do this or that"; "all they have for the poor is advice, and for that they probably send the Almighty a bill" (Trattner, 1989, p. 91).

The charity organization society (COS) movement fostered the development of social casework, and the settlement house movement set the stage for community organization. A contemporary of the COS movement, the settlement house movement differed in philosophy, approach, and goals. The COS philosophy treated indigence as the result of individual moral failure, while the settlement movement placed poverty in a broad social context. COS workers carefully investigated individual worthiness, while settlement workers focused their equally systematic research efforts on the social conditions of urban poverty. The primary goal of COS intervention, friendly visiting, aimed to improve the morals of the worthy poor. Settlement interventions did not distinguish between worthy and unworthy, and aimed to reduce class divisions and enhance living conditions in urban slums. The testy relationship that prevailed between COS workers and settlement workers continues today in the tension between social work professionals committed to individual treatment and those who advocate social change.

At the end of the nineteenth century the relief of poverty was largely a private affair, involving the pioneers of the social work profession in two movements. The COS movement aimed to reduce poverty through individual change, while the settlement house movement used a community organization model to attain the same goal. Public involvement in relieving poverty was generally limited to institutional care, provided in poorhouses and other settings for the "dependent, defective and delinquent" (Leiby, 1978). The role of government in poverty relief and amelioration would undergo dramatic changes in the next century.

AMERICAN APPROACHES TO POVERTY IN THE TWENTIETH CENTURY

The beginning of the twentieth century saw private charities assuming primary responsibility for the nation's poor. The role of government quickly expanded, however, and outdoor relief was widely adopted.

The change began with the 1909 White House Conference on Children, convened by President Theodore Roosevelt. Conference participants, 200 of the nation's elite, concluded that children should be cared for whenever possible in their own homes, and that the "home should not be broken up for reasons of poverty" (Trattner, 1989, p. 200). Like their contemporaries, conference participants were strongly opposed to outdoor relief. They stated that widows' pensions should be provided by private charities under the direction and supervision of the charity organization societies. In actual practice, however, many private agencies refused to give funds to women capable of working. Widows were forced to work, often for long hours at low wages, to support children they were unable to supervise. The result was maternal illness and child delinquency.

Advocates of widows' or mothers' pensions argued that it was ultimately less costly, in both human and economic terms, to provide public assistance to women with dependent children. This approach would preserve children from neglect, prevent juvenile delinquency, and protect the health of mothers. Proponents noted that the boom and bust nature of the industrial economy exposed workers' families to financial insecurity that jeopardized the well-being of children. Like Emily Morrison, they believed that mothers were performing a valuable service in caring for their children. Not only were they the best possible caregivers, but they did not belong in the workplace.

Social workers, especially those employed by private charity organizations, opposed widows' pensions. They protested against transforming voluntary, personal charity into an impersonal entitlement, arguing—in terms remarkably familiar today—that entitlements would undermine the work ethic of the poor. These arguments proved unsuccessful.

In April 1911, Missouri became the first state to enact a widows' pension law that provided cash assistance to mothers with dependent children. By 1935, all but two states—South Carolina and Georgia—offered public assistance to widows with dependent children. Over time, these programs were extended beyond widows to include other mothers raising children without spouses. A few recipients were single mothers with "illegitimate" children. Others were wives of men who were incapacitated, imprisoned, or otherwise unavailable to support their families. Assistance was conditioned by a "suitable home" provision, requiring the mothers to maintain healthy and supportive environments for their children. These widows' pensions set the stage for the passage of Title IV of the 1935 Social Security Act, which established a grant-in-aid program known then as Aid to Dependent Children.

THE DEPRESSION AND THE NEW DEAL. Prior to the Depression, only a few crusaders saw relief as a public responsibility. Some of these advocates sought a fundamental reorganization of the U.S. economy toward a socialist model. Others preferred mandatory social insurance to buffer the effects of capitalism. These were minority views, however. It took an economic calamity to shake the antipathy most Americans felt toward public assistance.

For some, including President Herbert Hoover, it would take more than economic calamity. Despite his personal background in relief work,[8] Hoover was

---

[8]The President organized a flood relief effort in the Mississippi Valley and was a relief administrator during World War I. As Secretary of Commerce in 1921, he organized a conference on unemployment relief. As a result of this background, he enjoyed widespread support from social workers in the 1928 election.

reluctant to intervene during the Depression. He felt the economy was basically sound, and as soon as confidence had been restored prosperity would return. Thus, in repeated messages he advised the public that the "worst was over." Hoover saw in federal relief the enslavement of the American people. Consistent with this philosophy, in December 1930 the President approved an appropriation of $45 million to feed the livestock of struggling Arkansas farmers, but opposed an additional $25 million to feed the farmers and their families. While the President postponed federal action, private charities around the country folded.

State and local governments did their best to shore up the failing private relief effort. The most notable effort was undertaken in New York. Then-governor Franklin D. Roosevelt had commissioned studies of the situation by the state's charity organization societies. He called a special legislative session to discuss the crisis, and New York became the first state to provide unemployment relief. Millions of dollars were passed on to local governments to provide subsidized work opportunities and relief. Roosevelt appointed a New York City social worker, Harry Hopkins, to direct the effort as head of the new "Temporary Emergency Relief Administration."

Roosevelt's philosophy stood in sharp contrast to President Hoover's viewpoint. Roosevelt saw relief as a matter of public duty, not charity. With this viewpoint, Roosevelt accepted the Democratic Party's nomination for president and defeated Hoover by a landslide in 1932.

The first order of business in Roosevelt's "New Deal" was emergency relief for the unemployed. The Federal Emergency Relief Act, signed into law in May 1933, established a series of grants-in-aid that were provided to the states through the Federal Emergency Relief Administration (FERA) under the direction of Harry Hopkins. Hopkins and Roosevelt agreed that all federal relief programs were to be operated by public agencies. They felt that provision of public subsidies to private agencies resulted in corruption and inefficiency. Thus, the relief and commodity distribution programs operated under FERA were administered by governmental units. Along with the FERA, a veritable alphabet soup of programs was created. Most emphasized work in exchange for relief, an approach that proved to be popular with Americans.

In addition to emergency relief measures, Roosevelt sought to establish a system of social insurance for workers. In 1934 he created a Committee on Economic Security (CES) to develop a proposal. The committee included four Cabinet members and Harry Hopkins. It was headed by the nation's first female Cabinet official, Frances Perkins, Secretary of Labor. Edwin E. Witte, a professor from the University of Wisconsin, served as the CES executive director. In January 1935, after six months of intensive deliberation, the committee delivered its outline for a social security program to the President.

Public assistance programs for children in single-parent homes, the blind, and the elderly that were established under the Social Security Act did not involve the federal government in the direct provision of relief. Instead, they established grant-in-aid programs under which revenue from the general fund was distributed to the states. The states then established relief programs that operated in accordance with regulations set at the federal level.

These grant-in-aid programs departed from the Poor Law principle of local responsibility in financing and authority, if not in distribution. Local authorities no longer used local funds to support local indigents. Financing came from federal revenues. Eligibility requirements and grant levels were determined by a federal agency. Local agencies were left to distribute relief under direction and guidance from federal authorities.

New Deal relief efforts touched millions but did little to end the Great Depression. All of the federal relief programs (FERA, the Civil Works Administration or CWA, and Works Progress Administration or WPA) ended before the hardships had passed. Even the establishment of Social Security did not stimulate recovery. It took World War II to pull the United States out of its most devastating economic crisis.

WORLD WAR II AND THE WAR ON POVERTY. World War II brought prosperity to a nation weary of hardship. Employment opportunities expanded, and as a result personal incomes rose for all workers, including women and minorities. To reduce discrimination in the defense industry, President Roosevelt issued the famous Executive Order 8802, forbidding "discrimination in the employment of workers in defense industries or Government because of race, creed, or national origin" (Trattner, 1989, p. 279). Rosie the Riveter became emblematic of the need for women to work in support of national defense.

The war ended in 1945, and for many the postwar years proved to be an unusually prosperous era. There were recessions (1948–49, 1953–54, 1957–58), but the post-war boom, with its increased demand for labor, led many to believe that poverty would simply "wither away" in the growing economy.

By the 1950s many argued that poverty had already disappeared. John Kenneth Galbraith was among them when, in 1958, he called the U.S. "The Affluent Society." Acknowledging the existence of poverty at the fringes of this society, Galbraith and others contributed to the widespread perception that poverty in the land of plenty was the result of inadequate skills and faulty personal choices.

Meanwhile the welfare rolls told a different story. Not only did the public assistance rolls grow, but their composition changed. Prior to Social Security, the elderly made up a majority of public assistance recipients. They were replaced by a new class of unemployed: former agricultural workers. Technological developments from 1940 to 1960 mechanized the nation's farms, increasing productivity and dramatically reducing the number of agricultural jobs available. Most of these were located in the South, and African-Americans were disproportionately represented in this group of the newly unemployed.

Some public programs for the poor were expanded during this era. In 1950 the "Aid to Dependent Children" (ADC) program (established with the 1935 Social Security Act) was amended to include "caretaker" grants for mothers of dependent children. Later, its name was changed to AFDC, "Aid to Families with Dependent Children." Social services were added to AFDC, and the Department of Health, Education and Welfare was created. The Social Security Act was further amended to include a new categorical program, "Aid to the Permanently and Totally Disabled."

With these expansions and the continued elimination of agricultural jobs, relief rolls continued to grow during the 1960s. Indeed, the number of people receiving public assistance more than doubled from 1960 to 1970, a period when the nation's population increased by only 12 percent. President Kennedy brought to his presidency a commitment to eliminate poverty, hunger, and unemployment. The young president inspired a sense that these ancient problems could be eliminated through determined intervention. But this spirit of optimism, like the Kennedy administration itself, would be short-lived.

When Kennedy took office in 1961, AFDC was expanded to include low-income two-parent families headed by an unemployed member. This new program, called AFDC-U (Aid to Families with Dependent Children—Unemployed parent) was designed to provide help to families who were ineligible for the program due to the presence of a "man in the home." AFDC-U was conceived as a temporary measure, and states were not required to participate.

The following year, the 1962 Public Welfare Amendments to the Social Security Act were signed into law. These measures provided federal support for state provision of social services (casework, job training, and other services) to AFDC recipients and echoed the belief of the COS movement that individual change was pivotal (perhaps even more important than material relief) in reducing poverty. Under the amendments, material relief and personal improvement were linked, and public assistance recipients found in their caseworker both an eligibility worker and a friendly visitor.

Public assistance was expanded through the 1964 passage of the Food Stamp Act. The Act provided for the distribution of vouchers to the needy for the purchase of food products. The Department of Agriculture was charged with administration of the program, which was seen by some as a way of reducing the impact of agricultural price supports on the poor.

The mid-sixties saw riots erupting in the slums of major cities. Unlike the anti-war riots that would follow, these riots represented protests against social conditions such as discrimination, unemployment, inadequate housing, and poverty. In 1966, welfare rights demonstrations broke out in cities across the nation. In their classic work *Regulating the Poor*, Piven and Cloward (1971) argued that the subsequent expansion of public relief programs was a response to social unrest, and hence the role of public programs (and the social workers who staffed them) was to maintain a status quo that relied on the oppression of the poor and minorities.

In response to the riots, President Lyndon B. Johnson established the Kerner Commission to investigate their causes and recommend ways to prevent future unrest. The Commission recommended creation of a federal jobs program for the unemployed.

President Lyndon B. Johnson declared an "unconditional war on poverty" in his 1964 State of the Union address, calling on Congress to support his "Great Society" programs designed to vanquish "the most ancient of mankind's enemies." These programs were established through the Economic Opportunity Act, which created a federal "Office of Economic Opportunity." They included the Volunteers in Service to America (VISTA), a domestic version of the popular Peace Corps; the Neighborhood Youth Corps, which provided jobs to unemployed teens; Operation Head Start, which offered preschool training to children; a Community Action Program designed to mobilize low-income communities to fight the causes and manifestations of poverty; and a program for rural families and migrant workers.

The War on Poverty was based on the belief that poor families needed little more than training and encouragement to better themselves. It did not offer money or jobs to the poor, but instead sent (middle-class) professionals to change their culture, values, and expectations.

The War on Poverty was minimally funded, due (Michael Harrington suggested) to the competing demands of another war in Vietnam. It also faced opposition from both ends of the political spectrum. Radicals like Saul Alinsky opposed the Great Society programs as "a macabre masquerade" (Alinsky, 1972). Conservatives opposed the expenditures involved. Disenchantment with the programs undermined the nation's brief confidence that interventions informed by social science could eliminate social problems. The failure of the War on Poverty would set the stage for the subsequent War on Welfare.

THE WAR ON WELFARE. In 1968 Richard Nixon won election by a wide margin. A staunch conservative, the new President saw in his election a mandate to dismantle the Great Society programs and criticize recipients of public assistance. This he did, with enthusiasm.

Although Nixon struck the first blows in the "War on Welfare," reforms proposed and enacted during his administration did more to enhance the status of the poor than had all the Great Society programs combined. He proposed to replace the federal-state AFDC program with a single federal program. His proposal, called the "Family Assistance Plan," would have created a federally guaranteed minimum annual income for families with children. It called for strict penalties and strong incentives to ensure that everyone who was able-bodied (including mothers of children younger than three years old) worked in paid employment.

The Family Assistance Plan (FAP), while not generous in its benefits, would have increased the incomes of AFDC recipients in poor Southern states. It also represented a significant philosophical change in public assistance, because it assigned primary responsibility to the federal government and provided a guaranteed minimum income for Americans.

Many liberals, including social workers, opposed the FAP. In part this opposition reflected their distrust of Nixon, but in an era of high unemployment, the plan's work requirements (dubbed "workfare" by opponents) struck many as ludicrous. Welfare rights activists thought the guaranteed minimum was too low, and they were concerned that the plan would lower benefits to welfare recipients in more generous states. Conservatives were unhappy with the expanded federal role proposed under FAP, and some objected to the notion of mothers with young children being forced to work. The President showed no commitment to the plan, and it eventually died in committee.

While AFDC remained unchanged, the Nixon era saw significant improvements in other public assistance programs. These included expansion of the Food Stamp program, the establishment of Cost of Living Adjustments (COLAs) for Social Security, the creation of an Earned Income Tax Credit (EITC) and the consolidation of three categorical assistance programs (Old-Age Assistance, Aid to the Blind, and Aid to the Permanently and Totally Disabled) into a single program called Supplemental Security Income (SSI). The Social Service Amendments (Title XX of the Social Security Act) also passed during this period, provided $2.5 billion to states to deliver social services to welfare recipients.[9] Notably, these expansions took place in an era of high unemployment (low demand for labor).

Following Nixon's resignation in 1974 in the wake of the Watergate scandal, Gerald Ford enjoyed a brief term as President. Best known for his unconditional pardon of Nixon, Ford presided over an era of economic "stagflation." Economic growth was stagnant, while unemployment climbed to its highest rate since 1941 (9 percent), and inflation was in double digits. The number of Americans living in poverty rose dramatically, and white, male-headed families emerged for the first time as a group at significant risk of living in poverty.

President Jimmy Carter contributed to the anti-welfare rhetoric of his day. In 1977, he proposed the Better Jobs and Income Program (BJIP), which would replace existing public assistance programs, such as AFDC, SSI, and food stamps, with a two-tiered system. For the able-bodied, the program would offer part-time subsidized jobs that paid the minimum wage or better. Those deemed unable to work included the aged, the blind, the disabled, and parents of children under 14 years old. They would receive a cash benefit more generous than that offered under existing public assistance programs. Unlike the FAP, Carter's proposal offered universal coverage (it was not restricted to families with children); benefits were more generous, and work exemptions extended to parents of children aged 3 to 14. But, perhaps most significantly, BJIP proposed to guarantee jobs for those able to work. This work guarantee was the source of most of the opposition from the conservative side of the political spectrum. Industry representatives feared that publicly subsidized jobs would compete with those available in the private sector. Liberals opposed the work requirement, dubbing the plan yet another attempt to impose "workfare" on welfare recipients. After introducing his plan in Congress, the President encountered other challenges (such as the Iran hostage crisis) that undermined his ability to pursue significant domestic policy initiatives.

Ronald Reagan, a movie actor and former Governor of California, swept into

---

[9]Title XX also marked the first time the federal government provided funding for social services to individuals with incomes above the poverty line. While welfare recipients received means-tested services, those with higher incomes could use Title XX services on a fee-for-service basis.

office with an overwhelming victory. Reagan declared that the war on poverty had been won, and he labeled welfare recipients as "cheats" and "free-loaders." Reagan argued that the federal government should not be in the business of providing welfare. That business, he felt, was best left to private charities in local communities. Thus began a 12-year period (two Reagan administrations, followed by one administration headed by Reagan's Vice President, George H. Bush) marked by tax cuts for the wealthy, ever-expanding defense budgets, and re-duced domestic spending.

Just before his re-election to a second term, President Reagan signed his "sweeping overhaul" of the nation's welfare system. The Family Welfare Reform Act, sponsored by Daniel Patrick Moynihan, had as its major provision the Job Opportunities and Basic Skills program (JOBS). The program revised, but did not fundamentally alter, the conditions of public relief. Under JOBS, all welfare recipients had to secure jobs or enroll in job training or educational programs. Mothers of children under age three were exempted from the work requirement. Those who did go to work were to receive support for one year to assist with child care and transportation expenses, and Medicaid coverage was extended for one year. The Act required states to participate in the AFDC program for two-parent households, dubbed "AFDC-UP" for AFDC—Unemployed Parent. It also included new procedures for collecting child support from non-custodial parents of welfare recipients. The basic premise of JOBS was that welfare recipients needed little more than training and motivation to become self-sufficient.

ENDING WELFARE AS WE KNOW IT. Unlike his predecessors, President Clinton presided over an era of relatively low unemployment. Like his predecessors, Clinton came into office promising to "end welfare as we know it." Unlike his predecessors, he did it. Clinton authorized the most sweeping welfare reform since the Great Depression: The Personal Responsibility and Work Opportunity Reconciliation Act (PRWORA) of 1996 (HR 3734).

The PRWORA was a significant provision in the Contract with America that was offered by Republican representatives to Congress in 1994. In the flush of victory, the new Republican majority took aim at a variety of federal entitlement programs, including food stamps, Medicaid, and AFDC, and proposed converting federal assistance into block grants. Through this vehicle, federal allocations could be reduced and state discretion over the programs increased.

The PRWORA was a comprehensive piece of legislation expected to reduce federal welfare expenditures by $54.5 billion by 2001 (Welfare Policy Organization, 1997). It eliminated the open-ended entitlement under AFDC, converting the aid to a block grant that provided time-limited assistance to needy families (TANF). It reduced food stamp benefits, prohibited most legal immigrants from receiving either SSI or food stamps (a measure that accounted for much of the anticipated budget reductions), and established more stringent eligibility requirements for children under SSI.

The PRWORA was amended through passage of the Balanced Budget Act of 1997. This measure restored SSI benefits to most non-citizens, established a $24 billion program that allows states to expand Medicaid eligibility or directly purchase health coverage for uninsured children, and set up a $3 billion welfare-to-work program for long-term welfare clients.

Ending a 50-year-old entitlement for needy children and their families, PRWORA was the most far-reaching welfare reform legislation since the New Deal. It reflected several of the values and beliefs outlined at the opening of this chapter. PRWORA established lifetime limits on public assistance, in response to the belief described above that welfare promotes dependency (the "pauperization" argument). It created strong work requirements for the receipt of assistance, and forced welfare recipients to develop job skills or enter the labor market. While these requirements may have reflected a desire to increase opportunities available to the poor (the human capital explanation), the Act also included restrictions on the type and duration of job training. The work requirements seemed tailor-made to ensure that welfare would not serve as an alternative to employment in a growing economy with high demand for laborers. The 20-percent exemption from lifetime limits established a class of "deserving" poor, leaving the states to define that group. Most states incorporated physical disability into that definition, suggesting that these individuals continue to be the legitimate focus of relief. At the same time, the Act established new categories of "undeserving" poor, including individuals with drug-related felonies, teenage parents who leave home, and legal immigrants.

PROGRAMS FOR AMERICA'S POOR

In this section we will examine five programs that serve America's poor: Temporary Assistance to Needy Families (TANF), Food Stamps, Housing Assistance, Medicaid, the Earned Income Tax Credit (EITC), and the Minimum Wage. The Supplemental Security Income program, which provides a minimal monthly benefit to the elderly, blind and disabled, was discussed in Chapter 3.

TEMPORARY ASSISTANCE FOR NEEDY FAMILIES (TANF)

Established with the 1996 passage of the Personal Responsibility and Work Opportunity Reconciliation Act, TANF consists of a federal block grant to the states. The program allows states to establish eligibility criteria, provided that their treatment of recipients is "fair and equitable." Under federal law, TANF benefits may be provided to low-income parents who have not reached the five-year lifetime limit on assistance and who are meeting federal work participation requirements. Assistance must be reduced if parents do not cooperate with official efforts to collect child support from non-custodial parents (usually fathers). Assistance must not be provided to individuals convicted of a drug felony or to parents under the age of 18 who are not living in an adult-supervised setting.

Using criteria of their own design, states may exempt 20 percent of their TANF caseload from the lifetime limit on assistance. TANF gives the states wide latitude in program decisions, but the program includes a "maintenance of effort" provision that requires states to devote 75 percent of the amount spent on AFDC in 1994 to the current TANF program.

The transition from AFDC to TANF has been fraught with controversy and ambiguity. Welfare advocates were horrified by the prospect of families being cut off abruptly from public assistance. Program recipients are often unaware of provisions that affect them, such as the measure that exempts victims of domestic violence from the requirement that they assist officials in collecting child support if doing so would present "undue hardship" or the 20-percent exemption that will allow some recipients to continue receiving assistance after passing the lifetime limit. The work participation requirements have been interpreted either broadly (to include a wide range of activities such as participating in mental health or substance abuse treatment) or narrowly (to include only paid employment). The use of "sanctions" also varies tremendously. In short, cash assistance has entered a period of transition in which decisions made at the state level will have greater impact on recipients' lives than was the case under the AFDC program.

FOOD STAMPS

Established under the Food Stamp Act of 1977, the Food Stamp Program is operated by the Department of Agriculture (DOA), and provides vouchers for the purchase of food items by eligible households. Established in 1964, it was designed to reduce the impact of agricultural price supports on the needy and to enable the poor to have nutritionally balanced diets. The costs of the program are borne primarily by the DOA, which covers 100 percent of benefit costs and 50 percent of administrative costs. The remaining administrative costs are borne by state and county governments, who are charged with administering the program.

Eligibility requirements are established at the federal level, are based on the Department of Agriculture's Thrifty Food Plan (similar to the Economy Food Budget on which the poverty threshold was based), and are approximately 100 percent of the federal poverty threshold. In 2001, the maximum net monthly income limit for an eligible family of four was $1,848. Households may have up to $2,000 in countable assets, such as a bank account. Homes and some vehicles are not included as countable assets. Households in which at least one person is over the age of 60 may have up to $3,000 in assets and retain their eligibility for food stamps (U.S. Department of Agriculture, 2000a).

The Food Stamp program has been criticized for providing inadequate benefits. The maximum monthly allotment for a household of four in the 48 contiguous states was $434 in 2001 (U.S. Department of Agriculture, 2000b). However, because the allotment is adjusted to reflect family income, the average monthly benefit is lower. In 2000, the average monthly allotment of food stamps was approximately $70 per person, or $177 per household (U.S. Department of Agriculture, 2001).[10]

Historically, only about half of Americans who are eligible for food stamps participate in the program (Castner & Cody, 1999). States' participation rates have varied tremendously. For example, in 1997, when national participation was at approximately 62 percent, only 45 percent of eligible residents of Nevada participated, compared to 92 percent of eligible residents of West Virginia (Mathematica, 2000).

Recent years have seen a nationwide decline in food stamp participation from 71 percent in 1994 to 62 percent in 1997 (Mathematica, 2000). The Department of Agriculture reported that participation in January 1998 dropped to 20.3 million participants, a decline of 14 percent from the previous year (Castner & Cody, 1999). This decrease can be attributed in part to changes made by 1996 welfare reform legislation (PRWORA). The 1996 Act changed the Food Stamp program in several ways: it reduced the level of benefits, denied benefits to most legal immigrants, and created time limits for receipt of benefits by able-bodied adults without children.[11] Approximately 6.73 million people have left the Food Stamp program since passage of the PRWORA. Other factors in low food stamp participation rates may include onerous procedures required to maintain food stamp eligibility. In some cases it can take hours to complete an initial application, and some states require re-certification every three months. Since most welfare offices are open only during the workday, low-income parents with jobs must leave work to secure and maintain their food stamps. Many conclude that benefits are not worth the time, effort, and humiliation involved (see Mathematica, 2000; Castner & Cody, 1999; Rosenbaum, 2000).

HOUSING ASSISTANCE

In the United States, housing is viewed not as an entitlement, but as a private commodity to be traded for profit in the real estate market. As a result, budget allocations for housing assistance programs consistently fail to meet the need, and low-income Americans who seek housing assistance confront waiting lists and complex bureaucratic requirements.

Federal housing assistance is provided through three programs that date back to the New Deal, when public housing was developed for low-income working families. Since that time, the structure of a federal program of low-income housing has evolved. That structure was in place by the mid-1970s. Federal programs include public housing: Public housing offers low-cost hous-

---

[10]Benefits for Alaska, Hawaii, and the U.S. territories of Guam and the Virgin Islands are higher, reflecting higher food costs in those areas.

[11]Able-bodied adults without children can receive food stamps for a maximum of three months in a three-year period, unless they meet certain work requirements.

ing to the poor and the disabled, Section 202 provides developers with incentives to build housing for the elderly and disabled, and Section 8 provides rent subsidies to low-income families.

PUBLIC HOUSING. Widespread federal involvement in public housing dates to the Great Depression. The National Industrial Recovery Act (NIRA) of 1933 provided federal funding for housing construction. But the focus of New Deal efforts was less on provision of housing for the poor than on creation of jobs for the unemployed. Public housing was made available to the working poor who lived in "intact" families. Unwed mothers were excluded from most housing units, and only a small percentage (usually 10 percent) of units were available to families on welfare.

World War II brought a serious housing shortage. The Federal Housing Administration (FHA) and GI home mortgage programs offered low-interest mortgages to middle-class persons and veterans. Members of Congress and welfare authorities argued that public housing should be reserved for those in greatest need. As a result, new policies lowered income limits for eligibility and prohibited discrimination against welfare families and unwed mothers.

By the mid-1960s, public housing in the United States had become a "war zone," replete with drug dealing and violent crime. Mildred Hailey was one of several resident leaders who advocated for reform in public housing. Reasoning that federal indifference and resident apathy conspired to create hellish living conditions, Hailey and others argued for returning control (and even ownership) of public housing to the residents. She took over the project she lived in, Bromley-Heath in Boston, and with an administrative board of fellow housing residents set out to manage and police the project. Since then, a growing number of public housing units have been purchased or managed by the residents themselves.

SECTION 202. Section 202 of the Housing Act of 1959 was passed to provide low-interest construction loans to nonprofit sponsors (such as churches and civic organizations) who were interested in expanding the supply of low-cost housing for the low-income elderly and disabled. Once constructed, a Section 202 housing development is operated by the nonprofit sponsor with federal oversight. The elderly have probably been the greatest beneficiaries of this program. In 1990, 70 percent of new Section 202 units were designated for elderly residents, with the remaining 30 percent for the disabled (Sonnenberg, Budget Analyst, Department of Housing and Urban Development, personal communication, 1993). There has been a substantial increase in the proportion of existing public housing units intended exclusively for the elderly. In 1960, units for the elderly made up only 3.2 percent of public housing stock. By 1988 the figure had grown to 26 percent (U.S. Department of Commerce, 1992).

SECTION 8. The Housing and Community Development Act of 1974 included Section 8 to provide rent subsidies for low-income families. Families eligible for

Section 8 benefits are given a voucher to cover a portion of their rent. Each family is expected to pay 30 percent of its income towards rent. The voucher covers the remainder of the rent, up to a pre-determined amount.

As Mulroy (1990) pointed out, Section 8 is frequently cited as "a great liberator," freeing low-income families from reliance on public housing, and from exorbitant housing costs. Because of limited funding, however, Section 8 reaches only a small fraction of low-income households. In 1980, The Office of Management and Budget estimated that only 8 percent of eligible households were receiving subsidies (U.S. General Accounting Office, 1980). The OMB report noted that "The Section 8 program may be likened somewhat to a lottery in which only a few strike it big. For those families fortunate enough to get into the program, many can be expected to stay in it for a long time" (U.S. General Accounting Office, 1980, p. 12). Although the number of vouchers available under Section 8 was increased during the Clinton administration, the program still falls short of meeting the housing needs of low-income Americans (U.S. Department of Housing and Urban Development, 1993 and 1999). Clients who do receive vouchers often find the program's procedures and regulations complex and difficult (Mulroy, 1990).

MEDICAID

Established under the 1965 Amendments to the Social Security Act, Medicaid provides health insurance to the nation's poor. Direct administration of Medicaid is carried out by each state, with federal matching funds meeting from 50 to 80 percent of Medicaid costs. States vary in their eligibility requirements. All cover recipients of TANF and SSI. States also vary in the services covered through Medicaid. Some services are required by federal law, including inpatient hospital services, outpatient hospital services, rural health clinic services, laboratory and X-ray services, skilled nursing facility (nursing home) services, and physician services. Optional services include prescription drugs, eyeglasses, dentures, diagnostic screening, and preventive care.

The majority of Medicaid recipients are mothers and children receiving TANF funds, but the bulk of the program's expenditures go to the care of low-income elderly and disabled persons because of the higher cost of medical care for the latter groups (see Chapter 5).

Under federal law, TANF recipients who leave the program by securing employment may retain their Medicaid coverage for up to six months. Thus, Emily (the subject of this chapter's case study) probably would be able to retain her Medicaid benefits for a brief period after securing employment and leaving TANF. The question in her case would be whether at the end of that period her employer would provide health coverage. If not, she would be faced with the likelihood of unreimbursed medical expenses for asthma-related medical care.

Most metropolitan areas require that Medicaid recipients enroll with a managed care provider. This requirement is a cost-control measure that may also improve health care access for the poor. On the other hand, the focus on cost control that is characteristic of managed care may introduce barriers that prevent the poor from accessing needed care. The advantages and disadvantages of Medicaid managed care are discussed further in Chapter 5.

EARNED INCOME TAX CREDIT (EITC)

Established in 1974, the Earned Income Tax Credit has become one of the nation's most effective and popular anti-poverty initiatives. The EITC is also relatively unknown, to the extent that it could be considered a "hidden entitlement." Some view it as a way to offset the regressive effects of the payroll tax on low-income workers (see Chapter 3 for a discussion of the payroll tax). It also rewards work and supplements the earnings of low-income families with children (Hoffman & Seidman, 1990; Phillips, 2001).

The EITC, which is administered by the Internal Revenue Service, provides a refundable tax credit to eligible taxpayers. For low-income families, the EITC consistently exceeds their federal income tax obligation. In such cases, the IRS would first apply the credit to any taxes owed, then send the remaining amount directly to the family. In fiscal year 2000, the program distributed approximately $30.4 billion, an amount that exceeded federal expenditures on TANF and roughly equalled the combined federal expenditures for food stamps and SSI. In some states (13, as of this writing) federal EITC benefits are supplemented by state Earned Income Credits (Coalition on Human Needs, 2000)

EITC is available to low- to moderate-income working families, with the greatest benefits going to families with children. It offers substantial assistance. In 1999, a qualifying family with one child could receive a credit worth as much as $2,312. This amount would have phased out completely when their annual income reached $26,928 (Coalition on Human Needs, 2000). Workers without children could have received up to $347 in 1999, with the credit phasing out at an income level of $10,200 (Coalition on Human Needs, 2000).

The EITC is a powerful antidote to poverty. In 2000, some 19.4 million taxpayers received EITCs, and the credit lifted an estimated 4.8 million individuals, including 2.6 million children, out of poverty. Porter and colleagues (1998) reported that the EITC has lifted more children out of poverty than all federal assistance programs combined.

Despite its advantages, the EITC has encountered criticism. First, the IRS has reported a 21 percent error rate in EITC payments, which has led some people to claim that it is simply another opportunity for the poor to "work the system." Second, because moderate-income workers experience a high rate of tax on earnings while the EITC is being phased out, opponents of the credit argue that the higher rates represent a disincentive to work. There is no evidence to support this view (Hoffman & Seidman, 1990).

MINIMUM WAGE

The minimum wage was established in 1938 through the Fair Labor Standards Act. According to a Department of Labor historian: "When he felt the time was ripe, President Roosevelt asked Secretary of Labor Perkins 'What happened to that nice unconstitutional bill you had tucked away?'" (Grossman, 1978). Evidently, Perkins's CMS 6.15 willingness to become Secretary of Labor was at least partly conditional on Roosevelt's willingness to advocate a law that would "put a floor under wages." So, in 1938, over outraged industrial opposition, the minimum wage was set at 25 cents per hour. The minimum wage is not indexed to inflation, so any increase requires congressional and presidential approval. Since its passage, the minimum wage has been raised 17 times, most recently (at the time of this writing) in 1997 when it rose to $5.15 per hour.

An estimated 12.5 million workers are affected by the minimum wage (U.S. House of Representatives, 1999). There are a number of exemptions. For example, youth (who are under 20 years of age) are subject to a sub-minimum wage during their first three months of employment. The law is enforced by the Wage and Hour Division of the Department of Labor.

Objections to increasing the minimum wage typically come from business representatives and conservative Republicans. Their predominant argument is that thousands of low-wage workers will lose their jobs. As one advocate argued on the Internet, "Studies suggest that for every 10 percent increase in the minimum wage, a minimum of 100,000 jobs are lost . . ." (Cox, 1997). There is no empirical evidence to support this claim.

SUMMARY OF ATTITUDES AND INTERVENTIONS

A major thread that runs through the history of poverty policy in the United States is the close connection between the values and beliefs discussed earlier in this chapter and interventions designed to prevent or alleviate poverty. When poverty represented an opportunity for comfortable people to secure their salvation, charity was given with an open hand and little concern for its impact. When poverty was viewed as a crime, the response was to impose punishment. If poverty serves to motivate the industrial labor force, it is important that relief not create a class of comfortable paupers. If there is a "culture of poverty," then the values and beliefs of children and adults with low incomes must be changed. If poverty is the result of limited opportunities, ensuring equal opportunity should relieve the problem. And, most recently, if poverty is caused by welfare, then "ending welfare as we know it" should reduce the suffering of the poor.

Another historical thread is the tremendous variety in Americans' beliefs about poverty. The poverty policies we live under reflect a combination of these beliefs. Indeed, Americans' beliefs about poverty are as heterogeneous as the poor themselves. The following section describes the current face of poverty in the United States, one that is increasingly made up of female-headed households with children.

THE REALITIES OF POVERTY
IN THE CONTEMPORARY UNITED STATES

During the War on Poverty, advocates and bureaucrats often took the position that "poor people are just like you and me, except they have less money." Interventions based on this premise offered education and job training in the expectation that these efforts would enable the poor to achieve self-sufficiency. Some benefited from this approach, but it did not stop the growth in welfare rolls. When conservatives took office in the 1980s they orchestrated a backlash that essentially said, "If poor people are just like you and me, then they should be expected to work!" So today's poverty interventions incorporate sanctions and pressures to move into jobs. The extent to which these interventions will succeed in reducing poverty depends to a large extent on the characteristics of individuals in poverty, particularly their ability to meet the demands of the labor market.

CHARACTERISTICS OF AMERICA'S POOR

If poverty is one of the risks, or costs, of membership in American society, its distribution reflects an important allocation principle. If the risks of poverty were randomly distributed, one might fairly argue that poverty is the result of personal idiosyncrasy or failure. John Rawls's "veil of ignorance" (discussed in Chapter 1) might then predict that the nation's policies would maximize the well-being of the poor. But Americans do not enter the world with equal risks of poverty. Indeed, one's risk of poverty is in some ways inversely related to the likelihood of serving in Congress. Several factors determine both probabilities, among them race, age, gender, residence, immigration status, and employment. Each of these factors is addressed below.

RACE. Although whites make up the largest group of Americans with incomes below the poverty threshold, they do not experience the nation's highest poverty rates. For example, in 1997 non-Hispanic whites represented 72 percent of the total U.S. population, but made up just under half (46.4 percent) of America's poor (Dalaker & Naifeh, 1997). In 1999, the poverty rate for non-Hispanic whites was relatively low (7.7 percent) compared to Hispanics (22.8 percent), African-Americans (23.6 percent), and Asians and Pacific Islanders (10.7 percent). The highest poverty rates in the United States are typically reserved for Alaska Natives and American Indians like Emily Morrison. In 1999 more than one in four (25.9

TABLE 4.2 POVERTY RATES FOR ETHNIC
POPULATIONS IN THE UNITED STATES, AS OF 1999*
(Overall Poverty Rate: 12.7%)

Race/Ethnicity	Proportion below Poverty
Non-Hispanic White	7.7%
Asian & Pacific Islander	10.7
Hispanic	22.8
African-American	23.6
American Indian & Alaska Native	25.9

*Source: U.S. Census Bureau, 2000a.

percent) of the nation's indigenous people had incomes below the poverty threshold (U.S. Bureau of the Census, 2000). These figures are presented in Table 4.2.

AGE. In America, children experience the highest risk of poverty. Whereas the overall poverty rate in 1997 was 13.3 percent, nearly one in five children under 18 (19.9 percent) lived in poverty in 1997. Young children are especially vulnerable to poverty, with 21.6 percent of children under the age of six living in households with incomes below the poverty threshold in 1997. The majority of young children living in families headed by a single woman (59.1 percent) lived in poverty. In sharp contrast, children in married-couple families had a 10.6 percent risk of poverty (Dalaker & Naifeh, 1997).

The elderly—those aged 65 and over—had a substantially lower risk of poverty (10.9 percent) in 1997 than children did. This does not mean that all of the nation's elderly are well-off. First, as mentioned previously, the poverty threshold for the elderly is lower than for other age groups. Second, a significant proportion (6.4 percent) of those over 65 years old had incomes between the federal poverty threshold and 125 percent of that amount. Thus, 17 percent of the elderly had incomes under 125 percent of the federal poverty threshold. In 1997 the threshold for an elderly couple was $9,712 (Dalaker & Naifeh, 1997).

Further, people who are very old experience rates of poverty that rival those of the very young. Almost one-fifth (18.4 percent) of those over the age of 85 years who lived in the community (not in nursing homes) had incomes below the poverty threshold in 1989 (U.S. Senate Special Committee on Aging, 1988). This rate is the highest found in any adult age group. When the near poor (those with incomes up to 125 percent of the poverty level) are included with the poor, the oldest old have had a higher rate of poverty (31.2 percent) than that observed among children (26.6 percent) (Bould, Sanborn & Reif, 1989). The risk of poverty is particularly high for very old people who live alone. Over one-third (35 percent) of older adults aged between 65 and 74 years who lived alone had poverty-level incomes in 1990, compared to 49 percent of those over the age of 85 (Siegel, 1996).

TABLE 4.3 STATE POVERTY RATES, THREE-YEAR AVERAGES: 1997–1999*
(National Average: 12.6 Percent)

State	Poverty Rate	State	Poverty Rate	State	Poverty Rate
New Mexico	20.8%	Oklahoma	13.5%	Maine	10.4%
District of Columbia	19.7	Florida	13.3	Michigan	10.3
Louisiana	18.2	Oregon	13.1	Delaware	10.1
Mississippi	16.8	North Carolina	13.0	Virginia	9.8
West Virginia	16.7	South Carolina	12.8	Vermont	9.6
Arkansas	16.4	Hawaii	11.9	Washington	9.2
Montana	15.9	Wyoming	11.9	Minnesota	9.1
New York	15.7	South Dakota	11.7	New Hampshire	8.9
Tennessee	15.6	Ohio	11.4	Iowa	8.7
Texas	15.6	Rhode Island	11.4	Alaska	8.6
California	15.3	Missouri	11.1	Colorado	8.6
Arizona	15.2	Nebraska	11.0	New Jersey	8.5
Alabama	15.1	Nevada	11.0	Wisconsin	8.5
Idaho	13.9	Massachusetts	10.9	Connecticut	8.4
North Dakota	13.9	Pennsylvania	10.6	Indiana	8.3
Kentucky	13.8	Kansas	10.5	Utah	7.9
Georgia	13.7	Illinois	10.4	Maryland	7.6

*Source: U.S. Census Bureau (2000b).

GENDER. Women experience a significantly higher risk of poverty than men, hence the phrase "feminization of poverty." Female heads of household had a 31.6 percent poverty rate in 1997, compared to a rate of 5.2 percent for married couples. Hispanic female heads of household had the highest rate (47.6 percent) compared to 39.8 percent for African-American women and 27.7 percent for white women (Dalaker & Naifeh, 1997).

RESIDENCE. Prior to 1994, the south had the nation's highest poverty rates. Since that time, however, that distinction has been shared with the western region. In 1997, both the South and the West had poverty rates of 14.6 percent, compared to 12.6 percent for the Northeast and 10.4 percent for the Midwest. These regional trends are mirrored in the state-level rates (see Table 4.3) (Dalaker & Naifeh, 1997).

The poverty rate in rural America once exceeded that in the nation's cities. Today that situation has reversed. The nation's highest poverty rates are found in the inner cities. In 1997, the poverty rate in central cities was 18.8 percent, compared to a suburban poverty rate of 9.0 percent for the same year. Rural poverty, measured as that "outside metropolitan areas," was 15.9 percent.[12]

---

[12]It is worth noting that until 1981, the poverty threshold for farm families was lower than for others. The rationale was that farm families had access to low-cost food.

IMMIGRATION STATUS. American citizens who are foreign-born have a slightly higher risk of poverty than those who are native-born. The poverty rate for naturalized citizens was 12.5 percent in 1997, compared to 11.4 percent for native-born citizens. Foreign-born individuals who have not attained citizenship have a substantially higher poverty rate. In 1997, 25 percent lived in poverty.

EMPLOYMENT. Having a job does not guarantee escape from poverty. Many Americans with incomes below the poverty level are employed. In 1997, among poor people 16 years old and over, 42 percent worked. But only 10 percent worked full-time, year-round. Among those with incomes above the poverty threshold, 70 percent worked and 45 percent had full-time, year-round employment (Dalaker & Naifeh, 1997). The Earned Income Tax Credit and the minimum wage are designed to improve the quality of life experienced by the working poor.

SUMMARY: CHARACTERISTICS OF AMERICANS LIVING IN POVERTY. It is clear that America's poor and near-poor are an extremely heterogeneous group, dominated by children in female-headed households. Those under 18 made up nearly 40 percent (39.7 percent) of America's poor in 1997. Many of the poor are white, and nearly half are employed. But racial minorities and those with either part-time or seasonal employment are extremely vulnerable to poverty. More of the poor live in the South than in any other region. In 1997, 38.6 percent of the poor lived in the South, while those living in the West experienced a similar risk of poverty. The nation's poor are concentrated in the central cities, which in 1997 housed 42.2 percent of those with incomes below the poverty threshold. Most (73.7 percent in 1997) of the poor live in families related by blood or marriage. Finally, although immigrants experienced somewhat higher risk of poverty, the vast majority (85.3 percent) of the poor were native-born (Dalaker & Naifeh, 1997).

INEQUALITY IN THE UNITED STATES

During the past 25 years, inequality has increased significantly in the United States. Between 1967 and 1973, income increased for most Americans, regardless of whether they were in the top income quintile (the fifth of the population with the highest incomes) or the bottom quintile (the fifth of the population with the lowest incomes). During this period, the Congressional Budget Office reports that the mean adjusted family income for those in the lowest quintile increased by 30 percent, while the mean adjusted family income for the highest quintile grew by 21 percent. Since 1973, this situation has changed markedly. Income for the bottom quintile has declined, while income for the highest has risen dramatically. Put simply, for the past two and a half decades, the rich have gotten richer and the poor have gotten poorer. While this growth in inequality slowed somewhat during the economic growth of the 1990s, it continued nonetheless (Bernstein et al., 2000).

Increases in inequality would be interpreted differently by adherents of each of the philosophical perspectives introduced in Chapter 1. The perspective of oligarchy would suggest that inequality is a natural, perhaps divinely inspired, method for ordering the social classes. From a libertarian perspective, inequality is the inevitable and even desirable result of a competitive economy, and governmental efforts to reduce inequality are wasteful and inappropriate. Philosophical liberals tolerate a certain amount of economic inequality if it does not jeopardize political equality. John Rawls, a contractual liberal, suggested that inequality was acceptable as long as those who were least well-off did not fall below an agreed-upon social minimum. The principle of "less eligibility," discussed earlier, would dictate that the level of support available through public assistance must not make a recipient as comfortable as he or she could be through employment. This principle helps us understand recent attacks on welfare.

Real wages in the U.S. declined dramatically from their peak in the late 1960s to the year the PRWORA passed (1996). Indeed, 1996 saw a low point in average hourly earnings that had not been seen for three decades. Figure 4.1, below, presents the average hourly earnings of U.S. workers in private settings. The earnings figures are adjusted for inflation and represent constant 1982 dollars. As the figure indicates, earnings rose slightly during the late 1990s.

At the same time, the gap between the poor and the middle class has diminished. The federal poverty threshold has increased relative to median family income. In 1970 the poverty threshold for a family of four was $3,968. This rep-

FIGURE 4.1 AVERAGE HOURLY WAGE FOR U.S. WORKERS, 1964–2001*

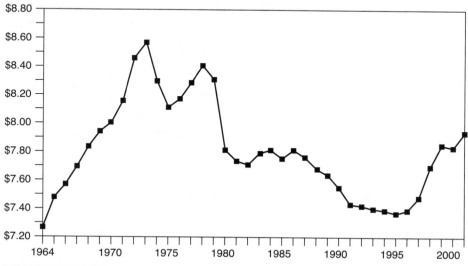

Source: Bureau of Labor Statistics.

*Earnings are in constant 1982 dollars.

resented 12 percent of the median income reported for all families. By 1990, the poverty threshold for the same family ($13,359) represented 37 percent of median family income. During the same period, the U.S. poverty rate increased slightly, from 12.6 percent to 13.5 percent. Not only do more Americans have below-poverty incomes, but the gap between "middle" (or median) income households and the poor has diminished.

The median income in 1990 was roughly three times the poverty threshold, whereas the median income twenty years earlier, in 1970, was nearly ten times the poverty threshold. Half of American households now find themselves earning no more than 300 percent of the poverty threshold. This places programs for the poor in a tenuous position. As middle-class Americans see their opportunities and conditions more closely resembling those of poor families, widespread support for public assistance to the poor has diminished. This is illustrated in Figure 4.2.

Thus, the past three decades have seen an erosion in the standard of living experienced by working-class Americans. This erosion is apparent both in wage declines and in the shrinking gap between the poverty line and the median household income. Under the principle of less eligibility, this drop must be accompanied by a corresponding drop in the standard of living available to those on public assistance. The 1996 welfare reform act is one approach to maintaining the distinction between workers and public assistance recipients.

FIGURE 4.2 POVERTY THRESHOLD AND MEDIAN HOUSEHOLD INCOME

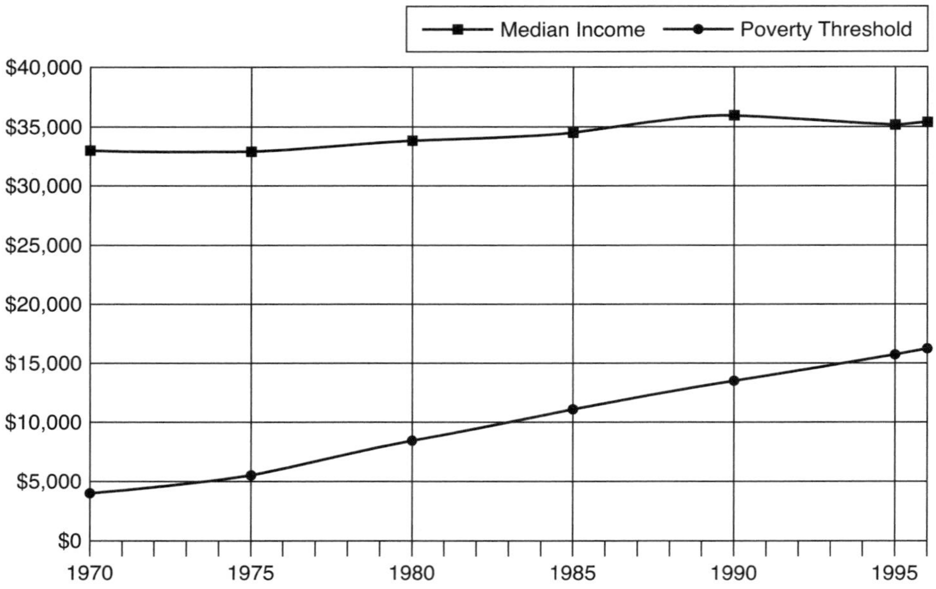

In addition to lack of resources, poverty brings "secondary risks" that further deteriorate the quality of life available to disadvantaged Americans.

"SECONDARY RISKS" OF POVERTY

America's poor are not just economically vulnerable. They are exposed to homelessness and violence to a much greater degree than other citizens of the United States. Further, they are frequently accused of "fraud," despite the relatively small economic impact of their fraudulent activities. In the following section, we will examine "secondary" risks that accompany poverty.

HOMELESSNESS. In the United States a house is a commodity, developed and traded for profit. A house can provide shelter and protection. A "home" provides continuity and a social context for adults and children, and those who become homeless lose more than shelter. They lose connection with their past, friends, and schools, and their place in a community. Two developments in the U.S. housing market have increased the vulnerability of low-income people. The first is a diminishing supply of low-cost rental housing; the second is a reduced federal commitment to housing assistance.

As we mentioned above, the majority of low-income families do not have access to federal housing assistance, and they fare poorly in the private housing market. Since the early 1970s, the supply of low-cost rental housing has been diminishing. Analyzing data from the Annual Housing Survey, Sternleib and Hughes (1981) reported that

> more than a million units, which in 1973 rented for less than $150 a month, literally disappeared from housing inventory. . . . Low-rent housing units are literally being removed, and the potential renter who can only afford low rent, finds the inventory available to him or her shrinking markedly (pp. 111–112).

Urban renewal efforts have cost the nation more than a million rooms in "Single-Room-Occupancy" (SRO) hotels. In recent decades, major cities such as New York have lost many of their SROs. Some buildings have simply been demolished. "Gentrification" has been another significant factor reducing the supply of low-cost housing. In 1984, Harrington described gentrification as "the process whereby the middle class and the rich take over the physically sound and architecturally charming housing of the poor" (Harrington, 1984, p. 119). "Public subsidies, such as tax abatements for refurbishment, have often subsidized this process. But there has not been a commensurate subsidy to provide housing for the displaced" (Harrington, 1984, p. 12). The supply of low-income housing continued to diminish during the 1990s. As HUD reported, between 1991 and 1997 the number of affordable rental units in the U.S. dropped by an estimated 372,000, which amounted to 5 percent of the nation's supply (U.S. Department of Housing and Urban Development, 1999).

As an inevitable result of declining supply, the cost of housing has increased. In recent decades the Consumer Price Index for shelter has consistently increased at a rate higher than the general Consumer Price Index. This trend continued during the economic prosperity of the 1990s, requiring low- and middle-income Americans to devote a greater share of their income to housing than they had in the past (U.S. Department of Housing and Urban Development, 1999).

Federal housing interventions attempt to bridge the gap between the financial resources of low-income Americans and the cost of housing, but recent decades have seen erosion in all three programs. This erosion was especially marked during the Reagan administration, when funding for public housing was severely reduced. Funds allocated went from $32 billion in 1981 to $6 billion in 1989 (Burton, 1992). The number of Section 202 units dropped from a high of 39,381 in 1978 to 7,281 in 1990 (Sonnenberg, personal communication, 1993). In a despairing note, Koebel complained in 1998 that "The failure of government to directly provide decent housing for low-income families is now accepted as a given" (Koebel, 1998, p. 3). Coupled with a tight housing market, government inattention to the housing needs of the poor contributes to increased homelessness.

Michael Harrington (1984) suggested that people without homes be called "uprooted" rather than "homeless." Harrington noted that major economic transformations have traditionally created "a floating population" of people whose role in the old economic order has disappeared. It is hard to precisely estimate the number of Americans who are homeless. Two methods yield very different results. The "point in time" approach asks how many people are homeless on a particular day (or night). Using this method, Burt (1992) suggested that at any given time approximately one-half million people were homeless during the late 1980s. This figure has been widely cited. The "period-prevalence" approach asks how many people have experienced homelessness during a longer period, usually either a lifetime or the past five years. A definitive study, completed in 1994 (Link et al., 1995) found that 6.5 percent of American adults (12 million people) had been homeless at some point in their lives.

Who are America's homeless? There are two distinct groups: single adults and families. Single adults are predominantly homeless men, among whom an estimated 20–25 percent suffer from severe and persistent mental illness (Koegel et al., 1996). The proportion who suffer from addiction disorders has been estimated at 22 percent (Koegel et al., 1996). Notably, studies have found that between 22 percent and 40 percent of homeless men are veterans (Waxman & Trupin, 1997; Humphreys & Rosenheck, 1995).

Families with children are the fastest-growing group, constituting approximately 40 percent of the nation's homeless (Shinn, 1997). A study commissioned by the U.S. Conference of Mayors reported that children represented about one-fourth of the urban homeless (Waxman & Trupin, 1997). A 1990 Ford Foundation study found that half of homeless women and children were fleeing abusive situations (Zorza, 1991).

VIOLENCE. Violent crime in the United States has become more prevalent in recent decades, and poverty leaves people especially vulnerable to aggression and victimization.[13] Indeed, consideration of broad trends in violence in the U.S. led Gurr (1989) to comment that increases in violence have typically been associated with "immigration, war and economic deprivation" (p. 12).

Social dislocation and extreme poverty create conditions ripe for violence. In the case of African-American men, poverty and race have interacted to leave them at tragically high risk for violence. During the nineteenth and twentieth centuries, African-American men were more likely than white men to be murdered and to commit murder (Short, 1997). The same trends have been observed in France and Germany, where marginalized immigrant groups experience higher rates of crime (Short, 1997). There is also some evidence that inequality is associated with higher homicide rates (Blau & Blau, 1982). As Michael Harrington (1984) argued, "Certain social and economic conditions—above all, the experience of becoming marginal, useless—create not a fate, but a greater likelihood that some (a minority) will turn to violent crime either as means to an end, a way of earning a living, or else as an act of sheer rage" (p. 189).

Violent crime is concentrated where marginalized groups are restricted to certain neighborhoods or communities, such as inner-city ghettos. Emily's experience as the resident of a low-income neighborhood illustrates this localization of violence. Her children and their friends could all provide first-hand accounts of incidents of violence in their community. Many of these incidents are gang-related. It is unclear why ghetto residents experience more violence. Possible explanations include lack of opportunity, few role models for success, higher residential mobility, family disruption, and cultural values that tolerate violence (Short, 1997).

WELFARE FRAUD

In 1992 the Committee on Banking, Finance and Urban Affairs estimated that food stamp fraud cost the nation $1 billion. A popular urban myth holds that food stamp recipients use their coupons to buy guns and drugs, and hundreds of Americans have heard that "a friend of a friend" saw a woman drive to the welfare office in a Cadillac. In reality, welfare fraud is neither as prevalent nor as straightforward as many Americans believe.

The Food Stamp program distributes more than $22 billion worth of food coupons each year. The Department of Agriculture estimated that in 1990 less than 1 percent of participants defrauded the program (usually by lying about eligibility), and approximately 5 percent of funds were lost to fraud. Those who benefit most from food stamp fraud are not participants but retailers. In the most common form of food stamp fraud, the retailer purchases the stamps for 65 to

---

[13]James F. Short (1997) argues, and I agree, that violent crime creates two victims: the perpetrator and the identified victim. Both lives are either ended or permanently disrupted by the experience.

85 percent of their face value and then turns them in for full reimbursement. While this practice frees the participant to spend the reduced amount on whatever he or she likes, the profit accrues to the retailer. In one of the largest cases, a retailer in Toledo, Ohio, improperly redeemed $7.2 million in food stamps. This individual had been convicted of food stamp fraud in 1984, but evidently never quit the lucrative practice (Cook, 1989). Dishonest retailers, not the poor, are those who benefit most from food stamp fraud.

Public assistance payments seem designed to produce fraud. Cash assistance consistently fails to raise family incomes above the poverty threshold. For example, in 1996, the average AFDC payment to a family of three ($499) was less than half of the federal poverty threshold for the same family ($1,043). In some states, the mean AFDC payment was barely a quarter of the federal poverty threshold. (U.S. Department of Health and Human Services, 1998). Even when in-kind assistance such as food stamps, Medicaid, and housing supports are included, families find it difficult to raise children with such limited resources. Many mothers secure other sources of income, a practice that (if unreported) constitutes welfare fraud (see Funiciello, 1993). Emily Morrison's babysitting is one example of this widespread practice.

From a broader perspective, the economic impact of welfare fraud pales in comparison with that of middle-class fraud. Middle-class fraud includes practices such as health care fraud and tax evasion that benefit members of the middle and upper classes, often at the expense of taxpayers. In 1992, the General Accounting Office reported to Congress that health insurance fraud (including that in the Medicare and Medicaid programs) cost an estimated 10 percent of the total health care dollars spent in the U.S., as much as $84 billion in 1992 alone (National Health Care Anti-Fraud Association—www.nhcaa.org). Common forms of Medicare fraud include billing for services not furnished, misrepresenting the diagnosis to justify payment, soliciting, offering or receiving a kickback, and "upcoding" (billing for more costly services than those actually delivered).

Tax evasion also takes its toll. Based on IRS data, the GAO reported that taxpayers ultimately pay about 87 percent of the taxes they owe. Groups vary in the extent of their tax evasion, with wage earners reporting 99 percent of their earnings, while self-employed workers report only 19 percent. The difference between taxes owed and those collected, called the "tax gap," has increased during the past decade. In 1981, the tax gap amounted to $76 billion, or 1.6 percent of the nation's Gross Domestic Product. By 1992, that figure had grown to $127 billion, or 2.0 percent of the GDP (U.S. General Accounting Office, 1994).

America's energetic pursuit of welfare fraud can hardly be attributed to its drain on the public purse. Even when the amount lost seems large, it is a small fraction of the amount lost to health insurance fraud and tax evasion. Yet welfare fraud raises the public ire in a way that tax evasion never could. Why is that so? Is it more corrupt for a welfare mother like Emily to be paid under the table for providing child care to her neighbors than it is for a businessman to conceal income from the IRS? Or is the public furor over welfare fraud just another vehicle for humiliating recipients of public assistance?

SUMMARY: WHAT DOES THE FUTURE HOLD FOR AMERICA'S POOR?

This chapter began with the case of Emily Morrison, a bright, articulate woman who has successfully raised several children with assistance from AFDC. Her success as a mother might in earlier eras have entitled her to public assistance. But in 1996, Congress and the President took definitive action to "end welfare as we know it."

Under current welfare law Emily Morrison, along with millions of other welfare recipients, will be encouraged to assume "personal responsibility" for her limited means. The nation's collective responsibility for low-income families and their children is now limited. Upon reaching their lifetime limits, former welfare recipients may retain food stamps, Medicaid, and housing assistance. But they will not have money to pay for basic necessities such as housing and clothes for themselves and their children.

The 1996 welfare reform legislation was put in place after the nation's working families had endured three decades of declining wages—a trend that threatened to reduce the incentive to work by diminishing the gap between workers and welfare recipients. In a capitalistic economy like that of the United States, diminished work incentive represents a significant economic threat. We suggested in this chapter that welfare reform reduces that threat, both by eliminating the choice between welfare and work, and by reducing the quality of life for those on welfare. Thus, PRWORA represents a "stick" approach to work incentive. An alternative "carrot" approach would focus on improving the quality of life for the nation's workers. Economic growth that leads to wage increases could accomplish this goal in the absence of public policy. Policy initiatives aimed at this goal could involve increases in the minimum wage, improved working conditions, and expansion of earned income tax credits.

Moving beyond a focus on work incentive, Walter Trattner (1989) ended his exhaustive survey of the history of the American welfare state by suggesting that "Perhaps a time will come anyway when most Americans will acknowledge—or be forced to acknowledge—what our colonial forebears simply took for granted, namely, that the poor will be with us, always, through no fault of their own, and that they, too, have a right to a healthy, happy, and secure life" (p. 342). Whether both the working poor and welfare recipients will be able to live "a healthy, happy, and secure life" in the United States remains to be seen.

DISCUSSION TOPICS

1. Consider the three conditions that facilitate collective action to address individual problems, as outlined in the introduction to Part II. The events of the Great Depression led many Americans to see poverty as an individual problem with "uncertainty of moment and magnitude." Does this view still hold? Do any of these conditions play a role in contemporary debates about welfare reform? Should they? Does poverty in the United States have any "external effects?"

2. Which of the philosophical conceptions of social justice presented in Chapter 1 is most influential in the structure of the U.S. welfare effort?

3. Emily Morrison's children seem to be doing well, and she attributes their well-being to her presence in the home. Do you think society should spend public resources to make it possible for poor mothers to stay home with their children?

4. Apply the five-question social justice framework presented in Chapter 1 to a proposal to increase the minimum wage. Once you have finished with question 5, add a sixth question: "Why do I believe this is/is not fair?" Consider how your personal philosophy and experiences have influenced your answer to question 5.

5. Does your state provide an Earned Income Tax Credit for low-income workers? If not, is this an agenda item for local poverty advocates? Why or why not?

6. Compare your state's poverty rate with the rate nationwide. Is it substantially different? If so, how would you explain the difference?

SUGGESTED RESOURCES

Barusch, A. S. (1994). *Older Women in Poverty: Private Lives and Public Policies*. New York: Springer Publishing Co.

Danziger, S., & Gottschalk, P. (1995). *America Unequal*. New York: Russell Sage Foundation.

Harrington, M. (1984). *The New American Poverty*. New York: Holt, Rinehart & Winston.

Katz, M. (1989). *The Undeserving Poor*. New York: Pantheon Books.

Kozol, J. (1991). *Savage Inequalities: Children in America's Schools*. New York: Crown.

Specht, H., & Courtney, M. (1994). *Unfaithful Angels: How Social Work Has Abandoned Its Mission*. New York: Free Press.

Trattner, W. I. (1989). *From Poor Law to Welfare State: A History of Social Welfare in America* (4th ed.). New York: Free Press.

www.census.gov/hhes/www/poverty.html—Maintained by the Bureau of the Census, this site is a good starting point for up-to-date information on poverty in the United States.

www.ufenet.org—This site is operated by United for a Fair Economy, an organization devoted to polices that reduce inequality in the United States. UFE is "grounded in the belief that our country would be a far more democratic, prosperous, and caring community if we narrowed the vast gap between the very wealthy and everyone else." The UFE web site offers an introduction to the organization and provides position papers on issues.

www.urban.org—Operated by The Urban Institute, a nonprofit organization, this site provides reports on social and economic problems.

www.welfareinfo.org—Operated by the Welfare Information Network, this site includes a variety of publications regarding welfare policies in the U.S.

5

Health Care

The health of the people is really the foundation upon
which all their happiness and all their powers as a
state depend.

BENJAMIN DISRAELI, JULY 1877

The role of government in health care has long been the subject of debate.
Early public health reformers met vigorous opposition when they proposed
what we now consider to be the most basic public health measures. Today the
role of government in the financing and delivery of health care is again under
dispute. At issue is the extent to which illness should be addressed through collective, as opposed to individual, action.

Allocation of health care is clearly a social justice issue, as is the extent to
which a patient should be held responsible for his or her illness and the cost of
its treatment. America's reliance on private-market solutions to health problems
has created a billion-dollar health care industry to serve economically productive
and affluent members of society. In the same nation, there are millions of workers who do not have access to the most basic forms of health care. Should health
care be treated as a social good, with no one permitted to fall below a minimal
standard? Is the private market the most efficient means of distributing health
care? Should individuals bear the risk (and the cost) of catastrophic illness? These
and related questions are considered throughout this chapter.

We will begin by considering the case of Tanya Johnson, a young woman
who contracted HIV from her boyfriend. Tanya's situation illustrates many of the
dilemmas of health care in the United States. We will trace the development of

public health interventions in the U.S., focusing on three major federal health agencies: the Public Health Service, the Children's Bureau, and the Veterans Administration. Next, we will look at the federal role in financing health care through Medicaid and Medicare, and the impact of this legislation on the private health care industry. The next section outlines the U.S. health care investment (in the form of health expenditures) and its return (in terms of infant survival and longevity). Returning to a national focus, we will then consider the health of vulnerable groups within the United States, considering the impact of class, race and gender. Emerging health needs are examined next, including the HIV epidemic, the return of tuberculosis, and the growing demand for long-term care. We will explore two fundamental policy dilemmas affecting health care in the U.S.: criteria for assigning risk and the use of the market to allocate health care. The chapter closes with brief consideration of contemporary health care reform proposals and the ways in which social workers can influence health care policy.

CASE STUDY ♦ TANYA JOHNSON

At the age of 24, Tanya Johnson is considered uninsurable due to a pre-existing condition. Tanya is HIV-positive. She sees herself as living with, not dying from, AIDS and refuses to view herself as a "victim" of the epidemic. Her situation illustrates many of the tensions experienced by people coping with chronic illness in the U.S. health care system.

A bouncy, attractive woman with long, curly auburn hair, Tanya describes herself as "perfectly healthy . . . I don't take medications and I have good t-cells and I have a low viral load. I do have symptoms. My lymph nodes are swollen a lot and inflamed and sometimes they ache. They don't hurt, they ache. And so I just take Motrin for it. I get fatigued very easily. I take Motrin for cramps, for chest pains, headaches. I'm a walking ibuprofen advertisement."

When she speaks to high school classes for the local AIDS foundation, she begins by saying, "My name is Tanya Johnson and I've had HIV for four years that I contracted from a very lovely sociopathic IV drug user." Tanya assured me that "he WAS [sociopathic]. He's in prison right now, as a matter of fact, so he's proven it." Tanya met her boyfriend at a party one night. "We'd gone to a party, and this guy was there, and he was friends with us" and so they started going out. "It just kind of happened. I'd go to his place and party sometimes, and it just happened one night. It wasn't like we dated or anything."

Tanya's boyfriend knew he had AIDS, but didn't tell her. "I'm not angry about this. 'Cause I'm not. It's my own fault, you know? I knew what I was doing, you know? And you have to take your own responsibility for yourself. I knew about safe sex and I knew about AIDS. I lost my virginity when I was 14, so I knew about all the precautions to take. I wasn't stupid. I was just crazy, I guess. I was immortal and I was on top of the world and nothing bad was ever going to happen to me. I was going to live forever, young, and beautiful, and THIN."

After Tanya and her boyfriend broke up, she learned that he had AIDS. "So I went to go to get tested. I'd been tested before so I knew the drill. I waited past the 90 days 'cause I kind of really didn't want to know. I invented all the reasons in the world why it couldn't possibly be, and then all the reasons why it could possibly be, and I. . . . you know? The flu-like symptoms that they tell you about. I didn't feel good for a whole month. I called for my test results, and I was getting off at 3:30 p.m. I says, 'Are my test results in?' She says, 'Yes, they are.' I says, 'Great. I'll be in after work.' She says, 'No.' She says, 'Come in tomorrow.' I says, 'No, I can come in right now.' She says, 'No, come in tomorrow. How about 4:00?' And by now I'm panicked, 'cause I just know. And I says, 'What time do you open?' She says, '9 a.m.' I says, 'I will be there at 9 a.m.' I did not sleep that night. Did not have sex with my boyfriend that night, you know. And of course I hadn't told him about any of this. The next morning I go in. And you know when I go in I have to sit and wait forever in the waiting room. And then I go in, and then . . . the lady that gave me the test took me into a room and there was another lady sitting there. And I just started crying. They didn't even have to tell. And the lady that was in with her, she's a case manager for the state. And she's a wonderful lady. She says, 'What are you going to do when you leave here?' I says, 'I don't know . . . go home . . . ' She says, 'Call your mom right now. Make an appointment and meet her for lunch and tell her,' and I'm like, 'Okay.' She didn't want me to leave the office and have nowhere to go."

Tanya is an only child. She told her mother over lunch, and her mom responded, "So, do you want to live forever?" "I says, 'Well . . . yeah. I kind of would like to. You know? I'm 21 years old!' I couldn't tell Dad. She told dad for me. I went home the next afternoon, and my dad came out of the bedroom, and my mom had told him, and he comes up to me and just gives me a big, huge hug then went back to his bedroom. He couldn't stay with me because he was, you know, just too choked up. He says, 'I love you' and walked back in his bedroom. My family's been great. Except for my Uncle James, and he doesn't talk to me or won't come anywhere near me."

Tanya works as an office manager for a small firm with ten employees. Tanya likes her job. "The people are really nice, which is amazing, 'cause you know, usually at jobs, people are so cruel. And I like what I'm doing." The people at work don't know that Tanya is HIV-positive. It is important to her that her employers not know about her condition, because she was fired from her last job because of her HIV status.

When she was diagnosed, Tanya had worked as a computer operator for Homebase for four and a half years. She had health insurance and a 401(k). After careful deliberation she decided to tell the manager. "I thought he was a nice guy. I've never been a good judge of character. I thought maybe he could help me in case I needed some time off. I told him in confidence. He then has a staff meeting. Tells all the staff managers, my supervisor, his office staff."

Tanya describes the result as "nightmarish." After a year, she was fired for failing to come in for a scheduled shift. The manager had scheduled her for back-to-back closing and opening shifts. She had frequently asked not to be given this kind of shift because it was too draining, and had been accommodated. "I requested, two weeks in advance, that the schedule be changed. I told the general manager, and he refused to change the schedule. 'Look,' I says, 'I'm not going to do this to myself. I know what will happen to my body if I do it . . . It'll make me sick. Do you want me to be sick? He told me I would just have to work it. Everybody worked back-to-backs. He says, 'You know, I get tired too. You don't see me calling in sick.' My God! He has no clue what tired means. And so I told him I wouldn't show up for the shift. So I worked the night shift, and in the morning I set my alarm and I called him, and I called in sick. 'Well, Tanya,' he says, 'we have a problem.' The next day I went to work and they suspended me. I knew they were going to fire me. Before I went in to work, they had taken my picture off the computer room door."

Tanya experienced a health crisis shortly after she was fired, and she talked to her doctor about the experience. Her doctor referred her to "an ACLU attorney," who found someone to take her case. Tanya's lawyer took the case on a contingency basis and will receive payment only when Tanya does. Now, after mediation and two hearings before the state industrial commission, Tanya has a ruling in her favor. The judge ruled, in essence, that Homebase failed to provide the reasonable accommodation due to Tanya under the Americans with Disabilities Act. When Tanya received her notice in the mail she was thrilled, not because of the money (back pay) she may receive, but because she had been vindicated. "They did something wrong and they hurt me, and so yeah, I'm fighting back . . . and if they'll do it to me, then they'll do it to someone else, you know? And I don't want someone else to go through what they put me through."

When she was fired, Tanya lost her health insurance. With her pre-existing condition, getting new insurance was "a complete nightmare." In fact, she hasn't had insurance coverage for four years. "I applied for it when my time came up. I filled out the paperwork and sent it in 'cause I wasn't going to give it to my employers. Well, at the same time my employer decided to change insurance companies. The gentleman that had sold us this insurance policy, I called him and I says, 'Norm, I'm gonna mail you my insurance application.' I says, 'When you get it, if there's a problem, call me. Not my supervisor.' He's all, 'Okay.' So about two days later he calls me. He goes, 'I got your application, and unfortunately we're gonna deny your entire group because of your application."

So Tanya's firm didn't include her in their group's applications. "'We're gonna do this,' he [her supervisor] says. 'If you can get insurance on your own, we'll pay 75 percent of the premium.' Which he didn't do." Instead, Tanya went to the State Department of Health, which ran a Health Insurance Premium program for people with AIDS, funded under the Ryan White Act. To enroll in the program, Tanya needed to verify that the employer's insurance firm had reached its "cap." Under state law, health insurers are required to cover a certain proportion of "uninsurables" before they can begin denying coverage. But the insurance firm in this case had not reached its cap. As it turned out, "The insurance company just basically said, 'We're denying you,' but they hadn't really reached their cap." So the company was required to insure Tanya. "If I hadn't had to have verification I never would have known and I wouldn't have insurance."

Tanya must wait a year for coverage of her "pre-existing condition." For care, she relies on the services provided under her state's Ryan White program, which she describes in glowing terms. Her case manager is "absolutely amazing," her physician's assistant is "wonderful," and her physician walks on water. At present, her care needs are limited to bi-annual testing and periodic treatment of emerging symptoms.

Tanya teaches HIV 101 to high school classes. Her new boyfriend recently accompanied her to one of these sessions. "The teacher, instead of putting Matt (that's my boyfriend) over on the side of the room—he was just gonna sort of sit and listen—he put his chair right next to me up front. So, Matt's sitting here, like okay, you know? And I go through my story and one of the kids asked, he says, 'Well, what does your boyfriend think about this?' And I said, 'I don't know, Matt, what do you think about this?' He's like, 'What?' and then they start asking him questions and I think it was a really good thing to have him there. He came off with this just suave, smooth answer . . . that's why I like him."

Matt recently moved in with Tanya, and they are talking about buying a house (or maybe a ranch) together and getting married. Tanya would rather not have children. "I did a talk, and a girl was very . . . 'Well, can't you adopt?' I said, 'It takes a lot of energy to raise a child, and that's energy I need for myself if I'm going to stay healthy. My body works a lot harder than normal people's bodies, just at rest . . . and I've never had a craving to have kids.'"

Tanya is exceptionally motivated, with a positive attitude toward life and toward coping with HIV. As she puts it, "I don't understand depression. I don't get depressed. I get angry sometimes at people. I get pissy and whatever. But I don't get depressed." She has made lifestyle changes to maintain her health: drinking distilled water, avoiding rare meat, reducing her alcohol intake, carefully washing fruits and vegetables, and avoiding over-exertion. "I figure it's easier to change my lifestyle now, while I'm healthy, than later, when I'm sick. IF I get sick, God forbid."

But a lot of people Tanya knows through the AIDS Foundation don't take care of themselves. "They don't enjoy their life. They still do drugs; they still drink. I have one friend who's not supposed to take his medication when he takes alcohol and drugs, so when he goes to parties, he doesn't take his medication." Tanya attributes her good health to lifestyle and attitude: "My basic frame of mind is to be happy."

When she was initially diagnosed, Tanya knew very little about what to expect from the disease. During the first few months she "wasn't thinking in terms of the future." She only thought she was going to die. But she has developed a new philosophy. "You know? It changes your whole outlook on life. I don't get upset about all the petty [things] . . . who squoze the toothpaste on the wrong side of the tube? These things aren't important. My family and my friends, those are my priorities. Enjoying my life is my priority. Everyone's going to die. AIDS is not the only thing that people die from. People die from all sorts of cancers, and accidents . . . natural disasters. Everyone is going to die. I'd kind of like to die with dignity."

DISCUSSION   Tanya's experience as an American who is chronically ill has been influenced by several public policies. Federal policies that have affected her include Medicaid, the Ryan White Care Act, and the Americans with Disabilities Act. State policies, such as the state regulation that requires health insurance providers to serve the uninsurable, have also directly affected Tanya's care.

In some respects, Tanya's experience parallels that of anyone with a chronic condition who seeks care in the U.S. health care market. She has gone for extended periods without health insurance. The care she receives is determined by the political will of

Americans. Should she become unable to care for herself, Tanya will rely on family and friends as long as possible, hoping to delay or avoid nursing home placement. Should she need long-term nursing care, Tanya will probably apply for Medicaid. Of course, she would be required to "spend-down" her personal resources to become eligible.

The stigma associated with AIDS often leads to hysteria and discrimination. When Tanya was fired, she had access to legal remedies provided by the 1990 passage of the Americans with Disabilities Act (ADA). Like most programs for people with disabilities, the ADA was not drafted with HIV-AIDS victims in mind. Nevertheless, disability policies such as the ADA and income supports like OASDI and SSI have become significant resources for this group, because HIV-AIDS is considered a disabling condition.

Tanya is distinctive in having access to effective drugs to mitigate the effects of HIV. She contracted AIDS after a tremendous increase in pharmacological research. She lives in an industrialized nation, which gives her access to treatment that is unheard of, and a life expectancy unparalleled in developing countries. Her treatment will be expensive, however. A three-drug regimen that includes a protease inhibitor costs approximately $12,000 to $16,000 per year (Farmer, 1996, p. 264).

The United States is one of only two industrialized nations that do not offer universal health coverage (Roemer, 1993). (The other nation without universal coverage is South Africa.) In the U.S. we depend on a private market to provide health care and health insurance. Perhaps as a result of the failures of that market, new laws are enacted each year to regulate the operations of insurers and providers. Indeed, the year after I met Tanya, the Health Insurance Portability and Accountability Act restricted the use of pre-existing conditions to deny coverage. Even today, however, Tanya must remain employed to maintain private health insurance. If she becomes impoverished, she will depend on public care.

THE HISTORY OF PUBLIC HEALTH INTERVENTIONS IN THE UNITED STATES

Most of us are familiar with the major medical breakthroughs of the twentieth century: the development of antibiotics, immunizations, and advanced surgical techniques. Less familiar, but perhaps more significant, have been advances in public health. The development of modern plumbing, for example, has improved the health status of populations throughout the world. In this section, we will focus on the development of public health interventions in the United States.

The development of public health policies and measures has been an integral part of the growth of the U.S. welfare state. Indeed, early public health reformers recognized the close connection between health and social conditions. Policy milestones include the 1912 creation of the Children's Bureau, the 1930 establishment of the Veterans Administration, the 1944 creation of the Public Health Service, the 1946 establishment of the Centers for Disease Control and Prevention, the 1953 creation of the Department of Health, Education, and Welfare, and the 1965 passage of Medicare and Medicaid.

Public health reformers in nineteenth-century America drew from the English approach to community health, seeing (perhaps more clearly than we do now) the close link between poverty and disease. Just as this nation imported major elements of the Elizabethan Poor Law, we also inherited the perspectives and procedures of Britain's "Sanitary Movement." Edwin Chadwick and other leaders of the movement advocated national oversight of sanitation in urban areas, government tracking of vital statistics, and local regulation of waste drainage and purification of drinking water. When their suggestions were initially presented to Parliament in 1844 and 1845, they were met with shocked protest. Many saw them as violations of private property rights and individual liberties. Nonetheless, a staunch group of reformers, most of them from privileged backgrounds, persisted and in 1848 secured passage of the Public Health Act, which empowered a General Board of Health to establish local boards of health throughout the nation. Under the Act, the establishment of a local board could be triggered either by petition of at least one-tenth of taxpayers in the area or when mortality over a seven-year period exceeded 23 people per 1,000. Local boards dealt with water supply, sewage, management of cemeteries, control of "offensive trades" (such as prostitution), and investigation of conditions affecting community health.

Like the British model, the American approach to public health focused on local, as opposed to national, efforts. Local boards of health assumed responsibility for a wide range of public health tasks, from regulation and inspection of public eating establishments, to maintaining vital statistics, to managing quarantines. Fee and Porter (1991) described their work as "a kind of rearguard action against the filth and congestion created by anarchic economic and urban development" (pp. 20–21).

But there was a role for the federal government. In his classic history of the field, George Rosen (1993) dates the U.S. government's first involvement in public health to the Marine Hospital Service. Established by Congress in 1798, the Service was designed to meet the health care needs of seamen. Crews of merchant vessels were integral to the commercial success of the nation. Because the seamen were not residents of any parish or town, however, the system of local responsibility left them without health care.

The Marine Hospital Service provided medical and hospital care to sick and disabled seamen. This care was financed through a monthly tax of 20 cents on each man's wages. The result was the world's first prepaid, comprehensive, medical and hospital insurance plan. The Treasury Department collected the fees, and the Service was placed under its jurisdiction. As a result, until 1935, most federal public health services operated under the Treasury Department.

Another federal health responsibility involved immigration. In America, as in Europe, human travel from an infected area served as the primary vehicle for spreading epidemics. So early attempts to control epidemics of cholera, yellow fever, typhoid, smallpox, and other diseases focused on immigrants, who were seen as bringing in foreign contagion which then spread like wildfire through overcrowded urban slums. In 1878, the National Quarantine Act gave the Marine

Hospital Service authority to inspect immigrants. At first, this screening was intended to bar "lunatics and others unable to care for themselves" but later extended to include "persons suffering from loathsome and contagious diseases." Federal involvement in public health continued to expand. In 1879, a National Board of Health was established to collect information, advise the federal government on public health issues, and devise a plan that gave special attention to quarantine procedures.

Meanwhile, the development of immunizations expanded the responsibilities of local health authorities. From 1880 to 1898, understanding of the causes of disease expanded tremendously, as scientists in Europe identified the specific organisms responsible for most of the infectious diseases of the time. Even before these organisms were described, researchers had observed that a mild case of disease could produce lifelong immunity. This observation was accompanied by experiments (often conducted on poor children) that attempted to produce immunity through injection of blood from an infected patient. Louis Pasteur is credited with establishing and developing the principle of prophylactic inoculation.

Developments in Europe were observed closely by public health scientists and officials in the United States, and soon laboratories were added to local public health departments. These laboratories performed diagnostic tests, conducted research, and provided vaccinations to community physicians. Their practical importance was soon well established, setting the stage for widespread acceptance of government involvement in public health.

FEDERAL HEALTH AGENCIES

Four types of federal health agencies emerged in the United States during the twentieth century (Hanlon & Pickett, 1979). These include the Public Health Service, the only national agency concerned with broad health issues; agencies that serve specific groups, such as the Children's Bureau, the Women's Bureau, the Administration on Aging, the Bureau of Indian Affairs, and the Veterans Administration; and agencies that deal with specific problems or programs, such as the Office of Education, Food and Drug Administration, Department of Agriculture, and Bureau of Labor Statistics. We will briefly review the history of three of the largest federal health agencies: the Public Health Service, the Children's Bureau, and the Veterans Administration.

PUBLIC HEALTH SERVICE

Most public health specialists consider the Public Health Service (PHS) the most important federal agency in the field. The PHS grew out of the Marine Hospital Service. In 1902, Congress recognized its expanded responsibilities by renaming it the Public Health and Marine Hospital Service and placing the agency under the direction of a Surgeon General. In 1912 the agency was again renamed, this time with the title it bears today, the U.S. Public Health Service. The 1935 passage of the Social Security Act charged the Service with providing grants-in-aid to states and territories to assist in establishing health services and training health personnel. In 1953, the Service moved from the Treasury Department into the newly established Department of Health, Education, and Welfare (HEW). In 1980, the Department of Education was established as a separate agency, and HEW was renamed the Department of Health and Human Services (HHS).

The Service involved the federal government in direct provision of medical care. Originally hospitals and clinics were established to serve those eligible for care (seamen, federal civilian employees who became ill in the line of duty, members of the Coast Guard, and anyone requiring immunization for yellow fever). Later, under the Indian Health Service, medical facilities for Native Americans and Eskimos were established. In time, direct operation of most hospitals and clinics was phased out.

Today the Public Health Service supports direct care by providing grants to other organizations that deliver the care. Through its Health Resources and Services Administration (HRSA), the PHS operates grant programs that finance the provision of primary and preventive care to medically underserved residents in the U.S. and its territories. Some services funded through these programs include black lung clinics for coal miners, prevention and primary care delivery at the U.S.–Mexico border, medical services to migrant farm workers, health care for native Hawaiians, comprehensive care to residents of public housing, and primary care and substance abuse services for the homeless. The PHS does directly deliver primary health care to people who are detained by the Immigration and Naturalization Service.[1]

CHILDREN'S BUREAU

Establishment of the Children's Bureau was debated for six years before Congress finally authorized it in 1912. With support from the National Consumers League, the National Child Labor Committee, and many women's organizations and church groups, the Bureau was created to serve as a center of research and education for the general welfare of women and children. It was placed under the Department of Commerce and Labor, signaling its early focus on regulation of child labor. Under the direction of Julia Lathrop, the Bureau was authorized only to investigate and report on health issues affecting children and their mothers.

But even this charge involved the Bureau's staff in controversial activities. One such activity involved maternal and child health. The Bureau's research revealed serious maternal and child health problems in rural areas, lending momentum to an emerging movement to establish maternal and child welfare programs through federal grants-in-aid. Opponents of this effort included the

---

[1]For more information about HRSA programs, see http://bphc.hrsa.gov/bphc/index_1.htm.

American Medical Association, Anti-Suffragists, the Sentinels of the Republic, and several other organizations, who saw the bill as a violation of personal, family, and states' rights and a step toward socialized medicine.

Nonetheless, in 1921 (the same year that Grace Abbott took over as director of the Children's Bureau) the Sheppard-Towner Act was passed, with the Children's Bureau assigned to administer the grants-in-aid. It is easy to imagine the enthusiasm with which Abbott and her staff of reformers set out to establish maternal and child welfare programs throughout the states. Bureau staff moved fast, and in the two years following passage of Sheppard-Towner fifteen states established programs.

The original Act included what we now call a "Sunset Clause," which provided for review and extension of its programs after five years. This clause gave opponents another opportunity to attack the Act and the Bureau. As a result of their efforts, a bill introduced to extend Sheppard-Towner for seven years failed, and a two-year extension passed. This defeat signaled the end of the program. After Sheppard-Towner expired, 35 states decreased appropriations for child hygiene, and nine states eliminated this funding entirely (Hanlon & Pickett, 1979).

This hiatus in child and maternal health programming did not last long, however. The 1935 Social Security Act not only restored the Sheppard-Towner programs but extended the Bureau's responsibilities to include not only maternal and child health but also services for crippled children, as well as child welfare services. These programs were administered by the Children's Bureau through grants-in-aid to the states.

Through subsequent decades the Children's Bureau continued to act on its original mandate to investigate and report on issues affecting children's welfare, and the programs and services under its auspices continued to expand. When World War II left wives and children of servicemen unable to pay for medical care, the Bureau alerted Congress to the situation and an Act for the Emergency Maternity and Infant Care for the Wives and Children of Servicemen was passed. In 1963 the Maternal and Child Health and Mental Retardation Planning Amendments (to the Social Security Act) provided federal support for state-run projects that offered comprehensive care for high-risk mothers and infants in low-income families. Two years later, the Social Security Act was again amended to allow for the development of comprehensive health services for children and youth. Funds were allocated for clinics, hospital care, and health education for low-income families.

The costs of the Vietnam War brought significant reductions in funding for these programs. Reorganization of the Department of Health, Education and Welfare separated the health and social welfare functions of the Children's Bureau. Health functions, such as prenatal care for low-income mothers, primary health care for their infants and children, and disease prevention programs, were assigned to the newly created Maternal and Child Health Program that operates today in the Public Health Service. The social welfare functions of the Bureau, including protective services and shelters for high-risk youth, child care for recipients of public assistance, and adoption services, are now lodged in the Administration on Children, Youth and Families within the Department of Health and Human Services.

Veterans Administration

Government provision for veterans in the United States can be traced to the Pilgrims. Following their war with the Pequot Indians, the Pilgrims passed a law providing that disabled veterans would be supported by the colony. Since then, expanded benefits for veterans have often been used as an inducement to join the military and as a reward for service. The first residential and medical facility for veterans was authorized by the federal government in 1811. After the Civil War, many states established medical and convalescent facilities for veterans. Treatment was provided for all diseases and injuries, whether or not they were service-related.

The current system of federal veterans benefits originated in 1917, when the U.S. entered World War I. Benefits included disability compensation, insurance, and vocational rehabilitation for the disabled. In the 1920s these programs were administered by three different federal agencies: the Veterans Bureau, the Bureau of Pensions, and the National Home for Disabled Volunteer Soldiers. These agencies were combined to form a single "Veterans Administration" in 1930, "to consolidate and coordinate Government activities affecting war veterans." The status of the VA was enhanced in 1989, when it became the Cabinet-level Department of Veterans Affairs. Upon creation of the new Department, President Bush said, "There is only one place for the veterans of America, in the Cabinet Room, at the table with the President of the United States of America" (VA Fact Sheet: www.va.gov/vafhis.htm).

The VA system grew from 54 hospitals in 1930, to 171 medical centers, more than 350 outpatient, community and outreach clinics, 126 nursing home care units, and 35 residential facilities in 1997. These facilities provide a broad spectrum of medical, surgical, and rehabilitative care.

Like most health care programs, the VA medical system has experienced dramatic cost increases in recent decades. Cost-containment attempts have included restrictions in the nature of medical coverage and in the population covered. For example, injuries and diseases that are *not* service-related are not always covered, and access to care is subject to a means test. Thus, VA health care has undergone a transition from being an entitlement for all veterans to a program that primarily serves low-income veterans. The transition has not been smooth, and in 1996 the GAO and others called for "VA eligibility reform." The 1996 passage of the Veterans Health Care Eligibility Act was an attempt to clarify and simplify eligibility requirements for VA health care. Under this Act, all veterans seeking health care can apply for enrollment in what the VA is calling a "Uniform Benefits Package." Health care will be allocated through enrollment priorities that are based on degree of disability and financial need.

FEDERAL FINANCING OF HEALTH CARE

While the Public Health Service, the Children's Bureau, and the Veterans Administration have all been involved in delivery of health care, the federal role now extends to health care financing as well. Through Medicaid and Medicare, federal funding is used to pay for care that is delivered by other providers. Medicaid finances care for low-income Americans, while Medicare provides coverage for workers who have become elderly or disabled. Both programs are managed at the federal level by the Health Care Financing Administration (HCFA) within the Department of Health and Human Services.

Health insurance was not widespread in the early years of the twentieth century. Most Americans simply purchased their care. As late as 1963, for example, only 56 percent of the elderly had hospital insurance (U.S. House of Representatives, 1990). Those who lacked coverage and financial resources either did without treatment or used community health clinics, which were few and far between. Some states provided limited support for meeting the medical needs of public assistance recipients and others deemed "medically needy" or "medically indigent."

Early reform efforts date to the Progressive Era, a period of economic prosperity and social reform lasting from roughly 1890 to the 1920s, when the American Association for Labor Legislation (AALL) campaigned for "sickness insurance" to cover workers and their dependents (Skocpol, 1995). The reformers' efforts were opposed by the American Medical Association and business interests. Ultimately the campaign, and the organization itself, were defeated. Theodore Roosevelt's Bull Moose Party proposed a national health insurance program in 1912, but more than 50 years went by before any form of national health insurance was established in the U.S. The 1965 passage of Titles IX and XX of the Social Security Act established Medicaid and Medicare. This Act passed despite the objections of the American Medical Association, which threatened to boycott both programs.[2]

There is some irony to AMA objections, because the passage of Medicare and Medicaid established a reliable financing mechanism for many of the services provided by its members. Both programs provided what is considered "indemnity" coverage, also known as "fee-for-service" insurance. Under this model, providers were reimbursed by the program for all services provided to program beneficiaries. In essence, the federal government wrote a blank check to providers—a situation that (as we will see) set the stage for a tremendous increase in expenditures for public health care. The establishment of Medicare and Medicaid financed tremendous growth in the health care industry, even as the programs triggered revolutionary improvement in access to care for the poor, the aged, and the disabled.

---

[2]The American Medical Association did not always oppose national health insurance. Indeed, the AMA supported early efforts in this area.

Medicaid

When Medicaid was established, the federal government had only limited involvement in health care for the poor. Nonetheless, there was some precedent for federal involvement. The Hill-Burton Act of 1946 allocated federal funding for hospital construction and required that hospitals receiving these funds provide care to the indigent. Further, the 1950 Amendments to the Social Security Act provided for some federal participation in meeting the medical needs of public assistance recipients.

Through Medicaid, "The poor were promised that they would soon have access to mainstream medical care and that health care was a basic right" (U.S. House of Representatives, 1990, p. 7). The program was established as a federal-state partnership, primarily funded through federal money, with a matching requirement for the states. Administration was carried out by the states, with federal regulation and oversight. Medicaid does not provide health care directly; instead, it reimburses providers for the cost of caring for low-income patients.

During Medicaid's first thirty years, the population covered by the program expanded. Initially Medicaid was provided only to recipients of public assistance. Later, states were required to cover all pregnant women and infants living in households with incomes up to 185 percent of the poverty line, as well as low-income persons with disabilities.

Partially as a result of the expanded beneficiary pool, the costs associated with Medicaid increased dramatically. Total expenditures more than doubled from 1988 to 1992. In 1991, Medicaid spent $88.6 billion to provide health care to 27 million low-income people. By 2001, the Congressional Budget Office projected federal spending at $115 billion (Congressional Budget Office, 2001). At the same time, matching funds for Medicaid consumed an ever-larger share of state budgets.

This growth in spending was not entirely due to new groups entering the beneficiary pool, however. As the Kaiser Commission on the Future of Medicaid (1993) argued, only one-third of the growth in cost was due to enrollment increases. Another third was attributed to medical price inflation and the remainder to state utilization of "Medicaid maximization strategies" designed to increase their federal Medicaid match. For example, states might transfer clients to Medicaid from state-funded programs for the medically indigent, effectively transferring a portion of the states' health care costs to the federal government.

MEDICAID COST CONTAINMENT. Concern about rising Medicaid costs has fueled efforts at cost containment. The past two decades have seen draconian attempts to reduce Medicaid costs. These have included adoption of a prospective payment system, reductions in provider payments, eligibility restrictions adopted through welfare reform legislation, and managed care.

In 1983 the Hospital Prospective Payment System was developed as part of these efforts. Instead of reimbursing hospitals for all reasonable costs, this system provides payment at a set rate for Diagnosis Related Groups (DRGs). Under prospective payment, a hospital would receive the same amount for every patient with a certain diagnosis, regardless of the services provided. Designed to promote greater efficiency, the use of DRGs has led to earlier hospital discharges. Advocates and service providers agree that the prospective payment system has led hospitals to discharge patients "quicker and sicker" (Fischer & Eustis, 1989). In 1989 the principle of prospective payment was extended to physician payments as well as hospital bills.

Medicaid has also been modified through reductions or freezes in provider payments. Cost containment pressure has led to consistent decline in provider payments under Medicaid. In 1990, Medicaid payments to physicians averaged 50 percent of their charges and 60 percent of the Medicare rate (Physician Payment Review Commission, 1991). The result of provider cuts was a drop in the number of physicians who were willing to serve Medicaid patients (Derlet & Kinser, 1994).

On August 22, 1996, President Clinton signed the Personal Responsibility and Work Opportunity Reconciliation Act (PRWORA). In addition to replacing Aid to Families with Dependent Children (AFDC) with a block grant program called Temporary Assistance for Needy Families (TANF), the Act had significant implications for Medicaid. TANF beneficiaries who lost aid because they refused to work can lose Medicaid coverage. Further, states were no longer required to cover pregnant women and children with incomes between 133 percent and 185 percent of the federal poverty level. Finally, non-emergency care for legal immigrants was substantially reduced. States were required to provide Medicaid to legal immigrants who had entered the country before January 1, 1997, as well as those who were veterans or on active military duty, refugees and some people granted asylum, and those with a 10-year work history. Legal immigrants who had entered the United States after January 1, 1997 were banned from Medicaid for five years.

MEDICAID AND MANAGED CARE. Although managed care has only recently become a household word, Medicaid beneficiaries have known about it for a long time. In 1981, the Omnibus Budget Reconciliation Act permitted state-level experimentation with Medicaid managed care. Arizona was the first state to require all of its Medicaid clients to enroll in managed care through its "Health Care Cost Containment System." Other states followed, and by 1996, 40.1 percent of Medicaid enrollees were in managed care programs (Zuckerman, Evans, & Holahan, 1997). These were primarily AFDC clients. Today all of the states except Wyoming require that some Medicaid recipients enroll with managed care organizations. The growth in Medicaid managed care is illustrated in Figure 5.1, below.

The tremendous growth in Medicaid managed care has not yet had a widespread effect on the program's elderly and disabled clients. A recent analysis estimated that of the $9.9 billion in Medicaid payments to managed care organizations in 1995, only 10 percent were for disabled beneficiaries and 1 percent were for elderly clients (Rowland & Hanson, 1996). Nonetheless, pressures to reduce Medicaid costs will inevitably force these clients into managed care.

FIGURE 5.1 MEDICAID ENROLLEES IN MANAGED CARE

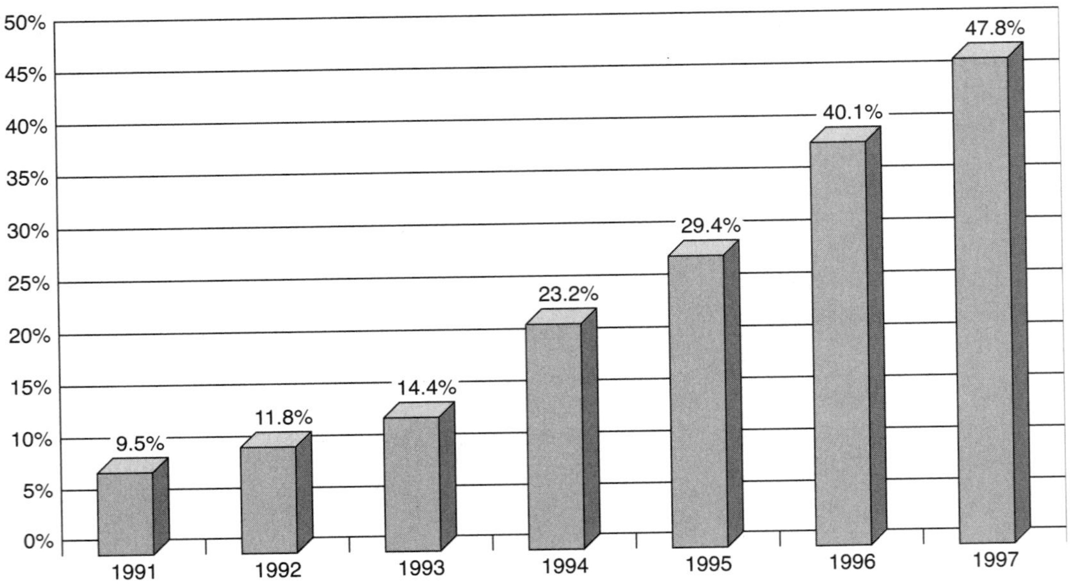

Source: Health Care Financing Administration (1998).

In the most common approach to Medicaid managed care, the state contracts with a managed care provider—typically a health maintenance organization (HMO)—to provide care for Medicaid clients on a "capitated" basis. Under capitation, the HMO receives a fixed amount for each Medicaid enrollee, regardless of the services provided.[3] Under HCFA's Freedom of Choice regulations, states are required to allow enrollees to choose their managed care providers.

The impact of managed care on Medicaid clients appears to be mixed. For some, managed care may improve access, because providers under contract with state Medicaid programs are not permitted to refuse enrollment to an eligible client (Rowland & Salganicoff, 1994). A few studies have assessed Medicaid clients' satisfaction with managed care. In general, AFDC clients in HMOs reported higher satisfaction with their care than those in traditional fee-for-service arrangements (Temkin-Greener & Winchell, 1991; Sisk et al., 1996).

The key to an effective system of Medicaid managed care lies in negotiation and monitoring of each state's contract with providers. The central role of state

---

[3]The term "HMO" was coined by analysts for the Nixon Administration and initially stood for "Health *Management* Organization." A last-minute change, solely for public relations, created the more user-friendly "Health *Maintenance* Organization." At the time, President Nixon was responding to what he announced was a "health care crisis" (Petchey, 1987).

health departments represents an opportunity for social work practitioners to ensure that the needs of consumers are addressed in these processes (see Perloff, 1996). As advocates and employees, social workers can ensure that the service mix, the provider choices, and the contract monitoring procedures are designed to address the needs of Medicaid clients who are required to enroll in managed care (see Rosenbaum, Hughes, Butler, & Howard, 1988). Further, social workers can increase the voice of Medicaid recipients in decisions related to managed care. As Perkins, Olson, and Rivera (1996) observed, "Recipients have tended to take a back seat when it comes to consumer involvement with the Medicaid program and its services" (p. 3). Mechanisms for increasing the influence of Medicaid recipients include consumer surveys, consumer representation on advisory boards, hotlines, and grievance procedures. A few states have established Medicaid managed care ombudsman programs, which are widely perceived as a useful way to encourage consumer involvement.

MEDICARE

The Medicare program differs fundamentally from Medicaid. It is not means-tested, and it provides health coverage to workers who are at least 65 years old or disabled and who are eligible for Social Security benefits. It is not operated as a federal-state partnership but is managed exclusively by the federal government. Medicare is not welfare for the disadvantaged, but an entitlement earned through participation in the work force. Despite these differences, the history of Medicare parallels that of Medicaid in many ways.

Prior to the 1980s, revisions to Medicare were characterized by expanded benefits and enhanced quality control. The 1972 Social Security Amendments added coverage for the disabled and people with end-stage renal disease. They also established Professional Standards Review Organizations (PSROs) as a vehicle for quality control. Benefit expansion was also part of the 1982 Amendments, which added hospice coverage. The same law replaced PSROs with Peer Review Organizations (PROs).

One recent effort to expand Medicare benefits was quickly repealed. In 1988, the Medicare Catastrophic Care Act (MCCA) provided for increased benefits (including prescription drug coverage), financed through a surtax on enrollees whose incomes were high enough that they owed federal income tax. Those who paid the surtax complained bitterly, arguing that they were being asked to do something required of no other segment of the population: pay for the care of others in their age group. Most MCCA provisions were repealed in 1989.

In recent decades, the costs of Medicare have grown exponentially, fueling efforts at cost containment. The Hospital Prospective Payment System described above has been applied to Medicare as well as Medicaid. DRGs have successfully reduced Medicare's hospital costs, and prospective payment has since been applied to services provided by physicians and other health care providers (Prospective Payment Assessment Commission, 1995).

Like Medicaid, Medicare has been modified through a variety of other budget controls. In the case of Medicare, these have extended beyond reductions or freezes in provider payments[4] to include increases in premiums and deductibles paid by beneficiaries. Despite these increases, the proportion of Medicare costs covered through premiums has dropped. In 1967, the Part B annual premium of $36 per enrollee accounted for 40 percent of the program's income. By 1991, the premium had increased to $359 per year, but accounted for only about one-quarter of program income (U.S. House of Representatives, 1990). The remaining cost of Part B is paid through general tax revenues.

Despite these efforts, the Medicare Trustees foresaw a fiscal crisis in the program. In 1996, the Trustees predicted that unless radical changes were made, the Hospital Insurance Trust Fund (which finances Part A of Medicare) would be depleted and outlays would exceed revenue by 2001. The economic growth of the late 1990s led the Trustees to revise their estimate considerably. In 2001 they reported that the date of projected depletion was 2029 (Rasell & Weller, 2001). Supplemental Medical Insurance (Part B) has also been the subject of fiscal alarm. This program is financed by premiums as well as an automatic allocation from general revenues. As the proportion of costs covered by beneficiary premiums has declined, the amount drawn from the general fund has grown—and with it, Congressional opposition to the program (Rasell & Weller, 2001).

MEDICARE AND MANAGED CARE. Some have attributed Medicare's rising costs to unrestrained utilization by the program's beneficiaries. Managed care was widely perceived as an effective way to control utilization and reduce costs. So in 1995, the Medicare Risk Program (now called "Medicare + Choice") was established to encourage beneficiaries to enroll in health maintenance organizations (HMOs). HMOs offer Medicare recipients lower out-of-pocket costs, while using managed care to control utilization.

HMOs are attractive to relatively healthy elders, who take advantage of the preventive care offered and who do not need much specialty care. The result is a phenomenon called "favorable selection," which refers to factors that encourage low-risk individuals to seek insurance from a particular provider. It is "favorable" to the insurance company in that it reduces the financial risk to the company. A contrasting phenomenon, "adverse selection," refers to factors that encourage high-risk individuals to seek insurance from a particular provider.

The experiment with managed care has not significantly improved the fiscal status of Medicare. Some argue that Medicare capitation rates paid to HMOs are too high for such a healthy subgroup of the elderly population (Butler, Lave, & Reuschauer, 1998). Others note that the cost savings achieved through reduced utilization may be less than the high overhead rates charged by HMOs, resulting in no net savings to the Medicare program (Brown et al., 1993). There is growing

---

[4]Freezes and reductions in Medicare's provider fees have led to a growing number of physicians declining to accept Medicare patients.

concern that favorable selection results in a "creaming" effect in which HMOs enroll the healthiest Medicare recipients, leaving high-risk elders in the fee-for-service system. Recent efforts to lower capitation rates to reflect the relative health of elders who enroll in HMOs have led growing numbers of HMOs to simply withdraw from the Medicare market. Indeed, by 2000 approximately 1 million Medicare beneficiaries had their HMO coverage cancelled (Hoffman, 2000).

GROWTH OF THE "HEALTH INDUSTRY"

Since the passage of Medicare and Medicaid, the United States has seen a dramatic concentration of private capital in what has come to be called the "health industry." Before the 1970s, for-profit health companies were largely confined to the pharmaceutical sector. By the mid-1980s hospitals had entered the for-profit sector, with profits exceeding those of drug companies. In 1987, for example, the largest for-profit hospital chains—Hospital Corporation of America, Humana, National Medical Enterprises, and American Medical International—each exceeded the sales of most pharmaceutical manufacturing firms (in excess of $3 billion). This growth was not confined to acute care. By 1990, twelve nursing home chains with total sales of $4.5 billion dominated the market, and 80 percent of nursing home facilities in the nation were proprietary.

The expansion of for-profit health care facilities left a shrinking role for non-profits, the traditional providers for the poor and under-served. Non-profit hospitals have typically provided a fuller range of health services than for-profits, and may be more responsive to community need. For example, most AIDS units are run by non-profits, as are the vast majority of trauma units. Yet in the 1990s non-profits were rapidly taken over by for-profits who were "gaining market share by buying out competitors, reducing excess capacity in their markets" (Cerne, 1995, p. 44).

As J. Warren Salmon (1995) observed, "No other nation in the world has witnessed as absolute or rapid a growth in health expenditures as has the U.S., and no other nation has such a for-profit presence in its health sector" (p. 22). Even Wall Street analysts have expressed concern with this trend. An analyst with Morgan Stanley suggested that "Ultimately we're going to see the formation of oligopolies, where each market or state will have three or four major players, and that's it. We're heading toward a utility model by the end of the decade, and at that point the government will have to step in" (Wagner, G., in Cerne, 1995, p. 42).

In the emerging for-profit health care industry, the public policy goal of reducing tax expenditures for health care conflicts with the private sector's drive for profits. This conflict might explain the limited success of cost-containment measures in health care programs. For example, when DRGs were introduced, the Senate Finance Committee monitored their impact on hospitals and in 1985 revealed that (1) 81 percent of hospitals made a profit on their Medicare accounts; (2) the average profit margin was 14.12 percent, compared to 3.3 percent in the rest of the service sector; and (3) the return on capital averaged 24 percent (compared to 14 percent elsewhere in the service industry). The Committee suggested that in one year Medicare had contributed $5 billion to company profits. Despite policies designed to reduce costs, much of the dramatic growth in the nation's private health care industry has been financed by Medicare and Medicaid.

PUBLIC HEALTH INVESTMENTS AND RETURNS

A major thread in the history of health interventions in the United States has been their tremendous growth. The twentieth century witnessed the expansion of public-sector programs to provide and finance health care. Agencies such as the Public Health Service, the Children's Bureau, and the Veterans Administration have provided care to vulnerable Americans. Two other threads are related to the nation's public-private partnership in health care. Two major programs were established to pay for the health care of the poor and the elderly: Medicaid and Medicare. These programs did not provide direct care, but offered reimbursement to providers. The availability of public financing contributed to dramatic growth in the private health care industry—growth that was marked by an increasing presence of for-profit companies. This thread of public subsidization of the private health care industry has emerged in the latter half of the twentieth century. It is related to a third thread, the conflict between the public sector's need to contain costs and the private sector's desire to maximize profits, which has surfaced in the past two decades as a tension in the U.S. health care system. In the next section we will examine health spending and health outcomes in America's hybrid public-private health care system.

HEALTH EXPENDITURES AND THE GDP

Health expenditures are typically measured both on a "per capita" basis (cost per person) and as a percent of the nation's Gross Domestic Product (GDP). Using either measure, the United States spends more on health care than any other nation in the world. In 1997, per capita spending on health care services was more than double that of other industrialized nations (Anderson, 1998). That year, the U.S. spent $4,090 per person for health care. This figure compares to a low of $1,347 in the United Kingdom. Among the 29 industrialized nations that belong to the Organization for Economic Cooperation and Development (OECD), the median per capita health care expenditure was $1,747 (Anderson, 1998).[5]

---

[5]Anderson's international comparisons also reveal that the average physician income in 1996 in the U.S. was $199,000. This makes the nation's doctors the most highly paid among eight countries (Japan, Germany, France, New Zealand, Australia, and the United Kingdom). Further, between 1960 and 1996, physicians in the U.S. had the greatest increase in their incomes.

TABLE 5.1 HEALTH EXPENDITURES
OF OECD MEMBER NATIONS

Nation	1960 Spending (Percent of GDP)	1997 Spending (Percent of GDP)
United States	5.2	13.6
Germany	4.8	10.4
France	4.2	9.6
Japan	3.0	7.3
Canada	5.5	9.3
Australia	4.9	8.3
New Zealand	4.3	7.6
United Kingdom	3.9	6.7
OECD Median	**3.9**	**7.6**

Source: Anderson (1998).

The Health Care Financing Administration reported that in 1999, U.S. health expenditures exceeded $1.2 trillion, or 13 percent of the Gross Domestic Product (Heffler et al., 2001). Table 5.1 compares health spending as percent of GDP for eight industrialized nations. This international comparison suggests that the United States has an extremely high rate of health expenditure. The proportion of the U.S. GDP committed to health care was approximately twice the median for 29 OECD nations.

From a global perspective, the United States ranks highest of the developed nations in health spending, both on a per capita basis and as a percent of the GDP. Do these high expenditures translate to favorable outcomes in the population's health? In the following section we will compare U.S. health outcomes with those of other countries.

HEALTH OUTCOMES: THE RETURN ON OUR INVESTMENT

The twentieth century witnessed tremendous improvements in Americans' health status. Life expectancy, a key indicator of well-being, increased by nearly 30 years, from 47.3 years in 1900 to 76.1 in 1999. This increased longevity is the direct result of improvements in public health and the decline of infectious diseases. These improvements have been especially helpful in reducing mortality among children under the age of five. In 1900, child mortality accounted for nearly a third (30.4 percent) of all deaths. That rate had dropped to 1.4 percent by 1997 (Centers for Disease Control, 1999). Thus, longevity trends as well as infant survival levels over the twentieth century suggest a substantial return on the nation's health expenditures. By comparison with health outcomes of other nations, however, the U.S. return is less impressive.

INFANT MORTALITY RATES. Infant mortality is a widely accepted measure of community health. The infant mortality rate (IMR) is usually measured as the number of infants who die before reaching one year of age, per 1,000 live births.

Data from 195 members of the World Health Organization permit international comparisons. Table 5.2 compares U.S. IMRs in 1978 and 1998 with those of seven other industrialized nations: Canada, Germany, France, the United Kingdom, Australia, Japan, and New Zealand.

Clearly the last twenty years have seen tremendous strides in infant health among these highly industrialized nations. Improvement in U.S. infant mortality rates, however, is not commensurate with health care expenditures. With seven infant deaths per 1,000 live births in 1998, the U.S. ranked highest among these nations, along with New Zealand and the United Kingdom, while Japan consistently reported the lowest IMR. Although the United States spends more on health care than the comparison nations, these expenditure have not translated into dramatically lower rates of infant mortality.

LIFE EXPECTANCY. A second measure of the health of populations is life expectancy. This measure reflects how long, on average, an individual of a specified age (usually a newborn infant) can expect to live. In addition to having considerably lower infant mortality, people living in industrialized nations have longer life spans. This increased life expectancy is often accompanied by a greater gender differential—in other words, the gap in life expectancy between men and women is bigger. Industrialized nations all reported gains in life expectancy in the last two decades of the twentieth century, as shown in Table 5.3.

Simple comparison of the health expenditures and health outcomes among industrialized nations reveals that the United States is at the top in terms of both per capita health spending and health spending as a percentage of GDP. Nevertheless, the nation is at or near the bottom in terms of infant mortality and life expectancy.

This observation could lead to two different conclusions. First, noting that the nation's relatively high health care expenditures are not associated with comparably high measures of health outcomes, one might conclude that the U.S.

TABLE 5.2 INFANT MORTALITY RATES (IMR) IN INDUSTRIALIZED NATIONS

Nation	1978 IMR	1998 IMR
Canada	12	6
Germany	15	5
United Kingdom	14	7
Australia	13	6
Japan	9	4
New Zealand	14	7
United States	14	7
France	11	6
WHO Average	**87**	**57**

Source: The World Health Report 1999 (World Health Organization, 1999).

TABLE 5.3 LIFE EXPECTANCY (LE) AT BIRTH IN INDUSTRIALIZED NATIONS

Nation	1978 LE		1998 LE	
	Males	*Females*	*Males*	*Females*
Canada	71	78	76	82
Germany	69	76	74	80
United Kingdom	70	76	75	80
Australia	70	77	75	81
Japan	73	78	77	83
New Zealand	69	78	74	82
United States	69	77	73	80
France	70	78	74	83
WHO Average	**60**	**63**	**65**	**69**

Source: The World Health Report 1999 (World Health Organization, 1999).

health care system is inefficient. This argument is often used in support of proposals to radically overhaul the system. A different conclusion is also possible, however. The United States is distinctive among industrialized nations in the diversity of its population. Rather than concluding that the entire system is inefficient, one might conclude that the system is inefficient with respect to disadvantaged groups within the population. Before considering the health status of vulnerable groups within the United States, we will briefly examine health conditions within developing nations. Consideration of infant mortality rates and life expectancy among these countries should help us keep in mind the relatively privileged position of residents of the industrialized world.

HEALTH OUTCOMES IN DEVELOPING NATIONS

The United States, like other industrialized nations, enjoys much lower infant mortality rates than developing nations do. Nations reporting the highest infant mortality rates in 1998 are listed in Table 5.4.

While this 20-year period saw improvements in IMR among developing nations, these rates continue to greatly exceed those observed in industrialized countries. With the exception of Afghanistan, all of the nations with the world's highest IMRs are located on the African continent.

Clearly, life expectancy at birth is influenced by infant mortality rates, as well as the health status of adults. Nations with high infant mortality rates, such as developing nations, also have shorter life expectancies. As in industrialized countries, women in developing countries enjoy greater life expectancies than men do. See Table 5.5.

The past two decades have seen improved life expectancies for most African nations. Two exceptions to this general rule are Rwanda and Malawi, both of which have been hit especially hard by the HIV-AIDS epidemic.

In the field of health care, life itself becomes a social justice issue. As indi-

TABLE 5.4 INFANT MORTALITY RATES (IMR) IN DEVELOPING NATIONS

Nation	1978 IMR	1998 IMR
Sierra Leone	192	170
Afghanistan	183	152
Malawi	177	138
Guinea-Bissau	176	130
Angola	161	125
Rwanda	133	124
Somalia	149	122

Source: The World Health Report 1999 (World Health Organization, 1999).

TABLE 5.5 LIFE EXPECTANCY (LE) AT BIRTH IN DEVELOPING NATIONS

	1978 LE		1998 LE	
Nation	*Males*	*Females*	*Males*	*Females*
Sierra Leone	34	37	36	39
Afghanistan	40	40	45	46
Malawi	42	44	39	40
Guinea-Bissau	36	39	43	46
Angola	38	42	45	48
Rwanda	43	47	39	42
Somalia	40	44	45	49

Source: The World Health Report 1999 (World Health Organization, 1999).

cated by the statistics in this section, survival can be a function of privilege. International comparisons demonstrate that longevity and infant survival are differentially distributed on the basis of a nation's wealth. In the following section we will examine the extent to which status is associated with differing health outcomes for people living in the United States.

VULNERABLE GROUPS IN AN AFFLUENT NATION

To a large extent, both health status and health care are socially allocated. Class, race, and gender often determine a person's risk of becoming ill. They can also affect the course of disease and a person's ability to secure needed treatment.

POVERTY AND HEALTH

Income affects health by determining the likelihood that one will contract a disease and by influencing the quality of care one will receive when ill. The net effect in the United States is poor health outcomes for citizens living in poverty. Among children, poverty has long been associated with low birth weight, increased infant mortality, and nutritional deficits (Rice, 1991). Poor adults experience significantly higher risk of AIDS and other infectious diseases. Finally, a history of exposure to health risks, environmental toxins, stress, poor nutrition, and limited preventive care can undermine the health of poor elders. Income also contributes to mental health, as the risk of depression has been linked to poverty (Amato & Zuo, 1992; Belle, 1984; Murphy et al., 1991).

Poor health outcomes among low-income groups may result partially from the stresses associated with living in poverty, but reduced access to health care certainly compounds the difficulties (Himmelstein & Woolhandler, 1995). Children in poverty experience limited access to preventive care (Kelly, Perloff, Morris, & Liu, 1993), and a combination of financial barriers, transportation, and cultural differences mitigates against their receiving treatment (Williams, 1993). Under the fee-for-service model, access for low-income groups has been problematic. As cost containment measures were applied to Medicaid, growing numbers of physicians (and nursing homes) refused to accept Medicaid patients (Barnes, 1984; Perloff, Kletke, & Neckerman, 1987).

RACE AND HEALTH

In a society where race is closely associated with class, it is difficult to distinguish the effects of race from those of class. Indeed, health policy analyst Vicente Navarro (1991) argued that in the U.S. class is a more powerful determinant of health than race (see also Fordyce, 1996). Indeed, observed differences among races in this country cannot be interpreted without reference to economic disparities and race-based oppression. Infant mortality is one example. The U.S. regularly documents race differences in the death rate for infants. In 1996 infant mortality was lowest for infants born to Asian and Pacific Islander mothers (5.2), followed by white (6.1), Native American (10.0), and African-American (14.1) mothers. The rate for Hispanic mothers (6.1) was similar to that for non-Hispanic whites, but the rate among Puerto Rican mothers was higher (8.6) (MacDorman & Atkinson, 1998). Yet, as we will see later in this chapter, when prenatal health care is readily available race-based differences in infant mortality decline considerably.

In some cases, race and class may interact to produce higher risk of illness. The incidence of type II diabetes, particularly in later life, is strongly influenced by race and class. The disease occurs more often among those with lower socioeconomic and educational levels (Overfield, 1995) and is most concentrated among African-Americans, Native Americans, and Hispanic Americans. Diabetes interferes with glucose metabolism, and can result in blindness, heart disease, strokes, kidney failure, amputations, nerve damage, and birth defects (U.S. Department of Health and Human Services, 1994a). In addition to genetic susceptibility, lifestyle considerations such as diet, lack of exercise, and limited access to preventive health care contribute to an individual's risk of contracting diabetes.

Long-term oppression can permanently influence the health of an ethnic group. For example, Tay-Sachs disease is dramatically more common among the Ashkenazi Jews, whose ancestors originated in Eastern Europe, than among other populations. This concentration has been attributed to the unique historical circumstances experienced by this group, including frequent migrations, numerous extermination attempts, dense concentration in urban ghettos, and periods of rapid population expansion and inbreeding (Fraikor, 1973). Tay-Sachs is an inherited condition characterized by very early onset, causing developmental retardation, paralysis, dementia, blindness, and death by age three or four (*Merck Manual*, 1992, p. 1051).

GENDER AND HEALTH

In this country there are consistent gender differentials in both mortality (likelihood of death) and morbidity (likelihood of illness). At any age, men have higher mortality rates, and women have greater morbidity (Hickey, Rakowski, & Julius, 1988). The gender difference in mortality yields a shorter life expectancy for men. This difference is projected to endure for at least another half-century (Grambs, 1989).

In later years, gender differences in morbidity translate into higher rates of acute illness among men and more chronic illness among women. Arthritis is much more common among women, while coronary heart disease more often strikes men (U.S. Senate Special Committee on Aging, 1988). Women develop late-onset diabetes at twice the rate of men (Dolger & Seeman, 1985). Older women also report more colds, infections, and stomach upsets than older men (Verbugge, 1985). Where men are more likely to suffer from hearing impairments, women are more apt to have vision problems (Verbugge, 1985). Finally, women are more likely than men to suffer from urinary incontinence (Mitteness, 1987). Our health system more effectively meets the acute care needs more commonly experienced by men than it does the long-term care needs more often experienced by women (Estes, C. L., et al., 1993).

Gender differences have also been observed with respect to mental health. Throughout life, women typically experience higher rates of both mild and severe depression (Herzog, 1989; LaRue, Dessonville, & Jarvik, 1985). This finding holds true regardless of the approach used to measure depression (Holzer, Leaf, & Weissman, 1985). Women's greater risk of depression has been linked to their greater risk of poverty (Feinson, 1991; Krause, 1986; Belle, 1984).

Although it is difficult to separate the effects of class, race, and gender on health outcomes, some generalizations can be made. Poverty is associated with increased risk of physical and mental health difficulties, as well as diminished access to care. Oppression can also make populations more vulnerable to disease. Finally, perhaps because they live longer than men, women experience greater chronic impairment and have greater needs for long-term care—needs that have long been neglected by our health care system.

UNINSURED CITIZENS

The United States is distinct among industrialized nations in the large number of citizens who lack health insurance. In 2001, for example, 43 million Americans, or 17 percent of the population under the age of 65, had no private or public health insurance (Lewers, 2001). (People over 65 are covered by Medicare.) An even higher proportion of the population has experienced sporadic lack of coverage. Among the eight industrialized nations considered above, only the United States has more than 1 percent of its population uninsured (Anderson, 1998).

Without health insurance, U.S. citizens lack access to both preventive care and routine treatment. Local health departments provide some preventive care, such as childhood immunizations, but preventive care for adults under the age of 65, such as mammograms, blood pressure screening, and cholesterol checks, is not routinely available. The routine treatment that insured Americans seek through their primary care physicians is also not available to the uninsured. This lack of access to preventive care and routine treatment contributes indirectly to the high cost of hospital care, because hospital emergency rooms deliver primary care to uninsured persons.

INFANT MORTALITY IN HARLEM

Fidel Castro visited Harlem in October 1995 and bragged that Cuba's infant mortality rate was not only the lowest in the Caribbean, but was lower than the death rate in Central Harlem. Castro and others argued that this difference demonstrated the failure of the U.S. economic system. Babies in Harlem, a low-income, primarily African-American neighborhood in New York City, were at least three times as likely to die in their first year as those in the rest of the nation, primarily of problems associated with low birth weight.

On August 11, 1998, the New York City Department of Health issued a press release reporting that infant mortality in the city had reached a "historic low."

More specifically, the press release stated that "In Central Harlem, the IMR plummeted by more than 56 percent, from 15.2 deaths per 1,000 live births in 1996 . . . to an IMR of 6.6 in 1997, below the Citywide average."

What could have produced this dramatic change? The Mayor's office, along with advocates and professionals working in Harlem, attributed the change to a federally funded effort that supported a series of initiatives: new drop-in centers where pregnant women could receive health education, counseling, workshops, and case management from pregnancy through their child's first year of life; a "Healthline" that provided information and referrals; an Adolescent Parent Education program that trained young parents; Child Health Plus, a subsidized insurance program for children; and Healthy Start, a federally funded effort that began in 1991 and focused on decreasing mortality in high-risk neighborhoods. These initiatives orchestrated the efforts of social workers, advocates, politicians, and health workers in a focused effort to improve health outcomes in a disadvantaged area. Their impact reveals the power of sustained effort and reminds us that social and health indicators are amenable to intervention. Inequality in health status and health care are not inevitable but the direct result of allocation decisions made every day, including policy choices made at various levels of government.

EMERGING HEALTH ISSUES

The health care needs of Americans have changed in recent decades, partly because of new outbreaks of contagious diseases and partly due to changes in the population itself. In addition to HIV, infectious diseases such as tuberculosis have resurfaced as public health concerns (see Garrett, 1994). Growing percentages of elderly persons in the general population, as well as among people with disabilities, have increased the demand for long-term care. These emerging health issues are addressed in the following pages.

HIV/AIDS

Human Immunodeficiency Virus (HIV) has created a global epidemic that threatens the very foundations of some nations. (Some experts suggest that Malawi may not survive as a sovereign nation because of widespread HIV infection.) In the United States, 548,429 people were diagnosed with AIDS between 1981 and December of 1996, with 362,004 deaths reported during the same period (National Institute of Allergy and Infectious Diseases, 1997). The characteristics of AIDS patients in the United States have changed in recent decades to include a growing number of women, children, and heterosexuals. Most children with AIDS are infected in utero, so the growth in pediatric AIDS cases has been attributed to the disease's expansion among women of childbearing age (Ploughman, 1995/1996). Indeed, women are the fastest growing sub-population among AIDS patients (Kaplan & Krell-Long, 1993; Diaz, 1991). In 1985, 7 percent of AIDS patients were female, and by 1994 the proportion had jumped to 18 percent

(National Institute of Allergy and Infectious Diseases, 1996a). The homeless population also has a high rate of HIV/AIDS infection (Stoner, 1995).

The prevalence of AIDS is highest among member of ethnic minority groups. The National Institute of Allergy and Infectious Diseases (1996b) reported that most AIDS cases in 1995 involved either African-Americans or Hispanics. The risk of AIDS in 1995 was six times higher among African-Americans (92.6 cases per 100,000 African-Americans) than among Caucasians (15.4 cases/100,000), and two times higher than among Hispanics (46.2 cases/100,000). Indeed, AIDS is the number-one killer of African-Americans between 25 to 44 years of age.

But epidemiological figures can obscure the social meaning of AIDS. As Peter Conrad suggested (1986), "AIDS is an illness with a triple stigma: it is connected to stigmatized groups; . . . it is sexually transmitted; and, like cancer, it is a terminal wasting disease. It would be difficult to imagine a scenario for a more stigmatizing disease" (p. 53). Since its discovery in the early 1980s, the disease has been associated with marginalized populations: homosexuals, drug users, Haitian immigrants, and Africans. Its early designation as "Gay-Related Immune Deficiency Syndrome" reinforced the notion that AIDS was the product of a deviant lifestyle. In contrast, some argue that AIDS is sustained and promoted by social and economic inequalities that force young women into prostitution and create ghettos that serve as breeding grounds for HIV (Farmer, 1996).

The growing number of "blameless" victims (those who, as Kimberly Bergalis said in her 1991 Congressional testimony, "didn't do anything wrong") has moved U.S. policy-makers to pay more attention to the disease. The primary legislative mechanism for funding prevention, treatment, and research on AIDS is commonly called the 1990 Ryan White Care Act, named after a teenage hemophiliac who died of AIDS in 1990. Services provided by the states through the use of these funds include health insurance programs that cover premiums for patients able to secure private coverage, drug programs that provide access to medication, and home-based health care. The subject of the case study at the beginning of this chapter, Tanya Johnson, received health care services and insurance funding through her state's Ryan White program.

Complications in the diagnosis and definition of AIDS interfere with government monitoring efforts and can restrict patients' access to treatment and income supports. Symptoms of AIDS differ among affected sub-groups. Children tend to display symptoms that resemble failure-to-thrive and developmental delays. Adults often develop rare cancers and infections. In women, AIDS may manifest as pelvic inflammatory disease, cervical dysplasia, and vaginal infections. Although Congress has refrained from listing conditions that make an individual eligible for disability benefits and protections available under the Americans with Disabilities Act (ADA), federal regulations and case law have clearly included AIDS as a legitimate disability (Stein, 1995). Therefore, appropriate diagnosis can provide protection against discrimination in employment and education, as well as income supports available under both Supplemental Security Income (SSI) and Social Security (OASDI).

Public spending on AIDS has increased dramatically in recent years. The FY2001 federal budget included $9.2 billion in discretionary spending on HIV/AIDS by the U.S. Department of Health and Human Services. This was up from the 1993 budget amount of $2.1 billion. In Medicare and Medicaid programs, spending for the care of HIV/AIDS patients increased from $1.6 billion in 1993 to $3.9 billion in 2001. By 2001, NIH funding for bio-medical research on AIDS was $2.1 billion, and services provided through the Ryan White Care Programs cost an estimated $1.7 billion (U.S. Department of Health and Human Services, 2000).

Meanwhile, Congress and state legislatures have seen recurring debates over policies related to AIDS. Mandatory testing, reporting, and partner notification have been debated. At present, AIDS testing is mandatory for prison inmates, prostitutes, immigrants, and military recruits (Hunter & Rubenstein, 1992). Mandatory partner notification has been debated, as has required testing of all pregnant women.

TUBERCULOSIS

Unlike AIDS, tuberculosis is a well-established killer of humans and was once the leading cause of death in the United States. TB, or "tuberculosis bacillus," is a chronic disease, caused by bacterial infection in the lungs. Symptoms include a bad cough that lasts longer than two weeks, pain in the chest, coughing up blood, weakness or fatigue, weight loss, chills, fever, and night sweats.

TB is much more contagious than AIDS, with airborne transmission when a person with active TB coughs, sneezes, or speaks. The immune systems of healthy people usually prevent widespread TB infection, walling off the bacteria in a small area of the lungs. This walled-off infection, called "latent TB," may be present throughout a person's life. People with compromised immune systems are more likely to develop full-scale infections upon limited exposure. A wide range of factors can weaken the human immune system, including HIV infection, chronic stress, malnutrition, substance abuse, low body weight, advanced age, diabetes mellitus, and several other diseases.

The number of TB victims in the U.S. peaked in 1992 at 26,673. During the Clinton years, the prevalence of TB declined. In 1998 the Centers for Disease Control reported a 32-percent drop in active cases to 18,361 (Centers for Disease Control, 1999). The CDC attributed this improvement to the TB control efforts undertaken during the interim. TB continues to be problematic among homeless and poverty-stricken groups, whose weakened immune systems leave them more vulnerable to infection. The treatment regimen can also present problems. Treatment typically involves use of multiple antibiotics over a period of several months. Since symptoms often disappear after a few weeks of treatment, it can be tempting for TB sufferers to discontinue treatment prematurely.

Recent years have also seen a dramatic increase in the number of cases of drug-resistant TB. In the 1940s and 1950s, 1 to 2 percent of TB cases showed drug resistance; in the 1960s and 1970s, that rate had risen to 3 to 5 percent. During the 1990s, drug-resistant strains began to appear much more often. Indeed, Roizman (1995) reported that "In New York City, where a variety of elements, including poverty, substance abuse, and deteriorating public health programs, combined to confound tuberculosis control, 33 percent of tuberculosis strains recovered in April 1992 were resistant to at least one drug, and 19 percent were resistant to two or more agents" (p. 137).

LONG-TERM CARE

The proportion of elderly people in the U.S. population is growing, and the life spans of people with disabilities have increased. These two trends are converging to produce tremendous growth in Americans' need for long-term care. The phrase once referred only to nursing home care but now encompasses the combination of in-home, outpatient, and residential care that is necessary to manage a chronic condition. The sheer number of Americans living in nursing homes has increased dramatically.

The widespread use and high cost of nursing home care have led many to advocate the expansion of intermediate alternatives to nursing home care (Estes, Swan, & Associates, 1993). This push for alternatives reflects the feeling that many nursing home residents do not require the intense level of medical care that is provided by a nursing home. Currently, both Medicaid and Medicare offer some funding for care provided in a patient's home. There has also been increased public recognition of the role played by family members in caring for people with disabilities. In 1999, this recognition led the Administration on Aging to introduce a National Family Caregiver Program as part of the reauthorization of the Older Americans Act. This $100 million program provides support to family members providing care.

FUNDAMENTAL DILEMMAS IN HEALTH CARE POLICY

Two fundamental dilemmas mark contemporary debates about health care in America. The first issue, involving how risk should be allocated, is clearly a social justice question. The second, perhaps more fundamental, issue is the extent to which the private market can reliably and efficiently deliver health care. The latter question has philosophical undertones as well as pragmatic considerations.

ASSIGNING RISK

In the context of health insurance, a primary issue is the question of who bears the risk, or who pays the cost in the event of a health catastrophe. Under federally operated social insurance programs such as Medicare and Medicaid, the nation essentially self-insures. Those who pay taxes bear the risk. In Richard Titmuss's view (1971), these social entitlements establish a moral community in which assistance from strangers replaces the one-on-one assistance of earlier times. The State serves as an intermediary, mandating and collecting insurance premiums, and allocating benefits.

When Medicaid recipients are required to enroll in managed care, the nation transfers the risk to the health care provider, typically a for-profit managed care organization or an HMO. Under capitation, Medicaid has limited its risk to the amount allocated for each client under the capitation agreement. In the event of health catastrophe, the HMO pays any additional cost.

Increasingly, managed care entities are passing the risk down the line to the physician through what is known as "Physician Incentive Plans." In some cases, physicians are paid on the basis of a capitated rate and are required to cover any additional costs above the designated reimbursement. In other cases, physicians who provide or authorize high-cost care run the risk of salary reduction through penalties or loss of bonuses. When financial incentives or disincentives are used to regulate or influence physicians' decisions, the "fiduciary responsibility" of physicians is jeopardized. Fiduciary responsibility in this case is the doctor's obligation to put the patient's interests first. Rodwin (1993) has argued that the amount of risk physicians be allowed to bear should be limited to 1 to 2 percent of base income and that organizational providers should be held liable for malpractice caused by underuse of services. Although the Health Care Financing Administration (HCFA) does require that managed care organizations report on their Physician Incentive Plans to the HCFA or the state Medicaid authority, there are currently no regulations limiting physician risk under Medicare and Medicaid contracts.

In health care there are two types of risk: financial risks and health risks. Financial risks are borne by the entity that pays unexpected expenses. Health risks, such as death or disability, are borne by the patient. Any type of health insurance separates health risk from financial risk in a way that, some argue, leads to overutilization of health care. To minimize their health risks, patients consume health services without even thinking about cost. Co-payments and deductibles attempt to stem this tendency by assigning part of the financial risk to the patient. Allocating the financial risk of illness is clearly a social justice issue. It is vital that policy practitioners in this area be prepared to effectively debate the fairness and desirability of assigning risk to the various entities involved: the patient, the physician, the HMO, the state, and the nation.

MARKET-BASED SOLUTIONS VERSUS PUBLIC PROVISION OF CARE

Fundamental to many debates about health care in the United States is the extent to which health care is a commodity amenable to delivery through the private market. Some, like Siminoff (1986), have argued that health care can never conform to the ideal of the competitive market. In order for the market to operate efficiently, consumers must be able to make informed choices among various providers. In these circumstances inefficient or inadequate providers will not be chosen and the process of selection will favor those who provide the best care for the best price. In the health care market, however, purchase decisions are not made by individuals but by their employers. The values and priorities of employers do not clearly mirror those of their employees. Another significant obstacle to rational consumer behavior is the difficulty of evaluating the quality of medical intervention. Few patients are able to consistently distinguish good from poor care. Finally, the life-and-death nature of health care decisions complicates the process of choosing a provider.

Others argue that regulation of the private market can solve these problems. Providers who fail to offer acceptable care are sanctioned by licensing and accrediting authorities. Thus, anyone offering medical care meets minimal requirements. Since cost is a significant concern today, the fact that employers may be more concerned about the cost of employee benefits than the quality of care may be seen as an advantage. Several states are considering the development of standardized "report cards" for HMOs and other managed-care providers to help consumers choose a provider that best meets their needs. Finally, public policy (through enforcement of antitrust laws) attempts to ensure that no single entity enjoys a monopoly in the health care market.

Although a libertarian argument might hold that the private market, left unchecked, will efficiently provide health care for all Americans, experience has shown that this is not the case. Left unchecked, the market provides health care only for those with the means to pay for it. Further, even those with the means to pay for care may lack the technical expertise to shop effectively for that care. The extent to which market-based solutions will be effective in delivering health care to all Americans remains to be seen.

These fundamental issues are pervasive in contemporary debates over how to reform the nation's system of health care delivery. Specific health care reform proposals are described below.

HEALTH CARE REFORM PROPOSALS

The contemporary debate over reform typically involves either incremental or comprehensive proposals. Incremental efforts retain the basic structure of the system but attempt to modify some components—for example, by regulating the insurance industry or encouraging the use of managed care. In contrast, comprehensive proposals would revise the system itself, typically by removing either public or private elements. Some proposals would eliminate the governmental role in health care, but "single-payer" proposals discussed below would eliminate the private market's role.

Through incremental measures, the United States attempts to strike a compromise between unbridled free-market delivery of health care and public control. Among these efforts are state and federal laws regulating insurance providers.

INSURANCE REGULATION

In 1996, Congress passed and President Clinton signed the Health Insurance Portability and Accountability Act (PL 104-191), also known as "Kassebaum-Kennedy" for the bipartisan team who introduced the bill. The law's best-known provisions limit pre-existing exclusions and improve the portability of health insurance. Under these provisions, insurers may impose only one 12-month exclusion period for any pre-existing condition treated or diagnosed in the previous six months. This limitation should ensure that any employee who maintains continuous health coverage will experience only one exclusion period in his or her lifetime. The law introduces the notion of "creditable coverage," requiring that individuals be given credit for their prior coverage when applying for a new plan. This means that the new plan will be prohibited from enforcing a waiting period for coverage of pre-existing conditions. Portability provisions allow people, under certain conditions, to purchase health insurance if they leave their jobs and seek coverage as individuals.

In a less-familiar provision, the law provides for "guaranteed issue and renewability." If an insurer sells policies to small businesses, the law requires the insurance company to sell its products to any small business. It also requires that insurers renew coverage for any group plan regardless of the health status of members of that group. This provision is important for people like Tanya, the subject of our case study. When her employer applied for coverage, the entire group's application was denied because of her HIV status. Indeed, many small employers have found their coverage terminated because of a high-cost individual. Under the Kassebaum-Kennedy legislation, insurers can neither terminate nor deny coverage in this way. This provision was implemented in response to many businesses, like Tanya's employer, that found their coverage cancelled because of one high-cost employee.

Kassebaum-Kennedy also established a small demonstration program testing the use of Medical Savings Accounts (MSAs). This controversial program allows people to maintain special savings accounts (MSAs) that are analogous to IRAs. Contributions to MSAs can be made by workers or their employers and are tax-deductible. Employees then purchase health insurance with high deductibles and use the MSAs to cover their routine health expenses. Opponents of MSAs argue that they will be used primarily by healthy individuals with taxable incomes. That would leave sicker people seeking insurance through traditional providers ("adverse selection") and increase the costs of their coverage.

The Kassebaum-Kennedy law represents a significant departure from the traditional approach to insurance regulation in the United States. Historically, insurance has been treated as a business to be regulated primarily by the states. Each state has an insurance official (often called the "Insurance Commissioner") who is charged with overseeing the solvency and market practices of companies doing business in the state. Observing the increase in insurer failures and in the number of companies that do business in several states or even several countries, however, many have begun to question whether states have the capacity to effectively regulate this global enterprise.

Managed Care[6]

Widely perceived as the solution to escalating health care costs, managed care is central to many incremental health care reform proposals. Definitions of managed care abound. Most reflect the professional training of the author. For example, one economist (Wells, 1995) explains that managed care is designed to "provide comprehensive health care for a defined population within an available budget." A physician, writing in the *Journal of the American Medical Association* (Miller & Luft, 1994), says, "Physician practice is what is managed in managed care" (p. 1512) and argues that selection and management of physicians is the single most important distinguishing feature. A researcher (Eisenberg, 1995, p. 1670) describes managed care as "a natural experiment in health care reform." Finally, Wall Street analysts view managed care as a promising investment option within the already profitable health care industry.

Even as federal policy is expanding the use of managed care by Medicaid and Medicare beneficiaries, Congress and the President have found it necessary to regulate the medical practices of managed care providers. For example, in 1997, the President signed an Act prohibiting what he termed "drive-through deliveries." Under the provisions of this Act, health care providers are prohibited from discharging a new mother after a hospital stay of less than 48 hours. The "Patients' Bill of Rights" is another effort to regulate managed care.

Single-Payer Proposals

Single-payer proposals advocate government provision of health care for all Americans. Advocates attribute the discrepancy between health "inputs" and health outcomes to a fundamental inefficiency that pervades the health care system. They argue that elimination of private health insurance providers would significantly reduce this inefficiency, partly by cutting administrative costs and overhead.

As anyone who has used health insurance in recent years can testify, the administrative complexity of the U.S. health care system is enormous. This complexity led the Office of Technology Assessment to conclude that conversion to a single-payer system could result in savings in excess of $47 billion 1991 U.S. dollars. These savings would result primarily from the simplified administrative procedures of a single-payer system (U.S. Congress, Office of Technology Assess-

---

[6]Terry Peak collaborated in the original research and drafting of the section on managed care.

ment, 1994). They would be more than sufficient to provide health coverage to everyone in the U.S. (Chamberlain, 1994).

Representatives of the health insurance industry vigorously oppose single-payer proposals. The health insurance industry spends millions of dollars in campaign contributions to ensure access to the nation's policy-makers, even as they conduct vigorous advertising campaigns to defeat reform proposals. These campaigns appeal to middle-class fears of losing access to high-quality care if the U.S. adopts a single-payer system. Despite evidence to the contrary, these lobbyists suggest that a single-payer system would create a federal bureaucracy that would prove even less efficient than the current system. They also argue that Canadians and Britons dislike their national health care systems, offering examples of middle-class consumers who, frustrated with waiting lists in their nations, travel to the U.S. for complex procedures such as coronary bypass surgery and hip replacements.

Despite the efforts of these powerful financial interests, a movement to support the single-payer alternative continues to gain strength in the United States. Several grassroots organizations promote this reform, including SPAN (Single-Payer Across the Nation), which was founded in 1994, and the Universal Health Care Action Network (UHCAN), established in 1992. From time to time, single-payer legislation is introduced in Congress. Given the nation's level of dissatisfaction both with managed care and with other forms of private health insurance, it seems likely that these reform efforts will continue.

SOCIAL WORK ROLES IN HEALTH CARE POLICY

Social workers have long been involved in U.S. health care policy as advocates, administrators, and practitioners. As director of the Children's Bureau, Grace Abbott took part in the establishment of programs for child and maternal health. Advocates in organizations such as Families USA work to ensure that the needs of the poor are taken into account in health care reform. On a daily basis, discharge planners struggle to find appropriate care arrangements for people leaving the nation's hospitals.

Today's health care system presents new challenges for advocates, administrators, and practitioners. In a variety of settings and a variety of roles, social workers strive to ensure that vulnerable populations receive the care they need. At the state level, social workers carefully monitor Medicaid managed care contracts. In clinics, hospitals, and other settings, social workers inform patients and their families of their rights and responsibilities. In community agencies they work with nurses to educate low-income and immigrant families in the use of new and established medical technology. In Congress and state legislatures, social workers continue in the tradition of the Children's Bureau, investigating and reporting the needs and concerns of vulnerable Americans. Finally, social work professionals find excellent opportunities for advocacy and community organization efforts in the grassroots movement for health reform.

SUMMARY: HEALTH CARE ISSUES
IN THE UNITED STATES

We began this chapter by discussing the life experiences of Tanya Johnson, a young woman who is living with HIV. Tanya's experiences have been influenced by several federal policies. She receives services through the Ryan White Care Act. When she was fired, she sued her employer for not complying with the requirements of the Americans with Disabilities Act. Insurance regulation at the state level helped her secure coverage, while the Kennedy-Kassebaum Act ensures that others will not face the same difficulties she experienced in seeking private health insurance.

We traced the development of the U.S. health care system, viewing it as a hybrid combining public regulation and financing with private delivery of services. The development of public-sector interventions was examined, as was the growth of the private "health care industry." One thread seen here is the contribution of public-sector financing to the growth of this private industry and a second is the tension between the public sector's need for cost containment and the private sector's drive for profitability. The nation's investment in health care was examined next, and international comparisons were used to assess health expenditures and health outcomes. The disparity between U.S. health expenditures and health outcomes was examined, particularly in relation to the failure of the system to serve vulnerable Americans. To pursue this idea further, the roles of class, race, and gender in health status and health care were considered, as were the experiences of uninsured Americans. Infant mortality in Harlem was discussed as a case example of the impact of sustained intervention on this health indicator. Then, following a discussion of emerging health needs, we addressed two fundamental dilemmas in U.S. health care policy: the problem of assigning risk, and implications of market-based delivery of health care. Contemporary health care reform proposals were considered briefly, followed by a review of the role of social workers in health care.

The United States and South Africa are unique among industrialized nations in that health coverage is linked, not to citizenship, but to employment. The resulting hybrid system has, in this country, resulted in inefficiencies that increasingly affect not only the poor, but the middle class as well. Rather than pursuing an increased public presence in health care delivery, the U.S. has expanded the use of managed care. The result has been consolidation in the health care industry to an extent that alarms even some stockbrokers. Consumer concerns have led to an attempt to balance the power of managed care organizations through federal regulation. Medicaid managed care brings this to the state level, as states struggle to ensure that the needs of these vulnerable Americans are met. Medicaid managed care represents a tremendous opportunity for social work intervention. By participating in state contracting, consumer advocacy, and care monitoring, social workers can make a tremendous contribution to the well-being of low-income Americans.

Health care reform is a continuous (if not steady) process in the United States. With a general understanding of the structure of our health care system, and a clear commitment to social justice, social work professionals can contribute to health care debates. By adding the profession's voice and supporting the client's voice on health care issues, social workers can make a direct contribution to the cause of social justice.

DISCUSSION TOPICS

1. Public acceptance of government provision of health care was advanced by the effectiveness of the immunizations developed and distributed by public agencies. This technological advance enhanced the stature of public health tremendously. Has there been any comparable development in the field of social welfare?

2. What roles do social workers play in the debate over health care in the United States? How do you feel about single-payer proposals? Do your views reflect your own background? Do they take into account the needs of vulnerable sub-groups in the U.S. population?

3. What ethical dilemmas is a social worker likely to encounter when working in a managed care setting? How might he or she resolve them?

4. If you had a choice, how would you assign risk among these entities: a Medicaid client (think of someone with whom you are familiar), a physician, an HMO, your state, and the federal government? Who should bear the greatest risk? Why? Should the client bear any risk? Why or why not?

5. Consider a health care proposal that is currently under debate. Is it incremental or comprehensive? Does it emphasize or support the public role in health care or that of the private market?

6. How would Tanya's experiences seeking health insurance have been different after the passage of the Health Insurance Portability and Accountability Act? Has the Act solved all the problems workers face with respect to private health insurance? What, if any, problems remain?

SUGGESTED RESOURCES

Estes, C. L., Swan, J. H., & Associates (1993). *The Long-Term Care Crisis: Elders Trapped in the No-Care Zone.* Newbury Park, CA: Sage Publications.

Navarro, V. (Ed.). (2002). *The Political Economy of Social Inequalities: Consequences for Health and Quality of Life.* Amityville, NY: Baywood Publishing.

www.cmwf.org — This site is maintained by The Commonwealth Fund, a foundation interested in health care issues. It offers some excellent reports on current policy issues.

www.hcfa.gov — This site is maintained by the U.S. Health Care Financing Administration. It is a good source of information on Medicaid and Medicare, including statistics and current policy developments.

www.who.int — Maintained by the World Health Organization, this site is a good starting point for international comparisons.

6

Mental Illness

Insanity is often the logic of an accurate mind overtaxed.

OLIVER WENDELL HOLMES

Americans aggressively pursue mental health, in what Fritz Perls called "an endless cycle of tortuous self-help exercises" (Derezotes, 2000). In colonial America, the pursuit of mental well-being was manifest in the popularity of advice columns and monographs. Later, the "mental hygiene movement" of the 1930s promised specific methods for achieving mental health. More recently, social workers have joined the "self-help" industry as active participants in the nation's pursuit of mental health, offering new means and approaches to personal improvement. With the possible exception of California, which once adopted self-esteem as a public policy goal, few governmental jurisdictions are involved in the pursuit of mental health. Instead, public agencies and public policies address the flip side of mental health: mental illness.

Prevention and treatment of mental illness are significant tasks for U.S. social policy. We will begin this chapter by reviewing the experiences of Rachel Sanders, a woman coping with a combination of depression and anxiety. After addressing the challenges of defining mental illness, we will examine values and beliefs about insanity. In later sections, we will trace the development of interventions for the mentally ill and examine contemporary realities of mental illness in the United States. The chapter closes with a discussion of emerging policy issues, including involuntary commitment, mandatory outpatient treatment, and insurance parity.

CASE STUDY ♦ RACHEL SANDERS

Rachel Sanders is a dynamic woman of 50-something. She works for her state's mental health authority, coordinating consumer advocacy efforts under a major federal grant. Rachel describes her job as "fantastic," and she clearly excels in her work. Yet, as Rachel points out, had she lived in the seventeenth century, she probably would have been "burned at the stake" during an episode of her illness.

Rachel has a brain condition known as "atypical bipolar disorder and panic disorder," which has presented as alternating bouts of severe depression with severe paranoia, mania, and acute anxiety attacks.

Rachel is the oldest of eight children. Her parents were devoutly religious, and family life revolved around her father's academic career, the children's artistic pursuits, and the family's religious activities. From the outside looking in, she said, theirs was envied as a model family. But privately, the children struggled to withstand their father's frequent violent rages. Rachel was the primary target of his brutal verbal and physical attacks. Rachel's mother didn't stop the abuse, possibly because she drew satisfaction from being the family comforter. When Rachel was 19, the family spent two years in South America where Rachel taught English as a second language to adults in a large international center. The family lived luxuriously, with many servants. This lifestyle gave the siblings time to socialize together and become far closer emotionally. Then Rachel's mother developed cancer. Rachel nursed her mother around the clock for the final four months of her life, and she was the only child present at her mother's death.

After a six-month stint traveling in Europe as a companion to a wealthy Frenchwoman, Rachel continued college as a fine arts major. She was an award-winning writer and watercolorist, concert pianist, and a National Merit scholar. During college, she experienced long episodes of depression during which she would "hide and sleep" rather than attending classes. Later, after the break-up of her first marriage, Rachel experienced debilitating panic attacks.

During college Rachel met and married a high-profile, good-looking entrepreneur from California, and the couple moved to Los Angeles. With the profits from their private corporation in international trade, they enjoyed first-class round-the-world travel and an opulent lifestyle in Marina del Rey. They kept twin pairs of expensive foreign sports cars, two private planes, and a 40-foot sailboat. In a spirit of adventure, Rachel took flying lessons and learned to pilot the boat. After a decade, when this marriage failed, she went into the real estate business. During this period, Rachel began to experience severe panic attacks.

The first attack, which occurred when she was age 32, started on a Sunday afternoon and lasted for eight hours. Rachel called 911, screaming, "I'm dying! I'm dying!" She thought she was having a stroke or a heart attack. Shorter attacks continued daily, and, quickly, Rachel's circle of activities began to shrink. Although she took Valium as prescribed, Rachel couldn't safely drive on the freeway, and eventually she could barely leave the house.

During this period she married an extremely kind, sensitive older man of independent means, but this second marriage ended amicably after less than three years. Faced with daily sieges of panic attacks, Rachel returned to her home town, where she received the emotional support of her siblings.

There, her life revolved around visits to the emergency room. She found an entry-level job at a hospital, and was on Valium for two and a half years. Then she learned about Xanax, and found that it more effectively controlled her panic attacks. Later, she returned to California and, as she put it, "got very grandiose." Rachel set up a corporation for international arts festivals and, as she said, "went through over a quarter of a million dollars of other people's money in less than 18 months."

Hoping to control her rising anxiety, she increased her intake of Xanax until she began to develop psychotic symptoms. She had never even heard of psychosis, and she firmly believed that people were trying to kill her. Finally, Rachel called a sister in Alabama and cried, "They're coming to get me." Within hours, her sister flew to California and, with a brother, committed Rachel to Long Beach General Hospital with severe depressive paranoid psychosis. She hadn't eaten or bathed in days. Rachel was put in restraints and spent five days on a locked ward. She recalls her hospitalization as mostly a negative experience, remembering aides who joked about her condition and the crowded facility. She was put on Stelazine and, when that started to pull her out of her psychosis, was transferred to a halfway house in Inglewood.

In retrospect, Rachel feels she was released to the halfway house too soon. There, she cowered in her room all night, peering out the window at people she thought were coming to kill her. For days, she refused medications, thinking they were poisoned. Finally, she said, a "big, boisterous black woman," who terrified Rachel, bullied her into taking her medication. What a difference it made! Soon she was whistling in the halls, and she was transferred to a residential care center in Watts where she stayed for six weeks. Rachel enjoyed the center, which had a grand piano in the recreation room that she would play for hours. Nonetheless, she was eager to leave the institutional setting. She took her medication regularly and convinced her sympathetic second ex-husband to let her stay with him. This arrangement didn't work well. She was heavily medicated and still severely depressed, not capable of much more than taking long walks by the ocean all day while her ex-husband was away. Finally, one of her brothers invited her to visit for Christmas. She ended up living with him and his extraordinarily supportive wife and children for a year and a half, working in a medical setting and learning to cope with her frequent bouts of extreme paranoid ideation.

Rachel eventually moved into an apartment of her own and found a stable position as a patient advocate in a clinic. She worked at the clinic for six years before recurrent panic attacks forced her to resign. She lived on her savings for a year and a half, caught in a downward spiral that she attributes to losing the validation and structure of working. This crisis led to her second hospitalization, which lasted five days.

When her health insurance ran out, Rachel asked to be referred by her private psychiatrist to a public clinic. There, her new therapist helped her apply for Medicaid and recommended that Rachel join a local mental health Clubhouse program. After a successful volunteer experience, Rachel entered a transitional employment program. She found a job as a receptionist with the state mental health authority. When a new administrative support position became available, Rachel moved into consumer programs, which set the stage for her current administrative job.

Rachel sees her therapist regularly at a community mental health center. After much adjusting of types and dosages of medications, she takes what her therapist calls "a sprinkle" of Xanax daily as a prophylactic to ward off panic attacks, accompanied by a small dose of anti-psychotic medication and Prozac. Rachel has become confident, both in her therapist and in her pharmaceutical regimen. Rachel describes her therapist, a nurse/MSW, as "extraordinarily deft." Her therapist is gifted with deep empathy, and Rachel thinks it helps that she is a woman of about her own age. With this level of care, Rachel is comfortable and happy. In fact, she describes this stage as "by far, the happiest time of my life."

Rachel occasionally has minor attacks of intense paranoia but is able to recognize them as such. After each one recedes, she experiences a warm feeling, "like you're coming back from a cold hell into a warm reality."

Rachel says, "You even learn to love your disease, as strange as that may sound. It forces you to develop compassion, and is a marvelous lesson." She is grateful for these lessons, and feels she wouldn't have been able to learn them any other way. The main problem she has encountered is the public's lack of knowledge about mental illness. She feels fortunate that she can remember every detail of her past psychotic episodes. Most consumers she works with don't have that degree of recall. For them, each episode is a new and terrifying experience.

As a leader among mental health consumers, Rachel has had the opportunity to discuss issues of concern at the state and national levels. She believes that in the consumer community she works with, there is some support for forced medication. Some of the mental health consumers she encounters have expressed reservations about side effects and the impact of mandatory medication on self-determination, but they feel the benefits of today's improved psychotropic medications override these considerations. Rachel is totally confident that the coming years will see the development of even more sophisticated medications for mental illness. Her state's consumers are also interested in gun control and housing. At least half of the people Rachel works with are upset about proposed restrictions on their ability to purchase guns. Arguing that they are statistically less violent than the general population, they believe such restrictions violate their rights. Those living on SSI and Social Security Disability Insurance (DI) find affordable housing scarce, and feel that the benefits of these programs are meager: "They want us to pay for the sin of having a mental illness." Mental health insurance parity is another big concern, which Rachel sees as primarily a state issue.

DISCUSSION   Given the timing, it is tempting to attribute Rachel's first bout with deep depression to the loss of her mother. While this event may have acted as a precipitating factor, Rachel explains her illness with reference to a combination of genetic and situational factors. She notes that severe depression and extreme cases of bipolar disorder are found on both sides of her immediate family, and that she suffered regular abuse during childhood that probably had an impact on her mental well-being. Her youngest brother was diagnosed with paranoid schizophrenia when he was seventeen and tried to commit suicide. He is now in his early 40s, living on DI and contributions from his siblings. Unlike Rachel, he has consistently resisted any mental health treatment.

Despite her struggles, Rachel feels fortunate. At times, she has lost most of her possessions, but she has never been homeless. She attributes this fact to the generosity of her siblings. Indeed, Rachel feels that without her family's enlightened support, she would not have survived her cycling illness. Rachel has achieved an astonishing reconciliation with the father who traumatized her so badly in childhood. She feels they probably will never be emotionally close, but they now have a peaceful and supportive relationship.

It is interesting to speculate on what might have happened if her childhood abuse had come to the attention of public authorities. Would Rachel have been removed from her parental home? Would the foster care system have provided the kind of supports that sustained Rachel through her episodes of illness? Would an experience with child welfare authorities have mitigated the impact of mental illness on her life? Without family supports, would Rachel have joined the ranks of the homeless mentally ill who now haunt the nation's towns and cities?

"Oh, worse than that!" Rachel sums it up emphatically. "I'm certain that without my artfully gifted professional treatment and enlightened support of my family and friends, I'd have been dead long ago!"

DEFINING MENTAL ILLNESS

The boundary between mental illness and mental health can be hazy. Consider the language of ordinary life. A mother exclaims to her children, "You are driving me crazy!" A student describes a party as "insane!" (meaning "great").

Definitions of mental illness vary in their emphasis. Some emphasize the biological component of mental illness, defining it on the basis of genetic configurations, neurological activity, or brain chemistry. Other definitions emphasize the behavioral component, treating mental illness as a failure of personality or personal development. During the 1960s and 1970s, mental health professionals such as R. D. Laing argued that mental illness was essentially a failure to conform. Thomas Szasz, a vocal proponent of this view, argued that mental illness was a "myth" and that the label "crazy" or "mentally ill" was applied as a sanction for violating social norms (Szasz, 1960).

In 1952, the American Psychiatric Association released the first edition of the *Diagnostic and Statistical Manual*, now in its fourth edition (the *DSM-IV*). This authoritative document reflects an ongoing effort to standardize psychiatric terminology that began during the 1920s. It defines mental illnesses in exquisite detail, based on cognitive, emotional, and behavioral indicators. The *DSM* has become a manifestation of the process through which mental illness is socially constructed. Its first edition reflected the view that mental disorders represented reactions or adaptations to psychosocial stressors. The *DSM-II*, issued in 1968, focused on describing psychiatric diseases. Its authors systematically eradicated all mention of "reactions" or "adaptation" from the manual. In 1980, the *DSM-III* was issued. This version has been described as a "paradigm shift" in American psychiatry. It represented a rejection of theoretical explanations and a return to the medical model of mental illness. Later versions of the *DSM* (the *DSM-IIIR* and the *DSM-IV*) are still dominated by the medical model of mental illness. They simply elaborate upon the classification schemes developed in the *DSM-III* (LaBruzza & Mendez-Villarrubia, 1994).

LaBruzza and Mendez-Villarrubia (1994) describe the *DSM*'s role in the social construction of mental illness as "diagnosis by consensus" (p. 38). The manual's treatment of homosexuality is illustrative. Homosexuality was listed as a mental illness in the first two editions of the *DSM*. During the 1960s and 1970s, gay rights groups were vocal in opposing this nomenclature, arguing that the difficulties experienced by homosexuals were caused by society, not by underlying mental pathology. In 1973, the American Psychiatric Association's board of trustees voted to delete homosexuality from the *DSM-II*. As LaBruzza and Mendez-Villarrubia noted, "With a single vote the APA cured millions of gay men and women in America of the 'mental illness' of homosexuality" (p. 21).

Addiction disorders also represent a definitional challenge in the field of mental health. Addiction to alcohol or illegal drugs, per the *DSM*, is considered a mental illness. Further, advocates for those who suffer from addiction emphasize its biological component, framing addiction as a *disease*. Nonetheless, the general public and many policy-makers view addiction not as a disease but as a moral failure.

As the length and complexity of the *DSM-IV* illustrate, mental illness is as intricate and varied as physical illness. We think of mental illness as a long-term condition that produces extreme emotions and behavior, such as depression or schizophrenia. But, as Mechanic pointed out, "some psychiatric conditions are like the flu or a gastrointestinal disorder; they are relatively short-lived and do not greatly disrupt one's life" (1999, p. 39). Indeed, as the field develops, the specificity with which we define mental illness will inevitably increase. Eventually, we may no longer speak of someone as having a "mental condition," but as having a specific diagnosis such as "bipolar disorder."

VALUES AND BELIEFS ABOUT MENTAL ILLNESS AND THE MENTALLY ILL

Even as defining mental illness has been a fluid process, society's attitudes toward mental illness have varied. In this section, we will examine several different perspectives on mental illness, suggesting that Americans have viewed it alternatively as eccentricity, sin, disease, and disability.

MENTAL ILLNESS AS ECCENTRICITY

In some contexts, mental illness is viewed as a sign of eccentricity, or difference. In artists this eccentricity may be seen as tolerable—even a sign of creativity. This attitude is most evident in the public response to artists who have mental diagnoses. Several of the nation's most creative artists have been diagnosed with depression or schizophrenia. (For a discussion of the relationship between creativity and insanity, and a list of artists who have been treated for mental illness, see Jamison, 1993.)

In other contexts, however, eccentricity is less readily accepted. This is often true in politics. At its extreme, a negative approach to eccentricity among politicians is seen when insanity is used by authoritarian regimes to silence political opposition. Thus, for example, political activists in China and other nations have been imprisoned, not as criminals, but as victims of mental illness. Their eccentric political views have been treated as evidence of insanity. The United States has limited tolerance for signs of mental illness among its politicians. Indeed, news of Thomas Eagleton's psychiatric treatment led to his replacement as McGovern's running mate in the 1972 presidential election. Thus, it was extremely courageous of Representative Lynn Rivers (D-Michigan) to publicly acknowledge in 1998 her own struggles with bipolar depression. The National Mental Health Association awarded Rep. Rivers its Legislator of the Year Award.

MENTAL ILLNESS AS SIN

During the early eighteenth century, mental illness was more often attributed to supernatural causes than to biological or social conditions. Cotton Mather, a Puritan minister, wrote prolifically on both mental and physical illnesses. As was typical at the time, he viewed madness as a consequence of sin (Grob, 1994). Treatment of madness took the form of prayer, repentance, and exorcism.

A clear distinction between mental and physical illness lies in the possibility that mental illness will be defined as "bad" or "sinful." People are rarely held responsible for contracting a physical illness. Treatment is provided as a matter of course, and incarceration is not even considered. But mental illness, with its problematic behavioral component, has invited judgments of this kind. We may wonder why the mentally ill person cannot simply "snap out of it," and certainly avoid "coddling" or encouraging the behavioral indicators of insanity.

MENTAL ILLNESS AS DISEASE

Recent years have seen a growing awareness of the biological component of mental illness, and with it, a widespread view of mental illness as disease. Still, our definition may be highly dependent on context.

David Mechanic (1962) has examined the definition of behavior as "sick" or "bad." He argued that "if the behavior appears to be peculiar and at odds with the actor's self-interests or with expectations of the way a reasonable person is motivated, the evaluator is more likely to characterize such behavior in terms of the sickness dimension" (p. 38, 1999). But if the behavior is in some way self-serving, it is more likely to be evaluated as "bad." Thus, a rich person who steals a loaf of bread is likely to be labeled "sick" or "crazy," while a poor person who does so will be labeled "bad."

Mental Illness as Disability

The notion of mental illness as a disability has direct significance for social policy, as it dictates eligibility for programs that serve the disabled. These entitlements include income maintenance through SSI and DI, as well as housing and rehabilitative services. Individuals whose mental illness renders them "unable to engage in any substantial gainful activity" (Social Security Administration, 2001) are eligible for monthly income through SSI and DI. They also have access to medical coverage, as SSI typically confers Medicaid eligibility, and those who are on DI for 24 months become eligible for Medicare coverage.

The label "disabled" cuts two ways. A mental patient who can persuade authorities that she is "permanently and totally disabled" will receive income support and medical coverage through these programs. In order to secure rehabilitative services, however, she may need to demonstrate that she can be rehabilitated. That is, she may be "totally" disabled, but not "permanently" disabled. Thus, an individual with a severe mental illness faces a quandary: is it better to give up hope of rehabilitation and gain a secure income, or to cling to hope and thereby gain access to rehabilitation? This quandary is a late twentieth-century development, reflecting the sophistication and fragmentation of the network of mental health interventions that have developed in the United States. The development of this network is described in the next section.

HISTORICAL DEVELOPMENT OF INTERVENTIONS FOR THE MENTALLY ILL[1]

In this section, we will trace the development of public interventions for the mentally ill in the United States. As we will discover, support for such interventions seems to ebb and flow in response to fluctuating enthusiasm for available treatment methods. During the Colonial period mental illness was often attributed to moral failure. Nonetheless, early records reveal collective responses to individual cases of mental disorder, perhaps because colonists recognized insanity as a danger to families and the community.

With the growth of cities, almshouses were established. Built to house the indigent, almshouses served as the first public institutional settings for the mentally ill. By the mid-eighteenth century, separate institutions for the insane were established.

---

[1]Much of the material in this section is based on Gerald Grob's 1994 book, *The Mad Among Us*, and David Rochefort's 1997 work, *From Poorhouses to Homelessness*.

The advent of new treatment methods fueled public optimism that mental illness could be cured. The result was expansion of both private and public mental institutions. Dorothea Dix contributed to this expansion through her crusading efforts on behalf of the insane.

As individuals with milder forms of mental illness recovered and were discharged, institutions were increasingly populated by individuals with chronic, sometimes incurable disorders. Mental health professionals turned to the prevention of mental illness through the mental hygiene movement, which was prominent in the 1920s and 1930s. This movement took psychiatrists and psychiatric social workers out of mental hospitals and into the community. It also shifted their focus from the mentally ill to people with emotional and adjustment problems that were seen as precursors of mental illness. The popularity of the mental hygiene movement, coupled with an emerging view of commitment as incarceration, set the stage for the community mental health movement and triggered deinstitutionalization of the mentally ill in the mid-1950s.

CARE OF THE MENTALLY ILL IN COLONIAL AMERICA

Living in close proximity to one another, American colonists were quick to recognize both the external effects and the unpredictability of mental illness. The impact of mental illness went beyond the victim's suffering, as Cotton Mather pointed out:

> These melancholicks do sufficiently Afflict themselves, and are Enough their own Tormentors. As if this present Evil World, would not Really afford Sad Things Enough, they create a World of Imaginary Ones, and by Medicating terror, they make themselves as Miserable, as they could be from the most Real miseries.
>
> But this is not all; *They Afflict others as well as Themselves, and often make themselves Insuportable Burdens to all about them.*
>
> In this Case, we must bear one anothers Burdens . . . (Jones, 1972, pp. 129–137) [emphasis added].

Further, one never knew who might be the next victim. Thus, in 1651, when Roger Williams exhorted his fellow citizens of Providence, Rhode Island, to care for a widow who was "distracted," he reminded them that "we know not how soone our wives may be widowes and our children Orphans, yea and our selves be deprived of all or most of our Reason, before we goe from hence, except mercy from the God of Mercies prevent it" (Grob, 1994, p. 13).

In colonial America, mental illness became a matter of public concern when it interfered with public safety or jeopardized survival. Indeed, one of the first laws governing care of the insane ordered the selectmen of Massachussettes to care for them "in order that they doe not Damnify others" (Grob, 1994, p. 7).

Public care of the mentally ill focused on meeting survival needs, but treatment was sometimes available. Therapies were eclectic, reflecting practitioners' varied notions about the causes of mental illness. Insanity was attributed to sin as readily as to extreme misfortune or digestive disturbances.

Richard Napier, an astrological physician of the era, treated thousands of patients for madness during his career. Treatments might include bleeding and purging. But Napier also used exorcism if he believed a patient was possessed, and environmental manipulation if he thought the trouble came from that source (Grob, 1994).

Depression was identified early in the nation's history, and its causes and treatments outlined in Robert Burton's famous 1621 work, *Anatomy of Melancholy.* Burton, himself a frequent victim of melancholy, advised a range of treatments, including social contacts (avoiding solitude), music, prayer, and medicines. The latter might consist of "a decapitated head of ram . . . boiled with cinnamon, ginger, nutmeg, mace and cloves," or "living swallows, cut in two and laid reeking hott onto the shaved Head," and "blood of an ass drawn from behind his ear" (Grob, 1994, pp. 9–10).

These treatments, while often effective, were seldom part of public interventions. They were provided to those who could afford them, or in individual cases where charity dictated relief of suffering. The notion of a "right to treatment" was not part of the dialogue about public responsibility for the mentally ill.

THE PROMISE OF THE ASYLUM

By the mid-eighteenth century, American understanding of mental illness focused more on personal and environmental influences and less on spiritual causes. During the age of enlightenment, belief in the potential for perfecting human beings—or at least improving their situations—increased general interest in curing mental illness.

With the growth of cities came the establishment of institutional settings for the mentally ill. Hospitals were available for those who could afford them, and almshouses were provided to those who were indigent. These almshouses initially combined the aged, young, infirm, and insane. Over time, however, efforts were made to separate the "distracted" from the rest of the population.

The nation's first public hospital designed exclusively for the insane, the "Virginia Eastern Asylum," was established in Williamsburg in 1769. The rationale for its establishment included both the need for early intervention and recognition of the external effects of madness. The Act that provided for the hospital stated in its opening clause that "several persons of insane and disordered minds have been frequently found wandering in different parts of this colony" and noted that "no certain provision" had "yet [been] made either towards effecting a cure of those whose cases are not become quite desperate, nor for restraining others who may be dangerous to society" (Hening, 1809–1823, vol. VIII, pp. 378–381).

During the latter part of the eighteenth century, public hospitals for the mentally ill proliferated, with a corresponding improvement in the care they provided. American institutions reflected a strong European influence. A Frenchman, Philippe Pinel, contributed to the expansion of the asylum by developing a new treatment approach. Based on exhaustive observations, he argued that bleeding and other practices generally were not effective. Pinel established what he called a *traitement moral,* or "moral treatment." Contrary to its name, Pinel's approach did not emphasize moral judgments or values. Instead, it offered a carefully structured environmental regimen in which the physician held complete authority. The goal was an institution in which physical abuse or neglect of patients was unheard of, and the environment was carefully structured to accomplish individual cures.

In England, William Tuke, a Quaker and merchant, applied Pinel's methods in the "York Retreat." The Retreat was established by Quakers in 1792 to serve the mentally ill. It established a well-considered regimen that was remarkably effective. The success of the Retreat contributed to a widespread belief that hospitals for the mentally ill could accomplish cures. This optimism set the stage for expansion of mental institutions throughout England and the United States.

Of course, high-quality care was costly, and private institutions were forced to serve an affluent clientele in order to secure adequate operating funds. Indigents were referred to public institutions where they would receive custodial care, if not the most sophisticated treatment.[2] The result was a class-based system of care in which the affluent were not forced to mix with members of the lower classes or immigrants from diverse ethnic backgrounds.

DOROTHEA DIX, "APOSTLE TO THE INSANE"

Enter Dorothea Dix (1802–1887), who has been called the "apostle to the insane." Ms. Dix was an educated woman from a middle-class family. Like many women from similar backgrounds, she found in social reform one of the few available outlets for her talents. Although she suffered illness and emotional trials, Dix was determined to contribute to society, observing that "life is not to be expended in vain regrets—self is not to be the object of contemplation—individual trials are not to be admitted to fill the mind to the exclusion of the sufferings of the *many*" (Brown, 1998, p. 76). When Dix was 39, she was invited to teach a Sunday school class at a jail outside of Boston. There, she found the insane housed with criminals in appalling conditions. Her outrage at this and similar conditions fueled a career in social advocacy.

Dix developed an effective methodology for her crusade to establish asylums for the mentally ill. She would travel to a state, visit prisons and almshouses, and prepare a petition or report outlining her findings. Dix met with policy elites and members of state legislatures to encourage establishment or expansion of the institutions in each state.

Like many advocates, she was not above exaggeration or hyperbole if it helped her cause. Some, like her fellow reformer Samuel Gridley Howe, saw her dramatic presentations as necessary to convey the urgency of her mission.

---

[2]Some public institutions did provide outstanding care. One of these was the Massachusetts State Hospital established by Samuel B. Woodward. This setting served as a model of effective treatment under public auspices.

Officials who ran the facilities raised strenuous objections, however. The administrators of the Danvers almshouse argued that Dix was in the facility for only five minutes and had then described "the high wrought fancies of [her] imagination, instead of the practical realities of life" (Brown, 1998, p. 95).

Howe linked the causes of insanity to the failings of social institutions, arguing that these failings dictated social responsibility for the insane. Dix, on the other hand, held that the causes were irrelevant. A deeply religious Unitarian, Dix argued the moral necessity of protecting the insane from the "predatory forces of society" (Brown, 1998, p. 93).

The expansion of public hospitals for the mentally ill continued for more than a century. Through the course of her career (1840–1860), Dix was instrumental in the founding or expansion of 31 asylums for the mentally ill (Brown, 1998). Within these new institutions, a new specialty called "psychiatric social work" was born. Paul Stuart (1997) traced its roots to 1907, when Massachusetts General Hospital assigned a social worker (Edith Burleigh) to its neurological clinic. Edith served as a liaison between the hospital and the community, supporting the treatment plans developed by the psychiatrist. Her work served as a model for other hospitals, which adopted the practice of hiring social workers to assist in the care of the mentally ill. Within most mental asylums a rigid hierarchy prevailed, in which psychiatrists enjoyed the highest status and the greatest decision-making authority. Second in status and authority were psychologists, with social workers a distant third.

The expansion of asylums for the mentally ill peaked in 1955, when they housed more than half a million Americans. Ironically, this growth destroyed the very feature that inspired it: the promise of a cure for insanity. Moral therapy and similar approaches were costly, and simply could not be sustained in over-populated, under-funded institutions. The gap between the reality of life in asylums and the promise of effective treatment widened, even as institutional populations grew. Cures were not unheard-of, but over time, intractable cases of chronic mental illness came to dominate the asylums.

Thus began a vicious spiral. The growing proportion of chronically mentally ill living in institutions belied the promise that the environment could be used to effect a cure. Without that promise, patients with transient or acute problems did not seek treatment in the institutions. This increased the proportion of intractable cases, including senile elderly patients, as well as victims of syphilis. The asylum became a place of despair—a last resort for those who had no other options.

COMMITMENT AS INCARCERATION

Even as Dorothea Dix was advocating for expansion of institutions, others argued that involuntary commitment of mental patients was incarceration without due process. In vivid support of this argument was the case of Elizabeth Packard. As Gerald Grob tells it,

Packard had been stricken at the age of nineteen with "brain fever" and spent six weeks . . . at the Worcester hospital in 1835. Four years later she married Theophilus Packard, a Protestant minister who was nineteen years her senior. An unhappy marriage was exacerbated by sharp religious differences. Elizabeth Packard adhered to a liberal theology, while her husband was a devout Calvinist who accepted the total depravity of humanity. When Packard refused to play the role of an obedient wife and expressed religious ideas bordering on mysticism, her husband had her committed in 1860 to the Illinois State Hospital for the Insane . . . where she remained for three years. After being released, she was confined by her husband in a locked room . . . a friend secured a writ of habeas corpus. In a trial that received national publicity, Packard was declared sane. She then spent nearly two decades campaigning for the passage of personal liberty laws that would protect individuals and particularly married women from wrongful commitment (1994, p. 84).

Elizabeth Packard was instrumental in establishing the National Association for the Protection of the Insane and Prevention of Insanity in 1880. On behalf of the mentally ill, this group advocated stricter standards for involuntary commitment and protection of patients' rights within institutional settings. In 1908, Clifford W. Beers wrote *A Mind that Found Itself,* which documented the indignities of institutional life and fueled the mental hygiene movement.

PREVENTING MENTAL ILLNESS: THE MENTAL HYGIENE MOVEMENT

Enthusiasm for "mental hygiene" flourished as the promise of the asylum faded. In essence, the mental hygiene movement took the business of mental health out of the realm of madness and into that of social adjustment and unhappiness. Its rationale was similar to that of the public health movement of the same era, and its proponents shared a similar zeal. They felt that adjustments in family life and social conditions would prevent the minor mental disturbances that, left untreated, could develop into incurable mental disorders (Rose, 1996; Richardson, 1989).

The National Committee for Mental Hygiene was founded in 1909 to promote the prevention of mental disorders, arguing that prevention is both easier and less expensive than treatment. Leading philanthropic agencies such as the Rockefeller Foundation contributed to efforts to identify the causes of mental illness. Childhood problems came to the fore as causal factors, and the mental hygiene movement came to focus on promotion of healthy child rearing practices. By 1930, the notion of mental hygiene was widely accepted. The 1930 White House Conference on Child Health and Protection declared childhood "the golden period for mental hygiene" (Richardson, 1989, p. 107).

Truancy and delinquency were seen as precursors of mental illness, and participants in the mental hygiene movement soon came to see the classroom as an ideal setting for preventive psychiatric work. Visiting teachers and psychiatric social workers served as on-site trainers and demonstrators in the public schools, "educating teaching staff into a different attitude toward children" (Richardson, 1989, p. 89). With funding from the Commonwealth Fund, child guidance clinics were established in eight U.S. cities to apply the principles of mental hygiene to the problems of childhood.

The most successful child guidance clinic funded by the Commonwealth Fund was established in Los Angeles. This clinic's focus was not on referrals from the courts or schools, but on children who were brought in by their parents or other relatives for adjustment-related problems. Children with mental retardation and established mental illness were referred elsewhere. Based on the popularity of the clinic, the state of California attempted to set up a statewide mental hygiene service (Richardson, 1989).

As mental health moved out of the asylum, the roles of mental health professionals changed. The field of community psychiatry was born, bringing psychiatrists out of mental institutions and into schools, courts, and even private homes. In child guidance and community education programs, social workers enjoyed higher status than they had been accorded in the rigid hierarchy of mental institutions.

The mental hygiene movement changed thinking about childhood, promoting the idea that childhood experiences were relevant to public policy because they contributed to mental illness in adulthood. Unfortunately, little research had been conducted on the precursors of mental illness. As a result, much of the work done by mental hygiene proponents, such as the campaign to reduce "bad mental habits," had a propaganda-like feel. Popular wisdom was promoted as solutions to complex psychiatric problems. As the idea of heredity surfaced as a popular explanation for insanity, proponents of mental hygiene became advocates for "eugenic" policies such as sterilization of the mentally ill.

The basic premise of the eugenics movement was that human characteristics and behavior were determined primarily by genetics. Thus, sterilization was seen as the ultimate means of preventing mental illness. Indiana passed the first law requiring sterilization of the mentally ill. Many states followed suit, and by World War II, 30 states had passed similar legislation. California was particularly active in pursuing this policy. Between 1907 and 1940, 18,500 mental patients were sterilized, half of them in the Golden State (Grob, 1994).

MENTAL HEALTH TREATMENTS DURING THE DEPRESSION AND WORLD WAR II

The period from 1929 to 1945 was a tumultuous one for mental health care in the United States. Resources available for institutional care were decimated by the Depression. But treatment innovations, primarily from Europe, again promised hope of cure. Some of the treatments used would strike us as bizarre today. For example, an Austrian psychiatrist, Julius Wagner-Jauregg, observed that mental symptoms sometimes disappeared in patients who developed typhoid fever. He drew blood from a soldier who had malaria and injected several patients. The results were promising, and he received a Nobel Prize in 1927 for this work. Fever therapy, or malaria therapy, became extremely popular in U.S. institutions and generated tremendous optimism that mental illness could be cured.

This optimism extended to other innovative approaches, such as insulin therapy, lobotomy, and use of electrical shock. The latter became extremely popular, and between 1935 and 1941 more than 75,000 patients received shock therapy. This figure compares to 18,608 who underwent psychosurgery between the years of 1936 and 1951 (Grob, 1994). Together, these therapies improved release rates for mental hospitals.

Events during World War II changed the mental health field. The war graphically demonstrated both the extent of mental illness among Americans and the influence of environmental stress. Over 1.75 million inductees were rejected by the military for psychiatric reasons (Grob, 1994). Despite this screening, many of the men who were sent into combat developed psychiatric symptoms. Military practitioners treated these men at the front, demonstrating that even extreme cases of what we might now call post-traumatic stress disorder (PTSD) can improve outside an institutional setting.

FEDERAL INVOLVEMENT IN MENTAL HEALTH

The end of World War II saw tremendous variation in the quality of care available through the nation's mental hospitals. In Kansas, the influence of the Menninger Clinic was felt soon after its founding in 1944. The Menninger brothers established an outstanding facility that continues to provide leadership in mental health. They also advocated for improved care in the state's public institutions.

Residents in other states were less fortunate. An exposé of Oklahoma mental institutions by Mike Gorman called "Oklahoma Attacks Its Snakepits" was published in Reader's Digest. It became the basis for a famous novel published in 1946, *The Snake Pit*, by Mary Jane Ward. This novel was adapted to create the screenplay for a popular motion picture that starred Olivia de Havilland.

Together, these media events increased concern for the quality of care in mental hospitals and triggered a call for increased federal involvement in mental health. The mental hygiene movement had already found a home in the federal government in 1930, when the U.S. Public Health Service created a Division of Mental Hygiene. Near the end of World War II, Robert H. Felix took over leadership of the Division. He is widely recognized as the leading force in the 1946 passage of the National Mental Health Act.

THE NATIONAL MENTAL HEALTH ACT OF 1946. The National Mental Health Act had three goals: to support research on psychiatric disorders, to train mental health personnel through fellowships and grants, and to provide grants to the states to establish clinics and demonstration programs. The Act also required states to establish a single state agency for planning and administration of federal mental health funds. Under the Act, the National Institute for Mental Health was established in 1949 as a branch of the Public Health Service. Robert Felix was its first director. One goal for NIMH leaders was to broaden the scope of mental health services beyond institutions. This community-based approach to treatment was more compatible with a public health approach to mental health. It served as the basis for the community mental health movement, which resulted in the discharge of thousands of mental patients from public facilities.

THE COMMUNITY MENTAL HEALTH MOVEMENT AND DEINSTITUTIONALIZATION

The idea of alternatives to traditional mental hospitals was not entirely new. In the mid-nineteenth century innovators like John M. Galt had advocated community-based care for the chronically mentally ill. In Illinois a model facility called Kankakee was constructed in 1877 to house the chronically mentally ill. It featured a decentralized plan, with small out-buildings to house patients. Its cost was about one third that of the larger centralized facilities. In 1885, Massachusetts had operated a small board and care program for the "harmless insane," and by World War II, eight states had similar programs. They proved less costly than institutional care, and advocates such as social worker Edith Stern suggested that the quality of care was better in family-like settings.

In the 1950s, new treatment technologies increased Americans' enthusiasm for community-based care. These technologies included new psychotropic drugs that promised to control some of the most problematic symptoms of mental illness. One such drug was chlorpromazine, marketed as Thorazine, which helped control the symptoms of schizophrenia. It was followed by tranquilizers and antidepressants.

Psychotherapies were also being developed during this period. The effectiveness of psychotherapies in combat situations set the stage for their eventual acceptance by the mental health community. Of course, they met with some skepticism. Nonetheless, approaches such as milieu therapy grew in popularity, and with them the idea that treatment of mental illness could be effective outside an institutional setting.

These changes set the stage for state legislation in support of community-based care. In New York, the Community Mental Health Services Act passed in 1954 to provide for state reimbursement of local mental health expenses. In 1957 California passed the Short-Doyle Act, which was designed to increase community services by providing for a state-local match.

Under the Kennedy administration, a federal plan for community mental health services was advanced. The first step in this plan was the 1961 release of the final report of the Joint Commission on Mental Illness and Health. This report outlined the results of an extensive study of mental illness and its treatment. It offered the administration an "Action for Mental Health" program that was both ambitious and expensive. The program would involve the federal government in diverse phases of mental health treatment, from prevention through after-care.

Kennedy established a Task Force on Mental Health under NIMH leadership. The Task Force advanced the concept of a comprehensive mental health center in each community that would provide a range of services. These mental health centers would eventually eliminate the need for mental institutions. The administration embraced this notion and held that the role of the federal government was not to operate the centers but to stimulate their establishment. Toward that end, the Mental Retardation and Community Mental Health Center Construction Act of 1963 provided a three-year authorization of $150 million for the construction of community mental health centers (CMHCs).

Americans brought to the construction of CMHCs the same level of enthusiasm with which they had endorsed the establishment of mental hospitals. President Kennedy gave a special message to Congress describing this "bold new approach" to the treatment of mental health and mental retardation. There was evidence that self-help models, such as those demonstrated by Fountain House in New York and Thresholds in Chicago (Beard, Propst, & Malamud, 1982) might help meet the needs of former mental patients. There was great hope that the mentally ill would be integrated into a welcoming community, with supportive services at hand. Two factors mitigated against the realization of this dream: the limited funding available for CMHCs and the very nature of serious mental illness.

During the 1960s and 1970s, the nation's fiscal resources were increasingly committed to the Vietnam War (Harrington, 1984). Only a limited amount of federal funding was available to construct CMHCs. Instead of the planned 2,000 centers, by 1980 only 754 were in place. Further, those CMHCs that were established did not effectively serve individuals with "severe and persistent mental illness" (SPMI). The centers were outpatient treatment centers, not residential facilities. They were based on the premise that patients would live independently in the community, perhaps with family members. But many patients with SPMI did not have families who were able to receive them. Family members were either unable or unwilling to cope with the challenges presented by their illnesses.

Nonetheless, the number of people living in public mental hospitals began to drop. In part, this reduction occurred because Medicaid provided a reimbursement mechanism for elderly to live in nursing homes. Many elders were simply transferred from state mental hospitals into nursing homes (Morrissey & Goldman, 1986; Roberts & Kurtz, 1987). During the 1960s the number of Americans living in nursing homes nearly doubled, from 470,000 to nearly 928,000.

The 1974 establishment of Supplemental Security Income (SSI) as a federal entitlement provided further rationale for releasing mental patients into the community. It was believed that this federal safety net would provide the financial resources necessary for the mentally ill to live independently. But the 1980 Disability Amendments changed the definition of disability for SSI eligibility and called for a review of SSI recipients every three years. Those who were disabled by virtue of mental illness were especially hard hit. Although they represented

11 percent of SSI recipients, they constituted 30 percent of those deemed ineligible for the program after these reviews (Grob, 1994).

Later presidents did not share Kennedy's enthusiasm for expanding the federal role in mental health. Johnson's Great Society emphasized poverty and related ills. Nixon opposed the use of federal funds to establish CMHCs, and he unsuccessfully attempted to terminate the program. The Carter administration formulated the Mental Health Systems Act to create a framework for service delivery, but it was unable to achieve full funding of mental health services. Reagan converted mental health and substance abuse programs into a block grant that existed only a short time.

During the 1960s and 1970s, patients' rights advocates raised the argument that involuntary commitment to a mental facility constituted incarceration without due process. Involuntary commitment procedures were successfully challenged in federal and state courts. The 1960s and 1970s saw several landmark events restricting involuntary commitment. In 1969, California passed the Lanterman-Petris-Short Act to discourage commitment and lengthy confinement. The *Lessard* decision in Wisconsin in 1972 established the due process rights of patients faced with commitment. Similar to the rights of individuals faced with criminal incarceration, they included the right to timely notice of charges, notice of right to a jury trial, aid of counsel, protection against self-incrimination, and use of an evidentiary standard "beyond a reasonable doubt." One of the most well-known cases resulted in the *Wyatt v. Stickney* decision, which in 1972 established patients' right to be treated in the "least restrictive setting" (Roberts & Kurtz, 1987).

Several advocacy groups, such as the National Mental Health Association, the National Alliance of Mental Patients, the Network Against Psychiatric Assault, and the Coalition to Stop Institutional Violence, emerged to support the civil rights of mental patients. One of the most enduring, the National Alliance for the Mentally Ill, was established in 1979 to advocate for patients' rights and attempt to reduce the stigma associated with mental illness.

Pressures to reduce public funding of mental hospitals, optimism about community treatment, and public aversion to incarcerating mental patients against their will converged in a movement to "deinstitutionalize" mental patients. Deinstitutionalization involved moving severely mentally ill patients out of public mental hospitals and then closing all or part of the hospitals. It has been termed "one of the largest social experiments in American history" (Torrey, 1997, p. 8). In 1955, the peak year for hospitalization of the mentally ill, 558,239 patients lived in the nation's psychiatric hospitals. By 1994 there were only 71,619 patients in public mental hospitals.

While the nation was transferring patients out of public mental hospitals, private psychiatric facilities were flourishing, as were the psychiatric wards of general hospitals. As David Mechanic (1999) noted, "Between 1970 and 1992, the number of nonfederal general hospitals with separate psychiatric services increased from 797 to 1,616" (p. 130). The growth of private facilities during this period was also dramatic. By 1992, these private facilities reported more than 1.7 million discharges for short stays (Graves, 1995). Private psychiatric facilities have continued to be a growth industry during the past few decades, catering to patients with insurance coverage and locating their services according to profitability rather than need. The care they provide typically involves short stays, and their patients are more likely to have affective disorders, such as depression. Public hospitals, by contrast, serve patients who need long-term care, including those with psychotic disorders, such as schizophrenia, and addiction disorders.

Clearly, deinstitutionalization did not represent a wholesale rejection of institutional treatment for mental illness. Low-income patients with intractable problems were released from hospitals, while those with private insurance and short-term difficulties had greater access to institutional care. Indeed, some have argued that deinstitutionalization would be more accurately termed "trans-institutionalization," because it involved the transfer of people with chronic mental illness from public mental hospitals to nursing homes and criminal justice facilities (Torrey, 1997).

MENTAL ILLNESS IN THE UNITED STATES TODAY

As we saw in the last section, several threads run through the history of mental health interventions in the United States. The first is a tension between the goals of the mental hygiene movement (prevention and health promotion) and the needs of the mentally ill. This thread runs through the social work profession, as many are attracted to practices and activities that promote mental health. Some, like Harry Specht, argue that this attraction drains needed resources from programs that serve the mentally ill. A second thread is the debate over the proper use of institutional or mandatory treatments for the mentally ill. Some argue that the use of these approaches should be minimized, as they infringe on the civil rights of patients. Others note the vulnerability of (and sometimes the threat posed by) mental patients, and suggest that at times the public's need for safety has greater priority than an individual's desire for freedom. In this section we will assess the realities of mental illness in the United States today.

Like physical illnesses, mental illnesses are not randomly distributed throughout the population. Cultural and social conditions influence a person's risk of mental illness, and people living in poverty experience a higher risk of mental disorder. In the following sections we will look at the distribution of mental illness in the U.S., exploring the association between mental illness, homelessness, and violence. Financing of mental health services is surveyed, and access to treatment examined. We then examine policies affecting social workers in the mental health system, focusing on licensure and the duty to warn. We will conclude the section by considering three emerging policy issues: involuntary commitment, mandatory outpatient treatment, and insurance parity.

THE PREVALENCE OF MENTAL ILLNESS

Two major national studies have been conducted under the auspices of the National Institute for Mental Health (NIMH) to determine the prevalence of mental illness among Americans. The first was conducted in the early 1980s. Called the Epidemiological Catchment Areas (ECA) study, it examined lifetime prevalence of major disorders in five communities: Los Angeles, California; New Haven, Connecticut; Baltimore, Maryland; St. Louis, Missouri; and Durham, North Carolina. While not strictly representative of the U.S. population, the sample numbered 20,000 and represented more than 1.6 million people living in these communities. The ECA study used a Diagnostic Interview Schedule based on the *DSM-III* to examine a wide range of disorders (see Robins & Regier, 1991).

The second prevalence study, conducted by NIMH in the mid-1990s, was called the National Comorbidity Study (NCS). This study surveyed more than 8,000 people, aged 15 to 55, in a widely dispersed sample designed to be representative of the U.S. population. Interviewers used a revised version of the instrument developed for the ECA study (see Kessler et al., 1994).

Results from the NCS suggested that mental illness is a common experience among Americans. Nearly half of the sample (49.7 percent) reported having had at least one psychiatric disorder in their lives, and almost a third (30.9 percent) had experienced at least one disorder in the 12 months prior to the interview (Kessler & Zhao, 1999).

Results also suggested that the most common psychiatric disorders among Americans are major depression and alcohol dependence. One in ten respondents reported having had an episode of depression in the 12 months prior to the interview, and 17 percent reported having had a bout with depression at some time during their lives. Similarly, 7 percent of the sample reported having been dependent on alcohol in the 12 months prior to the interview, and 14 percent reported a history of alcohol dependence. When addictive disorders were combined, they were more common than depression, with one fourth of the sample reporting at least one addictive disorder during their lives. Similar results were obtained when all the anxiety disorders were combined. Nearly one in five respondents (19.3 percent) reported having had an anxiety disorder in the 12 months prior to the interview. Other diagnoses, such as anti-social personality disorders (2.8 percent) and schizophrenia (0.5 percent), were considerably less common (Kessler & Zhao, 1999).

Comorbidity (the presence of more than one psychiatric disorder) is a significant concern for mental health practice and policy. As Kessler and Zhao (1999) noted, "Although a history of some psychiatric disorder is quite common among persons 15 to 54 in the United States, the major burden of psychiatric disorder in this age segment of our society is concentrated in a group of highly comorbid people who constitute about one sixth of the population" (p. 67). These individuals reported having had three or more severe psychiatric disorders. A typical pattern of comorbidity involved a combination of addiction with one or more other disorders.

SOCIAL CLASS AND MENTAL ILLNESS

From a social justice perspective, the distribution of mental illness among the population is of interest for two reasons. First, mental illness might be a symptom or result of social or economic disadvantage. Second, access to treatment (as a benefit of group membership) may be distributed on the basis of advantage, rather than need.

There is strong evidence of an association between mental illness and social class. The first epidemiological study documenting this association was conducted in 1934 at Johns Hopkins University. Researchers examined agency and hospital records to identify individuals with symptoms of mental illness. They concluded that there was an "unmistakable association between personality problems and low economic status, with the lowest income groups having about six times the number of problems as the highest income groups" (cited in Perry, 1996, p. 19). Their results were replicated in a series of studies across the country.

More recent studies have also documented the association between social class and mental illness. These include both the ECA study and the NCS described earlier. Both suggest that low socioeconomic status (SES) is associated with increased risk of mental illness in general, and with increased risk of depression, alcohol dependence, and schizophrenia, in particular (Holzer et al., 1986; Muntaner et al., 1998). Other studies have consistently reported higher rates of depression, schizophrenia, addiction, and other disorders among low-income populations (Dohrenwend, 1990; Eaton, 1985; Kessler et al., 1994; Robins et al., 1984). Gender and minority status are also associated with higher rates of some disorders.

Although the association between social and economic disadvantage and mental illness is well established, the underlying causal mechanism is unclear. It is difficult to determine whether the stresses associated with low SES cause mental illness (the "social causation" argument) or the disabilities associated with mental illness cause a person to move down the SES ladder (the "natural selection" argument).

There is virtually no empirical support for the natural selection argument, but many studies have documented the deleterious effects of economic, personal, and social stress on mental health. In 1973, Harvey Brenner published a famous study of the relationship between employment rates and mental hospitalization. He compared hospitalization rates for new cases of psychosis with employment rates in New York from 1910 to 1960 and found an inverse relationship. When the employment rate went down, admissions to treatment, especially among men, went up. When economic times improved, hospitalization rates declined. It is unclear whether the economic downturns actually caused mental illness. The economic stress may have simply exacerbated underlying conditions, overwhelming individuals' coping abilities. Nonetheless, the study did suggest an association between mental illness and economic conditions. Likewise, several studies have documented the adverse mental health consequences of unemployment (for example, Gray, 1985; Osipow & Fitzgerald, 1993).

More recent studies have also identified higher prevalence of mental illness in economically distressed populations. For example, Rand Conger conducted a series of studies of farm families in Iowa during the farm crisis of the 1980s. His results demonstrated a strong association between economic distress and psychiatric illnesses (Conger et al., 1994).

HOMELESSNESS AND MENTAL ILLNESS

The homeless mentally ill have become fixtures of America's urban landscape. They shuffle along city sidewalks, talking and gesturing to companions who are invisible to others. Attempts to estimate the proportion of mentally ill among the homeless have generated remarkably similar results, leading a 1990 Task Force of the American Psychiatric Association to conclude that the prevalence of severe and persistent mental illness among homeless people "ranges from 28 percent to 37 percent" (American Psychiatric Association, 1990). When alcohol and drug addictions are included, the proportion jumps to 75 percent or more (Torrey, 1997). If anything, these estimates are probably low, as mentally ill persons are among those most likely to refuse to be interviewed for surveys of this kind.

Homelessness, in itself, exposes people to an increased risk of victimization. The homeless who are mentally ill are especially vulnerable. Every major city in the United States has a horror story to offer (see Kates, 1985). Few studies have systematically documented the increased risk that mental illness brings to the homeless, yet common sense suggests that impaired thinking would undermine survival skills. Freezing to death in the winter is, as E. F. Torrey observed, "all too common" among homeless persons who are mentally ill (1997, p. 19).

Torrey links the increased incidence of homelessness among mentally ill persons directly to the deinstitutionalization movement, arguing that laws regarding civil commitment have become irresponsibly restrictive.

VIOLENCE AND MENTAL ILLNESS

Are the mentally ill more prone to committing violent acts than the general population? Perhaps the most definitive source of answers to this question is the ECA study discussed earlier. The survey included questions about violent acts, such as hitting or throwing things at someone, causing bruises or injury, fighting, and using a weapon. Individuals with severe mental illness were compared to those with no mental illness on these measures of violent behavior. Results suggested that people with a severe mental illness were more likely than people with no mental disorder to commit all of the violent behaviors examined. People suffering from schizophrenia were especially likely to have committed a violent act (Swanson et al., 1990). Similar results have been reported in numerous studies (Hodgins, 1992; Straznickas, McNeil, & Binder, 1993; Link, Andrews, & Cullen, 1992), including a survey of family members conducted by the National Alliance for the Mentally Ill (see Steinwachs, Kasper, & Skinner, 1992).

Media coverage of outrageous crimes committed by individuals suffering from severe mental illness supports the general perception that the mentally ill are dangerous. Indeed, in some communities acts of violence by individuals suffering from mental illness have triggered calls for measures that forbid the purchase of a gun by anyone with a mental diagnosis. As advocates for the mentally ill have pointed out, such measures unduly penalize Americans with mental illness. As in the general population, mentally ill persons who commit violent acts constitute a small minority.

Among the mentally ill, as in the general population, excessive use of drugs and alcohol substantially increases the risk of violence (Monahan, 1992; Link et al., 1992; Marzuk, 1996). Those who are likely to commit a violent act are also characterized by failure to take medications (Torrey, 1997). Indeed, the most common scenario found in media coverage involves an individual suffering from active psychotic symptoms who is not receiving treatment. Thus, the violent act may be as much a result of limited access to treatment as it is caused by the disease itself.

FINANCING AND ORGANIZATION OF MENTAL HEALTH CARE

A variety of mental health services and treatments is available in the United States. Together, they make up what researchers refer to as the "de facto mental health service system" (Regier et al., 1993; Surgeon General, 1999). The system has four components: the specialty mental health sector, the general medical/primary care sector, the human services sector, and the voluntary support network sector.

The specialty mental health sector is staffed by mental health professionals, such as psychiatrists, psychologists, psychiatric social workers, and psychiatric nurses. In this sector the bulk of services are provided in outpatient settings. Inpatient care is provided in special psychiatric units of general hospitals. Private psychiatric hospitals and residential treatment centers also provide care for troubled children and adolescents. Public-sector facilities include state and county mental hospitals as well as CMHCs. Just under 6 percent of adults, and about 8 percent of children and adolescents, use specialty mental health services in a year (Surgeon General, 1999).

Although it is not primarily designed to meet mental health needs, the general medical/primary care sector is an important component of the service delivery system. In 1999, the U.S. Surgeon General reported that more than 6 percent of the adult population use this sector for mental health care. The general medical sector often serves as an initial point of contact for adults with mental illness, and for some it is the only source of mental health services.

The human services sector is made up of social services, rehabilitation facilities, school-based counseling, prison-based services, and religious counselors. This sector is the primary source of mental health services for children, serving up to 19 percent of the population of children. Adults are less likely to use human services for mental health treatment. The NCS revealed that 5 percent of adults had accessed this sector.

The voluntary support network is made up of self-help groups and peer counselors. The 12-step program offered by Alcoholics Anonymous is an example of this type of service. The Surgeon General reported that this is a rapidly growing segment of the nation's mental health system. Nonetheless, it reaches few of those afflicted with mental illness. According to the ECA study, about 3 percent of U.S. adults used self-help groups in the early 1990s (Surgeon General, 1999).

In any given year, about 15 percent of the adult population and 21 percent of children receive mental health services through one or more of these sectors (Surgeon General, 1999). But many people who are afflicted do not receive treatment. In 1995, the National Advisory Mental Health Council estimated that of the 5.6 million Americans with severe mental illness, approximately 60 percent received treatment in any given year. That leaves roughly 2.2 million individuals with severe mental illness who do not receive treatment (Torrey, 1997). The fragmented mechanisms for financing mental health care leave many Americans without access to effective treatment.

FINANCING MENTAL HEALTH CARE. Mental health care is a billion-dollar industry in the United States. In 1996, approximately $37 billion was spent for the treatment of mental illness and addiction. This amount represented about 7 percent of total health spending. Just over half (53 percent) of mental health expenditures came from public sources, primarily state and local governments. The remainder was paid by private insurance firms (Surgeon General, 1999).

Insurance coverage of mental health treatment is complicated by the difficulty of determining what constitutes "medical necessity," and what is called the "moral hazard" problem of insurance. With respect to mental illness, the term "medical necessity" is hard to define. Is it medically necessary to provide psychotherapy to a professional who is in the throes of divorce? What if he or she suffers from schizophrenia? Problems of definition are complicated by the unpredictability of mental illness. Some patients may recover spontaneously without any treatment, while a lack of treatment may produce tragic results in others with the same diagnosis.

The term "moral hazard" refers to a tendency for consumers to overutilize mental health services if the services are covered by insurance. This concept has been applied to physical illness, but it has been a more significant concern for mental disorders. The argument here is that psychotherapy can be personally fulfilling and under some theoretical perspectives may require years of treatment. Companies have used co-payments and service limits to control overutilization.

Most funding for public mental health services comes from state and local governments. The federal role has increased with the establishment of Medicare and Medicaid, as well as new initiatives including the Community Mental Health Block Grant, Community Support Programs, the PATH program for the homeless mentally ill, and the Comprehensive Community Mental Health Services for Children and Their Families program. These public-sector sources fund services for people without private insurance for mental health services.

Among public sources of funding, Medicaid has been described as "the single largest and most important medical program affecting persons with severe and persistent mental illness" (Mechanic, 1999, p. 194). A joint federal-state program, Medicaid finances mental health services that vary tremendously from state to state. The differences are reflected in both coverage and expenditures per Medicaid recipient. With respect to coverage, for example, Rhode Island has been unusually inclusive. In 1994, that state covered 1,770 people for every 1,000 state residents with poverty-level income. In contrast, Nevada and Idaho covered 410 and 540 residents, respectively, for every 1,000 residents living in poverty. Expenditures also vary tremendously, ranging from states like New Hampshire, which spent an average of $10,654 per Medicaid user, to Tennessee, which spent only $1,899 per recipient (Health Care Financing Administration, 1996).

With expanded use of Medicaid waivers and increased interest in state-level control of the program, the services covered and extent of coverage result in tremendous disparities in service access.

ACCESS TO TREATMENT. Access to mental health treatment is clearly a social justice issue. Apart from the uneven availability of services described above, both income and race have consistently emerged as significant predictors of access to mental health treatment. Individuals who have private insurance coverage for mental health care are more likely than those without such coverage to receive treatment for a wide array of diagnoses. Moreover, people of color are less likely to receive treatment than members of the cultural majority.

For years, the racial disparity in service access has been explained by hypothesizing that minorities experience less mental illness. Recent studies (see Zhang & Snowden, 1999) have effectively refuted this claim. Although people of color experience mental illness differently, the overall prevalence of mental illness is comparable. Underutilization of mental health services by minorities may reflect a lack of minorities among mental health professionals, which results in language and cultural barriers to utilization. It may also reflect the economic disparity in access discussed above.

MANAGED CARE AND MENTAL HEALTH SERVICES. Managed care has become a vehicle for controlling not only health care expenditures but also the cost of mental health services. Managed care cost controls have been applied both to private insurance coverage and to Medicaid. Medicaid recipients in most states are required to enroll with managed care providers, but states vary in their treatment of mental health under managed care.

Two managed-care approaches have been applied to mental health: "carve out" and "capitation." Under a carve-out strategy, mental health services are treated separately from medical services. Thus, for example, an HMO or the state Medicaid authority may contract with local treatment providers for mental health care on a fee-for-service basis, while capitating medical services. Under capitation, the care provider receives a fixed amount per year for each Medicaid enrollee. Capitation of mental health services is extremely complicated due to the unpredictable trajectory and complex treatment requirements of mental illness.

Social Workers in the Mental Health System

Throughout the twentieth century, social workers played an important role in the nation's mental health system, even as mental health practitioners constituted a growing proportion of social workers. Social work professionals were involved in most aspects of the service delivery system, from institutional treatment to community care. Indeed, in the late 1990s NIMH noted that social workers provided the lion's share of mental health care in the United States. Two policies have had a direct impact on social workers in mental health practice: licensing and the duty to warn.

Licensing of mental health professionals has had a significant impact on the availability of mental health treatment. Insurance reimbursement is typically available only for services provided by licensed professionals, and in most states a license is required for the use of professional titles, such as "counselor" or "social worker." Physicians have generally resisted expanding the licensed activities of other professionals in the mental health field. Similarly, psychologists, social workers, and nurses frequently compete for the legitimacy afforded through licensing.

Social work licensing procedures vary from state to state. Candidates for licensure must demonstrate that they have completed educational and practice requirements, and they must successfully complete an examination. With a license they may practice independently or within agencies that are reimbursed by federal or private insurers. Few states accept licenses issued in other states, and there is no national license for social workers. The NASW offers a national *credential* for clinical social workers known as membership in the Academy of Certified Social Workers (ACSW). (The ACSW is not a professional license.)

The duty to warn, with its attendant duty to protect, was established by the 1976 *Tarasoff v. Regents of the University of California* decision and subsequent rulings. Mental health practitioners whose patients present a significant threat of violence are required to take whatever steps are reasonably needed to protect the intended victims. Many view this requirement as a threat to confidentiality that can undermine patients' trust. Of course, in most settings, practitioners must inform their patients of this duty. After an exhaustive review of research on the duty to protect, Appelbaum (1994) concluded that "The duty to protect has complicated life for some clinicians, but it may have made life safer for some potential victims; and it has by no means been the disaster some authorities feared" (p. 99).

EMERGING POLICY ISSUES

In recent years, several policy issues have emerged in the field of mental health care. Four of these are discussed in this section: public financial support for individuals with addiction, involuntary commitment of the mentally ill, outpatient commitment for the mentally ill, and insurance parity for mental health care.

INCOME MAINTENANCE FOR ADDICTS. The 1980s and 1990s saw growing numbers of Americans who were suffering from mental illness enrolling for SSI or DI benefits. This increase led policy-makers to worry that the programs are being abused. This concern has been especially prominent in relation to disability benefits for individuals disabled by addiction.

From 1972 to 1996, addicted individuals could only receive SSI or DI benefits through a payee, and they were required to participate in treatment. Nonetheless, during the early 1990s, the number of SSI recipients whose disability stemmed from addiction increased substantially, from 24,000 in 1990 to 131,000 in 1995, and over 200,000 in 1996 (Gresenz, Watkins, & Podus, 1998).

Some of this dramatic growth was due to "cost shifting" by states. In the early 1990s, several states encouraged substance abusers who were on state-financed General Assistance (GA) programs to apply for SSI benefits. In Illinois, for example, the state paid for psychiatric evaluations for substance abusers who applied for SSI, and financed a legal advocacy program designed to secure SSI benefits for this group (Katz, 1994). This strategy effectively shifted the cost of income maintenance for this group from the 100%-state-funded GA programs to SSI, which brings with it a federal match.

This growth brought concerns about possible misuse of both SSI and DI. An audit by the General Accounting Office suggested that despite the treatment mandates, only a minority of substance abusers who received SSI were in treatment (U.S. General Accounting Office, 1994a). Representative payees were also subjected to scrutiny. These were the individuals charged with managing recipients' checks and ensuring that the recipients were in treatment. Audits revealed that many payees were not suited for these tasks, some being themselves substance abusers and others being bartenders or liquor store owners (Cohen, 1994). This finding, along with the results of urinalysis of some cocaine addicts receiving SSI, strongly suggested that benefit checks were being used to purchase drugs and alcohol. Finally, rates of rehabilitation for substance abusers on both SSI and DI were extremely low (U.S. Department of Health and Human Services, 1994b).

Ultimately, these findings supported the general notion that addicts were using public funds, not to secure rehabilitation, but to support their drug and alcohol habits. As a result, in 1996, SSI and DI benefits for individuals disabled by drug or alcohol addiction were terminated. Aid recipients with other disabling conditions were allowed to appeal the termination of their benefits. This was the first time in the history of the Social Security program that the *cause* (rather than the extent or duration) of disability was used to deny eligibility.

In 1997, just over 209,000 individuals received termination notices, and 141,000 ultimately were cut off from SSI and DI (Gresenz, Watkins, & Podus, 1998). For these individuals, termination has meant more than the loss of monthly income. They were no longer subject to the treatment mandate, no longer had contact with their representative payees, and no longer had medical coverage. While some may return to their states' GA rolls, others will clearly join the ranks of the homeless and destitute.

INVOLUNTARY COMMITMENT. In America, some of the mentally ill have been confined against their will in institutions of various kinds since the nineteenth century. As early as 1806, the State of Virginia passed a law that permitted the involuntary commitment of mental patients. Justification for depriving these individuals of their liberty stems from two sources: the police power of the state and the concept of *parens patriae*, or "state as parent." Under this principle, the state is responsible for the care of those who are unable to care for themselves. Commitment cannot, however, be undertaken lightly. U.S. law views the deprivation of liberty as one of the most serious applications of governmental power. A person who might be deprived of liberty has the right to due process, as outlined in the Fourteenth Amendment to the U.S. Constitution.

The due process rights of the mentally ill were not well established nationally until 1975, when the Supreme Court ruling in *O'Connor v. Donaldson* clarified the conditions under which a state might commit someone for psychiatric care. The court found that: "a State cannot constitutionally confine . . . a nondangerous individual who is capable of surviving safely in freedom by himself or with the help of willing and responsible family members of friends" (Stavis, 1995). This decision has been widely taken to establish dangerousness (imminent danger to self or others) as a standard for involuntary commitment. This strict standard has come under scrutiny lately, as public concern for the untreated mentally ill has risen.

The National Alliance for the Mentally Ill (and others, as discussed by Torrey, 1997) have argued that this standard is too strict, preventing the state from protecting the mentally ill under the principle of *parens patriae*. NAMI has suggested that civil commitment should be used in the case of people who are "gravely disabled," regardless of their dangerousness (Stavis, 1995).

While civil commitment uses state coercion to compel those with mental illness to accept inpatient treatment, several measures have been established to compel or encourage the mentally ill to comply with outpatient treatment regimens. These measures include involuntary outpatient commitment, conditional release, and conservatorship/guardianship.

MANDATORY OUTPATIENT TREATMENT. The use of Involuntary Outpatient Commitment (IOC), or court-ordered treatment, has also been endorsed by NAMI. IOC procedures have been established in 35 states, with North Carolina as the pioneer (Torrey & Kaplan, 1995). Under IOC, a court orders a patient to comply with a specific outpatient treatment program. Thus, for example, a patient might be required to take his or her medications and to participate in regular outpatient therapy. Proponents argue that IOC improves the quality of life for mental patients, protects the community from patients who fail to comply with their medication regimens, and reduces the amount of time patients spend in mental hospitals. Opponents note that IOC deprives patients of the right to refuse treatment, requires excessive state intrusion, and is subject to abuse.

National surveys of IOC suggest that its effectiveness varies. Perhaps the most significant barrier to successful implementation has been the reluctance of community mental health centers to assume responsibility for IOC patients, particularly those who are noncompliant (Torrey & Kaplan, 1995). Difficulties also stem from failure to specify what happens to patients who do not cooperate with their treatment plans, as well as concerns about liability and cost (Mechanic, 1999).

Conditional release and conservatorship/guardianship have also been used to encourage treatment compliance. Under conditional release programs, patients' release from mental hospitals is based on compliance with an outpatient treatment regimen. Unlike IOC, conditional release is administered by the hospital superintendent, rather than the court. Conservatorship and guardianship are widely used in California (Torrey & Kaplan, 1995). Under this procedure, a third party is appointed by the court. This conservator or guardian can legally compel the patient to comply with a treatment program, or involuntarily commit the patient for institutional care.

INSURANCE PARITY. Until the 1970s, most insurance companies covered mental illness on a par with physical illness. Over time, companies found that their mental health costs were rising nearly twice as fast as their health care expenses. Mental health treatment looked like a "bottomless pit," with unreliable diagnosis and potentially unlimited demand. Insurers began to reduce both the number of psychiatric visits covered and the amount paid for the visits, and to establish "lifetime caps" on mental health care. By 1993, only 2 percent of private insurers offered parity for outpatient mental health treatment, and 20 percent offered parity for inpatient care (LaBruzza & Mendez-Villarrubia, 1994).

As private insurers have reduced their coverage for mental health, families and patients have reported difficulty securing needed care. The National Alliance for the Mentally Ill (NAMI) has reported cases of individuals exhausting their lifetime mental health benefits in a single hospital stay. NAMI and others argued that differential coverage of mental health care represents a form of discrimination against people with mental illness. So, with support from professional organizations such as NASW, NAMI launched a campaign to advocate for "insurance parity."

"Insurance parity" involves the use of government regulation to require insurers to offer the same benefits for mental disorders as they would for physical disorders. Parity applies to annual or lifetime limits, service or dollar maximums, co-payments, and deductibles.

State legislatures took the lead in striving for mental health parity. As early as 1975, New Hampshire was one of the first states to mandate parity for certain diagnoses. By 2000, 22 states had passed mental health parity legislation. Half of these (11 states) provided parity coverage for all mental illnesses and substance abuse, while the other half offered parity only for severe, biologically-based mental illness (Levin et al., 1998).

In 1996, the Domenici-Wellstone mental illness parity provision was adopted and signed into law. The law represents a small step towards parity. It requires that a plan providing a mental health benefit apply equal annual and lifetime limits to mental and physical illnesses. For example, private insurers may no longer set a $1 million lifetime limit for cancer patients and a $50,000 lifetime limit for mental illness. The law applies only to businesses with 51 or more employees, so it covers only a small fraction of the U.S. labor force. It does not require that health plans cover or maintain coverage for mental illness. Substance abuse or drug addiction are excluded from the parity requirement. The law does not require parity with respect to visit limits or managed care provisions. It does not apply to insurance plans sold to individuals. Finally, if a plan demonstrates that compliance results in an increased cost of at least 1 percent, the plan may be exempted from the parity requirement.

Critics of mental health parity offer several arguments. Some take a libertarian position, arguing that parity requirements represent inappropriate intrusion of government regulation into the private market. More compelling arguments focus on the potential impact of parity on the uninsured. Some argue that by increasing premiums, parity will move health insurance out of reach of the working poor. Finally, opponents have argued that parity requirements may lead companies to drop mental health coverage altogether.

SUMMARY: MENTAL HEALTH INTERVENTIONS AND ISSUES

At the beginning of this chapter we met Rachel Sanders and discussed her experiences coping with serious mental illness. We found that several factors have contributed to Rachel's success. Her family has the resources and commitment to sustain her. While she has at times lost all of her financial resources, Rachel has always been able to rely on family support. Finally, Rachel has a strong mind, as well as insight into the nature of her illness and its treatment. Many people with serious mental illnesses are less fortunate. Lacking family, finances, and (at times) insight, they rely on what we have termed the "de facto mental health system."

After considering Rachel's life experiences, we examined the challenges of defining mental illness, suggesting that the *DSM-IV* represents "diagnosis by consensus"—our best attempt to derive a working typology of mental illness. We then examined the values and beliefs that influence public reactions to mental illness and public policies for the mentally ill. We traced the development of mental health interventions in the U.S., closing with a critical review of the deinstitutionalization of mental patients. In the final section, we examined contemporary realities of mental illness in the U.S., including the association between class and mental illness, the financing and organization of mental health services, policy issues affecting social workers in the mental health system, the risks of homelessness and violence, and emerging policy issues.

Mental health policies bring several social justice issues to the fore. The allocation of mental health professionals is clearly a matter of distributive justice. When market forces determine this allocation, those who are most vulnerable may be left to fend for themselves. Clearly American mental health policy must distinguish between the seriously mentally ill (people with schizophrenia, manic-depressive illness, and other brain-related disorders) from the "worried well" (those who suffer from "quality of life" and emotional problems). The former would clearly fall under the rubric of "mental illness," and policies and services for them should be labeled accordingly. The latter are concerned primarily with "mental health." Torrey and others argue that "mental health" is a private, not a governmental concern, and scarce public resources should be reserved for "mental illness."

Need-based allocation rules can be problematic, however. Those who are most in need of care may lack insight into their illness. The tension between the liberty rights of the mentally ill and the public interest in their treatment is manifest in struggles over involuntary commitment. Mental health practitioners and policy-makers struggle to sustain a just balance between these competing goals.

As Morrissey and Goldman (1986) observed, the history of mental health interventions in the United States is marked by cycles of reform. The first cycle came with the development of moral treatment, and saw the expansion of the mental asylum. The second, marked by a focus on prevention, was the mental hygiene movement. The third cycle, the community mental health movement, resulted in the deinstitutionalization of mental patients. As Morrissey and Goldman (1986) observed, "Each reform began with the promise that early treatment in the new setting would prevent the personal and societal problems associated with long-term mental disability" (p. 11). As each reform failed to fulfill its exaggerated promise, however, public disenchantment increased and Americans became less willing to finance programs for the mentally ill.

These reform cycles obfuscate a fundamental reality in the field of mental health care: the fact that some people simply cannot survive without institutional treatment. When public support for mental health programming is limited, these individuals become like flotsam drifting through the streets of American commerce until they reach a shore.

DISCUSSION TOPICS

1. Why does the National Alliance for the Mentally Ill's handout entitled *Facts About Mental Illness* say that "Despite media focus on the exceptions, individuals receiving treatment for schizophrenia are no more prone to violence than the general public." Is this statement true?

2. What mental health services are available to your state's Medicaid recipients? What is the average expenditure per Medicaid recipient? Is mental health a "carved out" service in your state?

3. Should insurance companies be required to cover all mental diagnoses, or should parity requirements be restricted to severe diseases with organic components, such as schizophrenia or major depression?

4. What steps could a private or public insurer take to reduce the "moral hazard" problem without denying needed treatment to the mentally ill?

5. Apply the five-question social justice framework presented in Chapter 1 to a proposal to provide income supports to alcohol and drug addicts. Once you have finished with question five, add a sixth question: "Why do I believe this is or is not fair?" Consider how your personal philosophy and experiences have influenced your answer to question five.

6. The 1996 decision to deny SSI and DI benefits to addicts reflects a belief that they should assume personal responsibility for their disability. Can you think of other situations where the cause of a disability might be used to deny coverage (i.e., to enforce personal, as opposed to collective, responsibility)?

SUGGESTED RESOURCES

Appelbaum, P. S. (1994). *Almost a Revolution: Mental Health Law and the Limits of Change*. New York: Oxford University Press.

Mechanic, D. (1999). *Mental Health and Social Policy: The Emergence of Managed Care*. Boston: Allyn & Bacon.

Torrey, E. F. (1997). *Out of the Shadows: Confronting America's Mental Illness Crisis*. New York: John Wiley & Sons, Inc.

www.bazelon.org — This site is maintained by the Judge David L. Bazelon Center for Mental Health law. It offers advocacy and reports in support of the civil rights of the mentally ill.

www.mentalhealth.org — Maintained by the Center for Mental Health Services (CMHS) in the U.S. Department of Health and Human Services, this site offers a source for government reports and has links to other mental health sites.

www.nami.org — This site is maintained by the National Alliance for the Mentally Ill (NAMI), the nation's foremost advocacy group for mentally ill persons and their families. It outlines NAMI positions on emerging issues in the field. A great source for information on upcoming federal legislation.

www.ness.sys.virginia.edu/macarthur—Maintained by the MacArthur Research Center on Mental Health and the Law, this site is a good source of background on developments in the area.

www.surgeongeneral.gov/library/mentalhealth—In 1999, the Surgeon General issued a lengthy report on mental illness. This is a good source of general information on mental health services, epidemiology of mental illness, and the costs of mental illness.

PART III

Vulnerable Populations

DISCRIMINATION AND OPPRESSION

Within the mosaic of American life, each individual is in some sense a minority. Some groups in the United States have, however, been singled out to endure discrimination and oppression that members of the racial and cultural majority have been spared. Both *discrimination* and *oppression* have become "hot button" terms that are frequently misunderstood.

In a broad sense, *discrimination* means "the quality or power of finely distinguishing," but defined more narrowly, it means "making a difference in treatment or favor on a basis other than individual merit." Discrimination assumes policy relevance when it is based on *categorical* rather than *individual* characteristics, and when the difference in treatment occurs within a limited range of activities specified by law. Under United States law, several categories of persons are "protected," and discrimination directed toward individuals because of their inclusion in these categories is prohibited. In addition to race and national origin, protected categories include gender, religion, age, and disability.

As our discussions in this part of the book will reveal, social policy in the United States has at times been a tool for discrimination and oppression of vulnerable populations. Only in the nation's recent history have we come to expect government not only to refrain from discrimination but to take steps to eliminate it. These changes have triggered a backlash marked by claims of "reverse discrimination."

Although the term *discrimination* has neutral or even positive connotations in some contexts, *oppression* is negative by definition. Adams, Bell, and Griffin (1997) offered a working definition: "Oppression fuses institutional and systemic discrimination, personal bias, bigotry, and social prejudice in a complex web of relationships and structures that saturate most aspects of life in our society" (p. 4). It constrains a person's opportunities and restricts development and self-determination. It creates a hierarchical society in which privileged groups benefit from the subordination of other groups. It robs society of the talent and energies of thousands of people, even as it restricts individual opportunities for fulfillment.

Oppression leaves a group with limited or no access to resources or benefits. This is the case, for example, when the basic needs of children are neglected, when women earn wages that are consistently lower than men, when elderly people's vulnerabilities are ignored, or when racial minorities, gays, and lesbians are denied employment opportunities.

Oppression may operate in subtle ways. It occurs when a high school counselor discourages an African-American student from taking a college preparatory class, or a girl cannot imagine herself becoming President of the United States. Oppression also takes more obvious forms, as when the nation's Congress, through a "Defense of Marriage Act," declares that gays and lesbians shall not have the right to marry, or a corporation routinely promotes white employees over qualified minority candidates.

In its most insidious form, oppression invades the hearts and minds of the oppressed, persuading them to limit their expectations and moderate their demands for a just society. When this "internalized oppression" is operating, we see members of oppressed groups perpetuating stereotypes and punishing or ignoring those who question the status quo. We see poor people blaming themselves for their need for assistance, Native Americans dismissing other Indians as lazy alcoholics, or gays rejecting other gays for behavior that marks them as "too queer."

In Part III we will explore the experiences and status of five vulnerable subgroups of the U.S. population: children (Chapter 7), women (Chapter 8), elderly persons (Chapter 9), members of racial minority groups (Chapter 10), and gays and lesbians (Chapter 11). In each chapter, we will focus in depth on the population under consideration, beginning with a case study, then examining societal norms and beliefs regarding the group. The development of relevant policies and services will be considered, as well as emerging issues and concerns. The material in these chapters will provide the background required for students to apply the social justice framework described in Chapter 1 to emerging policy issues affecting these populations.

Rᴇꜰᴇʀᴇɴᴄᴇ

Adams, M., Bell, L. A., & Griffin, P. (1997). *Teaching for Diversity and Social Justice: A Sourcebook*. New York: Routledge.

7

Children

When the voices of children are heard on the green
And laughing is heard on the hill,
My heart is at rest within my breast
And everything else is still.

WILLIAM BLAKE
"Nurse's Song"

Children have played widely divergent roles in American society, from menial laborers to conscientious students, from innocent victims to dangerous villains. Once considered the private property of their parents, children are now almost public property. The well-established principle of *parens patriae* ("state as parent") indicates the compelling interest of the government in the welfare of the nation's children. Indeed, many now feel that "it takes a village" to raise a child, and that parents should not be expected to shoulder the responsibility alone.

In this chapter we will consider social policies that affect children in the United States. Following a case study of Lorenzo, a 15-year-old Hispanic boy, we will examine the treatment of children in diverse contexts. First, we will outline child labor and adoption policies in the United States. In the next section, we will focus on the development and reform of U.S. educational policies. Next, the victimization of children through poverty and violence will be addressed in a section on children as victims. In the fourth and final section of this kind, we will explore policies that treat children as villains. The chapter closes with a discussion of the role of social workers in programs that serve the nation's children.

CASE STUDY ◆ LORENZO MARTINEZ

Lorenzo is a vivid child, with jet-black hair and sparkling dark eyes. He has seen more of life than most 15-year-olds, and often has trouble understanding or interpreting his experiences. Lorenzo lives with his paternal grandfather and his grandmother (whom he affectionately calls "Nini"), his 14-year-old sister, and her four-month-old baby.

Lorenzo's family is of Mexican descent, and his grandparents speak both Spanish and English. They celebrate traditional Mexican holidays and watch Spanish stations on television. Lorenzo considers himself Mexican, but does not believe he has ever faced discrimination because of his heritage.

Lorenzo is the oldest of six children born to Margaret and Garcia Martinez. His mother was 14 years old when he was born, and his father was 16 years old. Both parents have been convicted on drug charges, and over the course of several years all six of their children have been removed from their home. Lorenzo blames his mother for his parents' drug problems, saying that his father tried to quit from time to time, but his mother was deeply embedded in a drug culture and made her living by selling drugs. He remembers his parents' home as "always filled with drugs." He said he used to eat the seeds as his parents sat at the kitchen table sorting and bagging marijuana for sale. He remembers an uncle making him "take a hit" off a joint when he was four, but says he didn't begin smoking regularly until he was in the sixth grade.

Lorenzo has not lived with his parents since he was in the third grade, when he moved in with his paternal grandparents. He says he doesn't know why he was moved, "It's just always been that way." A few years after he moved in with them his grandparents became his legal guardians. Lorenzo thinks this measure was required by his school. Like all of his siblings, Lorenzo is only supposed to visit his mother under supervision. He says he feels "pretty close" to his mom, however, and he goes to see her whenever he wants, with or without supervision. But she still has problems. A few months ago she had a baby with another man. The baby was born with drugs in his system and was removed from her custody.

Lorenzo is outgoing and enjoys being with his friends. He moved frequently during elementary school, but always had friends to hang out with. Since his father had been involved in a gang, he "courted" (jumped) Lorenzo into the same gang. Lorenzo was courted when he was 13, but has known this gang since early childhood. His girlfriend is the sister of one of his homeboys, and Lorenzo sees the gang as a way of life. He says all of his cousins, nephews, and acquaintances are involved in the gang, and that one of his favorite things to do is, "hanging out with my homeboys" and smoking marijuana.

In 1996, Lorenzo's father was murdered. Lorenzo is not sure why, but believes it was not gang-related. His father was involved in the gang, but a policeman told Lorenzo the murder was drug-related. This distinction seems important to Lorenzo, who is still a gang member, but not involved in selling drugs. Lorenzo was close to his dad and misses him. He remembers that his dad sometimes worked odd jobs in construction and attended technical school for a while. His mom used to work at fast food restaurants sporadically.

In sixth grade Lorenzo came to the attention of the local law enforcement authorities. He says he used to "get blazed" daily with his friends, and began to commit crimes. He has been convicted for shoplifting, carrying a weapon in school (brass knuckles), possession of a stolen vehicle, and probation violations (dirty urine analysis, breaking curfew, running away). He has been in a youth detention center on three separate occasions for one week each time, has spent five days doing community service (shoveling snow from sidewalks) and narrowly escaped a youth work camp when his uncle pled in front of the judge to have him sent instead to an inpatient psychiatric facility. He spent three weeks there in the winter prior to our interview, followed by a week in an outpatient program.

Although Lorenzo feels that he has been treated reasonably by the juvenile justice system, his grandmother disagrees. She said, "The system is a joke . . . these kids that have just minor offenses are treated worse than animals." Upon reflection, Lorenzo decided that the police don't give gang kids a second chance. "Once the police connect you with a gang you are automatically guilty of a crime. They seem to think that kids can never change."

Lorenzo strongly believes that kids could be kept out of the juvenile justice system if they knew more about "how awful it is." He thinks elementary school children should be taken on field trips to youth detention facilities, and that guest speakers should show slides of children there. He feels pictures or videos of "the bad stuff" will work, "get the kids at their sad times, when they're crying. . . . When you're in that cell, that's when it really hits you."

At the time of our interview, Lorenzo was on probation. He felt responsible for his behavior, saying "Everything I did I chose . . . I had a good home, good teachers at school . . . the only problems I had were ones I created." He also resolved to "stay clean" and leave the gang. Of course, Lorenzo knew that leaving the gang would be difficult. He expected to be given a hard time and to eventually get "jumped out." He was enrolled in an alternative high school, and planned to finish school there, where he hoped it would be easier for him to stay away from gang activities and drugs. He planned to stay with his girlfriend, and had just begun a job in the fast food business. Lorenzo's long-term goal was to be a therapist: "Once I saw that cool office I decided I wanted to kick back and eat M&M's all day!" He thought he might be able to get a football scholarship and attend college.

DISCUSSION   Lorenzo's extended family is clearly a strong resource in his life. His placement with grandparents is an example of "kinship care," an emerging practice in the child welfare system. Whenever possible, children who enter state custody are placed with members of their extended families. Lorenzo's grandparents had the resources and were willing to take him in, and his uncle argued on his behalf in juvenile court. He describes his grandparents' place as "a good home," and his grandmother appears deeply concerned about his experiences with the juvenile justice system.

On the deficit side of his equation are Lorenzo's parents. Clearly a troubled couple, they combined teenage parenthood, a gang lifestyle, and serious drug abuse in one dysfunctional package. One can only speculate about Lorenzo's experiences during the eight years when he was in his parents' care. But it is striking to note that his experience with counseling seems to have led Lorenzo, not to attribute his situation to childhood trauma, but to assume personal responsibility for following in his parents' footsteps. Perhaps this perspective reflects the attitudes he has encountered in a juvenile justice system that is increasingly inclined to blame (and punish) children for their misbehavior.

Lorenzo's life has been touched by two major components of the nation's child welfare system. First, child protective services intervened on behalf of Lorenzo and his siblings to remove them from their parents' home. In Lorenzo's case, the preference for kinship care brought him to a stable, supportive environment—his grandparent's home. Lorenzo's situation illustrates a potential advantage of kinship care. It afforded him access to the support of other members of his extended family, such as the uncle who intervened on his behalf in court.

The second child welfare component Lorenzo encountered was the juvenile justice system. Children of color, like Lorenzo, are disproportionately represented in all phases of the juvenile justice system, but particularly in detention facilities. Both Lorenzo and his grandmother felt that the system treated children—particularly those in gangs—like criminals, and that the police did not believe in a child's capacity to change. This treatment may reflect a growing tendency on the part of the justice system to emphasize punishment over rehabilitation when dealing with serious youth offenders. It may also reflect increased fear, on the part of the public and the police, that criminal acts by youth gangs are spiraling out of control.

Why did Lorenzo join the gang? Was it for a sense of belonging? For structure and a role? For economic advancement? For access to drugs? Because of his father's involvement? Specialists in gang behavior have identified each of these factors as potential reasons for youth involvement in gangs. Children in gangs commit roughly twice the number of crimes (especially violent crimes) as similarly "at risk" children who do not belong to gangs. They are, therefore, more likely than others to be labeled "villains" and to be subjected to the worst punishment the system has available.

In Lorenzo we see multiple problems: substance abuse, child abuse or neglect, gang involvement, and criminal behavior. His future, like that of other children in similar situations, will depend on the capacity and willingness of his family and community to invest resources in him, as well as on his own ability to change.

CHANGING IDEAS OF CHILDHOOD: FROM "LITTLE MEN" TO "FUTURE CITIZENS"

Society's views on childhood have changed over the centuries. Perhaps the most well-known work on the topic was *Centuries of Childhood*, by Philippe Aries (1962). Our discussion in this section draws heavily from his comparative study of modern and medieval families.

There was no place for childhood in the medieval world, where artists simply portrayed children as small-scale adults. This perspective prevailed throughout most of the ancient world as well. Aries observed that "the realistic representation of children or the idealization of childhood, in grace and rounded charms, was confined to Greek art" (1962, p. 34). Aries suggests that this lack of distinctive representation indicates that "childhood was a period of transition which passed quickly and which was just as quickly forgotten" (1962, p. 34).

From the twelfth through the fourteenth centuries, artists began to portray children, first in religious art and later in secular art. Children were depicted mingling with adults in a variety of settings depicting work, play, and relaxation. Aries suggested that this mingling indicates that the world of children was not separated from that of adults.

Nor were children treasured as individuals. Observing that portraits of children were rare, Aries noted that "childhood was simply an unimportant phase of which there was no need to keep any record." High mortality rates mitigated against forming strong attachments to young children. "The general feeling was, and for a long time remained, that one had several children in order to keep just a few" (Aries, 1962, p. 38). The death of a child was considered "necessary wastage," and it was not until the eighteenth century that this idea disappeared from Western thought.

Aries dates the transformation in attitudes towards childhood to the seventeenth century, when children began to appear in portraits, and family portraits began to be organized around children. Further, children's dress changed in this century, from imitation of adult clothing, to a distinctive style. This change was particularly evident for boys, as Aries noted: "The idea of childhood profited the boys first of all, while the girls persisted much longer in the traditional way of life which confused them with the adults" (1962, p. 61). With this transformation came two distinct approaches to children. The first, practiced within the home by children's caregivers, involved "coddling" and "playing" with the children—enjoying their antics, and giving them pleasure. The second, encouraged by public authorities and moralists, took children more seriously and encouraged discipline and direction. Thus children became, not only sources of amusement,[1] but future citizens to be given direction and education. The family became a vehicle, not only for the transmission of names and estates, but for the education of children. The concern of public and religious authorities of this era represents the early manifestation of a principle called *parens patriae*, or "state as parent," which recognizes that the government has a significant interest in children's upbringing.

---

[1]As sources of amusement, pre-pubescent children were often caressed and teased about their sexual organs in a manner that would be unacceptable today. An example comes from the diary of a sixteenth-century physician who wrote of Louis XII's childhood. When the child was one year old, the physician reported that "He laughed uproariously when his nanny waggled his cock with her fingers." Later the child copied the trick. He called a page and ". . . shouted, 'Hey, there!' and pulled up his robe, showing him his cock" (Aries, 1962, p. 100).

In time, the family and schools removed children from adult society, creating childhood as we know it—a sort of hiatus, a time of preparation and (for some) a time of fun. Given its emotional, moral, and intellectual importance, the modern family has much greater demand for privacy than the medieval one, and the distinction between private and public in modern life is much more clear.

CHILDREN AS ASSETS

Throughout history, children have often been viewed as assets. The idea of children as economic assets prevailed during colonial and post-colonial times, when children performed labor for their families and employers. Policies in the United States have diminished this role through the regulation of child labor. But modern children still constitute assets, most notably as the lynchpin for family-building. In this context, adoption policies have been influential.

CHILDHOOD IN COLONIAL AMERICA

The Europeans who settled in North America during the seventeenth century brought with them European views of children as little adults. Indeed, childhood in colonial America brought few special protections from family or government. Because of the contrast between the attitudes we now hold and those that prevailed in colonial America, many people have the impression that children were treated as property during that era. It probably would be more accurate, however, to say that they were viewed as economic assets.[2] Children's labor contributed to the family's well-being, and their fathers or masters (in the case of indentured servants and apprentices) had the legal right to their custody and control. Mothers in this era had no legal rights to their children if the father was alive, and very limited rights after his death. Fathers and masters had legal control over children. They were also legally responsible for the education and moral upbringing of children in their custody. The rights afforded to children themselves were limited. Misbehavior was severely punished. Some children found their way into poorhouses, and others were "sold" as indentured servants (Mason, 1994).

State involvement in the lives of children was limited but not unheard of. Criminal charges brought against adults for child abuse were recorded as early as 1655 (Watkins, 1990). During that year, a master in Massachusetts was found guilty of maltreatment that resulted in the death of his 12-year-old apprentice. He was punished severely. Bremner (1970) reported on other cases in which children were removed from homes that had been deemed unsuitable. It was more common to bring criminal charges against masters to whom children were appren-

[2]The exception to this statement is children born into slavery, who were treated as property to an extent not permitted with biological children and indentured servants.

ticed than against parents. Parents were charged only in cases of grievous abuse, described by Thomas as "punishment that was grossly unreasonable in relation to the offense, when the parents inflicted cruel and merciless punishment, or when the punishment permanently injured the child" (Thomas, 1972, p. 304).

Colonial America had no established authority charged with protecting children. Those responsible for enforcing criminal laws responded to crimes against children. Similarly, there was no systematic procedure for identifying children who were abused or neglected. No laws required observers to report incidents of child maltreatment. Cases came to the attention of the authorities through accidents of fortune: a visit from an especially public-spirited neighbor, the arrival of a census-taker, or a complaint from a teacher. This lack of a structure or a system of child protection persisted until the establishment of the New York Society for the Prevention of Cruelty to Children during the nineteenth century (this topic will be discussed later in this chapter).

CHILD LABOR: A TARGET OF REFORM

During the latter decades of the nineteenth century, reformers began to focus on child labor. This focus represented one small aspect of a much broader phenomenon. Since medieval times children had worked to help support themselves and their families, performing chores on a farm or in a home. It was not until their work took them into factories that children's labor drew public attention. In these more public settings, employers hired the youngest possible children to work the longest possible hours. The result was public revulsion. Labor unions, the Consumer's Union, and eventually even industrial management, went on record as opposing the practice. Some laws were passed by the states, but there was growing demand for federal legislation.

The Prohibition Party included a plank in its platform opposing child labor in 1872. Later, the Republicans, Democrats, and Progressives all went on record calling for a federal law against the employment of children. Child Labor was an early focus of the Children's Bureau, which documented the conditions in factories where children worked. A child labor bill was introduced by Senator Beveridge, a Republican from Indiana, in 1906.

The idea of the federal government interfering with the operation of business (by telling factory owners they could not hire children) was extremely controversial. Ten years after the first child labor bill was introduced, the Keating-Owen Bill was approved by Congress in 1916 and signed by President Woodrow Wilson. The bill declared it a misdemeanor to employ children under the age of fourteen as factory workers. The same Supreme Justices who established the principle of "separate but equal" (*Plessy v. Ferguson*) declared this statute unconstitutional. They also invalidated a second law that attempted to use the taxing authority of Congress to regulate child labor.

These Supreme Court rulings effectively derailed federal attempts to reform child labor practices. In response, the movement turned to state legislatures.

Today, laws governing child labor have been passed by all the states. Most states prohibit employment of children under the age of 14. Between the ages of 14 and 16, children may be granted work permits contingent upon their continued school attendance. Children over 16 may be employed in most states without restrictions.

It is important to note that these state-level reforms have taken place in the context of diminished demand for child labor. The role of children as economic assets to their families has largely been curtailed. In another sense, however, children continue to be viewed as assets. Many adults derive satisfaction and pleasure from being a mother or father, taking the responsibility for nurturing and guiding sons and daughters. Most often, children are born to the parents who raise them. In many cases, however, families are built or expanded through adoption. In the following sections, we will consider policies that influence the process of building families through adoption.

BUILDING FAMILIES THROUGH ADOPTION

Once stigmatized as the foundation of "abnormal" families, adoption has become widely accepted, both as a method for providing loving homes to needy children and as an approach to creating or expanding families. National policy controversies have erupted around two types of adoptions, however: those in which the children and adoptive parents are from different racial backgrounds, and those in which the parents are gay or lesbian.

TRANSRACIAL ADOPTION. Adoption across racial lines has become increasingly common in the last decade. In 1996, 11,340 children born outside of the United States were adopted by Americans (U.S. Department of State, 1998). Many of these adoptions were transracial, in that most of the children came into Caucasian homes from China, Korea, or Vietnam. Adoption of African-American children by white parents was rare prior to the 1964 Civil Rights Act. These adoptions increased to a peak in 1971, when 2,574 African-American children were adopted by white parents (Cox, 1994).

During the following year, the National Association of Black Social Workers (NABSW) expressed vehement opposition to the growing practice. They saw it as "an insidious scheme for depriving the black community of its most valuable resources: its children" (Day, 1979). Three years later, the number of transracial adoptions of African-American children dropped to 831 (Cox, 1994). Committed to the needs of the black community, NABSW argued that adoption agencies, both public and private, applied white, middle-class norms in evaluating prospective adoptive parents. As a result, they argued, African-American families were denied the opportunity to adopt, and African-American children were placed in white homes.

Two decades later, despite the fact that African-American families adopt at a rate 4.5 times greater than white families, the number of African-American children available for adoption continues to exceed the number of African-American families available as potential adoptive placements. In 1998, at least 110,000 foster children in the United States were waiting for adoption. Most (59 percent) were African-American (Maza, 1998). During the 1990s a consensus formed among child welfare professionals that agency policies and preferences against transracial adoption were denying African-American children permanent homes.

In 1994, President Clinton signed the Multi-Ethnic Placement Act (PL 103-382). The law is designed to "prevent discrimination in the placement of children in foster care and adoption on the basis of race, color, or national origin, to decrease the time children wait to be adopted, and to ensure agency recruitment of a pool of foster and adoptive parents who reflect the racial and ethnic diversity of the children available for adoption" (Pecora et al., 2000, p. 41). It established penalties for states that did not comply. Unfortunately, federal funds are not available to assist in recruiting minority families, either as foster or adoptive parents, and significant barriers persist. Among them is the lack of minority professionals within the child welfare system, the high proportion of single, low-income families within the African-American community, rigid requirements and fees, and pervasive institutional racism (Crumbley, 1999).

In 1994 (the year that MEPA passed), NABSW revised its position on transracial adoption:

> We believe that too many children are placed in foster care unnecessarily and that often they remain in foster care too long. . . . When all reasonable efforts have been made to keep the child and family together, and when family preservation, family reunification, and relative placement have failed, then, and only then, should we seek adoption. Adoption should be within the same race. Transracial adoption should only occur after clearly documented evidence of unsuccessful same-race adoption (Crumbley, 1999, p. 96).

The NABSW does not accept the argument that suitable adoptive families are not available in the African-American community. They argue that when an agency makes special efforts to recruit African-American families, same-race placement of African-American children can be as high as 94 percent (NABSW, 1994). As of 1998, however, 27 percent of African-American children who were adopted from foster care were placed in transracial situations (Crumbley, 1999).

ADOPTION BY GAYS AND LESBIANS. With the exception of the few states whose statutes specifically forbid the practice (Florida, Mississippi, and Utah in 2001), child welfare authorities throughout the nation confront thorny issues as they consider gays and lesbians as prospective adoptive parents. Ann Sullivan (1995) suggested that policy in this area be informed by two major trends in adoption. The first is the trend towards more inclusive adoption policies. Whereas several years ago only married Caucasians between 21 and 35 years of age who had no biological offspring were considered suitable adoptive parents, the opportunity to adopt children gradually has been extended to include unmarried women and men, people of color, disabled persons, older individuals, and families with children. In each case, adoptions have been controversial, with opponents questioning the suitability of the adoptive parents. The second trend is the growing number of children in the United States who are currently in foster care and eligible for adoption. In 1995, Sullivan suggested that these children numbered over 100,000.

Adoption by gay and lesbian persons runs counter to several myths: the idea that homosexual parents are likely to molest children sexually, that children adopted by homosexuals will be pressured to become homosexual, and that the children will be living in "immoral" environments. There is no empirical literature to support any of these claims. Indeed, perpetrators of child sexual abuse are predominantly heterosexual, and there is no evidence that the sexual orientation of a child is determined by that of his or her parent(s). Other opponents of gay/lesbian adoptions argue that the children will be teased by their peers from more traditional families due to the stigma attached to homosexuality. Of course, proponents of this argument can usually find anecdotal evidence of teasing or rejection by peers. Nonetheless, the social science literature shows no evidence of negative developmental effects. Indeed, the intolerance reflected in harassment of children in non-traditional homes may reflect dysfunction on the part of the *harassers*, rather than their victims.

The controversy that arises over transracial and gay/lesbian adoptions illustrates the powerful role ideology and values can play in social policy debates. Both supporters and opponents of these less-traditional approaches to family foundation can cite studies or cases in support of their positions. Of course, because it is not possible to randomly assign children to adoptive homes, it is impossible for social science to offer a definitive answer regarding the effects of transracial and gay/lesbian adoptions. As a result, these debates are slow to resolve—depending on political compromises and changing views about what constitutes a good family.

CHILDREN AS STUDENTS[3]

Philippe Aries (1962) discussed the establishment of schools as a force that defined and extended childhood for Western Europeans during the twelfth through seventeenth centuries. Girls were excluded from schools, but boys of various ages and classes were allowed to participate. Less formal and structured than modern schools, these institutions provided basic literacy skills and a smattering of Latin over periods that might extend as long as four or five years. The most well established were religious schools designed to prepare young boys for clerical careers. Another significant educational institution, dating back to the medieval period, was apprenticeship. Many boys learned a craft through a lengthy

---

[3]Most of the material in this section is drawn from H. G. Good's seminal work *A History of American Education*.

period of apprenticeship under a master. Indeed, in 1562, England passed "The Statute of Artificers," designed to force poor children into apprenticeships. This statute represented an early poverty prevention policy designed to reduce the children's need for public assistance during adulthood.

European immigrants brought the practice of apprenticeship to colonial America as a means of replenishing the skilled labor force. The first compulsory education law in colonial America involved apprenticeship. It was passed in 1642 by the Massachusetts Bay Colony. The Act required that the selectmen of each town attend to the "calling and employment of children" and "especially of their ability to read and understand the principles of religion and the capital laws of the country" (Good, 1962, p. 28). This education was to take place, not in schools, but as part of apprenticeship in homes and shops.[4] Schools were established in the colonies in a haphazard fashion that reflected the many other demands placed on communities. They operated irregularly, with terms seldom lasting more than three months. Curriculum was based on whatever reading and writing materials were at hand.

The Massachusetts Bay Colony passed an act in 1647 that attempted to establish educational consistency throughout the colony. The Act required that towns with at least fifty families maintain an elementary school (then called a "dame" school, because it was operated by a woman, often a widow). Towns numbering at least 100 families were required to provide a secondary school. Towns that failed to comply with the act were fined. Evidently some towns found it easier to pay the fine than to establish a school (Good, 1962). Similar laws eventually spread throughout the colonies. As towns grew, they were divided into school districts, each with its own governing board and elementary school. The practice of establishing school districts continues to this day.

Many of the great thinkers of revolutionary America (Thomas Jefferson, Benjamin Rush, Samuel Knox, and Noah Webster) viewed education as a fundamentally political endeavor. Education could secure liberty and democracy and set the stage for the nation's economic expansion. As Thomas Jefferson said of education's role:

> The object is to bring into action that mass of talents which lies buried in poverty in every county for want of means of development, and thus give activity to a mass of mind, which in proportion to our population, shall be the double or treble of what it is in most countries (Jefferson, 1817, pp. 94–95).

Education would help unify the states into a nation, but there was much debate over the form such education should take. Should it be centralized at the federal level or treated as a local endeavor?

The Tenth Amendment to the Constitution left education to the states and discouraged federal interference.[5] As a result, the nation's earliest statutes involv-

---

[4]Good argues that this law represented the beginnings of public involvement in children's upbringing in the New World.

[5]This does not prevent Congress from authorizing funds for educational endeavors.

ing education are found in state constitutions. Six of the new states included educational provisions in their constitutions. The most detailed was in Section 44 of the constitution of the state of Pennsylvania:

> A school or schools shall be established in every county by the legislature, for the convenient instruction of youth with such salaries to the masters, paid by the public, as may enable them to instruct youth at low prices; and all useful learning shall be duly encouraged and promoted in one or more Universities (Good, 1962, p. 88).

In this early stage of the nation's history, state efforts could supplement private schools, and some states provided free education for the poor. The notion of universal, free public education had not yet caught hold, however.

Free and universal public education was a uniquely American invention. It was more compatible with the nation's democratic ideals than the class-based systems that were in place in England and Europe. Because there was no model to follow, the establishment of the American school system was neither quick nor smooth. Indeed, during the nation's first few decades, there was no organized constituency who supported the concept.

The unionization of factory workers created the nation's first organized force for free public education. In 1828 (following the depression of 1819) the Workingmen's Party was organized in New York and Philadelphia. In Philadelphia, the party's initial advocacy efforts focused on the establishment of independent newspapers, libraries, and public lectures and debates. In 1829 the organization issued a report that addressed public education. It rejected the idea of providing free instruction only to the poor, and argued for free and universal elementary schools "in which teaching was not to be restricted to 'words and figures' but would also attempt to form rational self-governing character" (Good, 1962, p. 120). The report proposed the establishment of local school boards that were elected and answered to the people they served. The Workingmen's Party in New York had a socialist wing, and in 1825 party members proposed the establishment of free public boarding schools for all children as a vehicle for eliminating class differences in the new republic. Ultimately, the movement for public education expanded beyond the laboring classes to include advocates from diverse walks of life.

Opposition to public education came primarily from within the privileged classes. Some argued that apprenticeship made universal education both impossible and unnecessary. Others suggested that the laboring classes should work so that the rich could cultivate their minds. Many objected to the use of taxes to finance schools, seeing it as "an arbitrary division of the property of the rich with the poor" (Good, 1962, p. 122). Public schools, it was also argued, would be corrupt and inefficient.

Despite opposition, the public education movement grew, and after 1830 several states had expanded public education and retreated from their funding of private schools. Several cities (Philadelphia, Baltimore, and Cincinnati, for example) established public schools through special legislation passed prior to such action by the states. Eventually, however, state constitutions were amended (or established in newer states) to direct legislatures as the Illinois document does: "to provide for a thorough and efficient system of free schools whereby all the children of this State may receive a good common school education" (Good, 1962, p. 143).

States' public educational systems developed individually, in a piecemeal fashion. As a result there was considerable variation. The most striking variation involved the segregation of African-American children and Caucasian children in Southern educational systems (to be discussed later in this chapter). Over time, such regional differences have blurred, and a national pattern of public education has emerged (Good, 1962).

COMPULSORY ATTENDANCE LAWS

One aspect of the national pattern that we now take for granted is compulsory attendance. Massachusetts passed the first such law in 1852, requiring that children between the ages of eight and fourteen years attend school for 12 weeks each year. The law permitted exceptions for children of poor families, those who were ill, and those who were being "otherwise educated." Children were also excused from the 12-week requirement if local schools were not open that long. The law called for fines if parents did not comply, but punitive action was seldom taken. It was not until 1900 that compulsory attendance laws were enacted in a majority (32) of the states, and it was not until 1920 that all states required school attendance. Thus, it took 68 years for the movement for compulsory schooling to reach all of the 48 contiguous states.

Compulsory education was controversial for two reasons. First, many objected to the government interfering with the authority of parents. Several attendance laws were subjected to constitutional challenges. They were upheld consistently, with arguments reflecting the view that the state had a compelling interest in the education of children. The second objection was that these laws prevented children from working in industrial and farm settings, at a time when many parents relied on the labor of children to support their families.

Nonetheless, by 1918 all states had passed statutes requiring school attendance. Over subsequent years these laws have expanded the duration of required schooling and become more similar. Today most states require approximately nine months of regular attendance annually for children up to the age of 16.

AN EXPANDED FEDERAL PRESENCE

During the twentieth century the federal government began to exert more influence on public education. Federal involvement included the forced desegregation of Southern schools, subsidized higher education for veterans, and other financial supports for schools, such as the National School Lunch Program. Federal education programs are typically administered or supervised by the Department of Education, which was established by Congress in 1867 to provide educational information to state and local education authorities. Congress later reduced annual appropriations for the Department and downgraded it to an "Office of Education," later a "Bureau of Education" within the Department of the Interior. There it remained until 1929, when Herbert Hoover's National Advisory Committee on Education recommended the establishment of a Cabinet-level Department of Education.

DESEGREGATION. Late in the nineteenth century, after Reconstruction, seventeen southern states required that black and white children attend separate schools. Four other states permitted districts to engage in segregation. The U.S. Supreme Court supported the practice in an 1896 case (*Plessy v. Ferguson*). The case did not directly involve school segregation, referring instead to a Louisiana law that required separate railroad cars for African-Americans. The Court's opinion also involved the schools, however, stating that "separate and equal" facilities did "not necessarily imply the inferiority of either race," and cited "separate schools for white and colored children" as an illustration of the principle (Good, 1962, p. 577). With this judicial blessing, districts in the South and the North developed racially segregated schools.

In time it became abundantly clear that the separate schools for African-American and white children were hardly equal. African-American teachers were poorly paid, facilities were inadequate, and children's educational attainment suffered accordingly. On May 17, 1954, in its decision on *Brown v. Board of Education*, the Supreme Court reversed its earlier position, declaring that racial segregation in public education was unconstitutional. The court said, "We conclude that in the field of education the doctrine of 'separate but equal' has no place. Separate educational facilities are inherently unequal . . ." and concluded that segregation violated the equal protection guarantees provided by the Fourteenth Amendment.

The nation's progress toward school desegregation has been halting and remains incomplete. Twelve years after the Supreme Court decision, the U.S. Office of Education concluded that "the great majority of American children attend schools that are largely segregated—that is, almost all of their fellow students are of the same racial background as they are" (U.S. Commission on Civil Rights, 1967, p. 2). Decades later, Jonathan Kozol (1991) documented the abysmal conditions within inner-city schools that served children of color. Citizens' (sometimes violent) opposition to the court's decision has been well documented (see Bouma & Hoffman, 1968; Rubin, 1972; Damerell, 1968; Crain, 1968). A continuing challenge for U.S. educators has been the effort to ensure equal access to education for children of all races. The Head Start program represents an early-intervention approach to reducing inequality in American education.

HEAD START. One of the most significant federal investments in education has been Head Start. Established in 1965 to provide a comprehensive child development program for preschool children from low-income families, Head Start is managed by the Administration on Children and Families, within the U.S. Department of Health and Human Services. The program operates by extending grants to nonprofit and community organizations that administer the individual programs. In 1996, a total of 1,440 grantees provided Head Start services. Eligibility requirements vary, but the vast majority of spaces are reserved for chil-

FIGURE 7.1 Head Start Enrollment and Appropriation History

Fiscal Year	Enrollment	Congressional Appropriation
1966	733,000	$ 198,900,000
1967	681,400	349,200,000
1968	693,900	316,200,000
1969	663,600	333,900,000
1970	477,400	325,700,000
1971	397,500	360,000,000
1972	379,000	376,300,000
1973	379,000	400,700,000
1974	352,800	403,900,000
1975	349,000	403,900,000
1976	349,000	441,000,000
1977	333,000	475,000,000
1978	391,400	625,000,000
1979	387,500	680,000,000
1980	376,300	735,000,000
1981	387,300	818,700,000
1982	395,800	911,700,000
1983	414,950	912,000,000
1984	442,140	995,750,000
1985	452,080	1,075,059,000
1986	451,732	1,040,315,000
1987	446,523	1,130,542,000
1988	448,464	1,206,324,000
1989	450,970	1,235,000,000
1990	540,930	1,552,000,000
1991	583,471	1,951,800,000
1992	621,078	2,201,800,000
1993	713,903	2,776,286,000
1994	740,493	3,325,728,000
1995	750,696	3,534,128,000
1996	752,077	3,569,329,000
1997	793,809	3,980,546,000
1998	822,316	4,347,433,000
1999	826,016	4,658,151,000
2000	857,664	5,267,000,000
2001	n/a	6,199,812,000

Source: Administration for Children and Youth, DHHS, *Head Start 2001 Fact Sheet*—http://www2.acf.dhhs.gov/programs/hsb/about/fact2001/htm.

dren who meet federal income guidelines. Programs also vary in the types of services they offer. Head Start programs have some required components, including educational and social services for families. Most establish links with social service providers serving low-income families in their communities. Parent involvement is a hallmark of Head Start programs.

Head Start is an extremely popular program, and its budget has grown steadily, from $96.4 million in 1965 to its 1999 level of $4.44 billion (see Figure 7.1). Despite this growth, demand for the program continues to exceed the supply of available slots. In 1997, Head Start programs served approximately 800,000 children between the ages of three and five. Evaluation of the program has traditionally focused on the cognitive and academic achievements of the children involved. In some cases, results on these measures have been disappointing. More recently, studies of Head Start have considered its broader impact on the families and communities involved.

MODERN EDUCATIONAL REFORMS

Recent educational reforms have addressed two aspects of public education in the United States: school financing and school choice.

SCHOOL FINANCING. Throughout their history, American public elementary and secondary schools have been financed through local and state appropriations. Federal contributions typically represent only a small fraction of state budgets. State money comes from either general tax revenues or property taxes. The U.S. Department of Education reported that total funding for K-12 public education in the United States in 1999 was more than $300 billion, or 4 percent of the Gross National Product (less than a third of the amount that the nation spends on health care, a topic that was discussed in Chapter 5). Most of that amount comes from a combination of state funds (about 45 percent) and local taxes (another 45 percent). About 7 percent comes from federal sources, and 2.7 percent from private sources. Lotteries provide 2 to 7 percent of the states' contributions (Johnson, 1999).

Inequality has been a hallmark of school financing in the United States. In his landmark work, *Savage Inequalities*, Jonathan Kozol (1991) noted "a certain grim aesthetic in the almost perfect upward scaling of expenditures from poorest of the poor to richest of the rich within the New York City area: $5,590 for the children of the Bronx and Harlem, $6,340 for the non-white kids of Roosevelt, $6,400 for the black kids of Mount Vernon, $7,400 for the slightly better-off community of Yonkers, over $11,000 for the very lucky children of Manhasset, Jericho and Great Neck" (pp. 122–123).

The nation's approach to educational funding supports this inequality. The "foundation program" was introduced in the early 1920s to balance local control with state support for education. Under this approach, the initial funds required to operate public schools are drawn from a local tax based on the value of homes and businesses within the district. In affluent districts this amount is sufficient to meet the schools' needs. In less affluent districts, where the tax rate is the same, lower property values result in less revenue. State funds are then allocated to bring financial resources of the poorer districts up to the "foundation" level—a level that, in theory, is roughly equal to the amount used in the wealthy districts. Of course, the needs of poorer districts are often greater, as children experience higher rates of family dysfunction and community stress. Needs aside, poorer districts receive less funding because states set the "foundation level" to provide a bare minimum, not to establish an adequate educational foundation.

Kozol (1991) vividly documented the educational minimum provided for children in poor districts:

> Christopher approaches me at the end of class. The room is too hot. His skin looks warm and his black hair is damp. "Write this down. You asked a question about Martin Luther King. I'm going to say something. All that stuff about the dream means nothing to the kids I know in East St. Louis. So far as they're concerned, he died in vain. He was famous and he lived and gave his speeches and he died and now he's gone . . . don't tell students in this school about the dream. Go and look into a toilet here if you would like to know what life is like for students in this city." . . . I do as Christopher asked . . . Four of the six toilets do not work. The toilet stalls, which are eaten away by red and brown corrosion, have no doors. The toilets have no seats. One has a rotted wooden stump. There are no paper towels and no soap. Near the door there is a loop of wire with an empty toilet-paper roll (p. 36).

Disparities in school finance have resulted in lawsuits against states. One of the earliest was filed in Texas in 1968. In a class action suit (*Rodriquez v. San Antonio Independent School District*), plaintiffs charged that the unequal financing of education violated the equal protection clause of the U.S. Constitution. After years of litigation, the state was forced to change its method of school financing. Similar outcomes have been observed throughout the nation. Since 1972, more than 40 school finance cases have been heard in state Supreme Courts (Center for Education Reform, 1999).

LOTTERIES. No doubt, nineteenth-century educational reformers would be astonished by the current relationship between gambling and the public schools. In 1964, New Hampshire became the first state in the union to establish a state lottery. Since then, 36 more states and the District of Columbia have established lotteries (NASPL, 1999). Most states devote part of their lottery proceeds to education. In Georgia, lotteries support college funds called "Hope" scholarships. The practice of allocating some proceeds to education has increased public support for the lottery.

In no case does lottery funding provide a substantial portion of the educational budget. In California, less than 2 percent of the 1998 budget for public schools was drawn from the lottery (Education Data Partnership, 2001). As the government has moved into the gambling business, social workers and other helping professionals have become aware of gambling's toll. Compulsive gamblers have been compared to alcoholics in their capacity to ignore the costs of their problem behavior. Apart from the growing problem of compulsive gambling, professionals are concerned that those who participate in the lottery (the vast majority of whom lose money) come primarily from poor and working class backgrounds. Thus, the lottery is a regressive way to finance public education.

SCHOOL CHOICE: TUITION VOUCHERS AND CHARTER SCHOOLS. Traditionally, children in the United States have been assigned to the schools serving their neighborhoods. School choice reforms give parents the opportunity to select the schools that their children will attend. At its most basic level, school choice permits parents to send their children to any public school within the state. More complex and controversial school choice reforms include tuition vouchers and charter schools.

Under existing tuition voucher programs, the state or local school district provides parents with a portion of the educational funding allotted to their children and allows them to use these funds to enroll their children in the school of their choice. In some states, tuition vouchers can be used only for secular schools, while in other jurisdictions parents may use the vouchers to send their children to religious schools.[6] Voucher programs have been vigorously opposed by teachers' unions at local and federal levels. Opponents of the programs argue that they damage public schools by diverting needed funds and by draining away the most academically motivated students. As a result, they argue, schools in poorer districts will deteriorate even further.

Proponents argue that giving parents in low-income areas the opportunity to send their children to schools outside their neighborhoods equalizes educational opportunities and gives neighborhood schools the motivation to improve. School choice is the educational reform of preference for libertarians, most notably Milton Friedman (Friedman, 1955). According to Friedman, "A society that takes freedom of the individual, or more realistically the family, as its ultimate objective, seeks to further this objective by relying primarily on voluntary exchange among individuals for the organization of economic activity" (Friedman, p. 1). Libertarians argue that parents should be given vouchers and allowed to use them to purchase an education in any licensed school, public or private.

Whereas tuition vouchers address the "demand" side of the education equation, enabling parents to shop for schools, charter schools address the "supply" side. State legislatures provide for the establishment of special schools through a charter or contract that sets specific academic goals that must be met. These schools receive an allotment from the school district for students who choose to attend. Charter schools are, therefore, public schools. Exempt from district cur-

---

[6]The use of public funds to send children to religious schools has been subject to several court challenges. In a recent (1998) case, the Wisconsin Supreme Court ruled in favor of the practice.

riculum requirements and governance, they are managed by a charter board. The charter school concept was enthusiastically endorsed by the Clinton administration. President Clinton called for the establishment of 3,000 charter schools by 2000. Of course, the per-pupil allotment for charter schools is either the same amount as the established public schools or a lesser amount, and charter schools often face large start-up expenses to acquire buildings and purchase equipment. Therefore, their financial situation may be unstable. Opponents of charter schools argue that they are not feasible alternatives for low-income families, and that they siphon affluent and academically motivated students away from the traditional public schools.

CHILDREN AS VICTIMS

Children have probably been victimized by adults since the dawn of humankind, and non-perpetrating adults have ignored or been appalled by the neglect and abuse of children. The public response to child victimization in the United States has been marked by episodes of high interest, followed by extended periods of indifference or inattention. Children have been victims of both poverty and violence. In this section, we will first consider the victimization of children through poverty, then examine violence against children.

POVERTY AND CHILDREN, PAST AND PRESENT

In colonial times, children who were impoverished through parental death or other circumstances often were sold as indentured servants. In theory, this practice was designed to teach children a trade or skill, but more often indentured servants were assigned menial tasks and functioned essentially as slaves until they reached the age of release (21 or 24 for boys; 18 for girls). During indenture parents lost their custody rights, so children were sold only under dire circumstances. During the nineteenth century, institutional alternatives were established in major cities. Instead of being indentured, impoverished children were sent to orphanages, almshouses, or poorhouses.

A harbinger of change came in 1909, when James E. West, a friend of President Theodore Roosevelt who had been raised in an orphanage, persuaded the President to convene a "Conference on the Care of Dependent Children." The conference brought the needs of these children to national attention, setting the stage for the development of a public child-welfare system (Trattner, 1989). Its keynote statement proclaimed, "Home life is the highest and finest product of civilization . . . children should not be deprived of it except for urgent and compelling reasons" (Trattner, 1989, p. 194). The conference led to a reduced emphasis on institutionalization and an increased use of adoption and foster homes for children in need. It also was the first in a series of conferences of its kind, held every ten years until 1981, when it was canceled by the Reagan administration.

The U.S. Children's Bureau was established in 1912, three years after the first White House Conference on Children, despite fierce opposition from business interests who feared it would signal the end of child labor. They were prescient. Child labor eventually would become a significant issue for the Children's Bureau.

Julia Lathrop, a former Hull House resident and member of the Illinois State Board of Charities, took over as director of the agency. She chose infant mortality as the agency's initial focus. It seemed to be a relatively non-controversial issue. After all, if the federal government spent $1.25 million dollars a year for the Bureau of Animal Husbandry, shouldn't it devote some effort to care for the nation's children?

The matter quickly became controversial, however. In 1918, based on research by the Children's Bureau, Jeanette Rankin (the first woman to serve in the U.S. Congress) introduced the Sheppard-Towner Bill. The bill called for the federal government to offer grants-in-aid to states that would provide health care and education to disadvantaged mothers. Opponents accused Ms. Lathrop of being part of the recent Bolshevik Revolution and charged that the state was taking over both the raising and the medical care of children. Medical societies attacked the bill, its sponsor, and the staff of the Children's Bureau. In one of the debate's more vitriolic statements, Senator Thomas Reed of Missouri argued that if the bill passed, "female celibates would instruct mothers on how to bring up their babies" (Trattner, 1989, p. 199). Despite these views, after three years of debate and the ratification of the Nineteenth Amendment granting women the right to vote, the bill passed in 1921 and was signed by President Warren G. Harding.

Under its mandate, between 1921 and 1929 nearly 3,000 maternal and child health centers were established in 45 states (Trattner, 1989, p. 199). State health departments were strengthened, and infant and maternal mortality rates dropped significantly. Despite the Act's effectiveness, Congress refused to renew funding in 1929, bowing to the energetic opposition of both medical professionals and the new president, Herbert Hoover. Later, Title V of the 1939 Social Security Act would again establish federal grants-in-aid that enabled the Children's Bureau to resume its work in maternal and child health. This program operates today under the auspices of the Department of Health and Human Services.

Today, children in the United States face a higher risk of poverty than any other age group. Whereas in 2000 the general poverty rate was 11.3 percent, the rate for children was 16.2 percent, and for young children (those under six) the probability of living in poverty was 18 percent. Children of color, and those living in single-parent households, face even higher risks of poverty. For example, over half (54 percent) of African-American children under six were living in poverty (Center on Budget and Policy Priorities, 2001).

Modern policies regarding child poverty in the United States reveal a deep ambivalence. On the one hand, the notion of children suffering is unacceptable to most adults. Thus, the development of educational, health, and even social services for children in poverty seldom encounters serious opposition. On the other hand, the nation has long been inclined to blame adults for their indigence.

Most children in poverty are intimately linked to an adult in poverty. Therein lies the ambivalence that fuels controversies regarding income maintenance programs. If what it takes to move a child out of poverty is financial assistance to a member of the undeserving poor, the nation balks.

This ambivalence is evident in the history of income maintenance programs funded under the Social Security Act. Initially, Title IV of the act established a federal-state grant-in-aid program called Aid to Dependent Children (ADC). In 1962, the name of the program was changed to Aid to Families with Dependent Children (AFDC). This change reflected growing awareness of the role of the family in children's lives, and it also underscored the reality that aid was provided to families, not directly to children themselves. In 1996, the federal entitlement provided under AFDC was converted to a block grant called Temporary Assistance to Needy Families (TANF). As discussed in Chapter 4, the name change is the tip of the iceberg of the changes initiated by the TANF program. Nonetheless, it is important to note that the word "children" has, for the first time since 1935, been eliminated from the name of the income maintenance provision of the Social Security Act.

The implications of poverty for children are far-reaching. Children in low-income families face higher health risks because of the substandard quality of their housing and their limited access to health care. Their educational opportunities are also severely truncated. Finally, children in households with poverty-level incomes experience significantly higher rates of violence than those living in more affluent settings.

Vɪᴏʟᴇɴᴄᴇ Aɢᴀɪɴsᴛ Cʜɪʟᴅʀᴇɴ, Pᴀsᴛ ᴀɴᴅ Pʀᴇsᴇɴᴛ

The latter part of the nineteenth century was a time of outcry for public intervention in cases of child abuse and gross neglect. In 1875, the case of "Mary Ellen" brought child abuse to public attention and led to the creation of the New York Society for the Prevention of Cruelty to Children (NYSPCC). The case has become the stuff of myth, based on the false belief that in the absence of laws to protect children, those designed to protect animals were applied to protect a child. This myth has been repeated in several social work texts (i.e., DiNitto, 1995; Kadushin, 1974). Yet, as Watkins (1990) demonstrated, laws to protect children were on the books as early as the seventeenth century. What was lacking was an entity to assume responsibility for their enforcement. The NYSPCC became that entity, and during the first 20 years of its existence it intervened in over 230,000 cases, with enough impact to provoke criticism of its aggressive efforts to protect and rescue abused and neglected children.

Sallie Watkins (1990) presented the facts in the Mary Ellen case. In 1864, the infant was left with the Department of Charities by a woman who claimed to have no knowledge of how to reach her parents. She was indentured to a family at the age of 18 months. Mary Connolly was her mistress and her abuser. In 1873, Mrs. Etta Wheeler was visiting in poor neighborhoods when she heard complaints about a child being horribly abused. She posed as a census taker and investigated the situation in December 1873. Appalled by the child's condition, Mrs. Wheeler sought help from police and several charitable organizations before finding an ally in Mr. Henry Bergh, President of the New York Society for the Prevention of Cruelty to Animals. Mr. Bergh intervened in the case as a private citizen, not as a representative of the NYSPCA. The laws he invoked to remove Mary Ellen were those designed to protect people in custody. A judge issued a special warrant that led to Mary Ellen's removal from the home and the subsequent trial of her guardian, Mrs. Connolly. When searches for her parents proved unsuccessful, Mary Ellen was placed in the care of Mrs. Wheeler. She married at the age of 24, had two children, and lived into her 80s. Her abuser, Mrs. Connolly, was sent to a penitentiary for one year. Mary Ellen's experiences were important, not because they changed the laws regarding abuse of children, but because they raised public awareness of the problem and led to the establishment of the NYSPCC.

The NYSPCC was the first organization of its kind in the world, and the beginning of an "anti-cruelty" movement that spread throughout the U.S. and Europe. By 1910 more than 200 such societies had been established (Costin, 1992). The movement soon encountered a tension that to this day pervades the field of child welfare: the conflict between family privacy and child protection. The NYSPCC operated by aggressively removing children from homes and placing them in institutions. Institutionalization of children placed the organization in direct conflict with the deep-seated American preference for parental authority and family life. (This value was articulated in the famous resolution from the 1909 Conference on the Care of Dependent Children on home life mentioned earlier.) This conflict, coupled with social and economic conditions in the post–World War I period, drew attention away from the problem of child abuse. The ensuing period of indifference to the issue would last for several decades.

It ended in the 1960s, when child abuse was "discovered" yet again. This era was ushered in when a pediatric radiologist named John Caffey reported a new "syndrome" in infants that included subdural hematomas along with atypical fractures of limbs and ribs (Caffey, 1946). In 1962, C. Henry Kempe gave this condition a name: "battered child syndrome." With this label, child abuse resurfaced as a public concern (Kempe et al., 1962).

In its rediscovered form, child abuse was considered more a "medical" than a "social" problem. Responding to the advocacy of medical professionals, states quickly passed legislation dictating a public response to the abuse or neglect of children. Legislation was also enacted at the federal level. The Child Abuse Prevention and Treatment Act of 1974 established mandatory reporting procedures under which health and human service professionals were required to notify state authorities of suspected or known cases of child abuse or neglect. The Act also established the National Center for Child Abuse and Neglect, and it provided some funding to serve troubled families.

As a direct result of federal and state legislation, more cases of abuse and neglect came to the attention of authorities, and greater numbers of children were removed from their homes. In the case of Native American children the situation became especially egregious. As part of a campaign to "acculturate" Native American children the U.S. government and other authorities had developed a program of placing them in boarding schools.[7] These schools forced the children to wear the clothes, eat the food, speak the language, and practice the customs of the dominant culture. In the U.S., this practice continued from the late nineteenth century until the middle of the twentieth century. Although most boarding schools were closed by the 1960s and 1970s, the child welfare system continued a similar practice, as Native American children who were removed from their homes were often placed with Caucasian foster families. Critics saw foster placement as another attempt to eradicate the Native American culture— a practice that harmed the children the system was supposed to protect. In response to these concerns, the Indian Child Welfare Act of 1978 (PL 95-608) established tribal jurisdiction over Native American children who enter the child welfare system. Tribes exercise their jurisdiction in varying ways, but at a minimum the Act calls for the placement of Indian children in foster and adoptive homes that reflect the Indian culture, and for assistance (financial and educational) to enable the tribes to administer their own child welfare and family support services. (Recall that Emily Morrison, discussed in Chapter 4, became a foster parent for a Native American child at the request of the child's father.)

As the child welfare system matured, the practice of removing children from abusive and neglectful homes brought more children into foster care. Policymakers became concerned about this increase, noting that decades of research had illuminated flaws in the nation's foster care system. In the late 1950s, Henry Maas and Richard Engler (1959) had suggested that extended stays in foster care could produce behavior problems. Support for their view was offered at a 1963 conference sponsored by the Child Welfare League of America and the National Association of Social Workers. At this "Institute on Child Welfare Research," social scientists suggested that separating children from their parents and placing them in foster care was not always in the best interests of the child (Fanshel & Shinn, 1978). They documented an alarming phenomenon called "foster care drift," observing that children often languished for years in foster care, with little stability or planning for their future.

To address this problem, the 1980 Adoption Assistance and Child Welfare Act (PL 96-272) established clear procedures and timelines for the management of children who enter into state custody. Within 18 months of the child's placement, a dispositional hearing was to be held to place the child in the least restrictive, most family-like setting that was available and appropriate. States were required to make "reasonable efforts" to reunify families. Funds were provided for reunifi-

---

[7]Enrollment of Native American children in boarding schools was remarkably similar to the nineteenth-century practice of "placing out" developed by the Children's Aid Society, a topic that will be introduced in the section on children as villains.

cation services, which included a wide range of supportive activities, from parenting education and stress management to budgeting and case management. If progress toward reunification was not made, the law required states to begin "permanency planning" on behalf of the child. That is, the state agency was required to develop a plan for the permanent placement of the child in long-term foster care, guardianship, or (if parental rights were terminated) adoption. The law was codified as Titles IV-B and IV-E of the Social Security Act, and is still in force.

The 1980 law forced child welfare workers to make painful decisions. No longer could they wait and hope that abusive parents would change. Instead, for a limited time, workers became active partners with biological parents in an effort to preserve the family unit. Researchers and program administrators began to develop services and methods that would accomplish reunification. The "Homebuilders" program in the state of Washington was one model effort to support "family preservation," that is, the reunification of children and biological parents. This program developed a model that offered intensive services to families to prevent foster placement. Initial research on family preservation efforts was promising. Families were reunified and parenting was improved (Pecora et al., 1995).

The growing enthusiasm for family preservation led to the 1993 passage of the Family Preservation and Support Services Act (PL 103-66), which provided increased funding for reunification services. Each state received an amount of money based on the number of children receiving food stamps. Unfortunately, the Homebuilders model has proved hard to duplicate in other settings (Littell, 1995). Perhaps as a result, the nation's enthusiasm for family preservation seems to have reverted to an inclination towards child removal.

The Adoption and Safe Families Act of 1997 (PL 105-89) emphasized that the first priority for child welfare is the safety of children. While authorizing limited funding ($275 million in 1999) for family preservation, the law contains several provisions designed to encourage adoption, including incentive payments for states that exceed their average number of adoptions ($400 per adopted foster child); expanded health coverage for adopted children with special needs; new, shorter, 12-month timelines for permanency hearings and filing for termination of parental rights; and modifications in provisions requiring reasonable efforts to preserve and reunify families. Under these modifications, states need not make such efforts in cases that involve "aggravated circumstances" (including, but not limited to abandonment, torture, chronic abuse, and sexual abuse), cases in which parents committed (or aided, abetted, or attempted to commit) either murder or manslaughter of a child, cases involving felony assault that resulted in serious bodily injury to a child, and cases in which the parent's rights to the child's sibling have been involuntarily terminated. In essence, this law has established several categories of "undeserving" parents, and excused states from the responsibility to try to preserve their families. In these cases, states must hold permanency hearings within 30 days (not 12 months) of a child's removal.

The history of intervention in cases of child abuse or neglect in the United States reveals a profound ambivalence towards the parents involved—a tendency to see them either as victims or villains. The nation puts no restrictions on pro-creation.[8] Americans must complete more training to become drivers than to become parents. This would suggest a "right" to raise children—one that many would intuitively endorse. Some, due to mental illness, substance abuse, or poverty, are unable to fulfill their parental obligations. Motivated by enthusiasm for biological parenting, child welfare agencies have undertaken what in some cases has amounted to heroic measures to achieve "family preservation." On the other hand, some view abusive or neglectful parents as villains, not victims. This view supports prompt removal of children from abusive homes, as well as pun-ishment of the perpetrators. In some ways, it represents a return to the nation's nineteenth-century approach exemplified in the case of little Mary Ellen. Today, more children in the United States are dying because of violence than ever before. Many take their own lives, bringing youth suicide rates to unprecedent-ed high levels. Still others are the victims of homicide, too often at the hands of those charged with their care.

Homicides against children increased during the 1990s. In 1996, homicides of children aged five or under—most committed by parents or caregivers—reached a 40-year high (Wingfield, Petit, & Klempner, 1999). Homicide became the second leading cause of death for 15- to 19-year-olds and the leading cause for African-American males in this age range. The homicide rate for African-American men more than doubled between 1985 and 1996, from 46 per 100,000 to nearly 100. The rate for young white men was 12 per 100,000 (Wingfield, Petit, & Klempner, 1999).

From an international perspective, the U.S. has an unusually high rate of homicide against children. In 1994, the World Bank compared the rate of homi-cide against youth in 26 high-income nations. The rate in the U.S. was five times higher than in all of the other nations combined. Among the 26 nations studied, homicides accounted for 1995 deaths of youth under 15, of which 1,464 (73 per-cent) occurred in the U.S. (World Bank, 1994). Indeed, Dr. Paul Holinger (1994) reported that a comparison of World Health Organization countries revealed the nation's youth homicide rate was "at the top of the list." Only Mexico and the former USSR had comparable rates.

As Holinger et al. (1994) noted, suicide and homicide rates tend to be par-allel. Suicide rates for American children have quadrupled since 1950 (National Center for Health Statistics, 1998a). In 1996, the suicide rate among 15- to 19-year-olds was 9.7 per 100,000. Suicide was the second leading cause of death that year among white males aged 15 to 19, and the third leading cause for all teens and young adults (Wingfield, Petit, & Klempner, 1999). Suicide rates among children aged 10 to 14 years have also increased substantially in recent years (Centers for Disease Control, 1995). Although rates are highest for white males between the ages of 15 and 19 years, the suicide rates for African-American

---

[8]China is probably the only nation in the world in which most people seek government approval before becoming biological parents. Even in China, the practice is extremely unpopular.

males in this age group have increased dramatically. The World Bank (1994) reported that the suicide rate for children in the United States was two times higher than that in the other 25 high-income countries combined (0.55 compared with 0.27).

Attempts to explain youth suicide and homicide tend to focus on individual pathology. Studies have identified risk factors such as substance abuse and mental illness (Davidson & Linnoila, 1992; Blumenthal & Knupter, 1988; Klerman, 1987). Although these risk factors have clear implications for social work practice, they say little about the potential role of public policies in addressing these parallel trends. Yet research on the contribution of economic factors suggests an important role for social policy. As Holinger et al. (1994) and others have noted, "Poverty appears to be the most consistent underlying risk factor in communities with high homicide rates" (p. 150). Economic factors like unemployment are among the most important in determining both youth suicide and homicide rates. Clearly efforts to reduce poverty and economic vulnerability will have the secondary benefit of reducing the violence experienced by America's children.

CHILDREN AS VILLAINS

The Industrial Revolution brought overcrowding to U.S. cities, whose slums were notorious for producing "The Dangerous Classes" (a term Charles Loring Brace used to describe poor children living in the nation's cities). In 1853 Brace founded the Children's Aid Society, an agency that developed the practice of "placing out" poor urban children. Thousands of these children (most of whom were Roman Catholic) were sent to live on farms and work for families with "strong Christian (i.e., Protestant) values." This practice was harshly criticized. Brace attributed the criticism to "ignorant Roman Catholics" who spread rumors that the children were sold as slaves, given new names, and converted to Protestantism (Brace, 1872, p. 234). As a result, said Brace, the poor themselves opposed the practice. In his 1872 treatise on his work, Brace said, "Most distressing of all was, when a drunken mother or father followed a half-starved boy, already scarred and sore with their brutality, and snatched him from one of our parties of little emigrants, all joyful with their new prospects, only to beat him and leave him on the streets" (p. 235).

Opponents noted that the Children's Aid Society did not carefully investigate the foster homes, that the foster families sometimes mistreated the children, and that many of the children were never heard from again.

Over the course of 25 years, the Society removed 50,000 children from the streets of New York. Poor families protested the practice. The Roman Catholic Church charged the agency with using this practice to convert Catholic children to Protestantism. Later, many of the receiving states objected to having indigent youth dropped within their borders. Eventually, the practice of placing out was abandoned in favor of asylums.

Child Villains in Modern America

Today, many Americans still view some children as members of the "dangerous classes," and the nation's treatment of youth who commit crimes has cycled from a severe punitive approach to an emphasis on education and rehabilitation and back to punishment again.

Courts in early America did not differentiate between juvenile and adult offenders. The juvenile court movement of the nineteenth century (which coincided with emerging awareness of children as victims of abuse) led to the creation of separate courts and institutions for children that emphasized education and rehabilitation. Of course, given the widespread belief that the blame for delinquency lay with the individual child, these institutions often meted out severe punishment and extremely difficult living conditions.

Eventually the limitations of punishment as a deterrent became clear, and these institutions came to emphasize rehabilitation through the use of indeterminate sentences, probation and parole, and training and counseling. When offenders were released, they usually went straight into employment that had been arranged for them, and remained on parole so that their re-entrance into the community was carefully controlled. This system was applied in the New York State Reformatory at Elmira in the 1870s. Studies found four out of five of their "graduates" did not return to a penal institution. Soon other states established similar juvenile facilities.

The world's first full-fledged juvenile court was created in Cook County (Chicago) in July 1899 (Denver, Colorado established its juvenile court a year later). The aim was to reduce the stigma of juvenile crime and create new mechanisms for dealing with offenders. Hearings were informal, with no lawyers, oaths, or robes. The judge was in the role of a "parental guide," as defined by statute: "The care, custody, and discipline of the children brought before the court shall approximate as nearly as possible that which they should receive from their parents, and . . . as far as practicable they shall be treated not as criminals but as children in need of aid, encouragement and guidance" (Trattner, 1989, p. 118). Clearly this system depended heavily on the confidence of the public and legislators in the benevolence of juvenile court judges. The authority of these judges greatly exceeded that of judges in adult court. Later this approach was criticized as stripping children of their constitutional rights and placing them at the mercy of not-so-benevolent judges.

The *Gault* case, decided by the U.S. Supreme Court in May of 1967, dramatically changed the operation of juvenile courts. On January 8 at about 10 a.m., 15-year-old Gerald Gault and a friend were taken into custody by the Sheriff of Gila County, Arizona. (They were accused by a neighbor of making phone calls "of the irritatingly, offensive, adolescent, sex variety" (in re. Gault, 387 U.S. 1; 18 L. Ed. 2d 527; 87 S.Ct. 1428; 1967—available at http://funnelweb.utcc.utk.edu/~scheb/cases.html). At the time, Gerald was on probation as a result of having been with another boy who had stolen a wallet. Gerald's parents, both at work, were not notified that their son had been arrested. Gerald was taken to a detention facility. When the parents came home, they sent his older brother to look for Gerald and learned that he was in custody. The parents went to the detention facility and were told a hearing would be held the following day. There was no record of the hearing, and three to four days later Gerald was released, with no explanation. A note from the arresting officer indicated that the judge had set a date a week later for "further hearings on Gerald's delinquency." Gerald's mother requested that the woman who complained about her son be present at the hearing, but she was told that the complainant's presence was not necessary. At the end of the hearing, the judge committed Gerald as a delinquent to the State Industrial School "for the period of his minority [that is, until age 21]." The child was to be confined for years for making lewd phone calls, an offense that for an adult would result in a fine of $5 to $50 or not more than two months' imprisonment.

Concluding that "unbridled discretion, however benevolently motivated, is frequently a poor substitute for principle and procedure," the Supreme Court held that "neither the Fourteenth Amendment nor the Bill of Rights is for adults alone" and set forth procedural requirements for juvenile cases. These included timely notice of charges, the right of the child to legal counsel, the right to confront and cross-examine complainants, and protection against self-incrimination. At the same time that it imposed these due process requirements on juvenile courts, the Supreme Court upheld the constitutionality and desirability of other measures: the separation of juveniles from adult offenders, the practice of "sealing" juvenile records so they will not affect adult eligibility for civil service and other privileges, and the informality of juvenile court proceedings. These procedures remain in place today.

THE JUVENILE JUSTICE AND DELINQUENCY ACT OF 1974. The Juvenile Justice and Delinquency Act of 1974 (JJDP—PL 93-415) has become the vehicle for significant reforms of the juvenile courts. First, the act changed the courts' treatment of youth convicted of less serious offenses called "status offenses." Status offenses are crimes only when they are committed by youth. They vary from state to state, but typically include curfew violations, truancy, and failure to respond to parental authority. Until 1974, children who committed status offenses were incarcerated in detention facilities with those guilty of more serious crimes. The JJDP required states to separate status offenders from those guilty of criminal acts. As a result, as many as 40 percent of youths who were status offenders have been diverted from detention facilities (Clement, 1997).

In 1988, the JJDP Act was amended to address the disproportionate representation of minority youth (like Lorenzo, the subject of this chapter's case study) in the juvenile justice system. Unlike the diversion of status offenders, this initiative has been relatively unsuccessful. Both African-American and Hispanic youth have been disproportionately represented in the nation's detention centers. In 1991, 43 percent of those in detention centers were black, 35 percent were white, and 19 percent were Hispanic. Training schools are the most restrictive juvenile detention facilities. There, African-American youth represented 47 percent of the population. The general theme, as articulated by the Office of

Juvenile Justice and Delinquency Prevention, was that "In every state studied, minority males had a higher probability rate of incarceration before age 18 than their white peers" (Roscoe & Morton, 1994, p. 1).

Minority youth continue to be over-represented at all levels of the juvenile justice system. For example, in 1999 African-American youth made up 15 percent of the U.S. population under 18, yet they accounted for 26 percent of juvenile arrests, 32 percent of delinquency referrals to juvenile court, 41 percent of the juveniles detained in delinquency cases, 46 percent of juveniles in correctional institutions, and 52 percent of juveniles transferred to adult criminal court (Congressional Black Congress, 1999). As several studies have demonstrated, the over-representation of minority youth reflects the way they are "processed" in the juvenile justice system. Testifying before the House Subcommittee on Human Resources in 1986, Ira Schwartz reported that "minority youth now comprise more than half of all the juveniles incarcerated in public detention and correctional facilities in the United States . . . there is recent research showing that minority youth do not account for a substantially disproportionate amount of serious crime. However, minority youth stand a much greater chance of being arrested than white youth, and once arrested, appear to be at great risk of being charged with more serious offenses than white youth who are involved in comparable levels of delinquency" (Schwartz, 1986, p. 5). These remarks are echoed in several studies of the treatment of minority youth (see, for example, Leonard, Pope, & Feyerherm, 1995).

Oᴛʜᴇʀ Fᴏʀᴍꜱ ᴏꜰ Cʜɪʟᴅ Vɪʟʟᴀɪɴʏ

American children are still the "dangerous classes" when they engage in behavior that is threatening to the broader society. Emerging problems with child villains include teen pregnancy and youth gangs. When children become extremely threatening, the response of the nation's juvenile justice system is to "certify" them as adults so they can be tried and punished accordingly.

TEEN PREGNANCY. Teen pregnancy creates two high-risk children: a child-mother and an infant. The mother is less likely than older mothers to receive adequate prenatal care (National Center for Health Statistics, 1998b). She is also less likely to finish high school: only one-third of teen mothers receive high school diplomas (Maynard, 1996). Finally, teen mothers are likely to receive public assistance: nearly 80 percent of teen mothers rely on welfare at some point in their lives (Congressional Budget Office, 1990). Children born to teenage mothers have lower birth weights, are more likely to perform poorly in school, and experience greater rates of abuse and neglect (Wolfe & Perozek, 1997; Maynard, 1996; George & Lee, 1997). Sons of teen mothers are more likely to spend time in prison, while daughters of teens are more likely (like Lorenzo's sister) to become teen mothers themselves (Maynard, 1996).

The teen pregnancy rate in the United States peaked in 1991, at 116.5 pregnancies per thousand teens aged 15 to 19. It has declined in recent years, reaching a record low point of 94.3 pregnancies per thousand teens in 1997 (Ventura et al., 2001). Teen birth rates differ substantially from teen pregnancy rates. Births to American women aged 15 to 19 peaked in 1957 at 96 births per thousand. Teen births reached their lowest point (50 to 53 births per thousand teens) during the mid-1980s. During the 1990s the rate began to rise again, and in 1996 the National Center for Health Statistics reported a rate of 54.7 births per thousand teens (National Center for Health Statistics, 1998b). Teen pregnancy among Hispanic and African-American women is consistently higher than among Asian and Caucasian Americans (Ventura et al., 2001).

Like many issues in child welfare, the problem of teen pregnancy challenges the division between private, familial matters and matters of public interest. Most Americans believe teenagers should abstain from sex, but they also feel that sexually active teens should have access to contraception (Princeton Survey Research Associates, 1997). Most also believe that teens should seek information about sex and reproduction from their parents, but sometimes this does not happen. Teen pregnancy has consequences, not only for the family involved, but for the broader community. Recognizing the public interest in preventing teen pregnancies, public schools typically provide rudimentary education on sex and reproduction. These educational efforts often generate controversy. When they are coupled with proposals to educate teens about contraception—or even further, to provide them with contraceptive devices—the controversy can become overwhelming. Another delicate policy issue that bears on teen pregnancy involves abortions. Abortion is legal in the United States, but in about half of the states (22 in 1999) teenagers seeking abortions must have parental approval (Robinson, 1999).

YOUTH GANGS. Once confined to the urban core of a few major cities, youth gangs have been reported in every state in the nation. The Office of Juvenile Justice and Delinquency Prevention conducted Youth Gang Surveys in 1995, 1996, and 1997. The surveys were designed to gather general information about the prevalence of gangs, and they required the participation of thousands of police and sheriff's departments across the Nation. Respondents reported that in 1995 there were a total of 23,388 youth gangs in the United States, with an estimated 664,906 members. The 10 states reporting the most gang members were (in order) California, Illinois, Texas, Ohio, Indiana, New Mexico, Arizona, Florida, Nevada, and Minnesota. Respondents also noted the expansion of gangs into smaller cities, rural counties, and affluent suburbs (Moore, 1995).

Experts have identified several different reasons that youth join gangs. Observing that most of the nation's gangs originated in inner cities, some emphasize the role of poverty and hopelessness, suggesting that gang enterprise offers a chance for economic advancement. The recent expansion of gangs in affluent suburbs has led some observers (Monti, 1994) to emphasize the role of family dysfunction in gang involvement, noting that gang members often come from families affected by divorce, substance abuse, and abuse or neglect of children.

The gang, they suggest, becomes a surrogate family—one with clear roles, loyalties, and responsibilities.

Regardless of the reasons for joining, once children are part of a gang, they are widely feared. There is a rational basis for that fear. As the Office of Juvenile Justice and Delinquency Prevention (OJJDP) reported, "Gang members account for a disproportionate share of delinquent acts, particularly the most serious offenses" (Thornberry & Burch, 1997, p. 1). This observation stems from the Rochester Youth Development Study. Researchers followed a sample of 1,000 seventh- and eighth-grade boys and girls, primarily from high-crime areas. Interviewing children over a four-year period, they found that about 30 percent reported being a member of a street gang at some point prior to finishing high school. The same 30 percent committed 65 percent of the delinquent acts carried out by the entire group, including 70 percent of drug sales and 69 percent of violent crimes (Thornberry & Burch, 1997).

Often gang members commit delinquent acts while engaging in "gang enterprise": income-producing gang activities. A review of gang structure and activities prepared by Urban Dynamics (1999) indicated that the availability of cocaine and the ease with which it can be converted into "crack" has created an extremely lucrative business for gang members. Traditional gang enterprises, such as extortion, robbery and burglary, have been replaced by drug sales. The net effect for a hard-core gang member without a high school diploma can be a high, tax-free income that makes the minimum-wage job he or she might be able to perform in the legal economy seem laughable. As Barry Feld (1999) explained, "For many urban black youths, employment in the illegal economy provides an alternative to joblessness and poverty" (p. 197).

The nation's gang prevention efforts, largely orchestrated through law-enforcement authorities, have included the expansion of community-oriented policing efforts (COPS). Often police focus on "hot spots," such as public housing units, assigning extra patrol officers there. Other programs have mobilized community organizations to strengthen efforts to keep children in school. Still other communities have established physical blockades to prevent traffic from moving through areas with a high incidence of drive-by shootings. At the same time, youth convicted of serious gang-related offenses face extremely punitive treatment in the justice system.

CERTIFICATION OF SERIOUS YOUTH OFFENDERS AS ADULTS

The violent crimes committed by hard-core gang members have fueled public fear of serious youth offenders and given momentum to a movement to "get tough with these kids." One policy response has been the "waiver of juvenile court jurisdiction," or the "certification" of some youth offenders as adults. These processes remove the offender from the juvenile court system and place him under the jurisdiction of adult correctional authorities. Prosecution of youths as adults is based partly on a belief that these youthful offenders are not amenable to rehabilitation through the juvenile justice system, and partly because (in conjunction with the growing emphasis on "victim's rights") the idea of retribution has gained popularity in recent years. The net result is a series of policy decisions, beginning in the late 1980s, designed to move serious young offenders out of the juvenile justice system and into the criminal courts.

Typically a prosecutor will ask the juvenile court judge to "waive jurisdiction" in the case of a serious young offender who (1) is not amenable to rehabilitation and (2) represents a threat to public safety. States vary in the amount of discretion allowed the judge. In some cases, the age and seriousness of the offense might require that juvenile court jurisdiction be waived. For example, if a 15- or 16-year-old were to commit a murder the case would automatically be referred to the criminal (adult) court. Other states provide for "prosecutorial discretion," in which the prosecutor, not the judge, may decide whether to try the case in juvenile or adult court. An emerging focus in these procedures has emphasized not the age of the offender, but the nature of the offense. As a result, young children charged with heinous crimes have been tried in adult courts and sentenced to prison and to death.

International observers are appalled by the willingness of U.S. courts to impose the death penalty on children. The practice goes against provisions of the United Nations Convention on the Rights of the Child and several other international treaties. Nonetheless, the laws of 38 states and the federal government authorize the death penalty for murders committed by individuals who have not reached adulthood. Of those jurisdictions, 15 have selected 18 years as the minimum age for imposition of the death penalty. Four have set the minimum age at 17 years, and the remaining 20 use 16 as the minimum age. Between 1973, when a Supreme Court ruling revived the death penalty, and 1999, 180 juvenile death sentences were imposed. Among these juveniles, the vast majority (98 percent) were males. Four were females. Thirteen people were executed during this period for crimes they committed between the ages of 16 and 18. The states of Texas and Florida reported the greatest numbers of executions. As of June 1999, 70 people were on death row under sentences received for juvenile crimes. Among them, 30 (43 percent) were African-American, 14 (20 percent) were Latino, and 26 (37 percent) were Caucasian. The victims of their crimes were typically white adults (Streib, 1999).

VICTIMS OR VILLAINS?

In both child welfare and the juvenile justice system, ethnic minorities and low-income families are over-represented. This preponderance suggests that victim and villain are not polar opposites, but flip sides of the same coin—a coin molded by institutional racism and economic deprivation. From a social justice perspective, abusive parents and youthful criminals can be seen not as victims or villains, but as the inevitable result of systemic failures that may ultimately be corrected through social policy. In the following section, we will consider the role of social workers in social policies affecting the nation's children.

POLICY PRACTICE IN CHILD WELFARE: THE ROLE OF SOCIAL WORKERS

In some ways, twenty-first-century perceptions of children mirror nineteenth-century views. Children are once again viewed as part of the nation's "dangerous classes." At the same time, many of America's children face poverty, neglect, and abuse—even murder. Throughout the field of child welfare, there is a growing awareness that these phenomena are intertwined. The Child Welfare League of America has released a monograph called, "Breaking the Link Between Child Maltreatment and Juvenile Delinquency" (Child Welfare League of America, 1997). Researchers throughout the nation are documenting the close association between victimization of children and violence exhibited by youth. When society fails children, the results—for both the children and the society in which they live—are devastating.

Social work pioneers were aware of this relationship, and many focused their efforts on child welfare issues. Julia Lathrop, the first head of the Children's Bureau, Jane Addams, founder of Hull House, and others intervened on behalf of children who were victimized by the social conditions that impoverished their families. Today's social workers have the opportunity to continue the profession's long tradition of progressive advocacy on behalf of the nation's children. In the areas of child protective services, education, and juvenile delinquency, reasoned advocacy is needed as much today as it was in the nineteenth century[9]. In some ways, the tools for this advocacy effort remain the same: state-of-the-art research that documents conditions and evaluates programs, and passionate advocates who can communicate the implications of that research to policy-makers and the public. An emerging tool that is now available to child welfare advocates is the class action lawsuit.

Child welfare advocates throughout the nation have discovered the power of litigation for improving the policies and programs that affect the nation's children. The use of the courts for social advocacy was alluded to in the discussion of school finance, in which inequalities have been challenged by a series of class action lawsuits. These suits have also been used to improve services for abused and neglected children. Several state agencies in this field have been the subjects of class action suits, and a few have come under judicial supervision. This represents a new role for the judiciary, involving them in direct oversight of executive functions. It also frequently has the effect of increasing the funding available for child welfare services.

---

[9]There is a tendency among contemporary child welfare advocates to pit children's needs against those of the elderly. The nation has roughly twice as many citizens under the age of 18 as it does over the age of 65 (Pecora et al., 2000). Yet our financial commitment to the elderly (through Medicare, Social Security, and related programs) dwarfs our investment in children's education and care. See Chapter 9 for a discussion of the politics of intergenerational equity in the U.S.

SUMMARY: THE CURRENT OUTLOOK FOR AMERICA'S CHILDREN

The United States is a dangerous place for children. The nation's children face greater risks than those in most of the world's industrialized nations. In 1999, nearly one in five American children lived in a family with an income below the poverty threshold, giving the nation the highest child poverty rate in the developed world. The nation's infant mortality rate is high, compared with that of other developed nations. Finally, American children face an unparalleled risk of neglect, abuse, suicide and murder. This vulnerability represents a major thread in the nation's response to its children—the irony of children suffering such hazards in a nation of such wealth.

George Henry Payne observed that "the general history of the child . . . moves as from one mountain peak to another with a long valley of gloom in between" (Costin, 1992, p. 194). This description is particularly apt in relation to policies affecting America's children. Social workers in this field have long attempted to harness the energy and commitment of the peak periods to sustain the nation's children through extended periods of indifference.

Today, social workers in child welfare confront Herculean tasks. Aware of broad social trends that might preclude effective parenting, they help profoundly troubled people learn to raise their children. In a system that seems increasingly punitive towards low-income parents, they help judges, administrators, and policy-makers understand that the interests of a child frequently overlap with the rights of their parents. Aware of the educational failures that lead poor children to drop out of school and the economic transformations that have left them with no viable employment options, they strive to keep disadvantaged youngsters out of gangs. Facing public skepticism about the effectiveness of "throwing money at education," they sustain local, state, and federal support for Head Start.

In child welfare, social workers are the physical embodiment of the principle of *parens patriae*. They are the arms of the state, and as such they reach out to remove children from dangerous settings. The broader challenge now is to convert those settings to communities and homes capable of nurturing healthy human beings—to go from removing children from impoverished and neglectful settings to enriching those homes and communities for children and their families.

DISCUSSION TOPICS

1. What does your state constitution say about education? Has the state fulfilled its commitment in this area?

2. Do you think public child welfare agencies should allow gay and lesbian adoptions? If so, how should the agency manage public debate around the

issue? Should it quietly allow a few qualified gay and lesbian couples to adopt? Would it be better to hold public forums on the topic? If agency policies prevent adoption by gay and lesbian couples, is agency vulnerable to lawsuits?

3. Do you think school choice programs undermine public education? Who uses these programs? Are they serving low-income families? Why do you think the teachers' unions oppose vouchers?

4. What macro-economic and social trends do you think contribute to rising rates of youth violence in the United States? Have social policies contributed to the increase in violence by youths?

5. How have issues of diversity influenced child welfare policy in the United States?

6. Is there an established "right to parenthood" in the United States? Should everyone have the right to produce and raise biological children?

SUGGESTED RESOURCES

Feld, B. C. (1999). *Bad Kids: Race and the Transformation of the Juvenile Court.* New York: Oxford University Press.

Garbarino, J. (1992). *Toward a Sustainable Society: An Economic, Social, and Environmental Agenda for Our Children's Future.* Chicago: Noble Press.

Shelden, R. G., Tracy, S. K., & Brow, W. B. (1997). *Youth Gangs in American Society.* Belmont, CA: Wadsworth.

www.childrensdefense.org—The Children's Defense Fund considers itself "America's Strongest Voice for Children." This web site offers CDF reports and summaries on topics ranging from child care to gun control.

www.cwla.org—The Child Welfare League of America is the nation's oldest and largest nonprofit organization, committed to "developing and promoting policies and programs to protect America's children and strengthen America's families." Their web site offers a list of publications that can be browsed by subject, as well as current news on a wide range of issues related to child welfare.

www.ed.gov—The home page of the U.S. Department of Education offers a tremendous array of publications with an excellent search engine. A good source of general information and a good way to become familiar with the current administration's position on issues affecting education.

www.teenpregnancy.org—This site is maintained by the National Committee to Prevent Teen Pregnancy. It offers current reports on topics related to teen pregnancy in the U.S., as well as links to related sites.

8

Women

If I were asked . . . to what the singular prosperity
and growing strength of that people [the Americans]
ought mainly to be attributed, I should reply:
To the superiority of their women.

ALEXIS DE TOCQUEVILLE,
Democracy in America, III, 12

The status of women in the United States is neither singular nor static. A woman's situation is determined by factors apart from gender, such as culture, class, and sexual orientation. Therefore, it is probably more appropriate to speak of the "statuses" of American women. These "statuses" evolve and change in response to social movements and economic trends. Despite this diversity and flux, gender is pivotal in the allocation of resources, rights, and responsibilities in the United States and abroad. Thus, it is an important consideration in the pursuit of social justice.

After considering the life experiences of Annie Boone, we will examine the role of gender in the United States. Women's diverse roles—as wives and mothers, as workers, and as citizens—serve as the organizing framework for the chapter. For each of these major roles, the chapter traces the development of U.S. policies that have affected women, then examines contemporary issues. Emerging issues discussed include work force considerations, violence against women, the abortion debate, and child support. The chapter closes with a look at women in the social work profession.

Case Study ♦ Annie Boone

Annie works for a grassroots organization called JEDI Women (the same organization that helped Melissa, the subject of our case study in Chapter 1). Walking into its storefront offices, a visitor enters a beehive of activity. Men and women bustle through the main hall from office to office, displaying a sense of purpose and commitment. Annie serves as JEDI's lead organizer, a full-time (and then some) position that carries health benefits but no pension coverage. Her office is in the middle of all the activity, and she found it challenging to carve out time for our interview.

Annie is energetic and capable, with a rapid-fire style of speaking that can leave a listener struggling to catch up. With her face framed by brown curls that bounce when she gets excited, Annie dresses in jeans and appears much younger than her age (late thirties). She has testified before the state legislature and the U.S. Congress, and spoken to audiences numbering in the hundreds. She is often frustrated by the insensitivity of lawmakers, and shows contempt for women who don't understand life outside of their "Cinderella stories."

Hers is not a Cinderella story. Annie has experienced abuse at the hands of her father, her husband, and her son. She has raised four children on public assistance. Annie wrote an article about her experiences called "A Wedding Band Is a Never-ending Circle, and So Is Abuse" for the *Georgetown Journal on Fighting Poverty* (Vol. III, Fall 1995, pp. 13–16). In it she related that "I grew up thinking my only role in life was to become Betty Crocker—a good wife and a caring mother for my children. This message was inbred in me from the day I was born. A wife and a mother were all I ever wanted to be. I was never informed that . . . I should get as much schooling as I possibly could so that if something happened between my husband and myself, I could always take care of myself. The husband was the breadwinner of the family, and what he said went, whether you liked it or not. Women were to stay home, take care of their children, cook, and stay pregnant" (p. 13).

Annie's father was illiterate, but as she pointed out, "he turned out pretty good considering the situation. He ended up working for the Division of Motor Vehicles as a lab technician." Although he never abused his wife physically, he was very abusive with the children. His desire to control Annie was so powerful that he nailed her bedroom window shut and installed a lock on the outside of her bedroom door. As Annie said, "If he really wanted me in my bedroom, I was in my bedroom." She described one incident:

> You know, he loved me to death, but his violence was, like, out of control. I can remember when I came home late one time from school and . . . he was upset because I didn't clean my room. . . . When I came in the door he started yelling at me, so I went up to my room and I slammed my bedroom door. He came in there and he was just irate, and he started pulling all my clothes out of the drawers and . . . kicking me in the back, you know, with his steel-toed boots . . . abuse was pretty much the norm, you know.

Annie met her future husband, Jim, when she was 14. He wasn't violent before they married. "He was a sweetheart, you know, a charmer." The tension between Annie and her father escalated until "just about a half a year before I turned 16, I came home and all my stuff was on the front porch, and my dad said, 'I have just had enough. I don't want you around our house until you learn to abide by my rules.'" Annie decided to move in with her boyfriend. When her father threatened to file statutory rape charges against Jim and tell the police she had run away, Annie decided to get married. Annie said she "fit into being a wife rather easily." Jim wanted to have 12 kids. Annie worked, but Jim was unable to hold a steady job. He didn't enjoy work. He was "into drugs and alcohol too. So that kind of takes away your motivation to want to do things."

The first hint of trouble was Jim's desire to control Annie's contacts with her friends. He didn't want her to have friends, and the tensions between Annie and her parents escalated. His eventual physical abuse was no secret to Annie's parents. Annie relates, "I was pregnant with my oldest, and my ex-husband had beaten me up pretty bad, and I called home and I said, 'I need to come. I just need to come home.' . . . I didn't know at the time I was pregnant . . . I knew I was feeling really sick. I'm sure it was just morning sickness, but on top of him assaulting me and being in a strange environment . . . they sent me a plane ticket. . . . When I came back here, I had so much makeup on to cover up all the bruises, you know. I was just totally embarrassed by that and, um, I walked in the door and my mom said, 'You know, it'd be a really good idea if you'd go wash off that . . . makeup so we can see how bad you've been assaulted this time.'"

Annie's parents did not encourage her to escape the abuse. She explains, "They [imposed] a lot of their religious beliefs on me . . . women's roles in life were to stay married and have kids." In her article, Annie described the pivotal incident that led to her divorce: "One message my parents taught me well was that marriage is a commitment for life to be faithful. I was faithful, but was always accused of cheating with other men. I found out that my husband had gotten my roommate pregnant and that they were having an affair in my own home. After I confronted my husband about this and he admitted to having an affair with her, I was determined to leave. The violence was out of control . . . the next morning my family had five trucks out to my home and I was out of his life in less than one hour." Annie lived with her parents, briefly, and regretted bringing them into the "war zone." Jim stalked the house, picking fights with family and friends. Finally Annie applied for public assistance to secure a home for herself and her children. She did not tell the caseworker that she was a victim of domestic violence, and the caseworker did not ask.

Of course, Jim was not (and still is not) completely out of Annie's life. For some time after she left him, he stalked her. Over the years he has told the children that if it weren't for their mother, they could live as a family. This has been especially hard on the boys, generating resentment that translated into destructive behavior. Annie's second son, Jacob, has an attention deficit disorder and hyperactivity, as well as a conduct disorder. Annie feels some personal responsibility: "Watching my children and the pain they've gone through and kind of feeling like I inflicted some of that, you know. I made some bad choices about, you know, my life and having kids so young . . . I was never taught any of that."

Once she did leave, Annie found another source of stress in the caseworkers who entered her life. "Caseworkers, even though they want to sometimes help, they're not so helpful, you know, and I got so tired of all the caseworkers that wanted to make my life better and really what they were doing was creating more hassles for me, you know. . . . I asked the courts for help because my son was just out of control. Cops were at my house all the time. I felt like I was losing my sanity. I felt like I had to be around him 24/7, you know. And I was really striving for a better life . . . I'd get a job and I'd get laid off because, you know, he kept gettin' in trouble at school and I'd have to go and take care of his problems, you know . . . so I always kind of felt like we were a family at war, and it was something that always bothered me because I spent so much energy trying to diffuse all that anger, you know, and I felt like it was created by all the anger they'd seen at such a young age. And it just escalated as they got older . . . I mean, my sons had abused me quite a few times. . . . I did everything in the community that I could . . . because this was just becoming too overwhelming.

"Well, finally they appointed me this caseworker and she came out to my home. . . . So on her first appointment with me she comes to my house, and you know, I've cleaned everything from top to bottom because I'm afraid . . . you know, the system here is . . . to cause more havoc . . . when you walked in my house you smelled Pinesol and bleach. . . . And my girlfriend was sitting on the couch and this caseworker from hell walks in the door and says, 'I want you [to the girlfriend] to leave. This is a private meeting between me and Annie. And I really, Annie, want you to put that incense out, it's making my sinuses just go crazy.' And I thought, 'Oh God!' you know. 'I'm asking for help, not more destruction.' So, anyway, she sets up this plan for me and Jacob to abide by." The plan required that Annie spend all her time with her children, with no opportunity to get respite or continue her education. Annie finally convinced the caseworker that she needed to go to school.

Annie worked to become self-sufficient. "Even back when I left my husband, there were certain things that I'd do to try and become self-sufficient. Like, I didn't have a car at the time . . . the day care was ten blocks from me. That's a lot to walk with a four-year-old and little kids. So I had to take a bus that went from my house to downtown and then came back, for ten blocks. It took me two hours to get to school and two hours to get back every night." Ultimately, Annie received her GED and completed a clerk-typist program with straight B's. "That's not bad with four kids, you know."

On public assistance Annie received $563 per month to support her family of five. Among the continuing challenges she faced was difficulty laundering clothes. Usually she washed them in the tub and hung them "all over the house" to dry. On the few occasions that she could afford to use a laundromat, she walked, pushing a borrowed shopping cart full of her family's clothes. "That was so humiliating, you know?"

While on assistance, Annie had two destructive relationships. The first was with a man who bought her a car. He claimed that a case of malaria from his tour of duty in Vietnam had left him sterile. When Annie became pregnant, he insisted the child was not his. He was violent with Annie and one day took her car out and torched its interior. He finally moved out, and when Annie moved she lost touch with him. The second relationship lasted eight years. Bob was physically abusive, but as Annie explained, her self-esteem was so low that she thought she "deserved" the abuse. It was not until her work with JEDI had convinced her of her own worth that Annie was able to agree that Bob should leave.

Why didn't she just leave him? Or kick him out earlier? Annie believes that as long as benefits are inadequate, public assistance will leave women vulnerable to predatory men. A man who can contribute transportation, food, and even a little cash to the household may enable a woman who would otherwise become homeless to pay the rent or give her children a few "extras" like new clothes or a day at the movies. As a result, women on welfare may tolerate abuse that would be unacceptable to others.

"One day I heard about JEDI and I called Deeda and I talked to her . . . I said, 'You know, there's gotta be something wrong with this whole scenario.' She affirmed that I'm not the only woman out there that's going [through these difficulties]. . . . See, I'd tell myself that for years, is that I really felt like I was just born from hell or something because my whole life had been hell, you know . . . and Deeda's like, 'Uh-huh . . . There's a lot of injustice that happens to women,' you know . . . my first thing I ever did with JEDI was a protest. And I didn't know what they were going to do that day . . . I was just told that they were doing a news conference at the Capitol and that I should come. . . . I went to the Capitol and I was standing in the group and they were doing like a skit. And it all related to my life, and it was like, 'Whoa! This group's awesome. This is what I need!' . . . yeah, I was like 'I relate to this.' You know . . . the whole nine yards they're going through my life, one piece at a time . . . And I was like, 'This is too real,' and at the same time I kept thinking, 'God, I hope I don't get arrested out here being in this' . . . but the more involved I got, the more issues that I found that weren't just me, and that's when I decided that women really needed to be more vocal about what's going on with their lives." Annie told her children about her plans to speak out about the domestic violence she had experienced. At first her boys were angry about it, but the girls have participated in JEDI events and were pictured in a recent newspaper article about their mother's activism.

Annie is optimistic about her family's future. Her oldest son is showing signs of new maturity. During his senior year in high school, he has been attending school more regularly and Annie hopes he will graduate. Jacob is in a juvenile facility, "locked up for things that are really not his fault." But he has announced to members of his gang and opposing gangs that he isn't going to be involved in gangs anymore. Her oldest daughter called her father, "and she said, 'I'd never marry a man like you. I want somebody that's gonna be responsible and pay their child support if we ever got a divorce . . . I just don't think there's a man qualified to meet my expectations, so I don't think I'll ever get married. I'll just go to school.'" Annie's youngest daughter is "hanging around girls that are sexually active," but Annie plans to enroll her in a program this summer that educates teenagers about the harsh realities of single parenting. Annie hopes none of her children experience violence. "I just have a lot of expectations for my children and I hope that being with me has taught them something. If nothing else, to be vocal about what's going on."

For herself, Annie dreams of going to law school and working with victims of domestic violence. She has some money for college coming from her two years as a VISTA volunteer, and she anticipates that when her youngest child turns 18 she will be free to pursue this dream. Annie is enjoying a measure of financial security and independence for the first time in her life. She is dating a very nice man who doesn't drink, shows no signs of violence, and pays child support for his three children. Although she would certainly not rush into it, marriage is a possibility. But, as she points out, the relationship would have to be strong to endure the schooling she envisions for herself.

DISCUSSION   Like Annie, most women on public assistance have been victims of domestic violence. Estimates of the proportion of mothers receiving public assistance who have experienced domestic violence range from roughly half (Curcio, 1996) to more than two-thirds (Allard et al., 1997; Raphael, 1996). Violence forces many women and children to leave their homes and places them at the mercy of public and private service agencies. Further, as Annie suggested, women experiencing abuse are at greatest risk of injury and death after they have left home (Owens, 1999; Fleury et al., 1998).

Annie's experience with public assistance will not be shared in the future by women in her situation. She was on AFDC for 11 years. With current work requirements and lifetime assistance limits, women now must strive to secure employment as quickly as possible. (See Chapter 4 on income maintenance.)

Further, all states stipulate that mothers who are seeking public assistance must identify their children's father(s). This requirement enables the state to collect child support on the children's behalf. Mothers are allowed to keep a portion of the payments, and the rest is used to offset the cost of the family's welfare benefits (Garfinkel, 1992a). Although "good cause" exemptions to this requirement may be granted, they are rare (Pearson & Griswold, 1997). Thus, the state's interest in collecting child support from non-custodial fathers may further endanger women leaving abusive relationships.

Annie's training in clerical services prepared her to join the majority of employed women. Continued occupational segregation leaves most female workers in the service sector, often in jobs without benefits or pension coverage. Unlike 36 to 41 million Americans, Annie has health insurance. Like approximately two-thirds of working women, however, she does not have pension coverage. At the moment, Annie is enjoying the support and relative security of employment in a non-profit advocacy organization. She also has a long-term plan for financial security. Despite fears that going back to school may cost her the first healthy relationship she has ever had with a man, Annie is determined to earn the credentials necessary to secure her long-term financial well-being.

To understand the current status of women in American society, we will trace major policy developments that have affected women in three major roles: as wives and mothers, as citizens, and as workers.

WOMEN AS WIVES AND MOTHERS

A recurring thread in policies that affect women as wives and mothers is the fear that government intrusion will violate the sanctity of the home. Americans have always distrusted government intervention, and the notion that "a man's home is his castle" often runs counter to public policy efforts on behalf of women. To a great extent, early American public policy treated wives and mothers as the wards of their husbands. In this section, we will examine the impact of this perspective in several areas: property rights and credit, divorce, reproductive rights, and legal approaches to domestic violence and rape.

PROPERTY RIGHTS AND CREDIT

From the seventeenth through the early nineteenth centuries, married women were subject to a common-law doctrine called "coverture." This principle was based on biblical notions of the unity of spouses and simply held that a man and his wife were "one person in the law" (Rhode, 1989, p. 10). The "one," of course, was the husband. Wives could not hold, acquire, control, bequeath or convey property, enter into contracts, or initiate legal actions. Indeed, they could not legally withhold their wages from their husbands. The gender-based division of activity that was enforced by coverture had as its rationale a set of norms that have often been described by historians as the "doctrine of separate spheres." According to this view, women were best suited to private roles within the home, while men's character traits prepared them for public roles. Accordingly, women were legally barred from higher education, most professions, and public office. There were individual exceptions to these rules, such as women who operated taverns or were active in business. Often these women were viewed as acting as "agents" for their husbands.

As it turned out, strict restrictions on married women's property rights impeded commerce in the emerging nation. This was the case, for example, when a deserted wife could not sell her property or enter into contracts. Thus, beginning in 1839, state legislatures began to remove the most blatant restrictions on women's legal capacity. Several jurisdictions enacted married women's property acts, which granted wives certain powers. Nonetheless, even as late as 1970, men continued to be given preference over women in the selection of guardians, trustees, and executors of estates (*Reed v. Reed,* 404 U.S. 71, 1971).

Limitations on women's property rights contributed to restrictions on their ability to borrow money. As long as married women could not enter into contracts, they could not take out loans. Less than 30 years ago, many divorced women lacked credit records and thus were unable to borrow money. The Equal Credit Opportunity Act of 1974 prohibited discrimination in lending on the basis of sex. The Federal Trade Commission issued "Regulation B," which spells out the procedures for implementing the Act's provisions. Among these is the requirement that credit records for husbands and wives be maintained separately, each reflecting the experiences of the couple. Further, organizations must disclose the reasons whenever credit is denied. Although some women continue to have trouble securing credit to which they might be entitled, legal recourse is now available to them.

DIVORCE

Historically, the federal government has not been a major force in the development of family law in the U.S. As a result, divorce statutes vary from state to state. Further, many of the hard decisions in a divorce are made by individual judges using state law as a reference point. In this section, we will consider three aspects of divorce: the grounds under which it is granted, the division of marital resources, and the assignment of child custody. Divorce laws have undergone substantial changes in each of these areas.

The grounds under which divorce is granted have come full circle. Under Roman and early Anglo-American doctrine, consensual divorce (now known as "no-fault" divorce) was granted. Later, as divorce came to be seen as an ecclesiastic matter, the grounds for divorce were restricted. Early nineteenth-century American courts identified bigamy, impotence, and adultery as grounds for divorce. By mid-century, desertion and cruelty were added, although most courts did not identify "domestic chastisement" as cruelty. Although there was some liberalization over the years, most states applied these norms until the 1960s.

Class was a significant determinant of a couple's access to divorce. In New York, for example, where adultery was the only legal ground for divorce until 1966, wealthy couples either established residence in other states (like Nevada) that offered more liberal grounds or conducted elaborate courtroom charades to meet New York requirements. Less-affluent couples were left with separation as the "poor man's divorce."

Procedures for dividing marital assets, assigning alimony, and awarding child custody have reflected the social norms governing gender relations both within and outside of marriage. Most states are "common-law" property jurisdictions, in which spouses' earnings during marriage are treated as separate property rather than joint assets. This practice stood in contrast to "community-property" jurisdictions, which held that all property was jointly owned by both spouses. Until 1970, divorce within "common-law" jurisdictions significantly disadvantaged wives who did not work.

In 1970, the Uniform Marriage and Divorce Act was developed by the National Conference of the Commission on Uniform State Laws (NCCUSL), a deliberative body that develops and disseminates model legislation for consideration by state legislatures. Although the legislation has seldom been adopted in its entirety (Schneider, 1991), many provisions of the Act were incorporated by state legislatures. These included provisions requiring "equitable division" of marital resources. In many cases, this equitable division reflects the "one-third rule," in which wives are entitled to one-third of the property accumulated during the marriage. The husbands' greater share reflected their larger monetary contribution to the marital assets and ignored the wives' homemaking contributions.

In theory, a divorcing woman who did not receive substantial property might enjoy the security of lifetime alimony. In practice, however, as DiFonzo (1997) noted, "The most striking aspect of alimony was its scarcity" (p. 62). Data accumulated by the Census Bureau suggest that around the turn of the century (1897–1906) alimony was requested in 13.4 percent of cases and awarded in only 9.3 percent. Nationwide data from the turn of the century to 1922 suggest that the proportion of divorcing wives receiving alimony was consistently below 15 percent (Jacobson, 1959).

The divorce rate in the United States doubled during the 1960s and '70s, and courts increasingly used increased female participation in the labor force to avoid awarding alimony. Indeed, a stated goal of the Uniform Marriage and Divorce Act is to "minimize alimony as well as acrimony." As a result, alimony is seldom awarded except for brief rehabilitative periods.

The principles by which courts award custody of children reflect changing views of the roles of both fathers and mothers. Early Anglo-American doctrine gave custody to the father, who essentially had a property right in the child. During the Industrial Revolution the monetary value of a child's labor diminished, and American doctrine gradually evolved from "paternal preference" to "maternal presumption." Rather than giving priority to the father's rights, courts focused on the "best interests" of the child. Courts became unwilling to remove children "of tender years" from their mothers. For older children, the tendency was to focus on parental fitness. By the 1980s, two-thirds of states had officially abolished maternal preferences in favor of a more gender-neutral family law. Most had established some form of joint-custody legislation, and in contested cases, men were winning custody one-third to one-half of the time (Weitzman & Maclean, 1992).[1] During the early 1980s some states began adopting "primary caretaker presumptions," which grant preference to the parent who has been primarily responsible for attending to a young child's daily needs. Over time, then, custody provisions have gone from viewing children as property of the father, to viewing them as the developmental charges of the mother, to a more gender-neutral approach that emphasizes the caregiving function of the parent. Nonetheless, in the vast majority of divorces, primary custody of children is awarded to the mother.

CHILDREN AND DIVORCE. Reforms that have made divorce law more gender-neutral ironically may have also reduced women's bargaining power. Today, wives can no longer threaten to contest the grounds of the divorce or reveal proof of the husband's infidelity to get a better settlement. Similarly, the elimination of the presumption in favor of maternal custody may lead women to give up their property claims to avoid a stressful and protracted battle for custody of their children (Weitzman & Maclean, 1992). The loss of maternal preference has left women vulnerable when they do not conform to traditional stereotypes of the "good mother." Women who have had extramarital relationships or who are lesbian often risk losing their children. Further, some courts have been hostile to "overly ambitious" women whose careers absorb much of their energy and time, while others have refused custody to women without work interests on the grounds that they lack financial means. Nonetheless, in 90 percent of divorces custody is awarded to the mother, supporting the popular maxim: "In a divorce, men become single and women become single parents."

As single parents, most divorced women cannot rely on their children's father for support. Even when support is awarded, most divorced men fail to meet their obligations. In 1992, Irwin Garfinkel reported that "of women with

---

[1]As Deborah Rhode notes, a significant number of fathers who are denied legal custody of their children obtain de facto custody by abducting them.

children potentially eligible for child support . . . only six out of ten even have a child-support award . . . of those with child support awards, only half receive the full amount to which they are entitled, and over a quarter receive nothing. All told, more than half of the women potentially eligible for child support receive nothing" (p. 207 in Weitzman & Maclean, 1992). In recognition of this problem, legislation was enacted in 1975 that established the Federal Office of Child Support Enforcement and provided federal funding for states to establish offices for support enforcement. Further, the 1984 Child Support Amendments and Family Support Act of 1988 require states to implement child-support guidelines and automatic withholding of wages.

These and other measures have increased the amount of child support collected in the United States. The economic burden of child support is regressive, absorbing a greater proportion of the incomes of low-income fathers than of those who are well off. Nonetheless, stricter support enforcement translates into greater financial resources available to the children of divorce. (See Chapter 4 for discussion of child support collection and welfare benefits.)

REPRODUCTIVE RIGHTS

Humans have used measures to control fertility for several millennia, and only in modern times have birth control and abortion become emotionally charged political and moral issues. In the United States increased use of abortion and contraception coincided with the shift from a rural to an industrial economy. With this shift, children became less an economic asset than a potential impediment to a family's economic advancement.

THE DEBATES OVER ABORTION AND BIRTH CONTROL. According to Deborah Rhode (1989), early opposition to abortion and contraception stemmed from two concerns: first, that when sex was separated from procreation the result would be widespread promiscuity, venereal disease, and social instability; and the second, that if the "better" classes were able to control their fecundity while immigrants and working classes were not, the result would be an "inferior" race. Spearheading the opposition to abortion were physicians, who secured the high moral ground by arguing that abortion was unsafe for mothers, despite the fact that during the late nineteenth century (as today) abortion was considerably safer than childbirth. Physicians' opposition to abortion may have had an economic incentive. At the time, they had significant competition from midwives, in both reproductive health and obstetrics. Physicians' campaign against abortion included the myth that these "nefarious acts" were most often committed by midwives. Thus, their opposition may have been part of a larger effort to discredit lay health providers (Reegan, 1997).

In 1873, Congress passed the Comstock Law, which prohibited the distribution of information about contraception and abortion. Most states also passed statutes making abortion a felony. These statutes remained unchanged until the late 1960s. It is interesting to note that key actors in today's abortion debate were considerably less involved in the nineteenth century. For example, the Catholic Church did not begin to actively oppose the practice until late in the century. Some feminists of the era did not consider the issue of significant importance, and were reluctant to jeopardize the fight for suffrage over an issue they viewed as "too narrow . . . and too sordid" (Rhode, 1989, p. 204). During the early years of the twentieth century, some feminists openly opposed abortion, and most considered abstinence the appropriate measure for controlling fertility.

Margaret Sanger was the founder of a campaign for increased access to birth control during the early twentieth century. She was inspired to her advocacy efforts when she witnessed the death of an impoverished New York woman from self-induced abortion. Ms. Sanger's arguments for birth control did not emphasize feminist principles, focusing instead on hygiene and the prospect for "improving the race." She enlisted support from medical professionals by focusing on methods that could be controlled by physicians. In 1940, the term "family planning" was coined to shift the focus away from women's anatomy and sexual activity (Rhode, 1989, p. 205).

During the 1960s, members of the women's movement identified reproductive freedom as an essential right. At the same time, women had become more sexually active and were more often employed outside the home. The net result was an increase in the numbers of unwanted pregnancies and illegal abortions. Most estimates indicate that about 1 million abortions occurred annually, often performed under unsanitary conditions by unskilled practitioners. Thousands of women died each year, and many others suffered permanent injury. Their experiences served as the catalyst for efforts to liberalize abortion statutes.

In this context numerous polls attempted to weigh public sentiment regarding abortion. Results varied, but there was widespread public support for legalization of abortion, with varying figures depending on the circumstances. For example, support for abortion tended to be greater when respondents were asked to consider cases of rape or incest than when they were asked about its use as a method of birth control. In 1973, the Supreme Court heard *Roe v. Wade*, a case involving the constitutionality of a law prohibiting abortion except to save a mother's life. Justice Blackmun wrote the majority opinion that now governs women's access to abortion. That opinion concluded that during the first trimester of pregnancy the Fourteenth Amendment's guarantee of personal liberty implied a right to privacy "broad enough to encompass a woman's decision whether or not to terminate her pregnancy." Restrictions on that right required a compelling state interest in protecting either maternal or fetal life. At the time, the risk of abortion exceeded the risk of childbirth during the second and third trimesters, and fetal viability occurred during the third trimester. Thus, the Court permitted regulation of late-term abortion based on the state's interest in protecting life.

The decision, which satisfied neither feminists nor fundamentalists at the time, serves as the foundation for existing law governing women's access to abortion. It also set the stage for continuing debate.

The past two decades have seen a tremendous backlash against *Roe v. Wade*. Steady erosion in women's access to abortion probably began with the 1980 election of Ronald Reagan. During his tenure, President Reagan appointed half the federal bench and made three appointments to the Supreme Court, in each case attempting to select individuals who did not support *Roe v. Wade* (Melich, 1998).[2]

These appointments set the stage for two major Supreme Court decisions on the issue. In 1989 the Supreme Court upheld a restrictive abortion statute enacted in Missouri (*Webster v. Reproductive Health Services*). Then in 1992 the Court ruled that the usual standard applied to protection of constitutional rights ("strict scrutiny") did not apply to women's right to abortion. Instead, the court ruled that states could restrict access to abortion as long as the restrictions did not "unduly burden" the woman (*Planned Parenthood of Southeastern Pennsylvania v. Casey*).

A spate of restrictions have been passed by state legislatures, including mandatory waiting periods, parental notice and consent requirements, counseling requirements, and bans on "partial birth" abortions. In 1997, for example, 33 states enacted restrictions on abortion. In a few cases, these states have also expanded funding for programs that increase women's access to contraception, a measure seen by some as a practical approach to reducing the need for abortion. But public funding for contraception is itself controversial. Particularly controversial has been funding of programs that provide birth control education and contraceptive devices to teenagers.

Women's access to abortion has been further restricted by Congress. Generally these restrictions involve the use of federal funding for abortions. The restrictions are generally waived if the procedure is necessary to save a woman's life or if the pregnancy is the result of incest or rape. As of this writing, restrictions have been applied to the following groups of women: federal employees (whose insurance plans may not cover abortion); servicewomen stationed overseas (who may not obtain an abortion in a military medical facility); women in federal prisons (who may not use prison funds for abortion); women residing in the District of Columbia (who cannot use federal or local funds for abortion); and Medicaid recipients (who, under the "Hyde Amendment," may not use their health coverage for abortion). In each instance, the prohibition does not apply if the pregnancy is the result of rape or if the woman's life is endangered. Efforts to apply criminal sanctions to physicians who perform "partial birth" abortions were passed repeatedly in Congress and vetoed by President Clinton between 1996 and 2000.

Debates over reproductive rights are emotionally charged and typically leave little room for compromise. Opponents of legal abortion argue that a fetus of any

---

[2] Two of Reagan's appointees (Kennedy and O'Connor) did not prove to be as strongly opposed to *Roe v. Wade* as had been anticipated.

age should be seen as an innocent human being. They view abortion as murder, and a few go so far as to advocate violence against clinics and physicians. The notion of fetal rights leads not only to the view that abortion is murder, but also to the argument that maternal behavior that is damaging to the fetus should be prosecuted. So, some suggest, maternal drug use during pregnancy might be treated not only as a crime in its own right, but as an assault on a human being. This viewpoint has become an integral part of the platform of the Republican Party and serves as a key point of difference between most Republicans and most Democrats in the United States (Melich, 1998).

INVOLUNTARY STERILIZATION. The success of the family planning movement fueled a campaign for involuntary sterilization of thousands of poor and developmentally disabled women. With the development of relatively safe surgical sterilization techniques, states passed a wave of compulsory sterilization laws. These laws were reviewed and sustained in a 1927 decision by the Supreme Court (*Buck v. Bell*). The case involved the sterilization of Carrie Buck, the supposedly "feeble-minded" daughter of a "feeble-minded" mother. Carrie had just given birth in an institution to a feeble-minded child. Concluding that "three generations of imbeciles are enough" (Rhode, 1989, p. 205), Justice Holmes wrote the majority opinion supporting sterilization. As it turned out, evidence that Carrie was "feeble-minded" was equivocal, as the girl had been institutionalized to conceal her pregnancy, which was the result of a rape. Although the Supreme Court later cast doubt on the legality of the practice, it was used extensively by welfare officials who required "voluntary consent" to sterilization as a condition of receiving aid. Sterilization, particularly of poor minority women, continued until the 1980s, when it was curtailed by federal regulation.

PRESCRIPTION EQUITY. For years, private health insurance companies that provide coverage for prescription medications have denied coverage for contraceptives. In recent years, possibly owing to insurance coverage for the purchase of Viagra, the issue has come to the fore. Women's organizations, advocates, and several members of Congress have argued that companies that provide prescription coverage should not be allowed to exclude contraceptives.

There has been some progress towards prescription equity. In 1998, Congress extended contraceptive coverage to federal employees enrolled in the Federal Employees' Health Benefits Program. The following year, Senator Barbara Boxer and her colleagues introduced the "Equity in Prescription Insurance and Contraceptive Coverage Act." The text of the bill noted that "Private insurance provides extremely limited coverage of contraceptives: half of traditional indemnity plans and preferred provider organizations, 20 percent of point-of-service networks, and 7 percent of health maintenance organizations cover no contraceptive methods other than sterilization" [sec. 112, Findings (9)]. The Act did not reach the floor for a vote that year, but prescription equity will be "an issue to watch" at both state and federal levels in the early years of the twenty-first century.

VIOLENCE AGAINST WOMEN

Murder and assault of women have long been recognized as unacceptable, but only during recent decades have wife abuse and acquaintance rape been viewed as acts of violence. In this section we will look at domestic violence and rape as issues that continue to affect American women.

DOMESTIC VIOLENCE. Today wife-beating is condemned as domestic violence, but it was referred to as "domestic chastisement" in nineteenth-century America. Wife-beating was explicitly sanctioned by some early Christian ecclesiastics, who noted that "It was preferable for husbands to punish the [wife's] body and correct the soul than to damage the soul and spare the body" (Rhode, 1989, p. 238). Since husbands were legally responsible for their wives' behavior, common law recognized a husband's right to discipline his spouse, provided that he "neither kill nor maim her." A few American courts defined the boundaries of that right: a husband was permitted to whip his wife as long as he used a switch no thicker than his thumb. (The phrase "rule of thumb" comes from this stipulation.)

Divorce was an option only if the abuse was extreme and unprovoked. It was not available to women who continued to live with an abusive husband or who were judged to have "provoked" the abuse either through "passionate language" or refusal to have sexual relations. Because women had few formal or legal avenues for dealing with spousal violence, their best recourse was community disapproval. When the beating exceeded locally acceptable standards, a wife might seek assistance from family members or community leaders. This situation continued fundamentally unchanged until the late twentieth century.

On March 9, 1977, Francine Hughes was arrested for setting fire to her house while her ex-husband was sleeping. He died in the blaze, and she was charged with murder. During her trial she recounted her 12-year experience with an abusive husband, and the jury found Hughes not guilty by reason of temporary insanity. Her case, resulting in both a book (*The Burning Bed*, by Faith McNulty) and an NBC movie, contributed to a growing recognition of domestic violence as an issue of national concern.

The battered-women's movement, which had begun during the early 1970s, focused on providing refuge for victims and raising public awareness of the problem. For years, organizations such as the Salvation Army had provided shelter to battered women, but their primary focus was on the problems caused by alcoholism rather than on abuse. In 1973 women's advocates succeeded in opening the first shelters specifically designed for battered women: Transition House in Boston and Rainbow Retreat in Phoenix (Dobash & Dobash, 1992).

With these beginnings, a social movement to address domestic violence was born. Emerson and Russell Dobash (1992) have identified three general goals of the movement: "assisting victims, challenging male violence, and changing women's position in society" (p. 29). The number of organizations working to assist battered women grew exponentially. In 1977 there were 163 groups operating 130 shelters, and by 1989 the number of programs had reached 1,200, with shelters housing 300,000 women and children per year (Dobash & Dobash, 1992).

The battered women's movement moved from local and regional efforts to national initiatives in 1977, when a White House meeting was held to bring together activists and federal representatives. Within six months, the Commission on Civil Rights held hearings to consider whether battered women received equal protection under the law. Activists argued that because the legal system and police did not protect women, they were deprived of their liberty and property when forced to flee from abusive homes. More than 600 people attended the hearings, listening to presentations from 30 speakers. Among the issues discussed were law enforcement handling of domestic violence cases, oppression of women as a root cause of the violence, the potential for treating battering men, the incidence of husband-abuse, and federal funding for shelters.

The National Coalition Against Domestic Violence (NCADV) focused on attempting to secure federal funding for shelters. They encountered opposition in Congress from representatives who argued that government had "no business intruding into family disputes" (Rhode, 1989, p. 243). The Coalition secured the support of Rep. Barbara Mikulski, who introduced the Family Violence Prevention and Treatment Act in 1978. Despite support from the Carter administration, the bill failed, and after the 1980 election of Ronald Reagan its chances for passage diminished. Finally, during the 1983–84 congressional session, Mikulski condensed the bill and introduced it as an amendment to the Child Abuse Prevention and Treatment Act. It passed, providing states with $65 million over three years for abuse prevention and victim services, as well as $2 million each year for police training.

Today, the NCADV reports that at least four million incidents of domestic violence are reported and more than 3,500 women are killed by their batterers each year. The 1990s saw a dramatically increased federal response. The 1994 Violence Against Women Act expanded the funding available for training law enforcement officials, established interstate domestic violence as a federal crime, and confirmed that sex-based violence violates a woman's civil rights.[3] In 1996 President Clinton established the National Domestic Violence Hotline (1-800-799-SAFE) through executive order. In the first year and a half of its operation, the hotline received more than 120,000 calls.

RAPE. Unlike domestic violence, rape has long been recognized as a legal offense. However, it was primarily seen not as an offense against a woman but

---

[3]The Violence Against Women Act was declared unconstitutional by U.S. District Judge Jackson Kiser in Virginia, leading the National Organization for Women to argue that the judge's "bad" ruling is further evidence of the need for an Equal Rights Amendment.

as an affront to the men in her life—her father or husband. Based on a view of rape as a threat to the patrilineal system of inheritance, U.S. rape law "builds on a history of class, race, and gender biases" (Rhode, 1989, p. 245). The social status of both victims and assailants has traditionally been influential in determining the legal consequences of the crime. Thus, in the United States the rape of black women by white men was scarcely treated as a crime, while hundreds of black men were lynched when they were accused of raping white women (NAACP, 1969). Between 1945 and 1965, a death sentence was 18 times more likely for convicted black rapists with white victims than for any other combination (Rhode, 1989).

Women who charge strangers with rape have traditionally been subjected to a high level of scrutiny and a requirement that they demonstrate their resistance. Until the passage of "rape-shield" laws in the late 1970s, a woman's sex life was considered permissible evidence in court. Defendants used accounts of past behavior to establish that a woman was "unchaste" and probably had incited the rape through her behavior. Further, failure to energetically resist a rapist was interpreted by some courts as an indication of consent. Thus, women were victimized twice: once by a rapist and once by a legal system that insisted on putting rape victims on trial. Rape-shield laws prevent material regarding a woman's sexual history from being introduced by the defense during a rape trial.

Acquaintance rape does not correspond to the common understanding of the crime. Indeed, many women do not view forced sexual intercourse with a husband or date as a crime, so acquaintance rape often goes unreported. Nevertheless, under laws that are in effect in most states, sexual intercourse that is "accomplished forcibly, or by the threat of force without consent" (California penal code) is considered rape. The application and interpretation of this law often depends on the nature of a woman's relationship with the offender, as well as her sexual history. Rape shield laws do not apply if a woman has had previous sexual relations with the offender (Horney & Spohn, 1991).

For years, spousal rape simply did not exist as a crime. Under the principle of coverture, man and wife were one—and how could a man rape himself? Later arguments held that by getting married, women consented to intercourse upon demand and thus could not charge their husbands with rape. Opponents of prosecution of spousal rape continued to argue that the event itself was exceedingly rare and prosecution would involve the state as meddlers in "normal sexual relations" or voyeurs "behind the bedroom door" (Rhode, 1989, p. 250). Nonetheless, by 1990, 48 states had reformed their laws to include spousal rape. Successful prosecutions, while rare, have been reported (Wiehe & Richards, 1995).

During the past 25 years, the nation's laws have become less tolerant of violence against women. Two important reforms have been the rape-shield laws passed in the states in the 1970s and the 1994 Violence Against Women Act. Of course, these laws serve women who have already been victimized. Rape and the threat of violence hurt not only the women who are direct victims, but also women who constrain their movements and activities to avoid becoming victims.

American social policy has clearly influenced the costs and rewards incurred by women in their roles as wives and mothers. These laws reflect and influence broad changes in the social consensus about what constitutes justice in a family context. Today women can enjoy property rights and secure credit independently, regardless of their marital status. Divorce is available to more women than ever before. Public policy and public opinion have rejected the notion that a married woman should submit to "domestic chastisement." Women enjoy greater control over their reproductive futures than at any time in the past, and as we will see near the end of the next section, public policy has taken initial strides toward reducing the tensions experienced by mothers in the workplace.

WOMEN AS WORKERS

In the labor market a recurring challenge to public policies supportive of women has been Americans' belief (or hope) that if the free market is left unburdened by government regulation, it will ultimately provide fair conditions for all participants, be they male or female. In the workplace, American public policy has evolved from restricting women's job activities through "protective legislation" to prohibiting discrimination on the basis of gender.

A Brief History of Women in the U.S. Labor Force

A detailed history of women in the U.S. labor force is beyond the scope of this chapter. The interested reader will find material in Winifred Wandersee's *Women's Work and Family Values: 1920–1940*; Lynn Weiner's *From Working Girl to Working Mother: The Female Labor Force in the United States, 1820–1980*; Alice Kessler-Harris's *A Woman's Wage: Historical Meanings and Social Consequences*; and Susan Ware's (1981) *Beyond Suffrage: Women in the New Deal*. All of these sources were consulted extensively during the preparation of this section.

PROTECTIVE LEGISLATION FOR "WORKING GIRLS." The turn of the century has been characterized as the era of the "Working Girl." In 1890, roughly 19 percent of women, most of them young and single, were employed outside of the home, usually in domestic service. Critiques of female employment argued that women were rendering themselves either unfit or unable (if not unwilling) to assume their natural roles as wives and mothers (Weiner, 1985). In 1910 the U.S. Senate's study of employed women and children asked, "Is the trend of modern industry dangerous to the character of women?" (Kessler-Harris, 1990).

When women began entering the paid work force, they were routinely paid less than men who held the same jobs. For example, when the federal government bought its first typewriters in 1867, it established a classification for clerk typists. Within this classification, women received $600 per year, and men $1,200 per year (Simpson, 1985).

Working women of this era were excluded from most trade unions, so they established their own organizations. Unions in traditionally female occupations (laundresses, cap makers, and shoe workers) multiplied, and during the early 1900s the Women's Trade Union League was established to promote the formation of women's unions. Women also formed "protective leagues" to enhance working conditions and "abolish the sweatshop." Their successes prompted the development of protective legislation.

Protective labor laws were passed by states and municipalities in the post–World War I era amid rising concern that women were displacing men in manufacturing jobs. In the face of popular arguments that employment diminished women's reproductive capacity, the laws restricted the number of hours women could work and regulated the wages they could be paid.

The impact of the laws was debated. Some argued that wage requirements kept women out of middle- and upper-level positions. There were reports of women being fired as soon as they completed apprenticeships and became eligible for higher wages. Women complained that restrictions in the hours they could work further impaired their ability to compete effectively for jobs (Weiner, 1985).

Ultimately, the wage restrictions established by protective legislation were overturned by court rulings. In 1923 the Supreme Court overturned the wage regulations in the District of Columbia, invoking the freedom-of-contract argument (*Adkins v. Children's Hospital*; Weiner, 1985). Consequently, protective laws gradually were either overturned or disregarded.

WORKING MOTHERS AND THE NEW DEAL. The widespread movement of married women into the labor force emerged as a significant trend in the United States during the 1920s. Prior to this period, even in families with very low incomes, less than 25 percent of married women worked outside the home. African-American women were the conspicuous exception to this rule. At all economic levels, a much higher proportion of African-American wives and mothers worked. Wandersee (1981) argued that the increased employment of married women can be traced to an emerging ethic of consumption. With the emergence of mass marketing, the concept of an "American standard of living" became, as Wandersee put it, "[something] all could aspire to, many would attain, and some would never know" (p. 21). The changing character of home life also contributed. As the home was transformed from a unit of production to a unit of consumption, women who needed productive roles were forced to seek them outside the home.

Despite their presence in the labor force, women were excluded from most New Deal legislation that was enacted on behalf of workers. For example, the Fair Labor Standards Act, which regulated working hours, set a minimum wage, and prohibited child labor, specifically exempted domestic service from its provisions. The National Industrial Recovery Act, designed to "get industrial production moving again," covered only about half of employed women. Indeed, Wandersee notes that women who were most in need of protection—domestic laborers, laundresses not employed in laundries, and dressmakers not employed in factories—were among those explicitly excluded from the labor protections included in the Act (Wandersee, 1981). Most notably, the Social Security Act of 1935 excluded domestic workers, thereby precluding coverage for approximately 30 percent of working women (Wandersee, 1981).

Failure of the New Deal legislation to address women's needs reflected strong disapproval of employment among women, particularly those who were married. Disapproval and resentment were often articulated by the unions that worked with the Roosevelt administration to forge the New Deal. Central to their arguments were two concerns: (1) that working women would displace working men, and (2) that, by working, women jeopardized the natural order of civilization.

Samuel Gompers, head of the American Federation of Labor during this era, focused on the first concern when he said, "In industries where the wives and children toil, the man is often idle because he has been supplanted" (Kessler-Harris, 1990, p. 19). The second concern was expressed by a contributor to a labor journal called the *American Federationist*: "Woman's greatest security is to be found in the home, and where rests the security of women rests the security of life, the security of civilization" (Wandersee, 1981, pp. 69–70). Another labor paper argued that "sisters and daughters" should not leave home, even for congenial workshops and factories, and vowed to check this "most unnatural invasion of our firesides" (Abramowitz, 1996, p. 189).

Both concerns were expressed in a 1937 petition by the legislature of North Dakota. In it, legislators requested that the Department of Labor study the growing problem of "home-keeping" women entering paid employment.

> Whereas the employment of women in paid work outside the home has increased materially in recent years; and
>
> Whereas the home-keeping women going into commercial and industrial work was mentioned by the report of the Biggers Committee on National Unemployment as one of the causes of the unemployment problem; and . . .
>
> Whereas we all recognize the services rendered by the women of our homes in the building of character: Therefore be it
>
> Resolved, that the House of Representatives of the State of North Dakota, the Senate Concurring, hereby petition the . . . Department of Labor . . . to use its influence toward the securing of data on women employed outside the home . . . and thereupon to make a survey and a study of the problems of the home-keeping women, to find the reason for the tendency to leave home for commercial and industrial work and to make recommendations to reduce and, so far as possible, eliminate this tendency in modern living (*Congressional Record*, Vol. 84, p. 1271).

During the Great Depression, the federal government restricted the employment of married women in the civil service through Section 213 of the Federal Economy Act. In the interest of "spreading the wealth," this legislation prohibited more than one member of the same family from working in the civil service. Within a year, more than 1,600 workers lost their government jobs. Although the Act did not explicitly target women, three-fourths of those who lost their jobs were women. Nearly every state introduced bills to prevent employment of married women. Most Americans agreed with these practices, according to a 1936 Gallup poll (Abramowitz, 1996).

WORKING WOMEN AND THE GREAT SOCIETY. About three decades later, in 1964, President Johnson signed the first piece of congressional legislation that acknowledged gender discrimination as a significant social problem: Title VII of the Civil Rights Act. Popular myth holds that Title VII was introduced by an opponent of civil rights as a joke, or with the intention of scuttling the act completely. Indeed, the "sex" amendment (as it was known) was introduced by a Southern Democrat, Rep. Howard W. Smith of Virginia. While the Civil Rights Act was being debated on the House floor, Rep. Smith rose and offered a one-word amendment to Title VII, which prohibited discrimination in employment. The word was "sex," and it was intended to add women to the categories of individuals protected under the act. Evidently the amendment triggered several hours of "humorous debate," which Jo Freeman (1991) reported was later described as "Ladies' Day in the House." The amendment passed by a vote of 168 to 133. Freeman and other historians agree that Smith's motivation in introducing the amendment was not humor. Instead, she argues that he was responding to the tenacious lobbying of the National Women's Party (NWP). As we will discuss later in this chapter, the NWP also lobbied for the Equal Rights Amendment. Composed of an elite group of highly educated and well-off women, the NWP was a consistent force in the halls of the Capitol. They argued that sex discrimination was pervasive in the U.S. labor market, and if they did not succeed in persuading legislators to adopt their views they undoubtedly persuaded Congress that the NWP would not desist in its efforts. Thus, when Rep. Smith introduced the "sex" amendment he was bowing to pressure exerted by NWP.

As soon as the amendment passed the House, women's organizations throughout the nation organized to support it. Unlike the ERA, this provision received the endorsement of the Women's Bureau and the League of Women Voters. It passed the Senate and was signed into law, only to encounter the indifference of the Equal Employment Opportunity Commission (EEOC). The EEOC considered the inclusion of sex "a fluke" that was "conceived out of wedlock," and, as Jo Freeman notes (p. 164), "tried to ignore its existence" despite the fact that one-third of the employment complaints filed during the EEOC's first year of existence (1965) charged discrimination on the basis of sex.

The EEOC's indifference set the stage for the founding of the National Organization for Women (NOW). As Deborah Rhode (1989) tells it, NOW was founded during a 1966 National Conference of State (EEOC) Commissioners. Frustrated by the EEOC's tolerance of help-wanted advertisements that were clas-

Title VII of the Civil Rights Act of 1964

It shall be an unlawful employment practice for an employer. . . to fail or refuse to discharge any individual or otherwise to discriminate against any individual with respect to his compensation, terms conditions, or privileges of employment, because of such individual's race, color, religion, sex, or national origin; or. . . to limit, segregate or classify his employees or applicants for employment in any way which would deprive or tend to deprive any individual employee of employment opportunities or otherwise adversely affect his status as an employee, because of such individual's race, color, religion, sex, or national origin.

sified on the basis of sex, "twenty-eight disaffected conference participants each paid five dollars to join a group that Betty Friedan spontaneously christened NOW. Its purpose, as recorded on the most accessible napkin, was 'to bring women into full participation in the mainstream of American society now'" (Rhode, 1989, p. 58). NOW's first target was sex-classified help-wanted advertisements. Bowing to NOW's efforts, the EEOC eventually declared that the practice violated Title VII, a view that was upheld by the Supreme Court in 1973.

CONTEMPORARY WORK FORCE ISSUES

During the latter part of the twentieth century the United States witnessed phenomenal growth in the employment of women, including wives and mothers. In 1940, only 28 percent of adult women were in the labor force. By 1997, that figure had increased to 60 percent (Smith & Bachu, 1999). Many of these women were mothers. By 1992, most mothers of children under 18 (67.2 percent) were in paid employment (Women's Bureau, 1996). Even mothers of very young children were in the labor force. As of 1998, more than half (59 percent) of mothers of children one year old or younger were either working or looking for work (U.S. Census Bureau, 2000e).

Today, the majority of American women combine marriage, motherhood, and work. As a result, many policies and practices that affect women at work influence their other roles, just as resources to support their other roles affect women's ability to succeed in the labor market. Of course, a significant and growing minority of women do not marry and do not have children. A recurring challenge for U.S. public policy has been not only to enable the majority to combine family and work roles, but to do so without disadvantaging the minority who are pursuing a different life path.

In this section we will examine six issues that have emerged with the growth in women's employment: occupational segregation in the U.S. labor market, pay equity and comparable worth, family and medical leave, child care, women and pensions, and sexual harassment.

TABLE 8.1 OCCUPATIONAL DISTRIBUTION BY GENDER AND RACE*

Occupation	White		Black		Hispanic		Asian		Other	
	Male	*Female*	*Male*	*Female*	*Male*	*Female*	*Male*	*Female*	*Male*	*Female*
Executive, Administrative, and Managerial	14%	11%	6%	7%	6%	7%	13%	11%	7%	9%
Professional Specialty	12%	16%	6%	12%	5%	9%	19%	16%	7%	12%
Technician	4%	3%	2%	3%	2%	2%	7%	5%	3%	3%
Sales	12%	12%	6%	10%	7%	11%	11%	12%	6%	11%
Administrative Support (Clerical)	6%	26%	9%	25%	7%	24%	9%	22%	6%	24%
Private Household	.03%	.6%	.09%	2%	.1%	3%	.07%	.7%	.1%	1%
Service	8%	14%	18%	23%	15%	20%	13%	15%	14%	23%
Farming, Forestry, Fishing	4%	.8%	3%	.4%	7%	2%	2%	.5%	5%	1%
Manufacturing	19%	2%	14%	2%	19%	3%	11%	4%	22%	3%
Machine Operations	8%	5%	12%	10%	14%	14%	1%	10%	10%	9%
Transportation	6%	.8%	10%	1%	7%	.7%	3%	.2%	8%	1%
Laborers	7%	2%	12%	3%	11%	4%	4%	2%	12%	3%

*Figures represent the proportion of employed members belonging to each group (i.e., white male) that is found within each occupational grouping.

Source: U.S. Bureau of Census (1994). Summary Tape File 1, from 1990 Census (CD).

OCCUPATIONAL SEGREGATION IN THE U.S. LABOR MARKET. Occupational segregation permeates the U.S. labor market. While women have made inroads into traditionally male occupations, such as law and medicine, most continue to labor in occupations in which a majority of workers are women. Table 8.1 presents the proportion of workers in race and gender groups who labor in each occupational category.

Although women of all races work predominantly in clerical and service occupations, there are important occupational differences between white women and women of color. White and Asian women have substantially greater access to professional occupations than do black, Hispanic and Native American women. White women are more likely to be employed in sales positions, and black women are much more likely than others to work in private households.

With the passage of the Civil Rights Act of 1964, the federal government assumed a new position with respect to women's employment. Far from legislating gender discrimination, as was true in an earlier era, the Act prohibits it. Its implementation is largely dependent on the political views of the executive branch, with the Reagan and Bush administrations effectively curtailing activities in this area. Still, the Act itself represented substantial legislative progress toward a less segregated labor market.

PAY EQUITY AND COMPARABLE WORTH. The gender gap in wages no longer enjoys official sanction, yet it persists. In 1999, median earnings for women who worked full-time, year-round were only 72 percent of median earnings for men (National Committee on Pay Equity, 1999). Proponents of Human Capital Theory (discussed in Chapter 1) would argue that this difference, known as a "wage gap," occurs because women are less committed to their work, receive less education, have interrupted work histories, and fail to build up seniority on the job.

Most studies of the topic, however, have found that these human capital factors do not fully account for the gender difference in wages (Bergmann, 1971; Caputo, 1998; Malkiel & Malkiel, 1973; Mitchell, Levine, & Phillips, 1999; Oaxaca, 1975). As Senator Cranston noted,

> Variables such as attachment to the workforce, level of experience, education, job commitment, and similar factors have been examined in various studies. These studies have attempted to explain the difference in earnings between male and female workers, but they have generally been able to account for less than one-fourth and never more than one-half of the earnings differentials on the basis of different labor force participation patterns of male and female workers. Virtually every research study has concluded that there remains a large gap which can be explained only by the existence of discriminatory employment practices (*Congressional Record*, July 25, 1984, S9114).

Studies supporting Senator Cranston's views include Oaxaca (1975); Malkiel & Malkiel (1973); and Bergmann (1971).

The Equal Pay Act of 1963 required an employer to pay employees holding the same job the same wage. Title VII of the Civil Rights Act of 1964 went one step further, prohibiting wage discrimination on the basis of race, sex, religion, or national origin. A 1981 Supreme Court decision on pay scales for female prison guards in Oregon held that Title VII prohibits wage discrimination even when the jobs are not identical (*Gunther v. County of Washington*).

During the early 1980s, events in the state of Washington brought the high cost of gender discrimination to the fore. In December 1983, U.S. District Court Judge Jack Tanner ordered the state of Washington to raise salaries for workers in fields dominated by women in an effort to correct "pervasive" discrimination among state employees. The state was further ordered to pay back wages to women dating to the time the discrimination was identified. The decision was appealed, and the case was settled out of court.

This case became a catalyst for action at the state level, and other states have since adopted "comparable worth" plans or conducted comparable-worth studies. In these studies, jobs are evaluated on the basis of four categories: knowledge and skills, mental demands, accountability, and working conditions. Ratings are assigned within each category and a final score computed for each job. When wages in jobs with equal scores show consistent disparity, advocates argue that gender discrimination is the primary explanation. Rather than lowering the salaries of highly paid employees, remedies consist of increases to underpaid employees each year until their salaries approach parity.

Progress toward comparable worth reflects the longstanding American tradition of using public policy to remedy failures of the free market. The history of attempts to legislate comparable worth reveals profound resistance. At the heart of most objections is a belief that the free market, left unchecked, will eventually provide economic justice. As a result, federal legislation on comparable worth has been introduced, but to date nothing has passed. (For more information on comparable worth, contact the National Committee on Pay Equity, see Resources section at the end of this chapter.) Most progress towards pay equity has been made in the public sector, with cities such as Colorado Springs, Los Angeles, and San Jose, and states such as Minnesota and Washington implementing corrected pay scales for public employees.

FAMILY AND MEDICAL LEAVE. Today many women combine motherhood and work. More than 80 percent of working women are in their prime childbearing years (between the ages of 18 and 44). More than half of all mothers with babies one year old or younger are working or looking for work. Further, in 1991, 28.9 percent of all families with children were headed by a single parent, more than double the 1970 proportion of 13 percent (Mulroy, 1995; U.S. Census Bureau, 1991). It is no wonder that in the 1999 "Report on the American Workforce," the U.S. Secretary of Labor declared, "Since 80 percent of families now depend partly or fully on the paychecks of mothers . . . helping families deal with the competing needs of the home and the workplace must also be among our highest priorities" (Herman, 1999).

Issues related to pregnancy and child care can cause working mothers to take time off from their jobs or make a temporary switch to part-time work, but attempting to balance their roles as mothers and workers can put women at a disadvantage in the workplace. Interrupted employment can delay working mothers' career advancement and reduce their retirement income.

Until 1993, American women had only limited job protection when they became pregnant. What protection they did have dated to the Pregnancy Discrimination Act of 1978, which amended Title VII of the Civil Rights Act of 1964 to ensure that pregnant women would be treated the same as other employees. Essentially, the act required that states and employers extend temporary disability insurance policies to cover pregnant women.

The Pregnancy Discrimination Act was passed only after heated debate, with testimony against the bill claiming it would substantially increase costs to business, create unfair economic burdens, and even lead to increased discrimination against women of childbearing age. (See testimony of Francis T. Coleman, National Association of Manufacturers, U.S. Senate, April 26–29, 1977.)

In 1985 the first family and medical leave bill was introduced during the 99th Congress. Congress adjourned without voting on the bill. During the 100th Congress the bill was reintroduced and amended several times. During the 101st Congress, the bill was amended and passed both the House and the Senate. It was vetoed by President Bush on June 29, 1990. A House vote failed to override the veto. During the 102nd Congress, the bill was reintroduced and after some amendment passed both the House and the Senate. President Bush again vetoed the bill on Sept. 22, 1992. The Senate voted to override the veto, but the House did not. The Family and Medical Leave Act was introduced on January 21, 1993, passed both houses, and was signed into law by President Clinton on February 5, 1993 (PL 103-3). Thus, debate about family and medical leave continued through eight years and two presidential vetoes before passage of the act in 1993.

Under its current provisions, the Family and Medical Leave Act provides for up to 12 weeks of unpaid, job-protected leave per year—with uninterrupted health insurance coverage—for the birth or adoption of a child or the serious illness of the employee or an immediate family member. Businesses with fewer than 50 employees (a classification that includes most employers) are exempt. Employee eligibility is restricted to those who have worked 1,250 hours (25 hours per week) over the previous 12 months and who have worked at least 12 months. Employers may exempt key employees from coverage. Employees are required to provide 30 days' notice for foreseeable leaves and make a reasonable effort to schedule medical treatments to avoid unduly disrupting employers' operations. Employees must also provide medical certification justifying the need for the leave in the case of illness. Enforcement provisions parallel those of the Fair Labor Standards Act, with damages limited to double actual losses and a "good faith" exception granted to employers with reasonable grounds for believing they have not violated the Act.

CHILD CARE. At the beginning of the twenty-first century, the vast majority of mothers in the United States with children under 13 are employed. Their child care arrangements are, by and large, informal. As Hayes, Palmer, and Zaslow noted in a 1990 report, "The predominant form of non-parental care for all children 12 years old and under remains relatives" (p. 229). The next most common form of child care is "family day care," in which a woman (usually a neighbor) looks after children in her own home. "Most family day care homes appear to operate in an underground market in which prices are relatively low" (p. 230), and an estimated 10 to 30 percent of these homes are licensed (Hayes, Palmer,

& Zaslow, 1990). The widespread use of relatives and family day care continues today (Kilburn & Hao, 1996).

Federal initiatives in support of child care can take two forms: subsidies that compensate parents for child care expenses and direct payment for care. In recent decades, tax subsidies have assumed a growing proportion of federal child care expenditures. In 1972, 80 percent of federal child care dollars were targeted to low-income families through provider subsidies, such as Head Start and the Social Services Block Grant (SSBG) programs. By 1995, these programs accounted for about 69 percent of the total, while the child and dependent care tax credit (enacted in 1976) accounted for 25 percent of federal expenditures in this area. This tax credit represents the single largest federal expenditure for child care (Kilburn & Hao, 1996). Like any tax deduction, child care tax credits now offered by the federal government as well as many states have greatest value to those with the highest federal tax obligation—those who owe the most income tax.

Another innovation, established as part of the Economic Recovery Act of 1981, permits employers to establish "Flexible Spending Accounts" (FSAs) that allow employees to pay for their child care with "pretax dollars." Under these plans (regulated under Section 129 of the IRS code), employees specify their anticipated child care expenses up to $5,000 per year. The specified amount is withheld from gross salary on a regular basis and refunded upon presentation of receipts for child care expenses. Employers save Social Security and unemployment taxes on the portion of the salary allocated for child care. The Bureau of National Affairs (1984) reported that FSAs are one of the most popular types of employer benefits, expected to grow rapidly. Like the child care tax credit, this benefit is of greatest value to middle- and upper-income workers.

Federal interventions to expand child care availability to low-income women have applied direct expenditures to pay for care. Funding mechanisms have included TANF, Head Start, the Social Services Block Grant, and other preschool programs (Hayes, Palmer, & Zaslow, 1990; Kilburn & Hao, 1996). Federal programs also provide limited funding for infrastructure subsidies that enhance the supply and quality of available child care by financing increased training and wages for caregivers, improved standards and regulations, and extended resource and referral services.

WOMEN AND PENSIONS. The disadvantages women experience in the wage market pale by comparison to their lack of employer-provided benefits. As Crystal and Shea (1990) pointed out, "A 'good' job may be distinguished from less 'good' jobs more sharply by its benefits, such as pension entitlement, than by its salary. The holder of such a 'good' job is more likely to be well-educated, to have a long-term attachment to the job and employer, to be male and to be white" (p. 438).

Women have been treated differently from men by private pensions, both as workers and as workers' wives. Working women are less likely than men to even be covered by a pension. This contributes to the gender differential in retirement income among today's elderly. Women were historically paid lower pension benefits to reflect their greater longevity. Finally, among private employers there has been a tendency to view a wife's survivor coverage as her husband's responsibility.

Women are less likely than men to be covered by a pension during their working years, and as a result, less likely to have their retirement supplemented by pension benefits. This gender difference may be a key factor behind the greater incidence of poverty among elderly women than among elderly men (see Chapter 9). The tremendous post–World War II growth in private pensions led to higher retirement incomes for men who retired during the 1980s. As Radner (1991) noted, "Pension income was the only income type that was a substantial positive factor in the growth in mean total income of the aged" (from 1979 to 1989) (p. 11).

A gender gap in pension income persists, however. In today's elderly cohort, men are about twice as likely as women to receive private pension income. In 1996, only 18 percent of older women received pension benefits, compared to 34 percent of older men. Median pension income for these women was roughly half that of men with pension income (Johnson, 1999).

Some observers explain this gender gap by noting that the industries most likely to employ women (retail trade and nonprofessional services) are among those least likely to offer pension coverage. However, Korczyk (1993) argued that "Based on all characteristics other than earnings, women are still less likely to be covered by pensions than similarly situated men" (p. 28). In her analysis, the gender gap persisted among men and women who were similarly situated with respect to job tenure, industry, union membership, age, occupation, and firm size. She suggested that "Women's pension coverage lags behind that of men largely because the labor market treats women differently from men" (p. 32).

The gender gap in pension income should diminish for future cohorts of women. As a 1993 study reported, the gender gap tends to be less pronounced among younger workers. It was greatest in the 50 to 54 age group, in which 63 percent of male and 49 percent of female workers had pension coverage (Korczyk, 1993). Most studies of trends in pension coverage note that growing numbers of women workers have pension coverage (Evan & Macpherson, 1994; Wiatrowski, 1993). Of course, the extent to which increased coverage translates into higher retirement income remains to be seen.

In what might now be considered a historical quirk, both contributions and benefits under a private pension plan were once computed based on gender, with women required to contribute more and/or to receive lower monthly benefits. As Gohmann and McClure (1987) noted, the practice "seems economically logical," given women's greater life expectancy. Nevertheless, it is now illegal.

In 1978, the Supreme Court used Title VII of the Civil Rights Act of 1964 to conclude that employers could not require women to make larger contributions to a pension plan in order to receive the same benefits a man in their situation would receive (*City of Los Angeles Department of Water and Power v. Marie Manhart*). A 1983 decision extended this ruling to preclude offering lower monthly benefits to women employees (*Arizona Governing Committee for Tax-Deferred Annuity and Deferred Compensation Plans v. Nathalie Norris*).

Access to survivor's benefits is another significant pension issue for women. Prior to 1974, about one in five covered workers were in plans with no provision for survivors. For wives of workers, the death of a spouse therefore meant complete loss of pension income, as well as a one-third reduction in Social Security benefits. Further, wives of workers whose plans did offer survivors' benefits could be divested of those benefits without their knowledge or consent.

With the 1974 passage the Employee Retirement Income Security Act (ERISA), Congress accomplished the nation's first comprehensive pension reform legislation. Three subsequent laws have expanded ERISA protections: the Tax Equity and Fiscal Responsibility Act of 1982 (TEFRA), the Retirement Equity Act of 1984 (REA), and the Tax Reform Act of 1986. (These policies are also discussed in Chapter 9.)

Plans must now offer employees the opportunity to elect a "joint and survivor option," in which payments are made to survivors. This option must be provided at the time of retirement. Workers who select it opt for a reduction in their retirement income, in exchange for coverage that extends for the lifespan of their survivors. ERISA also requires that a spouse give "knowing consent" when the worker elects to forego the survivor annuity.

A growing number of retirees have opted for survivor coverage. In 1978, only 38 percent of married workers elected the survivor benefit option. By 1985 that figure had risen to 65 percent, and in 1989 as many as 80 percent of retiring married workers retained the joint and survivor annuity (U.S. General Accounting Office, 1992). Those who did not elect survivor protection were typically those with the lowest incomes. In 1989, only 45 percent of those with the lowest pension income (median of $354 per month) elected survivor coverage. By contrast, survivor coverage was chosen by 60 percent of those with mid-level incomes (median of $598 per month) and 74 percent of those at the highest level of pension income (median of $1,000 per month) (U.S. General Accounting Office, 1992). Clearly, women who could least afford to live without survivor protection were most likely to be forced to do so.

SEXUAL HARASSMENT. In 1991 many Americans were glued to their televisions, watching Anita Hill, a young law professor, testify that she had experienced sexual harassment at the hands of President Reagan's nominee to the Supreme Court. The experience contributed to a growing awareness of the issue of sexual harassment in the workplace. Since then, thousands of women and some men have filed lawsuits claiming they were sexually harassed. The result has been a potpourri of (sometimes contradictory) judgments and a growing number of "backlash" lawsuits by alleged perpetrators against companies from which they were dismissed.

What is sexual harassment? Current law recognizes two forms of sexual harassment. In "quid pro quo harassment," sexual favors are demanded in exchange for favorable treatment, or rebuffing sexual advances involves the risk of reprisal. Another form of harassment, recognized since a 1986 ruling by the

Supreme Court (*Meritor Savings Bank v. Vinson*) involves the creation of an "intimidating, hostile, or offensive" work environment. Both of these types of harassment are recognized by the Equal Employment Opportunity Commission as forms of sex-based discrimination. (See EEOC, "Guidelines on Discrimination Because of Sex," Title VII, Section 703—*Federal Register*, 45, April 11, 1980.)

Both forms of sexual harassment are prohibited by Title VII of the Equal Rights Act (Maypole & Skaine, 1983). Title IX of the Higher Educational Amendments of 1972 prohibits sexual harassment on college and university campuses. State laws governing assault and battery or infliction of emotional distress have been applied to cases involving hostile work environments (Thomas, 1991). Finally, most large employers and public agencies have established policies that prohibit sexual harassment and establish procedures for victims to pursue. Often these are "zero tolerance" policies, specifying that the slightest hint of sexual harassment will bring about disciplinary action.

In some cases, men who have been charged with sexual harassment have won large settlements against their former employers. Often these "backlash" cases charge that a man's First Amendment right to freedom of speech has been violated. In one 1993 case (*Silva v. University of New Hampshire*), a court reinstated a professor who had been suspended for using sexual metaphors in his technical writing class. Other backlash cases have resulted in large settlements awarded to men who were discharged on the basis of allegations of sexual harassment (i.e., *Mackenzie v. Miller Brewing Co.*).

Despite the array of policies and procedures designed to prevent and remedy sexual harassment, judicial practices and employment realities often prevent women from reporting incidents and pursuing legal remedies. In *Meritor Savings Bank v. Vinson*, the Supreme Court ruled that a victim's "sexually provocative" speech or dress was relevant to whether the conduct was offensive. This ruling opened the door to defenses that put women on trial for their relationships, behavior, and attire. Further, some courts have required that women demonstrate they resisted or complained about unwanted sexual demands. Thus, women who were in no position to refuse or complain may be denied access to legal remedies. In 1994, President Clinton signed the Violence Against Women Act, which restricts the extent to which a plaintiff's personal history can be brought in to defend against allegations of sexual harassment.

The EEOC and the courts have seen growing numbers of sexual harassment complaints. Between 1991 and 1998, the number of claims filed with the EEOC increased from 7,000 to 16,000 (Henetz, 1998).[4] Resolving these cases often

---

[4]Men, too, have been subjected to sexual harassment. In fact, a 1998 Supreme Court ruling (*Oncale v. Sundowner Offshore Services*) held that "The prohibition of sexual harassment does not necessarily speak to an individual's gender, but forbids behavior so objectively offensive as to alter the conditions of the victim's employment." Previous cases had been ruled discrimination as women were subjected to experiences that would not have occurred had they been men. In this ruling, the court focused on the severity and persistence of the harassment. Roughly 12 percent of the sexual harassment claims filed in 1997 involved male victims.

proves difficult, the body of case law regarding sexual harassment is contradictory, cases can degenerate into "he said/she said" allegations that are difficult to sort out, and there continues to be confusion regarding the distinction between harassment and discrimination.

As Yale University law professor Vicki Schultz has noted, it is important to keep in mind that prohibition of sexual harassment does not prohibit sexuality per se, but gender discrimination. The goal of this policy is to achieve equality in the workplace, not to prosecute people who tell off-color jokes (Schultz, 1998).

In summary, progress toward equal employment rights in the United States has been uneven at best. Attempts to expand government regulation of private employers confront deeply ingrained American beliefs about the fairness of the free market and the integrity of the entrepreneur. Public policy in this arena is often marked by ambivalence, reluctance, and denial. Nonetheless, our conceptions about what constitutes justice in the workplace have changed considerably. While pay equity may remain a distant goal, working women are no longer paid less simply because of their gender. Steps are being taken to reduce the career sacrifices that working women undergo when they become mothers. During retirement, many women enjoy the benefits assured by the nation's pension reforms. Finally, the costs of labor force participation need no longer include the risk of being subjected to unwanted sexual advances.

WOMEN AS CITIZENS

Initially, women were not considered "citizens" or even "persons" under the Constitution of the United States. As Deborah Rhode (1989) noted, "When the framers of America's founding documents spoke of men—of 'men . . . created equal' and 'endowed . . . with certain unalienable rights'—they were not using the term generically" (pp. 19–20). Women were not alone in this regard, sharing this exclusion with Native Americans (a Native American man was counted as two-thirds of a man in early censuses), and with African-Americans who were then held in slavery. Women's progress toward full citizenship in the United States has manifested itself in two major reform efforts. One effort was successful and the other was not. The first was the campaign for women's right to vote, and the second was the campaign for passage of the Equal Rights Amendment.

SUFFRAGE

The right to vote, or suffrage, which is considered the defining characteristic of full citizenship, was denied to American women until 1920. Women's suffrage was a long time coming. Signs of discontent surfaced as early as 1848, when the first convention to discuss women's rights convened in Seneca Falls, New York. Two years later, the National Women's Rights Convention, planned by Lucy Stone, Lucretia Mott, and Abby Kelley, drew one thousand people. Sixteen years later, suffragists presented petitions bearing 10,000 signatures to Congress, asking for an amendment prohibiting disenfranchisement on the basis of sex. During the same year, 1866, the American Equal Rights Association was formed to pursue voting rights for women and African-Americans. In 1868, when the Fourteenth Amendment was ratified, the word "male" was used for the first time to define a citizen for the purposes of voting. That same year, the first federal women's suffrage amendment was introduced in Congress.

During the years between introduction and passage of the Nineteenth Amendment, suffragists mounted a campaign that included marches and picketing, hunger strikes, fiery protests, and parades. At one especially clever protest in 1919, the National Woman's Party established a "watchfire for freedom" in which they burned every speech President Wilson had given about democracy. Suffragists were arrested by police, attacked by mobs, and reviled from many pulpits. Anti-suffragist organizations were formed and actively sought to prevent women from securing the right to vote.

Opponents of suffrage (many of whom were women of means) argued that it would jeopardize traditional values—allowing women to vote would run "counter to the dictates of biology, the experience of evolution and the will of the Creator" (Rhode, 1989, p. 14). They argued that domestic disaster would ensue. In a version of the "slippery slope" argument, anti-suffragists suggested that once women had the vote, they would want to enter the workplace, where mingling of the sexes would result in promiscuity. Thus, women's suffrage would pave the way to anarchy and free love. Others suggested that involvement in the public sphere would be hard to reconcile with the demands of the private sphere. Finally, some argued that either wives would vote the same way their husbands did—in which case their votes would make no difference—or wives would vote differently from their husbands, which would lead to domestic strife.

The suffrage movement found fertile ground during the settlement of the western part of the country. Wyoming granted women voting rights in 1869, while it was still a territory. Colorado followed 24 years later, adopting women's suffrage in 1893. Colorado was followed in quick succession by the states of Utah (1896), Idaho (1896), Washington (1896), and California (1911). By the end of 1914, women had voting rights in nine western states and Kansas. Six years later, the Nineteenth Amendment was ratified by 36 states and signed into law.

The Nineteenth Amendment to the Constitution

The right of citizens of the United States to vote shall not be denied or abridged by the United States or by any state on account of sex.

THE EQUAL RIGHTS AMENDMENT

Three years after the right to vote had been secured, the National Women's Party began working to establish a constitutional amendment protecting the civil rights of women. The Equal Rights Amendment (ERA) was authored by Alice Paul, head of the NWP. Its text read simply, "Equality of rights under the law shall not be denied or abridged by the United States or by any state on account of sex."

In 1923, the ERA was introduced in Congress by Senator Curtis and Representative Anthony, both Republicans;[5] Anthony was the nephew of suffragist Susan B. Anthony. In response to dogged lobbying by the NWP, the ERA was introduced in each subsequent session of Congress.

The ERA was opposed by most moderate women's organizations, including the League of Women Voters, The Women's Trade Union League, the National Consumers League, and the newly created Women's Bureau within the Department of Labor. Opponents feared passage would void protective legislation that restricted the number of hours women could be required to work and established minimum pay requirements for women.

The amendment was revived in 1967 with the establishment of the National Organization for Women (NOW), which pledged to battle for passage. Four years later, the ERA was approved without amendment by the House of Representatives. It had the endorsements of the National Education Association and the United Auto Workers. In 1972 the amendment passed the Senate. Although it passed both Houses with substantial margins, two Senators (Sam Ervin and Emmanuel Celler) were successful in setting a time limit of seven years for ratification.

With the clock ticking, NOW's campaign began. In light of Congress's overwhelming endorsement, the amendment seemed headed for early state ratification. Within months, 20 state legislatures had ratified it, often with minimal debate. It received a boost in 1973 with the endorsement of the AFL-CIO. During the late '70s, however, the ERA lost its momentum. Anti-ERA groups began to surface, such as Phyllis Schlafly's National Committee to Stop ERA.

Schlafly, herself a lawyer, worked for a right-wing organization and devoted her considerable energies to defeating the amendment. Flying throughout the nation, she became the spokesperson for traditional values. Arguments against the ERA held that women would lose their preferential treatment with respect to family and military obligations. Wives would be legally required to work; divorcing women would lose presumptions in favor of awarding them custody of small children; and women would be subject to the draft and forced into combat. The ERA, it was argued, would permit homosexual marriage and require unisex public bathrooms. Finally, the states' rights argument was raised by some who believed the amendment represented unwarranted intrusion of the federal government into the prerogatives of state governments.

In response to anti-ERA efforts, NOW organized a convention boycott of unratified states that was supported by more than 450 pro-ERA organizations. Participating organizations refused to schedule meetings or conventions in states that had not ratified the ERA. It was at this point in the struggle, on July 9, 1977,

---

[5]Members of the Republican Party supported the ERA well into the 1970s. The amendment was endorsed by the Party in its 1940 platform. Indeed, Republican support for women's concerns historically exceeded that of the Democratic Party. The reversal on the part of Republicans dates to the Reagan era, when systematic efforts by conservative Republicans effectively silenced the party's progressive element. The transformation of the party's positions vis à vis women is well documented in Tanya Melich's 1998 book, *The Republican War Against Women*.

that Alice Paul, author of the ERA, died at the age of 92. In 1978, with intense lobbying by women's organizations, the House of Representatives approved an extension of the ERA deadline to June 30, 1982.

The ERA battle extended (as many do) from legislatures to the courts, when in 1978 the Attorney General of Missouri filed an antitrust suit against NOW's boycott. A year later a federal judge ruled that NOW's activities were protected by the First Amendment and did not violate antitrust laws. This decision was upheld by the U.S. Court of Appeals, and the Supreme Court declined to hear Missouri's appeal. In the late 1980s the legality of NOW's boycott was established. In other court action, legislators from Idaho, Arizona, and Washington filed suit challenging the legality of the ERA extension and seeking to validate states' right to rescind their earlier approval of the amendment. The case was assigned to Judge Marion Callister, who held a high office in the Church of Jesus Christ of Latter-Day Saints (the Mormons). The church actively opposed the ERA, and Judge Callister ruled the ERA extension illegal and rescission legal. Seventeen days later, the Supreme Court granted a unanimous stay, prohibiting enforcement of the Callister decision.

Equal Rights Amendment

Equality of rights under the law shall not be denied or abridged by the United States or by any state on account of sex.

On June 30, 1982, the ERA was stopped three states short of ratification. Since then the amendment has been reintroduced in each session of Congress. Debate over the amendment continues, with opponents emphasizing that legislation of the past three decades has made the ERA unnecessary. Under this view, statutes such as Title VII of the Equal Rights Act of 1964, the 1963 Equal Pay Act, and the Equal Credit Opportunity Act of 1974 have provided remedies for the most glaring acts of discrimination against women. ERA supporters, including NOW, argue that the amendment is needed, if only for symbolic purposes, to put women squarely into the Constitution.

In this section we have considered two constitutional battles that have affected the status of women as U.S. citizens. The first, a fight for the right to vote, was a hard-fought victory; the second, a fight for the ERA, was an equally hard-fought defeat. In the final section of this chapter, we will consider the status of women in the social work profession.

WOMEN IN THE SOCIAL WORK PROFESSION

Many social workers devote themselves (like Deeda Seed in this chapter's case study) to the advancement of women. Within the profession itself, however, women experience the very discrimination that advocates struggle to eliminate. Most social workers are women. In 1995, 78.3 percent of NASW's 113,352 members were women (Gibelman & Schervish, 1997). But women social workers are consistently paid less than men. Results of a 1995 report mirrored earlier studies going back 20 years. With over 37,000 NASW members reporting, male social workers earned more than female social workers (Gibelman & Schervish, 1995). On average, women earned 89 percent of men's salaries. This difference holds at all levels within the profession. Men earn more than women even when they hold the same degree, share comparable job titles, and have the same number of years of experience. Indeed, a 1991 survey of social work faculty found that men with doctorates who held the rank of full professor earned more than women, even when rank, degree, publications, experience, and ethnicity were all controlled (Sowers-Hoag & Harrison, 1991). Clearly, as Gibelman and Schervish (1995) and others have noted, it is time for the profession to "get its own house in order" (p. 628).

SUMMARY: THE STATUS OF WOMEN IN THE UNITED STATES TODAY

Advertisements for Virginia Slims cigarettes used to annoy many women by declaring, "You've come a long way, *baby.*" Apart from the irritating "baby," the slogan has a ring of truth. Women in the United States have come a long way in a protracted struggle that has taken its toll. Progress has been achieved largely through the efforts of thousands of women and men who participated in one of the great social movements of our time, the "Women's Movement." This chapter began by recounting the experiences of Annie Boone, a twentieth-century woman who survived abuse to raise her children and build her own economic security. We chronicled the historical developments related to women's roles as wives and mothers, as workers and as citizens. We outlined the contemporary issues that face American women, and ended the chapter with a brief look at the position of women in the social work profession.

American women have achieved tremendous progress as wives and mothers, as workers, and as citizens. Today we can scarcely imagine being unable to vote, and the notion of coverture is inconceivable. The past half-century has seen progress in the rights of working women. Practices that were once condoned, such as differential pay scales for women and men in the same job, are no longer tolerated, and sexual harassment of women is prohibited. Like women in many other industrialized nations, American women have come a long way, but they continue to be over-represented among the nations' disadvantaged and victimized. Clearly, we still have a long way to go.

DISCUSSION TOPICS

1. To what extent do you think that genetic or physical differences between men and women contribute to their different roles and rewards in the U.S. workplace?

2. Is the notion of equal pay for comparable work compatible with your view of social justice?

3. Are low-income mothers among the "deserving poor"? Why or why not? Consider the U.S. welfare system—under what circumstances would low-income mothers be considered deserving in this context?

SUGGESTED RESOURCES

Bernikow, L. (1997). *The American Women's Almanac: An Inspiring and Irreverent Women's History.* New York: Berkeley Books.

Dobash, R. E., & Dobash, R. P. (1992). *Women, Violence and Social Change.* London & New York: Routledge Press.

Hoff, J. (1991). *Law, Gender, and Injustice: A Legal History of U.S. Women.* New York: New York University Press.

Rhode, D. (1989). *Justice and Gender: Sex Discrimination and the Law.* Cambridge: Harvard University Press.

www.dol.gov/dol/wb—Maintained by the Women's Bureau in the U.S. Department of Labor, this site offers information of interest to working women, not only in the U.S., but around the world.

www.feminist.com/fairpay—This site is maintained by the National Committee on Pay Equity (NCPE), which acts as a clearinghouse for pay equity news and information. The site offers NCPE publications and updates on data and activities having to do with fair wages.

www.now.org—The National Organization for Women provides an astonishing array of information through its web site. Visitors to the site can sign up to receive NOW action alerts.

www.owl-national.org—This site is home to the national office of the Older Women's League. It is an outstanding source of information on policy issues of importance, not just to older women, but to women of all ages.

9

The Elderly

Old age is an island surrounded by death.

JUAN MONTALVO

If old age is an island, it has been sparsely populated throughout most of human history. A few noteworthy individuals have always survived to an advanced age, but the aging of large numbers of people is a twentieth-century phenomenon. Today's elderly have been described as "modern pioneers,"[1] and nations throughout the world are seeking the best ways to provide for their needs and tap into their expertise.

As more people survive into old age, this demographic group is becoming more heterogeneous. Early in the twentieth century, age usually brought disease and indigence. Among today's elders, illness and poverty are less common. Many suffer from debilitating chronic conditions, but others compete in the Senior Olympics. Some of the nation's elderly (predominantly women, the very old, and minorities) live in abject poverty, but others number among the nation's most affluent and powerful. This diversity complicates the task of program and policy development, bringing into question the continued use of age as the basis of eligibility for public programs.

After discussing the life experiences of Sylvia Johnson, we will look at the treatment of the elderly in colonial America, then trace the development of public policies affecting this age group. The section on contemporary issues will begin with an examination of current attitudes towards the aged. Changing demographic realities are considered next, followed by a discussion of programs and policies for the elderly. Finally, we will consider the role of social workers in serving the nation's elderly.

---

[1]This phrase was used by Ethyl Shanas in her book by the same title.

CASE STUDY ◆ SYLVIA JOHNSON

Mrs. Sylvia Johnson, an 80-year-old African-American woman, lives 12 blocks from the White House in a D.C. public housing unit. I met her through a volunteer organization serving the elderly in her neighborhood. Wilma, the outreach worker, took me for an initial visit two days before my scheduled interview. At that time, Mrs. Johnson's one-room apartment was crowded with her homemaker, Wilma, Amy (a volunteer with a housing advocacy group), and me.

On the day of the interview, Wilma gave me detailed directions, including where to cross the street, and instructed me to "call in" as soon as I arrived so she wouldn't worry. I was one of only a few white people in the area. Homeless young men shuffled by, deciding not to bother asking me for money. Young men in cars zoomed down the street, making as much noise as possible. A few old people passed, walking as quickly as they could. Apartment units in the area were surrounded by wire fences, with bars on the windows at street level.

Entering the building, I was scrutinized by three men who had been in the foyer during my first visit. The security guard remembered me. Still, he reviewed my ID and told me to write my name, agency, destination, and arrival time on his sign-in sheet. After signing in, I took the elevator to the fourth floor, where the hall was totally deserted. Mrs. Johnson's apartment, like most in the building, bore the evidence of years of neglect. There were large holes in the walls where plaster had come off. Water ran continuously from the kitchen and bathroom faucets. Closet doors had come off their hinges and were propped against the wall. Walls carried several layers of grime, and cockroaches had the run of the place. The heating system worked, though, and the apartment was usually warm enough to keep a visitor in a light sweat.

Mrs. Johnson was heavy and had lost both legs and much of her eyesight to diabetes. She spent her time in a hospital bed, with blinds drawn. I entered the darkened room to find her lying in bed, the stumps of her legs against the foot of the bed, her head cocked to the side of her pillow, her eyes staring at the wall. She nodded slowly when I asked if she was OK.

Mrs. Johnson asked for some water. When I found a chipped mug and brought her water she said it was too cold. I offered some Ginger Ale I'd seen on the counter. She drank five cups, then said she was hungry. After inspecting the refrigerator I offered a bologna sandwich with mayonnaise. The bologna was open and dry in the refrigerator, not sealed in plastic. I found a plate and fixed the sandwich, while a half dozen cockroaches explored the counter. She ate eagerly, consuming all but the last corner of crust.

Mrs. Johnson did not have the strength to lift herself out of her bed. The mattress was covered with plastic, and she lay on the type of disposable absorbent towel called a "chuck" that is often used in hospitals. Under her bed two of these had been discarded, along with a crumpled hospital gown.

Mrs. Johnson had a homemaker who came four hours a day from Monday through Friday. Funding for this service was provided by Medicaid and the Older Americans Act. On weekends her son Louis gave what care he could. Louis drank too much, and some said he used crack. A few days before the interview he had been barred from the building for a year because he had assaulted a resident. Louis had no place else to sleep and had clearly spent the preceding night on Mrs. Johnson's sofa. The morning before I came he left, locking his mother in. When I called in, Wilma warned me not to stay "too long" because there would be trouble if Louis showed up. With Wilma's advice in mind, I put my tape recorder at the foot of the bed and began to talk with Mrs. Johnson about her life.

Sylvia Johnson was born in 1913 in Camden, South Carolina. She told me that she was the fourth of 12 children, all of whom were "mean." No one in town picked on them because they were all so mean. Her daddy was big—over 200 pounds. He worked in the construction trade. Her mother was pretty nice, but if you misbehaved she would "get daddy on you." What Daddy would do was never clear because Sylvia never dared find out.

Sylvia went to school and finished the 8th grade. While she was visiting her sister-in-law in D.C. she met her future husband, a much older man. She decided to quit school and marry him. People teased her about marrying someone old enough to be her grandfather, but Mrs. Johnson thought he was a good man to marry. He gave her money, and she'd never had money before. She was happy with her choice. "I had a good husband. . . . Well, like he know better than to try to beat me, you know."

Mrs. Johnson had four sons. Her children knew better than to make her mad because she was "mean as a dog." People didn't bother her much because she was so mean. "Mean as a dog." It's a phrase she used often to describe herself. Her sons grew up mean, and they protected their mama. She never worked. But her husband had jobs, and "things like that." They lived in a house on the edge of town. Then he died of "asthma, something like that." It made Mrs. Johnson cry to see him in such pain. Two of her sons died, too.

Midway through the interview I was startled by a loud knock on the door. Two police officers wanted to look in the closet for Louis's coat. They found the coat and examined it, then left. The closet was jammed full of men's clothes, with no women's clothes in sight.

Several people would have liked to see Mrs. Johnson moved to a nursing home. I asked her whether she would like to go someplace where people could take care of her and bring her food. She said, "No." As we talked she often mentioned that people didn't "bother" her. I asked whether they had bothered her in the hospital. "Oh no. They were nice." One woman brought her food, and when Mrs. Johnson didn't like it, she brought in some country food. Would Mrs. Johnson like to go someplace like a hospital? "No, because this is more like a home." Not that it was a home, just more like one. Mrs. Johnson clearly preferred the apartment over a nursing home.

Because Louis had been violent, several people had accused him of abusing his mother. This she denied. No one had ever hurt her, because she was so mean and her sons were so mean. "Louis? He wouldn't hurt his mama. He's a good boy."

Mrs. Johnson used to watch TV for the stories, but as her eyesight deteriorated she found it harder to follow the plots and just watched the pictures—despite their being out-of-focus.

What did Mrs. Johnson like best about herself? "I'm alive." Many people she knew were dead, but she wasn't, and she felt there must be a reason for that. Maybe because she helped people when she could. "Maybe there's . . . one star got in my hat . . . I was always . . . you know, nice to people. I used to take children, take care of 'em."

Mrs. Johnson considered herself neither unfortunate nor poor. "You know, I'm the richest somebody in the world . . . I thank God for bein' here, you know. I'm proud . . . a lot of folks . . . they're dead and gone." Reflecting on her life, she said, "It's all right, you know, like I've gotten married and everything and had a good life . . . I'm knowin' folks, you know, they're getting' married and they're just messed over and they get on welfare; but I did not go for none of that. . . ."

Did she think about death? "Hush your mouth." Did she worry about it? "No." Mrs. Johnson didn't worry about anything. Nor did she need anything. If she had more money she'd probably buy something but she wasn't sure what, because she hadn't bought anything in a long time. Mrs. Johnson didn't long for anything. But she would love to go back to the country with its cool, clean air.

DISCUSSION At the time of our interview, Mrs. Johnson seemed to be in dire straits. With severe functional limitations, an extremely low income, and limited family support, she depended on public services to meet her most basic needs. Most people who knew her—neighbors, the building security guard, and her outreach worker—would have felt more comfortable if Mrs. Johnson lived in a nursing home where she could receive 24-hour care. Medicaid would cover the costs of institutional care. But Mrs. Johnson did not want to go into a nursing home. She wanted to stay in the apartment.

Five months after our interview, Mrs. Johnson was still in the apartment. No steps had been taken to admit her to a nursing home. Her outreach worker doubted that this was even an option, given severe limitations on Medicaid beds in the area. Repairs to her apartment had not been made because funding for public housing in the District was limited. As her building manager explained, residents could enter all the repair requests they liked, but when there was no sheet rock, no plumbing supplies, "no nothing" in the warehouse, repair personnel could not do much.

Mrs. Johnson's situation combined lifelong poverty, family dysfunction, and severe health problems. But integral to her self-esteem was the fact that she had never been on "welfare." Her living circumstances made others uncomfortable. She lived in public housing in an impoverished neighborhood. We became aware of her situation because her neighborhood was served by an active home visiting agency. Surely other elders, equally dependent and equally neglected, were invisible because there was no outreach worker to knock on their doors twice a week.

DEFINING OLD AGE

Demographic and social changes have had a tremendous impact on the role and status of the elderly in the U.S., even to the point of changing what we *mean* by "the elderly." Like so many human categories, "old age" is socially constructed. Prehistoric people who survived past their reproductive prime possessed rare knowledge that may have helped their families survive periodic drought and crisis. They may have been considered "old" and "wise." During the colonial era, Americans had very short life expectancies, so the few who survived beyond 40 years were viewed as aged. By 1900, the U.S. life expectancy at birth had increased to 48 years, and the 3 million Americans who were older than 65 made up 4.3 percent of the population (Brody, 1971). By the turn of the century, the nation's definition of advanced age had extended by a few decades.

Reflecting modern retirement programs, senior organizations, and life expectancy, today's definition places the onset of old age between the ages of 50 and 80. Age-based policies and programs clearly influence this definition. At 62 an American is eligible to begin collecting Social Security benefits, but most wait to apply until age 65 when benefits are higher. Eligibility for programs funded under the Older Americans Act begins at age 60. Medicare eligibility begins at age 65. Senior organizations, themselves, contribute to our concept of when old age begins. Eligibility for membership in the American Association of Retired Persons (AARP) begins at 50 years of age. Life expectancy also contributes. Observing the growing proportion of Americans who were reaching the age of 65, Bernice Neugarten (herself in her 60s) coined the term "young old" to describe those from 65 to 75 years of age and "old old" to refer to those over 75. By 1996, Neugarten's "old old" had exceeded their life expectancies at birth. The U.S. life expectancy at birth that year was 76.1 years (National Center for Health Statistics, 1999). More recently, the term "oldest old" has been used to describe people over the age of 80. Perhaps someday centenarians (the nation's fastest-growing age group) will be termed the "incredibly old."

CULTURAL PERSPECTIVES ON OLD AGE IN COLONIAL AMERICA

Even as public policy relies on "objective" definitions of old age, it reflects popular beliefs and attitudes about the elderly. Before turning to the development of contemporary programs and policies for the elderly, we will briefly consider the status of the aged in early America, focusing on three groups: Native American elders, African-American elders, and European-American elders.

America's colonial era extended from the arrival of the Mayflower on November 11, 1620, well into the next century. Short life expectancies defined the experiences of the three main sub-groups. All three faced hostile environments. For Native Americans exposure to European immigrants radically decreased life expectancy by exposing them to diseases and war. African-Americans under slavery experienced extremely short life expectancies. The expected lifetime of a slave during this period has been estimated at 28 to 32 years (Mintz & Kellogg, 1988). Short life expectancies also marked the lives of early European immigrants. Life expectancy was particularly short in the South. As a result, there were few old people. Benjamin Franklin lived well into his 80s, but when he died in 1790 he had few age peers. Even as late as 1830, those over age 60 made up only 4 percent of America's population (Haber, 1983). This shorter life expectancy did not mean that *no one* reached extreme old age.

Indeed, there are recorded cases among Native American tribes of individuals who reached 95 to 103 years (Simmons, 1945), but they were the exceptions, not the rule. As we will see, culture was (and continues to be) a strong determinant of values related to age.

NATIVE AMERICANS

Respect for advanced age was an integral part of many Native American cultures. Legends illustrate the powers enjoyed by Indian elders, who were central figures in many stories of creation. Among the Hopi, two aged goddesses were believed to have created all living things, and an old Spider Woman is said to have invented arts and crafts (Simmons, 1945). The Menomini, Creek, and Omaha all have held that old men were the first recipients of magic powers and healing arts.

Tribal food taboos often served the interests of the elderly, reflecting their influence on this important aspect of the culture. The most choice, nutritious tidbits were withheld from the young. Elders often enforced (and, some claim, manipulated) these taboos. Among the Omaha, for example, the tender part of buffalo intestine was considered harmful to youths, and young people were warned against eating bone marrow. Old men warned that it would cause sprained ankles in the young and could only be eaten by those past their prime (Simmons, 1945, p. 27).

Native American groups varied in their response to those of advanced age. The Omaha Indians retained their elders in leadership positions long after they began to physically fail. For them, knowledge and experience were pivotal in determining an elder's status (Simmons, 1945).

Nevertheless, honor for the aged did not preclude abandoning those who became helpless. As Simmons (1945) observed, in times of need, some tribes were forced to euthanize or abandon their elders. He commented, "Among all people a point is reached in aging at which any further usefulness appears to be over and the incumbent regarded as a living liability. 'Senility' may be a suitable label for this. . . . All societies differentiate between old age and this final pathetic plight. Some do something positive about it. Others wait for nature to do it or perhaps assist nature in doing it" (p. 87). Native Americans, particularly those who were nomadic, were forced to abandon those who reached the "helpless stage" of life. Typically an elder would be left with a cache of supplies and fuel. The Omaha, for example, did not abandon their aged on the open prairie, but left them at a campsite with the promise of return. Less common than abandonment was euthanasia. Sometimes the Hopi, who placed a high premium on the elderly, would "help them to die" in an honorable, if violent, act of mercy.

Personal wealth often determined the quality of old age. Among the Navaho some elders accumulated wealth, both in the form of tangible goods (horses, sheep, cattle, and goats) and of intangible property, such as knowledge of medicinal herbs, healing ceremonies, and magic. Knowledge and healing powers could be exchanged for gifts or fees.

In most Native American tribes the aged poor were cared for. Among the Crow, for example, Curtis reported that "Sometimes one man killed as many as fifteen buffalo in a run. He would then cry, 'I do not take the arrows back, nor the skin'; it was then known that all but a few, which he kept for himself, were for the use of the poor old people who had come hurrying out from the camp when the butchering began. . . . After a hunt a broad, level stretch of land was dotted with dead buffalo, men butchering, old men hurrying to and fro receiving a piece of meat from this one and that . . ." (Simmons, 1945, pp. 21–22). The willingness of a tribe or clan to support dependent elders often depended on the availability of food. As Simmons noted, "among the Hopi no aged person needed to fear starvation *as long as his many relatives had food to spare* and he was able to go to their houses to eat" [italics added] (p. 23). It seems that a tribe's care of dependent elders depended at least in part on their ability to do so.

Gender also influenced the status of the elderly. Across tribes, gender differences in prestige tended to mirror those observed in relation to wealth. Where women had access to wealth, as in tribes with matriarchal patterns of descent, they enjoyed high status. It was more typical, though, for men to control wealth and have greater status than women. Simmons (1945) noted gender differences in the property rights of aged men and women: ". . . property rights of aged women show greater variations and seem to be more strongly influenced by the prevailing type of social organization" (p. 49). Women accumulated more property in groups characterized by matrilineal patterns of inheritance and descent. Women also fared better among groups that relied on collection, hunting, and fishing than among farmers and herders. Based on these observations Simmons concluded, "In the simpler beginnings aged women seem to have had a more nearly equal chance to acquire property, but with the development of society their mates and brothers have found it possible to get and to control more property" (p. 49).

Despite a general cultural disposition towards honoring age, the status of individual elders in Native American tribes was determined by knowledge and skill, wealth, and gender. Further, the treatment of needy elders was influenced, at least to some extent, by tribal resources.

African-Americans

The brutalities of slavery dictated short life expectancies for African-Americans who were kidnapped as young adults. Although those born in the colonies had somewhat longer life expectancies, slaves who survived to advanced age had no assurance of comfortable retirement. As Andrew Achenbaum (1986) reported, "If the law did not forbid it, some slaveowners 'emancipated' superannuated blacks, thereby 'freeing' *themselves* [italics added] of caring for elderly slaves. Others heartlessly banished their worn-out slaves like old horses to eke out an existence on their own" (p. 29).

Young African-Americans generally treated their elderly "aunts" and "uncles" with deference and support. As Frederick Douglass recounted,

"Uncle" Toby was the blacksmith, "Uncle" Harry the cartwright, and "Uncle" Abel the shoemaker . . . these mechanics were called "Uncles" by all the younger slaves, not because they really sustained any relationship to any, but according to plantation etiquette as a mark of respect, due from the younger to the older slaves. Strange and even ridiculous as it may seem, among a people so uncultivated and with so many stern trials to look in the face, there is not to be found among any people a more rigid enforcement of the law of respect to elders than is maintained among them (Gutman, 1976, p. 218).

Older slaves often exercised near-absolute authority over the younger members of their communities. Herbert Gutman tells of the following incident: "A white met an elderly man on a Mississippi plantation and learned from his owner that Uncle Jacob was a regulator on the plantation; . . . a *word* or a *look* from him, addressed to younger slaves, had more efficiency than a *blow* from the overseer" (p. 219). Older women were often appointed to care for children, teaching them prayers, hymns, and lessons along the way. As Leslie Owens suggests, "A beginning lesson was to respect slave elders, particularly the aged" (1976, p. 204).

The respect accorded to elderly members of slave communities may be traced in part to West African traditions, in which elders were repositories for information about family and community history, folklore, and ritual traditions (Gutman, 1976). The practice of referring to unrelated elders using familial terms was also adaptive. It helped create a "fictive" kin system among slaves that could help them to survive the separation of blood relatives (Owens, 1976).

It is unclear what status differentials were observed among elderly African-Americans. Possibly because of severe external oppression, there is no evidence of greater status being awarded either on the basis of possessions or gender.

EUROPEAN IMMIGRANTS

One persistent myth holds that European immigrants who reached advanced age in early America enjoyed high social status and strong family ties. Instead, as Carol Haber (1983) pointed out, "In early America . . . the relationship between age and honor was neither direct nor simple. For some, great age contributed to their high status; for others it led only to ridicule and neglect" (p. 9). Lacking programs and policies to define them as "old," nineteenth-century elders were judged by their individual attributes. Among Europeans, property, gender, and occupation were critical in defining a person's social status.

Elderly people who held sizable estates enjoyed commensurate prestige. Seating in early American town halls has been used by historians as a measure of social status. The best seats, those closest to the front, typically went to senior landholders. In an agricultural economy, where the primary means of securing a living was through the land, control of property implied social stature, as well as authority over family members. Thus, for example, an aged father might determine the timing of his son's or daughter's marriage. He might even select his child's spouse. But authority did not necessarily translate into affection. As Fischer (1977) noted, veneration "is a cold emotion." Younger generations may have respected the elderly, but the generations preserved an emotional distance.

A mother's authority and power derived almost exclusively from her spouse, and aged widows found themselves at the mercy of their children. To reduce mothers' vulnerability, some jurisdictions passed laws giving widows one-third of their husbands' estates. Husbands often went to great lengths to specify precisely what property was to be included in their wives' shares. For example, when Adam Deemus of Allegheny County, Pennsylvania, made a will in 1789, he left his wife "the privilege to live in the house we now live in until another one is built and a room prepared for herself if she chuses [sic], the bed and beding [sic] she now lays on, saddel [sic] bridle with the horse called Tom: likewise ten milch [sic] cows, three sheep . . ." (Haber, p. 20). Some went further, stipulating that children would receive their inheritance only after providing acceptable support and care to their mothers. Such was the case in Timothy Richardson's 1715 inheritance. He did not receive his father's estate in Woodburn, Massachusetts, until he agreed to "give, sign, and pass unto his mother, the widow of the diceased [sic], good and sufficient security . . ." (Haber, p. 20).

Many elderly Americans did not own large estates. In the absence of pensions or mandatory retirement laws, workers were expected to continue working as long as they could. The loss of occupation meant not only the loss of a livelihood, but also a decline in prestige as the retired worker gave up a principal means of social integration. Far from being an opportunity for leisure, retirement was the sign of impending poverty and possibly death.

Status differentials among European-American elders are fairly well documented and seem to have been determined by gender, wealth, and occupation. Nonetheless, like Native Americans and African-Americans, European immigrants had a general norm that supported respect for the aged. This norm would erode in subsequent years as attitudes towards the elderly shifted.

CHANGING PERSPECTIVES ON OLD AGE IN AMERICAN SOCIETY

Attitudes toward elderly *individuals* varied in colonial America as they do today. Nonetheless, most historians and social critics agree that values and attitudes were generally more positive toward the elderly *as a group* during the nation's formative years than they are today, suggesting a transformation in cultural values related to age. Some trace the advent of diminished respect for the elderly to the American Revolution (Fischer, 1977), while others date it within the last half of the nineteenth century (Achenbaum, 1978; Haber, 1983).

Signs of the transformation were apparent in several developments during the late eighteenth century (Fischer, 1977). First, seating in town meeting houses was revised. Age was no longer taken into account. Instead, desirable seats were assigned solely on the basis of wealth. Second, the nation's first compulsory retirement law was passed in New York in 1777. Third, census takers observed a shift in what is referred to as "age heaping." This process results in higher than expected population counts in certain age groups, and it is the cumulative result of individuals lying to census-takers about their ages. In early America people tended to report being older than they were, but after the revolutionary period census data revealed a bias toward reporting younger ages. Finally, some argued that the fashion in clothing during this era came to favor youth (Fischer, 1977).

Other signs date the transformation to the late nineteenth century, when popular and scientific writing came to describe the elderly as ugly and disease-ridden, rather than as stately and healthy. Paradoxically, the medical advances that contributed to longevity also focused attention on age-related disease and decline. As a result, instead of exalting their moral and practical wisdom, commentators began to equate age with illness and conclude that older people had nothing to contribute to society (Achenbaum, 1986).

What caused this transformation in attitudes? Many have concluded that industrialization established the lower status of elders in today's society (Achenbaum, 1986; Shanas, 1968). New practices in business and manufacturing technology stressed speed and efficiency, traits incompatible with the aging process. The industrial work force had few jobs that could accommodate the elderly, and thus between 1851 and 1861 the old experienced the greatest decline in both economic and occupational rank of any age group (Haber, 1983). Further, rapidly changing technology made the knowledge and skills of elderly workers obsolete. Younger workers no longer looked to their elders for training and advice.

But industrialization alone could not account for the reduced status of the elderly. As Fischer (1977) pointed out, in Japan—a nation that underwent rapid industrialization—the status of the elderly has remained quite high. Further, signs of diminished respect for elders appeared in the United States before the Industrial Revolution.

Several other factors may have contributed. The War of Independence may have brought not only a political revolution, but a revolution in ideas as well. Rejection of the old political order entailed rejection of traditional ideas that held age as the basis of prestige (Fischer, 1977). The accumulation of wealth may also have disrupted the practice of stratifying society by age. Wealth may have replaced age as a way of discriminating among people. New medical knowledge may also have contributed. As diseases and physical losses associated with age were documented, older people began to be seen as incapacitated and worthless (Achenbaum, 1986).

Finally, the elderly's diminished status may have been caused by changing relationships with their children (Haber, 1983). Parents in colonial times were seldom without children. The birth of the first grandchild followed closely or even preceded that of a couple's last child. As women limited their family sizes and planned the timing of childbirth, the line dividing generations grew more distinct and the "empty nest" became more common. With no children to raise, the older generation no longer had a central function. Urbanization tended to limit family size and diminish parental authority. In a city an older son who resisted his father's authority could simply leave home and find a job—an option that had not been available when the sole source of income was the family farm.

In sum, age alone did not determine the status or well-being of adults in early America. All three of the groups considered here showed evidence of a general norm of respect for the elderly. Native Americans typically expressed their veneration of the elderly through myths and food taboos, providing care for needy elders as resources permitted. Elders served as fictive kin among slave communities, assisting in the education and direction of younger slaves. Among European immigrants, the status of the elderly was closely tied to their control of property, and landed grandparents wielded authority over their offspring. The status of European-American elders showed signs of decline as early as the latter part of the eighteenth century. Historians hold different opinions regarding the cause of that decline, attributing it to revolutionary ideas, accumulated wealth, industrialization, urbanization, and changing family roles.

EARLY PROGRAMS AND POLICIES FOR THE ELDERLY

The programs and policies developed for indigent elders in the new nation reflected both American attitudes towards age and the nation's beliefs about poverty. European immigrant elders who fell into poverty were treated as poor, not old.

PUBLIC RELIEF FOR NEEDY ELDERS

To be old and poor in America has always been a precarious position. The township records of early colonies illustrate the status of indigent elders. In these documents, the wealthy are listed by both first and last names and the poor are called by their last name with the prefix "old." Thus, while "Thomas Moore" might be a man of means, his poor cousin would be referred to as "Old Moore."

Public relief for indigent elders in the United States was initially modeled on England's Elizabethan Poor Laws. These laws did not allow for differentiation on the basis of age. Indigent elders were treated the same as any other group of poor people. Their sustenance was the responsibility of the parish or local community, which provided either "outdoor relief" (money to pay rent or buy goods) or "indoor relief" (lodging in a poorhouse).

With urbanization, the population of cities increased, as did the number of indigents within a city's borders. Philadelphia, for example, saw dramatic growth in its poorhouse population. Prior to 1750, fewer than 50 paupers per year were admitted, but by 1815 this number had risen to 2,250. Roughly a third of these were destitute by virtue of old age (Haber, 1983), but age was not yet used to distinguish among the poor. Elderly people were lodged in the almshouse or poorhouse among the worthy poor—people who were disadvantaged through no fault of their own.

Beginning in the 1830s the notion of a homogeneous class of indigents was challenged. Reformers who served the urban poor became interested in more efficient use of their resources and decided to focus their efforts on those most capable of reform, "the redeemable poor." The elderly were not included in this category. In 1855, for example, the New York Association for Improving the Condition of the Poor declared that it would assist only five groups: industrious laborers; indigent widows and deserted wives with children; educated single females; the sick and the bereaved who would improve; and mechanics who suffered temporary loss of employment (p. 37, NYAICP annual report 1855, cited by Haber). The Association resolved "to give no aid to persons who, from infirmity, imbecility, *old age*, or any other cause are likely to continue unable to earn their own support and consequently to be permanently dependent" [italics added] (p. 38 of annual report). Urban Charity Organization Societies took the same position. In 1892, Amos Warner expounded on the hopelessness of work with the aged: "In work with the aged one is conscious that for the individuals dealt with there is no possibility of success" (Haber, 1983, p. 40).

Thus, while COSs and other philanthropies were sending young laborers back to rural areas and attempting to retrain or rehabilitate others, the elderly were confined to public almshouses. In time they made up a growing proportion of the almshouse population. By 1904, 53 percent of the residents in almshouses throughout the nation were over 60 years old (Haber & Gratton, 1994).

Over time, age came to be associated with destitution (particularly by charity professionals).[2] In 1902 Homer Folks, New York City's Commissioner of Charities, announced a new name for the city almshouse: the "Home for the Aged and Infirm." He intended to send the message that the residents of this facility were not the lazy able-bodied, but those who were simply too old or sick to earn a living. Institutional care was less expensive than outdoor relief for the aged, and so they came to be seen as the most appropriate setting for needy elders.

As "homes" or "asylums" were populated by the elderly and infirm, they took on a more medical focus. The line between hospital and almshouse blurred and "old-age homes" began to offer medical care in addition to room and board, thereby setting the stage for the expansion of facilities we now call "nursing homes."

---

[2]Three classic books illustrate this tendency to associate age with poverty: *Pauperism and the Endowment of Old Age* and *The Aged Poor in England and Wales*, both published in the 1890s and written by Charles Booth; and *Old Age Dependency in the United States*, published during the same era by Lee Welling Squier.

INFORMAL ASSISTANCE AMONG AFRICAN-AMERICANS

During the antebellum era many African-American elders lived in abject poverty. Unable to access the relief provided to European elders, African-Americans relied on informal community supports. Organizations known as "benevolent societies" were organized in collaboration with homes for the aged. These mutual-aid societies worked to keep blacks off public relief and to provide for a decent burial. Society members paid annual dues and in return were given sickness and death benefits, which could then be turned over to a home for the aged. For example, in 1864, Quakers and African-Americans founded the "Home for Aged and Infirm Colored Persons" in Philadelphia, to provide care for "worthy" and "exemplary" blacks "who in their old age from sickness of infirmity have become more or less dependent upon the charities of the benevolent" (Pollard, 1980, p. 231). For at least 27 years, the "Home" provided lodging and care to members of Philadelphia benevolent societies and, in return, the societies turned members' benefits over to the Home. The number of these societies mushroomed. Philadelphia alone had more than 100 societies serving more than 7,000 members (Pollard, 1980). During the latter part of the nineteenth century, the resources of benevolent societies were strained by the longevity of their members. Ultimately the societies were replaced by insurance firms with greater financial reserves. Nonetheless, the benevolent societies represented a significant resource for elderly African-Americans, serving as a hallmark of the community's response to need.

PUBLIC PENSIONS FOR VETERANS

The nineteenth century set the stage for many of our current approaches to care of needy elderly. Agencies that focused on the "redeemable poor" gave up on elders, reserving their energy and resources for young people with some hope of employment. Poor elders increasingly found themselves "warehoused" in institutional settings—precursors of today's nursing homes. One class of elders was favored by public policy initiatives, however: military veterans.

Public pensions for veterans were the nation's first federal retirement programs. In 1829 (100 years before the passage of the Social Security Act) federal legislation awarded pensions to veterans of the Revolutionary War. Notably, this act was passed 46 years after the end of the war, ensuring that few would collect the pensions and that those who did would be very old. Later, provisions were made for survivors of the War of 1812, the Indian conflicts, and the Mexican War to receive federal pensions. These pensions were funded through general tax revenues and did not represent a significant drain on the public purse.

This situation changed when Civil War veterans were added to the federal pension program. Their addition (only 25 years after Appomattox), meant thousands of potential recipients might receive pensions, placing a huge drain on public revenues. Faced with this potential drain, the U.S. Pension Bureau stressed that the money was only for those in dire need, establishing severe restrictions on eligibility. Applicants had to prove they were "suffering from a mental or physical disability of permanent character, not the result of their own vicious habits, which incapacitates them from the performance of manual labor in such a degree as to render them unable to earn support" (Haber, 1983, pp. 110–111).

Administration of these restrictions was complex. Physicians disagreed about the character and cause of disabilities, and many decisions were appealed and reversed. In 1904, Theodore Roosevelt officially included every aged veteran in the pension program and declared that those who reached the age of 62 would be considered half disabled; at age 65 they would be considered two-thirds incapacitated, and those over 70 would be considered totally disabled. Thus, chronological age replaced functional ability in determining who would receive a pension. This change dramatically eased the administration of the program, replacing physician examination with a simple review of birth records (Haber & Gratton, 1994). By establishing the ability of the federal government to operate a pension program, federal pensions for veterans set the stage for Social Security.

The threads revealed in this brief history reappear in the development of U.S. aging policies. Among threads still in effect are a tendency for publicly funded services to serve primarily the majority population, a willingness to make special provisions to meet the needs of veterans, the administrative complexity of using functional status as a measure of need, an inclination to apply institutional solutions to economic and social problems, and the impact of economic resources on a community's willingness to sustain indigent elders.

MODERN ATTITUDES TOWARD THE ELDERLY

International visitors to the United States often subscribe to the stereotype that Americans do not value or care for their elderly. They ask to see where the old people are "warehoused." Indeed, Americans' veneration of youth may reflect deep-seated hostility towards age. Robert Butler coined the term "ageism" to describe the negative stereotypes that can deprive an older American of opportunities and resources.

The nation's attitudes towards the elderly are complex, rooted in cultural norms that dictate respect for the aged and distracted by contemporary pressures to shunt elderly people aside. In this section we will consider two divergent views of the nation's elderly: "intergenerational equity" rhetoric that paints the elderly in negative terms, and a "productive aging" approach that does just the reverse.

INTERGENERATIONAL EQUITY

American attitudes towards the elderly have been influenced during the past few decades by a strident debate over "intergenerational equity." The term has become a catchword for political commentators predicting an "age war" or a "generational conflict" over the allocation of society's resources. According to this view, "greedy geezers" have taken up more than their share of public funds, and

America's youth have been deprived as a result. This argument is confined to the United States and has not been seriously advanced in any other nation (Kingson & Quadagno, 1997). It surfaced in a context of relative economic scarcity as U.S. economic growth slowed considerably during the 1970s, with limited increases in productivity and rising inflation.

Notably, the intergenerational equity argument was not advanced by advocates for children, but by an elite group of political and business leaders. In 1984, Senator Dave Durenberger (R-Minnesota) founded an organization called "Americans for Generational Equity (AGE)." This organization's goal was "to promote the concept of generational equity among America's political, intellectual and financial leaders" (Quadagno, 1989). Financial support for AGE came primarily from "banks, insurance companies, defense contractors, and health care corporations" (Quadagno, 1989, p. 360), and with that support the organization mounted an effective campaign of inflammatory propaganda that included articles with titles such as "Older Voters Drive Budget," "U.S. Coddles Elderly but Ignores Plight of Children," and "The Tyranny of America's Old" (Cook, 1996). AGE staff also wrote books, such as *Born to Pay* by Phillip Longman (1987). Although AGE no longer exists, it had a dramatic influence on the debate about public support for the elderly (Quadagno, 1989), and its work is being continued by the Concord Coalition, funded by Pete Peterson (Chair of President Clinton's Tax and Entitlement Reform Commission). Robert Binstock observed a broad shift in the portrayal of the elderly occurring around 1978. He suggested that until that time the elderly had been described using a "compassionate stereotype" that presented them as poor, frail, and needy. During the 1980s, however, the media, public commentators, and scholars began describing elders as rich, healthy, and politically powerful. This shift provided the foundation for an emerging stereotype that Binstock (1983) calls the "aged as scapegoat," in which a wide range of political, social, and economic problems is blamed on senior citizens.

PRODUCTIVE AGING: AN ATTITUDE SHIFT

During the decade of the 1990s, a growing number of professionals and academics in the field of aging began working to advance the concept of "productive aging." Their efforts, in part designed to counter the effects of the "greedy geezer" rhetoric, underscore the potential and the actual contributions of older adults. According to this view, the "new aged" are more healthy and more financially secure than any previous generation and, as a result, they are in a better position to contribute to the well-being of their families, their communities, and their society. Within this tradition, the elderly are portrayed as vital individuals who are eager for meaningful involvement (Perlmutter, 1990; Rowe & Kahn, 1998).

Central to this viewpoint is the notion that societal barriers, such as age discrimination in employment or inaccessible public buildings, make it difficult for elders to provide meaningful contributions. Thus, advocacy in the field of productive aging would focus on removing those barriers and increasing opportunities for engagement. This more positive view of the aged offers a sharp contrast to the critical view presented in the intergenerational equity rhetoric (Bass, Caro, & Chen, 1993; Butler, Oberlink, & Schechter, 1990; Morrow-Howell, Hinterlong, & Sherraden, 2001).

SOCIAL AND DEMOGRAPHIC FACTORS AFFECTING THE ELDERLY

Modern public policies reflect social and demographic realities as well as attitudes. In this section we will examine several factors that affect policies and programs for elderly Americans.

THE GRAYING OF AMERICA

The founders of major New Deal and New Society programs did not anticipate the impact of demographics on these programs. The twentieth century has seen an explosion in the number of elderly Americans. The U.S. is not alone in the "graying" of its population. Nations throughout the world are seeing dramatic increases in their aged populations; however, in the U.S. the situation is exacerbated by unusually high post–World War II birthrates that produced a "baby boom." The cohort of individuals born between 1945 and 1964 has moved through the system of age-based public services like a "pig in a python," and during the first half of the twenty-first century this generation is expected to accentuate the underlying growth in America's senior population. Figure 9.1 illustrates the growth in this age group.

FIGURE 9.1 PERCENT OF POPULATION 65 AND OLDER, 1900–2050

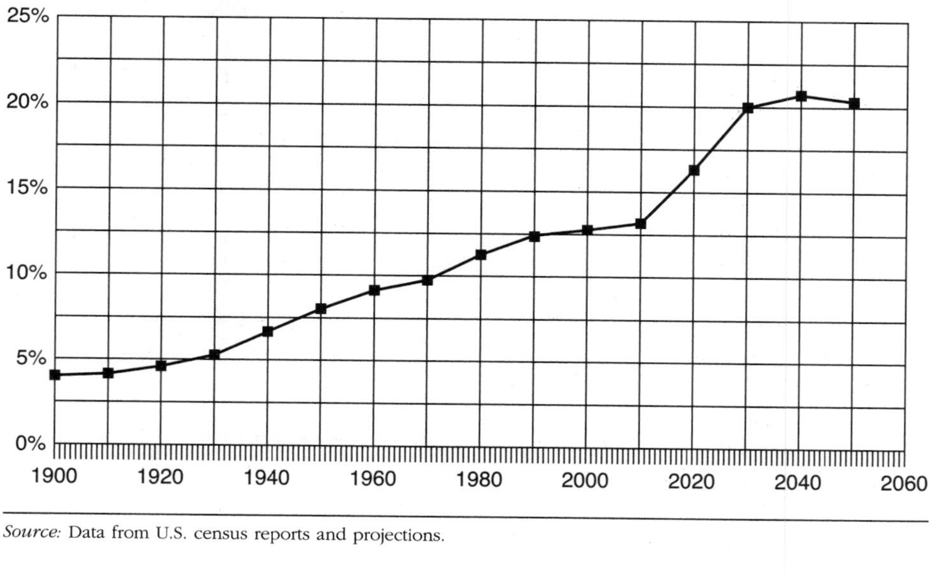

Source: Data from U.S. census reports and projections.

The baby boom was a temporary aberration in a long-term trend of declining fertility. It was followed in the 1970s by a new and more enduring demographic reality: the "baby bust." Fertility rates in the United States appear to have stabilized in the past three decades at levels well below those of any time in history. This trend is illustrated in Figure 9.2, below.

More Americans are surviving childhood, and greater numbers are living to advanced ages. These two trends have dramatically increased life expectancies. It has been estimated that in colonial America, life expectancy for the population as a whole was less than 40 years. By 1997, life expectancy for women born in the United States was 78.6 years, and for men 71.8 (see Figure 9.3). This trend toward increased life expectancy is largely attributable to public health measures that have reduced infant mortality.

Declining fertility and increased longevity have resulted in unprecedented growth in the nation's elderly population. In 1830 only 4 percent of the U.S. population was over 60 years of age. This figure slowly rose to 6.4 percent in 1900. By 1995, 33.5 million elders represented 12.8 percent of the U.S. population, or about one in every eight people. By 2030, that number is expected to more than

FIGURE 9.2 U.S. FERTILITY RATES

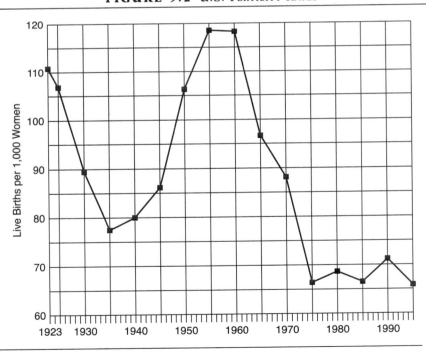

Source: National Center for Health Statistics, 1998.

FIGURE 9.3 HISTORIC TRENDS IN LIFE EXPECTANCY, 1900–1995

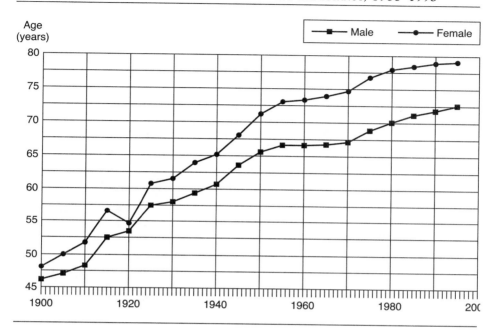

double, to 69.4 million elders, who will represent 20 percent of the population. In other words, by 2030 one in five Americans is expected to be over age 65. This growth will place unprecedented demands on programs that serve the elderly.

GROWING DIVERSITY

The aging population has increased not only in numbers but in diversity. The numerical growth has been dramatic. Between 1930 and 2000, the number of Americans 65 years of age and older increased by 414 percent. The fastest-growing subgroup within the elderly population has been the very old (75 and older). During the same period, the number of Americans in this group grew by 733 percent. Other fast-growing groups among the aged population have included people of color (624 percent increase) and women (506 percent).

As a result of these increases, growing proportions of the elderly population belong to these three subgroups (very old people, people of color, and women). In 1930, people 75 and older made up only 29 percent of the aged population. By 2000, that proportion had increased to 48 percent. Similarly, in 1930 women were 50 percent of the elderly, and by 2000 they represented 59 percent. Finally, people of color made up only 6 percent of the elderly in 1930, but by 2000 they

FIGURE 9.4 SUBGROUPS OF U.S. ELDERLY POPULATION

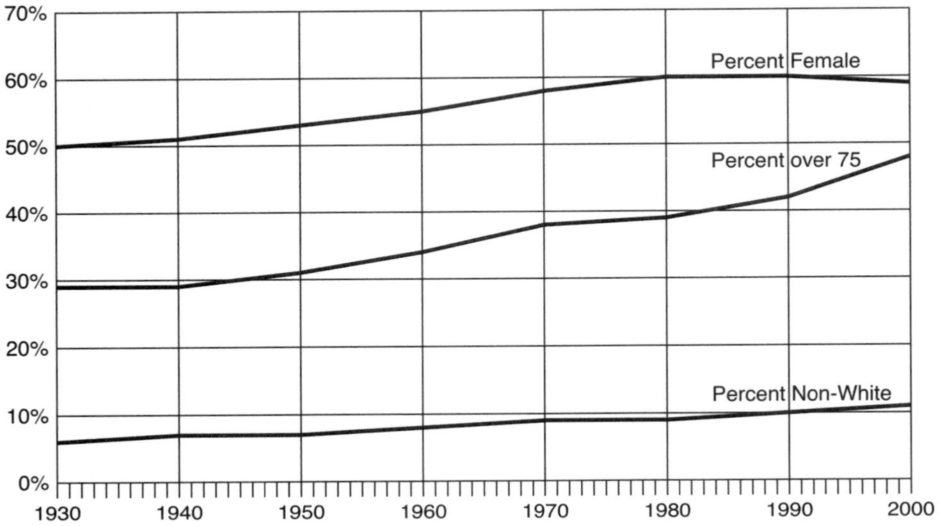

Source: *Statistical Abstract of the U.S.,* 1998.

FIGURE 9.5 POVERTY RATES AMONG THE ELDERLY, 1966–2000

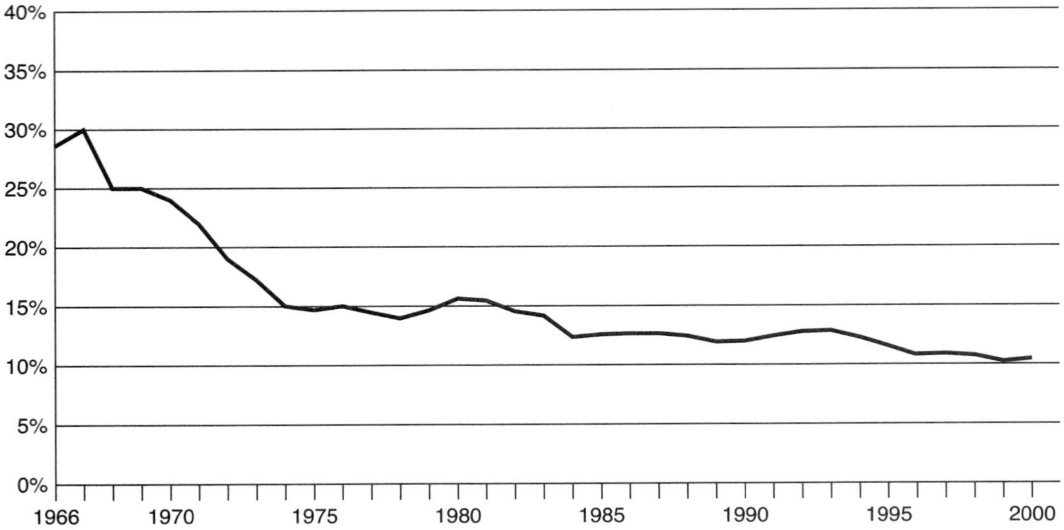

Source: U.S. Census Bureau, 2000.

amounted to 11 percent. Thus, not only has the number of elderly people in the United States been growing, but the elderly population includes greater proportions of these three subgroups. Figure 9.4 illustrates this shift in the composition of the nation's elderly population.

POVERTY AND AGE

While poverty among the elderly has diminished in recent decades (see Figure 9.5), longevity brings increased risk of financial vulnerability for Americans. With respect to the proportion of elders living in poverty, this country fares poorly by international comparison. In a 1993 study of eight Western industrialized nations,[3] researchers found that "The United States has everywhere the highest elderly poverty rates of the countries studied" (Smeeding, Torrey, & Rainwater, 1993, p. 7). Further, the sub-groups of the nation's elderly who are growing fastest—the very old, women, and people of color—are the same groups that face the highest risk of poverty.

The very old continue to have high rates of poverty. When the Department of Health and Human Services conducted a study of the economics of aging, they found that whereas 35 percent of those aged 65 to 74 had low incomes, *two-thirds* of those over 85 were financially vulnerable (Alecxih & Kennell, 1994). In 1991 the Senate Special Committee on Aging reported a poverty rate of 18.4 percent among those over 85 who lived in the community. This represented the highest rate of poverty found in any adult age group (U.S. Senate, 1991). Of course, women make up the majority of the nation's extremely old people.

Older women have almost higher risk of poverty than older men. In 1999, older women had twice the poverty rate of men over 65 years. The rate for women that year was 11.8 percent; for men, 6.9 percent (U.S. Bureau of the Census, 2000f). Older women living alone in the U.S. are consistently the poorest group among the aged, faring worse than older couples. The international study mentioned above reported that older women living alone in the United States "are not only the poorest group among the aged, they are also the only group with poverty rates significantly higher than those of non-aged population groups" (Smeeding, Torrey & Rainwater, 1993, p. 8). This comparative study reported that older women in the United States had the highest poverty rate. Other nations did not even come close. The reported rates for these nations are presented in Table 9.1.

TABLE 9.1 POVERTY AMONG OLDER WOMEN: INTERNATIONAL COMPARISONS

Nation	Poverty Rate	
	Single Women	*Couples*
United States	17.6%	6.0%
Canada	3.2	0.6
Australia	3.8	4.2
Germany	2.4	2.7
Sweden	1.7	0.2
France	0.8	0.7
United Kingdom	0.4	0.9
Finland	0.0	0.0

Source: Smeeding, Torrey, & Rainwater (1993).

[3]Nations studied include Canada, Australia, Sweden, France, Germany, the Netherlands, the U.S., and the United Kingdom.

Finally, members of racial and ethnic minority groups experience higher rates of poverty in their later years. In 1999, the highest risk of poverty among the elderly was experienced by African-American women, among whom more than a quarter (26.4 percent) had incomes below the poverty threshold (U.S. Bureau of the Census, 2000). African-American elders overall have the highest rates of poverty among the elderly. In 1999, the poverty rate for African-Americans over the age of 65 years was 22.3 percent, compared to an overall rate of 9.7 percent. Hispanic elders also experience elevated risk of poverty, with an overall rate of 20.4 percent in 1999. Gender and race differences in poverty rates among the elderly are illustrated in Table 9.2, below. Clearly, those who are most at risk of poverty are also most likely to benefit from anti-poverty programs.

Social Security has been termed the nation's most effective anti-poverty program. Its impact was demonstrated in a seminal study by the Center on Budget and Policy Priorities (Porter, Larin, & Primus, 1999). Researchers analyzed five years of census data (1993–1997) to determine the number of elders in each state who would have been poor if they had not had Social Security benefits. Results indicated that Social Security lowered the number of elders in poverty from 15.3 million to 3.8 million in 1997. Without Social Security, nearly half (47.6 percent) of the U.S. elderly population would have been poor. The study also revealed that 60 percent of those lifted from poverty by Social Security were women. Because women live longer than men, the fact that Social Security benefits are indexed to inflation is especially important to women.

TABLE 9.2 Poverty Among the Elderly: Gender and Race Differences

	Men	Women	Overall
White	5.7%	10.3%	8.3%
Hispanic	13.3	25.4	20.4
African-American	17.2	26.4	22.7
Overall	6.9	11.8	9.7

Source: U.S. Census Bureau (2000). Annual Demographic Survey, March Supplement, Poverty Status of People and Families by Selected Characteristics in 1999 (http://ferret.bls. census.gov/macro/032000/pov/new01_001.htm).

MODERN PROGRAMS AND POLICIES FOR ELDERLY AMERICANS

Current programs for the elderly that are woven into the Social Security Act were introduced in Chapter 3. These include Old Age and Survivor's Insurance, Medicare, Medicaid, and Supplemental Security Income. These programs are integral parts of the nation's safety net for the elderly. In the following sections we will consider three significant policies affecting the nation's elderly: the Older Americans Act, public policies governing private pensions, and the Age Discrimination in Employment Act. We will also look at health policy issues of particular relevance to the elderly.

THE OLDER AMERICANS ACT AND AGE-BASED SERVICES

The Older Americans Act (OAA) was passed just prior to the escalation of the Vietnam War and the economic downturns of the 1970s. It reflected a significant national commitment to meeting the needs of the elderly. Although its goals were exalted, its funding was limited. Nonetheless, the OAA established a national network of providers and governmental authorities charged with the care of the elderly. The structure of this network and some inherent tensions in OAA programs are discussed below.

Prior to the 1965 passage of the Older Americans Act (OAA), the elderly received limited social services through programs that had not been specifically designed for them. As early as 1950, President Truman initiated the first National Conference on Aging. Participants called for greater government involvement in meeting the needs of the elderly. Continuing interest led President Eisenhower to create the Federal Council on Aging in 1956 to coordinate federal activities related to aging. Successful passage of the Older Americans Act has been attributed to the 1961 White House Conference on Aging. The Conference brought experts on aging and advocates for the elderly to Washington, D.C., from across the nation, raising awareness of issues affecting the elderly. In 1962, Representative John Fogarty of Rhode Island and Senator Pat McNamara of Michigan introduced legislation to establish an independent U.S. Commission on Aging. The Kennedy administration objected to the creation of an independent agency. In 1963, the Act was re-introduced, this time proposing to set up an Administration on Aging under the Department of Health, Education and Welfare. Again, the proposal was defeated.

The 1965 proposal reflected the 1963 version, but the 1965 proposal received bipartisan support and the OAA was signed into law by President Johnson on July 14, 1965. In his remarks upon signing the bill, the President suggested the legislation would provide "a coordinated program of services and opportunities for our older citizens" (U.S. House of Representatives, 1988, p. 2). Of course, the goals of the Older Americans Act were considerably more lofty than the President suggested.

By means of partnerships between federal, state, and local authorities, the OAA established a network of 57 State Offices on Aging and 670 Area Agencies on Aging that effectively blankets the United States. OAA programs were placed under the jurisdiction of the Administration on Aging (AOA), a federal agency within the Department of Health, Education and Welfare (now Health and Human Services). Originally the head of AOA was a Commissioner on Aging who reported to the Secretary of HEW, but in 1993 Fernando Torres-Gil received a presidential appointment as the first Assistant Secretary for Aging. This appointment established the AOA as a more autonomous federal agency. The Act has been amended at least 12 times (Gelfand, 1988; U.S. House of Representatives, 1988).

The Act's initial funding was modest. In 1966, total appropriations under the Act amounted to $6.5 million. By 1988, this figure had grown to more than $1 billion, and the appropriation for fiscal year 2001 was more than $1.3 billion (U.S. House of Representatives, 1988; Administration on Aging, 2001).

A comparison of the 1966 and 2001 appropriations reveals the increasing complexity of programs operating under the Older Americans Act. The 1966 appropriations funded two categories: Title II, Grants for State and Community Programs on Aging ($5 million), and Title IV, Training, Research and Discretionary

Older Americans Act of 1965: Declaration of Objectives

. . . in keeping with the traditional American concept of the inherent dignity of the individual. . . the older people of our Nation are entitled to, and it is the joint and several duty and responsibility of the governments of the United States, the several states and their political subdivisions, and of Indian tribes to assist our older people to secure equal opportunity to the full and free enjoyment of the following objectives:

(1) An adequate income in retirement in accordance with the American standard of living.

(2) The best possible physical and mental health which science can make available and without regard to economic status.

(3) Obtaining and maintaining suitable housing, independently selected, designed and located with reference to special needs and available at costs which older citizens can afford.

(4) Full restorative services for those who require institutional care, and a comprehensive array of community-based, long-term care services adequate to appropriately sustain older people in their communities and in their homes, including support to family members and other persons providing voluntary care to older individuals needing long-term care services.

(5) Opportunity for employment with no discriminatory personnel practices because of age.

(6) Retirement in health, honor, dignity—after years of contribution to the economy.

(7) Participating in and contributing to meaningful activity within the widest range of civic, cultural, educational and training, and recreational opportunities.

(8) Efficient community services, including access to low-cost transportation, which provide a choice in supported living arrangements and social assistance in a coordinated manner and which are readily available when needed, with emphasis on maintaining a continuum of care for vulnerable older individuals.

(9) Immediate benefit from proven research knowledge which can sustain and improve health and happiness.

(10) Freedom, independence, and the free exercise of individual initiative in planning and managing their own lives, full participation in the planning and operation of community-based services and programs provided for their benefit, and protection against abuse, neglect and exploitation.

TABLE 9.3 2001 APPROPRIATIONS UNDER
THE OLDER AMERICANS ACT

Activity	Appropriation
Supportive services and senior centers	$325 million
National family caregiver support	125 million
Congregate meals	378 million
Home-delivered meals	152 million
State and local innovations	38 million
Preventive health services	16 million
Alzheimer's demonstrations	8.9 million
Grants to Indian tribes	23 million
Protection of vulnerable older Americans (ombudsman and elder abuse)	14 million
Program administration	17 million

Source: Administration on Aging, 2001.

Projects and Programs ($1.5 million). The 2001 appropriations are detailed in Table 9.3.

OAA PROGRAMS TODAY. The Older Americans Act established the administrative structure for the delivery of social services to the elderly. Under the authority of the AOA, each state and territory operates its own "state office on aging." The network is further divided into "Area Agencies on Aging." Thus, every jurisdiction in the United States has a designated authority responsible for programming for the elderly. This tremendous accomplishment can be attributed to (and is dependent on) a partnership of federal, state, and local governments. Eligibility for services funded under the OAA is based solely on age. Anyone aged 60 or over may participate, regardless of income or assets.

Under the Act, Area Agencies on Aging must avoid providing services themselves. Whenever possible they must contract with private and public entities. The funding formula for AOA programs is based on the proportion of the nation's elderly who reside in each state. As a consequence, states with large senior populations, such as Florida and California, enjoy higher AOA appropriations than states with relatively young populations, such as Alaska and Utah.

Funded by their appropriations, states sustain a network of OAA services. These services include those described in Title III of the Act:

1. **Access Services:** transportation, outreach, information, and referral;

2. **Supportive Services:** health (including mental health), transportation, housing repair, community-based services to prevent institutionalization, legal assistance, exercise programs, health screening, pre-retirement counseling, and "any other necessary services for the general welfare of the older people";

3. **Nutrition Services:** congregate meals in senior centers and home-delivered "Meals on Wheels."

In addition, a "National Caregiver Initiative" was passed in 2000 to provide services to family members caring for the nation's frail elderly.

TENSIONS SURROUNDING OAA PROGRAMS. Targeting of OAA services has been a source of tension in recent decades. As indicated above, the Act requires that services be made available to all Americans over the age of 60, regardless of their income or assets. Yet today's elderly are, on average, considerably more affluent than were the aged in 1965 when the Act was passed. As a result, OAA services often benefit elders who are members of the middle class.

The denizens of senior centers and recipients of congregate meal programs funded under the Act may not be those most in need of publicly funded assistance. Congregate meals are provided in senior centers and frequently offer socialization opportunities as well as a nutritional supplement. They have consistently been one of the AOA's most well-funded programs, yet congregate meals have been criticized as failing to serve cultural minorities and frail elders. The climate in most senior centers reflects the majority culture in the area.[4] While the environment is not overtly hostile to minorities, the activities, food, and atmosphere are often not familiar or welcoming. Similarly, frail elders—those who are most in need of assistance to maintain their independence—are unable to participate in congregate meals or senior center programs.

In response to this tension, the 1987 amendments to the Older Americans Act added Section 305 of Title III to require that states "(E) Provide assurances that preference will be given to providing services to older individuals with the *greatest economic or social need, with particular attention to low-income minority individuals* . . ." [italics added]. Subsequent appropriations have revealed an increased emphasis on cultural minorities and vulnerable individuals. Between 1986 and 2001, grants to Indian tribes more than doubled, going from $8.3 million to $23.5 million (U.S. House of Representatives, 1988; Administration on Aging, 2001). Programs serving frail and vulnerable elders were also initiated, including in-home services for frail elderly, elder abuse prevention, and long-term care ombudsman services. Most recently, the $125 million National Caregiver Support Program has been added to OAA programs. This program will offer assistance, training, and respite to family members caring for the frail elderly. Since the 1987 amendments, OAA programs have incrementally shifted resources and focus to those in greatest need. This shift may be, at least in part, a response to rhetoric that paints seniors as a population that exploits, but does not need, public assistance.

OAA programs are deeply affected by changing perceptions of the nation's elderly. When seniors are perceived as "greedy geezers," Americans become

---

[4]In some areas an entire catchment area might serve predominantly minority residents. This is the case, for example, when a city's African-American neighborhood has its own senior center. These centers tend to serve an African-American clientele, and congregate meals reflect the predominant culture in the surrounding neighborhood.

more critical of programs that use age-based eligibility criteria, particularly if these programs fail to meet the needs of the most vulnerable elders. The challenge for the network of age-based programs will be to respond credibly to this criticism while maintaining the integrity and political viability of programs funded under the Older Americans Act.

PUBLIC POLICIES AND PRIVATE PENSIONS

Most Americans are familiar with public programs such as the Older Americans Act, but they may be unaware of other significant policies that provide security to millions of elderly persons. These are the laws governing the establishment and operation of private pensions. The term "private" is a misnomer when applied to pensions. Few personal assets are as profoundly affected by public policy as pensions.[5] Although the first company pension plan was established in 1875 (by the American Express Company) most pensions were developed after passage of the Revenue Act of 1921. This law encouraged the development of private pensions by exempting both employer contributions and pension fund income from federal income taxes.

During the 1940s and 1950s private pensions mushroomed. The number of workers covered rose from about 4 million in the late 1930s to 10 million in 1950. This expansion was the result of wage and price controls imposed to control inflation during World War II. With wages capped, one of the few ways companies could attract qualified workers (themselves in limited supply) was to offer generous fringe benefits such as pensions and health insurance. Thus, two public policy initiatives—wage controls and tax deductions—set the stage for the expansion of private pensions.

There were several problems with the early pensions: (1) they tended to treat top executives much more favorably than regular employees; (2) workers often lost their benefits as a result of mergers, closures, and bankruptcies; (3) in some spectacular scandals, pension reserves were mismanaged and lost; (4) some workers were fired just months before they became eligible for a pension; and (5) workers' survivors (most of them widows) received no income from pensions upon the death of the worker.

In 1974 Congress addressed these problems by passing comprehensive legislation to regulate pensions. The Employee Retirement Income Security Act (ERISA) limited the number of years of employment an employer could require before a worker had the legal right to receive pension benefits—before the worked became "vested." It strengthened standards governing the management of pension funds. It restricted the extent to which employers could use pensions only to reward "key employees"—that is, highly paid executives. As discussed in Chapter 8, ERISA was amended in 1984 by the Retirement Equity Act to require

---

[5]See Schulz (1995) for a detailed discussion of private pensions.

that plans provide the option of a "Joint and Survivor Annuity." This stipulation provides a modicum of income security to survivors.[6]

Another major public policy affecting pensions was the 1974 establishment of the Pension Benefit Guarantee Corporation (PBGC). Created through Title IV of ERISA, The PBGC manages a mandatory insurance program for pension plans so that in the event of bankruptcy workers do not lose all of their pension rights. Prior to the establishment of the PBGC, workers lost their pensions if their employers went out of business. For example, when Studebaker terminated its pension plan in 1963, more than 4,000 auto workers lost part or all of their pensions (PBGC, 2001). When Braniff Airlines went out of business in 1982, however, the PBGC insured vested employees and provided benefits up to a maximum of about $1,500 per month (Shulz, 1995).

Although business representatives opposed each of these regulatory reforms, the laws have not slowed the growth of pensions. Twenty million workers were covered in 1960 and 35 million in 1979. By 1995, an estimated 42 million workers, roughly half of the labor force, were covered by pension plans (Schulz, 1995).

Of course, many workers are still not covered. Sixty percent of these workers are employed in trade and service industries. Key factors determining whether a worker will be covered are his or her union status and the number of people employed by the company. Almost all workers without pensions are not union members and work for firms with relatively few employees. Women and minorities are over-represented among workers who do not enjoy pension coverage. In the case study for this chapter, it is clear that Mrs. Johnson and her husband did not have pension coverage. (See Barusch, 1994, for a discussion of women and pension coverage.)

For elderly people, like Mrs. Johnson, who are financially vulnerable, any barriers to employment or promotion exact a tremendous cost. The elderly have traditionally been among the groups subjected to employment discrimination in the United States—a situation the Age Discrimination in Employment Act was designed to rectify.

AGE DISCRIMINATION IN EMPLOYMENT ACT. Prior to passage of the Age Discrimination in Employment Act (ADEA) in 1967, help-wanted advertisements could, and did, list age as a basis for hiring. The notion that "older workers need not apply" was widespread, and as James Schulz (1995) argued, may have been the basis for the longer periods of unemployment experienced by older men. The 1964 Civil Rights Act did not prohibit discrimination on the basis of age. But Congress did direct the Department of Labor to conduct a study of age discrimination. The following year, a report submitted to Congress revealed "a persistent and widespread use of age limits in hiring that in a great many cases can be attributed to arbitrary discrimination against older workers on the basis of age and regardless of ability" (Rich & Baum, 1984, p. 179).

---

[6]ERISA also enabled some employees to establish Individual Retirement Accounts.

The ADEA prohibits discrimination on the basis of age in hiring, discharge, compensation, benefits, and other terms of employment. Its stated purpose is to "promote employment of older persons based on their ability rather than age; to prohibit arbitrary age discrimination in employment; to help employers and workers find ways of meeting problems arising from the impact of age on employment" (Section 621, Congressional Statement of Findings and Purpose).

ADEA protections originally extended only to workers between the ages of 40 and 65, but the Act was amended in 1978 to cover workers up to age 69 and in 1986 to extend to workers of any age. The Act applies only to employers with 20 or more employees, and allows for discrimination when age is a "bona fide occupational requirement"—that is, when the employer can demonstrate a rational basis for the use of age-based decision-making. Typically such requirements have been applied to airplane pilots and air traffic controllers.

As Schulz (1995) noted, "It is difficult to determine the extent to which actual discrimination has in fact lessened" (p. 73). Between 1991 and 1995, an average of 17,000 complaints of age discrimination were filed each year with the Equal Employment Opportunity Commission (EEOC) (Administration on Aging, 1997). These complaints probably represent the tip of the iceberg, and it is fair to say that age-based discrimination remains an elusive social problem. Perhaps the ADEA's greatest impact is symbolic. The simple fact that age discrimination in employment is against the law of the land is, in itself, a statement of American values and expectations regarding the elderly.

HEALTH CARE FOR THE ELDERLY

Vigorous criticism of programs for the elderly appears against a backdrop of strong support for public efforts to meet the health care needs of this population. Medicare enjoys widespread support, even as the pressure for reform has grown. In the following sections we will examine issues related to health care for the elderly, including prescription drug coverage, long-term care, rationing health care by age, and assisted suicide.

PRESCRIPTION DRUG COVERAGE. When Medicare was established, pharmaceutical drugs were much less important to health care than they are today, and the proportion of health care dollars spent on medications was much less. Consistent with these realities, the program was not designed to provide coverage for medication expenses. Recent decades, however, have seen tremendous advances in the number and quality of medications available for a variety of chronic illnesses, and drugs have become integral to most treatment regimens. The elderly now spend more for medications than they once spent for all of their health care services combined (Crystal, Harmon, & Sambamoorthi, 2000). As a result, recent years have seen a growing call for Medicare coverage of prescription medications.

Early proposals called for financing the prescription benefit through increased payroll taxes, but more recent plans, such as those debated in the 1999 presidential election, would apply user premiums, subsidized through the federal budget surplus.

LONG-TERM CARE. As Joshua Weiner noted, "One of the great successes of the twentieth century has been the prevention and treatment of acute illnesses" (1996, p. 51). Unfortunately, this cannot be said of the chronic illnesses that affect millions of elderly Americans. While the vast majority of the nation's elderly have Medicare coverage for most of the costs of acute care, less than 1 percent of those over 65 have long-term care insurance (Kingson, 1996). Problems identified in the nation's long-term care system include its high cost and the resulting impoverishment of the elderly and their families; the use of Medicaid by the non-poor; the lack of alternatives to nursing home care; and the limitations of private long-term care insurance.

Nursing home care is expensive, averaging $37,000 per year (National Policy and Resource Center on Women and Aging, 1996). The costs of long-term nursing care can quickly impoverish an aged person. Once impoverished, the patient can turn to Medicaid for coverage. Many nursing homes will not accept Medicaid patients, however, and most states have introduced screening procedures to reduce their nursing home costs under Medicaid.[7]

Those who do enter long-term care face a risk known as "spousal impoverishment." Because Medicare provides only limited long-term care, older people who need extensive care must "spend down" to become eligible for Medicaid coverage. In other words, they must deplete their assets and use up their income until they meet Medicaid's eligibility limits. This process once left the patient's spouse in poverty. The Medicare Catastrophic Coverage Act of 1988 (MCCA) included provisions designed to address this problem. Under MCCA, state Medicaid programs were required to permit spouses to retain income up to a certain level—usually 150 percent of the federal poverty threshold. The spouse was also allowed to retain some of the couple's assets. Although most MCCA provisions were repealed, these spousal impoverishment measures remain in effect.

A growing number of more affluent individuals have transferred their assets to others in order to qualify for Medicaid coverage of their long-term care. This type of asset transfer is often accomplished through a legal instrument popularly known as a "Medicaid-qualifying trust." This practice has meant that state and federal funds reserved for medical care of the poor have been spent to cover the care of Americans who could afford to pay for it from their own assets. In response, both state and federal governments have introduced measures designed to reduce the number of individuals who become eligible for Medicaid after asset transfers.

---

[7]Most states require Medicaid applicants who apply for nursing home admission to be screened to ensure that the placement is appropriate. Individuals who request placement for primarily social reasons (such as the lack of a committed caregiver) or mental health reasons (such as depression) are denied admission.

MCCA and subsequent federal statutes have made laws governing the transfer of assets more stringent. Institutionalized patients are normally ineligible for Medicaid coverage if, within a "look-back period" of three years prior to applying for Medicaid, they disposed of assets for less than fair market value. This provision does not apply to a house transferred to a spouse or other relatives.[8]

The U.S. long-term care system has also been criticized for its "institutional bias." Apart from nursing homes, there are few publicly supported living arrangements available for the chronically ill.[9] Without adequate services in the community to serve the frail elderly, a growing number of elderly persons (like Mrs. Johnson) find themselves trapped in what Carroll Estes termed "the No-Care Zone." They require limited care and/or supervision, but are unable to secure Medicaid coverage unless they enter a nursing home. In an effort to address this problem, both Medicare and Medicaid programs have offered limited coverage for in-home health care.

As the high cost of nursing homes has affected growing numbers of Americans, private companies have begun to offer long-term care insurance. In the private long-term care market, the vulnerable consumer has limited protection. According to a 1991 study carried out by *Consumer Reports*, many insurance companies have resorted to fraudulent practices to sell long-term care policies. *Consumer Reports* found that "Not one sales agent properly explained the benefits, restrictions, and policy limitations . . ." (National Policy and Resource Center on Women and Aging, 1996). In addition to misleading sales practices, companies have introduced several undesirable features, such as premiums that increase with age, a clause that specifies that the policy is renewable only under certain conditions, or exclusion for "mental or nervous disorders" including Alzheimer's Disease (National Policy and Resource Center on Women and Aging, 1996). Most state agencies on aging provide consumer assistance in making long-term care insurance decisions.

RATIONING HEALTH CARE BY AGE. Some people advocate withholding medical care from the elderly, on the grounds that their care is expensive and their social contributions are limited. According to this view, the care of the elderly involves lavish expenditures for individuals who have little to contribute to society—a situation that is particularly galling in view of the unmet health needs of infants and children. Then-Governor Lamm of Colorado and others have suggested that medical treatment be withheld beyond a certain age (see Callahan, 1987, 1990). Through acceptance of a "natural life course," we might allocate scarce resources more effectively (Daniels, 1988). In a less diplomatic statement

---

[8]Medicaid eligibility is not affected by the transfer of a house to the following relatives: a spouse, a child under 21 years of age, a disabled or blind adult child, an adult child who lived in the house and cared for the patient for at least two years before the patient was institutionalized, or a sibling who has equity in the house and has lived in it for at least one year before nursing home placement of the homeowner.

[9]"Assisted Living" facilities are under development in several areas. These facilities offer an alternative to nursing home care for elders who need minimal assistance to live independently.

of the same view, Lamm has been widely quoted as arguing that old people "have a duty to die and get out of the way" (Slater, 1984, p. 1). By doing so, they would presumably free up money for the care of the young.

In opposition to age rationing of health care, Jahnigen and Binstock (1991) have argued that it is wrong to deny lifesaving care to a class of people defined only by their age. According to this view, clinical decisions about care should be based on individual considerations. As C. Everett Koop suggests, "Age is far too loose a criterion. Look at me. One of the main reasons I was rebuffed during my nomination to the office of surgeon general was because I was 'too old.' I was just a youngster of sixty-five . . . Of course, this did not sit very well with the man who nominated me. President Reagan had just passed his seventieth birthday" (Binstock & Post, 1991, p. ix). Opponents of age-based rationing suggest that denying health care on the basis of age would deny some people life or functioning for significant periods, at a cost not only to the elders themselves, but to their family members and friends. They further suggest that the fiscal crisis in health care is caused by systemic factors such as inflation in medical costs and technological development, rather than by the graying of America.

ASSISTED SUICIDE. Dr. Jack Kevorkian, a retired pathologist in Michigan, has probably done more than any individual to bring the topic of assisted suicide to public attention. Dr. Kevorkian has acknowledged assisting in the suicides of at least 92 people since 1990—most of them women, ranging in age from 26 to 89 (ERGO, 1998). In 1999, he was convicted of second-degree homicide for his involvement in the death of 52-year-old Thomas Youk.

Several organizations are working hard to secure legal protection for physicians who help patients commit suicide.[10] These advocates make several arguments in support of their cause. First, they suggest that the suffering associated with some terminal diseases is unbearable and cannot be relieved, stripping the patient of dignity and depriving his or her life of meaning. Second, advocates argue that physicians (like Dr. Kevorkian) are already helping patients commit suicide and that "de-criminalizing" their actions would open them to public scrutiny and ensure that decisions are made in a balanced way that protects the interests of terminally ill patients. Finally, they note that a nation such as the United States, which places a high value on individual dignity, should not deprive terminally ill persons of assistance in ending their lives. (See Orentlicher, 1996 for a detailed review of legal aspects of these arguments.)

Opponents[11] of assisted suicide offer several arguments. First, they argue that it is the duty of medical practitioners to relieve terminally ill patients of the suf-

---

[10]Groups that support assisted suicide include Americans for Death with Dignity, Choice in Dying, Death with Dignity, National Center, and Euthanasia Research and Guidance Organization.

[11]Opponents of assisted suicide include the Roman Catholic Church, Not Dead Yet, the International Anti-Euthanasia Task Force, and Americans Disabled for Attendant Programs Today.

fering attendant to their diseases. If physicians have an "easy out" in the form of assisted suicide, they will not make the heroic efforts necessary to relieve pain. Second, they suggest that assisted suicide is one step down a "slippery slope" that could lead to euthanasia of undesirable or disabled elders. Finally, they suggest that a terminally ill patient who is in unremitting pain is not competent to make an informed decision regarding the value or meaning of his or her life.

As of this writing, the legal status of assisted suicide is ambiguous. In November 1994, Oregon voters made theirs the first state in the nation to legalize physician-assisted suicide, passing Measure 16 by a slim margin (51 percent in favor and 49 percent opposed). The new law was immediately challenged by a group of patients who declared that it violated their constitutional rights. Federal District Court Judge Hogan ruled in their favor, issuing a permanent injunction against the law. In February 1997, the Federal Ninth Circuit Court reversed Hogan's ruling. The court did not rule on the constitutionality of the statute, but decided the patients did not have "standing" to bring the case. In October 1997, the Supreme Court refused to hear the case. Thus, the Oregon law stands, but its constitutionality is unclear. Few patients have used the law to commit suicide.

Two cases decided by U.S. Courts of Appeals offer contradictory opinions. In the first, *Quill v. Vacco*, three New York physicians and their patients challenged the constitutionality of that state's laws prohibiting physicians from providing drugs to hasten death. In April 1996, the U.S. Court of Appeals for the Second Circuit held that "physicians who are willing to do so may prescribe drugs to be self-administered by mentally competent patients who seek to end their lives during the final stages of a terminal illness" (*Quill v. Vacco* opinion, 1995, pp. 2–3). In contrast, the constitutionality of the State of Washington's law against physician-assisted suicide was upheld in a 1995 ruling by the U.S. Court of Appeals for the Ninth Circuit. The opinion states that the court found "no basis for concluding that the statute violates the constitution" (*Compassion in Dying v. State of Washington*, 1995, p. 4).

SOCIAL WORK WITH THE ELDERLY

The number of social workers qualified to serve the nation's elderly is insufficient to meet the demand for their services, and the need will become greater in the near future. Estimates by Greene (1989) and Petersen (1988) revealed that between 17,396 and 29,608 social workers were providing services to the nation's elderly. The Department of Health and Human Services has estimated that between 60,000 and 70,000 professionally trained social workers will be needed to serve older people and their families in the year 2020 (NIA, 1987). This estimate suggests the need for at least a threefold increase in the supply of social workers trained to work with elderly persons.

Few schools of social work offer specialized training in aging to their MSW students, however, and those that do find student interest to be low (Lubben, Damron-Rodriguez, & Beck, 1992; McCaslin, 1987). Unless the production of professional-level social workers prepared to serve the elderly increases, individuals from other fields such as nursing and gerontology will fill roles ordinarily reserved for social workers, such as case manager, counselor, discharge planner, and program administrator. Most social workers in aging find the rewards of working with the nation's elders greater than they anticipated.

SUMMARY: THE OUTLOOK FOR ELDERLY AMERICANS

Public provision for the elderly depends to a great extent on public attitudes. When "compassionate stereotypes" prevail, aging programs expand. In response to "greedy geezer" rhetoric, they contract. But apart from attitudes, the realities of age drive policies and programs.

Twenty-first century realities for this age group are complex. Foremost is its tremendous growth. The aging of the large baby-boom generation will place unprecedented demands on public programs for the elderly. Many in this cohort are economically well-off and will enjoy the accumulated benefits of an advantaged life, a phenomenon known as "cumulative advantage" (Crystal and Shea, 1990). These advantages will render suspect the use of age-based eligibility requirements for publicly funded benefits. As a result, programs ranging from Social Security and Medicare to services provided under the Older Americans Act will continue to undergo intense public scrutiny.

Among the elderly, we also see the cumulative effects of lifelong oppression, termed "cumulative disadvantage" (Crystal & Shea, 1990). Older minority women, like Mrs. Johnson, have extremely high rates of poverty. Age itself brings disadvantages. Even normal physical aging processes can leave a person dependent on health care to limit pain and disability. In the decades to come, a growing proportion of the nation's elderly will be composed of the very old, women, and minorities—the same groups that are most vulnerable to these disadvantages and most likely to depend on public programs and services. It is vitally important that social workers act as advocates for the interests of these disenfranchised and vulnerable elders.

DISCUSSION TOPICS

1. Consider Mrs. Johnson's experiences with public policies and programs. In what ways do they reflect the threads that were discussed in the historic sections of this chapter? What modern policies and programs have influenced her? In what ways do gender and race determine the resources available to Mrs. Johnson?

2. Federal, state, and local governments devote considerable resources to measures that assist older people. These measures range from health services to the popular "Meals on Wheels" programs. At the same time, many observers feel the nation has neglected the needs of vulnerable children. How would you justify spending public resources on programs for the elderly?

3. A central tension in OAA programs is the need to use scarce funds to serve those in greatest need, while the political viability of these programs stems from their middle-class constituency. If you were the director of a State Office on Aging, how would you respond to the mandate to serve those in greatest social and economic need?

4. Consider three elderly people, all of whom have incomes below the federal poverty threshold. Helen is a widowed homemaker who raised four children. Her children are all doing well, but her husband's terminal illness in the early 1980s has left her impoverished. Sandra worked all her life in a non-union factory. She has no pension and now is too disabled to work. Betty is a life-long alcoholic. Married three times, never for more than three years, she has moved from place to place working at low-paying jobs. She has two children, but doesn't know where they are. Describe the public income supports on which these individuals might draw. Now list these three individuals in order of priority—who has the greatest claim on public resources?

5. Medicare currently offers health coverage to elders of all income levels, and this coverage is better than the policies that low- and many middle-income workers could afford to purchase on their own. Does Medicare coverage entail a social justice issue? How would you propose to resolve it?

SUGGESTED RESOURCES

Achenbaum, W. A. (1986). *Social Security: Visions and Revisions*. Cambridge: Cambridge University Press.

Binstock, R. H., & Post, S. G. (Eds.). (1991). *Too Old for Health Care: Controversies in Medicine, Law, Economics and Ethics*. Baltimore: Johns Hopkins University Press.

Haber, C. (1983). *Beyond Sixty-Five: The Dilemma of Old Age in America's Past.* Cambridge: Cambridge University Press.

Hudson, R. B. (Ed.). (1997). *The Future of Age-based Public Policy*. Baltimore: Johns Hopkins University Press.

Kingson, E. R., & Berkowitz, E. D. (1993). *Social Security and Medicare: A Policy Primer.* Westport, CT: Greenwood Publishing Group.

Schulz, J. H. (1995). *The Economics of Aging* (6th ed.). Westport, CT: Auburn House.

www.aarp.org — The official site of the American Association for Retired Persons, this is a goldmine of information about aging. AARP's legislative issues link provides up-to-date information about issues that affect the elderly.

www.agingsociety.org—This is the site of the National Academy on Aging, a policy institute operated by the Gerontological Society of America (**www.geron.org**). The Academy's mission is to promote "education, research, and public understanding" on issues that affect the elderly. Its publications are well balanced and carefully researched.

www.aoa.dhhs.gov—Maintained by the U.S. Administration on Aging, this site is an excellent source of information on programs funded under the Older Americans Act.

10

Racial and Ethnic Minorities

E Pluribus Unum

Perhaps more than any other country in the world, the United States is a multicultural nation. For some, this diversity is a problem, forcing them to endure the presence of people who do not conform to their notions of propriety. When racial and ethnic minorities demand equal opportunities, those who can barely endure their presence may erupt in rage, committing atrocious crimes and spewing obscenities. Racial intolerance can be viewed as a national disease, with periodic outbreaks and remissions. But more insidious and pervasive than hate crimes is institutionalized racism: the more subtle form of discrimination that denies individuals access to basic necessities such as education, housing, and employment.

After considering the experiences and accomplishments of the Reverend France Davis at the beginning of this chapter, we will examine the roots of racism in the United States. Next is a brief overview of the history and status of the nation's largest minority groups: African-Americans, Hispanics, Asians, and American Indians. The history of these groups illustrates both the role of government as an agent of racial oppression and more recent demands for government to serve the interests of racial equity. Emerging policy issues are then considered, including U.S. immigration policy, affirmative action, hate crime legislation, English-only legislation, and standardized testing.

CASE STUDY ◆ **THE REVEREND FRANCE DAVIS**

When I called the Calvary Baptist Church to schedule an appointment with Reverend Davis, his booming voice greeted me from the answering machine: "It's a great day at Calvary Baptist. We have services every Sunday at 11:00, and we would love to see you there." With that welcome, I went on to request an hour of his time for an interview that would go into a book on social policy. I knew he was a busy man and I couldn't expect a leisurely discussion. This would have to be a highly focused interview.

I met Reverend Davis at his church office. The office was crowded with memorabilia from the Reverend's productive career. On the walls were beautiful drawings of African-Americans, a birthday card made by one of his children, a few inspiring quotes, and a picture of Reverend Davis from 1974 when he became pastor of the church. Piles of books were stacked on the floor. The furniture was worn, but the computer was state-of-the-art. As I arrived his secretary was leaving, so he warned me he would have to answer the phone himself. During our hour together, Reverend Davis received a dozen phone calls, all of them important, and all brief and to-the-point. Sometimes he would answer with "Grand Central Station . . ." which aptly described his office—Command Central for his urgent and important calling.

France Davis was born in 1946 in Georgia, the eighth of nine children. He grew up on a cotton and corn farm and attended African-American schools throughout his education. His parents were adamant that their children receive more education than they had. Mr. Davis had completed third grade, and Mrs. Davis had completed eighth grade. Both insisted that their children at least consider going to college.

Of his parents, Reverend Davis said, "Other people use celebrities as role models. I use my parents. . . . They modeled participation and involvement in the community and society in which I grew up." Although they were unable to register to vote during his early years, France's parents were always active in the affairs of their community, and when they were able to register, they participated in the electoral process. They set the stage for their son's success through their teaching and upbringing. Reverend Davis recalled, "They taught us early to strive for balanced living; to get oneself academically prepared, but also spiritually prepared and then economically, socially, and politically aware. The goal was always to be best, and as an African-American we were taught that to be the best you had to be twice as good as anybody else."

After finishing high school, he went to Tuskegee University in Alabama, the school founded in 1881 by Booker T. Washington. He started college in 1964 and became actively involved in the civil rights movement. He was part of Martin Luther King's Selma to Montgomery march and participated in student activities. He also wrote for the student newspaper, which gave him "a platform from which to talk about some of the issues."

Reverend Davis remembers his involvement in the civil rights movement as a great adventure. He had no support from his family; in fact, Rev. Davis believed that if his mother had known what he was doing she "would probably have disowned me . . . [at least] she would have tried to get me to quit." There was some danger involved. "There was the Klan, and even the Alabama National Guard with their confederate flag." But, as Reverend Davis put it, "I didn't have anything to lose. I didn't own anything, so no one could take anything away from me. I didn't have a job, so no one could fire me. . . ." Besides that, Rev. Davis was accustomed to the threat posed by hate groups, having grown up, as he put it, "in Klan country."

The greatest success Reverend Davis remembers from those days came in the march from Selma to Montgomery. The march "was a major achievement and undertaking in a place where the governor of the state had argued that admission to the white school would come over his dead body. So there was a sense of 'here we are, in his face' . . . we were right out in front of the Capitol building. He was probably standing at a window looking at us. We were in his face and there was a real sense of accomplishment."

Other efforts were not always successful. Once Reverend Davis and some of his fellow students went into Mississippi to register voters. They were turned back at the airport in Mississippi, as outside agitators. "We were turned away because we were outsiders . . . someone had told them we were coming, so they were there and they just put us on a plane back out. . . .We were always considered outsiders . . . one of the common strategies of the other side was to define certain people as outsiders and then to make them of no effect."

Overall, though, the civil rights movement was a deeply satisfying experience for Reverend Davis. "We had a great time at it, and got a lot done . . . there was a sense of being part of that which was causing change of a major structural part of our society. What we were changing was the ways laws were interpreted from 1896 with the *Plessy v. Ferguson* Supreme Court decision. We were pulling down strongholds that were related to that [decision] so it was a sense of accomplishment, but also a sense of adventure."

Forced to withdraw from college due to lack of funds, Reverend Davis joined the U.S. Air Force and served for four years during the Vietnam conflict. Of this experience, he said, "Life in the service was exciting and the travel in particular was educational. I probably learned more in four years of military travel and experience than I did in the previous years of college and high school. I saw the world in many ways and traveled to different countries. I saw the way people lived. So it was an opportunity to see people living all across the country and different places I never thought I'd be . . . to see how life was different, and as a result of that I concluded that there was no such thing as 'normal.' Everything is relative . . . what's normal for me is just that—therefore no one is inferior or superior." Reverend Davis learned to speak Thai, and he made friends in every community in which he lived.

After leaving the service, Reverend Davis entered several colleges in California. He says he "took school seriously, and enrolled in four colleges full-time." Somehow, Reverend Davis found time for involvement in the student movements at U.C. Berkeley. He also met his future wife during this period.

Then, in 1972, he was recruited by the University of Utah to serve as a teaching fellow. He describes his entry into the state as "difficult," reporting that he was "turned down for a place to stay . . . due to my skin color and cultural differences." His response reflected his personal commitment to social action. "As had been my custom before, I just decided to do something about it. I knew it wasn't right, and so I set about to take whatever action was necessary to get the person's attention." With the assistance of a University administrator, Reverend Davis "reminded them that they were contractors with the University. Second, we reminded them that it was illegal to discriminate against a person because they were of a particular skin color or culture." Reverend Davis's efforts were successful, and he was offered housing. He took some pleasure in turning down that offer. "The forces of the University were behind what I was talking about, and so with that understanding they backed off . . . they offered me, as a result of our pressure, any place that they had before it was done, but I, of course, refused." Reverend Davis accepted housing in the University's International House, and enjoyed a congenial year there before marrying and relocating into married student housing.

In 1974, the Reverend Davis was asked to "fill in" at Calvary Baptist when their pastor resigned and they were looking for his replacement. Reverend Davis said, "Since they haven't found anybody, I'm still filling in . . . that's the way it is." His "filling in" has been marked by accomplishments and victories. The congregation has outgrown its current building, and construction of a new one is set to begin "any day." The church sponsors several important community-service projects, including a 30-unit housing project for the elderly and a preschool reading program. His own volunteer activities have included organizing to establish a Martin Luther King holiday in the state and a Martin Luther King Boulevard in its capital city, as well as serving on numerous boards and commissions.

As a member of the Board of Corrections, the Reverend Davis has worked to reduce racial profiling by police departments. He is stopped by an officer once a month or more, usually in the daytime and sometimes at night. When the officers find out that the black man they just pulled over is a Baptist minister, they apologize. "They apologize when they find out that I have a name, credentials. But the unfortunate thing about that is that it suggests that people who don't have the credentials get a different kind of treatment. That's why I'm concerned about it." He says, "One of the problems with it [profiling] is getting anybody to admit that they're doing it . . . there aren't any hard facts being collected." Reverend Davis hopes for passage of a bill that will require police to collect data on the racial backgrounds of people they pull over and cite for traffic violations.

I asked Reverend Davis about the role of the church in social change. His reflections reveal similarities between the church's role and the values of the social work profession:

> I think first and foremost the role of the church is a spiritual role. It's designed to help people be all they can be from the inside out—to help them to come to grips with who they are themselves, to understand their own heritage and their own being. That's first and foremost the role of the church in any community. But in addition to that, whatever it is that causes people to hurt is where the church ought to be. So if people are hurting spiritually, if they hurt physically, or with regard to housing or economically or socially or politically . . . Fairness and justice issues are at the top of the table, and it is the role of the church to be the voice for the voiceless—to represent the lost, the least, and the last. Those three groups tend to have not much voice in the community, so it is the role of the church to help them be represented and to give them voice.

Reverend Davis feels that education is the primary tool for combating racial prejudice. "I think much of what people do in terms of racial hatred and the problems of discrimination is based in ignorance." In his role as church leader and advocate for the

African-American community, Reverend Davis has been the target of racial hatred. He has a file with vile hate mail that has come to the church, and the church building has been defiled with racist graffiti. These actions have led him to conclude that "some folk are just filled with meanness and hatred, and we have to find another way to deal with those. I don't know what that is."

Coping with racial hatred requires learning not to take it in and let it devour you. I asked Reverend Davis whether the hate mail enraged him. He replied, "I'm accustomed to it so it doesn't enrage me. I expect this horror—it's life as I've learned it. . . . It's upsetting though. As long as they leave it here at my office [it's not as threatening], but every now and then somebody finds out where I live and they take it to the house, leave it at the door . . . but I've lived with this since I was born. I was born in Klan territory."

His experiences with racial hatred do not influence the way Reverend Davis feels about people. "I've learned to just consider the source of events, and I rationalize that the person that does that sort of thing is just probably angry and frightened, so what they direct toward me is what they feel toward themselves. They just hate themselves, so they need the hate of somebody else. I refuse to participate in their games." Indeed, Reverend Davis believes that this is an important skill for African-American children to learn. In the church preschool program children are taught "not to take things personally, to rise above them."

Reverend Davis takes a long-term view of race relations in the United States. When I asked what it would take to heal race relations, he replied, "I think it's going to take a few generations passing off the scene, first of all. I think people of my generation and older are not likely to change much. So we're going to have to, as did the children of Israel in the Bible, die before we get to the Promised Land." He does not expect race issues to be resolved during his lifetime, but hopes "we can get more young people understanding that difference does not mean 'less than,' it's just difference. 'Variety,' as my Daddy would put it, 'is the spice of life.'"

Reverend Davis lists education as a top issue for the African-American community. His advice for advocates interested in race issues is to "help to ensure that everyone learns to read and write—that they have a fair chance to get a good education." He is concerned about discrimination in education and employment, noting that policies must "ensure that people who have been discriminated against, who have been left out, are no longer." He argues that "some creative mind has got to come up with something that does not create as much backlash as affirmative action." Another critical issue for the African-American community, in his opinion, is securing adequate, affordable housing.

By the end of our hour together I knew Reverend Davis needed to move on to his next commitment. It was time for me to get out of the way so he could get back to the important work at hand. It is the work of a lifetime—work that he takes very seriously—preparing for a time when racial hatred, discrimination, and bigotry are historical anomalies rather than daily experiences.

DISCUSSION   The Reverend France Davis is a role model and community leader. His parents raised him and his siblings in a stable, loving environment with high expectations and clear commitments. Like many parents who are members of minority groups, they told their children "You have to be much better than the others for your abilities to be recognized." They also taught their son to understand racial hatred in ways that were constructive, rather than self-defeating. They prepared their son, not only to survive in a racist world, but to strive for a better world. The result is a committed activist who has become indispensable to his congregation and his community.

Social policies have had a profound impact on Reverend Davis's life, even as he has influenced social policies. As he noted, his parents were unable to vote when he was small, and he attended segregated schools. The civil rights movement, of which he was an integral part, not only established African-American electoral rights, but tore down the "separate but equal" farce that resulted from the *Plessy v. Ferguson* decision. Housing policies also affected Reverend Davis. In retrospect, he felt that he would have been unable to secure housing as a young, African-American man in a predominantly white town, without the assistance and support of a University Vice President.

Racial profiling has also touched Reverend Davis's life, as it has touched the lives of many minority individuals. Racial profiling may not seem as noble a cause as voter registration, but we vote only once a year. Members of minority groups going about their daily business are stopped by police several times during the same period. Each time, they risk being cited or even arrested, possibly for something they didn't do.

Reverend Davis devotes his professional career to spiritual leadership and his civic volunteer career to social justice. Equal access to education and employment ranks high on his list of priority issues, as does housing access. But equally important, if less tangible, is his desire to work toward a society in which "difference is just that, difference."

DEFINING RACE AND ETHNICITY

Most scientists agree that race is a social construct with little basis in human genetics or biology (Cox, 1970; Fields, 1982; Wilson, 1996). The notion that there were "types" of humans, and the use of the word "race" to refer to those types, has been described as a European invention. Indeed, Wilson (1996) noted that "the word 'race'—meaning different human species—appeared in the English language at precisely the time Britain began to colonize other lands" (p. 48).[1] Although there is no evidence for genetically distinct races, anthropologists traditionally identified three broad types of human beings, distinguished by history and appearance: "Negroid," "Mongoloid," and "Caucasoid."

To say that race is not a natural, but a social, construct is not to underestimate its impact. Race has profound meanings in the United States, even if they are primarily social, cultural, and political (see Omi & Winaut, 1994; Gossett, 1965; Goldberg, 1993). During the early part of the nineteenth century, Alexis de Tocqueville (1835) observed the persistence of racial prejudice and division in the United States, speculating that the nation would inevitably experience a race war at some time in its future.

Ethnicity has been used in several contexts to single out groups that may not

---

[1]The beginnings of Britain's colonization of other lands can be traced to the late 1500s.

FIGURE 10.1 RACIAL COMPOSITION OF THE U.S. POPULATION: 2000

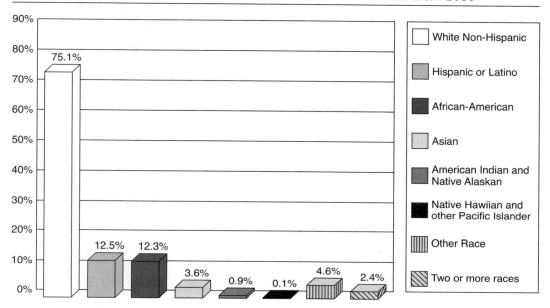

Source: U.S. Census Bureau (2001b). *Census 2000 Brief: Overview of Race and Hispanic Origin* (http://www.census.gov/population/www/cen2000/briefs.html).

be racially distinct, but are characterized by shared culture, common history, values, attitudes, and behaviors. Thus, for example, ethnicity was used to marginalize certain groups of European immigrants, such as Italians and Irish, who were sometimes referred to as "ethnics." It was used by Nazis in their persecution of Jews. Today the term *ethnicity* has lost much of its pejorative flavor, and is simply used to describe groups with distinctive cultural and historical traditions. Figure 10.1 presents the projected racial composition of the U.S. for the year 2000.

THEORIES ABOUT RACISM

Racism is based on the idea that some racial groups are "less intelligent, less virtuous, or less human than others" (Wilson, 1996, p. 39). It represents a system of ideas and beliefs that, when integrated into a culture, serve to justify racial oppression. Social scientists have speculated for decades concerning its roots. While some attribute racism to lack of familiarity or ignorance, others look to economic institutions for an explanation.

Those who use ignorance to explain racism argue that racism is simply an early stage in the historical process of cultural assimilation—the inevitable result of early contact between disparate groups. For example, Park (1974) argued that racial conflict surfaced in the early stages of cultural contact and receded with the process of assimilation. He identified four stages in the assimilation process: initial contact between racial or ethnic groups, competition between these groups, accommodation, and assimilation. The first two stages are marked by conflict and racism, which fades away in the later stages. Gordon (1964) elaborated on the later stages, arguing that assimilation proceeds in three stages: cultural assimilation (the minority culture is accepted or tolerated by the majority culture), marital assimilation (interracial marriages occur in large numbers), and prejudice-free assimilation (the final stage, when notions of racial superiority disappear).

Market theorists share the view that racism will simply disappear in their analysis of the impact of competitive forces on discriminatory practices. For example, Sowell (1981) argued that, in a free market, firms that discriminate against talented minorities pay a higher price for a less productive labor force. In a competitive market, this inefficiency should ultimately either eliminate these firms or force them to withdraw from their discriminatory practices. Of course, Sowell assumes a perfectly competitive market, in which minorities enjoy equal access to training and educational opportunities, labor unions do not organize to exclude minorities, and there is true competition.

In a sharply contrasting view, other theorists attribute racism to economic institutions, arguing, as Wilson (1996) does, that

> Racism is a modern historical phenomenon, grounded in alienating, exploitative, and oppressive economic arrangements. It arose in a particular stage in history, after the dissolution of feudalism, after the Protestant Reformation, and with the rise of a new economic order undergirded by the intense drive to accumulate wealth . . . it [this drive] fueled the genocide against American Indians and propelled the Atlantic slave trade. Modern racism emerged out of slavery and colonialism. These economic institutions created clear demarcation lines between the oppressed and the oppressor, which overlapped with color lines. The oppressed were not only separated from the oppressors, the oppressed were primarily people of color. The notion that people of color were of a different species and were inferior to the oppressors functions to legitimize the oppressive arrangement and to desensitize the dominant group to the plight of the oppressed (p. 37).

Wilson argues that racism evolves as the result of oppressive economic arrangements. It becomes the justification for the suppression of one group for the benefit of another. Support for this argument is found in the history of immigrant groups in the United States. When the Irish and the Jews immigrated, they lacked economic power and were characterized as an inferior race or culture. In time these groups, once seen as distinct sub-species of the human race, came to be assimilated and racial prejudice was, if not eliminated, at least reduced.

Class conflict theorists also attribute racism to economic sources, but instead of focusing on oppressive economic relationships they focus on competition between classes. This competition might take place between workers of different races, or between managerial and working classes. Noting a significant decline in racism during World War II, Willhelm (1970) argued that when the demand for labor increases, racism diminishes, and when jobs are scarce it increases. This argument does not explain the intense racism that marked the antebellum South, when slave labor was in high demand; nor does this labor-based approach explain this nation's efforts to exterminate American Indians.

THE ROLE OF GOVERNMENT: RACISM AND PUBLIC POLICY

Today we look to government to heal the divisions of racism and provide equal opportunity. But for much of its history the U.S. government was itself the agent of racist policies. Even leaders who professed belief in equality and liberty supported racist institutions. Stephen Douglass, a Democratic Senator in 1858, stated the prevailing view clearly when he said, ". . . this government of ours is founded on the white basis. It was made by the white man, for the benefit of the white man, to be administered by white men" (Loewen, 1995, p. 154).

From its very foundation, the U.S. government was an agent of race-based oppression. Even the most cursory review of U.S. history reveals centuries of government-sponsored and government-supported racial oppression. The question is not "whether" the U.S. government has been a racist institution, but what occurred to reverse this long trend. The same question applies to many state governments. This transition in the role of government did not occur magically or overnight, nor is it complete. Progress up to this point in time is chronicled in the following sections of this chapter.

THE HISTORY OF MINORITY GROUPS IN THE UNITED STATES

Minority groups in the United States today can be broadly categorized according to their historic origins. Some, like American Indians and "Californios," have ancestors who predated the arrival of Europeans. Most, like African-Americans, Chicanos, and Asian-Americans, originated in other countries, arriving in the U.S. after the European settlers. Of course, the largest racial minority in the U.S., making up 13 percent of the population in 1998 (U.S. Census Bureau, 1999) is African-Americans, whose ancestors were kidnapped and forced to come to this nation as slaves. Beginning with African-Americans, in the following sections we will briefly consider the historic treatment of racial and ethnic minorities in the United States. By understanding public policies and public attitudes towards racial minorities, social workers can help promote the development of culturally sensitive policies.

AFRICAN-AMERICANS

SLAVERY AND ITS AFTERMATH. During most of the seventeenth century, laborers on plantations in colonial America were indentured servants from Europe. Indeed, legal distinctions between these indentured servants and African slaves did not develop until the 1660s (Stampp, 1956). As Morgan (1975) noted, interracial marriages were common in the first half of the seventeenth century.

In time, the supply of indentured servants diminished, and the slave trade accelerated to the point where the population of African slaves exceeded the European population in southern colonies. Public policies of the late seventeenth century began to distinguish European servants from African slaves, meting out differential punishment for offenses. For example, in 1705, a Virginia law required dismemberment of "troublesome" slaves, while at the same time prohibiting masters from whipping European servants, naked, without a court order (Morgan, 1975). In one of the most brutal public policies recorded in the United States, several colonies enacted legislation mandating castration of slaves who made repeated attempts to escape.

With the American Revolution came revolutionary ideas of freedom and equality. While some were able to restrict their notions of freedom to white men, other revolutionary leaders found this more difficult. Thomas Jefferson was deeply opposed to slavery, authoring legislation in Virginia that allowed for the gradual emancipation of slaves. Yet, among his slaves, the only ones he freed were his children—and he did so upon his deathbed. He left their mother, Sally Hemings, enslaved for the rest of her life.

In states with the least economic investment in slavery, an abolitionist movement began and legislatures enacted laws to restrict or abolish slavery. These laws were enacted in New York, Massachusetts, New Jersey, Pennsylvania, Connecticut, and Rhode Island. Meanwhile, Southern leaders seized on the notion of property rights and individual liberty to argue that the government had no right to deprive them of their slaves (because they were property). In the South, black slavery was seen as a prerequisite to white freedom.

> **Thaddeus Stevens (1792–1868),** a white Republican senator from Pennsylvania, worked for racial equality throughout his career. At his request, he was buried in a cemetery that served both whites and African-Americans. His tombstone was a final chance to make his case. It says, ". . . finding other cemeteries limited as to race by charter rules, I have chosen this that I might illustrate in my death the principles which I advocated through a long life."

After the Revolution, the new Constitutional government was designed by men of property. Enumerating the wealth of the members of the Constitutional Convention, Dye and Ziegler (1996) estimated that nearly a third were plantation owners and slaveholders. In deference to their economic interests, not only did the Constitution not prohibit or restrict slavery, it included measures that reinforced the institution. For example, in population counts designed to establish congressional representation, each slave was to be counted as three-fifths of a person. The Constitution also required that runaway slaves who reached free states be returned to their owners upon demand. Article IV, Section Two, stated that "No Person held to service or Labor in one State, under the Laws thereof, escaping into another, shall, in consequence of any Law or Regulation therein, be discharged from such Service or Labor, but shall be delivered up on Claim of the Party to whom such Service or Labor may be due." Since slaves were recognized as property, the Fifth Amendment, which protected property from arbitrary governmental seizure, helped to sustain the institution of slavery. Finally, under the Naturalization Act of 1790, U.S. citizenship was defined in terms compatible with the European world view. The Act required applicants for citizenship to be of good character and "white."

The first federal involvement in abolitionist efforts came in 1808, when the international slave trade was banned. Even then, Congress did not alter the terms of domestic slavery. The Fugitive Slave Act of 1850 and the Dred Scott decision of 1857 established an obligation to return escaped slaves and denied equal citizenship to African-Americans.

State laws in the South not only treated slaves as property, they also restricted the activities of white residents in order to sustain the institution of slavery. Thus, for example, state laws prohibited whites—even slave owners—from teaching slaves to read or write. Owners were also prohibited from freeing their slaves unless the slaves left the state. Finally, interracial marriage, even between free adult blacks and whites, was strictly prohibited.

While the Civil War (1861–1865) did bring an end to slavery, it was not fought for that purpose. It was a war of independence for the South, and a struggle to maintain the Union for the North. Lincoln is reported to have said that slavery was acceptable, if that was what it took to sustain the Union. Because the war brought the promise of an end to slavery, hundreds of thousands of African-Americans contributed energetically to the Northern effort. For military and political reasons, the North's victory in the Civil War had to result in the end of slavery.

The post-war period was hardly one of racial equality. Southern landholders maintained their control over county and state governments and with the end of federal reconstruction, passed "Jim Crow"[2] laws designed to "keep Negroes in their place." The first Jim Crow law was passed in 1888 in Louisiana, declaring that African-Americans could not be seated with whites on railway cars. In addition to laws that sharply enforced racial segregation in public facilities, state and county laws established other oppressive practices, including the credit system used in sharecropping, debt peonage, convict leasing, segregated schools, and voting restrictions.

---

[2]Jim Crow was not a real person. The term is a pejorative way of characterizing African-Americans that was coined by a white minstrel named "Daddy Rice." He would blacken his face and dress in rags, then dance and sing while purporting to imitate African-Americans. His most popular song, "Jump Jim Crow," was an insulting parody of African-American culture.

CREDIT AND SHARECROPPING. Under sharecropping, those who worked the land owned very little, not even their tools. They paid a percentage of their crops as rent for their land, and borrowed tools and animals from the landowner. The credit system used in sharecropping was particularly onerous. Under this system, croppers received advances for their seed, supplies, and household goods. The interest rates charged on these advances were outrageous, ranging from about 53 percent to 71 percent (Mandel, 1992). In addition to the interest, landowners charged inflated prices for goods they sold to the croppers, who often had no alternative to the planter-owned stores.

DEBT PEONAGE. Under sharecropping and related practices, a landowner could virtually ensure a lifetime of debt for his tenants. Early in the twentieth century, nearly every southern state had a system of "debt peonage." Under state laws, the act of leaving the land without paying debts was defined as a form of labor fraud punishable by imprisonment. This legislation provided landowners with a pool of forced labor—tenants who could not leave the land because of their debts. The extent of debt peonage has been disputed. Some argue that the practice was rare and had died out by the Depression. But Daniel (1972) reported that it was not rare, and cited cases dating to the 1960s.

CONVICT LEASING. The practice of convict leasing has been described as "comparable to the worst horrors of slavery" (Wilson, 1996, p. 88). Under this system, landowners and other employers would bid on contracts to use convicts on chain gangs for their labor. The convicts, the vast majority of whom were African-Americans, had virtually no protection from abuse and lived in appalling conditions (Lichtenstein, 1996). They labored under the supervision of armed guards. Convict laborers had extremely high mortality rates. Camejo (1976) reported an annual mortality rate for convict laborers in the 1880s of one out of nine in Mississippi and one out of four in Arkansas. The practice died out by the 1940s, but chain gangs have been revived in several states in recent decades.

SEGREGATED SCHOOLS. Education is widely seen as a tool of empowerment, and thus race-based oppression has historically focused on denying educational access to African-Americans and other racial minorities. Prior to the Civil War, Southern states enforced laws that prohibited teaching an African-American to read or write. During reconstruction, federal efforts did not address equal access to education, and with the passage of Jim Crow legislation the Supreme Court became an ally of oppressive forces through its *Plessy v. Ferguson* decision.

Homer Plessy was a light-skinned African-American who purchased a first-class ticket on the East Louisiana Railway. When he tried to take his seat, he was ordered to go to the "colored" section. He refused to do so, and was jailed. The case was reviewed by the Supreme Court in 1896, and in its decision the Court held that "if Plessy be a colored man and be so assigned, he has been deprived of no property, since he is not lawfully entitled to the reputation of being a white man" (quoted in George, 2000, p. 7). The Court introduced the idea that "separate but equal" facilities were lawful, a principle that would have an enduring impact on the educational opportunities available to African-American children.[3]

Until the middle of the twentieth century, the nation's segregated educational system relegated African-American children to ill-equipped classrooms with outdated textbooks. Transportation and meal services available to white children were not provided in the "colored" schools. Access to higher education and professional training was severely limited. It was in this seriously under-funded system that Reverend Davis's parents were educated.

It was not until 1954 that the Supreme Court finally rejected the principle of separate but equal in its *Brown v. Board of Education* decision. On behalf of the National Association for the Advancement of Colored People (NAACP), Thurgood Marshall (later to become a Supreme Court justice) argued that segregation produced enduring damage in African-American children, scarring them for life with a sense of inferiority (an example of the "internalized oppression" discussed in the introduction to Part III). Chief Justice Earl Warren delivered the court's unanimous decision to order desegregation of the nation's schools.

Desegregation was not a simple matter. Three years passed before the school board in Little Rock, Arkansas, reluctantly concluded that they would have to desegregate their Central High School. Nine African-American children were hand-picked to attend the all-white high school. On Wednesday, September 4, 1957, the high school was surrounded by members of the National Guard and an angry mob. Eight of the children entered the school as a group under police protection. The ninth child, Elizabeth Eckford, did not have a phone and was not informed of the group's plans. She approached the school alone. Eckford vividly described the painful experience in her book *Growing Up Southern* (Mayfield, 1981).

VOTING RESTRICTIONS. Southern states established voting restrictions that disenfranchised large blocs of African-American voters. These included annual poll taxes that had to be kept current by anyone wishing to vote. Under these tax laws, an adult would be required to pay poll taxes for previous years as well as the current year before being allowed to register. Some jurisdictions required property ownership for voter registration, while others established complex literacy requirements. Some areas established poll taxes that applied only to African-Americans. African-Americans who did show up to vote were subject to harassment, intimidation, even violence. These measures kept millions of African-Americans, like Reverend Davis's parents, out of the voting booth until the civil rights movement of the 1960s.

---

[3]The *Plessy v. Ferguson* decision was not unanimous. Justice John Marshall Harlan wrote an eloquent dissent, stating that "The arbitrary separation of citizens, on the basis of race, while they are on a public highway, is a badge of servitude wholly inconsistent with the civil freedom and equality before the law established by the Constitution. It cannot be justified upon any legal grounds" (quoted in George, 2000, p. 8).

THE NEW DEAL. The New Deal, seen by many as a progressive movement towards equality, incorporated several provisions explicitly designed to maintain racial privilege. Roosevelt faced a solid bloc of white southern congressmen who refused to support any social security legislation that included blacks (Duster, 1996). As a result, the Social Security Act of 1935 excluded domestic servants and agricultural workers—jobs predominantly filled by African-Americans. The Wagner Act of 1935, which established the right of unions to collective bargaining, was revised to permit racial exclusion. Similarly, the 1934 National Housing Act exacerbated racial segregation in housing by permitting the use of race as a criterion for granting loans.

> **Dr. Charles Richard Drew (1904–1950)** became world-renowned for perfecting the technique for separating blood plasma from whole blood so it could be used more readily. Countless lives were saved. At the age of 45, Dr. Drew was injured in an auto accident in North Carolina. He was taken to a local hospital, which refused to treat him. The hospital was for whites only. Dr. Drew was African-American. He died from loss of blood.

THE CIVIL RIGHTS MOVEMENT. Two broad social and economic changes set the stage for the Civil Rights Movement of the 1960s: the migration of Southern agricultural workers to Northern cities, and the organizing experiences of African-American union members and leaders. Cotton prices dropped sharply during the first half of the twentieth century, and methods for harvesting and processing cotton were mechanized. As a result, hundreds of thousands of agricultural workers, many of them African-Americans, left the rural areas of the South and moved to urban areas in the North. They sought employment in industrial settings, often in union jobs.

This movement to urban settings provided opportunities for socialization and organization. Workers were no longer dependent on planters for employment and goods. It also brought a mandate to many of the nation's unions to support interracial solidarity.

LABOR UNIONS AND INTERRACIAL SOLIDARITY. The role of unions in the struggle for racial equality has been debated. Citing the example of racially exclusive unions, such as the American Federation of Labor (AFL) and the railroad unions, some argue that the racism of white members made unions hostile to African-American workers. Others suggest that racially exclusive unions were the result of pressure from local communities and from factory owners. Community hostility to racial integration took the form of anti-union violence. Several leaders of integrated unions, both African-American and white, were murdered or lynched with the cooperation of local law enforcement officials. Racism in unions was fostered when factory owners brought in African-American workers as strikebreakers.

The history of the union movement certainly provides examples of strong solidarity between white and African-American union members. The United Mine Workers of America (UMW) enrolled white and African-American members, as both races worked side-by-side in the coal mines of Appalachia. As Foner (1981) noted, African-Americans served in leadership roles at both local and national levels of the UMW. The Noble Knights of Labor, a federation of unions, was also deeply committed to racial solidarity, as was the International Workers of the World (IWW). These unions held integrated meetings, even in the South where local statutes prohibited such activities.

Thus, while some leaders and participants in the Civil Rights Movement came from churches and schools, others came from unions. They brought with them the methods and strategies of union organizing, as well as considerable financial support. The United Auto Workers, for example, contributed about $160,000 to the Southern Christian Leadership Conference to assist with bail expenses from the Birmingham demonstrations of 1963 (Flug, 1987; cited in Wilson, 1996).

The Civil Rights Movement effectively brought the federal government into the realm of race relations. Much civil rights legislation had the effect of negating state laws that supported racial oppression. The power of the federal government became a resource in the struggle for racial equality, frequently in conflict with state and local governments.

The era saw the passage of vitally important legislation. The Civil Rights Act of 1960 challenged voting discrimination. The Civil Rights Act of 1964 prohibited discrimination in public accommodations, employment, and programs receiving federal funds; the Voting Rights Act of 1965 prohibited discrimination in voting; and the Fair Housing Act of 1968 prohibited discrimination in housing. As a result of these statutes and accompanying court decisions, the role of the federal government shifted from racial oppression to the advancement of racial equity.

Ralph Bunche (1904–1971), African-American, negotiated the first cease-fire in the Middle-East, for which he received the 1950 Nobel Peace Prize.

CURRENT REALITIES. The progress of U.S. policies affecting African-Americans has been significant. Nonetheless, economic and health indicators show continuing race-based disadvantages.

African-Americans have lower median incomes and higher rates of poverty than other groups. As Figure 10.2 indicates, in 1999 the median household income for African-Americans was $25,000, compared to $40,600 for non-Hispanic white households. Similarly, as we saw in Chapter 4, the poverty rate for African-Americans was 23.6 percent in 1999, compared to a rate for non-Hispanic white Americans of 7.7 percent.

While African-Americans as a group do tend to have lower educational achievement, this does not completely explain the income differential. At comparable levels of education, African-Americans receive lower incomes than whites (Population Reference Bureau, 1999). For example, in 1998, the median earnings of a white worker with a high school diploma were 25 percent higher than those of an African-American worker with similar preparation (U.S. Census Bureau, 2000d). The same year, the median income for white workers with a bachelor's degree or more was 14 percent higher than the median income for African-American workers with similar preparation (U.S. Census Bureau, 2000d).

Household income for African-Americans is also influenced by household composition, as this group has a higher rate of female-headed households than whites and other minority groups in the United States. For example, in 1996, 47 percent of African-American households were headed by a single woman, compared to an overall rate of 18.2 percent for the nation. The rate for non-Hispanic whites was 13 percent that year, and the rate for Asian and Pacific Islanders was 13.2 percent (U.S. Census Bureau, 1997).

Health indicators offer another indication of race-based disadvantage. Life expectancy for a child born in the United States in 1997 was 76.5 years. The life expectancy for an African-American child born the same year was 71.2 years, while that of a white child in 1997 was 77.1 years (U.S. Census Bureau, 1999). In 1997, the infant mortality rate among African-Americans in the United States

FIGURE 10.2 MEDIAN INCOME BY RACE

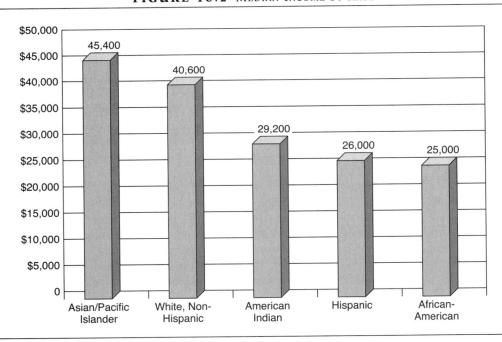

Source: Population Reverence Bureau (1999).

TABLE 10.1 OCCUPATIONAL DISTRIBUTION
OF AFRICAN-AMERICANS

	Percent African-American	
Occupation	*1983*	*1998*
Total Civilian Labor Force	**9.3**	**11.1**
Managerial and Professional Specialties	5.6	7.6
Aerospace Engineers	2.7	4.1
Social Workers	18.2	23.4
Technical, Sales and Administrative Support	7.6	11.1
Real Estate Sales	1.3	3.9
Postal Clerks	26.2	28.2
Service Occupations	16.6	17.6
Farm Operators and Managers	1.3	1.3
Private Household/Cleaners & Servants	42.4	15.4

Source: U.S. Census Bureau, 1999.

was more than twice the rate for whites. That year, 13.7 of every 1,000 African-American babies died before the age of one, compared to an overall infant mortality rate of 7.2 deaths per 1,000 and a rate of 6.0 per 1,000 for white Americans (MacDorman & Atkinson, 1999).

While recent decades have seen significant changes in the occupational attainment of African-Americans, the members of this group continue to be over-represented in service occupations and under-represented among managerial and professional specialties. This occupational distribution is illustrated in Table 10.1. Unemployment rates provide another indication of the labor-force experiences of Americans. In 1998, the unemployment rate for African-Americans was 8.9 percent, more than double the rate for white Americans, which was 3.9 percent (U.S. Census Bureau, 1999).

Although U.S. policies are no longer agents of direct, race-based oppression, a variety of factors contribute to continued disadvantage among African-Americans. These economic and health indicators are vivid indications of the legacy of racism in the United States.

HISPANICS

The term "Hispanic" refers to a person's ethnic and cultural origins. Hispanic Americans come from Spanish-speaking countries. Their history and culture reflect the global influence of Spain during its imperialist period. The Spanish (like other colonial powers) married members of the indigenous population of Spain's colonies. In Mexico, children of these mixed marriages were considered "mestizos" and possessed characteristics of the Spanish and the area's Indians. In Puerto Rico, the early decimation of the Indian population led the Spanish to bring in slaves from Africa. The resulting interracial marriages led some Puerto Ricans to identify themselves as black. Thus, "Hispanics" in the U.S. may have different racial identities and different experiences of U.S. racism. Puerto Ricans immigrating to New York may find themselves identified as black, whether or not they self-identify in this way. Their access to housing and jobs may more closely resemble that of African-Americans than it does other Hispanic groups.

The nation's Hispanic population has diverse origins and backgrounds. Some lived in the Southwestern United States before it was part of the United States. Others immigrated from Spanish-speaking areas, primarily Mexico, and more recently Latin America, Puerto Rico, and Cuba.

This diversity complicates our understanding of Hispanic claims on U.S. social policy. Should they be considered an indigenous group that has experienced disadvantage and oppression (and is therefore entitled to affirmative efforts to remedy past injustices), or should they be viewed as an immigrant group that, like other immigrant groups, can be expected to achieve economic and social parity in the process of assimilation? (See Chavez, 1991, for a discussion of this question.) Is policy needed to improve the status of Hispanics in the U.S.? Or will the process of assimilation inevitably improve it without public intervention? In the following sections we will consider the diverse histories of Hispanics in the U.S., looking at the experiences of Mexican-Americans, Puerto Ricans, Cubans, and immigrants from Latin America.

MEXICAN-AMERICANS. While other European nations were colonizing the northeastern region of what is now the United States, the Spanish government established its colonial presence in the southwestern region and Mexico. The Spanish encouraged the settlement of California, recruiting settlers from Mexico who were willing to move north. By the late eighteenth century the Mexican presence in California and the Southwest was well established.

Like Britain, Spain lost its American colonies by 1821, and Mexico became independent. At the time, the land area of Mexico was about twice what it is today, including the current states of California, New Mexico, Arizona, Texas, Colorado, Arizona, and Utah. Mexican society was rigidly hierarchical, with those who possessed Spanish land grants, the "Dons," enjoying a pastoral and aristocratic lifestyle and those at the bottom, the Indians, primarily responsible for the labor.

American visitors, and even settlers, were initially welcomed. As their numbers grew, and their intent to claim territory became clear, Mexico outlawed American immigration. Nonetheless, Americans continued to arrive as illegal immigrants, leading one Commissioner in Texas to declare, "The incoming stream of settlers is unceasing" (Takaki, 1993, p. 173).

This influx lasted until the Mexican-American War was declared in 1836. Conflict first broke out in Texas, where the Mexican government had outlawed slavery. This new policy enraged slaveholding Texans who, under the leadership of Sam Houston, forced the Mexican government to cede the state. The "Lone Star Republic" was established as an independent nation, with Houston as its leader.

The Texas victory was widely interpreted as an advance for the Anglo-Saxon race. Stephen Austin had declared war with Mexico inevitable, viewing it as a conflict between a "mongrel Spanish-Indian and negro race" and "civilization and the Anglo-American race." Similarly, Sam Houston declared the Lone Star Republic would reflect "glory on the Anglo-Saxon race" (Takaki, 1993, p. 174).

For Mexico, the war was devastating. The U.S. annexed Texas in 1845 and extended U.S. borders to the Pacific. In the 1848 Treaty of Guadalupe Hidalgo, Mexico lost Texas and the Southwest territories.

U.S. control of the area led to several measures designed to make life difficult for those of Spanish or Mexican descent. California passed a series of "Greaser Acts," declaring that those Spanish and Indian people who were not "peaceful and quiet" were vagrants subject to imprisonment. The acts also imposed a "Mexican Miners Tax" that required fees of all Spanish-speaking miners. Although the treaty's provisions afforded Mexicans the vote, poll taxes, language restrictions, and intimidation were used to reduce their political participation. Even the Dons were subject to oppression. Land holdings that derived from Spanish land grants were challenged by American squatters. The U.S. court review was a lengthy and expensive process, and even if their title was declared legitimate, owners frequently had to sell their land to pay legal expenses.

As a result of these and similar policies, Mexicans in California and the Southwest lost their property and their social standing, and those who stayed were reduced to the status of menial laborers. Even in these jobs, they encountered discrimination. Mexican workers in most industries (such as mining and railroads) were systematically paid less than "Americans" (whites) in the same jobs. A system of debt peonage was instituted, similar to that used to tie African-Americans to Southern farms. Living in company towns, many were forced to buy clothing, food, and other supplies from company-owned stores. The high price of these goods left workers so deeply in debt that they essentially became slaves to the company.

Over time, Mexican laborers organized into unions and declared strikes to improve working conditions. The strikes were supported by benevolent associations that were organized among Mexicans. These *mutualistas* helped members pay for hospitalization and funeral expenses, provided low-interest loans, and offered support in times of need. For example, when 3,500 miners (most of them Mexican) went on strike against the Clifton-Morneci mines, mutualistas provided food, clothing, and other supports to strikers. In this case, despite the use of the National Guard to break the strike, workers were successful at extracting a wage increase.

During the early twentieth century, as Mexican workers in the United States were struggling to achieve wage parity, Mexico itself was wracked by civil war. The Diaz government was overthrown in 1911 by Madeira, who was soon overthrown by General Victoriano Huerta. Huerta was forced into exile as two other generals battled the revolutionaries Pancho Villa and Emiliano Zapata. The war was especially hard on civilians, and thousands fled North to avoid starvation, torture, or murder.

The migration northward from Mexico would continue for decades. Mexican laborers were well received, particularly in Southern California and Texas, where they soon made up most of the construction and agricultural labor force. Differential pay scales persisted, and Anglo workers were typically paid more for the same work than Mexican immigrants, referred to as "Chicanos." Chicanos were also restricted to the most unskilled jobs and found it virtually impossible to move into managerial positions.

> **César Chávez (1927–1993)** organized the United Farm Workers to advocate on behalf of migrant workers. The UFW has been responsible for improved living conditions and benefits for migrant workers throughout the country.

There was tension around the education of Chicano children. Employers wanted to restrict their access to education to ensure a continued supply of cheap labor. Parents longed for their children to become educated so they would enjoy a better standard of living. Most school districts restricted educational opportunities of Chicano children, channeling them into technical and domestic classes. Some of the larger districts established separate schools for Chicanos similar to those provided for African-Americans in the South.

The Depression ended U.S. demands for Mexican labor, and a policy of "repatriation" was established. Chicanos who applied for welfare were given aid only upon agreeing to return to Mexico. Buses and boxcars were used to transport entire families—including children born in the United States—to Mexico. An estimated 400,000 Chicanos were "repatriated" during the Depression (Moquin, 1972).

In 1942, this inclination reversed, and the "Bracero Program" was introduced to encourage Mexican men to come north and work as contract agricultural laborers. Under an executive agreement between the U.S. and Mexico, approximately 350,000 men entered the U.S. to do agricultural work (Chavez, 1991). The program ended in 1960.

Meanwhile, the nature of Hispanic immigration to the United States began to change, as residents of Puerto Rico, Cuba, and Latin America relocated to this country.

IMMIGRANTS FROM CUBA, PUERTO RICO, AND LATIN AMERICAN COUNTRIES. Cubans are the second-largest group of immigrant Hispanics in the United States. Generally regarded as "elite" Hispanic immigrants, their ranks have included many landowners, professionals, and businessmen. Since the 1960s, Cubans have immigrated in waves. Unlike Mexican immigrants, who seek economic improvement, Cubans tend to be "political" refugees looking for a different political system.

Puerto Ricans are, in fact, citizens of the United States. Their island was ceded to the U.S. by Spain in 1898 and, although they cannot vote for President, they have been citizens since 1917. Migration from Puerto Rico swelled during the 1940s and 1950s, as young men left to serve in World War II and became aware of economic opportunities in the U.S. mainland. Today, nearly two-thirds of Puerto Ricans live on the U.S. mainland, primarily in New York (Chavez, 1991).

Latin American immigrants, primarily from the Dominican Republic, El Salvador, and Nicaragua, have increased the diversity of the U.S. Hispanic population. Many have fled political instability caused by the collapse of regimes (such as that in El Salvador) that were supported by the United States. In this situation, many immigrants had to struggle to secure refugee status, because recognition of their oppression meant indictment of the U.S.-supported regime.

CURRENT REALITIES. The nation's Hispanic population has changed. Today it is more heavily composed of immigrants than it was only three decades ago. Chavez (1991) reported that in 1970 barely one in five Hispanics was foreign-born, while by 1990 that figure had risen to more than a third. Where early Hispanic immigrants came almost exclusively from Mexico, more recent waves have brought migrants from Cuba, Puerto Rico, and Latin America (primarily El Salvador and Nicaragua). Mexican immigrants were primarily economic refugees, seeking to escape poverty. Refugees from Cuba and Latin America are primarily political refugees. They tend to include more professionals and members of landed classes. Nonetheless, these immigrants typically experience greater economic deprivation than second- and third-generation Americans of Hispanic descent (Chavez, 1991; Bean & Tienda, 1987).

Although the Hispanic population in the United States has grown increasingly diverse, broad economic and health indicators suggest the group as a whole continues to experience disadvantages. For example, as Figure 10.2 indicates, in 1999 the median income for Hispanic households was $26,000 compared to a median for white non-Hispanic households of $40,600. Similarly, as reported in Chapter 4, the poverty rate among the nation's Hispanic households was 22.8 percent in 1999, substantially higher than the rate for white non-Hispanic households, which was 7.7 percent (U.S. Census Bureau, 1999a).

Health indicators reflect the diversity of the Hispanic population. The National Center for Health Statistics (MacDorman & Atkinson, 1999) reported that infant mortality for some Hispanic groups was below the overall norm for the nation. In 1997, 7.2 of 1,000 infants born in the U.S. died before their first birthdays. Among Puerto Ricans, infant mortality was higher, at 7.9 per 1,000. Hispanics from Cuba and South America had an infant mortality rate of 5.5 per 1,000, and Mexican-Americans had a rate of 5.8 per 1,000. Life expectancy for Hispanics as a whole is generally comparable to or better than that of the white population. Among Hispanic men born in 1995, the projected life expectancy was 74.9, compared to 73.6 for white men. Hispanic women born in 1995 have a projected life expectancy of 82.2 years, compared to 80.1 for white women (Administration on Aging, 1999).

The occupational distribution of Hispanics is similar to that of African-Americans, in that Hispanics are over-represented in the lower-paying service occupations and under-represented in the more remunerative managerial and

TABLE 10.2 OCCUPATIONAL DISTRIBUTION
OF HISPANIC AMERICANS

Occupation	Percent Hispanic	
	1983	*1998*
Total Civilian Labor Force	**5.3**	**10.1**
Managerial and Professional Specialties	2.6	5.0
Lawyers and Judges	1.0	3.0
Social Workers	6.8	6.4
Technical, Sales, and Administrative Support	4.3	8.3
Securities and Financial Services	1.1	3.7
Teachers' Aides	12.6	13.5
Service Occupations	6.8	15.0
Protective Services: Supervisors, Police, and Detectives	1.2	6.0
Farm Workers	15.9	44.9

Source: U.S. Census Bureau, 1999.

professional roles. The occupational distribution of Hispanics in the U.S. is illustrated in Table 10.2. Unemployment among Hispanics in 1998 was nearly twice that of whites. The rate for Hispanics was 7.2 percent, while the rate for whites was 3.9 percent (U.S. Census Bureau, 1999).

ASIANS

Immigrants traveled across the Pacific in response to the demand for labor within the rapidly expanding economy of the western United States. The Chinese came first, entering California just before the Gold Rush of 1849. They were followed by large numbers of Japanese, whose emigration was carefully managed by their government. Immigrants from Korea, the Philippines, and other Asian and Pacific Island locations came in smaller numbers. In the following sections we will consider the experiences of Chinese and Japanese immigrants to the United States.

CHINESE IMMIGRANTS. Chinese immigrants came to this country in search of the "Gold Mountain," a land of beauty and wealth. Their native land was suffering from poverty and chaos caused by the "Opium Wars" with the British. To finance these wars, and to pay the large indemnities charged by Western imperialist powers, the Chinese (Qing) government imposed high taxes. Many farmers lost their land, and food shortages led to widespread famine.

During the latter half of the nineteenth century, hundreds of thousands of young Chinese men—primarily illiterate laborers—came to America. They were attracted by stories of countrymen who had spent a few years working in America and returned with fabulous wealth. These and related stories were propagated by labor brokers—entrepreneurs hired by American firms to recruit Chinese laborers. There is no evidence that Chinese men were kidnapped and brought to America as "coolies" (Takaki, 1993). Most stayed in California, but some made their way to Southern states, where they were viewed as an alternative to African-American labor.

Initially the Chinese were welcomed and their contributions appreciated. They did not represent a political threat, since the Naturalization Act of 1790 reserved citizenship for whites, and the Chinese immigrants did jobs that no white person wanted to perform. Chinese laborers worked in the mines under cramped and dangerous conditions. When mining became less profitable, they were hired by the railroads. As Chinn and colleagues (1969) explained, the Central Pacific Railroad line was a Chinese achievement. Again, Chinese workers labored under extremely difficult conditions, laying track through Donner Summit during the winter of 1866.

Thousands of Chinese (nearly one-fourth of California's Chinese population in 1869) went to live in San Francisco, where they established a thriving community known as "Chinatown" and helped the city to become a leading manufacturer. Chinese were also successful as agricultural laborers in California's Central Valley.

Their conspicuous effectiveness and relative success led to resentment on the part of white labor organizations, which lobbied for passage of the Chinese Exclusion Act in 1882.[4] The Act prohibited immigration by Chinese laborers. It was the first piece of immigration legislation that expressly forbade immigration from one nation.

Chinese continued to be targets of resentment, and eventually moved into self-employment, opening small businesses such as restaurants, grocery stores, and laundries. Chinese laundries represented an especially good niche for former laborers. Few white men viewed this occupation as an economic threat, as it was incompatible with their view of the male role. Yet laundry required only a minimal investment and did not demand high levels of skill or literacy. Laundry represented an excellent alternative to facing racial tension in the labor market.

Racial tension persisted in other venues, however, and Chinese were viewed as potential threats to the purity of the white race. In 1880, California passed a law prohibiting marriage between a white person and a "negro, mulatto, or Mongolian" (Osumi, 1982). These "anti-miscegenation" laws remained on the books in some states as late as 1998.[5]

Chinese immigrants were primarily male. For economic and cultural reasons, women did not emigrate from China. They had no value in the labor market and were accustomed to living within the narrow confines of their homes. Well-born Chinese women were nearly unable to walk, due to the practice of binding their

---

[4]The Chinese Exclusion Act was renewed in 1892 and extended indefinitely in 1902. Its effect ended with the passage of the Immigration and Naturalization Act of 1924.

[5]South Carolina and Alabama were the last states to eliminate statutes prohibiting interracial marriage. South Carolina did so in 1998, and Alabama in 1999. These laws had been declared unconstitutional by the U.S. Supreme Court in 1967.

feet into "rosebuds." A few Chinese men were able to bring their wives to the United States, and thousands of Chinese women were sold into prostitution. Nonetheless, the population of Chinese immigrants was predominantly male.

JAPANESE IMMIGRANTS. The Japanese immigration experience differed from that of the Chinese in several respects. First, it began later. The first wave of Japanese immigrants began to come to the U.S. in 1885, roughly 40 years after the beginning of Chinese immigration. Second, their country of origin was not a relatively undeveloped region but an emerging world power. Japan had defeated the Russians in 1905 and commanded a measure of respect for its military and economic potential. Third, while the Chinese government was not involved in emigration, Japanese emigration was carefully orchestrated and monitored by the Japanese government, which was ready to intercede diplomatically if its citizens were abused by the United States government (Daniels & Kitano, 1970). These differences led to a less difficult immigration experience for the Japanese, particularly as it was affected by federal policies.

These advantages did nothing, of course, to reduce the impact of American racism or mitigate the demands of the American economy on Japanese immigrants. Like the Chinese, the Japanese fled economic deprivation and, like the Chinese, they sought a better standard of living. Another similarity was the widespread belief, if not expectation, that Japanese emigrants were only temporarily residing in the United States.

Like the Chinese, the Japanese came to the United States as laborers. Thousands labored in the sugar cane fields of Hawaii, and others became agricultural laborers in California. The agricultural skills of the Japanese were considerable, and they introduced new techniques and crops to the fast-growing agricultural economy of California.

Unlike the Chinese, Japanese women emigrated to the United States to work alongside their husbands. In Japan they had already become accepted members of the industrial labor force, and a wife was an asset in the immigration process. As a result, the first generation of Japanese immigrants (the "Issei") settled and raised a second generation (the "nisei") of U.S.-born Japanese-Americans.

Like the Chicanos, Japanese immigrants saw education as the key to their children's advancement as Americans. Also like the Chicanos, the Issei encountered resistance in their attempts to secure a public education for their children. In San Francisco the resistance was especially strident. In 1906, in the middle of an anti-Japanese campaign by the *San Francisco Chronicle*, the Board of Education ordered all Japanese students (both native- and foreign-born) to attend the segregated "Oriental School" that had been established in Chinatown. Daniels and Kitano (1970) noted that the furor was disproportionate to the number of Japanese children in San Francisco schools: "Only a very few students were involved—at the time of the order there was a grand total of 93 Japanese students distributed among 23 different public schools, and 25 of them were native-born citizens" (p. 48).

The School Board's order created international uproar. The U.S. ambassador to Japan received official protests from the Japanese government, which maintained that the action violated treaties protecting the rights of Japanese citizens in the United States. President Theodore Roosevelt summoned the School Board to Washington and "with a combination of threats, pleas, cajolings, and promises, succeeded in having the school board rescind the offending order" (Daniels & Kitano, 1970, p. 48). Roosevelt also succeeded in persuading the California legislature to refrain from passing anti-Japanese legislation.

In return, Roosevelt exchanged a series of notes with the Japanese government that have come to be known as the "Gentlemen's Agreement." In it, the Japanese agreed to limit emigration of laborers and farmers to the United States. This concession quieted calls for national legislation to restrict Japanese immigration on the model of the Chinese Exclusion Act. The Gentlemen's Agreement did allow for wives to join their husbands in the U.S., and as a result thousands of "picture brides" made up the last of the Japanese immigrants. These women had long-distance arranged marriages to men with whom they had exchanged only photographs prior to meeting as man and wife in the United States.

Of course, the Japanese government's protection of its citizens in the United States did not pave the way to U.S. citizenship. In a telling example of judicial racism, the U.S. Supreme Court denied the citizenship petition of Takao Ozawa. In 1922, Ozawa (a graduate of the University of California and young man of good character and light complexion) petitioned for citizenship. The Court ruled that his complexion, however light, did not qualify as "white," and thus did not meet the criteria for naturalization, which limited applicants to "free white persons" and "persons of African descent." The Court ruled, in *Ozawa v. United States*, that "white" meant "Caucasian." As Daniels and Kitano (1970) reported, however, the same Court ruled "shortly thereafter, that an applicant from India, who was ethnographically a Caucasian although his complexion was of a mahogany hue" was not, in fact entitled to citizenship because, "White did not mean Caucasian at all, but meant, rather, 'white' as commonly understood" (p. 54). This court served as what Daniels and Kitano called "the last bulwark of racism" until its membership changed in the 1930s and 1940s through appointments by President Franklin Roosevelt.

CURRENT REALITIES. Asian and Pacific Islanders are typically grouped together by the Census, despite their heterogeneity. Economic indicators provide limited support for the popular notion that Asians represent a "model minority." For example, as indicated in Figure 10.2, the median household income of Asian and Pacific Island households in 1999 was higher than that of white households; $45,400, compared to $40,600. Nonetheless, as we saw in Chapter 4, the risk of poverty for Asian and Pacific Islanders remained somewhat higher than that of white households. The poverty rate for Asian/Pacific Island households was 10.7 percent in 1999, compared to a rate of 7.7 percent for white households. Clearly, while most Asian/Pacific Island households have attained economic parity, a few continue to experience economic disadvantage.

Two factors contribute to the higher median household income among

America's Asian population. First, the higher median income of Asian-Americans has been attributed to this group's higher likelihood of having more than two workers within a household. In 1997, 18 percent of Asian households had three or more earners, compared to 13 percent of white households (Population Reference Bureau, 1999). Second, Asian-Americans have a higher rate of business ownership than other minority groups. The rate among whites, measured as businesses per 1,000 in the population, is 80. The rate for Asian/Pacific Islanders is 68. Rates for other groups were considerably lower. Hispanics had a rate of 32 businesses per 1,000 population, African-Americans had 20, and Native Americans 19 (Population Reference Bureau, 1999).

Life expectancy and infant mortality among Americans of Asian and Pacific Island descent are generally favorable in comparison to the general population and to white Americans. Whereas the overall infant mortality rate in 1997 was 7.2 deaths per 1,000, the rate for Asian/Pacific Islanders was 5.0 per 1,000 births (MacDorman & Atkinson, 1999). Similarly, life expectancies for Asian and Pacific Islanders tend to be somewhat higher than those for the general population (National Women's Health Information Center, 1999).

AMERICAN INDIANS[6]

EARLY CONTACTS WITH EUROPEAN IMMIGRANTS. When Columbus encountered American Indians, he is quoted as having remarked:

> They [American Indians] are the best people in the world and above all the gentlest—without knowledge of what is evil—nor do they murder or steal. They are very simple and honest . . . none of them refusing anything he may possess when he is asked for it. They exhibit great love toward all others in preference to themselves. They would make fine servants. With 50 men we could subjugate them all and make them do whatever we want (Phillips and Phillips, 1992, p. 166).

When Europeans established their first colony in Virginia, the area was inhabited by an estimated fourteen thousand members of the Powhatan tribe (Takaki, 1993). For these agricultural people, corn was a dietary staple, as it was for many of the tribes encountered by the European immigrants. During what John Smith later called "the starving time" (winter of 1607), the Powhatans shared their food with the immigrants and taught them principles of survival. Later, the Iroquois Federation would teach the colonists important principles of governance by sharing "the Great Law of Peace" (see Figure 10.3).

In return, the Europeans declared Indians "heathens" and promoted their view of the race as "backward" and "savage." This view helped to justify the

---

[6]Some tribes object to the term "Native American," feeling that it is too broad and includes Native Hawaiians and other indigenous people in land now occupied by the United States. Today, many prefer the term "American Indian" for use when referring to indigenous tribes of the continental United States. Most natives of Alaska prefer to be referred to as "Alaskan Natives."

FIGURE 10.3 THE GREAT LAW OF PEACE*

Contrary to popular views of American Indians as savages, some of the English colonists recognized that they had developed effective methods for governance. Indeed, historians agree that the U.S. Constitution drew as much from the Indians as it did from the Europeans (Schaaf, 1990). Their argument is compelling in part because neither Britain nor other major originating nations had faced the challenge of uniting disparate political entities. In creating their new nation, the colonists faced just that challenge. Each colony had a distinctive history and culture, yet all needed to work together if the nation was to succeed. This challenge had been effectively addressed by tribal confederacies on the eastern seaboard of North America.

The Great Law of Peace governed a confederation of Iroquois tribes (also called the Haudenasaunee Six Nations). For centuries, these tribes strove for balance of power and supported the idea of the inherent rights of people, including freedom of speech and religion. Their council-based system of governance was of great interest to colonial leaders, including George Washington and Benjamin Franklin.

While serving as Indian Commissioner for Lancaster, PA, during the mid-1700s, Benjamin Franklin studied the Iroquois system of governance. In 1744, minutes of the Lancaster, Pennsylvania, Provincial Council reported that Onondaga leader Canasatego advised the council to form a league similar to the Iroquois confederacy, saying, "our Wise forefathers established Union and Amity between the Five Nations. This has made us formidable; this has given us great Weight and Authority with our neighboring Nations. We are a powerful Confederacy; and by your observing the same methods our Wise Forefathers have taken, you will acquire such Strength and power. Therefore whatever befalls you, never fall out with one another" (Friends Committee on National Legislation, 1987). Further, Schaaf (1990) noted that the "Albany Plan of Union," proposed by Benjamin Franklin in 1754, reflects the structures of the Iroquois confederacy's Grand Council. (Dr. Paul Wallace, an ethnohistorian, wrote extensively about the governance structures of the Iroquois and Algonquian peoples. See also Parker, 1916; Weatherford, 1988.)

On the 200th anniversary of the signing of the U.S. Constitution (September, 1987), a concurrent resolution to the 100th Congress set out to "acknowledge the contribution of the Iroquois Confederacy of Nations to the Development of the United States constitution and to reaffirm the continuing government-to-government relationship between Indian Tribes and the United States established in the Constitution." Senator Daniel Inouye and colleagues introduced the resolution.

*I am indebted to Russ Redner for introducing me to this material.

atrocities committed by the Europeans, who were eager to steal the land under cultivation by the Indians.

European interest in Indian lands initially stemmed from the popularity of tobacco in England. In 1613, the colony in Virginia sent its first shipment of tobacco to London. Within seven years, tobacco exports had increased to 60,000 pounds (Takaki, 1993). The Indians' already-cleared fields would, when converted to tobacco, produce riches for the immigrants. Europeans' lust for land, and their capacity for declaring other races "inhuman," set the stage for well-documented brutalities.

With the passage of the Naturalization Act of 1790, American Indians were classified as "domestic foreigners" and prevented from securing citizenship. The task of working with these internal nations was assigned to Congress through the Constitution, and affirmed later in the 1802 Indian Trade and Intercourse Act, which provided that no Indian land be ceded to the United States except through treaties with Congress.

European demands for cotton led to expansion into the southeastern part of the country. The states of Alabama, Mississippi, and Louisiana were carved out of Indian territory to facilitate the growth of cotton. Between 1814 and 1824, 11 "treaties of cessation" were negotiated, forcing tribes in this area to relocate to land west of the Mississippi. A popular justification for the appropriation of Indian lands was the argument that the Indians did not fully "use" the land.

Faced with the threat of extermination, the Indian nations fought back. The "Indian Wars" progressed, and violence by Indians was viewed both as evidence of their "savagery" and as justification for their annihilation. President Andrew Jackson (a veteran of the Indian Wars) encouraged this view, allowing states to appropriate Indian lands for distribution to white settlers in contradiction to the Indian Trade and Intercourse Act as well as an 1832 Supreme Court Ruling.[7] One example of Jackson's practice of ignoring federal law came when the state of Mississippi abolished the sovereignty of the Choctaw nation. The federal government then collaborated in the state's effort to deprive Choctaw of their land through the "Treaty of Dancing Rabbit Creek." Tribal leaders, threatened with extermination, had no choice but to approve the treaty, which required that Choctaw cede their land (10,423,130 acres) to the federal government and move west of the Mississippi.

Alexis de Tocqueville described the exodus of the Choctaws from Mississippi:

It was then the middle of winter and the cold was unusually severe; the snow had frozen hard upon the ground, and the river was drifting huge masses of ice. The Indians had their families with them, and they brought in their train the wounded and the sick, with children newly born and old men upon the verge of death. Three or four thousand soldiers drive before them the wandering races of the aborigines; these are followed by the pioneers, who pierce the woods, scare off the beasts of prey, explore the courses of the inland streams, and make ready the triumphal march of civilization across the desert (de Tocqueville, 1835, pp. 352–364).

The federal government made a profit from the sale of the Choctaw lands. Since this sale was in violation of their treaty, the Choctaws sued in federal court. In 1890 they were awarded a settlement of nearly $3 million, most of which went to pay their lawyers (Wright, 1928).

In one of many similar incidents, one-fourth of the Cherokee Nation died on the "Trail of Tears" as a direct result of betrayal and manipulation sanctioned by the President and the Congress. Cherokee lands covered what is now called Georgia. In 1829, the Georgia state government passed a law extending their authority to Cherokee lands. Aware that this action was a violation of federal law, Chief Ross of the Cherokee Nation wrote to President Jackson pleading for his

---

[7]Jackson is quoted to have responded to objections that he was acting in opposition to the Supreme Court ruling by saying, "Let the Supreme Court enforce its ruling."

protection. Jackson instructed his Indian commissioner, J. F. Schermerhorn, to negotiate a treaty to move the Cherokee. Schermerhorn presented the treaty to a Cherokee council that was carefully crafted to include only those Cherokee who were inclined to approve it. (Chief Ross was jailed for the occasion.) A tiny fraction of the Nation attended the Council. None of the tribal leaders was present. The treaty was ratified. Even some federal officials acknowledged it as a fraud. Nonetheless, Congress ratified the treaty, and the President approved it. And, as a result, most of the Cherokee Nation set out, in the middle of one of the worst winters on record, to re-settle west of the Mississippi on land they had never seen.

As the Western expansion progressed and railroads were built, the lands west of the Mississippi captured the imagination of the U.S. government and its citizens. The railroads made extensive use of public policy to advance their interests, securing the rights to millions of acres of land that lay adjacent to their tracks and fostering passage of the 1871 Indian Appropriation Act. This Act declared that "hereafter no Indian nation or tribe within the territory of the United States shall be acknowledged or recognized as an independent nation, tribe, or power, with whom the United States may contract by treaty" (Walker, 1874, p. 5). The Act denied the very existence of tribes as legitimate political units, eliminating the need to negotiate treaties and paving the way for the railroads' expansion. This Act was accompanied by federal policy that forcibly placed Indians on reservations, where they could be trained to become agricultural workers and eventually assimilated into the broader society.

Blanche K. Bruce (1841–1898) was the first African-American to serve a full term in the U.S. senate. Born a slave, Bruce was an ardent supporter of extending civil rights to Native Americans. Of the American experience, he said, "As a people, our history is full of surmounted obstacles. We have been scaling difficult problems for more than a hundred years. . . ."

Under the reservation system, land was assigned to the tribes, with the assurance that they would not be subject to attack by U.S. military forces as long as they were within reservation boundaries. Of course, the problem with the system was whites' insatiable appetite for Indian lands. Thus, in 1887, the Dawes Act, also known as "Indian Emancipation Act" was passed to eliminate the reservation system. White reformers believed that true assimilation would come only with private, not tribal, ownership of land. Under this Act, each Indian head of household who was at least one-half Indian would be given a 160-acre parcel. If a reservation had more parcels than households, the "surplus" parcels would be sold to white settlers. The net effect of the Act was removal of thousands of acres from the reservation system. Not only were "surplus" parcels sold, but individual settlers purchased or stole property from individual tribal owners. Tribal leaders recognized the threat the Dawes Act posed to tribal survival, and some, like Chief Lone Wolf of the Kiowas, went to court to argue that the parceling out of land was in violation of previous treaties. In 1903, the Supreme Court declared that the federal government could abrogate treaty provisions. This allotment procedure reduced Indian lands from 138 million to 48 million acres (Limerick, 1987).

In 1924, U.S. citizenship was conferred on all tribal members. Later, as part of Roosevelt's New Deal, Indians were offered an opportunity to regain tribal control of what remained of their reservation land through the 1934 Indian Reorganization Act (also known as the Howard-Wheeler Act). This law restored the political legitimacy of tribes (in the eyes of the U.S. government) and encouraged the maintenance of Indian culture on reservation lands. Reorganization meant that tribes would enjoy self-government on their lands, and that some funds would be allocated for purchase of additional tribal lands. The law included a provision that required ratification by a majority of tribal members. Most tribes did approve reorganization, but some (most notably the Navajo) chose to remain outside the system.

FORCED ASSIMILATION. General Richard Pratt's motto, "Kill the Indian, Save the Man," was the watchword of a movement to assimilate Indians by removing children from their homes and placing them in boarding schools, run either by the government or by messianic Christian denominations. Pratt founded the first Indian boarding school in 1879, the Carlisle Indian School, in Pennsylvania. Three years later, U.S. Indian Commissioner Thomas Morgan supported the effort, commenting that it was "cheaper to educate Indians than to kill them" (Kelley, 1999).

Tens of thousands of Indian children were placed in these schools. The children were subjected to a harsh daily schedule, with only limited time devoted to education and the remainder to hard labor. They were strictly punished for revealing any evidence of their cultures, such as carrying a medicine bundle or speaking their native languages. The children were trained to be domestic servants and agricultural laborers.

This assimilation program peaked in the U.S. in 1931, when nearly one third of Indian children were in boarding schools. It continues today in 52 boarding schools operated by the government. Most of these are located on the Navajo reservation. The schools are now managed primarily by Indians, many of whom are alumni. As a result, students can expect a less punitive, more culturally congruent experience (Limerick, 1987).

The horrors of Indian removal, the reservation system, and the Indian boarding schools are well documented, as is the duplicity with which U.S. officials treated Indian tribes. Between 1778 and 1871, some 370 Indian treaties were ratified by the U.S. Senate.[8] Many of them were later abrogated or ignored. This duplicity is well remembered by American Indians, and it colors their view of federal services and policies.

The betrayals committed by government representatives were not seen as "wrong" by most white U.S. citizens at the time they took place. Intelligent, well-

---

[8]These treaties are compiled in a volume entitled *Indian Treaties, 1778–1871*, available through the Diplomatic Branch of National Archives and Records Services, Washington, DC.

meaning people had been persuaded that Indians were less human than whites—that they were "savage." The whites' insatiable greed for Indian land stemmed from an economic system that allowed for the creation of immense private wealth at the expense of communal and environmental values. It was reinforced by religious values that emphasized the superiority of Christianity. Finally, it was fostered by a failure to see, as Reverend Davis said, that "Difference is just that, difference. Not better or worse, just different."

CURRENT REALITIES. Today, U.S. Indian policy is administered by the Bureau of Indian Affairs. Figures from the 2000 Census estimate an American Indian population of 2.4 million (U.S. Census Bureau, 2001a). For census purposes, an American Indian is someone who reports that he or she is an American Indian. The Bureau of Indian Affairs estimates that 1.2 million Indians live in, or adjacent to, a reservation. The BIA recognizes 550 tribes, including 223 village groups in Alaska. Since 1978, the BIA has received 150 petitions from various groups requesting tribal recognition. Seven of these groups have been officially recognized (www.doi.gov/bia/aitoday). American Indians speak 250 different tribal languages, and for most English is a second language.

Wilma Mankiller (1945–) organized the residents of the impoverished and demoralized three-hundred-family town of Bell, Oklahoma to develop a clean water supply that was connected to every house. She went on to be elected chief of the Cherokee nation.

Under current law, some 56.2 million acres of tribal lands are held in "trust" for Indians by the Secretary of the Interior. The federal government collects income on some Indian lands, through grazing and mineral leasing. This money is returned to the tribes as "trust income." It is not subject to federal income tax.

Tribes that are officially recognized by the federal government are viewed as "internal, dependent nations." As a result, most transactions on reservations are not subject to state income tax or sales taxes. Residents of reservations do not pay local property taxes. Indians living on reservation do have the right to vote in state and local elections. Several Western states (including Arizona and Utah) have attempted (so far unsuccessfully) to disenfranchise reservation residents within their jurisdictions.

Tribes are (understandably) sensitive about efforts to undermine their sovereignty, particularly by state governments. State efforts to regulate gaming on reservations were seen in this light. Accordingly, Indian advocates were alarmed by passage of the 1988 Indian Gaming Regulatory Act by Congress, which allowed for state regulation of gaming on reservations.

Another area that has been touched by sovereignty issues is child protective services. The 1978 Indian Child Welfare Act (ICWA) was designed to prevent removal of Indian children from their tribes and families. Under the ICWA, tribes have primary jurisdiction over Indian children who enter the child welfare system, and state authorities are required to give preferences to kin and tribes in finding homes for children who are removed because of abuse or neglect. Advocates complain that states are reluctant to designate children "Indian," claiming that even enrolled children living off-reservation are "not Indian enough" to be subject to ICWA provisions. Further, the Multi-ethnic Placement Act (passed in 1994) is seen as weakening the federal mandate to seek Indian homes for Indian children. (These Acts were discussed in Chapter 7.)

Today Native Americans, Alaskan Natives, and Aleuts represent an exceedingly small proportion of the U.S. population. In 2000, the Census Bureau identified 2.4 million Native Americans, representing less than one percent of the total U.S. population. Because the group is so small, Native Americans are frequently not included in annual reports issued by the Census Bureau. As a result, the most recent data available for this group still comes from the 1990 Census.[9] Available data provide a stark portrayal of the economic status of the first Americans. Whereas 76.5 percent of the overall U.S. population had completed high school, only 63.2 percent of Native Americans had comparable educational attainment. Similarly, the median household income for Indian households ($19,900) was about two-thirds of the overall 1990 median ($30,056). That ratio remained the same in 1999 estimates provided by the Population Reference Bureau. As indicated in Figure 10.2, the median household income for Native Americans was $29,200, compared to $40,600 for whites. Finally, as we saw in Chapter 4, in 1990 nearly a third (31.2 percent) of Native American households had incomes below the poverty threshold, compared to 13.1 percent of the overall U.S. population (U.S. Census Bureau, 1995).

POLICIES AFFECTING MINORITIES

The history of racial and ethnic minorities in the United States is rife with examples of prejudice and government-sponsored oppression. Has the nation moved forward in recent years? Has racism become a thing of the past? In this section we will examine policy developments in this area.

IMMIGRATION POLICY

Prior to 1882, the United States had an open immigration policy. Anyone could relocate to this developing nation. For just over a century, the nation has refined its immigration policy in pursuit of three goals: exclusion (excluding groups considered undesirable by the majority); economic advancement (promoting domestic economic interests); and humanitarian (providing a haven for the oppressed and permitting families to be together). Major milestones in U.S. immigration policy are summarized in Table 10.3.

---

[9]It is interesting to note that the report on the 1990 census data concerning the nation's Indian tribes was not released by the Census Bureau until 1995.

TABLE 10.3 LEGISLATIVE MILESTONES IN U.S. IMMIGRATION POLICY

Chinese Exclusion Act (1882)
- Suspended immigration of Chinese.
- Barred Chinese naturalization.
- Provided for deportation of Chinese who immigrated illegally into the U.S.

Immigration Act of 1891
- Provided for national control of immigration.
- Established Bureau of Immigration under Treasury.
- Provided for deportation of illegal aliens.

Immigration and Naturalization Act of 1924
- Imposed permanent numeric limit on immigration.
- Established national origins quota system (favoring Northern and Western Europeans).

Displaced Persons Act of 1948
- Allowed immigration of WWII victims.

Immigration and Naturalization Act of 1952
- Continued national origins quotas.
- Established quota for workers with needed skills.

Immigration and Nationality Act Amendments of 1965
- Repealed national origins quotas.
- Established seven-category preference system based on family unification and skills.
- Set 20,000 per country limit for Eastern Hemisphere.
- Imposed ceiling on immigration from Western Hemisphere (for first time).

Immigration and Nationality Act Amendments of 1976
- Extended 20,000 per country limit to Western Hemisphere.

Refugee Act of 1980
- Established permanent procedure for admitting refugees.
- Removed refugees as a category from preference system.
- Defined *refugee* according to international standards.
- Established process of domestic resettlement.
- Codified asylum status.

Immigration Reform and Control Act of 1986
- Instituted employer sanctions for knowingly hiring illegal aliens.
- Tripled employment-based immigration.
- Created diversity admissions category.
- Established temporary protected status.

1996 Immigration Acts
- Increased border patrols and barriers.
- Denied SSI and food stamps to legal immigrants.
- Denied most public services to illegal immigrants.

Sources: Fox & Passel (1994); Close Up Foundation (1998).

EXCLUSION. Early immigration restrictions such as the Chinese Exclusion Act of 1882 and the Immigration and Naturalization Act of 1924 were designed to exclude groups considered undesirable by the majority. As mentioned previously, the Chinese Exclusion Act suspended immigration from China. The Naturalization Act established a quota that favored immigrants from Western and Northern European nations. Based on the argument that immigrants from these nations were more readily assimilated, this Act responded to objections raised to immigration from Southern and Eastern Europe.

Ideology and sexual orientation have also been grounds for prohibiting immigration. Fear of communism led to the 1952 passage of the McCarran-Walter act, which prohibited immigration by people who subscribed to this ideology. This Act was overturned in 1990. Until 1990, U.S. immigration policy also allowed for the exclusion of homosexuals.

ECONOMIC ADVANCEMENT. Immigration policies explicitly designed to promote domestic economic goals surfaced in the Immigration and Naturalization Act of 1952, which established quotas for workers with needed skills. This practice is now a well-established part of U.S. immigration policy. Indeed, Microsoft's Bill Gates has argued against further restrictions on immigration, suggesting they would "prevent companies like ours from doing business in the United States" (Close Up Foundation, 1998).

Attempts to control the flow of illegal immigrants from Latin America and Mexico generally respond to concerns about the economic impact of immigrants, both as competition for U.S. laborers and as consumers of public services. In addition to the Repatriation and Bracero programs mentioned earlier in this chapter, these efforts include the Immigration Control and Reform Act of 1986, which established sanctions for employers who hired illegal aliens.

Concern over the cost of services provided to immigrants, particularly illegal immigrants, has led to policy restrictions on eligibility. Early policy on this topic came from the 1982 U.S. Supreme Court decision in the case of *Plyler v. Doe*. The court invalidated a Texas law that allowed school districts to charge tuition to illegal aliens whose children attended public schools. In its ruling (drafted by Thurgood Marshall) the Court held that depriving these children of education would ultimately prove costly to the government, as uneducated children were likely to rely on welfare in adulthood.

Political pressure to restrict public services to immigrants culminated in the 1996 welfare reform legislation, which would have denied SSI and food stamps to legal immigrants and excluded illegal immigrants from most public services. The ensuring uproar led to softening of some of the law's more draconian measures. The Balanced Budget Act of 1997 restored SSI eligibility to most legal immigrants who had lost it under the 1996 law. In 1998, PL 105-185 restored food stamp eligibility to some legal immigrants.[10] Nonetheless, the rights of immigrants, both legal and illegal, to receive public services that citizens take for granted are now open to dispute.

HUMANITARIAN GOALS. As the inscription on the Statue of Liberty proclaims, the nation was founded in part on the humanitarian principle of serving as a haven for the world's oppressed. Humanitarian goals were explicitly promoted in immigration policy after World War II, when Congress passed the

---

[10]The Balanced Budget Act was mentioned in Chapter 4.

Displaced Persons Act of 1948, to allow some of the war's victims to come to the United States. Later, the Refugee Act of 1980 established a procedure for admitting refugees, legally defining them as people who flee their home nations because of persecution "on account of race, religion, nationality, membership in a particular social group, or political opinion."

United States immigration policy is a fascinating example of the nation's response to diversity. It has frequently manifested the prejudices and superstitions of the political majority. At the same time, it is through immigration that the nation has attained, and continues to expand, its diverse cultural heritage.

AFFIRMATIVE ACTION

Cedric Herring (1997) offered a succinct definition of affirmative action: "Affirmative Action consists of activities specifically to identify, recruit, promote and/or retain qualified women and members of disadvantaged minority groups in order to overcome the results of past discrimination and to deter employers from engaging in discriminatory practices" (p. 6). This broad definition was made more specific by two major policy initiatives. The first was executive orders issued under the Kennedy, Johnson, and Nixon administrations requiring that firms doing business with the federal government engage in affirmative action. The second was Title VII of the 1964 Civil Rights Act, which prohibited discrimination by private employers and unions (Pedriana, 1999).

President Kennedy's Executive Order 10925 prohibited government contractors from practicing racial discrimination, and required that they take "affirmative action" to ensure that there was no discrimination. The order established the President's Committee on Equal Employment Opportunity (PCEEO) to enforce the law. Although other presidents had issued non-discrimination orders in the past, none had included the clause requiring "affirmative action." While establishing an obligation for employers to take action, the order did not specify what this might entail. In essence, it required that federal contractors "do something" without specifying exactly what "something" was. Only one specific action was required: employers had to maintain records of the racial composition of their work force.

Lockheed was the subject of the first complaint filed under order 10925. The NAACP complained that the company practiced blatant and pervasive racial discrimination. In response, the firm developed an aggressive "Plan for Progress" that included recruiting and training minority workers, reviewing promotion procedures, and establishing vocational programs for minorities in local schools.

"Plans for Progress" became a watchword for the PCEEO, and companies that voluntarily prepared these plans were guaranteed that they would not be subject to investigation. Many companies did so, but the results were consistently disappointing. An evaluation of the plans' impact, conducted by the Southern Regional Council, concluded that the plans were ineffective. Indeed, there was some evidence that firms completing the plans had worse records on equal employment than those that did not (Pedriana, 1999). Ultimately, the most influential feature of Order 10925 was its record-keeping requirement, which resulted in a "unique national profile of the employment distribution of race" (Graham, 1990, p. 60).

With support from the Kennedy administration, Congress passed Title VII of the Civil Rights Act of 1964. Enforcement of Title VII would move affirmative action out of the realm of vague, voluntary planning into an aggressive approach to equal opportunity that would become characteristic of the Johnson administration.

Title VII prohibited employment discrimination on the basis of gender or race, and established the Equal Employment Opportunity Commission (EEOC) to enforce the law. The phrase "affirmative action" was called for in cases of intentional violation. As Pedriana noted, the Title included the following language:

> If the court finds that the respondent has intentionally engaged in or is intentionally engaging in an unlawful employment practice . . . the court may enjoin the respondent from engaging in such unlawful employment practice, and order such affirmative action as may be appropriate . . . (Pedriana, 1999, p. 11).

Even this language was fairly broad, and it was left to the courts and the EEOC to interpret and implement the title. Central to their interpretations was defining "discrimination." The law prohibited, but did not define, the practice. Initial interpretations focused on discriminatory *intent*. Firms that intentionally and obviously discriminated on the basis of race were concentrated in the South, where separate locker, cafeteria, and washroom facilities were the norm, and where blacks were concentrated in low-paid employment. The approach based on intent was effective at eliminating these more obvious instances of discrimination.

Over time, a focus on institutional discrimination led to redefinition of the term to focus less on intent and more on the *consequences* of discrimination. Attention shifted to broader employment practices, such as seniority systems and employment testing, that led to racial inequality in the workplace. Indeed, under this view, employment discrimination was part of a broader pattern of oppression that included inferior educational opportunities, exclusion from informal job networks, and limited access to apprenticeship and mentoring opportunities.

Two federal court rulings supported a focus on consequences, rather than intent. In *Quarles v. Philip Morris*, the district court ruled against the company's argument that "the present consequences of past discrimination" were not covered by the Civil Rights Act, saying "Congress did not intend to freeze an entire generation of Negro employees into discriminatory patterns that existed before the act" (Pedriana, 1999, p. 16).

Then, in *Griggs v. Duke Power Company*, the Supreme Court unanimously ruled against the company's promotion requirement of a high school diploma and its use of employment testing. Establishing what is now known as "the Doctrine of Disparate Impact," the Court ruled that

> The objective of Title VII is plain from the language of the statute. It was to achieve equality of employment opportunities and remove barriers that have operated in the past to favor an identifiable group of White employees over other employees. Under the act, practices, procedures or tests neutral on

their face and even neutral in terms of intent cannot be maintained if they operate to "freeze" the status quo of prior discriminatory employment practices. . . . Congress directed the thrust of the Act to the consequences of employment practices, not simply the motivation (Pedriana, 1999, p. 17).

With the establishment of the doctrine of disparate impact, businesses that had racial and gender disparities in the workplace could be subject to costly and time-consuming litigation. To avoid litigation, many firms followed the EEOC's guidelines and developed voluntary affirmative action plans. These plans frequently included race-based hiring and promotion goals, now known as "quotas." Few firms were subject to court-ordered affirmative action, and those that were the subject of court mandates had fairly egregious discriminatory practices (Pedriana, 1999).

The use of quotas was much more common in enforcing presidential orders regarding government contractors. In 1965, President Johnson issued Executive Order 11246 to replace Kennedy's order 10925. This order created the Office of Federal Contract Compliance (OFCC) to enforce non-discrimination in government contracting. Under the order, firms were frequently required to set and meet hiring quotas. These requirements were especially controversial for construction firms, which traditionally segregated their trades along racial lines. These firms were required to set minority hiring goals in each of the trades, with the result being the much maligned practice of "hiring by the numbers."

President Nixon's contribution to affirmative action was substantial. Indeed, as Troy Duster (1996) pointed out:

> Nixon did more than any other president to promote and *institutionalize* affirmative action. While John Kennedy issued the initially limited executive orders in 1963, and while Lyndon Johnson had maneuvered through Congress the 1964 civil rights legislation that mandated selected forms in the workplace, it was Nixon who demanded and required that corporate America *institute programs* of affirmative action" (p. 41).

Insiders' accounts of the Nixon administration have argued that the President's motive was to drive a wedge in the traditional Democratic alliance of labor and blacks (see Erhlichman, 1982; Haldeman, 1994).

Both Title VII and the presidential orders governing federal contracting increased employment opportunities for minority workers. Probably the greatest impact of Title VII came with the courts' establishment of the Doctrine of Disparate Impact. Under this doctrine, even race-neutral practices that resulted in racial disparities were potential subjects of litigation. This led many firms to voluntarily adopt and implement affirmative action plans. The use of hiring quotas was most commonly a response to federal contracting requirements established under presidential orders.

The expansion of affirmative action occurred in an economic climate of expanded opportunity, and, as Duster (1996) and others (Quadagno, 1994; Ezorsky, 1991; Northrup, 1970) have argued, it worked. Affirmative action expanded minorities' access to employment, particularly in public-sector jobs and the building trades. Indeed, Duster (1996) argued that "It is empirically demonstrable that affirmative action provided a way out of poverty for hundreds of thousand, even millions, of poor blacks" (p. 56).

But by the late 1970s, unemployment rates had risen, real wages were declining, and the time was ripe for a backlash against affirmative action. This backlash was spearheaded by leaders in California (Nixon's home state), who argued that affirmative action was unfair to individuals. Other arguments have been devised against affirmative action:

- it stigmatizes women and minorities whose colleagues perceive them as having been hired, not for their qualifications, but to satisfy affirmative action quotas;

- it is no longer necessary, as discrimination in employment no longer exists;

- it results in "reverse discrimination" against men and whites;

- it does not help the "truly disadvantaged";

- it is ineffective.

At a time when jobs were disappearing and admission to California's public universities was increasingly competitive, these arguments were persuasive. Affirmative action received a serious challenge in the 1978 case of *Regents of the University of California v. Bakke*. In this case, a 37-year-old white engineer (Allan Bakke) had been twice denied admission to the University's medical school. The school reserved 16 of its 100 entering positions for minorities, and some of the 16 admitted when Bakke was denied had lower admissions scores than he had. The case was decided by the U.S. Supreme Court, in a split decision that represented a carefully crafted compromise.[11] The justices held that Bakke had been discriminated against, but it did not overthrow the use of race-based admissions (Ball, 2000).

Elimination of affirmative action was left to the political process. In 1995, The Regents of the University of California, under the leadership of Republican Governor Pete Wilson, voted to abolish affirmative action in college admissions. A year later, voters in California passed Proposition 209 by a narrow margin. This measure outlawed the use of race, sex, ethnicity, or national origin as a reason for discriminating against or granting preferential treatment to any person or group. Later, similar initiatives passed in Washington state (Initiative 200) and Florida (the "One Florida Initiative"). The University of Texas also abolished the use of affirmative action in its admissions program.

The dismantling of affirmative action was not initiated entirely by voters. President George H. W. Bush's appointments to the Supreme Court included Clarence Thomas, a conservative African-American who ardently opposed affir-

---

[11]The Supreme Court refused to order the University to admit Bakke, but he did obtain such an order through a California court. Bakke was admitted to the U.C. Davis Medical School, graduating in 1992.

mative action. President Bush also contributed through his veto of the 1990 Civil Rights Act.

Today the debate over affirmative action seems to be over. There is widespread consensus against the use of racial quotas in hiring, and the phrase itself has taken on negative undertones. As Reverend Davis explained, in our current political environment it will take a creative soul to devise a new approach to equal opportunity in employment that is both effective and politically feasible.

HATE-CRIME LEGISLATION

Under current federal law, crimes that occur because of a person's membership in a protected group (based on race, ethnicity, religion, or national origin) can result in more severe penalties. These crimes, called "hate" crimes, are seen as more grievous than others because they not only harm the immediate victims, but instill fear in vulnerable minorities. Although a 1969 statute offered federal prosecution of crimes against racial, ethnic, or religious minorities engaged in federally protected activities (such as voting or attending public school), most federal legislation in this area dates to the 1990s. During the Clinton administration several bills were introduced to apply hate-crime designations to crimes based on gender, disability, and sexual orientation. These did not become law. Recent federal initiatives in this area include:

- the Hate Crimes Statistics Act of 1990, which requires the Justice Department to gather and publish statistics on crimes motivated by prejudice based on race, ethnicity, religion, or sexual orientation;

- portions of the Juvenile Justice and Delinquency Prevention Act of 1992, directing the Office of Juvenile Justice Delinquency Programs to study hate crimes and develop prevention and treatment programs for perpetrators;

- the Hate Crimes Sentencing Enhancement Act of 1994, which calls for increased penalties when the crime is proven to be a hate crime;

- the Church Arson Prevention Act of 1996, making damage to religious property a federal offense;

- the Hate Crimes Prevention Act of 1998, which expanded federal jurisdiction to violent hate crimes and offered grants to state and local prosecutors to reduce hate crimes.

As of 1999, 42 states had passed hate crime statutes that mirrored federal law, allowing harsher penalties for crimes targeting people based on their race, ethnicity, religion, or national origin. About half of the state hate-crime statutes include sexual orientation.

Hate-crime legislation is controversial. Proponents argue that harsher sentences for hate crimes are just, because these crimes are more damaging than similar offenses not motivated by hate. They suggest that stiffer penalties may deter potential perpetrators. Opponents compare hate crimes to "thought" crimes, arguing that it is impossible to reliably demonstrate that a crime was motivated by hatred and that efforts to do so infringe on the right to freedom of speech (see Troy, 1998).

ENGLISH-ONLY LEGISLATION

English-only proposals surfaced in this country as early as 1780, when John Adams proposed that the Continental Congress establish an official academy to "purify, develop, and dictate usage of" English (ACLU, 1996). His proposal was rejected as undemocratic. With the 1803 purchase of the Louisiana Territory, President Jefferson tried to impose an English-only policy on French speakers in that territory. The uproar from the territory led to a quick retreat, and Louisiana entered the Union in 1812 as the only state with a non-English-speaking majority (Kloss, 1998). The Californios (Spanish speakers who resided in California when it was conquered) were much less successful. Although the state's constitution recognized Spanish language rights and guaranteed bilingual publication of state laws, the following year saw the Gold Rush. Spanish-speakers became a minority, and "greaser laws" were passed specifically to harass them (Leibowitz, 1969). "English only" became the law of the land in the new state of California. Finally, the forced assimilation of Native Americans into the English-only world involved taking Indian children to boarding schools far from home where they were punished for speaking their own languages.[12]

> In a vivid reminder of the benefits of language diversity, Navajo Marines in World War II used their language for top-secret communications. It was the only code the enemy was unable to break. The Navajo Code Talkers took part in every assault by the U.S. Marines between 1942 and 1945. They are recognized in a permanent exhibit on the Pentagon Concourse.

The "English-Only" movement re-surfaced in the 1980s, with proponents arguing that the English language was in need of legislative protection from the encroachment of other tongues and that "creeping bilingualism" threatened the very foundations of American culture. Legislation was advanced at the federal and state levels to restrict the use of minority languages for government business.

At the federal level, proponents of Official English have been political conservatives—the same people who favor immigration restrictions and would deny services to legal immigrants. In 1994 Republican leadership in the House of Representatives passed a measure that generally prohibited the use of languages other than English by the federal government. Threatened with a presidential veto, the measure died without Senate action (Crawford, 1992).

English-only proponents have been more successful at passing state legislation. At the time of this writing, legislation establishing Official English requirements has passed in most states.

---

[12]English-only efforts were also initiated in the U.S. territories of Puerto Rico and Guam. Less successful in Puerto Rico, these policies nearly eradicated the indigenous language of Guam.

Proponents of "English-only" legislation offer several arguments. First, they suggest that bilingual education delays or prevents acquisition of English by immigrants. They assert that immigrants today, unlike immigrants of the past, refuse to learn English and insist on government-sponsored bilingual programs. Second, they argue that the United States is at risk of becoming balkanized like Quebec or India. Idaho Senator Steve Symms introduced an English-only amendment to the U.S. Constitution, arguing that "countless hundreds of thousands have lost their lives in the language riots of India. Real potential exists for a similar situation in the United States" (Crawford, 1992, p. 395). Finally, proponents suggest that English is a "common bond" holding Americans of diverse backgrounds together.

None of these arguments is based on evidence, and most are designed to appeal to anti-immigrant and anti-minority emotions. Educational studies consistently demonstrate that language-minority students do better in school and learn English more quickly in bilingual or structured English immersion classrooms (Ramirez, Yuen, & Ramey, 1991). There is no evidence of language-based political organization (aside from the English-only movement) in the U.S. Finally, national pride in the U.S. tends to be more strongly associated with ideals such as individual freedom and achievement than with the English language. As James Crawford, who has studied the English-only movement for a decade, noted, "English-only arguments are so value-laden in their distaste for diversity, so crude in their analogies with other nations, so credulous about the power of social engineering, and so bereft of factual evidence that they are difficult to take seriously" (Crawford, 1996, p. 4).

Millions of Americans do take these arguments seriously, however. Scholars differ on the reasons for this phenomenon. Some argue that the movement attracts people with anti-minority sentiments and anxieties about cultural change (see Schmid, 1992). Others suggest that support for English-only is a direct result of national pride (see Citrin et al., 1990).

The effects of English-only legislation vary, depending on whether the laws simply declare English the official language or bar the use of minority languages. The official declaration of the prominence of English has had little practical effect, but some legislation passed by the states has banned bilingual ballots and bilingual instruction in public schools, some cities have passed ordinances prohibiting the use of minority languages in private signs, and some have eliminated the use of courtroom translation. These practices have all made life more difficult for non-English speaking immigrants (ACLU, 1996).

STANDARDIZED TESTING

On the surface, standardized tests appear race-neutral. Designed to measure general aptitude, most are not intended to promote discrimination. But the consequences of standardized testing consistently operate against racial and ethnic minorities.

The intelligence tests used today are based on the Stanford-Binet test, which emerged during the heyday of the "eugenics movement." This movement advanced the view that high intelligence, like other desirable traits, was genetically based and less present in "inferior" races. The creator of the Stanford-Binet test, Lewis Terman, used it to provide support for the notion that northern Europeans were superior to other races. He argued that high scores were correlated with moral behavior, and that the higher IQs of northern Europeans explained their economic dominance.

As mentioned above, employment testing was frequently used during the 1960s in hiring and promotion decisions. In addition to measuring proficiency in specific skills, these tests often purported to measure general aptitude or intelligence. Because of limited educational opportunities, minorities consistently did poorly on the tests. When the "intent" of the testing process was examined, the process appeared race-neutral; however, the "consequences" of the testing were disadvantageous to racial minorities. In 1966, the EEOC issued guidelines stipulating that tests with these consequences were in violation of Title VII of the 1964 Civil Rights Act unless the employer could demonstrate that they accurately predicted job performance.

SUMMARY: FUTURE PROSPECTS FOR MINORITIES IN THE UNITED STATES

In this chapter we have traced the history and current realities experienced by four of the nation's minority groups: African-Americans, Hispanics, Asians, and American Indians. A major thread in these histories is a shift in the role of public policy from the active promotion of race-based oppression to serving as an agent (to various degrees) of equal opportunity. Emerging debates about affirmative action, hate crimes, English-only legislation, and standardized testing have been explored. What remains is a brief discussion of the continuing role of race and ethnicity in the world's most diverse nation.

Over the past few decades, and particularly during the economic boom of the 1990s, many members of America's ethnic minority groups have moved into the middle class. For example, in 1997, more than one-fifth of Hispanic, American Indian, and African-American households had incomes over $50,000 (Population Reference Bureau, 1999). In 1999, just over one tenth of African-American households had incomes that placed them in the nation's highest quintile on the basis of income (U.S. Census Bureau, 2000c). These households typically have more than one earner, as minorities of all races continue to receive lower wages than whites with comparable education.

These statistics reflect a significant accomplishment, both for the United States as a whole and for the individuals involved. Economic advancement also tends to divide minority communities along class lines, fueling arguments that members of minority groups who are not economically successful are personally flawed. Some minority group members, frequently second- and third-generation members of successful families, have become vocal opponents of public income supports and affirmative action (see, for example Linda Chavez's 1991 work, *Out of the Barrio*). These advocates argue, in essence, "If I could make it, so can they." While race-based disadvantage is very real today, coming years may see erosion in the cohesiveness of racial and ethnic minority communities as class, rather than race, becomes the great dividing line of American society.

DISCUSSION TOPICS

1. Use the history of racial oppression by the U.S. to evaluate the two major theories of racism discussed in this chapter. Does history support the idea that racism is the result of ignorance or of market competition? What do you see as the roots of racism?

2. Do you think past injustices that do not result in present disadvantage (like the internment of the Japanese) entitle people to some kind of remedy? Is an apology in order? Economic reparation? To whom is it due? Should descendants of former slaves receive some kind of reparation? Why or why not?

3. Compare the educational experiences of the major minority groups discussed here. Do you think they have any bearing on the current status of these groups?

4. Consider the occupational distributions of African-Americans and Hispanics, as illustrated in Tables 10.1 and 10.2. What were the most significant changes in the occupations of these groups between 1983 and 1997? How would you explain these changes?

5. Do you think a class-based society is more or less just than one in which race is the basis of social allocations?

SUGGESTED RESOURCES

Mayfield, C. (Ed.). (1981). *Growing Up Southern: Southern Exposure Looks at Childhood, Then and Now*. New York: Pantheon Books.

Takaki, R. (1993). *A Different Mirror: A History of Multicultural America*. Boston: Little, Brown and Company.

Wilson, C. A. (1996). *Racism: From Slavery to Advanced Capitalism*. Thousand Oaks, CA: Sage.

Wright, M. H. (1928). The Removal of the Choctaws to the Indian Territory: 1830–1833. Chronicles of Oklahoma, VI, 2, 103–128.

www.airpi.org—The American Indian Policy Center is a non-profit organization that was founded in 1992 for the purposes of research, policy development, and education on Indian issues. The site offers some outstanding policy papers, written from an Indian perspective.

www.doi.gov/bia — This is the official web site of the Bureau of Indian Affairs, which is part of the Department of Interior. It offers some useful background information, written from a somewhat defensive posture.

www.eeoc.gov — This is the official site of the Equal Employment Opportunity Commission. It offers information on federal laws, background on the EEOC, instructions for filing a complaint, and news releases.

www.naacp.org — The National Association for the Advancement of Colored People describes itself as the nation's "largest and strongest civil rights organization." NAACP's site offers information about the organization, as well as news briefs and access to their magazine, *Crisis.*

www.splcenter.org — The Southern Poverty Law Center is a non-profit organization whose mission is to "combat hate, intolerance and discrimination through education and litigation." At the site, you will find information on current events and projects, "intelligence reports" on hate groups in the U.S., and educational material for teaching tolerance.

www.ufw.org — The United Farm Workers, now part of the AFL-CIO, continue their advocacy on behalf of migrant workers. At their site you will find action items, news releases, and inspiring quotes from UFW leaders.

11

Gays and Lesbians

I will scatter myself among men and women as I go.
I will toss a new gladness and roughness among them,
Whoever denies me it shall not trouble me,
Whoever accepts me he or she shall be blessed and shall bless me.

WALT WHITMAN,
"Song of the Open Road"

The struggle for equal rights for gay and lesbian Americans came to public awareness in 1969, when the New York City police raided a gay bar (Stonewall Inn) in Greenwich Village. The ensuing riots are seen by many as the beginnings of the gay rights movement. Since that time, most Americans have seen television coverage of annual "Gay Pride Parades" held in major cities throughout the country. These parades support a view of gays and lesbians as colorful, if eccentric, figures in the national landscape. Such vivid images can obscure the reality of daily life for Americans of minority sexual orientations. These realities include employment discrimination, legal barriers to marriage and adoption, losing custody of their children, and limited access to health and related benefits for partners.

In this chapter, we will examine social policies that affect gays and lesbians in America. After reviewing the life experiences of Mike, a gay man who is pursuing a career in social work, we will briefly outline the history of the gay rights movement in the United States, paying special attention to political initiatives that deny civil rights to lesbian and gay citizens. Next, we will consider legal barriers to marriage, adoption, and child custody and explore discrimination against gays and lesbians by employers and organizations. We will take a look at hate crime legislation, as well as social policy related to HIV/AIDS. The chapter concludes with an examination of the social work code of ethics as it relates to the struggle for gay rights.

CASE STUDY ♦ MIKE DIXON

Born during the early 1950s in Northern California, Mike has known he was gay since the age of eight or nine. He said, "I always felt 'different' from other kids, but I didn't really have a word for it. I did know that I shouldn't talk about it with anyone, and so I just kept whatever it was to myself." He has a vivid memory of the moment he realized he was gay. "I looked down and saw this older kid. He was swimming and only had shorts on. I got this overwhelming urge to grab him around the middle and hug him. . . . From that point on, I realized that I wasn't like the other boys I knew, but I didn't dare say why—even to myself."

Life in elementary school was rugged. Mike hated team sports, gym, and recess. Recess was especially awful "because that is when I would routinely get beat up by the bullies in school." But he loved working with his father and uncle in their heating business. "I used to go to work with them when I was a kid. I really loved doing this, and especially loved getting to 'do something' like rolling out pipe, soldering, digging holes for water pipes."

Mike said "things were a little better" when he got to high school. "The teachers were more intelligent, and I didn't feel like I was going to be picked on all the time . . . there were other kids like me—sort of brainy and withdrawn—and we hung out together." Still, he "got into drugs" in high school and nearly flunked out. Teachers identified him as an "underachiever," and eventually he graduated with a "low C" average. His sexual identity was not an important issue during high school. "I never had sex with anyone while I was in high school. I never even really thought about it. It never dawned on me that I could actually act on my desires—it was a hetero world, but even that was something that was taken for granted, and I didn't question why it was so." In retrospect, Mike said, "I have to say that I thought high school was a waste. I hated that place, and the conformist attitudes they tried to shove down my throat."

Mike graduated in 1968. After leaving home to attend college, he came out "to myself and a few other people I knew. I never came out formally to my parents." He felt that his mother "got it" without being told, but she never said anything. He said, "My father was kind of oblivious, and it turned out that he was completely cool about it when I came out to him around 1979, after my mother died." Mike's father liked all of his boyfriends, and took care to include them in invitations and celebrations. Of his only sibling, Mike said, "I came out to my sister around this time, and she didn't give a shit." Later his sister told him she resented his lifestyle, "Like being queer was about partying, spending money, and having a good time."

During college, Mike "met this guy in a class" and they moved in together. They didn't really consider themselves a "couple" because they were so different. "He was a real political hippie and I was a sort of brain-nerd-sass-ass-intellectual." Still, he had "a pretty good life for an 18-year-old" and they found jobs in a printing plant. Mike worked there for almost nine years, putting himself through college.

Mike enjoyed college very much. "I really liked the atmosphere of college, and was far more interested in what was going on in class, and in talking to the people I met there." But the prospect of being drafted and sent to Vietnam threw a shadow over this period of his life. When his deferment was changed and Mike received a new draft card, he had a horrible fight with his parents. He told them he planned to go to Canada if he was called to Vietnam, and "They did not understand that I didn't think it was my 'duty' to go off and get killed in Johnson's war. That was a confusing, almost psychotic time in my life. I went to work four nights per week, studied like mad so I wouldn't get kicked out of school, and just prayed that the draft board didn't call me."

Time passed, and the draft was replaced by the "lottery." Mike's number was 332. "That did it," he said, "I was free!" He graduated the next year, and moved to Holland with a friend he had met in school. The year in Holland was great. "We lived in Delft, I learned Dutch, and just spent all day hanging out and drawing pictures of old buildings. I lived on my 'retirement' check (some paltry union pension rebate) that they gave me when I quit the printing company." Then Mike got a call that his mother was dying. He flew back, and "she was dead within a week."

Mike stayed in the United States and enrolled to do graduate work in art. Here he met his "first boyfriend." He "met this kid on one of my drawing classes . . . we had a torrid affair that lasted about nine months . . . then he left me for a younger guy. . . . I was devastated. I spent the next year in an alcoholic isolation that only snapped when I got arrested for drunk driving . . . that sort of shocked me out of my swoon, but I never forgot that kid for 10 years." Mike got into therapy, an experience that changed his life and his outlook on himself.

Nonetheless, he said, "I think I was still in love with him [first boyfriend] when I moved in with my 'second' boyfriend, after I moved to San Francisco in 1980." He met "Bob" through a mutual friend, and they hit it off right away. "He had this idea that we should start a catering company—I was a good cook and he had worked in hotels and knew the business, somewhat. We borrowed $5,000 from a friend, bought a used van and a couple of cases of cocktail glasses, had some cards printed (at my old printing company), and we were in business. . . . We moved in together in 1981 and worked like dogs until he died in 1990."

The business was very successful. "We had the reputation of being one of the five top caterers in San Francisco, and we did it at the right time (the 80s) when people were spending money like it was water. We bought a huge house in the East Bay, with a pool. We went to Europe twice, went on long trips to New England and the South, went to Hawaii every winter for three weeks and generally lived as if there were no tomorrow."

But Mike's partner had AIDS. "When I think back on it, he must have had AIDS when we met. Then, in about 1985, he started to get 'opportunistic infections.' He got weaker and weaker, until finally he could not get out of bed without help. I kept the business together through his illness, and when I got a call during some job that he was not expected to make it through the night, I went and sat with him until he died. I went to Hawaii with his ashes . . . then I came back home. I put the house up for sale, sold the catering business, and just withdrew again."

Mike described the impact of AIDS on the San Francisco gay community, saying, "During this time about every male I knew died. I went to eight or ten "memorials" (funerals were considered un-PC) during that year and a half period. It was one a month for a while. I kept thinking, 'I'm next', but kept testing negative. One after another, everyone I knew died of AIDS. That period in San Francisco gay history is famous now—people started calling it the Plague, but that seemed too lighthearted, somehow. It was just awful. Everyone anyone knew was dying these hideous deaths. The gay community was trying to mobilize, but there was not a lot of organization. We were all grieving—no one's story was any more heartbreaking than anyone else's. We were all wrecks. Most people I knew got through a few deaths, and then they died themselves. Mayor Feinstein came and spoke at Bob's funeral. They were business friends, and she couldn't believe that "even Bob" would die. Straights just didn't get it. They seemed to just be unable to conceive of how huge it was, and of what it felt like to have your whole world die grisly deaths with only medical help and no social support other than that which we gave to one another. When we catered cocktail parties and dinners, I would overhear well-heeled straights saying things like, 'We have to do something about this! Pretty soon we are all going to get it if we aren't careful.' Little did they know—if some of those ladies knew what we knew about their husbands and sons, they would have been a little more respectful, I think."

After three years of "onslaught," Mike decided to move to the South with a friend, Tom. They bought a Civil War–era house in Tarboro, North Carolina, where, as Mike said, "We experienced no discrimination . . . in fact, it was the opposite. We got along with everyone, and even did some cooking (I wouldn't call it catering) around town. We knew everyone, and our house was a sort of central meeting place because it was right in the middle of town." Then, in 1995, Tom got really sick. "He knew what it was all about, and having seen dozens of his friends get sick too, he decided to forgo treatment and just let things 'take their course.' He was dead in two months, of acute sepsis and an encephalitic HIV infection. In other words, he went crazy, and then died of blood poisoning."

When Mike met his current partner through mutual friends in 1996, it was "love at first sight . . . we had everything in common except our age—he is 10 years younger than me. He and I felt like we had found the people we had been looking for all along. We still feel this way, and never get tired of each other's company. We are in love with each other, and that has a way of making the past make sense. I certainly don't regret a second of my past, and if our relationship now is the result of all that living I did, then it was well worth the wait. I cannot imagine being so lucky as to be living with someone so wonderful in such a mutually complementary way. Believe it or not, we have never had a major fight nor have we ever even had a negatively charged emotional exchange."

Rather than feeling oppressed or victimized, Mike feels that gay men are lucky and enjoy tremendous freedom. "I think society expects little of us, as a group. We don't have that onus of having to have kids if we don't want it, and we aren't expected to join that work-and-spend cycle that most heterosexual families are in. There is little outside pressure on our family (of the two of us and two dogs). We live our lives, pay our taxes and take care of the yard. The cars are in good repair, and once in a while we go on vacation to some nice place. We cook our own food, clean our own house, and maintain pretty good relationships with our neighbors."

He can cite very few experiences of discrimination. Once, after they knew Bob had AIDS, he and Bob applied for health insurance. "We knew he had AIDS, but the world hadn't caught up with the idea that it was truly a fatal disease. We applied for a small business policy, and they came over and interviewed us. The agent got it right away that we were a 'couple' and they turned down the application with no explanation. I called and asked them why, and they gave me some gobbledygook about being too small a business. I called the state office of consumer affairs, described the situation and asked for their advice. They said that we were definitely discriminated against (in the City of San Francisco, insurance companies were not allowed to discriminate on the basis of sexual orientation, even then), but they said that we would have an almost impossible time proving it. They knew that insurance companies were trying to weasel out of policies they had already written to gay businesses because of the fear of AIDS claims, and there wasn't anything they were willing to do about it."

Discrimination has not been an important influence in Mike's life. "I have bought and sold houses, lived in a small southern town, lived in a conservative suburb in the East Bay, traveled all over the place with other men, in short, done everything everyone else does, and I have never felt discriminated against personally."

In his late 40s, Mike decided to pursue a career in social work because, as he puts it, "It is one of the very few things we can do for each other that truly makes a difference in our lives (both the social worker's and the client's." In the MSW program he had what he describes as his first real experiences of feeling discriminated against. He said that "judgmental marginalization would be a better way to put it." In one class, a fellow MSW student announced that he would have trouble working with gay men, "because that would be like asking me to work with child molesters or rapists." Mike said he couldn't believe his ears. When the school administration did not respond appropriately, Mike took matters in his own hands. "I confronted the student later, and we had a meeting of the minds. In short, I told him that if he and his buddies made it uncomfortable for me in class, I was going to get an attorney and make it very uncomfortable for them and the school . . . that ended it."

His advice to a gay person dealing with discrimination is simply, "Get a lawyer. Even though we don't have the law on our side, the public humiliation of having everyone know that you bash fags is probably enough of a deterrent in this day and age. Especially at a university. I would tell them not to bother with the 'let's get together and talk about this' routine. Bigotry is bigotry and ought to be dealt with accordingly. You can be friends after you have a level playing field. For homosexuals the field is never level. We are a particularly hated minority, and it is an uphill battle . . . better to get the big guns right away, and save yourself the trouble of mediation in a world that does not really count you as a whole person anyway."

For Mike and his partner, the lack of a legal sanction for marriage is not a significant issue. "Who would want any authority regulating their material life, let alone their emotional life? We are together because we love each other, not because a state or a church has sanctioned our commitment. We are two men who choose to unite, and we are not trying to 'be like' the straight world because we are not straight." The same applies to restrictions on adoption and custody by gay and lesbian parents.

Possibly as an aftereffect of the trauma of the AIDS epidemic, Mike feels that the "mainstream" gay community is attempting to "normalize" their experience. "It is as if they are saying, 'We're just like you, but with this one tiny difference.' Neither Peter nor I believe that. We believe that we are not like the rest of the American culture—we are very different from it."

He believes homophobia is inevitable, and he attributes it in part to individuals' lack of clarity about their own sexuality and groups' need to define themselves as "right" by defining others as "wrong." His critique of social work education is biting. "I am shocked, almost on a weekly basis, at how little attention is paid to problems involving (or potentially involving) sexual orientation. I have sat through class after class and heard next to nothing about how things might seem from a sexual orientation other than heterosexual. Day after day, we tackle heterosexual family problems, heterosexual child problems, and heterosexual individual problems. All the intervention models seem to be constructed around heterosexual ideals and thinking. The sexual orientation angle has just been completely ignored. It is conservatively estimated that 8 to 10 percent of the population is lesbian, gay or mostly homosexually oriented bisexual . . . this is a huge minority. The 'out' representatives are perhaps less than a quarter of that—maybe 2 to 3 percent at most. This minority crosses all ethnic, cultural, and racial lines—it is a minority of everyone. Certain occupations and avocations have a larger-than-average representation of homosexuals. I think social work is one of them, and perhaps this accounts for the collective silence—lots of closet doors in this profession are tightly shut."

Mike says he "cannot envision a day when I (and those who come after me) will feel the real freedom of not being hated by someone, not for anything I have done or said, but simply because of who I am."

DISCUSSION   Mike's life experiences underscore the uniqueness of human experience and the difficulty of making broad generalizations about the homosexual population. As a member of the gay community of San Francisco, Mike experienced the overwhelming grief and pain of the HIV/AIDS epidemic. He drew strength and creativity from that experience, even as it brought repeated personal losses.

A self-professed "libertarian," Mike asks only that public policy not intrude on his personal life. For him, experiences of discrimination and laws that declare his lifestyle unacceptable have little relevance. Yet, as Mike readily acknowledges, these laws have a much different impact on members of the homosexual community who are attempting to raise children and who would like to pursue legal marriage. Mike sees hatred of homosexuality as inevitable, and expects little from public policies that strive to eliminate it.

Following a brief discussion of definitional issues, we will focus on U.S. policies related to homosexuality.

DEFINING HOMOSEXUALITY

Attraction between members of the same gender has probably always been an aspect of human sexuality. Homosexual activity (particularly among men) in ancient cultures, both Western and Eastern, has been well documented.

Homosexuality has been variously defined as "sin," "psychopathology," "preference," and "orientation." The term *homosexuality* was first applied in the mid-nineteenth century by the Viennese author Karoly Maria Benkert to refer to the "Uranians" described by Karl Heinrich Ulrichs in the 1860s. Ulrichs was a biologist in Hanover, Germany. Fascinated by findings of androgyny in early stages of human embryonic development, he concluded that homosexual attraction had congenital roots, and he identified what he called a "third sex" of people who were attracted to members of their own sex. In 1864, Ulrichs issued a pamphlet calling for legalization of same-sex marriage. In deference to the stigma attached to his theories about a third sex, Ulrichs used a pen name (Greenberg, 1988).

Public understanding of the causes of homosexuality has been closely associated with the treatment of homosexuals by public policy. The notion that homosexuality is caused by congenital events has two implications: first, it leaves homosexuals "blameless." Ulrichs's tolerant views stemmed from his belief that homosexuality was an inborn trait and that people who couldn't help being attracted to same-sex partners should not be punished. Second, it suggests that children (and other innocents) cannot be "converted" to homosexuality. The fear that children will be corrupted by exposure to homosexuals is frequently used in persecution campaigns. Advocates of more tolerant public policies generally adhere to the notion that homosexuality is an inborn trait, rather than an acquired characteristic.

Freud explained homosexuality in psychological rather than biological terms, placing its origins in early childhood experiences (Osborne, 1993). By attributing homosexual attraction to parenting, Freud helped expand the stigma of homosexuality beyond the individuals themselves to encompass their parents and families. Further developments in psychiatric theory would result in homosexuality being considered a form of psychopathology. This view was pivotal in the persecution of homosexuals, particularly by the Immigration and Naturalization Service. It persisted for decades, waning only with the 1973 decision by the American Psychiatric Association to remove homosexuality from its *Diagnostic and Statistical Manual.*

Contemporary theories of the causes of homosexuality incorporate aspects of biological determinism, childhood experiences, and behaviorism. There is evidence of genetic precursors, as well as embryonic influences that increase the likelihood of homosexuality. Similarly, childhood experiences and adult socialization have been seen as contributors. The precise factor or combination of factors that result in homosexuality has, so far, eluded detection (Suppe, 1994; Greenberg & Bailey, 1993). Nonetheless, advocates of both gay rights and gay persecution continue to base at least part of their rhetoric on categorical (frequently inaccurate) statements about the causes of homosexuality.

Ultimately, the causes of homosexuality are irrelevant to the case either for or against gay rights. As David Richards (1999) argued, persecution of individuals on the basis of any personal identity (gender, race, religion, or sexual orientation) is antithetical both to democratic values and to the nation's constitutional guarantees.

A Sexual Minority

Homosexuals, bisexuals, and transgendered[1] individuals are clearly a minority within the U.S. population. Mike mentioned a widely used estimate that this minority constitutes 8 to 10 percent of the U.S. population. The 10 percent figure probably comes from two Kinsey reports, *Sexual Behavior in the Human Male* (Kinsey, Pomeroy, & Martin, 1948) and *Sexual Behavior in the Human Female* (Kinsey, Pomeroy, Martin, & Gebhard, 1953). Based on his studies, Alfred C. Kinsey estimated that 13 percent of men and 7 percent of women engaged in sex primarily with same-gender partners for part of their lives. He went on to estimate that about 4 percent of men were exclusively homosexual throughout their lives. Although Kinsey's methods have been questioned (his study surveyed only volunteers, and thus he did not have a random sample), his figures were later duplicated in other studies (see Barnett, 1973; Michael et al., 1994).

Nonetheless, it is extremely difficult to precisely estimate the number of people who are homosexual. In 1992, Michael and colleagues surveyed a random sample of Americans about their sexual behavior. With a response rate above 80 percent, theirs is probably (as they claim) the most recent definitive study of the topic. Their results underscore some of the difficulties inherent in an effort to count homosexuals. The result varied, depending on whether attraction, behavior, or identity were considered. For example, about 6 percent of men in their study said they were attracted to other men; about 5 percent said they had had sex with another man since turning 18; and about 3 percent of men said they considered themselves homosexual or bisexual. Similarly, about 10 percent of women said they were attracted to other women; about 4 percent said they had had sex with another woman after age 18; and about 1.4 percent of women said they thought of themselves as homosexual or bisexual (Michael et al., 1994).

LEGAL ISSUES AFFECTING GAYS AND LESBIANS

A review of legislation affecting gays and lesbians reveals the role of state and federal government in the continued oppression of this minority group. In sharp contrast to racial minorities and even women, the government seems to have adopted a much more hostile posture toward homosexuals. This hostility is manifest in the issues considered here, which include sodomy laws, other anti-gay initiatives, the Defense of Marriage Act, legal issues in child custody and adoption, discrimination in employment, treatment of gays in the military, hate crime legislation, and policies related to HIV/AIDS.

---

[1]As defined by www.dictionary.com, *transgendered* means "Appearing as, wishing to be considered as, or having undergone surgery to become a member of the opposite sex."

SODOMY LAWS

Sodomy laws specifically forbid some physical expressions of affection between people of the same sex, even in the privacy of their homes. The nation's first sodomy law was enacted in Virginia in 1610 and carried the death penalty (Galas, 1996). Only 50 years ago, every state in the union had sodomy laws on the books. Today about a third of the states still have such laws, with penalties that include arrest and fines.

In 1986, sodomy laws were challenged in the *Bowers v. Hardwick* case. Michael Hardwick was arrested on sodomy charges after police entered his house to serve a traffic warrant and found him in bed with another man. Hardwick was convicted of sodomy and jailed. His lawyers appealed to the Eleventh Circuit Court of Appeals, arguing that the conviction violated Hardwick's right to privacy. Citing the importance of privacy in previous cases such as *Roe v. Wade*, they succeeded in overturning the verdict in the Eleventh Circuit. The State of Georgia appealed to the U.S. Supreme Court, which ruled against Hardwick. In a closely divided opinion (5–4), the court held that the right of privacy did not apply to homosexual conduct.

MORE RECENT ANTI-GAY INITIATIVES

The early 1990s saw anti-gay referendums in several states. These initiatives have been attempted in Arizona, Maine, Michigan, Missouri, Nevada, and Washington, where their supporters were unable to secure enough signatures to get them on the ballot. Anti-gay organizers were more successful in Colorado and Oregon.

COLORADO AMENDMENT TWO. The campaign to pass a Colorado initiative known as "Amendment Two" was spearheaded by a right-wing organization called Colorado for Family Values, an offshoot of the Traditional Values Coalition of Anaheim, CA, and The Eagle Forum (O'Rourke & Dellinger, 1997). The group used an argument against granting special rights to homosexuals. Opponents of the initiative argued that the issue was not "special rights" but basic civil rights. Amendment Two was designed to repeal existing state and local laws that protected gay people from discrimination and to ban all future laws that would have recognized claims by gay and lesbian people. Activists on both sides agreed that passage of Amendment Two would have historic impacts on the rights of gay and lesbian Americans.

The initiative passed by a margin of 53 percent to 47 percent, in November 1992. Many observers felt the public was ill informed about the Amendment. They suggested its passage reflected voters' opposition to "special rights," not their desire to deny gay and lesbian citizens basic civil rights. The Amendment did not go into effect. Nine days after it was passed, gay rights activists filed suit and sought an injunction against its enforcement. The injunction was granted in January 1993.

Amendment Two was declared unconstitutional by the U.S. Supreme Court in 1994, in a seminal six-to-one decision that is frequently cited as evidence of progress in gay rights. On *Romer v. Evans*, the Court ruled that Amendment Two violated the equal protection clause of the Fourteenth Amendment to the Constitution. Justice Kennedy wrote the opinion (echoing the dissent in *Plessy v. Ferguson*) that the Constitution "neither knows nor tolerates classes among citizens." The opinion found the argument that Amendment Two simply denied homosexuals "special rights" was "implausible," saying:

> The amendment imposes a special disability on those persons alone. Homosexuals are forbidden the safeguards that others enjoy and may seek without constraint. They can obtain specific protection against discrimination only by enlisting the citizenry of Colorado to amend the state constitution. . . . We find nothing special in the protections Amendment Two withholds. These are protections taken for granted by most people either because they already have them or do not need them; these are protections against exclusion from an almost limitless number of transactions and endeavors that constitute ordinary civic life in a free society (*Romer v. Evans*, p. 1627, cited by O'Rourke & Dellinger, 1997, p. 137).

The court found that Amendment Two inflicted "immediate, continuing, and real injuries that outrun and belie any legitimate justifications that might be claimed for it." Further, justices inferred that "the disadvantage imposed is born of animosity toward the class of persons affected" (O'Rourke & Dellinger, p. 138).

OREGON INITIATIVES. While the Supreme Court considered Amendment Two, another anti-gay rights measure was under development in Oregon. It was not the first effort of this type. As Douglass (1997) noted, "During a three-year period from 1991–1994, Oregon voters considered state and local ballot measures dealing with homosexuality on thirty separate occasions" (p. 17). The anti-gay measures introduced in Oregon were developed by an organization called the Oregon Citizens' Alliance (OCA).

The alliance had considerable success passing local initiatives. OCA introduced two statewide initiatives. In 1991, Ballot Measure 9 proposed to amend the Oregon Constitution to define homosexuality as "abnormal, wrong, unnatural, and perverse." The measure would have prohibited local and state governments from encouraging homosexual behavior and, like Colorado Amendment Two, would have prohibited state and local governments from extending civil rights protections to gays and lesbians. OCA's campaign suggested that homosexuality posed a threat to the state's children, and argued that gays and lesbians should have "no special rights." In this progressive state, opponents to the measure were many, and they were organized. Measure 9 was defeated by a 57–43 percent margin (Galas, 1996). Three years later, in 1994, OCA put Ballot Measure 13 before the Oregon voters. A toned-down version of the earlier initiative, Measure 13 was defeated by a 51–49 percent margin (Galas, 1996). The Oregon defeats coincided with voters in Idaho rejecting a similar measure, entitled variously "Stop Special Rights" and "Proposition One" (Levine, 1997). Since *Romer v. Evans*, anti-gay activists have ceased their efforts at the state level, turning their attention to federal initiatives such as the Defense of Marriage Act, described below.

MARRIAGE AND FAMILY FORMATION

Mike is not alone in feeling that his inability to marry does not represent a disadvantage. Rimmerman (2000) noted that "same-sex marriage is not a crucial issue for many [gay] movement members," and suggested that those for whom it is central represent the more conservative elements of the movement (p. 51).

But for many gay and lesbian Americans, the lack of legal sanction for a relationship has direct (and sometimes devastating) consequences. This is the case, for example, when a gay man's partner is critically injured in an accident and he is not permitted access to the intensive care unit because he is not a family member. It occurs when a lesbian who has lived with her partner for thirty years dies without leaving a will, and the partner is disinherited. It complicates the lives of homosexuals who cannot secure health insurance for their partners.

Legal marriage confers access to a wide range of rights and benefits. Its importance was recognized by the Supreme Court in 1967, when Chief Justice Earl Warren wrote a landmark opinion for the Supreme Court that said, "The freedom to marry has long been recognized as one of the vital personal rights essential to the orderly pursuit of happiness by free men. Marriage is one of the 'basic civil rights of man,' fundamental to our very existence and survival" (*Loving v. Virginia*, Supreme Court of the United States, 1967). This opinion struck down laws in 16 states that prohibited interracial marriage, and confirmed a "fundamental right" to marry.

Twenty-seven years later, three same-sex couples in Hawaii appeared in the local Department of Health to apply for marriage licenses. When a health official denied their requests, they filed suit. The case, known as *Baehr v. Lewin*, made its way to the Hawaii Supreme Court, which sent the case back to the lower court after ruling that under Hawaii's Equal Rights Amendment a standard of "strict scrutiny" must be applied to any measure depriving people of basic civil rights. The court found that the outcome in *Baehr v. Lewin* could not stand this level of scrutiny. The favorable decision did not establish a fundamental right to same-sex marriage, and it was invalidated through a subsequent amendment to the Hawaii Constitution banning same-sex marriages.

Vermont was more responsive. In 1997, several gay and lesbian couples filed a lawsuit after they were denied licenses to marry (*Baker v. State of Vermont*). Two years later, in 1999, the Vermont Supreme Court decided that current law discriminated against homosexual couples and ordered the legislature to correct the problem, either by allowing same-sex couples to marry or by establishing a parallel "domestic partnership" status in which couples could register their relationships and enjoy the same rights as heterosexual couples. The state legislature drafted a bill to establish "civil unions" for same-sex couples. After extensive hearings and debate, the bill was signed into law by Governor Howard Dean in April 2000. Dean was re-elected in November 2000 after what he described in his inaugural address as a "contentious" campaign.

Under the "full faith and credit" clause of the U.S. Constitution, states are required to recognize and enforce (give "full faith and credit" to) contracts established in other states. Anti-gay activists were concerned that civil unions registered in Vermont might be "exported" throughout the U.S. They initiated legislation at both the state and federal level to prevent this possibility. One of these state initiatives took place in the nation's most populous state, California.

In California, Proposition 22 was known as the "Knight Initiative" after state Senator Pete Knight, one of its ardent proponents. The initiative said, "Only marriage between a man and a woman is valid or recognized in California." This deceptively simple phrase sounds almost like a simple statement of fact. Its proponents argued that the initiative was not "anti-gay" but "pro-family," suggesting that it was possible both to support gay rights generally and to vote for this marriage initiative specifically. Their efforts were effective. The Knight Initiative passed in 2000 by a wide margin (61–39 percent). Prior to its passage, anti-gay activists had secured another significant victory at the federal level: the Defense of Marriage Act.

DEFENSE OF MARRIAGE ACT OF 1996. The Defense of Marriage Act (DOMA) was introduced during an election year (1996) by Representatives Steve Largent (R-Oklahoma) and Bob Barr (R-Georgia) in the House and Senator Don Nickles (R-Oklahoma) in the Senate. The bill passed both houses by overwhelming majorities and was signed into law (in the middle of the night) by President Clinton on September 21. DOMA does two things. First, it defines marriage for purposes of federal law as "a legal union between one man and one woman as husband and wife," and defines "spouse" as a "member of the opposite sex who is husband or wife." These definitions deny federal benefits, such as Social Security income, to partners in same-sex marriages. DOMA does not interfere with states' decisions about same-sex marriage, but it indicates that no state will be required to recognize a same-sex marriage that is legitimate in another state.

Advocates have questioned the constitutionality of DOMA, arguing that the "full faith and credit" clause of the Constitution cannot be superseded by federal legislation. Still others have held that the law is incompatible with the Supreme Court ruling in *Romer v. Evans*. Perhaps a legal challenge to DOMA will bring the matter before the Supreme Court for clarification.

The politics of same-sex marriage are similar to other civil rights battles in that a majority of Americans oppose extension of this right to a stigmatized minority. In 1967, when the Supreme Court struck down laws against interracial marriage, a majority of Americans opposed interracial marriage (Richards, 1999). Civil rights issues frequently involve protecting a vulnerable minority from the discriminatory views of the majority. In the United States, as recent history has shown time and again, the majority of the population is opposed to same-sex marriage. This opposition undoubtedly reflects deep-seated beliefs. As David Richards argued, "The prohibition of racial intermarriage was to the cultural construction of racism what the prohibition of same-sex marriage is to sexism and homophobia" (Richards, 1999, p. 163). In such battles, the political victories typically go to the majority, leaving the minority to resort to the courts for protection of their fundamental rights, including the right to raise their children.

CHILD CUSTODY AND VISITATION. Unlike Mike and his partner, many gay and lesbian Americans are (or would like to be) involved in raising children. It is difficult to estimate how many gay and lesbian parents live in this country, in part because many hide their sexual orientation. Estimates that have been offered suggest the number of children with gay or lesbian parents range from 6 million to 14 million (Harvard Law Review Editors, 1990).

Like marriage, parenting is widely considered a "fundamental right." The right to raise one's children has been affirmed in several Supreme Court cases (see *Meyer v. Nebraska*, 1923; *Pierce v. Society of Sisters*, 1925; *Lassiter v. Dept. of Social Services*, 1981). Yet discrimination against gay and lesbian parents is manifest in decisions regarding child custody and visitation following divorce proceedings, as well as adoption.

This discrimination reflects widely held beliefs that gay and lesbians are inadequate or inappropriate parents. Testimonials are frequently used to support this belief. Anti-gay activists ask unhappy children of gay and lesbian parents to elaborate on the difficulties they experienced while growing up. It is impossible to conduct a perfectly controlled and representative study comparing the parenting effectiveness of homosexuals and heterosexuals, but there is a growing body of evidence in the social science literature that sexual orientation predicts neither parenting ability nor children's sexual orientation (see Gottfried & Gottfried, 1994; Flaks et al., 1995; Patterson, 1995; Tasker & Golumbok, 1997). Nonetheless, the belief that homosexuals are unfit parents remains widespread, even among the nation's judiciary. Further, sodomy laws are frequently used as justification for denying parenting rights of homosexuals. In this case, the illegality of a couple's presumed sexual conduct is used as evidence of moral failure.

Three distinct approaches have been used by the courts to decide disputes regarding custody and visitation by gay and lesbian parents. These have been termed the "per se" approach, the "presumptive" approach and the "nexus" approach (Patterson and Redding, 1996; Stein, 1996).

The "per se" approach is no longer applied. Under this method, gay and lesbian parents were considered unfit, per se, as a matter of law (Patterson & Redding, 1996).

The "presumptive" approach is more common. Under this approach, a homosexual parent is simply presumed to be an unfit parent unless he or she can demonstrate that the child will not be exposed to any homosexual influences. In jurisdictions that take this view, any kind of homosexual connection might be sufficient to deny custody. A parent need not have a partner to be judged unfit. Simply belonging to a gay rights organization might result in loss of a child. This approach is still used in a few states (Patterson & Redding, 1996).

The most common approach, known as the "nexus" approach, begins from the position that a parent's sexual orientation is irrelevant to custody and visitation decisions. Before homosexuality can be discussed, a "nexus" or connection must be established between parenting and sexual orientation. In 1996, roughly half of the states applied this approach (Patterson & Redding, 1996).

ADOPTION. Gays and lesbians become involved in two types of adoption proceedings: "stranger adoption" and "second-parent" adoption. Stranger adoption occurs when a homosexual couple or individual offers to provide a permanent home to a child whose biological parents are unable or unwilling to do so. Such adoptions typically involve children in state custody who become available for adoption. Second-parent adoptions arise when the partner of a child's biological parent seeks legal recognition of his or her relationship with the child.

Despite growing numbers of children in state custody, some states do not allow cohabiting homosexual couples to adopt. In these states, gay and lesbian parents who live alone do adopt children, often by not disclosing their sexual orientation to authorities. A few states completely prohibit adoption by openly gay parents. In 1996, these included Virginia, Arkansas, Missouri, Florida, North Dakota, and others. In these jurisdictions, even private, second-parent adoptions by homosexuals are not allowed.

As is true of same-sex marriage, parenting by homosexuals taps into deep-seated prejudices among the American public. Most Americans believe homosexuals should not raise children (Patterson & Redding, 1996). Once again, the attitudes of an ill-informed majority deny members of a minority access to what many take for granted as a fundamental right.

DISCRIMINATION BY ORGANIZATIONS AND EMPLOYERS

The federal government openly discriminated against homosexuals in its civil service system until 1975. Gay men and lesbians could not work for the federal government, period. This meant that homosexuals who did have federal jobs were forced to conceal their sexual orientation. Disclosure meant immediate dismissal. Frank Kameny was the first federal employee to question this policy (Galas, 1996).

In 1957, Mr. Kameny worked as an astronomer with the U.S. Army Map service. He held a Ph.D. from Harvard and was well qualified for the position. But within a year after starting, he was fired because his supervisor suspected that he was gay. As Kameny told it,

I was called in by some two-bit Civil Service Commission investigator and told, "We have information that leads us to believe that you are a homosexual. Do you have any comment?" I said, "What's the information?" They said, "We can't tell you." I said, "Well, then I can't give you an answer. You don't deserve an answer. And in any case, this is none of your business." I was not open about being gay at the time . . . but I was certainly leading a social life. I went to the gay bars. . . . They issued a letter: They said they were dismissing me for homosexuality. I was in shock (Galas, 1996, p. 62).

Kameny waged a three-year battle to get his job back. His appeals to the Civil Service Commission, U.S. District Court, and the U.S. Court of Appeals were all denied, and the U.S. Supreme Court refused to hear his case. These defeats mobilized him for a lifetime of organizing. In the early 1960s, he began organizing gays in Washington, D.C., to battle employment discrimination. In 1975, these efforts paid off when the U.S. Civil Service Commission reversed its policy on homosexuals.

With the exception of the few states (11 in 2000) that include sexual orientation in their human rights statutes, employment discrimination against homosexuals is perfectly legal. A man or woman can be denied a job or a promotion, or fired, because he or she is homosexual. It is difficult to document the extent of employment discrimination against homosexuals. Nonetheless, survey results suggest that between 16 and 44 percent of gay and lesbian workers have experienced some form of employment discrimination (Badgett, Donnelly, and Kibbe, 1992; Human Rights Campaign, 2000). Gays and lesbians who work with children as teachers, counselors, and coaches are especially vulnerable in many jurisdictions. Job discrimination against homosexuals also takes the form of verbal harassment. Nearly a third (19 percent) of lesbians and gay men surveyed in 1991 reported experiencing verbal harassment (Comstock, 1991).

Laws governing employment discrimination on the basis of sexual orientation vary across the nation. Some openly homosexual teachers enjoy the protection of non-discrimination clauses that include sexual orientation, and others are subject to dismissal. A list of states that include sexual orientation in their non-discrimination statutes is included in Table 11.1.

To address the problem of discrimination by employers, gay rights activists have sought federal protection through the Employment Non-Discrimination Act (ENDA). This bill would prohibit employment discrimination on the basis of sexual orientation. ENDA was first introduced in 1994 by Senator Edward Kennedy, with about 30 co-sponsors in the Senate. It enjoys the support of the nation's largest labor union, the AFL-CIO,

TABLE 11.1 STATES THAT PROHIBIT DISCRIMINATION IN PRIVATE EMPLOYMENT ON THE BASIS OF SEXUAL ORIENTATION

Wisconsin (1982)
Massachusetts (1989)
Connecticut (1991)
Hawaii (1991)
Vermont (1991)
California (1992)
New Jersey (1992)
Minnesota (1993)
Rhode Island (1995)
New Hampshire (1997)
Nevada (1999)

Source: Van der Meade, 2000.

as well as numerous business interests. Hearings held in 1997 documented the effects of employment discrimination against gays and lesbians, and the bill was re-introduced in 1999. In its 1999 form, ENDA prohibits discrimination in hiring, firing, promotion, compensation, and other employment decisions on the basis of sexual orientation. ENDA would not apply to the military, religious organizations, or businesses employing fewer than 15 people. It specifically does not establish affirmative action for sexual minorities. The bill was introduced again in 2001, but it did not pass.

In addition to employment discrimination, homosexuals are subjected to discrimination in volunteer activities, most notably those sponsored by the Boy Scouts of America.

EXCLUSION OF GAY MEN AND BOYS FROM THE BOY SCOUTS OF AMERICA

The Boy Scouts' decades-long effort to exclude gay men and boys from the ranks of its volunteers culminated with the 1990 expulsion of James Dale by a New Jersey branch of the organization.[2] Dale had been a Boy Scout since 1978, when he was eight years old. As a high school senior, he had attained the rank of Eagle Scout. Before leaving for college in 1989, he applied for an adult membership. As a college student he was openly gay and became involved in gay rights activism. In 1990 his Boy Scout membership was revoked because the Boy Scouts "specifically forbid membership to homosexuals."

The Boy Scouts had a long-standing tradition of excluding gay men and lesbians, but New Jersey law prohibited discrimination on the basis of sexual orientation by public agencies and businesses. Arguing that they were a private organization, the Boy Scouts took the case all the way to the Supreme Court, which ruled in their favor in June 2000 (*Boy Scouts of America v. Dale*).

Although the Supreme Court's decision was widely held as a defeat for gay rights, communities throughout the nation have expressed their outrage by withholding support from the Boy Scouts. Several towns have held that since the Boy Scouts are a private organization they may not make use of public resources, such as educational and recreational facilities. Further, United Way chapters in some communities have either reduced or eliminated their support for the Boy Scouts.

Unlike homosexual marriage and parenting, most Americans oppose employment discrimination on the basis of sexual orientation. A survey conducted by the Human Rights Campaign found that 70 percent supported protections for gays and lesbians in the workplace. Similarly, an Associated Press poll conducted in 1996 indicated that 85 percent of Americans support equal rights in the workplace for homosexuals (Human Rights Campaign, 2001). This majority support suggests that a solution to employment discrimination could be pursued in the political arena, with ENDA becoming the law of the land.

---

[2]Mr. Dale's was one of several cases that resulted from the Boy Scouts' practice of denying membership to homosexuals.

GAYS IN THE MILITARY

In 1778, Lt. Gothold Frederick Enslin became the first man to be dishonorably discharged from the military for homosexuality. As testament to his shame, his sword was broken in half over his head. He marched out of Washington's camp at Valley Forge to the tune of a slow, melancholy drumbeat (Galas, 1996). The U.S. military had a clear policy of dishonorable discharge of homosexuals until the early months of the Clinton administration.

That policy was based on the view that homosexuality was a mental illness and that homosexuals were therefore "unsuitable for military service" (Shilts, 1993). In addition, the presence of homosexuals was believed to be bad for troop morale. These beliefs conflicted with a 639-page report prepared for the Navy in 1957. Known as the "Crittenden Report" after the chairman of the panel that wrote it, this document concluded that homosexuality did not interfere with effective military service. The report was not widely publicized until it "re-surfaced" in 1976 (Shilts, 1993).

Prior to the Clinton administration, literally thousands of people were forced out of the military because they were gay (Shilts, 1993). Until the 1970s these discharges were private affairs. Then, in 1975, Sergeant Leonard Matlovich decided to mount a challenge. A decorated Vietnam veteran, Matlovich was serving as a race relations instructor for the air force. He noted similarities between previous discrimination against blacks and current discrimination against homosexuals. In both cases, military authorities argued that the minority soldiers would prove untrustworthy and would threaten the morale of other soldiers. Matlovich felt his outstanding service record was proof against this assertion. The Air Force disagreed, and when Matlovich informed them of his sexual orientation, discharge proceedings began. Matlovich challenged the discharge in federal court but was unsuccessful. He appealed the adverse ruling to the U.S. Court of Appeals, which ruled in his favor and called for the Air Force to reinstate him. The Air Force was reluctant to do so, offering him a $160,000 cash settlement instead. Matlovich accepted the settlement, feeling that his case would not fare well in the U.S. Supreme Court. He died of AIDS in 1988. Matlovich's tombstone bears this inscription: "A Gay Vietnam Veteran—When I was in the military they gave me a medal for killing two men, and a discharge for loving one" (Galas, 1996).

Following Matlovich's lead, a growing number of young gay men and lesbians fought their military discharges. When Bill Clinton campaigned for President he promised to issue an executive order rescinding the ban on homosexuals in the military. After the 1992 election, the religious right began organizing, with strong support in the Senate Armed Services Committee, veterans' groups, and the Pentagon. The political costs of overturning the ban appeared overwhelming. The resulting compromise established "Don't ask, don't tell, don't pursue" as the military's policy on homosexuality (Rimmerman, 2000).

The compromise allows gays and lesbians to serve in the military, but it places restrictions on their behavior. They may not tell anyone they are homosexual, or engage in hugging, kissing, or dancing with someone of the same sex, even when they are off-duty. In 1994 the policy was challenged by six military personnel who were discharged. They argued that the policy violated their rights of free speech and equal protection. A U.S. District Court judge agreed with them and ordered the military to reinstate them (Galas, 1996).

The armed forces are one of the nation's largest employers and a bastion of anti-homosexual sentiment. Probably thousands of gays and lesbians are members of the military, devoting years (and even risking their lives) to protect this nation. Current policy allows them only a tightly closeted existence. The challenges to current policy will undoubtedly continue, and eventually a case may reach the Supreme Court.

ANTI-GAY VIOLENCE AND HATE-CRIME LEGISLATION

In 1978, Harvey Milk, San Francisco's first gay city supervisor, was murdered by Dan White. White also killed Mayor George Moscone, presumably for his support of gay rights. White had campaigned on an anti-gay platform, and he had been the only member of the board of supervisors to vote against the city's anti-discrimination ordinance.

Milk was one of the nation's early victims of anti-gay hate crimes. The FBI reports that violence against gays has escalated in recent decades. Only a few of these crimes come to public attention; a recent example is the 1998 murder of Matthew Shepard in Wyoming. Nevertheless, more than a thousand "bias-motivated incidents" against gays and lesbians are documented each year. In 1998, of the 7,755 "bias-motivated incidents" documented, 1,260 were based on sexual orientation (FBI, 1999).

Not all of these incidents represent severe violence, but the Southern Poverty Law Center (SPLC) noted a recent increase in murders of homosexuals. The SPLC reports that figures from the National Coalition of Anti-Violence Programs documented 14 anti-gay murders in 1996 and 33 in 1998. These statistics led the SPLC to conclude that "gay men and lesbians suffer from extraordinarily high levels of violence based on their sexual orientation" (SPLC, 1999).

The upsurge in violence against gay men and lesbians has triggered an effort to include sexual orientation in federal hate-crime legislation. In 1999, Senator Edward Kennedy, along with 39 Democrats and 5 Republicans, sponsored legislation that would have added gender, disability, and sexual orientation to federally protected categories. This bill has not passed. Current federal law does not address hate crimes against homosexuals, but such laws are on the books in 24 states, listed in Table 11.2.

Opponents of expanded hate-crime legislation cite concerns about infringement of freedom of speech. This argument has been central to the objections of conservative religious organizations and the ACLU. Supporters argue that stricter hate-crime legislation will help reduce violence and harassment, if not hate itself.

TABLE 11.2 STATES THAT INCLUDE SEXUAL
ORIENTATION IN THEIR HATE-CRIME STATUTES

Arizona	Kentucky	New Jersey
California	Louisiana	New York
Connecticut	Maine	Oregon
District of Columbia	Massachusetts	Rhode Island
Delaware	Minnesota	Tennessee
Florida	Minnesota	Vermont
Illinois	Nevada	Washington
Iowa	New Hampshire	Wisconsin

Source: Ontario Consultants on Religious Tolerance, 2001.

HIV/AIDS AND SOCIAL POLICY

As Mike's story illustrates, the HIV/AIDS epidemic has been devastating for the gay community. In addition to multiple losses, it spawned a wave of anti-gay sentiment that is sometimes manifest in the very policies that have emerged in response to AIDS.

The Centers for Disease Control reported that between 1981 and 1994, a total of 441,528 Americans were diagnosed with AIDS. During the same period, almost a quarter of a million (a total of 243,423) died of the disease (Galas, 1996). Most of those infected and killed were gay men.

Fear of contracting AIDS intensified discrimination against gay men. Many gay men who worked in food service and other fields that involved contact with other people were summarily fired. Others were denied housing or health care. Indeed, as we saw in Chapter 5, the discrimination spawned by AIDS extended beyond gay men to include anyone affected by the disease. Because of this discrimination the Americans with Disabilities Act of 1990 (ADA) provides specific protections for people with HIV/AIDS. The ADA prohibits discrimination in housing, health care, and employment, and it requires workplace accommodation for those who are ill.

Despite ADA protections, the fear of discrimination persists and the issue of AIDS testing has become controversial. Indeed, there is cause for concern. Extremists such as anti-gay activist Paul Cameron and former Ku Klux Klan leader David Duke have advanced outrageous proposals for responding to the AIDS epidemic. Cameron, for example, suggested a mandatory nationwide testing program for AIDS, with those testing positive either confined to their homes or detained in camps. Duke suggested that AIDS patients be tattooed (Galas, 1996).

HIV/AIDS testing evokes a tension between those committed to protecting the rights and privacy of patients and those worried about controlling the spread of the disease. Like California, most jurisdictions have responded by providing ready access to voluntary testing, with measures to ensure complete confidentiality of the results. To date, mandatory testing has been applied only to prison inmates, prostitutes, immigrants, and military recruits (Hunter & Rubenstein, 1992).

Programs for prevention and treatment of AIDS have also been controversial. Prevention efforts such as needle exchange and safe sex educational programs have drawn opposition for a variety of reasons, and thus they must rely on private sources for most of their funding. Funding for treatment and care of people with AIDS primarily stems from the Ryan White Care Act, which was discussed in Chapter 5.

SOCIAL WORKERS, SOCIAL JUSTICE, AND GAY RIGHTS

In the United States sexual orientation is used as the basis for denying a wide range of benefits, from marriage to employment. As we have seen in this chapter, individuals who identify themselves as gay or lesbian risk being denied benefits that heterosexuals take as a matter of right. The NASW Code of Ethics is clear on the profession's attitude towards discrimination on the basis of sexual orientation, stating that "Social Workers should not practice, condone, facilitate or collaborate with any form of discrimination on the basis of . . . sexual orientation."

Mike's experiences during his social work training were, sadly, not unusual. For some social workers the struggle for gay rights presents a dilemma. Their strong personal or religious beliefs against homosexuality may be in direct conflict with their professional obligation. This obligation goes beyond prohibiting active involvement in discriminatory conduct. It discourages "condoning" discrimination on the basis of sexual orientation. The challenge for these social workers is to limit the scope of their personal biases to ensure that these beliefs do not intrude into their professional lives.

SUMMARY: CURRENT AND FUTURE STATUS OF GAYS AND LESBIANS

Some have argued that gays and lesbians need not suffer from discrimination because their sexual orientation is "invisible." If they did not disclose that they were homosexual, they would not be subject to oppression or persecution. In essence, if they would just go back into the closet all would be well. Eskridge (1999) has called this "the apartheid of the closet." But life in the closet is stifling, lonely, and scary.

Gay men and lesbian women have made outstanding contributions to our nation's culture and our daily lives (see Table 11.3). In this chapter we have documented the role of federal and state policy in the oppression of homosexuals. Today, because of majority opinion, this minority continues to be denied fundamental rights, including in some cases the right to life itself.

Public opinion has been shifting, however. Growing numbers of Americans have voiced their objection to discrimination in employment and anti-gay vio-

TABLE 11.3 PROMINENT GAYS, LESBIANS, AND BISEXUALS

Leonardo da Vinci (1452–1519) A gifted artist, da Vinci is acclaimed for the beauty of his paintings and the novelty of his inventions. Little is known of his private life except that he was devoted to beautiful young men.

Christopher Marlowe (1564–1593) Heavily involved in political intrigue, Marlowe was a gifted playwright. His masterpieces include *The Tragicall History of Doctor Faustus* and *The Troublesome Raigne and Lamentable Death of Edward the Second.*

Walt Whitman (1819–1892) Whitman's poetry is widely interpreted as homoerotic, though he was silent on the topic of his own sexuality.

Peter Ilyich Tchaikovsky (1840–1893) Tchaikovsky's lasting compositions include Swan Lake, The Nutcracker, and The Sleeping Beauty. He was reportedly tormented by his homosexuality, but in his will Tchaikovsky named his companion Bob as his sole heir.

Oscar Wilde (1854–1900) Wilde's literary legacy includes *The Picture of Dorian Gray* and *The Importance of Being Earnest.* Wilde was prosecuted for sodomy and died in exile.

Jane Addams (1860–1935) A pioneer in the field of social work, Addams founded Hull House in Chicago. Her most intimate relationship was with Mary Rozet Smith, her companion for 40 years. The two traveled and lived together. Addams won the Nobel Peace Prize in 1931 for her leadership in the international women's peace movement.

Gertrude Stein (1874–1946) Stein's lifetime intimacy with Alice B. Toklas led her to personify lesbian identity for many during the early twentieth century and beyond. An author and critic, Stein enjoyed considerable influence within the artistic community.

Virginia Woolf (1882–1941) The author of literary criticism, novels, and plays, Woolf is probably best known for her collection of essays, *A Room of One's Own.* After suffering several nervous breakdowns, Woolf committed suicide by drowning herself.

Ruth Benedict (1887–1948) Benedict was a cultural anthropologist. Her partner and collaborator, Margaret Mead, may be a more familiar figure. Mead and Benedict worked closely together, and Benedict left a lasting mark on her field.

Tennessee Williams (1911–1983) Williams wrote plays that captured the American imagination, including *The Glass Menagerie, Cat on a Hot Tin Roof, Night of the Iguana,* and *A Streetcar Named Desire.* His partner, Frank Merlo, managed the chores of everyday life and thus freed Williams to write.

Alan Turing (1912–1954) Turing was a mathematician whose research and theoretical formulations set the stage for the development of the digital computer. He was arrested in Liverpool and charged with "Gross Indecency." The judge required him to participate in "organotherapy," an experimental treatment that involved administration of female hormones. Turing died of cyanide poisoning.

James Baldwin (1924–1987) Author of *Notes of a Native Son, Nobody Knows My Name,* and *The Fire Next Time,* Baldwin benefited from the support of his lover Lucien Happersberger.

Andy Warhol (1928–1987) Best known for his painting of a Campbell's Soup can, Warhol left a lasting mark on American contemporary art. Warhol was open about his sexuality, if reclusive in general.

Adrienne Rich (1929–   ) Described as "one of America's most important living poets," Rich has published critical essays on heterosexuality as a political institution.

Harvey Milk (1930–1978) Known as the first openly gay official elected in the U.S., Milk was a strong advocate for small business and minorities during his tenure as a San Francisco supervisor. Milk was murdered by Dan White.

Barney Frank (1940–   ) In 1987 Frank was serving his fourth term in the U.S. House of Representatives when a reporter asked him whether he was gay. Frank answered in the affirmative and braced himself for the end of his political career. Instead, he was reelected in 1988 by a strong majority.

Source: Russell, 1996.

lence. People with HIV/AIDS are no longer denied care on the grounds that, as Senator Jesse Helms said in his 1995 fight to reduce federal funding for HIV/AIDS, their "deliberate, disgusting, revolting conduct" was to blame for their illness (Galas, 1996, p. 84). Thus, there are some signs of progress. Whether it will continue depends in part on the will and ability of social workers to support the struggle for equal human rights for all Americans.

DISCUSSION TOPICS

1. Why do you think the Defense of Marriage Act was introduced in an election year? If you had been a gay rights advocate, would you have made heroic efforts to defeat the measure? Why or why not?

2. If you were advocating for gay rights, what would be your top-priority issue today? Why?

3. What are your state's laws concerning sodomy? Same-sex marriage? Adoption by gay and lesbian parents?

4. Does your university include sexual orientation in its non-discrimination policy? Does your city? Your state?

SUGGESTED RESOURCES

D'Emilio, J., Turner, W. B., & Vaid, U. (2000). *Creating Change: Sexuality, Public Policy, and Civil Rights.* New York: St. Martin's Press.

Richards, D. A. J. (1999). *Identity and the Case for Gay Rights: Race, Gender, and Religion as Analogies.* Chicago: University of Chicago Press.

www.hrc.org—The Human Rights Campaign is dedicated to promoting gay and lesbian rights. Their website offers action alerts and access to HRC publications. It is searchable.

www.ngltf.org—The National Gay and Lesbian Task Force is a leader in the struggle for gay rights. Their site provides news and issue alerts, as well as publications that offer useful background material on target issues.

www.indiana.edu/~glbtpol/—This site is maintained by Steve Sanders, of the College of Arts and Sciences at Indiana University. It is updated regularly, and offers excellent background material on issues of interest to sexual minorities in the U.S. It also has links to other major sites.

PART IV

Policy Practice and the Social Work Profession

CYCLES OF LIBERATION

Social workers advocating on behalf of the poor, the ill, and the insane confront the all-too-human tendency to distance themselves from misfortune. This tendency, coupled with the well-documented proclivity towards "blaming the victim," can lead to policies that distinguish between "us" and "them," with the latter group encompassing those who suffer from various kinds of problems.

Distancing strategies exclude victims of poverty, ill health and mental illness from the collective. This is the case, for example, when communities debate their level of responsibility for the homeless, asking, "Just how many of these people have come in from the outside?" Or when immigrants are declared ineligible for public support. Or when support for AIDS victims is withheld on the grounds that the disease is the result of sinful lifestyles. Finally, we see distancing when people suffering from addiction are denied benefits because they have failed in rehabilitation. When we set aside some people as non-members, Americans undermine the pursuit of social justice and weaken the collective.

Just as distancing is an important concept in our professional lexicon, liberation is integral to the pursuit of social justice. bell hooks (2001) described a "cycle of liberation" that includes personal empowerment, community building, and cultural transformation. Her views reflect a social work perspective, acknowledging the reciprocal relationships that exist between individuals and their environments.

Social workers tap into this cycle at various levels. We work at the interface of individual and community, applying empowerment strategies to transform lives and build communities. The experiences of Melissa (Chapter 1) and Annie (Chapter 8) clearly illustrate the personal transformation that can result from participation in community building. We also work towards cultural transformation when we follow David Gil's advice to question the inevitable and challenge the invincible. Among the case studies offered in this book, Reverend France Davis (Chapter 10) stands out as a person who has been directly involved in cultural transformation.

To facilitate liberation, social workers engage in a wide range of tasks, some of which fall under the heading of "policy practice." As we will see in Chapter 12, policy practice focuses on changing policy. As our case study, we will describe an advocacy effort on behalf of free public education. Next, we will discuss the philosophy and strategies of policy practice, offering a general perspective and specific advice based on conversations with advocates throughout the country.

Our perspective in Chapter 13 takes a speculative turn, considering the future of social welfare and exploring the trends, ideas, and politics that are likely to shape social policies in the twenty-first century. We will discuss two worldwide trends, globalization and rising inequality, and consider their implications for social justice. The chapter closes by examining contrasting visions of social welfare that stem from capitalist and socialist conceptions of justice.

REFERENCE

hooks, b. (2001). Feminism: A transformational politic. In P. S. Rothenberg (Ed.), *Race, Class, and Gender in the United States: An Integrated Study.* New York: Worth Publishers.

12

Policy Practice

We must complain, yes plain, blunt complaint, ceaseless
agitation, unfailing exposure of dishonesty and wrong—
this is the unerring way to liberty, and we must follow it.

W. E. B. DuBois, 1905

Aristotle was probably the first person to systematically examine the dynamics of persuasion. In the second volume of his three-volume work, *Rhetoric*, he described three components of effective persuasion: *logos*, reason based on content and logic; *pathos*, reason based on passion and emotions; and *ethos*, reason based on the merits and character of the speaker. Aristotle argued for moderate use of all three components.

Aristotle also set the stage for a philosophy of policy practice based on the concept of a "marketplace of ideas." He saw rhetoric as a vital aspect of the life of a community, and he believed that effective arguments would result in good decisions (Corbett, 1965). The marketplace of ideas can work effectively only when all voices are heard and all arguments are responsibly prepared. Modern advocacy is profoundly influenced by Aristotle's views. We rely heavily on the three components of persuasion, and any advocate would do well to remember Aristotle's philosophical approach to the "art of argument."

Our discussion of advocacy in this chapter draws on Aristotle's concepts to examine policy practice as a vital component of social work. It draws from the author's experiences in this area, as well as those of colleagues throughout the country. It is also informed by theory and research in the field of communication, which offers a veritable gold mine of advice and guidelines for advocates.

The chapter begins with a case study of an advocacy effort on behalf of "free public education" in the state of Utah. Next, we will introduce a definition of policy practice. Focusing on advocacy as a key element of policy practice, we will consider specific tactics for advocacy, including preparing and presenting arguments, negotiation and compromise, and the use of relationship. Ethical considerations are examined next, as we consider whether social workers have an ethical obligation to engage in advocacy, and we consider the ethical dimensions of common advocacy practices. The tactics described here can be applied in a variety of policy venues, from letters to the editor to testimony before Congress. For a lively primer on policy practice, see Nancy Amidei's book, *So You Want to Make a Difference* (1991).

Case Study ♦ Free Public Education[1]

In 1895, when Utah became a state, its constitution guaranteed each citizen a "free" public education, at least until the end of the eighth grade. Initially the practice of charging fees for "extras" provided by the public schools, such as uniforms and supplies for special art projects, seemed perfectly compatible with the constitutional mandate. In time enrollment grew and educational funding fell behind. Schools relied increasingly on fees to bridge the revenue gap. By the early 1970s, the use of fees had extended to include not only "extras" but basic necessities such as books and educational supplies. Local advocates became aware that the fees denied children from low-income families access to benefits available to those whose families who could afford to pay. Over the next 20 years, advocates from a statewide organization called Utah Issues employed a broad range of advocacy strategies to address the problem. Their efforts included individual advocacy, coalition building, careful research, and finally, litigation. The story of universal access to public education in Utah offers an instructive example of long-term advocacy for public policy.

Why are school fees a significant social justice issue? Irene Fisher, a key advocate in the early stages of the school fee effort, explained that the imposition of fees stigmatizes children from poor families by emphasizing class differences in a way that is personally and socially destructive. She explained, "When I grew up in South Dakota, no one knew we were poor. I was a cheerleader, and the school issued me a uniform just like everybody else. It may have been used in previous years, but so was everyone else's." In contrast, a low-income Utah parent wrote, "They threatened to withhold my daughter's grades and they always hounded her for money. I didn't have a job and we

---

[1]This account is based on interviews with advocates involved in the effort, and it draws heavily from a booklet by Bill Crim entitled *Sometimes You Need a Hammer: An Unfinished Story of Social Advocacy and Equal Educational Opportunity in Utah* (Salt Lake City: Utah Issues, 1994).

didn't have any money, but every couple of weeks they would pressure my daughter for the fees. She finally gave up and dropped out of school." Another parent explained that her son was arrested for shoplifting. He had stolen art supplies. His teacher had a special box of "poor kids' supplies" for children whose parents could not afford to pay the art supply fee. The boy stole supplies, rather than face the humiliation of using the supplies designated for "poor kids."

School fees were initially added to the funding equation of Utah's public schools as a way to fund enhancements to the educational and social experiences of students without requiring additional legislative appropriations. Once the seed was planted, the practice grew out of hand. Concerns surfaced as early as the 1930s, when the state legislature passed a bill requiring that public schools be free. Two years later, a state court interpreted the law, ruling that no fees could be charged for registration or tuition, and that all necessary supplies and books must be provided to students through grade 8. Although the law was clear, its enforcement mechanism was not. Schools continued to charge fees—sometimes in ways that were clearly illegal.

During the 1970s, the staff of Utah Issues began working on the school fee issue. With a mandate to advocate on behalf of the state's low-income population, the organization started working on a case-by-case basis, helping parents battle illegal fees. In time it became clear that individual advocacy efforts were insufficient, and the organization began holding workshops and conferences with affected parents, soliciting support from other advocacy groups, and preparing reports that the state legislature routinely ignored. The State Superintendent of Public Instruction was concerned about the issue, however, and issued a memo to local districts urging them to develop clear policies allowing for waiver of school fees depending on family circumstances. This memo and related documents became the state's policy on school fees.

At this point, it became clear that three realities affected advocates' progress toward their goals. First, even though school fees were harmful and often illegal, decision-makers believed their elimination was not feasible because of fiscal constraints facing the education system. Second, some policy-makers felt that the availability of waivers effectively solved the problem. Third, those within the educational system who were most concerned about fees—the State Superintendent of Schools and the State Board of Education—were state, not local, officials. Utah's strong commitment to local district autonomy limited their power and authority over local decisions related to fees.

These circumstances strained the energies and resources of the Utah Issues staff. They had to operate not only at the state level, but locally with forty individual school districts. Nonetheless, over the next several years, advocates held workshops with affected parents, helped parents plead their cases with local school personnel, and documented examples of continued harm.

Textbook fees emerged as a major target. Advocates tried during four State Legislative Sessions to obtain supplemental funding to permit elimination of textbook fees before finally getting a $2 million appropriation designated for that purpose in 1975. But local districts continued to charge textbook fees, and the State Board continued to resist pressure to intervene. 1981 saw a major setback, when the Utah Legislature passed a bill authorizing the sale and rental of textbooks to children in high school. A waiver provision was included in the law, but this was the first legislative sanction for fees for basic educational expenses. Advocates continued their efforts, but success seemed out of reach.

Perhaps as a result of this setback capping years of work, coupled with vital issues competing for the attention of poverty advocates, Utah Issues found itself in 1985 with progressively fewer collaborators on the school fee issue. Finally, no one else showed up at a key strategy meeting. The staff of Utah Issues decided to involve its Board of Directors in deciding how to approach an issue that mattered vitally but seemed to have lost its following. The Board chair, an attorney, keyed into the challenging but obvious legal implications of the issue and volunteered to work with the staff to investigate strategic options. Over the next year, the Board chair and staff developed and implemented a new phase of the school fee advocacy effort. The goal was to obtain statutory protections to reduce the harm done to low-income children through imposition of fees.

A legislative interim study committee was persuaded to investigate the school fee issue, and low-income public school students gained a handful of well-educated, committed legislators "on their team" who managed during the 1986 session to pass three laws. The first law required that waivers be made available to low-income children for any fees associated with school-sponsored activities. The second law mandated parental notification of the availability of waivers and the application process. The third law provided for local school board review and approval of all fees in a public meeting. The State Board of Education, in turn, was required to develop rules implementing the new laws, and a low-income advocate was able to move closer to the policy-making process by gaining a seat on the Board's School Fee Task Force. The presence of other child advocates on the Task Force offered the opportunity for successful coalition building on specific policy points.

All news that year was not good. Other legislative action took a forceful step toward solidifying the state educational system's tremendous reliance on school fees as a funding source. The body passed a resolution to place a question on the ballot asking voters whether they would approve of ending Utah's constitutional guarantee of free public education for children in grades 7 through 12. Fearful that extracurricular activities would be eliminated if fees were not charged, voters passed the ballot measure the following November. Over the next seven years, a Senator and two Speakers of the House attempted to repeat this action to remove free public education from the Constitution entirely, but these efforts were defeated. Public policy advocates and other legislators worked together to convince a majority that elementary school children were too young to face the painful experiences their older brothers and sisters endured.

The 1986 school fee law and resultant State Board policy provided new tools for advocates, who forged strong working relationships with State Office of Education staff charged with monitoring compliance over the next five years. Some parents reported success in securing fee waivers, but advocates continued to hear from parents that fees were not being waived, and that inadequate or inaccurate information was presented. Children were still excluded from school activities and denied school supplies.

In 1991, advocates launched a three-pronged research effort to quantify the extent of the problem. Committed to producing information that was both highly credible and reflective of the impact on children, they selected three approaches. First, professional standards and practices were used to conduct a survey of low-income parents concerning their children's experiences with school fees and the fee waiver process. Second, all local district fee policies were systematically analyzed to ascertain compliance with the 1986 laws and State Board Policy. Third, a history of the school fee issue was prepared to place the issue into a clearer context. The report, *School Fees in Utah: The Law and The Practice*, contained the findings and recommendations. The report was released to a broad audience. It left no question that the majority of local school districts had, even after five years, failed to meet the law's requirements, and that parents had many concerns about the impact of the waiver's failure on their children.

At the time that this research was going on, a number of parents contacted Utah Legal Services, which had hired an attorney experienced in school law. As the attorney investigated these parents' circumstances, he approached the State Superintendent of Schools about the policies and practices of the individual school districts involved. After many discussions and further study, he concluded that the Superintendent and State Board were caught in a dilemma. State appropriations for education were inadequate, leading local districts to rely on fees to cover the cost of their programs and activities. Although the State Board was aware of many violations, the philosophical principle of local governance was strong, the State Board had no relief to offer to districts if they waived fees for their many low-income, eligible students, and the State Board believed it had done all it could since 1986 to compel local districts to comply. When pressed, the Superintendent admitted to the attorney that it would take a lawsuit to change these parameters.

Thus, in July 1992, Utah Legal Services filed a class-action lawsuit against the Utah State Board of Education, the State Office of Education, and the State Superintendent of Schools in Third District Court. The lawsuit was commonly known as *Doe v. the Utah State Board of Education*. The judge immediately granted a preliminary injunction requiring that the State Board enforce state fee waiver statutes. The Board was ordered to withhold funds from schools and districts that were out of compliance.

The preliminary injunction increased pressure to resolve the school fee issue. As the State Office of Education's legal staff worked to prepare effective materials to help local districts determine how to achieve compliance with a complex snarl of fees, local school boards struggled to react to their economic dilemma. They were suddenly faced with a choice between economic sanction and substantial reduction in revenue by granting waivers. Some turned to their legislators, calling for necessary, long overdue appropriations. Other districts mounted efforts to evaluate the impact of fees and to ascertain their role in fulfilling the mission of the public schools. Some student groups pledged to raise funds to support low-income students' participation. Conversely, in a few areas, teachers and students feared their favorite activities might be eliminated, and lashed out at children known to be poor.

Attention in the education community turned in earnest to resolving the funding impetus behind school fees, and low-income advocates, education administrators, parents, and teachers worked together on strategies to obtain legislative support during the 1994 General Session. Backlash among some powerful legislators, resentful of the litigation and the assertive stance of the court, led to creation of a Legislative School Fee Task Force. Those selected for the task force were largely hostile to an appropriation to help districts cover fee waivers. The coalition of education advocates who supported waiver funding diligently attended six months of difficult meetings with this hostile group of legislators. The task force was preparing legislation to water down the waiver laws before the judge's permanent injunction was finalized, but that injunction, stronger than the first order, was released in October 1994. The Task Force disbanded angrily.

Although the outcome of *Doe v. the Utah State Board of Education* was a tremendous leap forward for low-income children, in social advocacy few victories are permanent. The underlying cause of schools' reliance on fees—limited state funding for education—still has not been addressed. Until it is resolved, school districts under financial pressure will be highly motivated to ignore waiver policies and impose fees in ways that are damaging and painful to low-income children.

DISCUSSION   This advocacy effort illustrates several basic principles of policy practice:

The struggle is long. Victories and setbacks must be understood in the context of a struggle that may extend beyond the lives of those involved at any given time. When the state constitution was drafted, someone thought to include a guarantee of free public education. This provision suggests that the issue of educational equity has been around since statehood. Clearly those who hunger for a "quick fix" will be disappointed in the advocacy arena. This doesn't mean progress is not possible, but that it may take a very long time—sometimes longer than we can bear.

Every individual counts. Despite—or perhaps because of—the magnitude of the struggle, each individual's efforts count. From the parents who called to complain and tell their stories, to lawyers who devoted their time to a class-action lawsuit, every effort was integral to the process. Not all individual contributions receive public recognition, but all are vital to the success of an advocacy effort.

Advocacy is rarely about "us vs. them." There is seldom a clear enemy to fight. Local districts in this example operated under impossible funding constraints. The State Board was hampered in its job by the overriding principle of local control of schools. The legislature struggled to stretch tax dollars as far as possible. At most, these entities can be accused of lack of consideration for vulnerable children, not of intentional evil. It is tempting, but counter-productive, to label an organization "them" and to dismiss its employees and volunteers as "the enemy."

Just as social policy includes laws, court opinions, and regulations, social advocacy takes place in all of these arenas. Many people think of advocacy as lobbying for legislation or program budgets. These efforts represent only one piece of the advocacy pie. Every bit as influential as the high-profile individual who testifies before legislative bodies and files lawsuits is the detail-oriented person who monitors the drafting of regulations and gently, but firmly, suggests revisions on behalf of vulnerable individuals.

WHAT IS POLICY PRACTICE?

Just as "individual practice" attempts to change individuals, "policy practice" focuses on changing policy. Although the two are closely entwined, policy practice does not *always* involve advocacy. It encompasses a range of activities that, while they sometimes overlap, can be loosely categorized in four groups: assessment and analysis, coalition building, advocacy, and empowerment.

Social workers engage in policy practice when they strive to master the laws and regulations that govern the services they provide to clients. This aspect of policy practice involves basic assessment. Social workers who critically analyze a court opinion for its potential implications for their clients are involved in policy assessment at an advanced level. A policy practitioner who is engaged in advocacy might employ a wide range of tactics, from preparing an argument in favor of expanded services for the disabled to building a coalition of organizations concerned about child welfare. Finally, when community organizers educate residents in a low-income neighborhood about the problem of racial profiling, they are engaged in the "empowerment" aspect of policy practice. In this chapter we will explore tactics and considerations relevant to each of these four aspects of policy practice: assessment and analysis, coalition building, advocacy, and empowerment.

RESEARCH FOR POLICY PRACTICE: ASSESSMENT AND ANALYSIS

While it is not possible for an advocate to know *everything* about the topic under consideration, it is vital that he or she include Aristotle's element of *logos* and be prepared to answer certain basic questions:

- How many people are affected by the problem or issue under consideration?
- What are they like (demographics such as age, race, sex, income, residence)?
- How long has this problem or issue been present?
- What is its history? Have there been previous efforts to address this concern? How well did they work?
- How do other jurisdictions (countries, states, communities) deal with this issue? What successes have they had?
- What are your recommendations or proposals to address the problem? Is there evidence that they will work?
- What do key authorities say about the issue? Who are potential allies and opponents?

Previous chapters of this book have offered material for the assessment and analysis of social policy in specific fields (poverty, health, mental health) and for specific populations (children, women, the elderly, racial and cultural minorities, gays and lesbians). Additional material can be obtained through a variety of sources, including books and professional journals, colleagues who have been working in the area, and Internet search engines. Some of the best policy analysis is done by professional public policy organizations, such as the Urban Institute or the Center for Public Policy and the Budget. The best of these treat social justice as an integral component of their missions and conduct credible legal and social research.

Remember that there are some quality controls in professional books and literature—an editor, and in most cases other reviewers, have examined the material for accuracy and relevance. There are no such controls on the World Wide Web. As a general rule, government web sites provide the most reliable and valuable information. These can be identified by the ".gov" in the URL. Educational web sites are usually reliable sources, but they should be viewed with greater caution than the government sites. The URLs of educational sites end with ".edu." Material drawn from other types of sites should be used only with scrutiny. (For an excellent discussion of criteria for evaluating web sources, see Vernon & Lynch, 2000.)

Although assessment and analysis can be conducted and reported without a direct link to advocacy efforts, they are essential components of effective advocacy. In the following section we will consider the advocacy component of policy practice, drawing from the experiences of policy practitioners, as well as communication theory and research on persuasion.

ADVOCACY SKILLS

Mark Ezell (2001) offers the following definition of advocacy: "Advocacy consists of those purposive efforts to change specific existing or proposed policies or practices on behalf of or with a specific client or group of clients" (p. 23). Drawing on assessment and analysis, advocates use a variety of tactics to accomplish their goals. Three of the most widespread advocacy skills are examined here, including the use of arguments, compromise, and relationship. These skills are profoundly influenced by the three components of persuasion identified by Aristotle. Arguments must be based on careful reasoning and solid research (*logos*). They must be presented in a way that engages the audience's passions (*pathos*). Finally, in all areas, advocates must preserve their professionalism and credibility (*ethos*).

Preparing, Composing, and Delivering Arguments

Persuasion, or argument, is central to advocacy. Three steps are involved in the use of argument: preparation, composition, and delivery.

PREPARATION: SPEAK TO THE AUDIENCE. "Speaking to the audience" sounds ludicrously simple but actually requires considerable analysis, empathy, and skill. Communication specialists describe this process as "constructing a receiver profile" (Johnston, 1994). Advertising firms spend millions of dollars building a profile of the "targets" of their persuasive efforts. Social advocates can increase their effectiveness by devoting time and thought to similar considerations. The advocate must identify the target audience and gear presentations to this group. The preparation process is complicated by the strong likelihood that any argument will be presented to multiple audiences. Several of these audiences, such as those charged with making a decision, are of primary importance, while others, such as fellow advocates, may have less importance. Nonetheless, the key to effective persuasion is winning over as much of the audience as possible.

Constructing a receiver profile is an exercise in perspective-taking. O'Keefe and Shepherd (1987) identified four developmental levels in perspective-taking. At the first level, no attempt is made to determine the target's needs or interests; at the second, the advocate communicates his or her own needs, without regard to those of the target; at the third level, the advocate is familiar with the target's position and has prepared counter-arguments designed to change the target's mind; at the fourth level the advocate focuses on the target and elaborates on the advantages to the target of taking the desired action (Johnston, 1994).

Operating at the fourth and highest level of perspective-taking requires knowledge of the basic demographic characteristics of a target, as well as his or her beliefs, attitudes, and values. The most effective persuasion optimizes the similarity between the persuader and the target, on as many relevant dimensions as possible. Thus, for example, an advocacy team appearing before an all-male legislative committee might do well to include at least one man among the presenters. Further, the most persuasive presentations emphasize the similarity in beliefs, attitudes, and values between the advocate and the target.

For example, a report on the effects of school fees on low-income families will be read by several discrete groups: the media, school board authorities, state legislators, the families themselves, and other advocates. The report must be written in a way that will speak credibly to all of these groups, but the primary target may be state legislators considering a bill that will expand the use of school fees. The report should carefully "speak" to legislators' rather predictable needs. This calls for impeccable accuracy; concise but well-supported argument; avoidance of moralizing or blaming; and clear presentation of a solution to the problem. The report should acknowledge the constraints that legislators may face in adopting a solution, perhaps acknowledging that "No one wants to increase taxes, and we all want to support our schools." The next step is to help legislators understand that we can and must support schools without stigmatizing, discouraging, and damaging children from low-income families.

Advocates can tap into core American values to increase the likelihood that their audience will identify with them and be prepared to receive their message.

TABLE 12.1 CORE AMERICAN VALUES

Puritan and pioneer morality: hard work, honesty, self-discipline, and cooperation

Individuality: personal integrity, the value of the life of even one person, personal rights

Achievement and success: personal success, money, self-made achievement, social status

Change and progress: new and improved, future and present always better than past, change for better

Ethical equality: all equal before God, all vote, etc.

Effort and optimism: no problem too big

Efficiency, practicality, and pragmatism: getting things done

Rejection of authority: power of individual; freedom and rights over duties and obligations

Science and secular rationality: reason, control, prediction

Sociality: networking

Material comfort: happiness can be bought

Quantification: bigger, faster, more, longer, quantity over quality

External conformity: popularity, social status

Humor: leveling influence

Generosity and consideration: welfare, benevolence

Patriotism: loyalty to values of America over loyalty to nation of origin

Source: From D. Johnston, *The Art and Science of Persuasion,*©1994. Reprinted with permission of the McGraw-Hill Companies.

Steele and Redding (1962) conducted a study of American values. Their results, which were remarkably similar to those identified in a 1940 study, continue to have relevance today (see Table 12.1).

By appealing to these values, an advocate can generate agreement and identification in a wide range of target audiences. Of course, for a given argument, only some of the core values might apply, and audiences vary in the strength with which they embrace each core value. Advocates should identify the most important core values held by their target audience. An advocate speaking before a group of social workers, for example, should include "appreciation for diversity" as a core value held by his or her audience. Someone appearing before the Chamber of Commerce might emphasize the contributions of free enterprise to our way of life.

It is important to be subtle and judicious in any appeal to the values of an audience. Any audience will be offended by manipulation or pandering. Condescension or an underlying message that the audience is ignorant or unfeeling is an immediate turn-off. Frequently an advocate's moral outrage on behalf of clients leads her to alienate an audience by demonizing anyone who does not share her fervor.

COMPOSING THE ARGUMENT. Three strategies can be used to enhance the effectiveness of most policy-related arguments: anticipating opposing arguments, using authority, and integrating analytic material (facts and figures) with anecdotal material (stories and symbols).

As a general rule, advocates should anticipate arguments that will be made by the opposition and address them. Within the field of communication this is called using a "two-sided" argument. Two-sided arguments present one perspective and then anticipate counter-arguments. They are contrasted with "one-sided" arguments, which present only the perspective the speaker is advocating.

Some advocates argue that it is simpler to offer one-sided arguments, noting that a risk in two-sided arguments is that you will work against yourself by presenting the opposing argument. But most summaries of communication research on this issue suggest that one-sided arguments should be used only under limited circumstances, such as when the audience is already in favor of your position, is easily confused on the issue, or is not aware of the opposition (Johnston, 1994; O'Keefe, 1992). The final case, in which the audience is unaware of opposition, should be treated with care. If a one-sided argument is presented and the audience *becomes* aware of the opposing point of view, an advocate can lose both the argument and her credibility.

An Approach to Avoid When Composing Arguments

We have all heard "slippery slope" arguments. When we were young, our teachers may have told us, "If I do this for you, I'll have to do it for all of the children." More sophisticated forms of this argument surface in contemporary debates such as the controversy over assisted suicide. Opponents argue that permitting assisted suicide for the terminally ill will lead to euthanasia of the disabled or even the unattractive. Slippery slope arguments have what my grandmother used to call "ear appeal." They sound good. They make sense at first blush. But upon careful consideration they are seldom persuasive. Indeed, a good debater can undermine his opponent's credibility by pointing out that he or she has used a slippery slope argument.

Generally an advocate is advised to anticipate the opposition and present a two-sided argument. Communication scholars suggest this approach when the audience is sophisticated, aware of contradictory positions, and not already in agreement with your position (Johnston, 1994). Social advocates should generally anticipate opposing arguments and, at a minimum, acknowledge the existence of opposing views. Effective arguments not only anticipate opposing arguments, but present counter-arguments that will essentially "inoculate" their audiences against persuasion by the opposition.

In the school fees debate, advocates supporting waivers should anticipate that their opponents will argue that some parents will misuse the program, claiming waivers when they do not really need them. This argument might be defused by suggesting a simple certification process under which children eligible for free school lunches are automatically eligible for fee waivers.

Advocates rely on authority to persuade. Their authority might stem from the care and accuracy of their observations (*logos*) or their personal credibility (*ethos*). Thus, an advocate's personal or professional experiences, or even academic credentials, might contribute to her authority. Other sources are scientific, moral, or political authorities. Legal authority for an argument can stem, as we have seen, from a variety of sources including the state and federal constitutions. Community leaders might also contribute authority to an argument.

Understanding one's audience can also influence an advocate's use of authority. The selection of authorities can either alienate or impress, depending on the audience. A group of secular humanists are likely to be more susceptible to the authority of well-done research than to religious authority. Colleagues might be impressed by the use of professional experience. State legislators in the Bible Belt might be persuaded by a well-chosen Biblical passage.

Another Approach to Avoid When Composing Arguments

Policy-makers, representatives of the media, and the public-at-large have grown impatient with what I call "Ain't it awful?" arguments. These arguments outline, in exquisite detail, the horrible conditions an advocate has discovered—and they stop at that point. Although such a presentation can reflect a tremendous amount of effort and study, it leaves an audience feeling frustrated and impotent. Advocacy presentations should generally close with at least one specific recommendation that is likely to address the problem. At a minimum, the person presenting the complaint should recommend further study of the problem that has been identified. Beyond this, discussion of possible solutions—particularly those that have proven effective in different settings or with similar problems—is always advisable.

A corollary to the observation that most arguments are presented before multiple audiences is the requirement that arguments speak to people using multiple communication devices. While some members in an audience will be intrigued and impressed by the *logos* of an argument—the facts and figures—others will find them dull or incomprehensible. Those who are either bored or intimidated by careful statistical analysis may perk right up when *pathos* is brought in through a strong, illustrative example.

The importance of examples or stories is underscored by research in the field of communications. O'Keefe's (1992) review of research on the effectiveness of examples as compared to statistics suggested that examples are generally more effective with all but the most sophisticated audiences. This is consistent with Douglass's (1997) analysis of the nearly effective anti-homosexual campaign of the Oregon Citizen's Alliance (OCA) in 1993. Douglass wondered how such an unsophisticated campaign could have led to the near-passage of Measure 9, an effort to amend Oregon's constitution to define homosexuality as "abnormal, wrong, unnatural and perverse" and to prohibit extension of civil rights to lesbians and gays. After careful study, he concluded that the OCA's effective use of narrative (even without compelling analytic arguments) was the key to their success in securing a 47 percent "yes" vote on Measure 9. [See also Fisher (1987) for documentation of the persuasive effectiveness of narrative.]

The value of symbols, such as graphic illustrations, should not be ignored. An effective presentation will incorporate multiple approaches to communication: facts and figures, illustrative examples, and symbols. This multi-faceted approach will engage a diverse audience and employ both *logos* and *pathos* to set the stage for successful persuasion.

SUCCESSFUL DELIVERY. Many social workers find oral presentation of their arguments stressful, particularly when it occurs in a formal setting such as a legislative hearing. We struggle with our own fear, and experience awkwardness in dealing with physical aspects of the setting, such as microphones and cameras. There are many self-help books available to help people overcome their fear of public speaking (i.e., Hoff, 1988).

While discussing this topic with my social work students, I have invited a consultant to address my classes. He teaches politicians about public speaking. His best advice is to concentrate on your intent. Keep your energy and your presentation totally focused on the message you plan to deliver. Remember that everything else is peripheral. I like to develop presentations with three to five points, and use the time prior to delivery to breathe deeply and review those points.

Organization of an oral presentation should be informed by research on memory. People remember what is said first and last, and they tend to forget what happened in the middle. A simple rule of organization is, "Tell them what you will say. Say it. Then tell them what you said."

Use of a written script should be viewed as a last resort. If you are going to be in front of television cameras or hundreds of people, the likelihood of severe stage fright is high and a script is a useful tool. Otherwise, an outline with key points and evidence should suffice. Use of a script generally leads to a lifeless presentation.

Any contact with the audience that acknowledges their nonverbal communication can enliven a scripted presentation. If the audience laughs or looks skeptical, a speaker should acknowledge their reaction and incorporate it into the presentation. This degree of responsiveness will involve the audience and make the presentation more like a dialogue than a lecture.

Presentations can also be made in writing. Format is a vital component of all persuasive communication. Advocacy speeches and documents should be organized and concise. All policy reports should include a one- to two-page executive summary for use by members of the press who have limited time and need quotable material. The executive summary will also help legislators pressed for time, who are simply unable to read every report they receive. Policy-makers invariably appreciate a summary of key policies in the area, objective facts and figures, and clear recommendations. All audiences appreciate a table of contents and clear, jargon-free language.

Thus far, our discussion has focused on the more formal aspects of advocacy, such as public debate and presentation. Another element goes on "behind closed doors" and involves advocates in negotiation and compromise. A vital consideration in many advocacy efforts is when to hold out for an ultimate goal and when to accept a compromise. The decision to compromise is never easy, and it can be extremely controversial. In the following section we will consider some factors involved in compromise.

NEGOTIATION AND COMPROMISE

Politics has been called "the art of compromise," and most advocacy efforts at some point involve it. Effective compromises are crafted to provide each party something highly valued while asking that each give up something of lesser value. The net result is an increase in overall satisfaction. Preparation for compromise is an exercise in clarification of values. This exercise involves identifying one's own values ("What is our 'do or die' position?") as well as anticipating the values of the opposition ("What is *their* 'do or die' position?"). Both questions may require careful consideration.

Tedeschi and Rosenfeld (1980) offered a useful (and more technical) approach to analyzing positions in negotiation. They suggest that all parties have a "status quo point," a "resistance point," and a "level of aspiration." If the negotiations fail, both parties will be at their "status quo point" and might as well not have engaged in any discussion. The "resistance point" is analogous to what I have called the "do or die" position. It is the minimum results required for the parties to reach an agreement. The distance between these two points, technically called the "bargaining range," is the crux of the negotiation. If that distance is too great, negotiations will fail. If not, the outcome will depend on the skill and power of the negotiators. The "level of aspiration" is what each party hopes will come from the negotiation. Both will be satisfied if they come close to this level. These three potential outcomes have been called a bargainer's "utility schedule" (Tedeschi & Rosenfeld, 1980). In a compromise, both parties should be advised at a minimum to clarify their own positions and ideally to estimate the positions of any other parties involved.

A coalition of organizations or individuals engaged in advocacy may come to the effort with different goals and priorities. Since most advocacy efforts involve more than one person, effective communication about priorities is an important part of the planning process.

Unless an advocate has become familiar with the opposition, either through repeated exposure or through inside information, it will be difficult to anticipate their priorities. Therefore, a first stage in the process of negotiation is usually an exchange of information concerning goals and priorities. This exchange may not be framed as such, but a proposed "informational meeting" might have, as its hidden agenda, an opportunity to introduce a compromise.

Frequently, in the heat of an advocacy effort involving a coalition, a decision-maker will approach one member of the coalition and offer a deal. The advocate is asked, on behalf of the coalition, to agree to a compromise. An advocate once told me, "This goes with the territory." Thus, it is vital for all members of a coalition to understand who is and who is not empowered to negotiate on behalf of the coalition. Agreement on this point should be an early item on any coalition's advocacy agenda.

USE OF RELATIONSHIP

Social workers have long understood the pivotal importance of "relationship" or "rapport." As the case example at the beginning of this chapter illustrated, advocacy is not about allies and enemies. It is about people, and today's opponent may be tomorrow's ally. While it is tempting, and sometimes emotionally gratifying, to cast the opposition as evil demons, this approach is ultimately detrimental to an advocate's effectiveness. A dispute, debate, or disagreement is an opportunity to build a relationship with the opposition. Social advocates seldom have the financial resources to influence policy with money, but our capacity to establish and maintain relationships can be every bit as effective as the perks delivered by corporate lobbyists.

Social Exchange Theory offers a useful perspective for understanding relationships in the policy arena. Within this framework, "reciprocity" is the glue that holds society together. Reciprocity is, simply, "giving what is due." It is the sense that a favor entails an obligation to reciprocate. Social workers frequently are given opportunities to do favors: when a policy-maker asks for information or advice, a candidate asks for a contribution or an endorsement, a colleague asks for moral support, or an administrator asks for supportive testimony. These requests are opportunities to build relationships. Over the course of a professional career, a social worker gives and receives assistance to the point where she and her contacts forget who owes whom.

Some exchange theorists argue that friendship is simply a reciprocal relationship that has reached this point. Both parties feel vaguely indebted to the other, and each would help the other without hesitation—partly to fulfill a sense of obligation but partly "because that's what friends do."

In addition to this kind of "exchange-based" relationship, advocates enjoy the opportunity to build alliances based on mutual interests and shared respect. A long-term commitment to building supportive relationships will tremendously enhance an advocate's effectiveness. Sometimes this commitment requires separating the messenger from the message—letting someone know that while you disagree vehemently with his or her views you are extremely fond of him or her as a person. I have often seen state legislators debate vigorously, almost to the point (I thought) of coming to blows. After the debate, in quieter quarters, I have seen the same people check in with each other, apologize for their excesses, and affirm their commitment to the relationship. This capacity to sustain relationship through controversy is vital to effective advocacy.

BUILDING AND MAINTAINING COALITIONS

In a pluralistic democracy, a coalition of several groups can be extremely powerful. The challenge for advocates is first to identify potential coalition partners and then to establish clear guidelines for maintaining the coalition.

Potential coalition partners are groups and key individuals who share an advocate's goal. A coalition is not a marriage—these groups need not necessarily be personally or philosophically compatible. Despite their differences, however, they can work together to achieve a common goal. My first job taught me about unlikely partners in coalition. I was employed by the Oregon Environmental Council to organize a coalition of diverse interests that would focus on maintaining stream-flows (keeping water in rivers). Our first task was to identify those parties who shared our interest in keeping water in rivers. As it turned out, the "Water Action Coalition," as it was eventually called, united the efforts of Native Americans, commercial fishermen, sports fishermen, and environmentalists. These groups were frequently on opposite sides of the fence on other issues, but when it came to minimum stream flows they united into a remarkably effective organization. On a much grander scale, the civil rights movement involved a powerful coalition of religious and labor leaders from both white and African-American communities. These leaders demonstrated that they could transcend their differences and work together for civil rights.

Although common goals are an essential ingredient, a sense of shared purpose may not be enough to make for smooth coalition action. At some levels coalition building can become an intensely personal business. People who disrespect or loathe each other can make difficult coalition partners. An organization known for its confrontational tactics and extreme positions may not be able to build an effective coalition, just as an individual advocate known for alienating or embarrassing the opposition may not be able to do so. Coalitions are built and maintained by moderates whose positions and tactics are palatable to most potential partners—people who get along well with others. This does not mean that the more extreme personalities or groups cannot instigate a coalition, but only that they may have a harder time facilitating ongoing operations or recruiting potential partners.

Coalitions require care and tending. Roles must be carefully defined. For example, it is vital that partners agree about how they will make decisions, what types of issues they will (and will not) address, how partners will be informed about developments, and who is (and is not) empowered to speak on behalf of the coalition. A general rule of coalition maintenance is "When in doubt, talk it out." Particularly in the early stages of their development, coalitions need both routine ways to communicate (i.e., monthly meetings) and emergency routes of conversation (i.e., e-mail, phone trees). The emergency routes are useful when a partner identifies the need for immediate action, enabling him or her to contact coalition members for their feedback and agreement prior to committing the coalition to a course of action.

EMPOWERMENT IN POLICY PRACTICE

Social advocates are frequently seen as self-serving. Our opponents argue that when we advocate for increased program budgets or supports for the poor we are actually trying to enhance our professional stature and line our purses. Indeed, as Pat Powers noted (Hardcastle, Wenocur, & Powers, 1996), an advocate's credibility is greatest when either she or a member of her family has been directly affected by the policy under consideration. For example, a former welfare mother or the sister of a person with a disability brings personal credibility to an advocacy effort. This credibility can be more influential than professional experience and degrees, moral and legal authority, and good science put together. Unfortunately, the same forces that generate personal credibility with regard to social problems (poverty, disability, prejudice, and discrimination) work against effective involvement in the policy arena. That is why empowerment is a vital component of policy practice and a crucial element of social change.

We can empower people by helping them secure the knowledge, skills, resources, and opportunities to advocate for themselves. When Utah Issues held workshops to inform parents about the school fee issue and waiver regulations, it empowered parents by providing knowledge. When a social worker coaches a welfare mother through testimony before the state legislature, the client is empowered by acquiring new skills. When an activist hunts down a bus to transport children from low-income families to a march on the capital, he is empowering people by securing resources. When a bureaucrat suggests that clients be represented on an advisory committee, she empowers clients by securing an opportunity for them to speak out on behalf of themselves.

While direct advocacy tends to place social workers on the firing line of controversial social issues, empowerment allows them to operate in the background. Advocacy generates clear results—either successes or failures. The results of empowerment efforts, by contrast, are seldom immediately apparent. Sometimes organizations and individuals who find the confrontational aspects of social advocacy unpleasant or abhorrent will find empowerment efforts perfectly acceptable. For example, a foundation that would never fund lobbying efforts may be willing to support client education. Similarly, a public official who would oppose expansion of welfare benefits may support a program to enhance the communication skills of welfare recipients, making it more likely that they will be able to secure jobs.

ETHICAL ISSUES IN POLICY PRACTICE

Some people think of politics and policy practice as sordid activities. This perspective is sometimes used to justify deviating from ethical standards. In his now-classic work, *Rules for Radicals*, Saul Alinsky (1972) offered another rationale for deviation. Alinsky argued that in social activism, as in war, the ends justify the means. He felt that the power differential between social advocates and policy-makers was so huge that advocates were justified in "suspending the rules" of ethical conduct to achieve important policy victories.

It is important to keep in mind, however, that Alinsky was writing in a different era of social advocacy—a war truly *was* being fought, and advocacy was a life-or-death proposition. Further, Alinsky was writing for activists who were excluded from the realm of policy decisions. Unlike most of Alinsky's street-level activists, social work advocates are professionals. We have colleagues in most state legislators, and to a great extent we are *insiders* in the policy arena. The power differential between social work advocates and some policy-makers may be substantial, but it is never big enough to justify deviating from the rules of ethical communication.

In this section we will consider several ethical aspects of policy practice, asking first whether social workers have an ethical obligation to engage in advocacy, then exploring the ethical dimensions of two common practices: "sharpening the message," and "using clients." We will then explore issues of confidentiality and conclude the section by describing the characteristics of ethical persuasion.

IS ADVOCACY AN ETHICAL OBLIGATION?

Mark Ezell (2001) observed that the NASW Code of Ethics includes several statements that may support an ethical obligation to do advocacy:

- Social workers should advocate for living conditions conducive to the fulfillment of basic human needs and should promote social, economic, political, and cultural values and institutions that are compatible with the realization of social justice (Ethical Standard 6.01).

- Social workers should engage in social and political action that seeks to ensure that all people have equal access to the resources, employment, services, and opportunities they require to meet their basic human needs and to develop fully (Ethical Standard 6.04(a)).

- Social workers should act to prevent and eliminate domination of, exploitation of, and discrimination against any person, group, or class on the basis of race, ethnicity, national origin, color, sex, sexual orientation, age, marital status, political belief, religion, or mental or physical disability (Ethical Standard 6.04(d)).

The wording of these statements suggests that social workers are strongly encouraged, but not required, to undertake these activities and goals. The operative word here is "should." Had that word been replaced with "must" or "will," the Code could be interpreted differently. Nonetheless, policy practice represents a powerful means for carrying out the professional mission of promoting social justice and human well-being.

SHARPENING THE MESSAGE

The practice of "sharpening the message" or "getting to the gist" is common in story-telling (Gilovich, 1991). We weed out extraneous details, narrowing down our presentation to include only those critical facts that convey our message in the most efficient way possible. Dorothea Dix probably used this approach in her many presentations on the treatment of the insane. She "sharpened" her message, and as a result was (perhaps rightly) accused of exaggeration and outright lies.

Modern advocates often do the same thing, seeking and presenting information that supports their case, while ignoring contradictory facts. This common practice has both ethical and practical ramifications for social work professionals. Social workers have a clear ethical prohibition against deceit. The NASW Code of Ethics includes several statements that emphasize the importance of truthfulness. Integrity is identified as a core value of the profession, and the Code requires that "social workers behave in a trustworthy manner."

Does this prohibition against deceit *require* us to present facts that do not support our position? The line between "sharpening the message" and deceit may be fuzzy, but both practices threaten the credibility of social advocates.

In the advocacy arena, social workers have little to offer but professional and personal credibility. We do not give huge campaign contributions. We seldom control committee assignments or large numbers of votes. Instead, we strive to represent the disenfranchised and the vulnerable in a way that is credible, balanced, and persuasive. As professionals, social workers should emphasize balance and accuracy in our advocacy efforts, even at the risk of delivering a message that is less focused or dramatic than we might like.

USING CLIENTS

Involving clients in advocacy also brings social work practitioners into delicate ethical territory. For some clients, like Annie Boone (Chapter 8), the opportunity to become involved in advocacy is empowering and transformative. For others, however, it may be terrifying, humiliating, and personally destructive.

How can a practitioner determine whether it is "ethical" (as opposed to advisable) to involve a client in an advocacy effort? The concept of "self-determination," a core social work value, provides some direction here. When a client chooses to enter into an advocacy effort, with full knowledge of what this effort is expected to entail, that client is exercising his or her right to self-determination. The social worker's obligation is not to protect the client from discomfort or to promise immediate results, but to inform the client—insofar as possible—what can be expected.

A typology proposed by Martin Buber offers another way to judge the ethics of client involvement. Buber suggests that we can hold two distinct attitudes towards other people, an "I-thou" attitude or an "I-it" attitude. An "I-thou" attitude recognizes the individuality of the other, and treats him or her as person worthy of respect. An "I-it" attitude treats the other as an object designed to serve the communicator's selfish needs (Friedman, 1960). Ethical client involvement requires that clients be treated with respect and that communication be characterized by honesty and directness, without the use of power or subordination. It is vital that clients never be treated as a means to an end. The advocacy effort must not "use" clients, but "engage" them in a mutual effort to achieved a shared goal.

A practitioner cannot always tell how the client will respond to advocacy experiences, but it is essential to make sure the client is as informed as possible about what to expect from involvement. A social worker who worries that she might be "using" a client should ask herself whether the client was able to make an independent decision about involvement, and whether the social worker has done all she could to inform the client what to expect, both of the advocacy experience itself and of its potential results.

KEEPING CONFIDENCES

Advocacy is a public act, in a public arena where one should assume that "there are no secrets." This may seem to be a strange assumption, since we know on its face that it is probably not true. Nevertheless, it is a useful assumption to live by. Whenever an advocate finds himself thinking, "I bet he/she will never find out about it," the advocate is probably taking a risk that could jeopardize a relationship or worse. In policy practice it is best to assume that every word you utter and every act you commit will become public knowledge. Advocates live in fish bowls, and the more controversial the cause, the more transparent the bowl.

A corollary to "there are no secrets" is the danger of receiving confidences. When you are engaged in policy practice, people may offer to share confidences with you. They may offer secrets so tantalizing and interesting that it is hard to resist hearing them. Resist you must, however, simply as an act of personal protection. Consider this: if this person is willing to tell you this secret, how many other people have been told? And even if you are not the one who reveals it, how can you ensure that no one else will? Thus, unless you have a strong relationship with someone in the political arena, it is best to avoid these "dangerous confidences."

Of course, it goes without saying that if you do accept someone's confidence you must guard it carefully. Sometimes it is unclear that something is being told "in confidence." Most of us have had the painful experience of inadvertently revealing a confidence we thought was common knowledge. When someone tells us something that seems sensitive or newsworthy it is important to ask that person, "Am I free to pass this on and give you as the source? Or would you prefer that I hold it in confidence?" This practice is an excellent way to strengthen trust in a relationship.

CHARACTERISTICS OF ETHICAL PERSUASION

Within the marketplace of ideas, ethical persuasion is a two-way process, with expectations for both advocate and listener. Johnston (1994) offered a summary of the expectations of both communicators in an ethical exchange, as shown in Table 12.2.

In an advocacy exchange, both advocate and listener are responsible for ensuring that the debate about social issues results in the best possible decision. Both parties share an obligation to ensure a civil, fair-minded interaction.

Clearly, advocates cannot control the behavior of their audiences—and audiences sometimes misbehave. It takes only a short time in the advocacy trenches to encounter a listener who is more intent on humiliating the advocate than on hearing a new perspective. Indeed, most experienced advocates can tell horror stories of public attacks by legislators or elected officials.

TABLE 12.2 CHARACTERISTICS OF ETHICAL PERSUASION

1. Persuaders are clear, direct, and honest about their intentions.

2. Communicators promote mutual respect and mutual satisfaction of goals, rather than self-interests.

3. Communicators use strategies that confirm others and preserve the dignity of others.

4. Communicators seek input and elaboration from each other.

5. Persuaders avoid the use of active deception and the withholding of relevant information, except when the truth may cause significant harm to others.

6. Communicators listen and critically process each other's messages.

7. Communicators welcome and explore dissent.

8. Communicators analyze their own and others' biases without defending or threatening their own or others' egos.

9. All participants in the persuasion process share the ethical responsibility of persuasive outcomes and respond to each other with resoluteness and openness.

10. Communicators weigh opinions equally, rather than on the basis of individual power or status.

11. Communicators assess probable consequences of their message on others.

12. Communicators employ persuasion to celebrate the human qualities of diversity, personality, intelligence, passion for beliefs, humor, and reasoning.

13. Communicators encourage social discussion and social contact.

14. Communicators critically challenge claims of certainty and truth.

15. Decisions are subject to revision over time.

16. The relative power of the persuader and the receiver determines the degree of ethical responsibility.

17. Communicators maintain free speech, but the probability of harmful consequences guides the ethical decision to produce a persuasive message.

Source: Reprinted with permission from Johnston, 1994, p. 72.

It is difficult not to take attacks personally, but that is exactly what an advocate must do. I believe it is helpful for beginning advocates under attack to ask themselves "why" the official is behaving in this way. He or she may be grandstanding, or playing to a constituency that is hostile to your position. He or she may be threatened by your effectiveness. He or she may be in a bad mood. It also helps to recall that public attack is a violation of the "rules of engagement," and the attacker's colleagues probably view it that way. They may be embarrassed by the attack. Indeed, a virulent and irrational attack by an opposing legislator may advance an advocate's cause better than his or her own arguments![2]

LEGAL CONSIDERATIONS IN POLICY PRACTICE

Some readers of this book may be independently wealthy and engage in social work purely as philanthropy. The rest of us will be using other people's money. Such use imposes legal obligations. Often technical rules are difficult to understand, remember, and apply. You will find it useful to remind yourself, from time to time, who is providing the funds for your activity, and what those persons expect of you. Social advocates often find themselves working for the government or for public charities. Some of the limitations on these groups are discussed below.

THE HATCH ACT

The Hatch Act is a federal statute that was passed in 1939 to regulate the political activity of civil servants. Its primary focus was ensuring that federal employees did not use the power or resources of their offices to promote political candidates. The Act was amended in 1993 to allow some political involvement by federal employees. The Hatch Act also applies to employees of private, state, and local organizations whose activities are financed by federal loans or grants (i.e., Head Start employees). Most states have adopted provisions similar to the Hatch Act for state employees.

Employees who are covered by the Hatch Act are not permitted to do any of the following things:

- Use their official authority or influence to affect an election;
- Solicit or discourage political activity of anyone with business before their agency;
- Solicit or receive political contributions;
- Be candidates for public office in *partisan* elections;

---

[1]Sometimes a beginning advocate may feel under attack when legislators or officials are asking questions the advocate cannot answer. In such situations, it is best to admit ignorance and offer to find the answer and provide it to the questioner later.

- Engage in political activity while on duty, in a government office, wearing an official uniform, or using a government vehicle;
- Wear partisan political buttons while on duty.

The key to Hatch Act compliance is avoiding misuse of the power or authority of the government office. The Act certainly does not rule out all political involvement by government employees. They can, for example, serve as candidates in *non-partisan* elections (e.g., school board), register and vote as they choose, contribute money to political organizations, attend fundraising functions, be active and hold office in a political party or club, and campaign for or against candidates in partisan elections.

PRESERVING TAX-EXEMPT STATUS

Groups that rely on public support usually seek to qualify for tax-deductible contributions. Such groups are described in Section 501(c)(3) of the Internal Revenue Code and are therefore often referred to as "501(c)(3) organizations." Donors can usually make contributions to such organizations free of estate and gift tax as well as federal and state income tax.

These attributes "stretch" the donor's dollars. Suppose Mr. A is willing to part with $100 of his personal wealth to support your organization. If he makes a gift of $150 dollars and receives a tax deduction of the same amount he may "save" $50 in taxes, so he is out of pocket only $100 while your organization receives $150 in revenue. Special provisions in the tax code can help stretch contributions in a variety of ways. These include special treatment for appreciated property, private foundations, charitable remainder and charitable lead trusts (including trusts established during life and by will), charitable annuities, and "endowment funds" (usually mutual funds) permitting current deductions for future contributions. If you become involved with the "development" (fundraising) side of your organization, you may need to learn more about these provisions.

The extra $50 from Mr. A, along with the other money and benefits, comes from the government. Naturally there are "strings attached." A few organizations are unwilling to accept the strings. They may still be non-profit entities and often are tax-exempt [the organization pays no income taxes by virtue of Internal Revenue Code Sections 501(c)(4) to 501(c)(22)]. However, unless the rules of Section 501(c)(3) are followed, there will be no "stretching" from donor tax deductions.

Perhaps the most famous example of a non-profit organization that decided to forego 501(c)(3) status is the Sierra Club. This group was formed for summer treks in the mountains and preservation of the lands visited. In the mid-1960s the Sierra Club found itself fighting to preserve the Grand Canyon from dams. The organization lobbied Congress to oppose reclamation projects proposed by state and local governments. Using government funds to influence legislation, particularly legislation supported by other governments, raises serious issues. The

Sierra Club decided, in effect, to stop taking government handouts. It gave up its 501(c)(3) status.

Social advocates are likely to find themselves in a similar position. You may be trying to persuade legislators or other policy-makers to take actions opposed by other parts of government. Here are some of the rules that apply:

A 501(c)(3) organization is one in which "no substantial part of the activities . . . is carrying on propaganda or otherwise attempting to influence legislation . . . and which does not participate in, or intervene in (including the publishing or distributing of statements) any political campaign on behalf of (or in opposition to) any candidate for public office."[3] For public charities that wish to engage in limited political activities, Congress has provided what is known as a "Conable[4] election," or "safe harbor"[5] that may offer greater ability to act with less risk of challenge. The "Conable election" may be selected by filing a form with the IRS.[6]

Under the safe harbor (or Conable election) clause, certain activities are explicitly permitted without the need to report them as lobbying. The following activities are included:

- making available results of nonpartisan analysis, study, or research;

- providing technical advice or assistance to a political body in response to a written request from such body;

- appearances before or communications to legislative bodies which affect the existence of the organization, its powers and duties or its tax exemption; and

- communication between an organization and its members with respect to legislation of interest to the members, other than efforts to encourage members or others to attempt to influence legislation.

Under the Conable election, any communication with a government official or employee who is not a member of the legislative body considering action (e.g., a staff member or executive) is permitted as long as it is not intended to influence legislation.

Influencing legislation (lobbying) includes attempts to influence the opinion of the general public or any segment of the public or any legislative body. It includes matters before local government bodies and extends to any initiative, referendum, constitutional amendment, motion, resolution, or bill.

---

[3]Code § 501(c)(3).

[4]The Conable election, which is found in Section 501(h) of the Internal Revenue Code, is named after Barber Benjamin Conable, Jr., a Congressional representative for the state of New York from 1965 to 1985.

[5]Code §§503(h) and 4911.

[6]Currently made by filing Treasury Form 5768.

Under the Conable election, the amount of "influencing legislation" that can be done is clear, relatively easy to calculate, and once determined, allows the organization to make informed choices about its activities. It knows that when it is really critical to "lobby" (or influence legislation) it can do so without fear of jeopardizing its tax status. The amount that can be spent to influence legislation is based on an organization's total budget, not including fundraising expenses, and may not exceed $1,000,000 per year regardless of the budget. The amount of permitted expenditure for an organization is called its "Lobbying Nontaxable Amount." If the limits on this amount are "normally" exceeded by 150 percent, the organization will lose its 501(c)(3) status.

The preceding discussion is a summary of current law, which may change. Details have been omitted. You may wish to consult Internal Revenue Service Publication 557, *Tax Exempt Status for Your Organization*. The Alliance for Justice, located in Washington, D.C., also helps non-profits understand laws governing their advocacy efforts. There are also separate laws in many states that govern the activities and require reporting by any entity that engages in lobbying.

While you should be aware of these laws, don't let them distract you from your mission. Laws are like the rules of a game. They control, to an extent, how you advocate, but they need not and should not affect your long-term goals.

SUMMARY: QUESTION THE INEVITABLE AND CHALLENGE THE INVINCIBLE

David Gil (1998) criticized most frameworks for policy analysis, arguing "that major aspects of prevailing institutional and cultural realities tend to be treated as 'constants' rather than as 'variables'" (pp. 117–118). Gil urges social workers to question contextual factors that most people take for granted. Today these might include the "right" of corporations to make a profit or the inevitability of zero-sum budgeting.[7] Too often, social advocates are stymied by opponents who argue that their proposals would "cost too much money." Keeping their values in sight, social workers can question these inevitables or constants, noting that failure to solve a social problem may ultimately prove more costly, or arguing that the amount spent on humanitarian values is dwarfed (as it is in most community budgets) by the amount committed to economic development or even transportation infrastructure.

---

[7]Zero-sum budgeting assumes that increased funding in one human service area must be offset by reduced funding in another area. In some settings (such as personal budgeting), this approach is appropriate and necessary, but in the complex arena of federal (or even state) budgeting, it can artificially restrict the range of options available for advocates. Along these lines, it was astonishing to witness how quickly after September 11, 2001, Congress found billions of dollars to bail out the airline industry and mount a military response. Prior to the terrorist attacks, a budget request of such magnitude would have faced stiff opposition.

In this chapter we have provided some tools for policy practice, perhaps best summarized as "questioning the inevitable and challenging the invincible." Our examination of the school fee controversy illustrated some important themes in policy practice:

- *The struggle is long.* Social advocates usually strive for extremely high goals such as "the elimination of injustice." We must celebrate the victories and acknowledge the setbacks without losing sight of our long-term objectives.

- *Every individual counts.* Each contribution to an advocacy effort is important and deserves acknowledgment.

- *"Us vs. Them" does not apply here.* There is no evil conspiracy to deprive minorities and disadvantaged Americans of the means to live. Sometimes people take opposing positions, but that does not mean they are enemies. The better you understand the reasons for their position, the more effectively you will be able to address their opposition.

- *Social policy is more than legislation.* It is easy for advocates to focus on getting a bill passed and forget that beyond passage of legislation they must consider regulations created by the executive branch, budgets that limit program services, and judicial opinions that may alter a bill's impact. Effective advocacy happens in all three branches of government.

Beyond these themes, in this chapter we introduced a philosophical view of policy practice as participation in a marketplace of ideas. We discussed Aristotle's suggestion that effective persuasion incorporates *logos, pathos,* and *ethos,* offering specific tactics for advocacy, coalition-building, and client empowerment. We considered ethical issues in policy practice and argued that responsibility for effective debate is shared by the advocate and the audience. The chapter closed with a brief review of major legal considerations governing policy practice by social workers, and with an exhortation to *question the inevitable, and challenge the invincible.*

Advice from Advocates

Be accurate.
Be honest.
Be credible.
Build relationships.
Protect confidences.
Form alliances.
Celebrate victories.
Reframe defeats.

DISCUSSION TOPICS

1. You are the director of a small anti-poverty organization, and you have been invited to join a well-established welfare-rights coalition. After agreeing to join, you find the coalition's tactics are so confrontational that your continued participation risks alienating some of the organizations that have given your organization money. What should you do?

2. A local bank that vigorously (and, you think, unethically) opposed your efforts to increase the supply of affordable housing last year offers to give your organization a significant amount of money for its organizing efforts this year. Would you take the money? Why or why not?

3. The homeless shelter in your town has hired you to do a study of "repeaters"—that is, people who come back to the shelter over and over but don't seem to change their lives. The shelter director sees these people as a problem, and wants to identify them early and keep them out of the shelter. Your results suggest that these "repeaters" tend to have intractable problems, such as substance abuse and mental illness. When you submit your report, the director calls and withdraws his previous invitation for you to present it before the board of directors. What, if anything, should you do?

4. The band director from an inner-city school asks for your advice. The band has been invited to compete in a prestigious contest. The director has enough money to buy new instruments. The band's current instruments are old and dented and cannot produce good music. However, she does not have funds for new uniforms for everyone. She is thinking about asking students to purchase their own uniforms, except for those who cannot afford them. What are her alternatives? What factors should she consider in making her decision?

5. Describe how you would incorporate Aristotle's three components (logos, pathos, and ethos) into a policy presentation on school fees or some other topic of interest to you.

SUGGESTED RESOURCES

Amidei, N. (1991). *So You Want to Make a Difference: Advocacy Is the Key.* Washington, DC: OMB Watch.

Ezell, M. (2001). *Advocacy in the Human Services.* Belmont, CA: Brooks/Cole.

Fisher, R. (1991). *Getting to Yes: Negotiating Agreement Without Giving In.* New York: Penguin.

Hoff, R. (1988). *I Can See You Naked: A Fearless Guide to Making Great Presentations.* Kansas City, MO: Andrews and McMeel.

Schneider, R. L., & Lester, L. (2001). *Social Work Advocacy: A New Framework for Action.* Belmont, CA: Brooks/Cole.

www.advocacy.org—Devoted to "strengthening the capacity of social and economic justice advocates," this site provides selected articles from a related journal "ChangeExchange," and opportunities to order books and network with other advocates.

www.afj.org—The Alliance for Justice strives to "strengthen the public interest community's ability to influence public policy and foster the next generation of advocates."

Their web site offers information about IRS regulations and laws governing non-profits, access to their publications, advocacy alerts, and job announcements.

www.osc.gov—This is the official site of the Office of Special Counsel, an excellent source for information about compliance with the Hatch Act (Reference: 5 U.S.C. chapter 73, subchapter III, as amended; 5 CFR part 734; PL 103-359 Section 501(k)).

www.policy.com—This site is operated by SpeakOut.com, a non-partisan Internet activism portal. With a trendy appearance, the site has "activism centers" that provide news articles on a variety of topics, abstracts of articles, opportunities to chat, and some fun surveys. The site is updated daily.

13

The Future of Social Welfare and Social Work

> The past is never dead.
> It's not even past.
>
> WILLIAM FAULKNER

Today's social work students can expect to practice well into the twenty-first century. Their work will be influenced by threads that extend deep into the history of the United States—threads that have been described throughout this book. Our focus in this chapter will be speculative, as we consider trends, ideas, and politics that are likely to shape social welfare and social work practice.

EMERGING TRENDS

Two emerging trends—globalization and rising inequality—will define the context of social work practice in the decades to come.

GLOBALIZATION

The term "globalization" refers to the flow of capital, labor, technology, and information across national borders. Taking this process to its theoretical extreme would mean that movement across national boundaries had become as easy as movement within a country. This point has not yet been reached; nonetheless, advanced communication and transportation technologies have enhanced the flow of information and goods between countries, and national boundaries have become less significant. Within a global context, the social justice issues we think of as primarily domestic concerns, such as distribution of income and wealth, will assume new depth and require greater sophistication.

Social workers concerned with issues of poverty may well focus on global inequities in the distribution of wealth and income. International organizations such as the United Nations may become major employers of social workers as they attempt to resolve global conflicts and reduce human suffering. The policies of the International Monetary Fund (IMF) and the World Bank may be the focus of mainstream social work advocacy efforts. Finally, the World Trade Organization could become the target of social workers' research and advocacy efforts as social workers, like other Americans, struggle to assess the true impact of the WTO's efforts. These international organizations are discussed below.

THE UNITED NATIONS. The most widely known of the major international organizations, the United Nations (UN), was founded during the aftermath of World War II, on October 24, 1945. The UN's original membership included 51 countries, and its stated purpose was "preserving peace through international cooperation and collective security" (see www.un.org/overview/brief.html). Today, with 189 member nations, the UN includes nearly every country in the world.

The UN is made up of six main entities. Five are located in the UN headquarters in New York. They include the General Assembly, the Security Council, the Economic and Social Council, the Trusteeship Council, and the Secretariat. The sixth entity, the International Court of Justice, is located at The Hague, Netherlands.

The General Assembly serves as a kind of parliament to the UN, with representatives from all member nations. Each nation has one vote, and decisions are made through either simple or two-thirds majority votes. During the Assembly's 2000–2001 session, its representatives considered a wide range of topics, including globalization, nuclear disarmament, development, protection of the environment, and consolidation of new democracies. Assembly decisions are not binding, but do carry the moral authority of the UN.

The Security Council is primarily responsible for maintaining peace and security. It includes 15 members: five permanent members (France, China, the Russian Federation, the United Kingdom, and the United States) and ten elected by the General Assembly for two-year terms. Decisions by the Security Council require nine affirmative votes, and a decision may be vetoed by any one of the five permanent members.

A natural home for future social work practitioners, the Economic and Social Council carries on the UN's economic and social work. The Council addresses issues such as social development, the status of women, crime prevention, drug trafficking, and environmental protection. Its activities are primarily cooperative enterprises with non-governmental organizations (NGOs). This council has 54 members who are elected from the General Assembly for three-year terms. It holds a major conference in July of each year.

The Trusteeship Council meets rarely, as its work is mostly complete. It was formed to provide international supervision to 11 Trust Territories administered by 7 member states. By 1994, all the Trust Territories had become independent or self-governing. The last one to achieve independence was the Trust Territory of the Pacific Islands, administered by the United States.

The Secretariat conducts the work of the United Nations. With a staff of approximately 8,900, the Secretariat maintains its major office in New York, with other locations in Geneva, Vienna, and Nairobi.

The International Court of Justice, also known as the World Court, arbitrates disputes between UN member nations. Nations are not obligated to participate in World Court proceedings, but those who do participate are obligated to comply with the Court's rulings.

The UN promotes the cause of social justice in large part by encouraging political independence of areas formerly under colonial rule. Through its "Declaration on the Granting of Independence to Colonial Countries and Peoples" the UN has focused world opinion and attention on the status of former colonies. Since the UN was founded in 1945, hundreds of millions of people have moved towards independence. In 1945, 750 million people lived in non-self-governing territories. Today, that number is approximately 1.3 million. The UN also led a 30-year campaign to end apartheid in South Africa and held a World Conference Against Racism, Racial Discrimination, Xenophobia, and Related Intolerance in South Africa in September 2001. The United States did not participate in conference deliberations, objecting to the inclusion of the Israeli-Palestinian conflict and reparations for the trans-Atlantic slave trade as agenda items.

To relieve suffering, the UN provides emergency assistance in the wake of natural disasters and environmental emergencies. Humanitarian aid is also provided through UN refugee programs and food assistance.

The United States plays a pivotal role in the activities of the UN, both as a permanent member of the Security Council and as an important source of financial support for UN activities. Not all Americans support this role, and congressional ambivalence about the UN sometimes has taken the form of measures to postpone payment of the nation's dues.

INTERNATIONAL FINANCIAL ORGANIZATIONS. Like the UN, the International Monetary Fund (IMF) was established in the wake of World War II, in 1946. The IMF's purpose is "to promote international monetary cooperation, exchange stability, and orderly exchange arrangements; to foster economic growth and high levels of employment; and to provide temporary financial assistance to countries to help ease the balance of payments adjustment" (see http://www.imf.org/external/about.htm). Most of the nations in the world (a total of 183) belong to the IMF, which provides loans through the World Bank.

The World Bank is a source of development loans to Third World nations. These loans amount to approximately $16 billion each year, and current loans involve over 100 nations. World Bank loans are controversial, as they usually provide financing for major projects such as dams, roads, and power plants.

Critics argue that these development loans enrich the elite while providing only social dislocation to the vulnerable.

Also controversial are the Structural Adjustment Programs (SAPs) that are imposed as conditions for receiving loans. Critics argue that these conditions, which are designed to strengthen free markets in developing nations, actually decrease public investment in social services, education, and health care. SAPs might call, for example, for a nation to reduce its taxes on imported goods and increase interest rates. By opening local markets to imports, tax reductions disadvantage local producers. Similarly, while increased interest rates combat inflation, they make it difficult for small borrowers to secure needed capital.

Although the IMF and the World Bank have "poverty reduction" as a stated goal, both organizations have acknowledged that increased global inequality has accompanied economic globalization. Critics such as Global Exchange have argued that these international financial organizations contribute to inequality by undermining public investment and increasing the wealth of the world's elites.

THE WORLD TRADE ORGANIZATION. The World Trade Organization (WTO) entered the consciousness of most Americans in December 1999, when violence rocked the streets of Seattle. The violence of the Seattle demonstrations may have distracted observers from their fundamental message, which was a critique of the WTO.

The WTO was established in 1994 as a result of a round of negotiations held in Uruguay under the General Agreement on Tariffs and Trade (GATT), as "the only international organization dealing with the global rules of trade between nations. Its main function is to ensure that trade flows as smoothly, predictably, and freely as possible." Representatives of member nations participate in trade negotiations held under the auspices of the WTO, which are then submitted to congresses for domestic ratification (for additional information on this topic, see http://www.wto.org/english/thewto_e/thewto_e.htm#intro).

Critics argue that the ratification of trade agreements should require the two-thirds vote required to ratify international treaties. Instead, the U.S. Congress typically ratifies them by a simple majority vote.

The WTO argues that it strengthens the international economy and breaks down barriers among people by facilitating trade. The WTO has been a fierce advocate for the free market on international levels. Critics argue that the WTO is the agent of international corporations and that it undermines democratic processes. They suggest that the WTO promotes a "race to the bottom" in the areas of labor and environmental protections (see http://www.globalexchange.org/economy/rulemakers/TopTenReasons.html).

RISING INEQUALITY

Fundamental to debates about international financial organizations is the impact of globalization on inequality. The twentieth century was a time of rising inequality throughout the world. The difference between resources consumed by the world's richest countries and those consumed by the poorest grew, particularly during the second half of the century. Similarly, per-capita incomes in the richest nations grew, while the proportion of income received by inhabitants of the world's poorest nations declined during the latter half of the twentieth century. Globalization has been linked to this increasing gap between residents of rich and poor nations (Woodward, 1998). During the same period, however, life expectancies throughout the world increased with the expanded use of public health measures. The increase in life expectancies may support the argument that increased inequality is necessary to produce economic growth that ultimately improves the lives of all, including the disadvantaged.

Just as inequality among nations increased during the twentieth century, inequality among individuals in the United States increased dramatically during the century's last decades. Indeed, inequality in the United States was greater at the beginning of the twenty-first century than it had been since the government began monitoring the income gap in 1947 (Blumberg, 1980). This trend accelerated through the 1980s and persisted (but slowed) during the economic growth of the 1990s. The net effect of the past two decades on family income was to slightly decrease the income of the poor, leave middle-income families with minimal income growth, and to tremendously increase the incomes of the most affluent. As the CBPP reported, "Nationwide, from the late 1970s to the late 1990s, the average income of the lowest-income families fell by over six percent after adjustment for inflation, and the average real income of the middle fifth of families grew by about five percent. By contrast, the average real income of the highest-income fifth of families increased by over 30 percent" (Bernstein et al., 2000, p. vii).

The causes of increased inequality in the United States are not hard to identify. Researchers have documented stagnation in the lower and middle levels of the wage scale, accompanied by tremendous growth in the wages of highly-paid employees (Burtless, 1999; Bernstein et al., 2000). Similarly, economic booms that increase investment income tend to provide benefits to the affluent. Public policy also contributes to inequality. When policy-makers unravel the safety net, fail to raise the minimum wage, or diminish labor protections they further disadvantage low-income Americans. Tax structures at the local, state, and federal levels can accelerate the trend toward greater inequality.

As a result, the United States today is a nation of extremes. In 1999, about 144,000 Americans enjoyed annual incomes in excess of one million dollars, and some reported incomes higher than $100 million (IRS, 1999). As Mantsios (2001) observed, "It would take the average American, earning $34,000 per year, more than 65 lifetimes to earn $100 million" (p. 170). On the other end of the spectrum, 13 percent of Americans, including one-fifth of American children, lived in households with incomes below the federal poverty threshold in 1999 (Mantsios, 2001).

A recent study by the Center on Budget and Policy Priorities (CBPP) reported that "In the United States as a whole, the poorest 20 percent of families had an average income of $12,990 in the late 1990s, while the average income of families in the top 20 percent of the income distribution was $137,490, or more than

10 times as large" (Bernstein et al., 2000, p. ix). By contrast, the comparable ratio in Japan and Germany was 4 to 1 (World Bank, 2000).

The consequences of inequality, as distinguished from the effects of poverty, are difficult to tease out. There is some evidence that inequality has an independent effect on public health. One study reported that mortality and illness are higher in nations with above-average inequality than in those with comparable poverty rates but lower inequality (Burtless, 1999). Growing inequality can also result in greater geographic separation of rich from poor, a factor that contributes to inequalities in housing, public services, and schools (Bernstein et al., 2000). More difficult to measure are the effects of inequality on the cohesiveness of American society. As the wealthy grow unable to fathom the plight of the poor, the poor become less able to believe in the American dream that hard work will pay off.

Michael Harrington once observed that "America has the best-dressed poverty the world has ever known" (1962, pp. 12–13). Those who support the notion that "a rising tide lifts all boats" note that a significant proportion of the nation's poor own televisions, microwaves, and even automobiles. Some note that poor families in the United States have larger living spaces than the average family in Japan. Whether these possessions compensate for the lack of decent schools, safety, and health care is open to discussion.

The philosophical perspectives introduced in Chapter 1 offer distinctive approaches to understanding and responding to inequality. These views, and their implications for the future of public social policy, are discussed below.

IDEAS ABOUT SOCIAL JUSTICE

PHILOSOPHICAL PERSPECTIVES REVISITED

Four major perspectives on social justice were introduced in the first chapter of this book: oligarchy, libertarian, liberal, and socialist. These philosophies are reviewed briefly below, with an emphasis on attitudes toward inequality and implications for government interventions.

The philosophy of oligarchy is fundamentally conservative, holding that one's position in society is either divinely ordained or genetically determined. According to this view, social inequality is inevitable and perhaps even desirable. The government may be called upon to maintain the social order, but it would certainly not be expected to intervene to reduce inequality.

Libertarian views differ considerably with respect to the social order but are similar regarding inequality. Libertarians hold liberty as the highest social value, and their views on social issues consistently reflect that perspective. A rigid social order is anathema to libertarians, but inequality is not. Indeed, some libertarians argue that the presence of extremely rich citizens balances out the power of government, protecting liberty by preventing authoritarian governments. The idea of using government to reduce inequality is incompatible with a libertarian philosophy, as it would inevitably involve the government forcing the rich to give up their property. A student of mine once commented, "Libertarianism is a cold philosophy. It holds that your suffering is an acceptable price to pay for my liberty." While this summary may overstate the case—libertarians are, at least in principle, willing to suffer in defense of liberty—it sometimes rings true as we consider libertarian positions on social issues.

Liberal philosophies offer a contrasting perspective on inequality and the role of government. Contractual liberals emphasize the well-being of society's least-well-off, arguing that inequality is acceptable only to the extent that it enhances the lives of the poor. John Rawls supported the use of government to sustain a "social minimum" for all citizens. Utilitarian liberals reach a similar conclusion through a different route. According to this view, optimizing the well-being of society as a whole requires some redistribution of wealth. Recall that under John Stuart Mill's vision the millionth dollar has less value to a rich man than the hundredth dollar has to a poor man. Thus, the use of government to redistribute that dollar from rich to poor is justified as a vehicle for increasing societal well-being.

Socialists offer a fundamental critique of the free market, arguing that the exploitation of laborers to produce greater wealth for those who hold capital will ultimately result in a rejection of capitalism. A socialist may applaud increased inequality in a capitalist economy, viewing it as the harbinger of a future communist state. On the other hand, a Marxist who adopted a less long-term perspective might find abhorrent the presence of need in an affluent society. He or she might feel some conflict between supporting the downfall of capitalism and trying to meet the immediate needs of those who are suffering.

In the U.S. and worldwide, these philosophical perspectives are evident in debates over the proper role of government and international authorities. The libertarian view is applied by the World Trade Organization, which is organized around the premise that freedom in the marketplace will improve society. A liberal perspective in support of the IMF and World Bank may argue that, while development loans initially increase inequality, they will eventually raise the poor above a minimal level of subsistence. A Marxist viewpoint may be critical of UN relief efforts, suggesting they do little to accomplish the fundamental economic reforms necessary to liberate the working class. In the United States, each of these views has at various times and to varying degrees informed the development of the social welfare system. In the following section we will examine two divergent perspectives on future developments in the U.S. social welfare system.

CAPITALIST AND SOCIALIST VISIONS OF SOCIAL WELFARE

In Western industrialized nations, two dominant economic philosophies offer contrasting interpretations of the social welfare state. The first, "welfare capitalism," takes a capitalist economy as a given and emphasizes the role of social welfare in support of that economy. The role of social policy in this view is to function as "the enabling state," facilitating individual contributions to economic productivity. The second view, "post-industrial socialism," de-emphasizes the role of the market in human life, viewing the social sphere as more important. According to this view, the role of social policy is to facilitate the expansion of the social sphere, thereby liberating modern workers from economic pressures and demands.

THE ENABLING STATE. Gilbert and Gilbert (1989) illustrate the approach of welfare capitalism in one of the most coherent visions of the future of social welfare. Observing that public welfare expenditures leveled off in the 1970s, and noting the growing use of government lending and tax deductions to accomplish the goals of social policy, these authors argue that the welfare state "has been transformed into the *enabling state.*" They suggest that in the enabling state, "social welfare transfers are interlaced throughout the fabric of modern capitalist society" (p. xii). According to this view, public resources should be used to encourage and support private responsibility. In a distinctively American approach, the enabling state would optimize the efficiencies and vitality of the private market while encouraging individual decisions in support of social policy goals. The risk, of course, is that the most vulnerable Americans will be left behind. Noting that "there is a tendency for this movement to dilute protection and aid for the weakest, most disadvantaged members of the community," the Gilberts argue that public policy must "temper the increasing concern for private responsibility with greater tolerance for public purpose" (pp. 185–186).

The enabling state is a fundamentally capitalist view of the role and objectives of government. Government still serves the purposes of the market, and a primary purpose of social policy is to support personal responsibility in the economic sphere of life. A sharply contrasting view is offered by academics who describe themselves as post-industrial socialists.

THE BASIC INCOME. A socialist critique of the welfare state has been offered by Baker (1987), who suggested that "the present welfare state is a compromise which serves many interests. It helps people in need, but it also helps to keep them in their place. It is a system of support but also of control" (p. 10). Thus, the modern welfare state is seen as an agent of inequality and a device for sustaining an exploitative economic system. Socialist critiques extend to the free market, noting that it exploits workers and destroys both the environment and the social cohesion of a nation. The task of socialism, then, is to free the laborer from the market.

Post-industrial socialists advocate expansion of the social sphere of life. As Gorz (1994) explained, "The societal objective of productivity gains must be to bring about a contraction of the sphere governed by economic calculation and an expansion of the self-determined, self-organized spheres of activity in which human facilities can develop freely" (Gorz, 1994, p. 20). According to this view, the technological developments of the twenty-first century could bring about "the end of work-based society" (Little, 1998, p. 19). Indeed, as a central tenet, post-industrial socialism rejects the strong link between work and the resources necessary for survival.

A parallel argument about the impact of the market on the social life of Americans comes in Robert Putnam's book, *Bowling Alone* (2000). In an exhaustive analysis, Putnam argues that recent decades have seen a decline in "civic engagement and social capital." This observation is based on declines in American's participation in a wide range of activities, including political, volunteer, religious, civic, and informal social events. Putnam traces these changes to the dominance of the economic market and "materialism." He goes further, suggesting that they destroy neighborhoods and families, leaving children in jeopardy. Putnam draws an analogy to the end of the nineteenth century, when the "Gilded Age" was marked by dramatic economic growth and threats to social ties. Calling for a return to "social capitalism," Putnam suggests that modern reformers draw inspiration from the early twentieth-century Progressives, who restored to the nation a measure of social commitment. His incremental approach falls short of the more far-reaching proposals of post-industrial socialists to establish a "basic income."

The notion of a "basic income," advanced by neo-Marxists, was actually introduced by Thomas Paine in his work, *Agrarian Justice* (1795). The basic (or citizen's) income is a universal, unconditional benefit provided to all members of a society regardless of their work or household status. Supporters argue that the basic income would enhance productivity, in part by eliminating poverty and its attendant social and physical costs, but also by ensuring that those who choose to work (not to avoid poverty, but to increase their affluence and contribute to society) would be better qualified and more motivated. For example, Offe and colleagues (1996) argued that

> It does not seem too far-fetched to assume that in wealthy industrial societies, employees who are accorded the right to withdraw from paid work without penalty and at the cost of only loss of income (but not poverty!) will as a result be better motivated, better qualified, and in a better physical and psychic condition to engage in it (for then they would be choosing it 'voluntarily') than those from whom this choice is withheld, and who must consequently work knowing that nonengagement in paid work (or the failure of an attempted engagement in it) carries the threat of material need and social stigma (p. 219).

Some, like Gorz (1985) and Atkinson (1996) have argued that a basic income is not sufficient to restore equity and community to post-industrial societies. Gorz suggests that, in addition to a more equitable distribution of income, society should provide an equitable distribution of the opportunity to contribute through work. In Gorz's view, an overall reduction in the number of hours worked should accompany the basic income to ensure that no one who is willing to work lacks the opportunity. In another variation on the basic income proposal, Atkinson (1996) suggested that some kind of "social contribution" be the condition for receiving the benefit. This contribution might entail being a good parent, a skilled artist, or an educated voter. Thus, rather than a "basic" income, the social welfare system would provide a "participation benefit."

Welfare capitalism and post-industrial socialism offer sharply contrasting visions. Certainly the enabling state is most compatible with the realities of twentieth-century America. But the new century will offer new opportunities, even as it demands new visions. Social workers may apply the notion of a basic income in their efforts to advance the cause of social justice. Of course, the practicality of any social welfare proposals will be largely determined by political realities.

SUMMARY: CHANGING POLITICS

The end of the twentieth century brought Americans a renewed enthusiasm for capitalism. The dissolution of the Soviet Union, the opening of Chinese markets, and the longest peacetime economic expansion in U.S. history all seemed to signal a victory for the nation's dominant economic philosophy. This victory may have quieted the American left, and it certainly gave impetus to what some consider the "third wave" of American conservatism. With the 1994 election of a Republican majority in the House of Representatives, the nation seemed poised for a return to the laissez-faire politics of the nineteenth century. The Republican revolution was short-lived, however, and the "compassionate conservatism" of the current presidential administration sounds remarkably like early twentieth-century Progressivism. George W. Bush's 2001 inaugural address is illustrative:

> While many of our citizens prosper, others doubt the promise—even the justice—of our own country. The ambitions of some Americans are limited by failing schools and hidden prejudice, and the circumstances of their birth. And sometimes our differences run so deep, it seems we share a continent, but not a country.
>
> We do not accept this and will not allow it. Our unity, our union, is the serious work of leaders and citizens in every generation. And this is my solemn pledge: I will work to build a single nation of justice and opportunity. . . .
>
> In the quiet of American conscience, we know that deep, persistent poverty is unworthy of our nation's promise. And whatever our views of its cause, we can agree that children at risk are not at fault. Abandonment and abuse are not acts of God, they are failures of love. . . .
>
> Where there is suffering, there is duty. Americans in need are not strangers, they are citizens; not problems, but priorities; and all of us are diminished when any are hopeless.

The President's rhetoric seems to recognize the problems of the disadvantaged and to promise steps to advance social justice. His use of this rhetoric may not predict his future decisions, but it does suggest that he recognizes the power and attraction these ideas hold for the American electorate. Indeed, it may indicate, as E. J. Dionne (1996) argued, that American Progressives "only look dead."

Dionne, like Putnam, drew analogies between this turn of the century and the last. He suggested that during the economic transformation of the early twenty-first century Americans will look to a new Progressivism to restore a balance between the economic and the social spheres of life. Dionne articulated a clear agenda for the New Progressives: "to succeed, a New Progressivism must be genuinely and not simply rhetorically new. Its task is to restore the legitimacy of public life by renewing the effectiveness of government and reforming the workings of politics . . . The New Progressives are those who accept the need to make another large economic transition, but know that the transition will be successful only if government acts creatively, and with a strong concern for social justice" (pp. 16, 277). Dionne's charge to Progressives may be equally relevant to social work professionals.

CALL TO ACTION

On September 11, 2001, American awareness of global issues was forever changed by the murder of thousands of civilians. Terrorists attacked the citadels of U.S. economic and military power in a gesture of hatred unlike any the world had ever witnessed. Our nation's struggle to understand and respond to these attacks highlights many of the issues we have explored in this book. Some will attribute the violence to the "evil" tenets of Islamic fundamentalism. They will label Muslims and Arabs "other" and use this as an excuse for oppression. But those who look beyond simple explanations will find themselves reflecting on what social justice means in a global context, asking whether rich nations—out of "enlightened self-interest," if nothing else—have an obligation to meet the basic needs of the world's disadvantaged. They will ask whether the United States can responsibly withdraw from any international dialogue on oppression or social justice.

Speaking to the realities of a new century will require social workers to become conversant not only with the traditional programs and policies of social welfare, but also with domestic tax and financial policies and with global debates about independence and accommodation. We must look beyond labels and rhetoric. We must offer a vision of social welfare that is compatible with economic and political conditions, even as it advances the cause of social justice. We can draw inspiration from the Progressives of the past, but we must forge our own path, which will require unprecedented ingenuity. Our success will be measured on individual and global scales, as we work to eliminate the *causes* of hatred and build a world that offers "liberty and justice for all."

DISCUSSION TOPICS

1. Noting that most of the poor in the U.S. have living space that is larger than that of the average Japanese family, some would argue that America's poor are not disadvantaged. Do you agree or disagree with this statement? Why?

2. The twentieth century was marked by rising inequality, both globally and within the United States. Yet life expectancies and, some would argue, the quality of life of the disadvantaged increased during this period. Does this improvement support the notion that inequality is the necessary price for expanding the economic pie? What are the implications of this observation for economic policies aimed at redistributing the nation's wealth?

3. Do you think the "enabling state" accurately describes the role of the U.S. government in social welfare? Why or why not?

4. Dionne (1996) suggested that it is important for the New Progressives to "embrace the dual concepts of freedom and community." What does this statement mean? Are freedom and community compatible? Does community membership entail responsibilities and roles that limit individual freedom?

SUGGESTED RESOURCES

Loeb, P. R. (1999). *Soul of a Citizen: Living with Conviction in a Cynical Time.* New York: St. Martin's Griffin.

www.un.org — The web site of the United Nations offers a wealth of information about international issues, as well as links to other international organizations.

www.imf.org — This site is maintained by the International Monetary Fund. In addition to a description of IMF activities, it provides research and statistics about economic issues and a link to The World Bank's site (**www.worldbank.org**).

www.wto.org — This site provides a fairly one-sided look at the mission and activities of the World Trade Organization.

www.globalexchange.org — For a critical look at the activities of the IMF and the World Bank, visit this site, which is maintained by a human rights organization called Global Exchange. Founded in 1988 in San Francisco, Global Exchange is designed to increase global awareness in the United States.

References

Abramowitz, M. (1996). *Regulating the Lives of Women: Social Welfare Policy from Colonial Times to the Present*. Boston: South End Press.

Achenbaum, W. A. (1978). *Old Age in the New Land: The American Experience Since 1790*. Baltimore: Johns Hopkins University Press.

Achenbaum, W. A. (1986). *Social Security: Visions and Revisions*. Cambridge: Cambridge University Press.

Administration on Aging. (1997). Age discrimination: A pervasive and damaging influence (http://www.aoa.gov/factsheets/ageism.html).*

Administration on Aging. (1999). *Aging into the Twenty-First Century* (http://www.aoa.dhhs.gov/aoa/stats/aging21/health.html).

Administration on Aging. (2001). Older Americans Act Appropriation Information (http://www.aoa.gov/oaa/oaaapp.html).

Alecxih, L., & Kennell, D. (1994). *The Economic Impact of Long-Term Care on Individuals*. Washington, DC: HHS (http://aspe.dhhs.gov/daltcp/reports/ecoimpes.htm).

Alinsky, S. (1972). *Rules for Radicals: A Pragmatic Primer for Realistic Radicals*. New York: Random House.

Allard, M. A., Albelda, R., Colten, M. E., & Cosenza, C. (1997). *In Harm's Way? Domestic Violence, AFDC Receipt, and Welfare Reform in Massachusetts*. A Report from the University of Massachusetts, Boston.

Altmeyer, A. J. (1963). The Development and Status of Social Security in America. In G. G. Somers (Ed.), *Labor, Management and Social Policy: Essays in the John R. Commons Tradition*. University of Wisconsin Press (http://www.ssa.gov/history/aja1963.html).

Amato, P. R., & Zuo, J. (1992). Rural poverty, urban poverty and psychological well-being. *Sociological Quarterly, 33*(2): 229–240.

American Association of Retired Persons. (1993*). The AARP Public Policy Agenda, 1993: Toward a Just and Caring Society*. Washington, DC: AARP.

American Civil Liberties Union. (1996). *English Only: ACLU Briefing Paper* (http://www.aclu.org/library/pbp6.html).

American Psychiatric Association. (1990). *Psychiatry and Homeless Mentally Ill Persons. Report of the Task Force on the Homeless Mentally Ill*. Washington, DC: American Psychiatric Association.

Amidei, N. (1991). *So You Want to Make a Difference: Advocacy Is the Key*. Washington, DC: OMB Watch.

Anderson, G. F. (1998). Multinational comparisons of health care: Expenditures, coverage, and outcomes (http://www.cmwf.org/programs/international/ihp_1998_multicompsurvey_299.asp).

Appelbaum, P. S. (1994). *Almost a Revolution: Mental Health Law and the Limits of Change*. New York: Oxford University Press.

Applebaum, R. P. (1989, May–June) The affordability gap. *Society, 26*(4): 6–8.

---

* Addresses of web sites mentioned in this text may have changed since the manuscript was written.

Aries, P. (1962). *Centuries of Childhood: A Social History of Family Life.* (Translated by Robert Baldick.) New York: Vintage Books.

Aristotle. From Chapter V of *Aristotle's Ethics for English Readers*, rendered from the Greek of the *Nicomachaen Ethics* by H. Rackham (1943). Reprinted with permission in Sterba, 1980.

Atkinson, A. (1996, Jan.–March). The case for a participation income. *Political Quarterly, 67*(1).

Badgett, L., Donnelly, C. & Kibbe, J. (1992). *Pervasive patterns of discrimination against lesbians and gay men: Evidence from surveys Across the United States.* New York: National Gay and Lesbian Task Force.

Baker, J. (1987). *Arguing for Equality.* London & New York: Verso.

Ball, H. (2000). *The Bakke Case: Race, Education and Affirmative Action.* Topeka: University Press of Kansas.

Ball, R. M. (1996). Medicare's roots: What Medicare's architects had in mind. *Generations, 20*(2): 13–18.

Banfield, E. C. (1968). *The Unheavenly City.* Boston: Little, Brown.

Barnes, K. (1984, Nov.). Battles in Medicaid: Patients win access to quality care. *Dollars and Sense, 101:* 12–14.

Barnett, W. (1973). *Sexual Freedom and the Constitution.* Albuquerque: University of New Mexico Press.

Barusch, A. S. (1994). *Older Women in Poverty: Private Lives and Public Policies.* New York: Springer Publishing Company.

Barusch, A. S. (1995). Programming for family care: Mandates, incentives and rationing. *Social Work, 40*(3): 315–322.

Bass, S. A., Caro, F. G., & Chen, Y. (Eds.). (1993). *Achieving a Productive Aging Society.* Westport, CT: Greenwood Publishing Group.

Bean, F., & Tienda, M. (1987). *The Hispanic Population of the United States.* New York: Russell Sage.

Beard, J. H., Propst, R. N., & Malamud, T. J. (1982). The Fountain House model of psychiatric rehabilitation. *Psychosocial Rehabilitation Journal, 5:* 47–53.

Beers, C. W. (1908). *A Mind that Found Itself: An Autobiography.* Garden City, NJ: Doubleday, Doran, and Co.

Bell, L. A. (1997). Theoretical foundations for social justice education. In M. Adams, L. A. Bell, & P. Griffin (Eds.), *Teaching for Diversity and Social Justice: A Sourcebook.* New York: Routledge.

Belle, D. (1984). Inequality and mental health: Low-income and minority women. In L. E. Walker (Eds.). *Women and Mental Health Policy* (pp. 135–150). Beverly Hills, CA: Sage.

Bergmann, B. R. (1971). The effect on white incomes of discrimination in employment. *Journal of Political Economy, 79:* 294–313.

Berkowitz, E. D. (2000). *Disability Policy and History: Statement before the Subcommittee on Social Security of the Committee on Ways and Means.* (July 13, 2000) (http://www.ssa.gov/history/edberkdib.html).

Bernstein, J., McNichol, E., Mishel, L., & Zahradnik, R. (2000). *Pulling Apart: A State-by-State Analysis of Income Trends.* Washington, DC: Center on Budget and Policy Priorities. Economic Policy Institute (http://www.cbpp.org/1-18-00sfp-part1.pdf).

Binstock, R. H. (1983). The aged as scapegoat. *The Gerontologist, 23:* 136–143.

Binstock, R. H. (1985). Perspectives on measuring hardship: Concepts, dimensions, and implications. *The Gerontologist, 26:* 60–62.

Binstock, R. H., & Post, S. G. (Eds.). (1991). *Too Old for Health Care? Controversies in Medicine, Law, and Ethics.* Baltimore: Johns Hopkins Press.

Blau, J. R., & Blau, P. M. (1982). The cost of inequality: Metropolitan structure and violent crime. *American Sociological Review, 47:* 114–129.

Blumberg, P. (1980). *Inequality in an Age of Decline.* New York: Oxford University Press.

Blumenthal, S., & Knupter, D. J. (1988). Overview of early detection and treatment strategies for suicidal behavior in young people. *Journal of Youth and Adolescence, 17*(1): 1–23.

Bould, S., Sanborn, B., & Reif, L. (1989). *Eighty-five Plus: The Oldest Old.* Belmont, CA: Wadsworth.

Bouma, D. H., & Hoffman, J. (1968). *The Dynamics of School Integration: Problems and Approaches in a Northern City*. Grand Rapids, MI: Eardmans.

Brace, C. L. (1872). *The Dangerous Classes of New York and Twenty Years' Work Among Them*. New York: Wynkoop & Hallenbeck Publishers. (Reprinted in 1973 by NASW Press.)

Bremner, R. H. (Ed.). (1970). *Children and Youth in America: A Documentary History, 1600–1865*. (Vol. 1). Cambridge, MA: Harvard University Press. (Cited by Watkins, 1990.)

Brody, E. M. (1971). Aging. In *The Encyclopedia of Social Work* (pp. 55–77). New York: National Association of Social Workers Press.

Brown, R. S., Clement, D. G., Hill, J. W., Retchin, S. M., & Bergeron, J. W. (1993). Do health maintenance organizations work for Medicare? *Health Care Financing Review, 15*(1): 7–23.

Brown, T. J. (1998). *Dorothea Dix: New England Reformer*. Cambridge, MA: Harvard University Press.

Burt, M. (1992). *Over the Edge: The Growth of Homelessness in the 1980s*. New York: Russell Sage Foundation.

Burtless, G. (1999). Growing income inequality: Sources and remedies. In H. J. Aaron & R. D. Reischauer (Eds.), *Setting National Priorities: The 2000 Election and Beyond*. Washington, DC: Brookings Institution Press.

Burtless, G., & Saks, D. (1984). The Decline in Insured Unemployment During the 1980s. Unpublished Brookings Institution Report to the Department of Labor, March. (Cited by McMurrer & Chasanov, 1995).

Burton, C. E. (1992). *The Poverty Debate: Politics and the Poor in America*. Westport, CT: Greenwood Press.

Butler, R. N., Oberlink, M. R., Schechter, M. (Eds.). (1990). *Promise of Productive Aging: From Biology to Social Policy*. New York: Springer.

Butler, S., Lave, J., & Reuschauer, R. D. (1998). *Medicare: Preparing for the Challenges of the 21st Century*. Washington, DC: National Academy of Social Insurance. (Distributed by Brookings Institution Press.)

Caffey, J. (1946). Multiple fractures in the long bones of infants suffering from chronic subdural hematoma. *American Journal of Roentgenology, 56:* 163–173.

Callahan, D. (1987). *Setting Limits: Medical Goals in an Aging Society*. New York: Simon & Schuster.

Callahan, D. (1990). *What Kind of Life: The Limits of Medical Progress*. New York: Simon & Schuster.

Camejo, P. (1976). *Racism, Revolution, Reaction, 1861–1877: The Rise and Fall of Radical Reconstruction*. New York: Monad.

Caputo, R. K. (1998). Discrimination and pension income among aging women. *Journal of Aging and Social Policy, 10*(2): 67–83.

Castner, L., & Cody, S. (1999). *Trends in FSP Participation Rates: Focus on September 1999* (http://www.fns.usda.gov/oane/MENU/published/FSP/FILES/trends97.pdf).

Center for Education Reform. (1999). *Frequently Asked Questions About School Choice* (http://www.edreform.com/faq/faqsc.htm).

Center on Budget and Policy Priorities. (2001*). Poverty Rates Fell in 2000 as Unemployment Reached 31-Year Low* (http://www.cbpp.org/9-26-00pov.htm).

Centers for Disease Control. (1995, April 21). Suicide among children, adolescents, and young adults—United States, 1980–1992. *MMWR Weekly, 44*(15): 289–291 (http://www.cdc.gov/epo/mmwr/preview/mmwrhtml/00036818.html).

Centers for Disease Control. (1999, Aug. 27). Progress towards the elimination of tuberculosis—United States, 1999. *MMWR Weekly, 48*(33): 732–736 (http://www.cdc.gov/epo/mmwr/preview/mmwrhtml/mm4833a2.htm).

Cerne, F. (1995, Mar. 20). Streetwise. *Hospitals and Health Networks,* 38–46.

Chalfant, H. P. (1985). *Sociology of Poverty in the Unites States: An Annotated Bibliography*. Westport, CT: Greenwood Press.

Chamberlain, E. (1994, Nov./Dec.) Blues for single-payer. *The Humanist, 54*(6): 3–7.

Chambers, D. E. (1982). The U.S. Poverty Line: A time for change. *Social Work, 27*(4): 354–358.

Chavez, L. (1991). *Out of the Barrio: Toward a New Politics of Hispanic Assimilation.* New York: Basic Books.

Child Welfare League of America. (1997). *Breaking the Link Between Child Maltreatment and Juvenile Delinquency.* Washington, DC: CWLA.

Chinn, T., Lai, H. J., & Choy, P. (1969). *A History of the Chinese in California.* San Francisco: Chinese Historical Society of America.

Citrin, J., Reingold, B., Walters, E., & Green, D. P. (1990). The Official English Movement and the symbolic politics of language in the United States. *Western Political Quarterly, 43*(3): 553–560.

Clement, M. (1997). *The Juvenile Justice System: Law and Process.* Boston, MA: Butterworth-Heinemann.

Close Up Foundation. (1998). U.S. Immigration Policy (http://www.closeup.org/immigrat.htm).

Coalition on Human Needs. (2000). Earned Income Tax Credit (EITC) (http://www.chn.org/eitc/ib-eitc.htm).

Cohen, W. S. (1994). *Tax Dollars Aiding and Abetting Addiction: Social Security Disability and SSI Cash Benefits to Drug Addicts and Alcoholics.* Investigative Staff Report of the Minority Staff of the Senate Special Committee on Aging.

Compassion in Dying v. State of Washington. (1995). United States Court of Appeals for the Ninth Circuit Opinion (http://www.rights.org/~deathnet/ninth_circ.html).

Comstock. D. (1991). *Violence Against Lesbians and Gay Men.* New York: Columbia University Press.

Conger, R., Elder, G. H., Lorenz, F. O., Simons, R. L., & Whitbeck, L. B. (1994). *Families in Troubled Times: Adapting to Change in Rural America.* New York: Aldine De Gruyter.

Congressional Black Congress. (1999). Open letter to Senator Trent Lott (http://www.cjcj.org/254/cbcletter.html).

Congressional Budget Office. (1990). *Sources of Support for Adolescent Mothers.* Washington, DC: CBO.

Congressional Budget Office. (2001). *An Analysis of the President's Budgetary Proposals for FY 2001* (http://www.cbo.gov/showdoc.cfm?index=1908&sequence=3&from=5).

Conrad, P. (1986, Summer). The social meaning of AIDS. *Social Policy 17*(1): 51–56.

Cook, D. (1989). *Rich Law, Poor Law.* Philadelphia, PA: Open University Press.

Cook, F. L. (1996). Can Public Support for Programs for Older Americans Survive? (http://www.northwestern.edu/IPR/publications/nupr/nuprv01n1/cook.html).

Corbett, E. P. J. (1965). *Classical Rhetoric for the Modern Student.* New York: Oxford University Press.

Corson, W., & Nicholson, W. (1988). *An Examination of Declining UI Claims during the 1980s.* Unemployment Insurance Occasional Paper 88-3 (U.S. Department of Labor).

Costin, L. B. (1992). Cruelty to children: A dormant issue and its rediscovery, 1920–1960. *Social Service Review, 66:* 177–198.

Cox, J. (1997). *The Ugly Truth About the Minimum Wage* (http://www.self-gov.org/cox02.html).

Cox, M. W. (1994). *Make Adoption Policies Colorblind* (http://majorcox.com/columns/adoption.htm).

Cox, O. (1970). *Caste, Class, and Race: A Study in Social Dynamics.* New York: Monthly Review Press.

Crain, R. L. (1968). *The Politics of Desegregation: Comparative Case Studies of Community Structure and Policy-Making.* Chicago: Aldine Publishing Co.

Crawford, J. (1992). *Language Loyalties: A Sourcebook on the Official English Controversy.* Chicago: University of Chicago Press.

Crawford, J. (1996). Anatomy of the English-only movement: Social and ideological sources of language restrictionism in the United States. *Conference on Language Legislation and Linguistic Rights.* University of Illinois at Urbana-Champaign (http://ourworld.compuserve.com/homepages/JWCRAWFORD/anatomy.htm).

Crim, B. (1994). *Sometimes You Need a Hammer: An Unfinished Story of Social Advocacy and Equal Educational Opportunity in Utah.* Salt Lake City: Utah Issues.

Crumbley, J. (1999). *Transracial Adoption and Foster Care: Practice Issues for Professionals.* Washington, DC: Child Welfare League of America.

Crystal, S., Harmon, J., & Sambamoorthi, U. (2000). *Out-of-Pocket Health Care Costs Among Older Americans.* Washington, DC: The Urban Institute (http://ur.rutgers.edu/medrel/pocketcosts/pocketshort.html).

Crystal, S., & Shea, D. (1990). Cumulative advantage, cumulative disadvantage, and inequality among elderly people. *The Gerontologist, 30:* 437–443.

Curcio, W. (1996). *The Passaic County Study of AFDC Recipients in a Welfare to Work Program: A Preliminary Analysis.* Passaic County, NJ: Passaic County Board of Social Services.

Dalaker, J. & Naifeh, M. (1997). U.S. Bureau of the Census, Current Population reports, Series P60–201. *Poverty in the United States: 1997.* Washington, DC: U.S. Government Printing Office.

Dalton, H. (1925). *Some Aspects of Inequality of Incomes in Modern Communities.* London: Routledge.

Damerell, R. G. (1968). *Triumph in a White Suburb: The Dramatic Story of Teaneck, N.J., the First Town in the Nation to Vote for Integrated Schools.* New York: Morrow.

Daniel, P. (1972). *The Shadow of Slavery: Peonage in the South, 1901–1969.* Chicago: University of Illinois Press.

Daniels, H. (1988). *Am I My Parents' Keeper? An Essay on Justice Between the Young and the Old.* New York: Oxford University Press.

Daniels, R., & Kitano, H. H. L. (1970). *American Racism: Exploration of the Nature of Prejudice.* Englewood Cliffs, NJ: Prentice-Hall.

Davidson, L. & Linnoila, M. (1992). Risk factors for youth suicide. *International Social Work, 35*(1): 91–93.

Davis, K., & Moore, W. E. (1967). Some principles of stratification. In R. Bendix & S. M. Lipset, *Class, Status and Power: Social Stratification in Comparative Perspective* (2nd ed.). London: Routledge.

Day, D. (1979). *The Adoption of Black Children: Counteracting Institutional Discrimination.* Lexington: Lexington Books.

Derezotes, D. (2000). Personal Communication. Professor, Graduate School of Social Work, University of Utah.

Derlet, R. W., & Kinser, D. (1994, Sept. 29). Access of Medicaid recipients to outpatient care. *New England Journal of Medicine, 331*(13): 877–878.

DeRosier, A. H. (1970). *The Removal of the Choctaw Indians.* Knoxville: University of Tennessee Press.

De Swaan, A. (1988). *In Care of the State: Health Care, Education, and Welfare in Europe and the U.S.A. in the Modern Era.* New York: Oxford University Press.

De Tocqueville, A. (1835). *Democracy in America,* Vols. I and II. Reprinted in 1996 in New York by Harper & Row.

Diaz, E. (1991, Dec./Jan.). Public policy, women, and HIV disease. *SIECUS Report,* pp. 4–5.

DiFonzo, J. H. (1997). *Beneath the Fault Line: The Popular and Legal Culture of Divorce in Twentieth-Century America.* Charlottesville, VA: University Press of Virginia.

DiNitto, D. M. (1995). *Social Welfare: Politics and Public Policy* (4th ed.). Needham Heights, MA: Allyn & Bacon.

Dionne, E. J. (1996). *They Only Look Dead: Why Progressives Will Dominate the Next Political Era.* New York: Simon & Schuster.

Dobash, R. E., & Dobash, R. P. (1992). *Women, Violence and Social Change.* London & New York: Routledge Press.

Dohrenwend, B. P. (1990). Socioeconomic status (SES) and psychiatric disorders: Are the issues still compelling? *Social Psychiatry and Psychiatric Epidemiology, 25:* 4–47.

Dolger, H., & Seeman, B. (1985). *How to Live with Diabetes* (5th ed.). New York: Norton.

Douglass, D. (1997). Taking the initiative: Anti-homosexual propaganda of the Oregon Citizens' Alliance. In S. L. Witt & S. McCorkle (Eds.), *Anti-Gay Rights: Assessing Voter Initiatives* (pp. 3–32). Westport, CT: Praeger.

Dreyfuss, R. (1996, May–June). The biggest deal: Lobbying to take Social Security private. *American Prospect, 26:* 72–75.

Duster, T. (1996). Individual fairness, group preferences, and the California strategy. *Representations, 55:* 41–58.

Dworak, R. J. (1980). *Taxpayers, Taxes, and Government Spending: Perspectives on the Taxpayer Revolt.* New York: Praeger.

Dye, T. R., & Ziegler, L. H. (1996). *The Irony of Democracy: An Uncommon Introduction to American Politics.* Belmont, CA: Wadsworth.

Eaton, W. W. (1985). *Epidemiologic Field Methods in Psychiatry: The NIMH Epidemiological Catchment Area Program.* Orlando, FL: Academic Press.

Education Data Partnership. (2001). *EdFact: A Primer on School Finance* (http://www.ed-data.k12.ca.us/Finance/SF_Prime2.asp).

Ehrlichman, J. D. (1982). *Witness to Power: The Nixon Years.* New York: Simon and Schuster.

Eisenberg, J. (1995). Economics. *Journal of the American Medical Association, 273* (21): 1670–1671.

Eskridge, W. N. (1999). *Gaylaw: Challenging the Apartheid of the Closet.* Cambridge: Harvard University Press.

Estes, C. (1981). *The Aging Enterprise.* San Francisco, CA: Jossey-Bass.

Estes, C. L., Swan, J. H., & Associates. (1993). *The Long-Term Care Crisis: Elders Trapped in the No-Care Zone.* Newbury Park, CA: Sage Publications.

Euthanasia Research and Guidance Organization. (1998). *Dr. Jack Kevorkian* (http://www.efn.org/~ergo/dr.k.html).

Evan, W. E., & Macpherson, D. (1994). *Trends in Individual and Household Pension Coverage. Final Report Submitted to Department of Labor.* Contract No. 41USC252C3 (available online: http://www.sba.muohio.edu/evenwe/res%20papers/trends%20in%20ind%20and%20hh.pdf).

Eysenck, H. J. (1973). *The Inequality of Man.* London: Temple Smith.

Ezell, M. (2001). *Advocacy in the Human Services.* Belmont, CA: Brooks/Cole.

Ezorsky, G. (1991). *Racism and Justice: The Case for Affirmative Action.* Ithaca, NY: Cornell University Press.

Families USA. (1995). *Hurting Real People: The Human Impact of Medicaid Cuts.* Washington, DC: Families USA (http://epn.org/families/fahurt.html).

Fanshel, D., & Shinn, E. B. (1978). *Children in Foster Care: A Longitudinal Investigation.* New York: Columbia University Press.

Farmer, P. (1996). Social inequalities and emerging infectious diseases. *Emerging Infectious Diseases, 2* (4): 259–271.

Federal Bureau of Investigation. (1999). *Crime in the United States: 1998.* Washington, DC: FBI, U.S. Department of Justice.

Fee, E., & Porter, D. (1991). Public health, preventive medicine, and professionalization: Britain and the United States in the nineteenth century. In E. B. Fee & R. M. Acheson (Eds.), *A History of Education in Public Health: Health That Mocks the Doctors' Rules.* Oxford: Oxford University Press.

Feinson, M. C. (1991). Reexamining some common beliefs about mental health and aging. In B. B. Hess & E. W. Markson (Eds.), *Growing Old in America* (4th ed.) (pp. 125–136). New Brunswick: Transaction.

Feld, B. C. (1999). *Bad Kids: Race and the Transformation of the Juvenile Court.* New York: Oxford University Press.

Fields, B. (1982). Ideology and Race in American History. In J. M. Kousser and J. M. McPherson (Eds.), *Region, Race, and Reconstruction: Essays in Honor of C. Vann Woodward* (pp. 143–177). New York: Oxford University Press.

Fischer, D. H. (1977). *Growing Old in America.* New York: Oxford University Press.

Fischer, L. R., & Eustis, N. N. (1989). Quicker and sicker: How changes in Medicare affect the elderly and their families. *Journal of Geriatric Psychiatry, 22*(2): 163–191.

Fisher, G. M. (1997, Spring). Setting American standards of poverty; A look back. *Focus* [newsletter of the Institute for Research on Poverty], *19*(2): 47–52 (http://www.ssc.wisc.edu/irp/pubs/foc192.pdf).

Fisher, W. F. (1987). *Human Communication as Narration: Toward a Philosophy of Reason, Value, and Action*. Columbia, SC: University of South Carolina Press.

Flaks, D. K., Ficher, I., Masterpasqua, F., & Joseph, G. (1995). Lesbians choosing motherhood: A comparative study of lesbian and heterosexual parents. *Developmental Psychology, 31:* 105–114.

Fleury, R. E., Sullivan, C.M., Bybee, D.I., & Davidson, W.S. (1998). "Why don't they just call the cops?" Reasons for differential police contact among women with abusive partners. *Violence and Victims, 13*(4): 333–346.

Flora, P. (Ed.). (1983). *State, Economy, and Society in Western Europe, 1815–1975: A Data Handbook. Vol. I: The Growth of Mass Democracies and Welfare States*. Frankfurt: Campus Verlag.

Flora, P., & Heidenheimer, A. J. (Eds.). (1981). *The Development of Welfare States in Europe and America*. New Brunswick and London: Transaction.

Foner, P. S. (1981). *Organized Labor and the Black Worker, 1619–1981*. New York: International Publishers.

Fordyce, E. J. (1996, Apr.–June). Urban mortality: Race or place? *Statistical Bulletin, 77*(2): 2–10.

Fox, M., & Passel, J. S. (1994). *Immigration and Immigrants: Setting the Records Straight*. Washington, DC: Urban Institute (http://www.urban.org).

Fraikor, A. L. (1973). *An anthropological analysis of Tay-Sachs disease: Genetic drift among the Ashkenazim Jews*. Boulder, CO: University of Colorado Press.

Freeman, J. (1991). How "sex" got into Title VII: Persistent opportunism as a maker of public policy. *Law and Inequality: A Journal of Theory and Practice*, pp. 163–184.

Friedman, M. (1955). The role of government in education. In Robert A. Solo (Ed.), *Economics and the Public Interest*. Princeton, NJ: Trustees of Rutgers College.

Friedman, M. S. (1960). *Martin Buber: The Life of Dialogue*. New York: Harper Torchbook.

Friedman, M. (1962). Excerpt from *Capitalism and Freedom* reprinted with permission in Sterba, 1980.

Friedman, M., & Friedman, R. (1979). *Free to Choose*. New York: Harcourt Brace Jovanovich.

Friends Committee on National Legislation. (1987, Aug./Sept.). With all due respect to the "founding fathers": Indian contributions to the U.S. Constitution. *Indian Report* (http://www.fcnl.org).

Funiciello, T. (1993). *Tyranny of Kindness: Dismantling the Welfare System to End Poverty in America*. New York: The Atlantic Monthly Press.

Galas, J. (1996). *Gay Rights*. San Diego, CA: Lucent Books.

Galbraith, J. K. (1958). *The Affluent Society*. Boston: Houghton Mifflin.

Gans, H. (1971, July–Aug.). The uses of poverty: The poor pay all. *Social Policy, 2*(2): 20–24.

Garfinkel, I. (1992). Child-support trends in the U.S. In L. J. Weitzman & M. MacLean (Eds.), *Economic Consequences of Divorce: The International Perspective* (pp. 205–218). New York: Oxford University Press.

Garfinkel, I. (1992a). *Assuring Child Support: An Extension of Social Security*. New York: Russell Sage Foundation.

Garrett, L. (1994). The Coming Plague: Newly Emerging Diseases in a World Out of Balance. New York: Farrar, Straus & Giroux.

Gelfand, D. E. (1988). *The Aging Network: Programs and Services*. New York: Springer.

George, C. (2000). *Life Under the Jim Crow Laws*. San Diego, CA: Lucent Books.

George, R. M., & Lee, B. J. (1997). Abuse and neglect of children. In R. A. Maynard (Ed.), *Kids Having Kids: Economic Costs and Social Consequences of Teen Pregnancy* (pp. 181–203). Washington, DC: The Urban Institute Press.

Gibelman, M., & Schervish, P. H. (1995). Pay equity in social work: Not! *Social Work, 40*(5): 622–629.

Gibelman, M., & Schervish, P. H. (1997). *Who We Are: A Second Look*. Washington, DC: NASW Press.

Gil, D. G. (1998). *Confronting Injustice and Oppression: Concepts and Strategies for Social Workers*. New York: Columbia University Press.

Gilbert, N., & Gilbert, B. (1989). *The Enabling State: Modern Welfare Capitalism in America*. New York: Oxford University Press.

Gilder, G. (1981). *Wealth and Poverty*. New York: Basic Books.

Gilovich, T. (1991). *How We Know What Isn't So: The Fallibility of Human Reason in Everyday Life*. New York: Free Press.

Gohmann, S. F., & McClure, J. E. (1987). Supreme Court rulings on pension plans: The effect on retirement age and wealth of single people. *The Gerontologist, 27:* 471–477.

Goldberg, D. T. (1993). *Racist Culture: Philosophy and the Politics of Meaning*. Cambridge, MA: Blackwell.

Good, H. G. (1962). *A History of American Education* (2nd ed.). New York: Macmillan.

Gordon, M. (1964). *Assimilation in American Life: The Role of Race, Religion, and National Origins*. New York: Oxford University Press.

Gorz, A. (1985). *Paths to Paradise: On the Liberation from Work*. London: Pluto Press.

Gorz, A. (1994). *Capitalism, Socialism, Ecology*. London: Verso.

Gossett, T. (1965). *Race: The History of an Idea in America*. New York: Oxford University Press.

Gottfried, A. E., & Gottfried, A. W. (Eds.). (1994). *Redefining Families: Implications for Children's Development*. New York: Plenum Press.

Graetz, M. J., & Schenk, D. H. (1995). *Federal Income Taxation: Principles and Policies*. Westbury, NY: The Foundation Press.

Graham, H. D. (1990). *The Civil Rights Era: Origins and Development of National Policy 1960–1972*. New York: Oxford University Press.

Grambs, J. D. (1989). *Women Over Forty: Visions and Realities*. New York: Springer.

Graves, E. J. (1995). *1993 Summary: National Hospital Discharge Survey. Advance Data from Vital and Health Statistics,* No. 264. Hyattsville, MD: National Center for Health Statistics.

Gray, G. (1985). National Commission on Unemployment and Mental Health. *Resource Papers to the Report of the National Mental Health Association Commission on the Prevention of Mental-Emotional Disabilities*. Alexandria, VA: National Mental Health Association.

Greenberg, A.S., & Bailey, M. J. (1993). Do biological explanations of homosexuality have moral, legal, or policy implications? *Journal of Sex Research, 30*(3): 245–251.

Greenberg, D. F. (1988). *The Construction of Homosexuality*. Chicago: The University of Chicago Press.

Greene, R. (1989). The growing need for social work services for the aged in 2020. In B. S. Vourlekis & C. G. Leukefeld (Eds.), *Making Our Case: A Resource Book of Selected Materials for Social Workers in Health Care* (pp. 11–17). Silver Spring, MD: National Association of Social Workers.

Gresenz, C. R., Watkins, K., & Podus, D. (1998). Supplemental Security Income (SSI), Disability Insurance (DI), and substance abusers. *Community Mental Health Journal, 34*(4): 337–350.

Grob, G. N. (1994). *The Mad Among Us: A History of the Care of America's Mentally Ill*. New York: The Free Press.

Grossman, J. (1978, June). Fair Labor Standards Act of 1938: Maximum struggle for a minimum wage. *Monthly Labor Review,* 22–30.

Gurr, T. R. (1989). The history of violent crime in America: An overview. In T. R. Gurr (Ed.), *Violence in America: The History of Crime*. Newbury Park, CA: Sage.

Gutman, H. (1976). *The Black Family in Slavery and Freedom, 1750–1925*. New York: Pantheon Books.

Haber, C. (1983). *Beyond Sixty-Five: The Dilemma of Old Age in America's Past*. Cambridge: Cambridge University Press.

Haber, C., & Gratton, B. (1994). *Old Age and the Search for Security: An American Social History*. Bloomington: Indiana University Press.

Haldeman, H. R. (1994). *The Haldeman Diaries: Inside the Nixon White House*. New York: G.P. Putnam.

Hanlon, J. J., & Pickett, G. E. (1979). *Public Health Administration and Practice*. St. Louis: Mosby.

Hardcastle, D. A., Wenocur, S., & Powers, P. R. (1996). *Community Practice: Theories and Skills for Social Workers*. New York: Oxford University Press.

Harrington, M. (1962). *The Other America*. New York: Macmillan.

Harrington, M. (1984). *The New American Poverty*. New York: Holt, Rinehart & Winston.

Harvard Law Review Editors. (1990). *Sexual Orientation and the Law*. Cambridge, MA: Harvard University Press.

Hayek, F. A. (1960). Excerpt from *The Constitution of Liberty* reprinted with permission in Sterba, 1980.

Hayes, C. D., Palmer, J. L., & Zaslow, M. J. (1990). *Who Cares for America's Children? Child Care Policy for the 1990s*. Washington, DC: National Academy Press.

Health Care Financing Administration. (1996). "Medicare and Medicaid Statistical Supplement." *Health Care Financing Review*. Baltimore, MD: U.S. Department of Health and Human Services.

Heffler, S., Levit, K., Smith, S., Smith, C., Cowan, C., Lazenby, H., & Freeland, M. (2001). TRENDS: Health Spending Growth up in 1999; Faster growth expected in the future. *Health Affairs, 20*(2): 193–203 (http://www.healthaffairs.org/archives.htm).

Henetz, P. (1998, March 15). "Getting to the Roots of Gender Discrimination." *Salt Lake Tribune.*

Hening, W. W. (Ed.) (1809–1823). *The Statutes at Large: Being a Collection of All the Laws of Virginia from the First Session of the Legislature in the Year 1619* (13 vols., Richmond, VA), cited by Grob, 1994, p. 20.

Herman, A. (1999). Report on the American Workforce. Secretary of Labor (http://stats.bls.gov/opub/rtaw/message.htm).

Herring, C. (Ed.). (1997). *African Americans and the Public Agenda: The Paradoxes of Public Policy*. Thousand Oaks: Sage Publications.

Herrnstein, R., & Murray, C. (1994). *The Bell Curve: Intelligence and Class Structure in American Life*. New York: Free Press.

Herzog, A. R. (1989). Physical and mental health in older women: Selected research issues and data sources. In J. A. Hendricks (Ed.), *Health and Economic Status of Older Women* (pp. 35–91). New York: Baywood.

Hickey, T., Rakowski, W., & Julius, M. (1988). Preventive health practices among older men and women. *Research on Aging, 10,* 315–328.

Himmelstein, D., & Woolhandler, S. (1995). Care denied: US residents who are unable to obtain needed medical services. *American Journal of Public Health, 85*(3): 341–344.

Hodgins, S. (1992). Mental disorder, intellectual deficiency, and crime. *Archives of General Psychiatry, 49:* 476–483.

Hoff, R. (1988). *I Can See You Naked: A Fearless Guide to Making Great Presentations*. Kansas City: Andrews and McMeel.

Hoffman, S. D., & Seidman, L. S. (1990). *The Earned Income Tax Credit: Antipoverty Effectiveness and Labor Market Effects*. Kalamazoo, MI: W.E. Upjohn Institute for Employment Research.

Hoffman, W. (2000). The trouble with Medicare HMOs: Health plans say money is the key but critics see other problems. *ACP-ASIM Observer* (an electronic journal published by the American College of Physicians-American Society of Internal Medicine, available at http://www.acponline.org/journals/news/dec00/medicarehmos.htm).

Holden, K., & Smeeding, T. (1990). The poor, the rich, and the insecure elderly caught in between. *The Milbank Quarterly, 16:* 227–239.

Holinger, P. C., Offer, D., Barter, J. T., & Bell, C. C. (1994*). Suicide and Homicide Among Adolescents*. New York: Guilford Press.

Holzer, C., Shea, B., Swanson, J., Leaf, P., Myers, J., George, L., Weissman, M., & Bednarski, P. (1986). The increased risk for specific psychiatric disorders among persons of low socioeconomic status. *American Journal of Social Psychiatry, 6:* 259–271.

Holzer, C. E., Leaf, P. J., & Weissman, M. M. (1985). Living with depression. In M. R. Haug, A. B. Ford, & M. Sheafor (Eds.), *The Physical and Mental Health of Aged Women* (pp. 101–116). New York: Springer.

Horney, J., & Spohn, C. (1991). Rape law reform and instrumental change in six urban jurisdictions. *Law and Society Review, 25*(1): 117–153.

Human Rights Campaign. (2000). *State of the Workplace for Lesbian, Gay, Bisexual, and Transgendered Americans: 2000* (http://www.hrc.org/worknet/publications/state_workplace/2000/sow2000.pdf).

Human Rights Campaign. (2001). Hewlett-Packard, General Mills, and others back federal employment non-discrimination bill (http://www.hrc.org/worknet/workalert/2001/0408/article01.asp).

Humphreys, K. & Rosenheck, R. (1995). Sequential validation of cluster analytic subtypes of homeless veterans. *American Journal of Community Psychology, 23*(1): 75–98.

Hunter, N., & Rubenstein, W. (1992). AIDS and civil rights: The new agenda. *AIDS and Public Policy Journals, 7*(4): 204–208.

Internal Revenue Service. (1999). *Statistics of Income Bulletin, Summer 1999*. Washington, DC: GPO (cited by Mantsios, 2000).

Jacobson, P. H. (1959). *American Marriage and Divorce*. New York: Rinehart & Company.

Jacoby, R. (1975). *Social amnesia: A critique of conformist psychology from Adler to Laing*. Boston: Beach Press.

Jahnigen, D., & Binstock, R. H. (1991). Economic and clinical realities: Health care for older people. In R. H. Binstock & S. G. Post (Eds.), *Too Old for Health Care: Controversies in Medicine, Law, Economics and Ethics*. Baltimore: Johns Hopkins University Press.

Jamison, K. R. (1993). *Touched With Fire: Manic-Depressive Illness and the Artistic Temperament*. New York: Macmillan.

Jefferson, T. (1817). Letter from Thomas Jefferson to Mr. Correa, Nov. 25, 1817. In *The Writings of Thomas Jefferson* (Washington Ed. 1854). Cited by U.S. Commission on Civil Rights, 1967.

Jensen, A. R. (1973). *Educability and Group Differences*. London: Methuen.

Johnson, H. L. (1999). Minds and money: The challenge to public education. *Response* (http://gbgm-umc.org/Response/articles/challenge.html).

Johnson, R. W. (1999). *The Gender Gap in Penson Wealth: Is Women's Progress in the Labor Market Equalizing Retirement Benefits?* Washington, DC: The Urban Institute (http://www.urban.org/pubs/retirement/brief_1.html).

Johnston, D. D. (1994). *The Art and Science of Persuasion*. Boston: McGraw-Hill.

Jones, G. W. (Ed.). (1972). *Cotton Mather, The Angel of Bethesda*. Barre, MA: American Antiquarian Society and Barre Publishers (pp. 129–137). (Cited by Grob, 1994, p. 10).

Kadushin, A. (1974). *Child Welfare Services* (2nd ed.). New York: Macmillan.

Kaiser Commission on the Future of Medicaid. (1993). The Medicaid Cost Explosion: Causes and Consequences. Baltimore, MD: Kaiser Family Foundation.

Kaiser Family Foundation (1998). Medicaid and Managed Care (http;//www.kff.org - Nov. 18, 1998 - #2068).

Kammerman, S., & Kahn, A. (1987). *The Responsive Workplace: Employers and a Changing Labor Force*. New York: Columbia University Press.

Kaplan, M., & Krell-Long, L. (1993). AIDS, health policy, and ethics. *Affilia, 8*(2): 157–170.

Kates, B. (1985). *The Murder of a Shopping Bag Lady*. New York: Harcourt Brace Jovanovich.

Katz, H. J. (1994, Feb. 19). Statement before the Subcommittees on Social Security and Human Resources of the House Committee on Ways and Means. *Hearing on Exploring Means of Achieving Higher Rates of Treatment and Rehabilitation Among Alcoholics and Drug Addicts Receiving Federal Disability Benefits*. 103rd Congress, 2nd Session. (Cited by Gresenz, Watkins, & Podus, 1998).

Kelley, M. (1999, April 28). "American Indian boarding schools: 'That hurt never goes away.'" CNEWS—Canada's Internet Network (http://www.canoe.ca/CNEWSFeatures9904/28_indians.html).

Kelly, M. A., Perloff, J. D., Morris, N. M., & Liu, W. (1993). Access to primary care among young African-American children in Chicago. *Journal of Health and Social Policy, 5*(2): 35–48.

Kempe, C. H., Silverman, F., Steel, B., Droegemueller, W., & Silver, H. (1962). The battered child syndrome. *Journal of the American Medical Association, 181:* 17–24.

Kessler, R.C., McGonagle, K. A., Zhao, S., Nelson, C. B., Hughes, M., Eshleman, S., Wittchen, H. U., & Kendler, K. S. (1994). Lifetime and 12-month prevalence of DSM-III-R psychiatric disorders in the United States: Results from the National Comorbidity Survey. *Archives of General Psychiatry, 51:* 8–19.

Kessler, R. C., & Zhao, S. (1999). The prevalence of mental illness. In A. V. Horwitz & T. L. Scheid (Eds.), *A Handbook for the Study of Mental Health: Social Contexts, Theories, and Systems* (pp. 58–78). Cambridge: Cambridge University Press.

Kessler-Harris, A. (1990). *A Woman's Wage: Historical Meanings and Social Consequences.* Lexington, KY: University of Kentucky Press.

Kijakazi, K., Primus, W., & Greenstein, R. (1998). *Understanding the Financial Status of the Social Security System in Light of the 1998 Trustees' Report.* Center on Budget and Policy Priorities (http://www.cbpp.org/424socsec.html).

Kilburn, M. R., & Hao, L. (1996). *The Impact of Federal and State Policy Changes on Child Care in California.* Rand Corporation Report (http://www.rand.org/publications/CF/CF123/kilburn/).

Kingson, E. (1996). Ways of thinking about the long-term care of the baby-boom cohorts. *Journal of Aging and Social Policy, 7* (3–4): 3–23.

Kingson, E. R., & Berkowitz, E. D. (1993). *Social Security and Medicare: A Policy Primer.* Westport, CT: Greenwood Publishing Group.

Kingson, E., & Quadagno, J. (1997). Social Security: Marketing radical reform. In R. B. Hudson (Ed.), *The Future of Age-Based Public Policy.* Baltimore: The Johns Hopkins University Press.

Kinsey, A. C., Pomeroy, W. B., & Martin, C. E. (1948). *Sexual Behavior in the Human Male.* Philadelphia: W. B. Saunders Co.

Kinsey, A. C., Pomeroy, W. B., Martin, C. E., & Gebhard, P. H. (1953). *Sexual Behavior in the Human Female.* Philadelphia: W. B. Saunders Co.

Klerman, G. L. (1987). Clinical epidemiology of suicide. *Journal of Clinical Psychiatry, 48* (supplement): 33–38.

Kloss, H. (1998). *The American Bilingual Tradition* (2nd ed.). Washington, DC: ERIC, Clearinghouse on Language and Linguistics.

Koebel, C.T. (1998). Nonprofit Housing: Theory, Research, and Policy. In Koebel, C.T. (Ed.), *Shelter and Society: Theory, Research and Policy for Nonprofit Housing* (pp. 3–20). New York: State University of New York Press.

Koegel, P., Burnam, M.A., & Baumohl, J. (1996). The causes of homelessness. In J. Baumohl (Ed.), *Homelessness in America.* Phoenix: Oryx Press.

Korczyk, S. M. (1993). *Why Has Women's Pension Coverage Improved?* Paper presented at the 1993 meeting of the Eastern Economic Association.

Kozol, J. (1991). *Savage Inequalities: Children in America's Schools.* New York: Crown Publishers.

Krause, N. (1986). Stress and sex differences in depressive symptoms among older adults. *Journal of Gerontology, 41:* 727–731.

LaBruzza, A. L., with Mendez-Villarrubia, J. M. (1994). *Using DSM-IV: A Clinician's Guide to Psychiatric Diagnosis.* Northvale, NJ: Jason Aronson Inc.

LaRue, A., Dessonville, C., & Jarvik, L. F. (1985). Aging and mental disorders. In J. E. Birren & K. W. Shaie (Eds.), *Handbook of the Psychology of Aging* (pp. 664–702). New York: Van Nostrand Reinhold.

Leibowitz, A. H. (1969). English literacy: Legal sanction for discrimination. *Notre Dame Lawyer, 45*(7): 7–76.

Leiby, J. (1978). *A History of Social Welfare and Social Work in the United States.* New York: Columbia University Press.

Leighninger, L. (1990). Professionalism in British and American social work. *Current Research on Occupations and Professions, 5:* 29–42.

Lemann, N. (1986, June and July). The origins of the underclass. *Atlantic Monthly,* 31–55 (June) and 54–68 (July).

Lenroot, K. (1960). A Quarter-Century of Service to Children (http://www.ssa.gov).

Leonard, K. K., Pope, C. E., & Feyerherm, W. H. (Eds.). (1995). *Minorities in the Juvenile Justice System.* Thousand Oaks, CA: Sage Publications.

Levin, B. L., Hanson, A., Coe, R. D., & Taylor, A. (1998). *Mental Health Parity: 1998 National and State Perspectives*. Tampa, FL: Louis de la Parte Florida Mental Health Institute, University of South Florida (http://www.fmhi.usf.edu/institute/pubs/pdf/parity/parity98.pdf).

Levine, D. (1997). The Constitution as rhetorical symbol in Western anti-gay-rights initiatives: The case of Idaho. In S. L. Witt & S. McCorkle (Eds.), *Anti-Gay Rights: Assessing Voter Initiatives* (pp. 33–50). Westport, CT: Praeger.

Lewers, D.T. (2001). AMA: Uninsured Americans Constitute a National Health Crisis. Statement before the House Ways and Means Health Subcommittee, April 4, 2001 (http://www.ama-assn.org/ama/pub/article/1617–4463.html).

Lewin Group (1998). *Policy evaluation of the effect of legislation prohibiting the payment of disability benefits to individuals whose disability is based on drug addiction and alcoholism. Interim report, April 28, 1998* (http://www.ssa.gov).

Lewis, O. (1965). *La Vida*. New York: Harper & Row.

Lichtenstein, A. (1996). *Twice the Work of Free Labor: The Political Economy of Convict Labor in the New South*. New York: Verso.

Limerick, P. N. (1987). *The Legacy of Conquest: The Unbroken Past of the American West*. New York: Norton.

Link, B. G., Andrews, H., & Cullen, F. T. (1992). The violent and illegal behavior of mental patients reconsidered. *American Sociological Review, 57:* 275–292.

Link, B., Phelan, J., Bresnahan, M., Stueve, A., Moore, R., & Susser, E. (1995, July). Lifetime and five-year prevalence of homelessness in the United States: New evidence on an old debate. *American Journal of Orthopsychiatry, 65*(3): 347–354.

Littell, J. (1995). Debates with authors: Evidence or assertions? The outcomes of family preservation services. *Social Service Review, 69:* 344–351.

Little, A. (1998). *Post-Industrial Socialism: Towards a New Politics of Welfare*. London: Routledge.

Loewen, J. (1995). "Gone With the Wind": The Invisibility of Racism in American History Textbooks. In *Lies My Teacher Told Me* (pp. 137–170). New York: Simon & Schuster.

Longman, P. (1987). *Born to Pay: The New Politics of Aging in America*. Boston: Houghton Mifflin.

Lubben, J. E., Damron-Rodriguez, J. A., & Beck, J. C. (1992). A national survey of aging curriculum in schools of social work. *Geriatric Social Work Education, 18:* 157–171.

Lubbers, J. S. (1998). *A Guide to Federal Rulemaking*. Washington, DC: Government and Public Sector Lawyers Division of the American Bar Association.

Maas, H. S., & Engler, R. E. (1959). *Children in Need of Parents*. New York: Columbia University Press.

MacDorman, M. F., & Atkinson, J. O. (1998). *Infant Mortality Statistics from the 1996 Period Linked Birth/Infant Death Data Set, 46*(12). Supplement. Washington, DC: National Center for Health Statistics.

MacDorman, M. F., & Atkinson, J. O. (1999). *Infant Mortality Rates Vary by Race and Ethnicity*. Washington, DC: National Center for Health Statistics (http://www.cdc.gov/nchs/data/nvs47_23.pdf).

Malkiel, B. G., & Malkiel, J. A. (1973). Male-female pay differentials in professional employment. *American Economic Review, 63:* 693–705.

Mandel, J. (1992). *Not Slave, Not Free: The African American Economic Experience*. Durham, NC: Duke University Press.

Mantsios, G. (2000). Class in America: Myths and Realities. In P. S. Rothenberg (Ed.), *Race, Class, and Gender in the United States: An Integrated Study* (5th ed.) (pp. 168–182). New York: Worth Publishers.

Marx, Karl. 1888. Excerpt from the *Communist Manifesto,* first published in English by Friedrich Engels, reprinted with permission in Sterba, 1980.

Marzuk, P. M. (1996). Violence, crime, and mental illness: How strong a link? *Archives of General Psychiatry, 53:* 481–486.

Mason, M. (1994). *From Father's Property to Children's Rights.* New York: Cambridge University Press.

Mathematica. (2000). Reaching those in Need: Food Stamp Participation Rates in the States (http://www.mathematics-mpr.com/3rdLevel/fins2ndbrochurehot.htm).

Mayfield, C. (Ed.). (1981). *Growing Up Southern: Southern Exposure Looks at Childhood, Then and Now.* New York: Pantheon Books.

Maynard, R. A. (Ed.). (1996). *Kids Having Kids: A Robin Hood Foundation Special Report on the Costs of Adolescent Childbearing.* New York: Robin Hood Foundation.

Maypole, D.E., & Skaine, R. (1983, Sept./Oct.). Sexual harassment in the workplace. *Social Work, 28*(5): 385–390.

Maza, P. L. (1998). Personal communication, cited by Crumbley, 1999.

McCaslin, R. (1987). Substantive specialization in masters level social work curricula. *Journal of Social Work Education, 23*(2): 8–18.

McLeod, H. R. (1995, Spring). The sale of a generation. *American Prospect.*

McMurrer, D. P., & Chasanov, A. B. (1995, Sept.). Trends in unemployment insurance benefits. *Monthly Labor Review,* 30–39.

Mechanic, D. (1962). Some factors in identifying and defining mental illness. *Mental Hygiene, 46:* 66–74.

Mechanic, D. (1999). *Mental Heath and Social Policy: The Emergence of Managed Care.* Needham Heights, MA: Allyn & Bacon.

Melich, T. (1998). *The Republican War Against Women.* New York: Bantam Books.

Menefee, J. A., Edwards, B., & Schieber, S. J. (1981, June). Analysis of nonparticipation in the SSI program. *Social Security Bulletin, 44:* 3–21.

Merck Manual of Diagnosis and Therapy (16th ed.). (1992). Rahway, NJ: Merck.

Michael, R. T., Gagnon, J. H., Laumann, E. O., and Kolata, G. (1994). *Sex in America: A Definitive Survey.* Boston: Little, Brown, and Company.

Mill, J. S. (1863). Excerpt from *Utilitarianism,* Chapter V, reprinted in Sterba, 1980.

Miller, R., & Luft, H. (1994). Managed Care Plan performance since 1980: A literature analysis. *Journal of the American Medical Association, 271*(19): 1512–1516.

Mintz, S., & Kellogg, S. (1988). *Domestic Revolutions: A Social History of American Family Life.* New York: The Free Press.

Mitchell, O. S., Levine, P. B., & Phillips, J. W. (1999). *The Impact of Pay Inequality, Occupational Segregation, and Lifetime Work Experience on the Retirement Income of Women and Minorities.* Washington, DC: AARP (http://research.aarp.org/econ/9910_women_1.html).

Mitteness, L. S. (1987). The treatment of urinary incontinence by community living elderly. *The Gerontologist, 27:* 185–193.

Monahan, J. (1992). Mental disorder and violent behavior. *American Psychologist, 47:* 511–521.

Monti, D. J. (1994). *Wannabe: Gangs in Suburbs and Schools.* Cambridge: Blackwell Publishers.

Moon, M. (1990, Summer). Public policies: Are they gender neutral? *Generations,* 59–63.

Moore, J. P. (1995). *Highlights of the 1995 Youth Gang Survey.* Office of Juvenile Justice and Delinquency Prevention (OJJDP) (http://www.ncjrs.org/).

Moquin, W. (1972). (Ed.). *A Documentary History of Mexican Americans.* New York: Bantam Books.

Morgan, E. (1975). *American Slavery, American Freedom: The Ordeal of Colonial Virginia.* New York: Norton.

Morrissey, J. P., & Goldman, H. H. (1986). Care and treatment of the mentally ill in the United States: Historical developments and reforms. *Annals of the American Academy of Political and Social Science, 484:* 12–27.

Morrow-Howell, N., Hinterlong, J., & Sherraden, M. (Eds.). (2001). *Productive Aging: Concepts and Challenges.* Baltimore: Johns Hopkins University Press.

Moynihan, D. P. (1969). *Maximum Feasible Misunderstanding.* New York: The Free Press.

Mulroy, E. (1990). Single-parent families and the housing crisis. *Social Work, 35:* 542–546.

Mulroy, E. A. (1995). *The New Uprooted: Single Mothers in Urban Life*. Westport, CT: Auburn House.

Muntaner, C., Eaton, W. W., Diala, C., Kessler, R. C., & Sorlie, P. D. (1998). Social class, assets, organizational control, and the prevalence of common groups of psychiatric disorders. *Social Science and Medicine, 47*(12): 2043–2053.

Murphy, J. M., Olivier, D. C., Monson, R. R., Sobol, A. M., et al. (1991). Depression and anxiety in relation to social status: A prospective epidemiologic study. *Archives of General Psychiatry, 48*(3): 223–229.

Murray, C. (1994). *Losing Ground: American Social Policy, 1950–1980*. New York: Basic Books.

Mutchler, J. E. (1990). Household composition among the nonmarried elderly. *Research on Aging, 12*(4): 487–506.

National Association for the Advancement of Colored People (NAACP). (1969). *Thirty Years of Lynching in the United States, 1889–1918*. New York: Arno Press.

National Association of Black Social Workers. (1994). *Position Statement: Preserving African American Families*. Detroit: Author.

National Association of Social Workers (NASW). (1999). *Code of Ethics of the National Association of Social Workers*. Washington, DC: NASW. [Approved by the 1996 NASW Delegate Assembly and revised by the 1999 NASW Delegate Assembly.]

National Center for Health Statistics. (1998a). *Births, Marriages, Divorces, and Deaths for August 1998. National Vital Statistics Report, 47*(14). Hyattsville, MD: Author.

National Center for Health Statistics. (1998b). Teen Birth Rates Down in All States: New Government Report on Teenage Birth Rates Includes State Rates by Race and Ethnicity (http://www.cdc.gov/nchs/releases/98news/98news/teenrel.htm).

National Center for Health Statistics. (1999). Birth, Infant Mortality, and Life Expectancy: 1980–1998 (http://www.cdc.gov/nchs/SSBR/023tab.htm).

National Committee on Pay Equity (1999). Fact Sheet: The Wage Gap: 1999 (http://www.feminist.com/fairpay/f_wagegap.htm).

National Institute for Mental Health (NIMH). (1992, May 8). *Social Work Research and Development Centers: Program Announcement,* NIH Guide, *21*(17) (http:www.nimh.gov/grants/research/920078.cfm).

National Institute of Allergy and Infectious Diseases (1996a). *Fact Sheet: Women and HIV Infection*. National Institutes of Health (http://www.niaid.nih.gov/factsheets/womenhiv.htm).

National Institute of Allergy and Infectious Diseases (1996b). *Fact Sheet: Minorities and HIV Infection*. National Institutes of Health (http://www.niaid.nih.gov/factsheets/Minor.htm).

National Institute of Allergy and Infectious Diseases. (1997). *Fact Sheet: HIV/AIDS Statistics*. National Institutes of Health (http://www.niaid.nih.gov/factsheets/aidstat.htm).

National Institute on Aging, National Institutes of Health (1987). *Personnel for Health Needs of the Elderly Through the Year 2020*. Washington, DC: U.S. Department of Health and Human Services (DHHS-NIAH Pub. No 87-2950).

National Policy and Resource Center on Women and Aging. (1996). "A big decision for women: Should I buy long-term care insurance?" *Women & Aging Letter, 1*(6) (http://www.heller.brandeis.edu/national/ind.html).

National Women's Health Information Center. (1999). *Women of Color Health Data Book* (http://www.4woman.gov/owh/pub/woc/toc.html).

Navarro, V. (1991, Sept.). Class and race: Life and death situations. *Monthly Review, 43*(4): 1–13.

North American Association of State and Provincial Lotteries. (1999). *Lottery History* (http://www.naspl.org/history.html).

Northrup, H. R. (1970). *Negro Employment in Southern Industry: A Study of Racial Policies in Five Industries*. Philadelphia: Industrial Research Unit, Wharton School of Finance and Commerce, University of Pennsylvania.

Nozick, R. (1974). *Anarchy, State, and Utopia*. New York: Basic Books.

Oaxaca, R. (1975). Sex discrimination in wages. In O. Ashenfelter & A. Rees (Eds.), *Discrimination in Labor Markets* (pp. 124–151). Princeton, NJ: Princeton University Press.

Offe, C., Muckenberger, U., & Ostner, I. (1996). A basic income guaranteed by the state: A need of the moment in social policy. In C. Offe (Ed.), *Modernity and the State: East, West.* Cambridge: Polity Press.

Office of Management and Budget. (1997). A-133 Compliance Supplement—Unemployment Insurance (http://www.whitehouse.gov/OMB/circulars/a133_compliance/17225.html).

Office of Management and Budget. (2001a). *A Citizen's Guide to the Federal Budget: Budget of the United States Government, Fiscal Year 2001* (http://w3.access.gpo.gov/usbudget/FY2001/guidetoc.html).

Office of Management and Budget. (2001b). *Federal Resources in Support of Social Security* (http://www.whitehouse.gov/omb/budget/fy2002/bud15.html).

Office of the Parliamentarian, U.S. House of Representatives. (2001). *How Our Laws Are Made.* Washington, DC: Government Printing Office. (Stock number 052-071-01326-1. ISBN 0-16-050434-1.)

O'Keefe, B. J., & Shepherd, G. J. (1987). The pursuit of multiple objectives in face-to-face persuasive interactions: Effects of construct differentiation on message organization. *Communication Monographs, 54:* 396–419.

O'Keefe, D. (1992). *Persuasion: Theory and Research.* Newbury Park, CA: Sage.

Okin, S. (1989). Excerpt from *Justice, Gender and the Family* reprinted with permission in Sterba, 1980.

Oliver, M. L., & Shapiro, T. (1990). Wealth of a nation: A reassessment of asset inequality in America shows at least one third of households are asset poor. *American Journal of Economics and Sociology, 49*(2): 129–152.

Omi, M., & Winaut, H. (1994). *Racial Formation in the United States: From the 1960s to the 1990s* (2nd ed.). New York: Routledge.

Ontario Consultants on Religious Tolerance. (2001). *U.S. Hate Crimes: Definitions, Information, and Legislation* (http://www.religioustolerance.org/hom_hat1.htm#st).

Orentlicher, D. (1996, Aug. 29). The legalization of physician-assisted suicide. *New England Journal of Medicine, 335*(9): 663–667.

O'Rourke, S. P., & Dellinger, L. K. L. (1997). *Romer v. Evans:* The centerpiece of the American gay-rights debate. In S. L. Witt & S. McCorkle (Eds.), *Anti-Gay Rights: Assessing Voter Initiatives* (pp. 133–140). Westport, CT: Praeger.

Orshansky, M. (1965). Counting the poor: Another look at the poverty profile. *Social Security Bulletin, 28*(1): 3–29.

Osborne, R. (1993). *Freud for Beginners.* New York: Writer's and Reader's Publishing.

Osipow, S. H., & Fitzgerald, L. F. (1993). Unemployment and mental health: A neglected relationship. *Applied and Preventive Psychology, 2:* 59–63.

Osumi, M. D. (1982). Asians and California's Anti-Miscegenation Laws. In N. Tsuchida (Ed.), *Asian and Pacific American Experiences: Women's Perspectives.* Minneapolis: Asian/Pacific American Learning Resource Center and General College, University of Minnesota.

Overfield, T. (1995). *Biologic Variation in Health and Illness: Race, Age, and Sex Differences.* New York: CRC Press.

Owens, L. H. (1976). *This Species of Property: Slave Life and Culture in the Old South.* New York: Oxford University Press.

Owens, M. J. (1999). Battered women and their children: A public policy response. *AFFILIA: Journal of Women and Social Work, 14*(4): 439–459.

Paine, T. (1795). *Agrarian Justice* (http://www.ssa.gov/history/paine4.html).

Park, R. (1974). *The Collected Papers of Robert Ezra Park.* New York: Arno.

Parker, A. C. (1916). *The Constitution of the Five Nations or the Iroquois Book of the Great Law.* Albany, NY: A.C. Irocrafts, reprinted by Iroquois Reprints.

Patterson, C. J. (1995). Lesbian mothers, gay fathers, and their children. In A. R. D'Augelli & C. J. York (Eds.), *Lesbian, Gay, and Bisexual Identities Across the Lifespan* (pp. 262–290). New York: Oxford University Press.

Patterson, C. J., & Redding, R. E. (1996). Lesbian and gay families with children: Implications of social science research for policy. *Journal of Social Issues, 52*(3): 29–50.

Pearson, J., & Griswold, E. A. (1997). Child support policies and domestic violence. *Public Welfare, 55*(1): 26–32.

Pecora, P., Fraser, M., Nelson, K., McCroskey, J., & Meezan, W. (Eds.). (1995). *Evaluating Family-Based Services*. Hawthorne, NY: Aldine de Gruyter.

Pecora, P., Whittaker, J. K., Maluccio, A. N., & Barth, R. P. (2000). *The Child Welfare Challenge: Policy, Practice and Research*. New York: Aldine de Gruyter.

Pedriana, N. (1999). The historical foundations of affirmative action, 1961–1971. *Research in Social Stratification and Mobility, 17:* 3–32.

Pension Benefit Guarantee Corporation. (2001). Pension Benefit Guarantee Corporation: History (http://www.pbgc.gov/about_pbgc/history/hptext.htm).

Perkins, J., Olson, K., & Rivera, L. (1996). *Making the Consumers' Voice Heard in Medicaid Managed Care: Increasing Participation, Protection and Satisfaction* (Report on Required and Voluntary Mechanisms). National Health Law Program (http://www.healthlaw.org/pubs/19970128consumersvoice.html).

Perlmutter, M. (Ed.). (1990). *Late Life Potential*. Washington, DC: Gerontological Society of America.

Perloff, J. D. (1996). Medicaid managed care and urban poor people: Implications for social work. *Health and Social Work, 21*(3): 189–195.

Perloff, J. D., Kletke, P. R., & Neckerman, K. M. (1987). Physicians' decisions to limit Medicaid participation: Determinants and policy implications. *Journal of Health Politics, Policy, and Law, 12*(2): 221–235.

Perry, M. J. (1996). The relationship between social class and mental disorder. *The Journal of Primary Prevention, 17*(1): 17–30.

Petchey, R. (1987). Health maintenance organizations: Just what the doctor ordered? *Journal of Social Policy, 16*(4): 489–507.

Petersen, D. A. (1988). *Personnel to Serve the Aging in the Field of Social Work*. A report prepared by the Andrus Gerontology Center, University of Southern California, Los Angeles, CA, and the Association for Gerontology in Higher Education, Washington, DC.

Phillips, K. R. (2001). *Who Knows About the Earned Income Tax Credit?* Washington, DC: Urban Institute (http://newfederalism.urban.org/html/series_b/b27/b27.html).

Phillips, W. D., & Phillips, C. R. (1992). *The Worlds of Christopher Columbus*. Cambridge, UK: Cambridge University Press.

Physician Payment Review Commission (1991, April). Annual Report to Congress: 1991. Washington, DC: Author.

Piven, F. F., & Cloward, R. A. (1971). *Regulating the Poor: The Functions of Public Welfare*. New York: Pantheon Books.

Ploughman, P. (1995/1996). Public policy versus private rights: The medical, social, ethical, and legal implications of the testing of newborns for HIV. *AIDS & Public Social Policy Journal, 10*(4): 182–204.

Pollard, L. J. (1980, Sept.). Black beneficial societies and the Home for Aged and Infirm Colored Persons: A research note. *Phylon, 41*(3): 230–234.

Population Reference Bureau. (1999, Sept.). America's racial and ethnic minorities. *Population Bulletin, 54*(3) (http://www.prb.org/pubs/population-bulletin/bu54-3/income_wealth_poverty.htm).

Porter, K. H., Larin, K., & Primus, W. (1999). *Social Security and Poverty Among the Elderly: A National and State Perspective*. Washington, DC: Center on Budget and Policy Priorities (http://www.cbpp.org/4-8-99socsec.htm).

Porter, K., Primus, W., Rawlings, L., and Rosenbaum, E. 1998. *Strengths of the Safety Net: How the EITC, Social Security and Other Government Programs Affect Poverty.* Washington, DC: Center on Budget and Policy Priorities.

Princeton Survey Research Associates. (1997). *National Omnibus Survey Questions About Teen Pregnancy,* for the Association of Reproductive Health Professionals and the National Campaign to Prevent Teen Pregnancy. Washington, DC: Author.

Prospective Payment Assessment Commission. (1995). PPRC Annual Report to Congress, 1995. Washington, DC: Government Printing Office.

Putnam, R. D. (2000). *Bowling Alone: The Collapse and Revival of American Community.* New York: Simon & Schuster.

Quadagno, J. (1989). Generational equity and the politics of the welfare state. *Politics and Society, 17:* 360–376.

Quadagno, J. (1994). *The Color of Welfare: How Racism Undermined the War on Poverty.* New York: Oxford University Press.

Quadagno, J., & Meyer, M. H. (1990, summer). Gender and public policy. *Generations,* 64–66.

Quill v. Vacco. (1995). United States Court of Appeals for the Second Circuit No. 60—August term, 1995 (http://www.law.pace.edu/lawlib/legal/us-1...diciary/second-circuit/test3/95-7028.html).

Quinn, J. F., & Mitchell, O. S. (1996, May–June). Social Security on the table. *American Prospect, 26:* 76–81.

Radner, D. B. (1991). Changes in the incomes of age groups, 1984–89. *Social Security Bulletin, 54:* 2–18.

Ramirez, J. D., Yuen, S. D., & Ramey, D. R. (1991). *Final Report: Longitudinal Study of Structured English Immersion Strategy, Early-Exit, and Late-Exit Transitional Bilingual Education Programs for Language-Minority Children.* San Mateo, CA: Aguirre International.

Raphael, J. (1996). *Prisoners of Abuse: Domestic Violence and Welfare Receipt.* A second report of the Women, Welfare and Abuse Project. Chicago: Taylor Institute.

Rasell, E., & Weller, C. E. (2001). *Trust funds' rainy day postponed, again: Trustees' reports provide no justification for radical changes in Social Security and Medicare.* Washington, DC: Economic Policy Institute (http://www.epinet.org).

Rawls, J. (1971). *A Theory of Justice.* Cambridge: Harvard University Press.

Reegan, L. J. (1997). *When Abortion Was a Crime: Women, Medicine and Law in the United States, 1867–1973.* Berkeley: University of California Press.

Regier, D. A., Narrow, W., Rae, D., Manderscheid, R., Locke, B., & Goodwin, F. (1993). The de facto U.S. mental and addictive disorders service system: Epidemiological Catchment Area prospective one-year prevalence rates of disorders and services. *Archives of General Psychiatry, 50:* 85–94.

Reynolds, B. C. (1963). *An Uncharted Journey: Fifty Years of Growth in Social Work.* New York: Citadel Press.

Rhode, D. (1989). *Justice and Gender: Sex Discrimination and the Law.* Cambridge: Harvard University Press

Rice, D. P. (1991). Ethics and equity in U.S. health care: The data. *International Journal of Health Services, 21*(4): 637–651.

Rich, B. M., & Baum, M. (1984). *The Aging: A Guide to Public Policy.* Pittsburgh: University of Pittsburgh Press.

Richards, D. A. J. (1999). *Identity and the Case for Gay Rights: Race, Gender, and Religion as Analogies.* Chicago: University of Chicago Press.

Richardson, T. R. (1989). *The Century of the Child: The Mental Hygiene Movement and Social Policy in the United States and Canada.* Albany, NY: State University of New York Press.

Richmond, M. (1917). *Social Diagnosis.* New York: Russell Sage Foundation.

Rimlinger, G. V. (1971). *Welfare Policy and Industrialization in Europe, America, and Russia.* New York: Wiley.

Rimmerman, C. A. (2000). A "friend" in the White House? Reflections on the Clinton Presidency. In J. D'Emilio, W. B. Turner, & U. Vaid (Eds.), *Creating Change: Sexuality, Public Policy, and Civil Rights* (pp. 43–56). New York: St. Martin's Press.

Roberts, A. R., & Kurtz, L. F. (1987). Historical perspectives on the care and treatment of the mentally ill. *Journal of Sociology and Social Welfare 14*(4): 75–94.

Robins, L. N., Helzer, J. E., Weissman, M. M., Orvaschel, H., Gruenberg, E., Burke, J. D., Jr., & Regier, D. A. (1984). Lifetime prevalence of specific psychiatric disorders in three sites. *Archives of General Psychiatry, 41:* 949–956.

Robins, L. N., & Regier, D. A. (Eds.). (1991). *Psychiatric Disorders in America: The Epidemiological Catchment Area Study.* New York: Free Press.

Robinson, G. (1999). Parental Consent/Notification for Teen Abortions (http://www.religioustolerance.org/abo_pare.htm).

Rochefort, D. A. (1997). *From Poorhouses to Homelessness: Policy Analysis and Mental Health Care* (2nd ed.). Westport, CT: Auburn House.

Rodwin, M. (1993). *Medicine, Money and Morals: Physicians' Conflicts of Interest.* Oxford, England: Oxford University Press.

Roemer, M. I. (1993). *National Health Systems of the World, Volume II: The Issues.* New York: Oxford University Press.

Roizman, B. (Ed.). (1995). *Infectious Diseases in an Age of Change.* Washington, DC: National Academy Press.

Roscoe, M., & Morton, R. (1994). *Disproportionate Minority Confinement.* Office of Juvenile Justice and Delinquency Prevention (OJJDP) (http://www.ncjrs.org/txtfiles/fe-9411.txt).

Rose, N. (1996). Psychiatry as a political science: Advanced liberalism and the administration of risk. *History of the Human Sciences, 9*(2): 1–23.

Rosen, G. (1993). *A History of Public Health* (expanded edition). Baltimore: Johns Hopkins University Press.

Rosenbaum, D. (2000). Improving access to Food Stamps: New reporting options can reduce administrative burdens and error rates. Washington, DC: Center on Budget and Policy Priorities (http://www.cbpp.org/9-1-00fs.htm).

Rosenbaum, S., Hughes, D., Butler, E., & Howard, D. (1988). Incantations in the dark: Medicaid, managed care and maternity care. *Milbank Quarterly, 66*(4): 661–693.

Rosenheck, R. (1996). Homeless veterans. In J. Baumohl (Ed.), *Homelessness in America.* Phoenix: Oryx Press.

Rowe, J. W., & Kahn, R. L. (1998). *Successful Aging.* New York: Pantheon Books.

Rowland, D., & Hanson, K. (1996). Medicaid: Moving to managed care. *Health Affairs, 15*(3): 150–152.

Rowland, D., & Salganicoff, A. (1994). Commentary: Lessons from Medicaid—Improving access to office-based physician care for the low-income population. *American Journal of Public Health, 84*(4): 550–552.

Rubin, I. S. (1998). *Class, Tax, and Power: Municipal Budgeting in the United States.* Chatham, NJ: Chatham House Publishers.

Rubin, L. B. (1972). *Busing and Backlash: White Against White in a California School District.* Berkeley, CA: University of California Press.

Ruggles, P. (1990). *Drawing the Line: Alternative Poverty Measures and Their Implications for Public Policy.* Washington, DC: Urban Institute Press.

Russel, P. (1996). *The Gay 100: A Ranking of the Most Influential Gay Men and Lesbians, Past and Present.* Secaucus, NJ: Citadel Press.

Saleebey, D. (1990). Philosophical disputes in social work: Social justice denied. *Journal of Sociology and Social Work, 17*(2): 29–40.

Salmon, J. (1995). A perspective on the corporate transformation of health care. *International Journal of Health Services, 25*(1): 11–42.

Schaaf, G. (1990). *Wampum Belts and Peace Trees: George Morgan, Native Americans and Revolutionary Diplomacy.* Golden, CO: Fulcrum Publishers.

Schmid, C. (1992). The English-only movement: Social bases of support and opposition among Anglos and Latinos. In J. Crawford (Ed.), *Language Loyalties: A Sourcebook on the Official English Controversy* (pp. 202–209). Chicago: University of Chicago Press.

Schmid, C. (1996). New immigrant communities in the United States and the ideology of exclusion. *Research in Community Sociology, 6*(39): 67.

Schneider, C. (1991). Discretion, rules, and law: Child custody and the UMDA's best-interest standard. *Michigan Law Review, 89:* 2215–2298.

Schultz, V. (1998). Reconceptualizing Sexual Harassment. *Yale Law Review, 107*(6).

Schulz, J. H. (1995). *The Economics of Aging* (6th ed.). Westport, CT: Auburn House.

Schwartz, I. (1986, June 19). Testimony Before the House Subcommittee on Human Resources.

Segalman, R., & Basu, A. (1981). *Poverty in America: The Welfare Dilemma.* Westport, CT: Greenwood Press.

Shanas, E. (1968). *Old People in Three Industrial Societies.* New York: Atherton Press.

Shilts, R. (1993). *Conduct Unbecoming: Gays and Lesbians in the U.S. Military.* New York: St. Martin's Press.

Shinn, M. (1997). Family homelessness: State or Trait? *American Journal of Community Psychology, 25*(6): 755–769.

Short, J. F. (1997). *Poverty, Ethnicity, and Violent Crime.* Boulder, CO: Westview Press.

Siegel, J. (1996). *Aging into the 21st Century. Factors in Program Participation and Dependency.* Report prepared for the National Aging Information Center.

Siminoff, I. (1986). Competition and primary care in the US: Separating fact from fantasy. *International Journal of Health Studies, 16*(1): 57–69.

Simmons, L. W. (1945). *The Role of the Aged in Primitive Societies.* New Haven, CT: Yale University Press.

Simpson, P. (1985, Oct.). If the wage system doesn't work, fix it. *Working Woman,* 118–159.

Sisk, J. E., Gorman, S. A., Reisinger, A. L., Glied, S. A., DuMouchel, W. H., & Hynes, M. M. (1996, July 3). Evaluation of Medicaid managed care: Satisfaction, access, and use. *Journal of the American Medical Association, 276*(1): 50–55.

Skocpol, J. (1995). *Social Policy in the United States: Future Possibilities in Historical Perspective.* Princeton, NJ: Princeton University Press.

Skocpol, T. (1996). *Boomerang: Clinton's Health Security Effort and the Turn Against Government in U.S. Politics.* New York: Norton.

Slater, W. (1984, March 29). Latest Lamm remark angers the elderly. *Arizona Daily Star,* p. 1.

Smeeding, T. J., Torrey, B. B., & Rainwater, L. (1993). *Going to Extremes: An International Perspective on the U.S. Aged.* Working Paper 87, Luxembourg Income Study.

Smith, K. E., & Bachu, A. (1999). Women's labor force attachment patterns and maternity leave: A review of the literature. *Working Paper No. 32.* Population Division, U.S. Census Bureau, Washington, DC.

Social Security Administration, Office of Research, Evaluation, and Statistics. (1998). *Income of the Population 55 or Older, 1996* (http://www.ssa.gov/statistics/incpop55/1996/).

Social Security Administration. (1999). *Social Security and Supplemental Security Income Disability Programs: Managing for Today, Planning for Tomorrow* (http://www.ssa.gov/policy/pubs/dibreport.html).

Social Security Administration. (2000). *2000 OASDI Trustees Report* (http://www.ssa.gov/OACT/TR/trib.html).

Social Security Administration. (2001a). *Old-Age and Survivors Insurance Trust Fund, Calendar Year Operations* (http://www.ssa.gov/OACT/STATS/table4a3.html).

Social Security Administration. (2001b). Chapter 5: Cash disability benefits and related disability protection. *Social Security Handbook* (14th ed.). Washington, DC: U.S. Government Printing Office. SSA Publication No. 65-008—ICN 958392 (http://www.ssa.gov/OP_Home/handbook/handbook.05/handbook-0507.html).

Social Security Administration. (2001c). *Formula for the Primary Insurance Amount* (http://www.ssa.gov/OACT/COLA/BenForm.html).

Southern Poverty Law Center. (1999, Spring). *Intelligence Report: Hate Crimes: Serious Violence Against Gays Said to Rise* (http://www.splcenter.org/intelligenceproject/ip-4j10.html).

Sowell, T. (1981). *Markets and Minorities.* New York: Basic Books.

Sowers-Hoag, K. M., & Harrison, D. F. (1991). Women in social work education: Progress or promise? *Journal of Social Work Education, 27:* 320–328.

Specht, H., & Courtney, M. (1994). *Unfaithful Angels: How Social Work Has Abandoned Its Mission.* New York: Free Press.

Stampp, K. M. (1956). *The Peculiar Institution: Slavery in the Ante-Bellum South.* New York: Vintage.

Stavis, P. F. (1995). Civil Commitment: Past, Present, and Future. An address by Paul F. Stavis at the National Conference of the National Alliance for the Mentally Ill, Washington, DC, July 21, 1995 (http://www.cqc.state.ny.us/cc64.htm).

Steele, E., & Redding, W. C. (1962). The American value system. *Western Speech, 26:* 83–91.

Stein, T. (1995). Disability-based employment discrimination against individuals perceived to have AIDS and individuals infected with HIV or diagnosed with AIDS: Federal and New York Statutes and case law. *AIDS & Public Policy Journal, 10*(3): 123–139.

Stein, T. J. (1996). Child custody and visitation: The rights of lesbian and gay parents. *Social Service Review,* 435–450.

Steinwachs, D. M., Kasper, J. D., & Skinner, E. A. (1992). *Family Perspectives on Meeting the Needs for Care of Severely Mentally Ill Relatives: A National Survey.* Arlington, VA: National Alliance for the Mentally Ill.

Sterba, J. (1980). *Justice: Alternative Political Perspectives.* Belmont, CA: Wadsworth Publishing Co.

Sternleib, G., & Hughes, J. (1981). *The Future of Rental Housing.* New Brunswick, NJ: Center for Urban Policy Research, Rutgers.

Stoner, M. (1995). Intervention and policies to serve homeless people infected by HIV and AIDS. *Journal of Health and Social Policy, 7*(1): 53–68.

Straznickas, K. A., McNeil, D., & Binder, R. L. (1993). Violence toward family caregivers by mentally ill relatives. *Hospital and Community Psychiatry, 44:* 385–387.

Streib, V. L. (1999). *The Juvenile Death Penalty Today: Death Sentences and Executions for Juvenile Crimes, January 1973–June 1999* (http://www.law.onu.edu/faculty/streib/juvdeath.htm).

Strouse, J. (1998, Nov. 23). The brilliant bailout. *New Yorker,* 62–77.

Stuart, P. (1997). Community care and the origins of psychiatric social work. *Social Work in Health Care, 25*(3): 25–36.

Sullivan, A. (1995). Policy issues. In *Issues in Gay and Lesbian Adoption: Proceedings of the Fourth Annual Peirce-Warwick Adoption Symposium.* Washington, DC: Child Welfare League of America.

Suppe, F. (1994). Explaining homosexuality: Philosophical issues, and who cares anyhow? *Journal of Homosexuality, 27*(3–4): 223–268.

Supreme Court of the United States. (1937). Opinion in *Helvering et al. v. Davis* (http://www.ssa.gov/history/supreme1.html).

Supreme Court of the United States. (1967). Opinion in *Loving v. Virginia* (http://www.bowdoin.edu/~sbodurt2/court/cases/loving.html).

Surgeon General. (1999). Mental Health: A Report of the Surgeon General (http://www.surgeongeneral.gov/library/mentalhealth).

Swanson, J. W., Holzer, C. E., Ganju, V. K., & Jono, R. T. (1990). Violence and psychiatric disorder in the community: Evidence from the Epidemiologic Catchment Area surveys. *Hospital and Community Psychiatry, 41:* 761–770.

Sweeney, J. (1999, June 24). *Statement by AFL-CIO President John Sweeney on the Employment Non-Discrimination Act* (http://igc.org/prideatwork/enda.html#2).

Szasz, T. (1960). The myth of mental illness. *American Psychologist, 15:* 113–118.

Takaki, R. (1993). *A Different Mirror: A History of Multicultural America*. New York: Little, Brown and Company.

Task Force on Social Work Research. (1991). *Building Social Work Knowledge for Effective Services and Policies*. Washington, DC: NASW.

Tasker, F., & Golumbok, S. (1997). *Growing Up in a Lesbian Family: Effects on Child Development*. New York: Guilford Press.

Tedeschi, J. T., & Rosenfeld, P. (1980). Communication in bargaining and negotiation. In M. E. Roloff & G. E. Miller (Eds.), *Persuasion: New Directions in Theory and Research*. Beverly Hills: Sage Publications.

Temkin-Greener, H., & Winchell, M. (1991). Medicaid beneficiaries under managed care: Provider choice and satisfaction. *Health Services Research, 26*(4): 509–529.

Thomas, C. S. (1991). *Sex Discrimination in a Nutshell* (2nd ed.). St. Paul: West Publishing Co.

Thomas, M. P. (1972). Child abuse and neglect: Part 1. Historical overview, legal matrix, and social perspectives. *North Carolina Law Review, 50:* 293–349 (cited by Watkins, 1990).

Thornberry, T., & Burch, J. H., II. (1997). *Gang Members and Delinquent Behavior*. Office of Juvenile Justice and Delinquency Prevention (OJJDP) (http://www.ncjrs.org/txtfiles/165154.txt).

Titmuss, R. (1971). *The Gift Relationship*. New York: Pantheon Books.

Torrey, E. F. (1997). *Out of the Shadows: Confronting America's Mental Illness Crisis*. New York: John Wiley & Sons, Inc.

Torrey, E. F., & Kaplan, R. J. (1995). A National Survey of the Use of Outpatient Commitment. *Psychiatric Services, 46:* 778–784.

Trattner, W. I. (1989). *From Poor Law to Welfare State: A History of Social Welfare in America*. New York: Free Press.

Troy, D. E. (1998, Oct. 19). Rule of law: Hate crime laws make some more equal than others. *Wall Street Journal* (http://www.aei.org/ra/ratroy3.htm).

Urban Dynamics (1999). *Gangs 101* (http://www.lincolnnet.net/users/lrttrapp/block/gang101.htm).

U.S. Census Bureau. (1930 and 1998). *Current Population Reports*, series P-25.

U.S. Census Bureau, U.S. Dept. of Commerce. (1991). *Current Population Reports, Population Characteristics, Series P-20, No. 458. Household and Family Characteristics: March 1991*. Washington, DC: Government Printing Office.

U.S. Census Bureau. (1995). *Selected Social and Economic Characteristics for the 25 Largest American Indian Tribes: 1990* (http://www.census.gov/population/socdemo/race/indian/ailang2.txt).

U.S. Census Bureau. (1997a). *Selected Characteristics of Families by Type, Region, and Race of Householder* (http://www.census.gov/race/black/tabs97/tab06.txt).

U.S. Census Bureau. (1997b, March). Poverty statistics on population groups. *Current Population Survey*.

U.S. Census Bureau. (1999). *Statistical Abstract of the United States*. Washington, DC: U.S. Department of Commerce.

U.S. Census Bureau. (1999a). *Money Income in the United States: 1999* (http://www.census.gov/hhes/income/income99/incxrace.html).

U.S. Census Bureau. (2000a). *Poverty Rate Lowest in 20 Years, Household Income at Record High*. Department of Commerce News Release (http://www.census.gov/Press-Release/www.2000/cb00-158.html).

U.S. Census Bureau. (2000b). *Poverty 1999: Percent of People in Poverty by State: 1997, 1998, and 1999*. Data from Current Population Surveys (http://www.census.gov/hhes/poverty/poverty99/pv99state.html).

U.S. Census Bureau. (2000c). *Selected Characteristics of Households and Families by Quintile* (http://www.census.gov/hhes/income/dinctabs.html).

U.S. Census Bureau. (2000d). Table 8: Income in 1998 by Educational Attainment for People 18 Years Old and Over, by Age, Sex, Race, and Hispanic Origin: March 1999 (http://www.census.gov/population/socdemo/education/p20-528/tab08.txt).

U.S. Census Bureau, U.S. Dept. of Commerce. (2000e). *Record Share of New Mothers in Labor Force, Census Bureau Reports* (http://www.census.gov/Press-Release/www/2000/cb00-175.html).

U.S. Census Bureau. (2000f). Current Population Reports, "Poverty in the United States: 1999," P60-210, issued September, 2000.

U.S. Census Bureau. (2001a). *Resident Population Estimates of the United States by Sex, Race, and Hispanic Origin: April 1, 1990 to July 1, 1999, with Short-Term Projection to November 1, 2000.* Population Estimates Program. Population Division (http://www.census.gov/population/estimates/nation/intfile3-1.txt).

U.S. Census Bureau. (2001b). *Census 2000 Brief: Overview of Race and Hispanic Origin* (http://www.census.gov/population/www/cen2000/briefs.html).

U.S. Commission on Civil Rights. (1967). *Racial Isolation in the Public Schools.* Washington, DC: Government Printing Office.

U.S. Congress, Office of Technology Assessment. (1994, Sept.). International comparisons of administrative costs in health care (BP-H-135). Washington, DC: U.S. Government Printing Office (http://www.ota.nap.edu/pdf/data/1994/9417.PDF).

U.S. Department of Agriculture. (2000a). Food Stamps: Income Chart (available online: http://www.fns.usda.gov/fsp/MENU/APPS/ELIGIBILITY/income/INCOMECHART.HTM).

U.S. Department of Agriculture. (2000b). Food Stamps: Allotment Chart (http://www.fns.usda.gov/fsp/CHARTS/ALLOTMENTCHART.HTM).

U.S. Department of Agriculture. (2001). Food Stamps: FAQ's (http://www.fns.usda.gov/fsp/menu/faqs/faqs.htm).

U.S. Department of Commerce, Economics and Statistics Administration, Bureau of the Census. (1992). *Statistical Abstract of the United States, 1993* (112th ed.). Washington, DC: Government Printing Office.

U.S. Department of Health and Human Services, Social Security Administration. (1992, Sept. 4). *Supplemental Security Income Modernization Project: Final Report; Notice* (Federal Register). Washington, DC: Government Printing Office.

U.S. Department of Health and Human Services. (1994a). *Diabetes Overview.* Washington, DC: Government Printing Office.

U.S. Department of Health and Human Services. (1994b). Office of the Inspector General. *Requirements for Drug Addicts and Alcoholics on SSI,* OEI-01-94-00110.

U.S. Department of Health and Human Services. (1998*). Aid to Families with Dependent Children: The Baseline* (http://aspe.hhs.gov/hsp/AFDC/afdcbase98exhib.htm).

U.S. Department of Health and Human Services, Social Security Administration. (1999). *Annual Statistical Supplement to the Social Security Bulletin, 1999.* Washington, DC: Social Security Administration.

U.S. Department of Health and Human Services. (2000, June 5). *HHS Fact Sheet: Clinton Administration Record on HIV/AIDS* (http://www.thebody.com/hhs/clinton.html).

U.S. Department of Housing and Urban Development. (1993, Oct.). *Creating Communities of Opportunity: Priorities of U.S. Department of Housing and Urban Development: Executive Summary.* Washington, DC: HUD.

U.S. Department of Housing and Urban Development. (1999). *The Widening Gap: New Findings on Housing Affordability in America* (http://www.hud.gov/library/bookshelf18/pressrel/afford/afford.html).

U.S. Department of State, Immigration and Naturalization. (1998). *Statistics on Foreign-Born Adopted Children.* Washington, DC: Author.

U.S. General Accounting Office. (1980). *Section 8 Subsidized Housing: Some Observations on Its High Rents, Costs and Inequities* (Report to Congress by the Comptroller General of the United States, CED-80-59). Washington, DC: Government Printing Office.

U.S. General Accounting Office. (1992, February). *Pension Plans: Survivor Benefit Coverage for Wives Increased After 1984 Pension Law.* (Report to the Chairman, Sub-committee on Retirement Income and Employment, Select Committee on Aging, House of Representatives, GAO/HRD-92-49). Washington, DC: Government Printing Office.

U.S. General Accounting Office. (1994a). *Social Security: Major Changes Needed for Disability Benefits for Addicts.* Washington, DC: Government Printing Office. GAO/HEHS-94-128.

U.S. General Accounting Office. (1994b). *Tax Gap: Many actions taken but a cohesive compliance strategy needed.* (GGD 94-123) (http://www.unclefed.com/GAOReports/gao94-123_sum.html).

U.S. General Accounting Office. (1995). *Supplemental Security Income: Recent Growth in Rolls Raises Fundamental Program Concerns.* Washington, DC: USGPO (GAO/T-HEHS-95-67).

U.S. Health Care Financing Administration. (2001). *Managed Care Trends* (http://www.hcfa.gov/medicaid/trends00.pdf).

U.S. House of Representatives, Select Committee on Aging, Subcommittee on Human Services. (1988). *Older Americans Act: A Staff Summary.* Washington, DC: Government Printing Office. (Comm. Pub. No 100–683.).

U.S. House of Representatives, Select Committee on Aging. (1990). *Medicare and Medicaid's 25th Anniversary—Much promised, accomplished, and left unfinished.* (Committee Publication No. 101–762. Washington, DC: Government Printing Office.

U.S. House of Representatives. (1999). Hot Topic: Minimum Wage. A report from the Democratic Leadership (www.house.gov/democrats/ht_min_wage.html).

U.S. Office of Personnel Management. (1997). *Federal Civilian Workforce Statistics: Employment and Trends as of November 1996.* Washington, DC: U.S. Government Printing Office.

U.S. Senate, Special Committee on Aging. (1988a, Feb. 26). *Developments in Aging,* Vol. I. Washington, DC: Government Printing Office.

U.S. Senate, Special Committee on Aging. (1988b). *Aging America* (1987–88 ed.). Washington, DC: U.S. Department of Health and Human Services.

U.S. Senate. (1991). *Aging America: Trends and Projections.* (A report of the Special Committee on aging, in collaboration with American Association of Retired Persons, Federal Council on Aging, and the U.S. Administration on Aging). Washington, DC: U.S. Government Printing Office.

Van der Meade, W. (2000). *Legislating Equality: A Review of Laws Affecting Gay, Lesbian, Bisexual, and Transgendered People in the United States.* New York: National Gay/Lesbian Task Force.

Van Tassel, E. F., with B. H. Wirtz and P. Wonders. (1993). *Why Judges Resign: Influences on Federal Judicial Service, 1789 to 1992.* Federal Judicial History Office.

Ventura, S. J., Mosher, W. D., Curtin, S. C., Abma, J. C., & Henshaw, S. (2001). Trends in pregnancy rates for the United States, 1976–1997: An update. *National Health Statistics Reports, 49*(4). Hyattsville, MD: National Center for Health Statistics (http://www.cdc.gov/nchs/data/nvsr/nvsr49/nvsr49_04.pdf).

Verbugge, L. M. (1985). An epidemiological profile of older women. In M. R. Haug, A. B. Ford, & M. Sheafor (Eds.), *The Physical and Mental Health of Aged Women* (pp. 41–64). New York: Springer Publishing Co.

Vernon, R., & Lynch, D. (2000). *Social Work and the Web.* Belmont, CA: Wadsworth.

Wagner, G., cited in F. Cerne. (1995, Mar. 20). Street wise. *Hospital and Health Networks,* 38–46.

Wakefield, J. (1988, June). Psychotherapy, distributive justice, and social work. Part 1: Distributive justice as a conceptual framework for social work. *Social Service Review,* pp. 187–210.

Walker, F. A. (1874). *The Indian Question.* Boston: J. R. Osgood.

Wandersee, W. D. (1981). *Women's Work and Family Values: 1920–1940.* Cambridge: Harvard University Press.

Ware, S. (1981). *Beyond Suffrage: Women in the New Deal.* Cambridge, MA: Harvard University Press.

Watkins, S. (1990). The Mary Ellen Myth: Correcting Child Welfare History. *Social Work, 35*(6): 500–503.

Waxman, L., & Trupin, R. (1997). *A Status Report on Hunger and Homelessness in America's Cities: 1997.* Washington, DC: U.S. Conference of Mayors.

Weatherford, J. (1988). *Indian Givers: How the Indians of the Americas Transformed the World.* New York: Crown Publishers.

Weil, A. (1997). *The New Children's Health Insurance Program: Should States Expand Medicaid?* Washington, DC: Urban Institute (Paper A-13 in "New Federalism" series) (http://newfederalism.urban.org/html/anf_al13.htm).

Weiner, J. M. (1996). Managed care and long-term care: The integration of financing and services. *Generations, 20*(2): 47–52.

Weiner, L. Y. (1985). *From Working Girl to Working Mother: The Female Labor Force in the United States, 1820–1980.* Chapel Hill: University of North Carolina Press.

Weitzman, L. J., & Maclean, M. (1992). *Economic Consequences of Divorce: The International Perspective.* Oxford, England: Clarendon Press.

Welfare Policy Organization. (1997). *Comparison of Prior Law and the PRWORA Statute.* Reference Library: Federal Laws and Regulations (http://www.welfare-policy.org/aspesum.htm).

Wells, K. (1995, Sept.). Proceedings of the NIMH Conference on Service Research in Washington, D.C.

Wiatrowski, W. J. (1993). Factors affecting retirement income. *Monthly Labor Review, 116*(3) (http://stats.bls.gov/opub/mlr/1993/03/art2abs.htm).

Wiehe, V. R., & Richards, A. L. (1995). *Intimate Betrayal: Understanding and Responding to the Trauma of Acquaintance Rape.* Thousand Oaks: Sage.

Willhelm, S. (1970). *Who Needs the Negro.* Cambridge, MA: Schenkman Publishing Co.

Williams, D. D. (1993). Barriers to achieving health. *Child and Adolescent Social Work Journal, 10*(5): 355–363.

Wilson, C. A. (1996). *Racism: From Slavery to Advanced Capitalism.* Thousand Oaks, CA: Sage Publications.

Wilson, W. J. (1987). *The Truly Disadvantaged.* Chicago: University of Chicago Press.

Wingfield, K., Petit, M., & Klempner, T. (1999). *Mortality Trends Among U.S. Children and Youth: An Issue Brief.* Washington, DC: Child Welfare League of America.

Wolfe, B., & Perozek, M. (1997). Teen children's health and health care use. In R. A. Maynard (Ed.), (1996), *Kids Having Kids: Economic Costs and Social Consequences of Teen Pregnancy* (pp. 181–203). Washington, DC: The Urban Institute Press.

Women's Bureau, U.S. Dept. of Labor. (1996, Sept.). *Facts on Working Women.* No. 96-2.

Woods, J. R. (1989). Pension coverage among private wage and salary workers: Preliminary findings from the 1988 Survey of Employee Benefits. *Social Security Bulletin, 52:* 2–19.

Woodward, D. (1998*). Globalization, Uneven Development, and Poverty: Recent Trends and Policy Implications.* Social Development and Poverty Elimination Division, United Nations Development Programme (available online: http://www.undp.org/poverty/publications/wkpaper/wp4/wp4-wood.PDF).

World Bank. (1994). *World Development Report.* New York: Oxford University Press, 251–252.

World Bank. (2000). *World Development Report, 1999/2000: Entering the 21st Century.* Herndon, VA: World Bank Publications.

World Health Organization. (1999). *The World Health Report 1999* (http://www.who.int.whr/1999/index.htm).

Wright, M. H. (1928). The removal of the Choctaws to the Indian Territory: 1830–1833. *Chronicles of Oklahoma,* V1, 2, 103–128.

Zedlewski, S. R., & Meyer, J. A. (1987). *Toward Ending Poverty Among the Elderly and Disabled: Policy and Financing Options.* Washington, DC: The Urban Institute.

Zhang, A. Y., & Snowden, L. (1999). Ethnic characteristics of mental disorders in five U.S. communities. *Cultural Diversity and Ethnic Minority Psychology, 5*(2): 134–146.

Zorza, J. (1991). Woman battering: A major cause of homelessness. *Clearinghouse Review, 25*(4): 421.

Zuckerman, S., Evans, A., & Holahan, J. (1997). *Questions for States as They Turn to Medicaid Managed Care.* Number A-11 in Series, "Issues and Options for States." Urban Institute (http://newfederalism.urban.org/html/anf_a11.htm).

Name Index

Subject Index